T5-DIE-566

Racial and Ethnic Relations in America

Volume III

Politics and racial/ethnic relations in Canada - Zoot-suit riots

SALEM PRESS, INC.
PASADENA, CALIFORNIA   HACKENSACK, NEW JERSEY

Managing Editor: Christina J. Moose
Research Supervisor: Jeffry Jensen
Acquisitions Editor: Mark Rehn
Photograph Editor: Karrie Hyatt
Editorial Secretary: Andrea E. Miller

Project Editor: Rowena Wildin
Manuscript Editors: Rowena Wildin, Robert McClenaghan
Research Assistant: Jun Ohnuki
Production Editor: Joyce I. Buchea
Design and Layout: James Hutson

Some of the essays in this work originally appeared in the following Salem Press sets: *American Indians* (1995), *American Justice* (1996), *Ethics* (1994), *Great Events from History: North American Series* (revised edition, 1997), *Identities and Issues in Literature* (1997), *The Sixties in America* (1999), *Survey of Social Science: Psychology Series* (1993), *Survey of Social Science: Sociology Series* (1994), and *Women's Issues* (1997).

∞ The paper used in these volumes conforms to the American National Standard for Permanence of Paper for Printed Library Materials, Z39.48-1992(R1997)

Library of Congress Cataloging-in-Publication Data

Racial and ethnic relations in America / editorial board Carl L. Bankston . . . [et al.].
    p. cm.
    Includes bibliographical references (p.   ) and indexes.
    Contents: v. 1. Ability testing—Ethnic enclaves — v. 2. Ethnic entrepreneurship—Political correctness — v. 3. Politics and racial/ethnic relations in Canada—Zoot-suit riots.
    ISBN 0-89356-629-2 (set : alk. paper). — ISBN 0-89356-630-6 (vol. 1 : alk. paper). — ISBN 0-89356-634-9 (vol. 2 : alk. paper). — ISBN 0-89356-635-7 (vol. 3 : alk. paper)
    1. North America—Ethnic relations Encyclopedias.   2. North America—Race relations Encyclopedias.
I. Bankston, Carl L. (Carl Leon), 1952-   .

E49.R33   2000
305.8'00973—dc21   99-29348
                                                                                                    CIP

First Printing

PRINTED IN THE UNITED STATES OF AMERICA

Racial and Ethnic Relations in America

Contents

Photo Credits in Volume III

Racial and Ethnic Relations in America

Politics and racial/ethnic relations in Canada

> **Significance:** Canada is a land of ethnic and cultural diversity. It has also been a land of communities with a conservative tradition. Although the United States broke with Britain and Europe, Canada's British and French maintained a slow and cautious evolutionary milieu, which included loyalty to their respective British and French homelands.

By the time James Wolfe captured Quebec in 1759, the sixty thousand French Canadians living there had become a distinct community. For 150 years, they had been an outpost of the French Empire and had carried the French flag and Catholic cross within sight of the Rocky Mountains. To ensure the loyalty of the French in Canada, the British Quebec Act of 1775 was passed, granting the French special status to retain their feudal landholding system and establishing church and civil law. The French Canadians were in essence a nation. In this way, both the British and French communities maintained a tradition of respect for authority, continuity, and the rights of collective communities. The role of governmental authority was widely accepted by both communities, and in the case of the French, the role of government was reinforced by the clergy, who administered most educational, health, and social service institutions. The clergy also gave influential advice on how to vote in certain matters, advocated a high birthrate, stressed an agricultural economy to counter the homogenizing effects of industry, and encouraged loyalty to constituted authority.

Most of the events affecting ethnic issues that occurred before World War I concerned the French and aboriginals. The economic development of the northlands was a large factor in ending the nomadic hunting life of the aboriginals. By 1945, poverty and disease on the reserves were so rampant that it was apparent that the system was a reproach to Canadian policy and had to be changed.

French Canadians

The 1885 execution of Louis Riel, Jr., separatist leader of the Metis (whose ancestry is both aboriginal and French, and a sense of minority grievance promoted the development of French nationalism. Many French Canadians farmed and worked in the timber trade up to 1890. The coming of hydroelectric power, the wood-pulp industry, and manufacturing plants, combined with a reduction in available workable land, brought French Canadians to the cities. By 1921, Quebec was the most urbanized and industrialized of all Canadian provinces; however, the new enterprises were owned or controlled by English Canadians or U.S. businesspeople. The result of the influx into the cities was not only a "second conquest of Quebec" but also a clash of the old with the new that destroyed the myths by which French Canadians had survived—that the Roman Catholic mission and agriculture were the basis for a virtuous life. Workers soon realized that those traditional values were an obstacle to progress. The clash of old and new came to a head under the regime of Quebec premier Maurice Duplessis, who was in power from 1936 to 1939 and 1944 to his death in 1959. Duplessis was a conservative who retained the enterprise system in Quebec, assisted greatly by British and U.S. businesspeople and investors.

Rise of Ethnic Politics

After the end of World War II, ethnic politics began to dominate Canadian society. Aboriginals received greatly improved health care as a result of the Indian Act of 1959, which provided greater Indian influence in decision making. As a result of protests, all Indians were given the franchise to vote in 1960.

In Quebec, the gap between the French and English Canadians widened and opinions crystallized. The industrialization of the province created a desperate need for reforms. Some people felt these reforms could be achieved within the federal system, while others felt that Quebec needed a special status or independence. Some social revolutionaries, inspired by refugees from Algeria and Cuba, resorted to terrorism. Bombings began in 1963 and continued sporadically. French and English Canadians felt such actions were "un-Canadian," but they illustrated both the social ills of Quebec and the ties of the French intellectuals to the outside world.

In October of 1970, with the kidnapping of James Cross, British trade commissioner in Montreal, and Pierre Laporte, minister of labor and immigration, in Quebec, the province government called for federal help. The War Measures Act was invoked, and troops moved into Quebec, civil liberties were suspended, and around five hundred people were arrested. Few of those arrested were charged or convicted. Although Cross was released unharmed, Laporte was murdered, and his killers were found and convicted. Although a majority of Canadians and Quebecers approved of the federal action, many civil libertarians believed that the invocation of the War Measures Act and the suspension of civil liberties was too severe a course of action.

Postwar Immigration

Besides the plight of the aboriginals and rise of French separatism, large-scale immigration after World War II challenged Canada's social structure. Traditionally immigration had been limited to British and American nationals, except in the mid-1920's, when central and eastern Europeans were recruited to farm the vast Canadian prairies and work in extractive industries. As the demand for labor eased, antiforeign sentiment increased, and Canada closed its doors to non-British and American immigrants. After 1945, Canada again needed laborers, and immigration restrictions were loosened. First, displaced people arrived from war-torn Europe. Then, in the 1950's, Canada experienced its greatest influx of immigrants. The majority were from Europe, but a sizable number were from southern Europe, particularly Italy, Greece, and Portugal. This change in immigration patterns started a new phase in the character of Canadian society. Those of British and Irish descent dropped to 43.8 percent and those of French heritage to 30 percent of the nation's population. Those of other descent rose to 26.4 percent—a social change that stimulated the rise of nationalism in Quebec.

The Establishment of Multiculturalism

In 1965, the Royal Commission on Bilingualism and Biculturalism was set up to examine the strained relations between Canada's two charter groups, the French and the English. The commission was besieged by organized ethnic communities demanding that their ethnocultural heritages be accorded equal status in the nation-building process. The politicians, made aware of the fact that one-third of all Canadians were neither British nor French in origin, acknowledged this third

Distribution of Ethnicity in Canada, 1997 Estimates
(percentage)

British	40.5
French	26.6
German	8.1
Italian	3.3
Ukranian	3.1
Dutch	2.9
Aboriginal	2.8
Scandinavian	2.2
Polish	2.0
Chinese	1.4
Black, Jamaican, Haitian, Other Caribbean	1.2
Jewish	1.1
South Asian	1.0
East and Southeast Asian	0.9
Portuguese	0.8
Other	2.3

Source: Statistics Canada.

force in Canadian society. In response, Prime Minister Pierre Trudeau established the official policy of multiculturalism within a bilingual framework in 1971. The purpose of this policy was to encourage members of all ethnic groups in Canada to maintain and share their languages and cultural heritages with other Canadians. The goal was to build personal and collective confidence among all ethnic groups and thus promote tolerance of diversity and positive intergroup attitudes.

The Multiculturalism Act was passed in 1988. This legislation expanded the policy of multiculturalism from an attempt to meet the needs of mainly European immigrants and their descendants through cultural programs and activities and language and heritage education to an effort to combat prejudice and discrimination and promote the full and equal participation of ethnic minorities in all aspects of Canadian society, including mainstream economic, political, and cultural life.

Concerns of Multicultural Canada

Canada is a country of cultural and ethnic diversity. Besides the aboriginals (1.5 percent) and the founding communities, the French (26.6 percent) and British (40.5 percent), the nation contains a wide range of ethnic groups, including large numbers of Germans (8.1 percent), Italians (3.0 percent), Dutch (2.9 percent), Ukrainians (3.1 percent), Polish (2.0 percent), Scandinavians (2.2 percent), Chinese (1.4 percent), blacks, Jamaicans, Haitians, and other Caribbeans (1.2 percent), Jews (1.1 percent), South Asians (1.1 percent), East and Southeast Asians (0.9 percent), Portuguese (0.8 percent), and others (2.3 percent). Almost 10 percent of the population are visible minorities, persons other than aboriginals who are nonwhite. Those officially designated as visible minorities by the Canadian government are blacks, Chinese, Filipinos, Japanese, Koreans, Latin Americans, other Pacific Islanders, Indo-Pakistanis (or South Asians), Southeast Asians, West Asians, and Arabs. The visible minority population is expected to double by the year 2020.

The aboriginals, which include North American Indians, Inuit, and Metis, have suffered because of prejudice and discrimination. In 1991, 4 percent of Canada's population of more than 29 million claimed aboriginal ancestry, double the 1981 figure. Experts project that those reporting aboriginal ancestry will increase to 4.5 percent by the year 2016.

Concerns about the future of race and ethnic relations in Canada include the strained relations between the French and English Canadians, the poor treatment of native people, and the increased prejudice against visible minorities. In addition, ethnic diversity—and the possibility of conflict—is increasing in Canada. Groups with very different, sometimes opposing, cultural and religious practices are expected to get along; however, under the policy of multiculturalism, they are also encouraged to maintain their unique cultural background while sharing in the Canadian experience. Some groups bring with them histories of conflict from their region of origin that should not become part of the Canadian fabric. Another problem is that resources are scarce, and at some time, Canadians may come to view multiculturalism as a luxury they cannot afford. On the other hand, it may be that embracing multiculturalism is the only way Canada can survive.   *Arthur W. Helweg*

Core Resources

J. W. Berry and J. A. Laponce's *Ethnicity and Culture in Canada: The Research Landscape* (Toronto: University of Toronto Press, 1994) provides a good analysis of the current situation of multicultural Canada. Angie Fleras and Jean Leonard Elliotto's *Multiculturalism in Canada: The Challenge of Diversity* (Scarborough, Ontario: Nelson, 1991) and Leo Driedger's *The Ethnic Factor: Identity in Diversity* (Toronto: McGraw-Hill Ryerson, 1989) are superb descriptions and analyses of multiculturalism in Canada.

See also: Aboriginal Canadians; African Canadians; Anglophone; Asian Indians in Canada; Bilingualism in Canada; Chinese Canadians; Employment in Canada; European immigration to Canada: 1867-present; Francophone; French Canadians; Indian-white relations: Canada; Japanese Canadians; Metis; Multiculturalism Act; Multiculturalism in Canada; October crisis; Official Languages Act; Racial and ethnic demographics in Canada; Racial/ethnic relations in Canada; Reserve system of Canada; Riel Rebellions; Separatist movement in Canada; Sikhs in Canada; Visible minority allophones in Canada.

Politics of hate

The politics of hate uses the "language of hate," the code words that politicians and other public officials use in place of overtly racist language, to manipulate white voters' anxieties and gain their votes.

Alabama's segregationist governor George Wallace pioneered the politics of hate approach during the 1968 presidential primaries, when his fiery rhetoric received substantial support in Democratic primaries in Wisconsin, Indiana, and Maryland. More mainstream politicians realized that Wallace had substantial appeal to urban, blue-collar whites who lived in areas adjacent to expanding black communities and who felt that their interests were being subordinated to those of black Americans. Presenting himself as a populist fighting against elitist, hypocritical liberals, Wallace associated his approach with anticommunist rhetoric, reformu-

lated his defense of segregation as a stand for states' rights, and derided the federal government's efforts at busing to promote integration of the public schools, specifically condemning the U.S. Supreme Court.

Since Wallace, other politicians have used similar strategies to galvanize and direct voters on the basis of fear without appealing directly to racism. During the 1968 campaign, Richard Nixon avoided direct mention of race, while promising to restore "law and order" and "local control" of schools. Blaming "permissive," "indulgent," liberal policies for student antiwar uprisings, urban riots, and the creation of a "criminal" class of the "hardcore unemployed" financed by "middle-class" tax dollars, he linked race and disorder.

The effectiveness of George Bush's 1988 campaign strategy demonstrated how deeply racist narratives still permeated the nation. Trailing Michael Dukakis in polls, Bush resorted to a series of advertisements focused on Willie Horton, a black felon, who, while on furlough, had raped a white woman. The Bush campaign thereby manipulated the tendency of much of the president's constituency to link race with fear of crime in this classic instance of hate politics.

In the 1994 congressional races, the religious right's program to "restore family values" used the language of hate to support diverse agendas such as antigay legislation, exclusionary immigration policies, and reduced public assistance. Republican House members called for an end to "entitlement status." Attempting to disparage the Democratic Party, they attacked with coded terms from a list which included "sick," "traitors," "corrupt," "cheat," "devour," "self-serving," and "criminal rights."

                        Trudi D. Witonsky

See also: Hate speech; Horton, Willie, incident; Racial propaganda; Racism: changing nature of; Stereotype.

Poll tax

Poll taxes existed in the United States from the earliest colonial times. They were usually quite small and did not act to discourage many people from voting. In the years following the Civil War (1861-1865), the poll tax system was refined in the southern states for the purpose of disfranchising black voters. The tax remained small, but it had to be paid during every election in which the potential voter might have voted. This tax effectively disfranchised nearly all black voters. Because the election laws in the United States are made by state governments, a constitutional amendment was needed to do away with poll taxes. In 1964, the Twenty-fourth Amendment abolished the payment of such taxes as a condition for voting in federal elections.   *Robert Jacobs*

See also: Disfranchisement laws in Mississippi; Jim Crow laws; Voting Rights Act of 1965.

Poor People's March on Washington

Martin Luther King, Jr.'s Poor People's Campaign, carried out after King's death, was a major mass-participation event designed to dramatize to the nation and the government the plight of the poor. By 1967, King had come to see the Vietnam War and the War on Poverty as inseparable issues: The war overseas was taking needed money and government attention away from the more important goal of ending poverty in the United States. The Poor People's Campaign was designed to demonstrate the problem of poverty vividly and graphically by bringing thousands of poor Americans to Washington, D.C., to camp and lobby.

Organizing for this massive march on Washington was interrupted while King went to Memphis in support of a sanitation workers' strike. While there, he was assassinated, the event stunning the movement and the nation. The Southern Christian Leadership Conference (SCLC), now led by Ralph Abernathy, decided to carry out King's Poor People's March in his honor and memory. From all parts of the nation, thousands of poor people of all races set out for Washington, arriving five weeks after King's death. They built Resurrection City, a campground-city, on the Washington Mall.

In the few weeks of its existence, Resurrection City provided "freedom schools" and free food and medical care for its poor residents. Demands were made on the government through such actions as marching to the Department of Agriculture and demanding an end to American hunger in a land of such plenty. Jesse Jackson, a longtime member of the SCLC and King associate, came into prominence, leading marches and giving speeches. Running a city sapped all the energy from the SCLC, however; the group had no time to plan other actions and no clear agenda. Then it began to rain. The rain and mud made life in Resurrection City miserable, and the protesters soon had to abandon the project.

A few government actions can be attributed to the Poor People's Campaign—provision of food to some of the country's neediest counties, some funding for low-income housing, and additional funds for the Office of

Jesse Jackson (standing in front of police officers) addresses a group of demonstrators during the Poor People's Campaign in Washington, D.C., in May, 1968.

Economic Opportunity—but, in general, the campaign had only very limited success. *Lisa Langenbach*

See also: Civil Rights movement; King, Martin Luther, Jr., assassination; Southern Christian Leadership Conference; Student Nonviolent Coordinating Committee.

Popé's Revolt

> **Significance:** This August 10, 1680, uprising against European colonial authority ensured the survival of Puebloans as a distinct people.

The first permanent European colony in Pueblo territory was established by Juan de Oñate in 1598. The jewels and gold of the fabled Seven Cities of Cíbola had proven to be a myth, but the Spanish still intended to settle the land. Franciscan friars came to seek converts to Catholicism, the civilian authorities and settlers to seek their fortunes in mining, trading, and ranching. The entire Spanish system was based on the need for American Indian labor. In order to get it, the Spanish imposed the *encomienda* system, which gave large land grants to holders, known as *encomanderos*. The part of this program known as *repartimiento* bestowed upon the *encomanderos* the right to the labor of any nearby natives. Annual taxes also were collected from the natives in the form of produce, textiles, or other resources.

Spanish Brutality

The Spanish were able to impose these measures by access to guns and horses and frequent displays of force. Harsh physical punishments were meted out for even slight infractions. The Franciscans—who recognized no belief system except their own and thus felt justified in exterminating Pueblo religion—saved the most extreme measures for natives practicing their traditional beliefs. Father Salvador de Guerra, in 1655, had an "idolator" at Oraibi whipped, doused with turpentine, and burned to death. Even missing the daily Mass could bring a public flogging.

This unrelenting assault on native beliefs and practices was the single greatest cause of Popé's Revolt, also known as the Pueblo Revolt. The people believed that harmony within the community and with the environment was maintained through their relationships with a host of spirit figures called kachinas. They communicated with the kachinas at public dances and in ceremonies conducted in their circular churches, called kivas. It seemed no coincidence to the natives that when priests stopped these practices, things began to go wrong.

Severe droughts, famine, Apache raids, and epidemics of European diseases reduced a population of fifty thousand in Oñate's time to seventeen thousand by the 1670's. Three thousand were lost to measles in 1640 alone. At times between 1667 and 1672, people were reduced to boiling hides and leather cart straps for food. The abuse of women and sale of slaves to work the silver mines of Mexico made it seem that the moral as well as the physical universe was collapsing. Calls were made to return to the old ways.

In 1675, forty-seven Puebloans were arrested for practicing their religion. All were whipped, three were hanged, and one committed suicide. One deeply resentful survivor was a Tewa medicine man for San Juan Pueblo named Popé. Incensed by this oppression, he began planning retribution, but his task was formidable.

The Spanish label "Pueblo" obscured the fact that these people were not of one tribe, but members of a collection of autonomous villages that cherished their independence and rarely acted in unison. Although they shared many cultural features, three major language families were represented in the Rio Grande area alone: Zuñi, Keresan, and Tanoan. The latter had three distinct dialects of its own: Tiwa, Tewa, and Towa. Hopi villages of Uto-Aztecan speech lay farther west. Previous revolts had been localized affairs and were suppressed quickly.

In hiding at Taos Pueblo, fifty miles north of the Spanish capital at Santa Fe, Popé began building a multilingual coalition. He enlisted the great Picuris leader Luis Tupatú, a Tiwa speaker who was influential in the northern Rio Grande pueblos; Antonio Malacate, a Keresan spokesman from pueblos to the south; the Tewa war leader Francisco El Ollita of San Ildefonso; and

many others. His role becoming more messianic, Popé claimed inspiration from spirit contacts. Gradually, a plan emerged to expel the Spanish from Pueblo territory entirely.

The Revolt

The time came in August of 1680. Runners were sent out bearing knotted maguey cords, each knot representing one day. The uprising was to begin the day the last knot was untied. Governor Antonio de Otermín was told by informants that that day was August 13, but Popé had advanced it to August 10 and the Spanish were caught completely by surprise. Just nine miles north of Santa Fe, the citizens of Tesuque killed Padre Juan Pio early that morning as he came to gather them up for Mass, and upheaval soon swept the countryside as eighty years of frustration came to a boil.

Lieutenant Governor Don Alonso Garcia led soldiers on a sweep to the south of the capital and encountered such destruction that he organized the survivors for evacuation south. They left for El Paso del Norte (now Juarez) on August 14. The next day, Governor Otermín found himself besieged in Santa Fe by five hundred Puebloans who demanded that he free any slaves and leave the territory. He responded by attacking, but when the opposition increased to more than two thousand warriors and Otermín's water supply had been cut, he abandoned the capital. On August 21, Otermín led more than a thousand settlers south, meeting Garcia's group on September 13, and the whole bedraggled column reached El Paso on September 29.

Four hundred civilians and twenty-one of thirty-three priests had been killed. To undo their conversions, baptized Puebloans had their heads washed in yucca suds. A new kachina entered the pantheon of Pueblo spirit figures known among the Hopi as Yo-we, or "Priest-killer." In the years following the revolt, the coalition began to unravel, as drought, disease, and Apache raids continued to plague the tribes. Popé, who had become something of a tyrant himself, died in 1688. In 1692, Spain reconquered the area, and the new governor, Don Diego José de Vargas, entered Santa Fe on September 13.

Consequences

The Pueblo Revolt did much more than dispel the stereotype that Puebloans were unassertive and peaceful farmers who could not unify. It also was much more than a twelve-year respite from colonial oppression. It catalyzed transformations in Native American cultures in many directions. Large numbers of Spanish sheep came into the hands of the Navajo, forming the core of a new herding lifestyle. Weaving skills, possibly passed along by Puebloans fleeing Spanish reprisals, soon turned the wool into some of the world's finest textiles. Previously forbidden horses, now freed by the hundreds, became widely traded. Within a century, tribes such as the Nez Perce, Cayuse, and Palouse to the northwest, Plains Cree to the north, and Sioux, Cheyenne, and others to the east became mounted. With the mobility to access the great bison herds of the Plains, the economic complex that became the popular image of the Native American evolved.

The continued importance of the Pueblo Revolt to all Native Americans was demonstrated during the tricentennial of 1980. Cultural events celebrating the "First American Revolution" were held all across the United States. The revolt was seen as a symbol of independence and religious freedom. It was also recognized that some Puebloans who chose to settle with Otermín at El Paso in 1680 subsequently had lost most of their language, arts, and customs. After three centuries, the Puebloans see their ancestors' revolt as a key reason for their survival as a distinct people.   *Gary A. Olson*

Core Resources
Charles W. Hackett's *Revolt of the Pueblo Indians of New Mexico and Otermín's Attempted Reconquest, 1680-1682* (2 vols.; Albuquerque: University of New Mexico Press, 1942), translated by Charmion Shelby, is the definitive report on the subject. Pam Hait's "The Hopi Tricentennial: The Great Pueblo Revolt Revisited" (*Arizona Highways* 56, September, 1980) is a beautifully illustrated exploration of Hopi culture. Joseph Hill's "The Pueblo Revolt" (*New Mexico Magazine* 58, June, 1980) is an overview of the subject, with nine illustrations. James K. Page, Jr.'s "Rebellious Pueblos Outwitted Spain Three Centuries Ago" (*Smithsonian* 11, October, 1980) contains good observations on the revolt's modern significance. Robert Silverberg's *The Pueblo Revolt* (Lincoln: University of Nebraska Press, 1994) is based mainly on Hackett's earlier work.

See also: Indian-white relations: United States.

Positive ethnocentrism

For all humans, the very long and complex process of acquiring culture through socialization leads to the development of prejudices about other groups or cultures that are seen as different. Consequently, ethnocentrism is a general belief, and frequently a demonstrated practice, that one's group or culture is superior to that of others.

Ethnocentrism has both positive and negative functions. Positive ethnocentrism, as defined by sociologists Joe R. Feagin and Clairece Booher Feagin in the fifth edition of their textbook *Racial and Ethnic Relations* (1996), is "characterized by a loyalty to the values, beliefs,

and members of [one's] own group." Positive ethnocentrism permits individuals to derive personal benefit from belonging to what they perceive as a superior group or culture and may also provide individuals with a particular identity, which otherwise they would not have. Positive ethnocentrism may also integrate an otherwise indistinct group, providing members with a strong sense of belonging, a sort of consciousness of kind, one that may even justify their sociopolitical actions against other groups.

Of course the problem with positive ethnocentrism is that it may encourage and even become a rationale for attempting to change other groups by whatever means deemed necessary, even annihilation. Positive ethnocentrism does nothing to permit people to accept the ways of others whom they see as different.   *John Alan Ross*

See also: Cultural citizenship; Ethnocentrism; Stereotype.

Poverty and race

Significance: The poverty rate measures the fraction of families who do not have sufficient income and therefore lack a decent standard of living. When a large fraction of a particular racial or ethnic group finds itself in poverty, other people often place little value in that group.

When a large proportion of a particular racial, ethnic, or other minority group is poor, the group is generally looked down on by the majority of the population. This has negative consequences for race relations and for the entire society. This reaction perpetuates poverty and leads to feelings of resentment and hostility among the impoverished minority group. Aristotle, the ancient Greek philosopher, noted in his *Politics* that "poverty is the parent of revolution and crime." The 1968 Kerner Commission Report pointed to inner-city poverty amid general affluence as a major cause of urban violence and rioting in the United States during the late 1960's.

In the early 1960's, Mollie Orshansky of the Social Security Administration developed the methodology that is used to measure poverty in the United States. Using Department of Agriculture nutritional studies, Orshansky found the minimum food requirements for households of different sizes and types. She then estimated the cost of purchasing this food. From surveys, Orshansky knew that households spent around one-third of their income on food. To derive a poverty line for a family of a particular size, Orshansky multiplied the cost of that size household's minimum food requirements by three. Each year, poverty lines are raised to reflect the increase in prices during the prior year. The poverty rate is defined as the percentage of families or individuals who fall below the poverty line. Poverty rates have been calculated for different racial groups as well as the general population.

Estimates of Minority Poverty

According to U.S. Census Bureau estimates, African Americans and Hispanics are around three times more likely to be poor than non-Hispanic whites. In 1996, 11.2 percent of whites were poor, yet nearly 30 percent of African Americans and almost 30 percent of Hispanics were poor. This nearly three-to-one ratio has changed very little over time. In 1980, 10.2 percent of whites were poor, compared with 32.5 percent of blacks and 25.7 percent of Hispanics. In 1970, 9.9 percent of whites were poor, and 33.5 percent of blacks were poor; and in 1959, 18.1 percent of whites were poor, and 55.1 percent of blacks were poor.

This mother and her daughters sew a quilt in their home in Gee's Bend, Alabama, in 1937. A disproportionate number of African Americans and Latinos in the United States are poor.

Native Americans have experienced some of the highest poverty rates in the United States. In the late 1960's, Native Americans had poverty rates of around 74 percent. However, federal antipoverty programs directed at Native Americans cut this figure to around 25 percent by the late 1970's, about the same as for African Americans and Hispanics.

Causes of High Poverty Among Minorities

Many scholars have attempted to explain why minorities have such high poverty rates. Their answers have included prejudice and discrimination in the job market, cultural or behavioral traits, single-parent families and illegitimate children, urban ghettos, a lack of adequate education or business skills, and language barriers.

Prejudice and discrimination in the labor market is one prominent explanation. Because African Americans and members of other racial minorities cannot get good jobs, they are forced to accept low-wage, menial positions. Moreover, these jobs provide little opportunity for advancement and for workers to develop skills. Many of these jobs are unstable, which means the workers often lack a source of income for part of the year. Gunnar Myrdal's groundbreaking work *An American Dilemma: The Negro Problem and Modern Democracy* (1944) blamed high rates of African American poverty on a cumulative process in which prejudice and discrimination reinforced each other. Sociologist William J. Wilson updated Myrdal's cumulative analysis by arguing that discrimination also leads to feelings of inferiority and causes African Americans to adapt in dysfunctional ways.

A second explanation focuses primarily on cultural or behavioral traits. The cultural explanation for poverty was first set forth in Louis Wirth's *The Ghetto* (1929). Wirth considered the urban mode of life too difficult for people with rural backgrounds. Therefore, when rural southern African Americans migrated to the urban North, crime and alienation became more prevalent as employment diminished. A similar thesis appears in Nicholas Lehman's *The Promised Land* (1991).

A common view in the early twentieth century was that high rates of African American poverty were caused by the numerous single-parent families and large numbers of illegitimate children, which were usually blamed on African American racial characteristics. Edward Frazier's *The Negro Family in the United States* (1939) countered this view and argued that the overall status of the black family was shaped by prevailing economic and social conditions. Slavery destroyed African cultural patterns, and emancipation maintained the matriarchal system that developed under slavery. The migration of African Americans to the North further undermined communal institutions and community pressure that helped keep African American families intact.

More recent work has focused on the problem of African Americans living in urban ghettos. Wilson blames this problem partly on historical discrimination. However, the real blame, according to Wilson, lies with economics and demographics. When the U.S. economy shifted from manufacturing to services, it produced high unemployment rates in urban cities. This exacerbated the problems generated by the flow of African American migrants from the rural South and the rapid growth of young minorities in central cities. Sociologist John Kasarda, likewise, sees the decline of manufacturing and the rise of the service economy as causing the poverty of urban blacks. However, he notes another aspect to the problem: African Americans are less likely to move to areas experiencing job growth. In part, he says, this is caused by racial discrimination, which keeps African Americans from moving to the suburbs, and in part, it is because African Americans lack the skills and education required by the new service jobs.

Since the Coleman Report (1966) documented racial segregation in American schools and proclaimed that education in the United States was separate but unequal, differences in the quality of education have figured prominently in explanations of why racial minorities are more likely to be poor. If minority children receive a poor education, they are unlikely to leave school with the skills needed for high-paying jobs.

Another problem facing racial minorities is their lack of business experience and management skills. They also lack access to capital, making it hard for them to start their own businesses. Another problem is that businesses catering to racial minorities are less likely to be successful and make money when they cater primarily to low-income individuals.

Many Hispanics face additional problems involving language and culture. The inability to speak English well reduces some Hispanics' ability to get jobs and receive a decent education. Cultural differences make some Hispanics critical and distrustful of the values and interests of the dominant culture in the United States and suspicious of social institutions such as the government and schools. Their differences have led to discrimination against them in the job market. Native Americans, like Hispanics, have some cultural differences that may reduce their ability to obtain high-paying positions.

Policy Solutions

There are probably as many suggestions for reducing the racial disparity in poverty as there are theories of why minority racial groups are more likely to be poor. Many scholars have looked to desegregation in education as a means of improving the incomes of minorities and thereby reducing their high poverty rates.

Another approach has focused on labor market policies to increase the wages of minorities, to help minorities get better or higher-paying jobs, and to improve the job training that they receive both before and after employment. This approach has supported affirmative action as a means of combating discrimination in the labor market. It has also supported raising the minimum wage so that those with jobs are more likely to earn wages above the poverty line.

An American Dilemma

In *An American Dilemma* (Harper & Brothers, 1944), Gunnar Myrdal, winner of the Nobel Prize in Economics in 1974, describes the "American dilemma" as a moral conflict between American ideals of equality and fairness and the treatment accorded African Americans. Most of this classic work is devoted to an in-depth examination of the poverty facing African Americans in the early 1940's and how this condition has been brought about by how white Americans treat African Americans. Myrdal argues for the existence of a "vicious circle," or cumulative process, in which white prejudice and black economic conditions mutually cause and reinforce one another. Prejudice and discrimination keep blacks in an impoverished state, which in turn supports white prejudices. For example, discrimination in education means that African Americans are less likely than whites to become doctors. Discrimination in education means that African Americans are less knowledgeable about health. In addition, blacks make less money and therefore cannot spend as much on medical care. For all these reasons, blacks receive less adequate medical treatment and are in poorer health than whites. Consequently, blacks find it harder than whites to obtain and keep a job; with lower incomes, black education and health suffer further. The only practical solution, according to Myrdal, lies in broad-minded American institutions such as schools and churches propagating the American ideals of equality and fairness and bringing pressure to bear against racial prejudice. Myrdal proposed expanding the role of the federal government in the areas of education, housing, and income security. Laws making it easier for African Americans to vote were another way he suggested to break the cycle of discrimination and prejudice. Incorporating blacks into the labor movement would help both U.S. labor and African Americans. Finally, Myrdal advocated a full-employment policy so that blacks migrating to northern and western cities from the rural South could find jobs and become integrated into the postwar industrial economy.

A third approach has been to work on developing minority businesses and to teach minorities entrepreneurial skills. Another approach has focused on spurring economic growth, assuming that growth will lead to more jobs and higher incomes. Finally, beginning in the 1970's, a great deal of debate arose over government welfare programs and whether they can be made an effective antipoverty tool. Some experts argue that government benefits reduce work incentives and hurt the very people they are intended to help. Others argue that government benefits have always been inadequate to bring families above the poverty line. *Steven Pressman*

Core Resources

Mollie Orshansky's "Consumption, Work, and Poverty," in *Poverty as a Public Issue*, edited by Ben B. Seligman (New York: Free Press, 1965), explains how poverty is calculated in the United States. Poverty data can be found at the Census Bureau's Web site (www.census.gov). The Coleman Report, *Equality of Educational Opportunity* (Washington, D.C.: Government Printing Office, 1966), documents the separate and unequal education received by black and white children. Edward Frazier's *The Negro Family in the United States* (Chicago: University of Chicago Press, 1939) is a classic early study of African American poverty. *The New Urban Reality*, edited by Paul Peterson (Washington, D.C.: Brookings Institution, 1985), is one of the best contemporary studies of the causes of African American poverty and contains important articles by Kasarda and Wilson. *Inequality at Work: Hispanics in the U.S. Labor Force*, by Gregory DeFreitas (New York: Oxford University Press, 1991), provides a good description of the Hispanic poverty problem. *American Indians and Federal Aid*, by Alan Sorkin (Washington, D.C.: Brookings Institution, 1971), presents a great deal of information on Native American poverty, although some of it is a bit outdated. A more recent analysis is contained in Matthew Snipp and Gene Summers's "American Indians and Economic Poverty," in *Rural Poverty in America*, edited by Cynthia Duncan (New York: Auburn House, 1992). For additional information on antipoverty policies, see the collection *Fighting Poverty: What Works and What Doesn't*, edited by Sheldon Danziger and Daniel Weinberg (Cambridge, Mass.: Harvard University Press, 1986). The *Encyclopedia of Political Economy*, edited by Phil O'Hara et al. (New York: Routledge, 1998), contains several excellent introductory essays on race that are connected to the question of why certain groups of people are poor.

See also: Discrimination: racial and ethnic; Economics and race; Employment among African Americans; Employment among American Indians; Employment among Latinos; Employment in Canada; Prejudice: effects; Welfare reform: impact on racial/ethnic relations; Welfare's impact on racial/ethnic relations.

Power elite

Significance: In 1956, C. Wright Mills introduced the notion of the power elite—the interconnected leaders of political, economic, and military institutions in American society. This analysis offers insight into class and race relations in the contemporary United States.

The concept of a "power elite" in modern American society involves the idea that the leaders of a combination of economic, political, and military institutions together wield tremendous power and control over society. Each of the separate institutions within these areas of society possesses its own ruling class. Formal groups of Pentagon officials, including generals, admirals, and appointed officials, govern the military hierarchy. Likewise, boards of directors provide both leadership and control for the large corporations that dominate the economic sphere, along with institutions such as the securities markets, the Federal Reserve Board, the banking system, major pension funds, and other large sources of capital. Within politics, elected officials join with career bureaucrats and other appointees to direct the national government. Each of these institutions creates its own elite group of leaders, and each of these elite groups exercises considerable power and influence over a variety of affairs within American society.

The Power Elite Concept

Sociologists have identified a high degree of overlap among these distinct elite groups, and C. Wright Mills, in his influential book *The Power Elite* (1956), coined the term that has been widely used to describe them. The power elite concept points to several characteristics of the overlapping elite groups. The members of the power elite tend to share many life experiences, such as education and class notions of responsibility. Many of them know one another, even across institutional lines. For example, politicians and corporate executives not only create policies that affect one another's institutions but also socialize together, share loyalties to the same schools, join the same clubs, attend the same functions, and contribute to the same causes. Also, members of the power elite possess extensive personal resources in addition to their control over larger societal resources.

As the power elite in the United States has grown in influence, traditional institutions such as family, education, and religion have assumed lesser roles in determining values and orientations. In the case of education, advanced degrees do not confer or limit membership in the power elite. Even when certain affiliations arise between graduates of certain universities (especially Ivy League law schools), more importance may well be attached to membership in certain campus clubs reserved for elites than to factors such as academic performance and degrees earned. Likewise, regional concerns diminish in comparison with the national (and international) perspectives of the elites, who tend to be urban (or suburban) rather than rural in their perspectives.

The presence of a power elite correlates with the creation of celebrity. Some persons attain high celebrity and name recognition through their personal wealth, their corporate leadership, their political position, or their military prominence. Again, this celebrity is related not to any sort of objectively measured "success" but rather to power and influence. The corporate chief executive officer (CEO) who turns the highest profit ratios is not necessarily a member of the power elite, but the chairs of the largest corporations probably are. Similarly, politicians do not receive celebrity for high efficiency or great service, but instead for their ability to persuade and influence others with power. Celebrities become well known throughout the culture, both inside and outside their particular group of institutions. For example, many Americans do not know the names of their own senators or congressional representatives, but most could name several prominent politicians from other states who have attained the celebrity accorded those members of the power elite who seek it.

The American power elite forms an entrenched class of leaders. Though celebrity attaches itself to many of them, most work behind the scenes, attaining celebrity for only brief periods of time if at all. Examples include a corporate lawyer who wields extensive power over decades but gains fame only during a cabinet appointment late in life. Even though partly enshrouded, the power elite controls most sectors of social existence. The interlocking nature of the power elite allows for interchange between different sorts of institutions, maintaining and strengthening the power of each. This cooptation of elites from one field to another furthers the connections between different sectors of power.

In theory, the United States government contains a series of checks and balances. The typical understanding of government that emphasizes checks and balances between different branches of the federal government, however, fails to recognize the interlocking nature of political, economic, and military power throughout the society. The same economic entities that exert direct financial influence on the lives of many citizens not only participate in the military-industrial complex but also donate sizable funding to the political campaigns of congressional and presidential candidates. This reduces the effectiveness of any true balances within the political system itself. At the same time, the power elite fractures the nonpowerful classes into dispersed minority interests. This appearance of pluralism obscures the power of the elite, who often exercise their power subtly through the creation of a mythical "common interest" of the majority, against which the minority interests are doomed to fail. Such a common interest often does not reflect the wishes of any true majority but instead serves as an expression of the power of the dominant group. The mass media, controlled by the same interlocking forces of the power elite, play an increasingly significant role in the creation of such "majority" opinion. They become lenses that control public perceptions of reality and create public desires. This in turn creates "public opinion."

Context

Mills's development of the concept of the power elite followed earlier notions of power systems within American society and reacted against them. The nineteenth century political philosopher Alexis de Tocqueville provided an early statement on American power; he emphasized the affiliational elements and the possibility of social mobility. Despite the great degree of accuracy in his description of the postrevolutionary United States, Tocqueville's analysis grew seriously out of date as power became more entrenched in the hands of a few and as social mobility declined. During the early twentieth century, other notions of power became prevalent. Conservative theorists often devised conspiracy theories that rooted power in devious groups of hidden actors working for personal gain. Mills, however, argued that the United States is ruled by a class or group of power elites with interlocking but not synonymous goals. At the same time, liberal theories of power emphasized the importance of common people and thus the impotence of power groups to affect public opinion. Mills asserted the naïveté of such positions and demonstrated that these views obscured and justified the true nature of power in American society.

The notion of the power elite also drew on other social concepts. Against many eighteenth century social theories, the power elite model assumes the irrationality of social actors, seeing them as influenced more by power than by thought. This incorporates essentially Freudian ideas about human behavior into a larger model of social action and organization. Likewise, the power elite model assumes that ideas about reality are socially conditioned. Because members of the power elite occupy social positions of influence, they can affect people's assumptions about reality and thus enhance their own capacity for power.

Power elite models maintain a certain popularity within sociology, and they are evolving as studies continue. These models will need to give greater attention to the processes by which power elites reorganize themselves internally and to the related processes by which the power elite brings about (and reacts to) social change. The power elite joins disparate groups from different social institutions such as politics, the economy, and the military; not all elites are equals. Not all elites experience the same opportunities for upward mobility or horizontal mobility into other social institutions. Thus, the internal organization of the elites needs further study. At the same time, some power elite models tend toward static functionalism, overemphasizing the ability of elite groups to maintain their systems of privilege. This overstatement can limit understanding of how elites not only cause change but also must react to changes in the social situation.   *Jon L. Berquist*

Core Resources

Anthony Giddens's *The Constitution of Society: Outline of the Theory of Structuration* (Berkeley: University of California Press, 1984) connects power with the larger theory of structuration, which is the process by which social structures develop. Gerhard E. Lenski's *Power and Privilege: A Theory of Social Stratification* (New York: McGraw-Hill, 1966) argues that position and private property are the only two sources of power. *Power* (New York: New York University Press, 1986), edited by Steven Lukes, provides easy access to many of the key writings in contemporary discussion of power and thus offers a good introduction to the issues in the current evaluation of power elite models. Lukes's *Power: A Radical View* (London: Macmillan, 1974) provides an essential discussion of the connections between power and conflict, interpreting instances of power as disclosures of latent conflict. C. Wright Mills's *The Power Elite* (New York: Oxford University Press, 1956) is the most important study on the topic of the power elite; Mills provides a strong analysis of the different segments of elites within the power elite and gives excellent descriptions of the process of the power elite's historical development in American society. Kenneth Prewitt and Alan Stone's *The Ruling Elites: Elite Theory, Power, and American Democracy* (New York: Harper & Row, 1973) emphasizes political and ideological dimensions, perhaps to the detriment of economic issues. Alexis de Tocqueville's *Democracy in America*, translated by Henry Reeve (New York: Schocken Books, 1961), first published in 1835, provides the classic study of social structure, power relationships, and the high degree of social mobility in the postrevolutionary United States.

See also: Black middle class/black underclass relations; Caste model; Class theories of racial/ethnic relations; "Classless" society; Economics and race; Marxist models; Poverty and race; Structural assimilation.

Powwows

A powwow is a way for Native Americans to meet together to share traditions through dancing, singing, and visiting with old and new friends. The Ponca tribe of Oklahoma was the first to practice this ceremony, as early as 1804. The songs and dances are reminders to the Indian people of their old ways and rich heritage. Although dance styles and content have changed, their meaning and importance have not. The dances and colorful outfits worn by the dancers have evolved over time, indicating that the native American culture is not stagnant, but a vibrant, changing way of life. Powwows are held all across the North American continent, from small towns such as White Eagle, Oklahoma, to some of the largest cities, including Los Angeles. They can take place anywhere, from pastures to convention centers, and they occur all year-round.

Powwows serve as one of the main cultural activities of Native Americans, and they make the participants feel good physically, mentally, and spiritually. Many native American people are convinced that powwows promote Indian culture and tradition and help to dispel stereo-

Singers beat a drum as dancers circle around them at a powwow in Springfield, Missouri.

types. On the other hand, some native Americans and many people of other cultures and races believe that powwows are ceremonies from past history that act as a source of controversy to enhance typical stereotypes of Indians.

Alvin K. Benson

See also: American Indian dance and music; American Indian stereotypes.

Prejudice and discrimination: Merton's paradigm

> **Significance:** Merton's paradigm shows that prejudice does not always lead to discrimination and suggests that discrimination is not always directly caused by prejudice.

"Prejudice" and "discrimination" are crucial terms in the study of race and ethnic relations. In general discourse, they are often used as if they were interchangeable, but they actually denote distinct phenomena. Prejudice involves attitudes, thoughts, and beliefs about members of different groups (such as ethnic, racial, religious, or political groups). Discrimination, on the other hand, is action, either overt or subtle, that treats members of different groups differently.

Prejudice may be expressed in various ways, through negative terms, slurs, or jokes that denigrate members of ethnic or racial groups. Prejudice may also be expressed in discriminatory actions—hence the popular linkage between the terms.

Discrimination may take overt forms, as in an employer's refusal to hire an Italian American or African American because the employer thinks that all people of Italian or African descent are incompetent, basing this perception on stereotypes rather than on an objective appraisal of the applicant's qualifications. Discrimination also appears in the form of institutional discrimination or racism, which is a denial by society's institutions of opportunities and equal rights to individuals or groups; this type of discrimination may be unintentional. A crucial point, and one that was long unrealized, is that individual prejudice does not necessarily express itself in discrimination; moreover, discrimination may result from causes other than prejudice.

Merton's Paradigm

Sociologist Robert K. Merton proposed a typology or paradigm in 1949 regarding the relationship between prejudice and discrimination. Merton's work was influential in clarifying these distinctions and in expanding the definition of discrimination to include institutional and unintentional discrimination. This paradigm appeared in an article entitled "Discrimination and the American Creed." Merton attempted to show that, although prejudice and discrimination are related, one does not necessarily cause the other. Merton identified four categories of people according to how they rate on a scale of prejudicial attitudes and discriminatory behavior.

The "unprejudiced nondiscriminators," or "all-weather liberals," are low in both prejudice and discrimination. People in this category usually believe firmly in the equality of all people, and they try to practice this belief. Yet committed as they are to equality, they often do have some shortcomings, according to Merton. For one thing, the all-weather liberals tend to be removed from reality, in the sense that they do not experience face-to-face competition from members of minority groups for limited resources.

The second category consists of "unprejudiced discriminators," whom Merton also calls "fair-weather liberals." Fair-weather liberals are low in prejudice, but they tend to discriminate against other people when it is expedient, as when it is profitable to do so. In Merton's words, this person's expediency may take the form of holding his or her silence and thus implicitly acquiescing in expressions of ethnic prejudice by others or in the practice of discrimination by others. This is the expediency of the timid: the liberal who hesitates to speak up against discrimination for fear he or she might lose status or be otherwise punished by his or her prejudiced associates. In South Africa, for example, under the rigid racial caste system of apartheid that existed until 1994, many whites who themselves were not prejudiced remained silent about the injustices of apartheid, under which the white minority maintained privileges and absolute control over society. The fair-weather liberals did not condemn the system simply because they were benefiting from it.

The third category of Merton's paradigm involves people who do not believe in equality. These are "prejudiced nondiscriminators," whom Merton identified as "fair-weather illiberals" and called "timid bigots." They discriminate if there is no sanction against it; their discriminatory practices are situational. In the early 1930's, social scientist Richard LaPiere conducted a study in which he traveled in the United States with a Chinese couple to see how much discrimination they would encounter; prejudice against Asians was still quite strong at that time. LaPiere and his companions received warm treatment at nearly all motels, hotels, and restaurants they visited; only once were they refused service. Six months later, LaPiere sent a questionnaire to all the establishments, asking whether they would accept Chinese people as guests or customers. To his surprise, more than 90 percent of the responses revealed prejudiced attitudes and said that they would refuse service to them. This is a clear example of how prejudice does not necessarily translate into discrimination. A similar test was conducted in the 1950's with a black couple, and similar results were obtained. People seem to be able to adjust their actions and attitudes according to what sociologist W. I. Thomas called the "definition of the situation."

The final category in Merton's paradigm is the "prejudiced discriminators," also called "active bigots." These people are high in both prejudice and discrimination. They openly express their beliefs and do not hesitate to discriminate publicly. Sociologist Thomas F. Gossett presented a good example of such people, noting that in 1932 a Southern Baptist leader refused to sit at a banquet table at a meeting because a black person was present. Since court decisions and civil rights legislation in the 1950's and 1960's outlawed discrimination, active bigots in American society have found it more difficult to practice individual discrimination. Hate groups such as the Ku Klux Klan, for example, continue to espouse their prejudiced views, even on national television, but when evidence of discriminatory actions is uncovered, legal cases are filed against the perpetrators. According to the social distance scale, active bigots tend to show a high degree of intolerance for, and unwillingness to accept, members of out-groups such as racial and ethnic minorities.

Context

The assumption of many people before the 1940's that prejudice was the single cause of discrimination was challenged when Merton introduced his paradigm in 1949. Since the 1950's, both social scientists and civil rights activists have made marked progress in confronting discrimination. Instead of focusing only on prejudice as the cause of discrimination, many scholars and activists have broadened their perspectives. Prejudice and discrimination have been viewed in various lights and attacked in various ways. Activist Paula Rothenberg, in her work *Race, Class, and Gender in the United States: An Integrated Study* (1992), brings to light various facets of prejudice and discrimination. She also calls attention to the use and internalization of words that subtly perpetuate prejudice, such as "culturally deprived" and "underdeveloped," which tend to be misleading as well as reflective of the attitude that only the dominant culture is acceptable and others are inferior. Awareness of how language can perpetuate prejudice and discrimination is another way of confronting the problem of racism. A broad analysis of the ways prejudice and discrimination actually exist in society, as in the case of Merton's paradigm, shifts the focus from blatant and intentional expressions of racism to all forms of discrimination—some unintentional,

some incorporated into the institutions of society—in the day-to-day functioning of society.   *Rejoice D. Sithole*

Core Resources

Christopher Bates Doobs's *Racism: An American Cauldron* (New York: HarperCollins, 1993) explores how racism influences individuals' behaviors and attitudes without their being aware of it. Joe R. Feagin and Clairece Booher Feagin's *Racial and Ethnic Relations* (5th ed., Englewood Cliffs, N.J.: Prentice-Hall, 1996) discusses important basic concepts and theories as well as various social and ethnic groups. Thomas F. Gossett's *Race: The History of an Idea in America* (New York: Schocken Books, 1971) is rich in historical background on the American racist ideology and its influence in all social institutions. S. Dale McLemore's *Racial and Ethnic Relations in America* (3d ed., Boston: Allyn & Bacon, 1991) includes detailed discussion of minority groups and well-documented and footnoted summaries of research studies. Martin N. Marger's *Race and Ethnic Relations: American and Global Perspectives* (2d ed., Belmont, Calif.: Wadsworth, 1991) takes a broad and comparative approach. Paula S. Rothenberg's *Race, Class, and Gender in the United States: An Integrated Study* (2d ed., New York: St. Martin's Press, 1992) is one of the best integrated texts on racism, sexism, and classism.

See also: Discrimination: direct institutionalized; Discrimination: intentional vs. unintentional; Prejudice and stereotyping; Prejudice: effects; Prejudice: reduction.

Prejudice and stereotyping

Significance: Prejudice consists of negative attitudes toward certain groups and members of groups based on classifications such as gender, race, and religion. Stereotyping is rigidly believing that individuals have certain traits simply because they belong to a particular group. Discrimination, often fueled by prejudice and stereotypical thinking, is behavior that leads to the denial of basic rights and opportunities.

Prejudice, stereotyping, and discrimination are three closely related but distinct phenomena. Prejudice is literally a "prejudgment"—a belief about something or someone that is based on assumptions rather than on actual experiences. Strictly speaking, a prejudice may be either for or against something, but in common usage it refers to a dislike of all the members of a particular group, such as a racial, ethnic, religious, gender, or age group. Sociologist Gordon Allport defined prejudice as "an antipathy based upon a faulty and inflexible generalization." A crucial point is that a prejudice is an attitude, not a behavior.

A stereotype might simply be defined as one of the "inflexible generalizations" to which Allport referred. Stereotyping is the attributing of certain characteristics to people simply on the basis of their membership in a group. Stereotypes are oversimplified and rigid mental images; they may contain a "kernel of truth," but that kernel is overwhelmed by the false generalization that has grown around it. One of the interesting things about stereotypes is that people tend to continue to believe them even when they are presented with evidence that refutes them. People often discount their own observations, shrugging them off as "exceptions to the rule." Stereotypes therefore can be extremely persistent.

Prejudice and Discrimination

Discrimination, in contrast to prejudice, refers to behavior: the denial of basic rights and/or opportunities to members of certain groups based on such surface variables as race, age, gender, religion, or disability. An interesting finding of a number of studies of prejudice and discrimination—and one that surprised the researchers who first noted it—has been that prejudicial attitudes do not necessarily result in discriminatory behavior. Many people who state their dislike of a particular ethnic group, for example, in practice treat them with equality and civility. Moreover, discrimination can have causes other than prejudice; institutional discrimination may be unwittingly practiced by people working for institutions who are unaware that their policies and actions are discriminatory. Nevertheless, prejudice and the stereotyping that helps reinforce it can lead to discriminatory behavior as well as to the commission of hate crimes and other harmful, violent, and even fatal acts.

Prejudice and stereotyping have led to the sociological phenomena of exclusion and, in some cases, elimination of certain groups from "mainstream" society. In the United States, for example, a combination of prejudice and economic greed led to the near extinction of the American Indian population, the previous mainstream culture of the Americas, between the seventeenth and twentieth centuries. Other groups, such as women, African Americans, Hispanics, and Asians, have also felt the brunt of prejudice at various times in the history of the United States. The effects of prejudice are destructive both to the individuals who suffer violence or psychological harm as a result of discrimination and to the integrity of society as a whole.

This Thomas Nast cartoon depicts three minority groups—Chinese Americans, American Indians, and African Americans—who were the subject of stereotyping and prejudice.

Causes of Prejudice

A number of sociological theories have speculated about the causes of prejudice. Socialization—the process of teaching people (particularly as children) the knowledge and attitudes of a group or society—has been implicated as a cause of prejudice. Adults in society pass on their prejudicial beliefs to impressionable children. Thus, prejudicial attitudes are learned. Another theory on the cause of prejudice involves the principle of relative deprivation; relative deprivation is the gap between people's expectations and their actual condition or situation. When people see themselves as relatively deprived, they experience frustration and may look for scapegoats on which to blame their situation (a situation that is usually a result of a number of interrelated, complex causes). Historically, minority groups such as women or ethnic minorities have been "scapegoated," or blamed for someone else's economic or social misfortunes. A number of sociologists have also observed that competition increases prejudice, stereotyping, and discrimination. Muzafer Sherif, a sociologist, conducted studies showing how boys at a boys' camp could learn prejudice very quickly. The boys became biased and hostile when they were divided into groups and intergroup competition was introduced into their activities.

Social conformity is another concept that has been used to explain the cause of prejudice. Social norms—the expectations for behavior in a culture—define what kinds of behaviors or attitudes are acceptable. Thomas F. Pettigrew demonstrated this idea in the 1950's when he found that people from the South became less prejudiced toward African Americans when they were in the Army. The Army had norms that accepted blacks, so prejudice and discrimination were reduced in that social context. Robert A. Baron, a social psychologist, has written about theories that hypothesize conditions in which prejudice may occur. Baron (as well as many others) believes that periods of economic hardship and scarce resources can contribute to the occurrence and intensity of various types of prejudice. In the field of social psychology, this premise forms a part of what is known as "realistic conflict theory."

A growing body of research illustrates that class status has a profound effect on both influencing and buffering prejudicial beliefs and expectations. The interdisciplinary text *Race, Class, and Gender: An Anthology* (1992), by Margaret Andersen and Patricia H. Collins, contains a variety of articles that illustrate the intricate interplay of race, class, and gender in human experience. The text notes, for example, that racial and ethnic bias has been found to exist even among mental health professionals, a group of professionals who should be objective and neutral in their work.

There is no one single cause for the perpetuation of prejudice. Rather, sociologists believe that prejudice and stereotyping are socially determined and that multiple methods of transmission are involved.

Context

Social psychologist Gordon Allport's *The Nature of Prejudice* (1954) is considered a classic book on prejudice. It elaborates Allport's approach to prejudice, an approach consistent with contemporary perspectives because of the emphasis on cognitive factors such as categorization and cognitive bias. According to Allport, there are two forms of prejudice, personal prejudice and group prejudice. Allport's model involves in-group and out-group

distinctions. In 1979, Pettigrew proposed the "ultimate attribution error," an extension of Allport's theory. Pettigrew suggests that people tend to look favorably on the actions of people in their in-group (those whom they perceive to be like them) and attribute negative motives to the same actions by out-group members. If an in-group member observes an out-group member committing a negative act, the in-group member is likely to attribute the action to a concrete factor such as genetic makeup. If, on the other hand, an in-group member observes an out-group member doing something positive, he or she may attribute it to luck, the individual's being an exception to the rule, the particular situational context in which the behavior occurred, or a high level of individual motivation and effort.　　*Karen M. Wolford*

Core Resources

Gordon W. Allport's *The Nature of Prejudice* (Cambridge, Mass.: Addison-Wesley, 1954) is a classic social psychological book on prejudice, with an emphasis on cognitive factors such as categorization and normal cognitive bias. *Issues in Diversity: Voices of the Silenced* (Acton, Mass.: Copley, 1990), edited by Mary Stuck, presents a series of well-chosen articles that review historical and sociological phenomena related to the problem of oppressed groups in American society. Gail E. Thomas's *U.S. Race Relations in the 1980's and 1990's* (New York: Hemisphere, 1990) explores issues involving racial stratification and education, occupational mobility, economics, and cultural pluralism; special attention is paid to the neglect of the problems of the American Indian population.

See also: Discrimination; Prejudice and discrimination: Merton's paradigm; Prejudice: effects; Prejudice: reduction.

Prejudice: effects

> **Significance:** The effects of prejudice include discrimination, low self-esteem, demoralization, racial self-hatred, helplessness and lack of control, social ostracism, social avoidance, lack of opportunities, and political underrepresentation.

Prejudice can be defined as a global view or attitude about a group of people; prejudicial views are characterized by their inflexibility, and they are usually considered to be negative and directed toward minority or out-groups. The effects of prejudice in American society, and throughout the world, are generally considered devastating, not only to the individuals who suffer injustice, humiliation, and violence as a result of discrimination based on prejudice but also to the integrity of society as a whole. Groups such as the Ku Klux Klan and other white supremacy groups attempt to promote segregation, prejudice, and discrimination, at least partly as a way of promoting a dominant status for whites. Most people realize that this is both unconstitutional and unfair. Since people have no choice over the race, religion, or gender into which they are born, it is unjust to judge persons solely on the basis of biological givens such as skin color, hair color, facial structure, gender, or other such characteristics. Almost everyone has experienced some prejudice or discrimination and can understand its negative effects on self-esteem and self-image.

Types of Prejudice

A classic book on prejudice that came from the field of social psychology is Gordon Allport's *The Nature of Prejudice*, published in 1954. His approach to prejudice is still considered contemporary because of his emphasis on cognitive factors such as categorization and normal cognitive bias. There are two broad categories of prejudice, personal prejudice and group prejudice. Allport's model involves in-group and out-group distinctions. In an extension of Allport's theory, Thomas F. Pettigrew proposed the "ultimate attribution error" in an article he published in 1979. Pettigrew suggests that people tend to favor the actions of people in their in-group (those whom they perceive as being "like them") and attribute negative motives to the same actions by out-group members. If an in-group member observes a negative act by an out-group member, the in-group member is likely to attribute the action to genetics or some other concrete factor. On the other hand, if an in-group member observes a positive act by an out-group member, he or she may attribute the act to luck, an exception to the rule, high motivation and effort, or the particular situational context in which the behavior occurred.

Experimental Studies

A study published in 1947 by Kenneth Clark and Mamie Clark on color preference for dolls in preschool children showed that even very young children of color preferred the "white" dolls to those representing their respective race or skin color.

In the 1970's, Jane Elliott conducted an experiment with elementary school children in which she instructed the brown-eyed children to sit in the back of the room and told them they could not use the drinking fountain. Blue-eyed children were given special privileges such as extra recess time and extra lunch helpings. The two groups of children were told not to interact with each other. Elliott belittled and berated the brown-eyed children, and their academic performance faltered. The favored blue-eyed group belittled the brown-eyed children more than the teacher did. After several days, roles were reversed, and the negative effects of prejudice were repeated. Eventually all the children disliked one another, demonstrating the destructive effects of status inequalities based on something as superficial as eye color.

Conflict Theory

Donn Byrne, a social psychologist, has written about theories on the conditions under which prejudice may develop. Byrne and others believe that periods of economic hardship and scarce resources characterized by lack of availability of food and jobs can contribute to the occurrence and intensity of various types of prejudice. In the field of social psychology, this premise is part of what is known as "realistic conflict theory." Indeed, throughout history, in periods of resource scarcity and political unrest, the unfair effects of prejudice have flourished. From the mid-fifteenth and sixteenth centuries until the present, racial and religious prejudice leading to discrimination has resulted in violence against different ethnic and religious groups in what has been a worldwide phenomenon. From the United States to the various republics that, until 1992, made up the Soviet Union, and from Northern Ireland to South Africa, these problems have been significant. Efforts made by countries to achieve internal peace and stability have been difficult, at best, given climates of religious or ethnic intolerance and economic hardship.

Effects on Inter-Class Relations

Class status is one factor that has been found to have a profound effect on prejudicial beliefs and expectations. In the 1940's, an epidemiological study of psychopathology, or mental illness, called the Midtown Study was initiated in Manhattan in New York City, and results were published in the 1960's. A number of stereotypes about lower-class patients which suggested they were incapable of achieving insight into their problems, unable to ask for psychological help, and unable to examine their motives or moods were disputed by this research. In fact, the research showed that lower-class patients did want to achieve psychodynamic understanding and insight into their problems. The research also showed that the patients of lower socioeconomic status had less access to treatment facilities than their higher-class counterparts.

Racial and ethnic bias has been found to exist even among mental health professionals, a group of professionals who should, by definition, be objective and neutral in their work; however, very little research has been published in this area. Some investigators found no evidence of racial bias upon diagnoses assigned by clinicians who were of different racial backgrounds. Others found that white, middle-class psychiatrists who recorded fewer symptoms for black patients as compared with white patients nevertheless concentrated on the more unusual or bizarre symptoms of the blacks. This practice resulted in the psychopathology of the black patients appearing more severe than the psychopathology of the white patients. Researchers and clinicians have noted that white patients have been given the label neurotic and that black or Puerto Rican patients have been given the label schizophrenic for similar behaviors. Social psychologist Leonard Derogatis and others caution that race and social class designation are the most prominent indicators of psychological assessment and symptom presentation.

Effects on Disabled Persons

Prejudice that has become widespread takes forms that are sometimes referred to as "isms": racism, classism, sexism, ageism, heterosexism, able-bodiedism, and so on. The prejudicial attitudes held regarding people with disabilities, of which there were more than 36 million in the United States in 1986, have been found to be one of the most insidious forms of misunderstanding. In American society, those with emotional or learning disabilities (the invisible disabilities) often suffer the worst misunderstanding and discrimination caused by ignorance, perpetuation of myths, social ostracism, and avoidance of contact. It is known that people without disabilities have demonstrated lack of empathy, avoidance of social interaction, lack of eye contact, and lack of respect for disabled persons. Research has shown that even disabled persons hold negative attitudes toward other disabled persons if the others have a disability different from their own. In reality, those who are physically disabled have been found to have strong self-concepts and good social interaction skills and have often been more able to provide support to others than the other way around.

Effects on Women

During the medieval period, women were also victims of prejudice, including some who simply were homeless or had a "sharp tongue" as well as some who were probably mentally ill. All told, this period of religious persecution, led by religious male patriarchs of the time (mostly representatives of the church), resulted in hundreds of thousands, perhaps millions, of people being tortured and put to death. A key thesis underlying this massive prejudice and persecution was that the Roman Catholic Church opposed women's sexuality. Sexuality was seen to be insatiable in women, and lust was thought to be uncontrollable. This prejudice was so strong that everything from bad crops to miscarriages was blamed on certain women. These women were persecuted as witches, as seen in the Salem witchcraft trials in colonial America. Males were often thought to be immune to witchcraft or possession by the devil because Jesus was a man; men were therefore usually seen as protected from this evil influence.

Effects on Social Policy

The women's movement (originating in the 1900's), gay and lesbian liberation movement, patients' rights movement, and the Civil Rights movement have all mitigated the effects of prejudice. As these organized political groups have gained more support, each has been instrumental in consciousness-raising; reducing prejudice, social inequity, and social injustice; and increasing political, educational, and economic opportunity for their members. Affirmative action programs continue, although they have met with criticism that they go beyond the goal of correcting inequity in hiring practices. Some people believe that these policies have led to a social phenomenon referred to as reverse discrimination; however, others believe that certain groups, such as Latinos, African Americans, and Native Americans, have suffered long-term damaging effects from discrimination and therefore need the help of affirmative action programs. For example, Spanish-speaking children in the United States experience language-related difficulties that limit their educational and work opportunities. Bilingual education is one possible avenue to maximize these children's educational opportunities and future economic opportunities.

Social class and cultural distinctions also continue to bring opportunity to some people while eliminating opportunity for those of lower socioeconomic status. Many black children and other minorities have been locked into a cycle of poverty and hopelessness that impairs educational progress and motivation at a very early age. Although some progress had been made with the funding opportunities for offspring of low-income families (such as Head Start programs), designed to pave the way for success in higher education, many programs are cut in times of economic hardship, when people need them the most. This then perpetuates a cycle of poverty, with prejudice leading to economic hardship for affected groups. The term "feminization of poverty" has been used to describe the economic impact of low-wage, menial jobs on women in the United States, Puerto Rico, and other nations. Newspapers and television news frequently report acts inspired by prejudice, such as "hate crimes" against minorities. Violations of the civil rights of minorities still occur, leading to public outcries for examination and correction of the racial inequalities in American institutions and society.   *Karen M. Wolford*

Core Resources

Robert A. Baron and Donn Byrne's *Social Psychology: Understanding Human Interaction* (4th ed., Boston: Allyn & Bacon, 1989) contains an excellent chapter titled "Prejudice and Discrimination: The Costs of Hating Without Cause." Gordon W. Allport's *The Nature of Prejudice* (Reading, Mass.: Addison-Wesley, 1954) emphasizes cognitive factors such as categorization and normal cognitive bias, an approach that is still contemporary by today's standards. *America's Troubles: A Casebook on Social Conflict* (Englewood Cliffs, N.J.: Prentice-Hall, 1969), edited by Howard E. Freeman and Norman R. Kurtz, presents first-person essays that bring home to the reader the significant impact of bias on individuals, groups, and society.

See also: Discrimination; Prejudice and discrimination: Merton's paradigm; Prejudice and stereotyping; Prejudice: reduction.

Prejudice: reduction

> **Significance:** Several approaches to the reduction of prejudice have been studied over the years. Intergroup contact, the introduction of a common enemy, the crossing of social categories, and the presentation of information in the media are all strategies that have been considered in the effort to reduce prejudice. Evidence regarding the effectiveness of these strategies is mixed, and research has been directed toward examining the specific mechanisms underlying prejudice reduction.

Gordon Allport defined prejudice as an attitude toward the members of an out-group in which the evaluative tendencies are predominantly negative. It seems self-evident that the reduction and elimination of prejudice stands as one of the largest and most pressing real-world problems confronting psychology. Several different approaches to the reduction of prejudice have been examined.

Each of these approaches to prejudice reduction is derived from one or more of the suspected root causes of prejudice. Numerous explanations have been offered in attempts to account for prejudice. For example, some people believe that individuals develop negative attitudes toward other groups that are perceived as competing with their own group. Alternatively, it is possible that differences in familiarity with one's own group and other groups can lead to differential perceptions and evaluations of the two groups. Prejudice might also develop as people grow up and learn from others about the features of different groups, especially if the features depict negative characteristics for certain groups. Finally, social thinking might inherently involve categorization processes that often lead people to divide the world into "us" and "them." The different strategies

designed to reduce prejudice generally focus upon one of these concerns and try to reduce that specific concern in the hope of reducing prejudice.

The Contact Hypothesis
One of the most obvious and most heavily researched techniques for reducing prejudice is exemplified by what is called the "contact hypothesis": that association with persons from a disliked group will lead to a growth of liking and respect for that group. Scholarly considerations of this basic idea can be traced back at least to the 1940's; for example, it can be found in Robin Williams's 1947 book *The Reduction of Intergroup Tensions*. It is the seminal work of Allport, however, that is generally credited with being the classic formulation of the contact hypothesis. Allport, in 1954, developed a taxonomy of relevant factors necessary for contact to be successful in reducing prejudice. These factors emphasized the nature of the contact experience, and they included the frequency and duration of contact, the relative status of the two groups, and the social atmosphere of the contact experience. Some studies have demonstrated a reduction of prejudice toward the out-group, whereas other studies have shown that contact actually increases prejudice among members of the majority group along with causing a decrease in self-esteem and an increased sense of isolation among members of the minority group. Part of the difficulty may stem from the differences between intended contact and actual levels of contact. For example, Donald Taylor and his colleagues have argued that intergroup contact is often avoided. One study showed that black and white students in a desegregated school "resegregated" themselves into ethnic groups during classroom activities and recess. Thus, the general emphasis has shifted from "whether the contact hypothesis is valid" to "under what conditions, and in what domains, is the contact hypothesis valid."

A variant of the contact hypothesis in the context of desegregated schools is the cooperative team intervention. In this type of intervention, small groups of school children, including children of two ethnic groups, are assigned to complete a task in which they need to cooperate in order to succeed. Sometimes these small groups are later put into competition with other similar groups. Norman Miller and Gaye Davidson-Podgorny (1987) have shown that this type of cooperative team intervention is generally effective in reducing prejudice, at least in terms of attitudes toward out-group classmates.

Belief Congruence Intervention
An alternative approach is known as the belief congruence intervention. According to this strategy, prejudice and intergroup hostility are driven by the assumption that members of the out-group hold beliefs that are

different from those held by the in-group. Therefore, if it can be learned that members of the out-group are actually more similar to the in-group, then members of the out-group might be liked more and prejudice will be diminished. This approach is illustrated by Rachel Dubois's (1943) "neighborhood festival," in which members of different ethnic groups talk about nostalgic memories of childhood, holidays, and so on. The goal is for participants to recognize that group experiences, customs, and meanings are in fact remarkably alike and that different ethnic groups actually share membership in a broader commonality. Although this intervention sounds very appealing, its success rests upon a problematic assumption: The perceived differences between groups are illusory, and learning about intergroup similarities in beliefs will bring people to a more enlightened enjoyment of one another. If there are fundamental differences between the central beliefs of two groups (for example, as between Catholics and Protestants in Northern Ireland, or between Arabs and Jews in the Middle East), then the belief congruence approach is unlikely to be successful.

Finally, the role of the media in maintaining or reducing prejudice should be considered. Research has shown that ethnic minority groups are sometimes portrayed in negative ways in the news media and popular entertainment. While little research has examined the prejudice-reducing effects of the media, it is reasonable to speculate that more positive portrayals of ethnic minorities in the media might make a substantial contribution in the future to the reduction of prejudice. In line with this possibility, research by Fletcher Blanchard and his colleagues has found that exposure to the normative influence of other people expressing antiracist views can increase an individual's expression of antiracist views.

Studying Prejudice

Understanding prejudice and developing strategies to reduce it have long been major concerns of social psychologists. Techniques used for studying prejudice, however, have changed over the years. Earlier research relied heavily on observing the outward behavior of one group's members toward another group's members and analyzing people's responses on surveys. The development of computers and other sophisticated experimental techniques has enabled researchers to probe more deeply into the specific cognitive workings that may result in prejudice. This has helped illuminate a number of intriguing features about prejudice.

For example, Patricia Devine (1989) has shown that what distinguishes unprejudiced people from prejudiced people is not that unprejudiced people automatically respond in nonprejudiced, egalitarian ways. Rather, both prejudiced people and unprejudiced peo-

ple may engage in automatic, learned responses of negative evaluation toward stereotyped out-groups. The unprejudiced people, however, are able to engage controlled cognitive processes that thwart the expression of these undesirable prejudiced responses. Viewed in this way, Devine suggests, prejudices may be likened to bad habits, and the replacement of prejudiced responses with nonprejudiced responses can be likened to the breaking of such a habit.

The work by Devine illustrates a key ingredient in all the various efforts to reduce prejudice. The way people learn and process information about groups may inherently lead to differential perceptions and evaluations of these groups. Because of a need to simplify and organize information, these differential perceptions and evaluations may be incorporated into stereotypes, which may be negative for some groups. As discussed by Brian Mullen (1991), in order for a technique for reducing prejudice to be successful, it must take this cognitive processing of information about different groups into consideration.

There does not seem to be any magic solution to the problem of prejudice. It seems apparent, however, that people need to be aware at some level of the cognitive biases that can develop. Therefore, becoming consciously aware of the biases in thinking about certain groups may be an important first step in the effort to reduce prejudice.   *Craig Johnson and Brian Mullen*

Core Resources

Gordon W. Allport's *The Nature of Prejudice* (Reading, Mass.: Addison-Wesley, 1954) is the classic statement of prejudice and the contact hypothesis. *Contact and Conflict in Intergroup Encounters* (Oxford, England: Basil Blackwell, 1986), edited by Miles Hewstone and Rupert Brown, describes the results of specific contact experiences between particular groups in a wide variety of settings, including Northern Ireland, Israel, Germany, Quebec, and South Africa. James M. Jones's *Prejudice and Racism* (Reading, Mass.: Addison-Wesley, 1972) provides an insightful discussion into the effectiveness and ineffectiveness of various strategies for addressing the problems of prejudice and racism. *Groups in Contact: The Psychology of Desegregation* (Orlando, Fla.: Academic Press, 1984), edited by Norman Miller and Marilynn Brewer, considers theory and research on the effects of desegregation, particularly in schools in the United States. Brian Mullen's "Group Composition, Salience, and Cognitive Representations: The Phenomenology of Being in a Group," in *Journal of Experimental Social Psychology* (27, no. 4, 1991) discusses a model of the cognitive mechanisms that drive stereotyping and prejudice.

Donald M. Taylor and Fathali M. Moghaddam's *Theories of Intergroup Relations: International Social Psychological*

Perspectives (2d ed., Westport, Conn.: Praeger, 1994) examines intergroup relations in various settings. Cooperative team intervention is the subject of Norman Miller and Gaye Davidson-Podgorny's "Theoretical Models of Intergroup Relations and the Use of Cooperative Teams as an Intervention for Desegregated Settings," in *Group Processes and Intergroup Relations*, edited by C. Hendrick (Newbury Park, Calif.: Sage, 1987). Rachel Davis DuBois's *Get Together Americans: Friendly Approaches to Racial and Cultural Conflicts Through the Neighborhood-Home Festival* (New York: Harper & Brothers, 1943) outlines an approach to reducing prejudice. Patricia G. Devine's "Stereotypes and Prejudice: Their Automatic and Controlled Components." (*Journal of Personality and Social Psychology* 56, no. 1, January, 1989) examines how prejudiced and nonprejudiced people differ.

See also: Contact hypothesis; Discrimination; Prejudice and discrimination: Merton's paradigm; Prejudice and stereotyping; Prejudice: effects.

President's Committee on Civil Rights

Like many white people of his time, U.S. president Harry S Truman inherited the racial attitudes of his southern ancestors. He attended segregated schools in Missouri and regarded segregation as normal and desirable. He used what people today consider offensive racial language and once claimed that blacks belonged in Africa, not America. Yet when he became president in 1945, Truman rose above his racist heritage and responded to African American demands. As a successful politician, he had learned to work with African American political groups and to understand the necessity of serving all his constituents. He disliked social mixing among people of different races, but he believed that African American people had the right to equality under the law and deserved equal opportunity.

At the end of World War II, racial tension rose as African Americans tried to cement economic and social gains they had made during the war. Racial violence increased. For example, in February, 1946, a South Carolina policeman blinded an African American veteran still in uniform, and in July, two more veterans were killed in Monroe, Georgia. In addition to domestic racial problems, the Cold War was beginning to destroy the wartime alliance between the United States and the Soviet Union. The two superpowers began to divide the world between them and to compete for the allegiance of Asian and African peoples. Truman, recognizing the negative image presented by American segregation, said,

"The top dog in a world which is 90 percent colored ought to clean his own house."

On December 5, 1946, Truman issued Executive Order 9008 to create the President's Committee on Civil Rights and filled the fifteen-member committee with prominent Americans who were sympathetic to civil rights. It was a high-profile committee that included important businessmen, educators, labor leaders, and members of the African American community. On October 29, 1947, in a document entitled *To Secure These Rights*, the committee recommended establishment of a civil rights division in the Department of Justice, a commission on civil rights, and a fair employment practices committee. It urged Congress to strengthen existing civil rights statutes, pass an antilynching law, and provide new protection for voting rights. To move toward desegregation, the committee said, the government must discontinue federal funding to private and public bodies that practiced discrimination, prohibit discrimination in private employment and in health services, and seek court action to end restrictive covenants in housing.

These recommendations established the civil rights platform for Truman and his successors. In 1948, Truman issued Executive Order 9980 to forbid discrimination in federal government employment and Executive Order 9981 to integrate the armed forces. Under Truman's direction, the Justice Department entered *amici curiae* briefs in court cases to back the National Association for the Advancement of Colored People (NAACP) and others in their assaults on the legal edifice that supported segregation. It took many years before the vision expressed in *To Secure These Rights* started to become reality, but the report moved civil rights to the forefront of the national reform agenda. *William E. Pemberton*

See also: Desegregation: defense; Discrimination: racial and ethnic; Military desegregation; Race riots of 1943.

Proclamation of 1763

The Proclamation of 1763, issued by the British crown, attempted to draw a line between American Indian lands and the American colonists; ultimately it added to the discontent the colonists felt toward English rule.

British officials hoped that this decree would end the problems associated with colonial western expansion, a problem exacerbated when Britain drove France from the interior of North America at the conclusion of the American phase of the Seven Years' War. With the Proclamation of 1763, officials hoped to resolve Anglo-Indian misunderstandings dating back more than a decade.

John Pownall was the primary author of the Proclamation of 1763. At the time, Pownall was undersecretary to the Board of Trade. In drafting his proposal, he relied on a series of letters he had received from his brother, Thomas. Thomas Pownall had originally gone to New York as secretary to Sir Charles Hardy. When Hardy died later that year, Pownall found himself without a job. He became the "eyes and ears" of the Duke of Halifax, a newly arrived British commander. In this unofficial capacity, he attended the Albany Congress of 1754 and met the major figures in Anglo-Indian affairs: William Shirley, William Johnson, John Lydius, and George Croghan.

As an edict, the proclamation attempted to do three things. First, it forbade colonial governments from surveying and issuing patents for lands lying beyond the headwaters of any river feeding the Atlantic Ocean. Imperial officials hoped that the proclamation would end the colonists' constant attempts to gain western lands. Officials wanted to slow the pace of western expansion because they thought western settlers were the most difficult colonists to control. Indeed, royal officials blamed these frontiersmen for the outbreak of Pontiac's Rebellion. Second, the decree prevented private individuals from purchasing Indian lands. Third, the proclamation organized four new British colonies: the island of Grenada, Quebec, East Florida, and West Florida. By outlining these three areas, imperial officials formally defined the "Indian country" for the first time.

Once the proclamation was implemented, the Crown expected the British military and Indian superintendents to enforce the measure. Even though both military and Indian department officials supported the plan, the proclamation was much easier to write than to implement. The difficulty with implementation concerned what colonial governments and land companies such as the Ohio Company of Virginia had already done. Virginia had already promised this western land to veterans of the Seven Years' War, and the Ohio Company patent lay in the region now closed to settlement. The Proclamation of 1763 shows clearly how colonial objectives and imperial policy were in conflict.

The proclamation also contained a clause that undermined the hopes of imperial officials from the beginning. When issued, the proclamation included an exception to the acquisition of western lands. Retiring military personnel could secure between 50 and 5,000 acres, depending upon their rank. This exception fueled colonial discontent with the edict. Equally important, any Indian group could still sell land to speculators in the future. In 1763, no one viewed this flaw as fatal because London officials considered the Proclamation of 1763 a temporary expedient. This temporary line would allow Indian agents to negotiate a more lasting settlement. Other events and issues undermined the hopes of officials in drawing this boundary, however, so the promise implied in the Proclamation of 1763 was never realized.

See also: Indian-white relations: Canada; Indian-white relations: United States.

Progressive inclusion theory of assimilation

The progressive inclusion theory of assimilation is a theory of the way minority groups interact with, and become part of, a dominant society. This process is called assimilation and involves the incorporation of different ethnic groups into the fabric of the larger society. One version of assimilation, known popularly as the melting pot theory, entails the loss of an individual's ethnic identity in the process of assuming the identity of a member of the dominant society. In this case, the idea of a "hyphenated person" (such as an African-American) is impossible, because assimilation and pluralism (the notion that ethnic, racial, and cultural diversity can continue to exist in an ideal society) are seen as mutually exclusive.

An alternative view of assimilation has been articulated by sociologists Milton Gordon and Talcott Parsons, who believe that the progressive inclusion of ethnic and racial minorities can occur—that, over time, members of these groups can attain full rights of citizenship not only legally but in fact and daily experience as well—while simultaneously vestiges of ethnic identity can persist over time. In other words, these sociologists contend, assimilation and pluralism are not necessarily antithetical. Gordon, for example, contends that cultural assimilation can occur without structural assimilation, which means that while ethnics adopt the values and behavioral patterns of the dominant society, they do not necessarily abandon their own ethnic institutions and neighborhoods. For Parsons, the pluralistic character of modern societies is not a problem for assimilation. Citizenship becomes the key criterion for national solidarity, and thus ethnic differences can be accommodated by this larger, more encompassing sense of collective identity. Parsons viewed this as an evolutionary process characteristic of modern societies in general.   *Peter Kivisto*

See also: Assimilation: cultural and structural; Assimilation theories; Cultural pluralism; Melting pot theory; Pluralism vs. particularism; Structural assimilation.

Proposition 187

Proposition 187 was developed in the early 1990's as California and the United States were experiencing major economic changes and social problems. Worries

Opponents to Proposition 187 hold a mock funeral for the initiative and California governor Pete Wilson during a November, 1994, rally in Los Angeles.

about increased taxation and unemployment were added to concerns that violence, illegitimate births, and welfare dependency were increasing. Some members of conservative organizations raised fears that the new wave of immigrants would not easily assimilate into the dominant culture.

In 1994, Dan Lungren, running for attorney general, Michael Huffington, who later lost to Senator Dianne Feinstein, and Governor Pete Wilson, running for reelection, all offered an answer to voters as to why California's citizens were insecure: Too much tax money was being spent on illegal immigrants. Proposition 187, a proposed law, would make illegal immigrants ineligible for publicly financed social services, education, and nonemergency health care. Proponents of this initiative argued that, by making false documentation a felony, it would prevent illegal immigrants from coming to the United States to take jobs from U.S. citizens. Furthermore, the threat of arrest would prevent pregnant foreign women from crossing the border, illegally, to give birth in the United States.

This call to limit immigration was also reflected in the platforms of many Republicans across the country who soon would take control of the U.S. House and Senate. A disproportionately large white voter turnout in California on election day, November 8, 1994, may have contributed to the 59 percent of voters who approved of this initiative; its preamble declared that Californians were suffering "economic hardship caused by the presence of illegal aliens" and from their criminal activity.

Lawyers were successful in getting an immediate hold placed on most provisions of Proposition 187 until federal courts could examine its merits. Not blocked, however, were the provisions making it a felony to manufacture or use false documents.

On November 20, 1995, federal judge Mariana Pfaelzer ruled against major portions of Proposition 187. She argued that federal laws regarding immigration cannot be overridden by state laws and that it would be illegal to ask people who sought to attend public schools or to receive health and welfare services about their immigration status; she did not extend her argument to include higher education benefits. Judge Pfaelzer's decision permitted the state to deny benefits to illegal immigrants only in those programs that are fully funded by the state; that is, where no federal funds are involved. Although Proposition 187 was essentially gutted by Judge Pfaelzer's ruling, the decision faced further appeals.

One argument against Proposition 187 is that because U.S. employers want low-wage workers who will tolerate poor working conditions—such as migrant farmworkers or textile factory workers—employers will continue to entice Mexicans to come to the United States to find work. Therefore, it would be wrong to deny immigrants and their families the basic health, educational, and social services that they need. Others have pointed out that if immigrants are denied these basic services, the larger society will inevitably experience a host of related economic and social problems.

Another argument made against Proposition 187 is that immigrant laborers from Mexico and elsewhere make significant contributions to the U.S. economy, other than through the work they do for their employers, including the Social Security and other taxes that they pay.

Grace Maria Marvin

See also: Illegal aliens; Latino stereotypes; Politics of hate; Undocumented migrant/worker; Welfare reform: impact on racial/ethnic relations; Welfare stereotypes.

Proposition 209

Proposition 209, the California Civil Rights Initiative (CCRI), was a measure to amend the California state constitution that appeared before California voters on the November, 1996, election ballot. Proposition 209 proposed that the state should "not discriminate against, or grant preferential treatment to, any individual or group on the basis of race, sex, color, ethnicity, or national origin in the operation of public employment, public education, or public contracting." This proposal did not affect preferential treatment practices of private firms or private educational institutions in the state.

In the weeks leading up to the election, a heated public debate developed over the CCRI. Ward Connerly, a black businessman from Sacramento who led the campaign for the CCRI, and other supporters claimed that the measure's intent in prohibiting discrimination and preferential treatment was in accord with the desires of those involved in the Civil Rights movement of the 1960's to create a society in which everyone, regardless of gender or skin color, would be guaranteed equal treatment under the law. The opposition to Proposition 209 included a wide variety of organizations, such as the state chapters of the National Association for the Advancement of Colored People and the American Civil Liberties Union (ACLU). Opponents argued that the CCRI was a deceptive measure whose true intent was not revealed by its language. As they saw it, although Proposition 209 did not explicitly mention the words "affirmative action," the purpose of the proposition was not to end discrimination or preferential treatment but rather to end state-supported affirmative action programs in California. This, they argued, would actually lead to increased, rather than decreased, discrimination against women and African American, Latino, and other California minorities, and cause setbacks in the educational and employment gains achieved by these groups as a result of affirmative action programs.

On election day, Proposition 209 passed by a vote of 54 percent to 46 percent. It was immediately challenged in the California courts, and an injunction was issued against its enforcement. Those who challenged the CCRI argued that it violated the equal protection clause of the Fourteenth Amendment by denying some groups, namely women and racial minorities, preferential treatment but not denying it to other groups, such as military veterans. In April, 1997, the U.S. Court of Appeals affirmed the constitutionality of the CCRI, and the injunction against the CCRI was lifted in August, 1997. In a "Save the Dream" march led by the Reverend Jesse Jackson, thousands rallied in the streets of San Francisco to protest the lifting of the injunction. Although the ACLU attempted to take the appellate court decision to the Supreme Court, toward the end of 1997, the Court declined to review the measure. Pete Wilson, the governor of California and a supporter of Proposition 209, took a major step toward implementing it in March, 1998, by officially ending the enforcement of preferen-

tial treatment for firms owned by women or minorities engaged in state contracting.

By mid-1998, the full impact of Proposition 209 had yet to be determined. At the University of California, Berkeley, for example, the number of African American and Latino students accepted for admission in the entering class of spring, 1998, declined by more than 50 percent, while the proportion of white and Asian American students accepted for admission rose. These changes followed decreases in the preceding year in African American and Latino admissions to the University of California law and business schools. To what extent these declines in minority enrollments were the direct result of the passage of Proposition 209 and to what extent they were brought about by the implementation of a 1995 decision by the University of California Board of Regents to discontinue gender and racial preferences in admissions is difficult to determine.   *Diane P. Michelfelder*

See also: Affirmative action; College admissions.

In 1996, Jesse Jackson speaks out against Proposition 209, which was designed to end affirmative action in California.

Proslavery argument

> **Significance:** The proslavery argument served as an intellectual bond among Southerners who saw slavery as a moral institution.

In the quarter-century preceding the Civil War, Southerners advanced a wide range of arguments and theories—some old, some new—to justify the institution of chattel slavery. The distinctiveness of proslavery thinking during the years before the Civil War lay less in its content than in its tone or spirit. Defenders of the South's "peculiar institution" were no longer on the defensive; their mood was no longer apologetic. Unlike most of their predecessors, they did not merely tolerate slavery; they defined it as a moral institution and many glorified it. They took the offensive on behalf of slavery partly in response to the attacks of Northern abolitionists. Perhaps the primary objective of their aggressive proslavery campaign was to dispel the doubts of Southerners as to the justice of slavery and to offer compelling proof to nonslaveholders and slaveholders alike that slavery found sanction in religion, science, and morality, forming an essential part of a civilized economic and political order.

Post-1830 proslavery discourse borrowed from a variety of sources, many of which had been used before immediate abolitionism posed a new threat to slavery. Proslavery apologists pointed to the existence of slavery in biblical times and throughout most of history, as well as to the notion of entailment, which blamed the introduction of slavery on the British and predicted social catastrophe should slavery be abolished. These arguments continued to dominate the thinking of most proslavery writers in the 1830's, as evidenced, for example, in Thomas R. Dew's *Review of the Debate in the Virginia Legislature of 1831 and 1832.* Although this was once treated as the first work of the new proslavery discourse, later historians have seen it as the culmination of the earlier, less affirmative phase of proslavery writing in the South. Dew's work, which was widely read, asserted that slavery was a preferred way of compelling efficient labor in the hot states of the lower South, the harbinger of the notions of perpetual slavery developed by later Southern apologists.

The Response to Garrison

Traditionally, historians have understood post-1830 proslavery as a reaction to the publication of William Lloyd Garrison's journal *The Liberator* (1831-1865), which marks the onset of immediate abolitionism, and the fear spawned by Nat Turner's slave rebellion in Southampton County, Virginia. Both events occurred in 1831, but other issues intensified proslavery writing and abolitionist discourse during the 1830's.

Proslavery polemics seem to have escalated along a continuum, rather than suddenly appearing after 1831. Two interrelated themes characterized this escalation of Southern proslavery. The first was a reaction to the abolitionist mail campaign of 1835, in which Northern abolitionists attempted to flood the South with literature arguing that slavery was immoral. In response, Southern ministers and denominations took the lead in denouncing the moral foundations of abolitionists. Virulent anti-abolitionism became a major feature, perhaps the single constant, in Southern proslavery. Southerners denounced abolitionism as incendiary, a wanton and dangerous interference with Southern safety. Southerners construed abolitionists as intent upon fomenting rebellion among Southern slaves, and were also infuriated by the "Gag Rule" in Congress, which persuaded Northerners that Southerners would trample on the First Amendment or any other right to preserve slavery.

The second theme involved a defense of slavery more ideological in tone, which blended biblical literalism with conservative social theories, some of which were quite popular among New England Federalists during the early nineteenth century. This strain of thinking challenged industrial economics and modern reform

The drawing depicts a lively debate over slavery in the U.S. Congress. In the pre-Civil War years, Southerners launched an aggressive defense of the institution of slavery.

movements, asserting that a stratified social order produced the best society possible. A heavy lace of paternal imagery, which threaded together honor and social responsibility, gave ornamentation to this new proslavery fabric. In the hands of John C. Calhoun, this two-pronged argument proved that slavery was not an evil, as the abolitionists claimed, but "a good—a positive good," "a great blessing to both races," and "the great stay of the Union and our free institutions, and one of the main sources of the unbounded prosperity of the whole."

Typical of thinkers who championed this phase of proslavery writing was Thornton Stringfellow, a Baptist minister of Culpepper County, Virginia, whose *Brief Examination of Scripture Testimony on the Institution of Slavery* argued that slavery enjoyed "the sanction of the Almighty in the Patriarchal Age . . . that its legality was recognized . . . by Jesus Christ in his kingdom; and that it is full of mercy." Godly Southerners, Stringfellow maintained, should withdraw from abolitionists, whose moral notions must originate from some other source than the Bible. In a speech before the U.S. Senate in 1858, James Henry Hammond of South Carolina held that African American slaves provided the "mud-sill" of society, whose labor was necessary but whose mean estate made essential their exclusion from the political process. Slavery was essential to free "that other class which leads progress, civilization and refinement" for more enlightened endeavors. Fortunately, the senator observed, the South had found African Americans perfectly adapted to serve as the "very mud-sill of society and of political government," "a race inferior to her own, but eminently qualified in temper, in vigor, in docility, in capacity to stand the climate, to answer all her purposes."

The Prewar Era

During the 1850's, other Southern writers embraced more extreme proslavery theories, although these attracted more interest from historians in the twentieth century than from nineteenth century advocates. Henry Hughes, of Port Gibson, Mississippi, drew upon the infant discipline of sociology to buttress his proslavery views. He described slavery as "Ethical Warranteeism," in which the slave labored for a master in return for food, clothing, and shelter. Josiah Nott, of Mobile, Alabama, embraced the theory of polygenesis, holding in *Types of Mankind* that African Americans resulted from a separate creation and were not *Homo sapiens*. Others compared Southern slavery with free labor in the North. In *Sociology of the South* (1854) and *Cannibals All!* (1857), for example, Virginian George Fitzhugh suggested that the Northern states would have to adopt some form of slavery to control the immigrant working classes, or else face moral and social chaos. Free labor, he asserted, produced class warfare in the North, while slavery permitted social harmony in the South. Southern masters had moral obligations toward, and were predisposed to kind treatment of, their slaves; Northern factory owners discarded their laborers at whim.

Most Southerners adhered to the less extreme argument based on the Bible and Plato. The proslavery argument became a justification for the entire Southern way of life, whose culture, social structure, and economy were believed to depend upon the institution of slavery. Its ubiquity helped bind Southerners together and produced the remarkable degree of unity among them in the days following the election of Abraham Lincoln in 1860 and his call for troops in April, 1861. Undoubtedly, the intensity and unanimity with which Southerners defended slavery had much to do with the fact that they had come to identify the system of slavery with Southern society as a whole and with their place in the Union.

Anne C. Loveland, updated by Edward R. Crowther

Core Resources

William S. Jenkins's *Pro-Slavery Thought in the Old South* (Chapel Hill: University of North Carolina Press, 1935), the oldest monograph on proslavery thinking, remains a useful starting point. Drew Gilpin Faust's *The Ideology of Slavery: Proslavery Thought in the Antebellum South, 1830-1860* (Baton Rouge: Louisiana State University Press, 1981) is an excellent anthology of proslavery writing augmented by a thoughtful introductory essay. William W. Freehling's *The Road to Disunion: Secessionists at Bay, 1776-1854* (New York: Oxford University Press, 1990) shows the complex uses Southerners made of proslavery thinking and why a degree of intellectual unity was vital in a South divided against itself. Larry E. Tise's *Proslavery: A History of the Defense of Slavery in America, 1701-1840* (Athens: University of Georgia Press, 1987) shows that proslavery thinking existed in both Northern and Southern states.

See also: Abolition; Bleeding Kansas; Civil War; Compromise of 1850; Fugitive slave laws; Kansas-Nebraska Act; *Liberator, The;* Lincoln-Douglas debates; Missouri Compromise; *Scott v. Sandford;* Turner's slave insurrection.

Psychological theories of intergroup relations

Significance: Theories of intergroup relations examine the processes that underlie relationships between individuals belonging to different groups; these theories provide insights into conflict, ethnocentrism, self-esteem, and leadership.

The major psychological theories of intergroup relations include Freudian theory, equity theory, relative deprivation theory, social identity theory, realistic conflict theory, and the "five-stage model" of intergroup relations. The three theories listed first are the most "reductionist" in that they attempt to reduce intergroup relations to the level of intra-and interpersonal processes. In contrast, social identity theory, realistic conflict theory, and the five-stage model provide explanations at the level of intergroup processes.

Freud's Influence

Although Sigmund Freud did not develop a formal theory of intergroup relations, his writings on hostility and aggression have had a historic influence on most of the major intergroup theories. Freud presented an irrationalist account of group processes, arguing that conflict arises out of the irrational feelings and emotional needs of in-group members, rather than as a result of differences between the material interests of groups.

Freud proposed that feelings of both love and aversion are involved in emotional ties between individuals. Group members are bound together by the ties of love that link them all with the group leader. The corresponding feelings of hate do not disappear, but are displaced onto out-groups. Freud believed that it is possible for ties of love to bind a number of people together as long as there are some other people left over onto whom hatred can be displaced. The most likely targets for such displaced aggression would be out-groups that are dissimilar.

Thus, for Freud, the key to understanding relations between groups lies in the nature of relations within groups, particularly relations between group members and the leader. Freud believed that the only groups worth considering are groups with leaders, because without leadership the group cannot be cohesive and effective in action.

Equity Theory

Equity theory is also reductionist in its account of intergroup relations, but, in contrast to the Freudian model, equity theory presents a picture of humans as rational beings. The main focus of equity theory is relations between individuals, but it also has implications for intergroup relations. The starting premise is that individuals strive to maximize rewards for themselves, but this "selfishness" is pursued within the norms of justice prevalent in society.

Individuals are assumed to feel distressed when they do not achieve justice in their relationships. Justice is achieved when the ratio of a person's inputs and outcomes is equal to that of the other person in the relationship. When this ratio is not equal, justice can be restored by adjusting the inputs and outcomes, either psychologically or in practice, to arrive at equity.

What makes equity theory a psychological theory rather than simply a model of economic exchange is that it is *perceived* justice that is assumed to determine relations between group members. For example, the relations between a minority group and a majority group may in actual practice by very unequal, but the ratio of inputs and outcomes for the two groups may be seen to be equitable by both groups; this perceived equality is what determines behavior.

Relative Deprivation Theory

Similar in its emphasis on purely psychological determinants of relations between groups is relative deprivation theory. This theory focuses on the conditions associated with feelings of discontent among disadvantaged individuals and, by implication, groups. Feelings of satisfaction are not assumed to be primarily determined by objective conditions, but rather by one's perceptions of one's own situation relative to that of others. Theorists disagree about the exact conditions required in order for relative deprivation to be experienced; however, two generally accepted preconditions for feelings of discontent are that individuals must, first, feel they deserve to attain a better situation and, second, believe it possible to do so.

Social Identity Theory

A major European theory, and one that has inspired much research since the 1970's, is social identity theory. This theory focuses on groups with unequal power and predicts the conditions in which people will feel motivated, individually or collectively, to maintain or change their group membership or the relations between their in-group and the out-groups. Social identity theory assumes that individuals are motivated to achieve and maintain a positive and distinct social identity. Specifically, this means that individuals will want to be members of groups that enjoy high status and are distinct in some important ways.

Social comparisons between the in-group and out-groups allow individuals to determine the extent to which the in-group provides them with a satisfactory social identity. In conditions in which the social identity of individuals is unsatisfactory and "cognitive" alternatives to the present intergroup situation are perceived, individual or collective forms of action will be taken toward achieving a satisfactory social identity. These actions range from redefining an in-group characteristic, as suggested by the slogan "black is beautiful," to direct intergroup confrontation. When cognitive alternatives are not perceived, disadvantaged group members may attempt to improve their social identity by individual mobility, or by simply comparing themselves with other members of the in-group and avoiding comparisons with members of higher-status groups.

The Five-Stage Model

The five-stage model of intergroup relations focuses on how disadvantaged and, to a lesser extent, advantaged group members cope with inequality. It assumes that all intergroup relations pass through the same developmental stages in the same sequential manner. During stage one, group stratification is based on rigid categories such as sex or gender. At stage two, there emerges the concept that individual effort and ability can determine group membership. It is assumed that upward social mobility will be attempted by members of the disadvantaged group, first on an individual basis, and this takes place at stage three. When individual mobility is blocked, however, during stage four, talented members of the disadvantaged group will engage in "consciousness raising" in order to try to mobilize the disadvantaged group as a collectivity. At stage five, if the challenge made by the disadvantaged group is successful and the two groups become fairly equal, there will be a healthy state of intergroup competition. If inequality persists, however, then the process of intergroup evolution begins again at an earlier stage in the five-stage cycle.

Realistic Conflict Theory

A rational and materialistic picture of intergroup relations is offered by realistic conflict theory, which addresses how conflicts arise between groups of fairly equal power, the course they take, and their resolution. At a first step, group cohesion and identity evolve as people cooperate in working toward shared goals. Intergroup conflict arises when groups interact and compete for scarce resources, such as territory or status. Conflict can be turned into peace, however, through the adoption of "superordinate goals." An example would be an environmentally safe world, a goal that is beneficial to all humankind but that cannot be achieved without the cooperation of all societies.

Other Theories

The similarity-attraction hypothesis and the contact hypothesis are not major theories, but they should be mentioned in any discussion of intergroup theories. The assumption that similarity leads to attraction and, by implication, that dissimilarity leads to dislike underlies several of the major theories. The contact hypothesis, in its simplest form, assumes that under certain conditions, liking increases as a result of increased contact between people.

The Study of Intergroup Theories

Within the general domain of psychology, intergroup theories constitute a subdiscipline of social psychology. The major books that have reviewed intergroup theories have all noted that intergroup relations is still a relatively neglected topic in social psychology. The main reason for this is that social psychology has tended to be reductionist and to seek to explain all social behavior by focusing on processes within and between individuals, rather than within and between groups.

The personal histories of researchers have undoubtedly been important factors in the development of intergroup theories. For example, many of the major theories were initiated by researchers who were themselves outsiders in one way or another and who thus had firsthand experience of prejudice. These include Freud, a Jew who lived in Vienna most of his life and had to flee to escape the invading Nazis at the start of World War II; Sherif, a Turk who moved to the United States after experiencing political problems in his home country; and Henri Tajfel, a Jewish refugee from Eastern Europe who found a home in England after World War II.

Research on intergroup relations has also been influenced in important ways by minority movements such as the "ethnic revival" and the women's liberation movement. As early as the 1940's, African American psychologists highlighted the negative impact of prejudice on African American children. Later the Black Power movement and the revival of ethnicity generally led to a greater focus on psychological research in the treatment of ethnic minorities. Similarly, since the 1960's there has been a greater concern for women's issues, which has led to more emphasis on minority-majority relations. For example, the issue of how the majority influences the minority, a major topic in mainstream research, has been turned on its head to become "how the minority influences the majority."

Intergroup theories should also be considered in the context of superpower conflicts. From the 1940's until the late 1980's, the United States and the Soviet Union were considered to be superpowers of fairly equal military strength. Not surprisingly, much of the research and several of the major intergroup theories, such as realistic conflict theory, dealt with competing parties of equal strength. The focus on unequal parties came with the more recent theories, particularly social identity theory, developed in the 1970's, and the five-stage model, developed in the 1980's.

There are indications that intergroup relations is receiving more attention from psychologists and that it is gaining a more prominent role in mainstream research. This trend is likely to continue, in part as a result of the changing demographic characteristics of North American society, in which the "minorities" will soon become the numerical majority. *Fathali M. Moghaddam*

Core Resources

Willem Doise's *Groups and Individuals: Explanations in Social Psychology* (Cambridge, England: Cambridge University Press, 1978) critically discusses intergroup research, particularly the work of Sherif and Tajfel. *Eliminating Racism: Profiles in Controversy* (New York: Plenum Press, 1988), edited by Phyliss A. Katz and Dalmas A. Taylor, discusses the challenges society faces in the area of race relations. Donald M. Taylor and Fathali M. Moghaddam's *Theories of Intergroup Relations: International Social Psychological Perspectives* (New York: Praeger, 1987) discusses each of the major intergroup theories. *Psychology of Intergroup Relations* (Chicago: Nelson-Hall, 1986), edited by Stephen Worchel and William G. Austin, presents the work of leading European and American researchers.

See also: Contact hypothesis; Prejudice: effects; Psychology of racism; Relative deprivation theory; Social identity theory.

Psychology of racism

> **Significance:** Students of racism examine the phenomenon of negative attitudes and behavior by members of the majority toward those who belong to racial and ethnic minorities. The topic of racism, which straddles the boundaries between social psychology and sociology, is connected with the study of intergroup relations, cognition, and attitudes in general.

The social and psychological study of prejudice and discrimination, including prejudice and discrimination against African Americans, has a long history; the term "racism," however, did not enter the language of social psychology until the publication of the Kerner Report of 1968, which blamed all-pervasive "white racism" for widespread black rioting in American cities. Although usually applied to black-white relations in the United States, the term is also sometimes used with regard to white Americans' relations with other minority groups such as Asian Americans or Latinos, or to black-white relations outside the United States, for example, in Britain, Canada, or South Africa. Most of the studies and research on racism, however, have focused on white racism against blacks in the United States.

The Causes of Racism

Racism is seen by many social psychologists not as mere hatred but as a deep-rooted habit that is hard to change; hence, subvarieties of racism are distinguished. Psychoanalyst Joel Kovel, in his book *White Racism: A Psychohistory* (1970), distinguishes between dominative racism, the desire to oppress blacks, and aversive racism, the

desire to avoid contact with blacks. Aversive racism, Samuel L. Gaertner and John Dovidio find, exists among those whites who pride themselves on being unprejudiced. David O. Sears, looking at whites' voting behavior and their political opinions as expressed in survey responses, finds what he calls symbolic racism: a resentment of African Americans for making demands in the political realm that supposedly violate traditional American values. Social psychologist James M. Jones distinguishes three types of racism: individual racism, the prejudice and antiblack behavior deliberately manifested by individual whites; institutional racism, the social, economic, and political patterns that impersonally oppress blacks regardless of the prejudice or lack thereof of individuals; and cultural racism, the tendency of whites to ignore or denigrate the special characteristics of black culture.

Where Dovidio and Gaertner find aversive racism, Irwin Katz finds ambivalence. Many whites, he argues, simultaneously see African Americans as disadvantaged (which creates sympathy) and as deviating from mainstream social norms (which creates antipathy). Such ambivalence, Katz contends, leads to exaggeratedly negative reactions to negative behaviors by an African American, but also to exaggeratedly positive reactions to positive behaviors by an African American. He calls this phenomenon ambivalence-induced behavior amplification.

The reasons suggested for individual racism are many. John Dollard and others, in *Frustration and Aggression* (1939), see prejudice as the scapegoating of minorities in order to provide a release for aggression in the face of frustration; in this view, outbursts of bigotry are a natural response to hard economic times. Muzafer and Carolyn Sherif, in *Groups in Harmony and Tension* (1953) and later works, see prejudice of all sorts as the result of competition between groups. Theodor Adorno and others, in *The Authoritarian Personality* (1950), view prejudice, whether directed against blacks or against Jews, as reflective of a supposedly fascist type of personality produced by authoritarian child-rearing practices. In *Racially Separate or Together?* (1971), Thomas F. Pettigrew shows that discriminatory behavior toward blacks, and the verbal expression of prejudices against them, can sometimes flow simply from a white person's desire to fit in with his or her social group. Finally, both prejudice and discrimination, many psychologists argue, are rooted in those human cognitive processes involved in the formation of stereotypes.

Stereotyping

Stereotypes are ideas, often rigidly held, concerning members of a group to which one does not belong. Social psychologists who follow the cognitive approach to the study of racism, such as David L. Hamilton, Walter G. Stephan, and Myron Rothbart, argue that racial stereotyping (the tendency of whites to see blacks in some roles and not in others) arises, like any other kind of stereotyping, from the need of every human being to create some sort of order out of his or her perceptions of the world. Although stereotypes are not entirely impervious to revision or even shattering in the face of disconfirming instances, information related to a stereotype is more efficiently retained than information unrelated to it. Whites, it has been found, tend to judge blacks to be more homogeneous than they really are, while being more aware of differences within their own group: This is called the out-group homogeneity hypothesis. Whites who are guided by stereotypes may act in such a way as to bring out worse behavior in blacks than would otherwise occur, thus creating a self-fulfilling prophecy.

Why is stereotypical thinking on the part of whites about African Americans so hard to eliminate? The history of race relations deserves some of the blame. Some mistakes in reasoning common to the tolerant and the intolerant alike, such as the tendency to remember spectacular events and to think of them as occurring more frequently than is really the case (the availability heuristic), also occur in whites' judgments about members of minority groups. In addition, the social and occupational roles one fills may reinforce stereotypical thinking.

Pettigrew contends that attribution errors in explaining the behavior of others may have an important role to play in reinforcing racial stereotypes. The same behavioral act, Pettigrew argues, is interpreted differently by whites depending on the race of the actor. A positive act by a black person might be ascribed to situational characteristics (for example, luck, affirmative action programs, or other circumstances beyond one's control) and thus discounted; a positive act by a white person might be ascribed to personality characteristics. Similarly, a negative act might be ascribed to situational characteristics in the case of a white person, but to personality characteristics in the case of a black person. The tendency of whites to view the greater extent of poverty among blacks as solely the result of lack of motivation can be seen as a form of attribution error.

The Study of Racism and Prejudice

Although the study of racism per se began with the racial crisis of the 1960's, the study of prejudice in general goes back much further; as early as the 1920's, Emory Bogardus constructed a social distance scale measuring the degree of intimacy members of different racial and ethnic groups were willing to tolerate with one another. At first, psychologists tended to seek the roots of prejudice in the emotional makeup of the prejudiced individual rather than in the structure of society or the general patterns of human cognition. For many years, the study of antiblack prejudice was subsumed under the study of prejudice in general; those biased against blacks were thought to be biased against other groups such as Jews, as well.

In the years immediately following World War II, American social psychologists were optimistic about the possibilities for reducing or even eliminating racial and ethnic prejudices. Adorno's *The Authoritarian Personality* and *The Nature of Prejudice* (1954), by Gordon Allport, reflect the climate of opinion of the time. Allport, whose view of prejudice represented a mixture of the psychoanalytic and cognitive approaches, used the term "racism" to signify the doctrines preached by negrophobe political demagogues; he did not see it as a deeply ingrained bad habit pervading the entire society. Pettigrew, who wrote about antiblack prejudice from the late 1950's on, cast doubt on the notion that there was a specific type of personality or pattern of child rearing associated with prejudice. Nevertheless, he long remained in the optimistic tradition, arguing that changing white people's discriminatory behavior through the enactment of civil rights laws would ultimately change their prejudiced attitudes.

The more frequent use by social psychologists of the term "racism" from the late 1960's onward indicates a growing awareness that bias against blacks, a visible minority, might be harder to uproot than that directed against religious and ethnic minorities. Social psychologists studying racial prejudice shifted their research interest from the open and noisy bigotry most often found among political extremists (for example, the Ku Klux Klan) to the quiet, everyday prejudices of the average apolitical individual. Racial bias against blacks came to be seen as a central, rather than a peripheral, feature of American life.

Responses to surveys taken from the 1940's to the end of the 1970's indicated a steady decline in the percentage of white Americans willing to admit holding racist views. Yet in the 1970's, the sometimes violent white hostility to school busing for integration, and the continuing social and economic gap between black and white America, gave social psychologists reason to temper their earlier optimism. The contact hypothesis, the notion that contact between different racial groups would reduce prejudice, was subjected to greater skepticism and ever more careful qualification. Janet Ward Schofield, in her field study of a desegregated junior high school, detected a persistence of racial divisions among the pupils; reviewing a number of such studies, Walter Stephan similarly discerned a tendency toward increased interracial tension in schools following desegregation. The pessimism suggested by field studies among younger teenagers was confirmed by experiments conducted in the 1970's and 1980's on college students and adults; such studies demonstrated the existence even among supposedly non-prejudiced people of subtle racism and racial stereotyping.

Yet while social psychological experiments contribute to an understanding of the reasons for negative attitudes toward blacks by whites, and for discriminatory behavior toward blacks even by those whites who believe themselves to be tolerant, they do not by any means provide the complete answer to the riddle of racial prejudice and discrimination. Unlike many other topics in social psychology, racism has also been investigated by journalists, historians, economists, sociologists, political scientists, legal scholars, and even literary critics. The techniques of social psychology surveys, controlled experiments, and field studies provide only one window on this phenomenon.   *Paul D. Mageli*

Core Resources

Gordon W. Allport's *The Nature of Prejudice* (Cambridge, Mass.: Addison-Wesley, 1954) contains one of the earliest expositions of the contact hypothesis and one of the earliest treatments of the relationship between prejudice and stereotyping. *Prejudice, Discrimination, and Racism* (Orlando, Fla.: Academic Press, 1986), edited by John F. Dovidio and Samuel L. Gaertner, collects essays on aversive racism, racial ambivalence, stereotyping, symbolic racism, and cultural racism. Irwin Katz's *Stigma: A Social Psychological Analysis* (Hillsdale, N.J.: Lawrence Erlbaum, 1981) reports on subjects' reactions to both blacks and people with physical disabilities and develops the notion of ambivalence-induced behavior amplification. *Towards the Elimination of Racism* (New York: Pergamon Press, 1976), edited by Phyllis A. Katz, contains particularly good essays on racism in small children, psychological approaches to intergroup conflict, aversive racism experiments, and opposition to racial reform. *Prejudice*, by Thomas F. Pettigrew, George M. Frederickson, Dale T. Knobel, Nathan Glazer, and Reed Ueda (Cambridge, Mass.: The Belknap Press of Harvard University Press, 1982), presents a concise and clearly written review of the social psychological literature on prejudice and racism up to 1980. Walter G. Stephan and David Rosenfield's "Racial and Ethnic Stereotypes," in *In the Eye of the Beholder: Contemporary Issues in Stereotyping*, edited by Arthur G. Miller (New York: Praeger, 1982), is a good critical review of the social psychological literature on whites' and blacks' stereotyping of each other.

See also: Contact hypothesis; Individual racism; Prejudice: effects; Prejudice: reduction; Psychological theories of intergroup relations; Racism: history of the concept; Symbolic racism.

Public Law 280

During the early 1950's, federal Indian policy returned to the goal of promoting the assimilation of Indians into American society. Tribes were considered to be major barriers to this end, and a number of policies were developed to reduce their influence. One of these measures was Public Law 280, which sought to place tribal Indians under the jurisdiction of the laws of the states in which they resided. This marked a significant change in the legal status of Native Americans, for while Indians had long been subject to federal law, they usually had been considered to be subject to their own tribal courts when on reservations. Like other measures of the 1950's, Public Law 280 sought to undermine those aspects of Indians' legal status that set them apart from other Americans.

Passed by Congress in August, 1953, Public Law 280 authorized state courts to assume civil and criminal jurisdiction of all Indian lands in the states of California, Minnesota, Nebraska, Oregon, and Wisconsin. (Three reservations were excluded by name in the act.) Furthermore, other states were allowed to extend jurisdiction over reservations if they desired by making the necessary changes in their laws or constitutions. A few limits were placed on state powers: States could not levy property taxes on reservations or exercise jurisdiction with regard to Indian water rights. By 1968, nine additional states had extended jurisdiction over Indian lands within their borders.

Public Law 280 was very unpopular with American Indians, who saw it as a drastic limitation on the tribal right of self-government that had been enacted without their consent. (President Dwight D. Eisenhower had objected to the lack of a provision for tribal consent but had signed the act when Congress refused to amend it.)

Indian resentment of the act helped to persuade Congress to amend its provisions in the changed atmosphere of later years. The American Indian Civil Rights Act of 1968 included provisions (known collectively as the Indian Bill of Rights) that were intended to safeguard Native American rights. One section altered Public Law 280 to require Indian consent before future extensions of state jurisdiction. States were also allowed to return jurisdiction to tribes. Public Law 280 was further limited in its impact by the Indian Child Welfare Act (1978), which gave tribal courts exclusive jurisdiction over child custody cases on reservations.

Though Public Law 280 initially was regarded as a major threat to tribal self-government, modification of the law lessened its potential for restricting tribal authority. Some states found that they preferred to avoid the expense involved in extending legal jurisdiction, while some tribes found it useful to ask the states to provide law and order. By the late twentieth century, the law was being used in a somewhat more cooperative manner that took Indian opinions into account.   *William C. Lowe*

See also: American Indian Civil Rights Act; American Indians in the justice system; Termination resolution; Tribal sovereignty.

Puerto Rican Legal Defense and Education Fund

The Puerto Rican Legal Defense and Education Fund (PRLDEF), a nonprofit civil rights organization, was founded in 1972 to protect and promote the legal rights of Puerto Ricans and other Latinos and to provide guidance and financial assistance to Latinos interested in legal careers. The New York City-based organization employs a staff of approximately twenty.

The PRLDEF was founded by a group of Puerto Rican leaders (including Jorge L. Batista, Victor Marrero, and César A. Perales) for the purpose of providing advocacy and educational programs for Latino communities. The organization's primary aim is to ensure equal protection under the law for Puerto Ricans and other Latinos by challenging discrimination in education, employment, health, housing, political participation, and women's rights.

The PRLDEF has successfully pursued a number of landmark cases, several of which have reached the U.S. Supreme Court. In 1972, a PRLDEF suit gave rise to the case *Aspira of New York v. Board of Education of the City of New York*, which, by leading to the Aspira Consent Decree, helped obtain the right to bilingual education for Latino children with limited English proficiency. The PRLDEF's pursuit of *Pabón v. Levine* (1976) helped to secure the right of Spanish speakers to have unemployment insurance services and materials, such as hearings and claims forms, provided in the Spanish language. These and other PRLDEF-filed cases have played an important role in shaping language-based discrimination rulings in the United States.

PRLDEF lawsuits against the New York City police, fire, and sanitation departments have led to increased Latino representation in civil service jobs in those departments. The PRLDEF has also worked to provide low-income housing for Latinos and has challenged discrimination in public and private housing projects.

The PRLDEF's Voting Rights Project has worked successfully to increase the number of Latino elected officials at the federal, state, and local levels in the U.S. Northeast. The organization has filed lawsuits and complaints with the U.S. Department of Justice against ger-rymandering, or the practice of strategically dividing voting districts to favor a particular political party or interest group. In addition, by providing internships, mentoring programs, Law School Admissions Test (LSAT) preparatory classes, and scholarships, the PRLDEF also has played an important role in expanding the number of Latino and other ethnic minority attorneys in the Northeast. In 1998, the PRLDEF merged with New York's Institute for Puerto Rican Policy.

Glenn Canyon

See also: League of United Latin American Citizens; Puerto Rico.

Puerto Rico

> **Significance:** The special political relationship between Puerto Rico and the United States has helped to make Puerto Ricans one of the largest Latino groups in the U.S. mainland.

On July 25, 1952, the flag of Puerto Rico was raised in ceremonies marking the creation of the Associated Free State, or Commonwealth, of Puerto Rico. This was the culmination of more than fifty years of efforts to define the relationship between the island and the United States. Luís Muñoz Marín, soon to become the first governor of Puerto Rico, had led efforts to establish the commonwealth. However, there was, and remains, opposition by Puerto Ricans who favor full independence and from others who wish Puerto Rico to become the fifty-first state in the Union. The plebiscite in 1952 and subsequent votes have continued to produce a majority that favors commonwealth status.

The U.S.-Puerto Rico Connection

The United States obtained Puerto Rico from Spain as a result of the Spanish-American War of 1898. Previously, Puerto Ricans had urged Spain to reform its colonial administration, and some had sought independence from Spain. With U.S. troops occupying the island after the war, responsibility for administering the island was placed in the hands of the War Department until 1900. In that year, Congress passed the Foraker Act, which established an island government headed by a governor appointed by the president. A legislature was established: Puerto Ricans could elect representatives to a Council of Delegates; the upper chamber was appointed by the United States president. This local body had advisory powers only, and most decisions regarding the island were made in Washington, D.C. There, an elected representative from Puerto Rico could sit in the House of Representatives but could not vote on legislation in the full House. Puerto Ricans finally obtained U.S. citizenship in 1917, when the Jones Act was passed by Congress. It also allowed Puerto Ricans to elect representatives to both houses of their island legislature. Not until 1947 could they elect their own governor.

The two most influential individuals in Puerto Rico's search for political identity were Pedro Albizú Campos and Luís Muñoz Marín. Albizú Campos was educated in the United States and joined Puerto Rico's Nationalist Party in 1927. Becoming president of the party in 1930, he led it into opposition against U.S. control and sought alliances with other Latin Americans. Lacking support at the polls, however, Albizú Campos became more radical. In 1936, he was accused of plotting to overthrow the federal government in Puerto Rico and was sent to a federal prison in Atlanta.

Luís Muñoz Marín also was determined to bring self-government to Puerto Rico, but became convinced that this goal would be best achieved through continued association with the United States. Muñoz and his Popular Democratic Party won the first election for governor in 1947 and began negotiations with the United States to recognize the islanders' desires for their own constitution. The Nationalist Party opposed Muñoz and favored complete independence. Pro-independence supporters were angered by the administration of Harry S Truman's collaboration with Muñoz and the passage of Public Law 600, authorizing a constitutional convention. In the fall of 1950, they attacked a prison in Rio Piedras, stormed the governor's mansion, and tried to assassinate President Truman in Washington, D.C. The attacks were unsuccessful but highlighted divisions among Puerto Ricans over the island's future. The violence led to a state of emergency and the mobilization of the National Guard, which took over the University of Puerto Rico and stormed the home of the Nationalist Party leader. Dozens of people were killed in the fighting. Albizú, having served his sentence and returned to Puerto Rico, was again arrested.

In June, 1951, Puerto Ricans went to the polls to elect members of a constitutional convention. Seventy delegates from Muñoz's Popular Democratic Party, fifteen supporters of statehood, and seven who favored independence were elected.

The Constitutional Convention

The constitutional convention met in 1951-1952 and produced a document that identified Puerto Rico as an Associated Free State, a unique relationship that allowed Puerto Ricans to benefit from U.S. citizenship but gave them the opportunity to elect their own island government. Falling somewhere between a state and a colony,

Puerto Rico can elect its own governor, a twenty-seven member senate, and a fifty-one member house of representatives. Puerto Ricans may not vote in U.S. presidential elections, and their representative in Congress may not vote on legislation on the floor. This places restrictions on Puerto Rico, because any changes to the island's status may be approved only by Congress.

When the constitution was sent to the United States Congress for approval in 1952, there was much debate and changes were proposed to provisions that differed from the U.S. Constitution. Eventually, Congress passed the legislation, and President Truman signed it into law, establishing Puerto Rico as a Commonwealth in Association with the United States.

Puerto Ricans in the United States

The question of the island's status was complicated by the continued migration of islanders to the United States. Approximately seventy thousand Puerto Ricans lived in the United States, mostly in New York, before World War II. Continued population growth on the island and cheaper transportation by airplane brought more Puerto Ricans to the United States in the years after the war. By 1987, there were more than two million Puerto Ricans in the United States, with more than half of that number in New York City and environs. By the 1990's, there were more Puerto Ricans in New York City than in the island's capital city of San Juan.

As United States citizens, Puerto Ricans may move freely anywhere within the United States mainland, as well as back and forth to the island. More and more Puerto Ricans have chosen to migrate to the mainland, but many, whose native language is Spanish, find that adaptation to the new language and culture is not easy. Many Puerto Ricans study English and speak it well, but those who first come to the United States often encounter a period of adjustment. In addition to language difficulties, Puerto Ricans often encounter racial discrimination in the United States. Although the Puerto Rican community has transformed parts of New York City and many other cities of the Northeast, many Puerto Ricans maintain strong ties to their island. Their participation in both lands is part of the unique identity the island and its people feel, and is reflected by the reluctance of many Puerto Ricans to sever the bonds created by commonwealth status. *James A. Baer*

Core Resources

Raymond Carr's *Puerto Rico: A Colonial Experiment* (New York: Vintage Books, 1984) deals with the status of Puerto Rico and the policies and platforms of major Puerto Rican political parties. Arturo Morales Carrion's *Puerto Rico: A Political and Cultural History* (New York: W. W. Norton, 1983) is a thorough evaluation of Puerto

Rico's history and a detailed account of Puerto Rico's emergence in the mid-twentieth century as a commonwealth. Ronald Fernandez's *The Disenchanted Island: Puerto Rico and the United States in the Twentieth Century* (New York: Praeger, 1992) is a detailed account of political ties between Puerto Rico and the United States. *Colonial Dilemma: Critical Perspectives on Contemporary Puerto Rico* (Boston: South End Press, 1993), edited by Edwin Meléndez and Edgardo Meléndez, includes chapters on contemporary politics, the economy, and feminism. Karl Wagenheim's *Puerto Rico: A Profile* (New York: Praeger, 1970) provides an overview of Puerto Rico's history and economy.

See also: Jones Act of 1917; Latinos in the United States; Puerto Rican Legal Defense and Education Fund; West Indian Americans.

Push and pull factors

Because migration is costly and stressful, people migrate only when there is a strong incentive to do so. This may occur because conditions where they live have become unusually bad, and they feel a "push" to leave. On the other hand, conditions may appear unusually good somewhere else, and they feel a "pull" toward that location. Often a combination of "push" and "pull" factors motivates migration, but the "push" factor usually is necessary for migration to be seriously considered.

Traditionally, religious and political persecution have been powerful push factors. The New England Puritans and the Pennsylvania Quakers fled religious persecution by coming to North America. Persecution of Jews in czarist Russia in the nineteenth century also motivated thousands to flee farther west. Adolf Hitler and Joseph Stalin escalated such persecutions in the 1930's and 1940's, culminating in the torture and deaths of millions of Jews during the Holocaust and Soviet pogroms. In the 1990's, refugees fled from tyrannical regimes in Africa, the Balkans, and the Middle East. U.S. immigration policy has given favored status to people who can show they have been victims of such persecution.

The push may also arise from unfavorable economic circumstances. Potato famines in the 1840's led to a mass exodus from Ireland and the Scandinavian countries, bringing many migrants to North America. Within the United States, the mechanization of cotton cultivation in the 1940's and 1950's greatly reduced the need for field hands in the South, causing thousands of African American families to move to the industrial North. The latter was a gradual process whereby the improvement in agricultural productivity reduced the number of people needed to produce food and fiber, leading to migrations from farms to towns and cities.

The strongest pull factors have been economic. People often move to locations where they expect to find good jobs and comfortable incomes. North America has exerted this kind of pull on the rest of the world since the mid-nineteenth century. Initially the great attraction was the vast abundance of fertile and relatively cheap land. By 1900, however, American manufacturing industries were also eager to employ relatively cheap and docile immigrant labor. Railroads, land speculators, and factory owners all sent recruiters to Europe to encourage immigrants.

The United States has continued to exert this kind of pull, partly because its labor market is relatively free from apprenticeship regulations and monopolistic labor union restrictions on who can be hired. The clearest evidence is the flood of migrants coming northward from Mexico, who in addition have been "pushed" by poor economic conditions and a lack of jobs in their mother country. A strong pull in the 1990's arose as American firms actively recruited people with computer skills, mostly from Asia. Immigration preferences are given to people with scarce job skills.

Finally, an important pull results from the desire to be reunited with family members. In the early 1990's, about half of all legal immigration into the United States involved spouses, children, or parents of U.S. citizens.

Paul B. Trescott

See also: Great Migration; Immigration and emigration; Irish Americans; Jewish Americans; Latinos in the United States.

Q

Quotas

A "quota" is a minimum or maximum number allowable, such as the ceiling on the number of automobiles that Japanese manufacturers once agreed to export to the U.S. market. In ethnic and race relations in the United States, the term has acquired an odious reputation as a means to limit the selection of meritorious persons in personnel matters.

After World War II, many well-trained Jewish high school students applied for college with test scores so high that they were fully qualified for admission to the very best colleges. Parents of alumni from those same colleges, finding the competition exceedingly difficult for their children, pressured the colleges to establish quotas in order to limit the number of Jews admitted. These quotas were later rescinded under pressure from many quarters. However, in the 1980's, when well-qualified Asian students achieved very high test scores for admission to colleges in California, a similar informal quota system was established, only to be abolished when word leaked out that academic standards were being compromised.

In the 1970's, with the advent of affirmative action, federal enforcement agencies began to insist that employers work toward desegregating the workforce by becoming aware of the percentage of qualified workers of each race for each job category. Employers were asked to establish the goal of having their businesses ultimately mirror the hiring patterns of the labor market as a whole, based on such labor market surveys as are found in the decennial census. Timetables for accomplishing this desegregation were to be based on turnover statistics and estimates of business expansion. Federal agencies also encouraged educational institutions to follow the same process of establishing goals and timetables in admissions.

Although federal guidelines insisted that goals and timetables were not quotas, in practice employers and educational institutions implemented affirmative action in such a way that quotas resulted, infuriating qualified white job seekers and college aspirants. Litigation resulted, culminating in the definitive *Regents of the University of California v. Bakke* (1978), in which the Supreme Court of the United States declared quotas, unless rationally based, to be unconstitutional. Even though Congress adopted a provision of the Public Works Employment Act that set aside 10 percent of all federal construction contracts for minority firms, the Supreme Court struck down the concept of a rigid quota in *Adarand Constructors v. Peña* (1995), holding that strict scrutiny must be applied to all race-conscious decision making, even that undertaken by Congress, and therefore a rational basis must be demonstrated in selecting 10 percent rather than some other figure.

In the late 1990's, affirmative action quotas were allowable when there was a logical basis. If specific harm to an ethnic or racial group is demonstrable, a court-approved remedy involving a quota must be tailored to the precise quantitative extent of that harm.

Michael Haas

See also: *Adarand Constructors v. Peña;* Affirmative action; *Bakke* case; Censuses, U.S.; College admissions; Set-asides.

R

Race as a concept

Significance: Eighteenth century racial concepts, with little if any scientific basis, molded modern racial classification and gave rise to stereotypes of superior and inferior peoples. Distortions of Charles Darwin's theory of evolution were used to justify imperialism as well as genocide. Today, ethnicity, not race, is used in understanding the complex phenomenon of human variation.

Although human societies from earliest times were aware of differences between themselves and other societies, the concept of race is a relatively modern construct, first developed in the late eighteenth century. The ancient Greeks had no word even remotely resembling race. Aristotle's classification system of Genus, Species, Difference, Property, Accident (which helped earn him the title of father of biology) contributed to the founding of racial classification systems. Aristotle himself believed that climate caused physical differences in humans. Like other ancient Greeks, he also believed in slavery. However, for Aristotle, slavery was a matter of virtue, not race. The most virtuous had leisure time for active involvement in politics.

Medieval and Early Modern Concepts
The Middle Ages in Europe was a land-locked age, with little reason to speculate on race. Yet, much ethnocentrism existed. Prussians, Irish, Lombards, and a host of others were portrayed in unflattering ways. By 1100 and the era of the Crusades, particularly venomous language was used to describe the followers of Islam. Jews also were subject to verbal and physical attacks, increasing with a vengeance after the bubonic plague epidemic in 1348. Yet when the word "race" was used in the Middle Ages, it was to refer to the pure lineage of some noble family. Racial theory itself did not emerge in the Middle Ages.

The age of exploration opened Europeans to a world of other human types, causing a debate about whether Indians and black Africans were men or beasts. The famous chemist and physician, Paracelsus, described Europeans as children of Adam, and found blacks and other races to have separate origins. Such separate origin theories were cut short when the papacy, in the mid-sixteenth century, condemned the separate origin of humanity theory as heretical. In 1565, French historian and political theorist Jean Bodin divided the world into Scythian, German, African, and Middler, according to skin color and basic body features. Bodin's primitive classification scheme was still far more advanced than that of Cambridge historian Raphael Holinshed, who wrote in 1578 about races of giants as well as races devoted to sorcery and witchcraft. During the age of the Counter-Reformation and witch-hunting (1550-1650), references to evil races grew, and at least in popular literature, black became viewed as a sign of the devil. With the beginning of the scientific revolution, classification became more in line with Bodin's schema. In 1684, François Bernier described four human races: European, Asian, African, and Lapp.

Racial Taxonomies
The term "race" was first used to classify humanity in 1775, when Johann Friedrich Blumenbach, a German professor of medicine, created a taxonomy dividing humanity into five separate races: Caucasian, Mongolian, American, African, and Malay. Each was described in terms of skin color, cranial size and shape, and other physical characteristics. Blumenbach used the term Caucasian for European, and he believed that the most beautiful people in the world lived in the Caucasus region. Devoting much attention to skull size, Blumenbach founded what would later be the pseudoscience of craniology and phrenology. In his classification system, Blumenbach built on the earlier work of Swedish botanist Linnaeus (Carl von Linné). In his *Systema Naturae*

> **race** . . . a group or set, esp. of people, having a common feature. . . . A tribe, nation, or people. . . . The fact or condition of belonging to a particular people, ethnic group, etc.

Source: New Shorter Oxford English Dictionary (Oxford: Clarendon Press, 1993).

(1758), Linnaeus divided humans into four groups defined by skin color, personality, and moral traits. Hence Europeans were "fair, gentle, acute, and inventive," while Asiatics were "haughty and covetous." Although Blumenbach and Linnaeus were early scientists, writing long before evolution or genetics were concepts, their classification systems became firmly embedded in scientific taxonomies and accepted as gospel in the public mind—despite the fact that Blumenbach used "race" as a convenient label and nothing more.

Blumenbach and Linnaeus were writing during the Enlightenment, when philosophers, historians, and political scientists were also toying with human classification themes. In 1749, the Count de Buffon defined six separate groupings of men, viewing all other races as variations of what he termed the "White Race." In 1775, the famous philosopher Immanuel Kant defined four races—Hunnic, White, Negro, Hindu—but viewed all races as having a common origin. Yet ten years later, Kant was further speculating about special powers of each race that could be evoked or suppressed as new conditions demanded.

Romantic Pseudoscientific Concept

Enlightenment thought tended to deal with universals. As a whole, the eighteenth century racial theorists viewed humanity as one distinct species. Their taxonomies were subdivisions of related peoples. It was the nineteenth century Romantics, with their stress on the unique and particular, who transformed taxonomies of race into vitriolic concepts of racism.

Johann Fichte (1762-1814), a student of Kant, argued that Germans inherited superior biological qualities through their blood. Fichte believed that these blood characteristics destined Germany to produce a nation unsurpassed in moral and social order. Similarly Johann Gottfried von Herder (1744-1803) pointed to different races having different inner qualities, and historian Barthold Niebuhr in his *History of Rome* (1828) viewed the German tribes as being powerful enough to conquer Rome because they, unlike the Romans, had maintained their racial purity. German racial concepts also influenced contemporaneous English and American thought. In 1850, English historian Robert Knox published a series of lectures entitled *The Races of Man*, in which he attempted to show that all scientific and cultural advances, and even civilization itself, were a manifestation of race. Similarly, American historian William H. Prescott extolled the Anglo-Saxon virtues that shaped the American character, and Francis Parkman praised the German race for its masculine qualities.

Many nineteenth century scientists joined the Romantics in identifying culture with race. Georges Cuvier, a leading French zoologist, argued that Caucasians created the highest civilization and, by right, dominated all others. For him, Mongolian peoples could only create static empires, and blacks remained in a state of barbarism. Cuvier introduced the concept of "fixity of type" to explain why different races were predestined to follow different developmental paths. In *Natural History of the Human Species* (1848), Charles H. Smith, an anatomist and a friend of Cuvier, classified three racial types based on the size of the brain. In the United States, Samuel George Morton collected hundreds of skulls and poured mustard seeds into each skull to calculate the skull's volume. He called this new science craniometry and published his conclusions in the influential *Crania Americana* (1839), which listed brain capacity from most (Caucasian) to least (black), with Amer-Indians falling somewhere in between.

The most powerful pre-Darwinistic racial theorist was Joseph-Arthur de Gobineau, called the father of racist ideology because of his stress on the inferiority and superiority of certain races. His *Essay on the Inequality of the Human Races*, published between 1853 and 1855, stressed that the races were physically, mentally, and morally different. For him, the white race was unsurpassed in beauty, intelligence, and strength. It was a natural aristocracy. Of the peoples in the white race, he

In the eighteenth century, Johann Friedrich Blumenbach classified humanity into five racial categories. He used the term "Caucasian" for Europeans because he believed the people who lived in the Caucasus region were the most beautiful.

found the Aryan to be the most advanced, and the German to be the foremost developed of the Aryans. Gobineau, interested also in the decline of civilizations, found race mixing to be a major cause. It is not surprising that the young Adolf Hitler found Gobineau fascinating.

Darwinism and Race

The advent of Charles Darwin's theory of evolution in 1859 shattered old racial concepts but opened the way for new ones. Darwin viewed all humans as belonging to the same species and had little to say about race except that all species change over time and that human subspecies had crossed repeatedly. If anything, he found that the similarities among humans far outweighed any differences.

However, the social and racial Darwinists who adapted Darwin's ideas had a lot to say. Francis Galton, a cousin of Darwin, coined the term "eugenics." He concluded that there are grades of races and grades of humans in each race. By 1883, Galton was popularizing the idea that social agencies were responsible for improving the racial qualities of future generations.

The Herculean mind of Herbert Spencer used evolution, natural selection, and survival of the fittest to explain practically everything in the universe, including race. In his travels he viewed Papuans, Australian aborigines, and African tribesmen, all of whom were classified as primitive, childlike, and of little intelligence. Spencer had a tremendous impact on other scholars and on the educated public. By the end of the century, Rudyard Kipling would write his famous poem "The White Man's Burden," classifying colonial peoples as "half-devil and half-child."

Another famous Darwinist was Henrik Hackle, who traced life from an organic broth in the oceans to the emergence of humankind. In his *Riddle of the Universe* (1899), Hackle found racial differences to be of paramount importance. He found "lower" races such as the Hottentots destined for extinction, while Negroes were labeled as incapable of higher mental thoughts. Hackle taught at the University of Jena. One of his students, Joseph Chamberlain, was destined to be British Secretary of State for Colonies.

A powerful writer, Chamberlain synthesized nineteenth century trends in his works on race. He found race to be everything; the germ of the culture, art, and genius of a people ran in its blood. Therefore, any race that allowed its blood to be mixed with that of others was destined to fall. In his own time, Chamberlain saw a major battle taking place between Teutons and Jews. However, the awakening of the Teutonic spirit in this battle was a great turning point in history that would lead to a new Europe and a new future world order. Hitler honored Chamberlain as a great world thinker and acted

on many of his conclusions. The carnage that resulted made overt racial concepts unfashionable in the post-1945 world.

Counterattack Against Racial Classification

Racial taxonomies should have been greeted with skepticism from the beginning. Scientist Chevalier Lamarck had shown that species change over time as their living environments change; however, the implications of his conclusions were ignored. The noted anthropologist Franz Boas challenged the rampant Darwinism of his time and demanded proof from his colleagues that race determines mentality and temperament. During the 1940's, Ashley Montagu claimed race was invented by anthropologists as an artificial concept and did not make sense in light of the hybridization of humanity over many millennia. Finally in 1964, the United Nations Educational, Scientific, and Cultural Organization (UNESCO), using the worldwide work of anthropologists and scientists, concluded that there is no such thing as a pure race, making it difficult to place humanity into clear-cut categories. UNESCO stated that because of the great mobility of humanity over time, no national, religious, geographical, linguistic, or cultural group in the modern world constitutes a race.

The majority of anthropologists find "race" to be a mystical and imprecise term that does not come close to explaining the tremendous biodiversity in humanity. They prefer, instead, "ethnicity," a term that encompasses people's language, religion, and geography and recognizes the existence of several hundred ethnic groups. The old divisions of Asian, African, European, American (Amer-Indian) have come to be viewed as mainly geographic terms. As populations continue to intersperse, even these geographic terms for humanity are becoming increasingly obsolete.   *Irwin Halfond*

Core Resources

Ivan Hannaford's *Race: The History of an Idea in the West* (Baltimore, Md.: The Johns Hopkins University Press, 1996) provides a thorough analysis of racial concepts from the ancients to the Renaissance and a detailed view of the racialization of the West from 1684 to 1996 in part II. Michael Banton's *Race Relations* (New York: Basic Books, 1967) presents a clear picture of the development of racial concepts in world societies. Two chapters are devoted to racial concepts in the United States. Banton's study *The Idea of Race* (London: Tavistock Publications, 1977) should also be consulted for a topical approach to racial concepts. Thomas Gossett's *Race: The History of an Idea in America* (New York: Oxford University Press, 1997) analyzes how racial concepts affected and were affected by developments in the United States. The concluding chapter provides an analysis of the counter-theorists who fought against rigid racial classifications. *The Concept of Race*, edited by Ashley Montagu (New York: Free Press, 1964), provides essays by ten leading anthropologists. Many of the essays, although dated, are still of value.

See also: Ethnicity and ethnic groups; Race formation theory; Racism: history of the concept; "Scientific" racism; Social Darwinism and racism; White "race."

Race card

The term "race card" refers to the practice of bringing up the issue of race or racial identity—usually African American—as an explanation or motivation for a certain circumstance or situation. To "play the race card" is to claim that an individual's race is the reason the person has been treated a certain way or has ended up in a particular situation.

The race card forces issues to be drawn along racial lines. Many minority members, especially African Americans, believe that it is erroneous to discuss a "race card" as if race were significant only in certain cases and could be "played" to gain an advantage. Others maintain that minority members use the issue of racism to win support or simply to evade responsibility for their actions. These critics view the race card as an excuse or negotiating ploy that people of color use when they find themselves in an unfavorable situation. They believe that race is being conveniently brought up at certain times to maximize support even if race is irrelevant to the issue at hand.

Defense lawyer Johnnie Cochran (right) has been accused of using the race card in the 1995 trial of O. J. Simpson (center).

Whether playing the race card is a legitimate move is a matter of perspective and often depends on the situation. During the O. J. Simpson trial, defense lawyer Johnnie Cochran was accused of playing the race card when he implied that Simpson was wrongfully accused of murder and set up simply because he is African American. *Erica Childs*

See also: Crime and race/ethnicity; Criminal justice system; Simpson, O. J., trial.

Race-neutrality

In the United States, overt racism has been on the decline since the 1940's. Most anthropologists and biologists now avoid classifying people into races. Although genetic differences among population groups do exist in the form of phenotypes (outward characteristics such as skin color, eye color, or hair types), these differences have not been shown to be significant at the basic level of molecular DNA (genes) and hence do not affect personality, intelligence, or any ability that significantly relates to social behavior. Therefore, the social significance of race is limited to how the members of a society draw unwarranted conclusions from the physical differences between peoples, meaning that race is a social construct.

Because democracy is evidenced not only by the legal framework of the United States Constitution but also by the real relations among the people governed by that law, social justice dictates that in a true democracy the role of race should be ignored when choices and decisions that matter to everyone are made. True race-neutrality means eliminating racial stereotypes and banning any preferential treatment on the basis of race. In a race-neutral America, equal opportunity and equal justice for all should, some argue, be sufficient to protect the rights of all races and ethnic origins without resorting to any form of race-conscious public policy. As a result, in the 1990's, many members of the United States Congress and state legislators began a movement to terminate affirmative action programs on the basis that America is approaching race-neutrality, or becoming a "color-blind" nation. Others argue that race and racism continue to have indelible impacts on social justice and that the notion of a race-neutral society, at least for any foreseeable future, is a smokescreen used by those who wish to put an end to equal-opportunity programs.

Alvin K. Benson

See also: Affirmative action; "Color-blind" society; Equality of opportunity; Genetic basis for race; Race as a concept; Racism: changing nature of.

Race relations cycle

> **Significance:** Park developed his theory of the race relations cycle in the early twentieth century to explain the process by which societies incorporate racially and ethnically diverse peoples into one social entity. Park's cycle consists of four progressive stages: contact, competition, accommodation, and assimilation.

In the 1920's, Robert E. Park's theory of the race relations cycle provided a new direction away from pseudo-scientific racialist theories and toward more scientific views of race and race relations. The theory hinges on an assumption that assimilation of minorities into a society's dominant culture is desirable—both for the minorities and for the dominant culture—and that it is also inevitable, proceeding through four consistent, irreversible stages: contact, competition, accommodation, and assimilation.

Park's Four Stages
Park describes the first stage of race relations, *contact*, from the vantage point of Europeans who, as they migrated into new territories, came into contact with peoples who seemed alien in their appearance and behavior. Contact and conquest, according to Park, form a natural part of the process of building a civilization. Park admitted that, as European peoples migrated into areas inhabited by other societies, they disrupted the sociocultural organization of those societies. They then replaced the indigenous social institutions with their own. He describes the processes accompanying the formation of the new social order as the unavoidable outgrowth of the migration, expansion, and amalgamation (intermarriage and reproduction) of peoples. As Park saw it, race relations develop as the natural product of migration and conquest; in this view, society is like a living organism that struggles to maintain balance, or "equilibrium." The absorption of new groups, then, is merely part of the society's attempt to reestablish this social equilibrium.

Park defined the second stage, *competition*, as the struggle of a racial group to perpetuate itself, or to continue to exist. Competition can be cooperative when it is based upon a division of labor that provides people with roles that suit them. Competition can also be accompanied by conflict, however, when different races or ethnic groups are first brought together. This conflict can be lessened through time as the different peoples come to have greater contact with each other and become attached to the moral order of the larger society.

Park defined the third stage, *accommodation*, as the inevitable result of the isolation felt by immigrants or racial minorities. They respond to this isolation by desiring to play an active role in the larger society. They also become aware of the "social distance" (the lack of intimacy, understanding, or influence between individuals and groups in society) that prevents their acceptance into that society. Driven to achieve higher social status, they become self-conscious of their differences from members of the dominant society. This social distance, according to Park, may last a long time, reinforced by established social customs and forming equilibrium. Eventually, however, social distance dwindles, making assimilation possible.

To Park, the final stage, *assimilation*, was a natural feature of what he called "civilized" society. In fact, he believed that a civilization is formed through the process of absorbing outside groups. Like other European and Euro-American sociologists, Park assumed that urbanization and modernization would break down ties based on family, race, and ethnicity. The breakdown of these ties, he believed, would free the individual to participate in modern civilization. Park believed that the United States was a democratic meritocracy—a society in which individuals could achieve upward mobility based on their innate abilities and in which caste and race distinctions would ultimately disappear.

Park on Prejudice
Nevertheless, Park acknowledged that for people of color, assimilation, while inevitable, would take time to achieve. Although he held the dominant society to be a meritocracy, he believed that prejudice would hinder assimilation. He did not consider the difference between white ethnic groups and racial ethnic groups highly significant. Rather, he believed that, to the extent that there was difference, it was attributable to the race *prejudice* confronting people of color because of their "racial uniform," the physical appearance that they could not alter. Park saw prejudice against intermarriage as a particular problem, because his theory required assimilation not only in a cultural sense but in a physical, biological sense as well, through intermarriage and reproduction (what Park termed "amalgamation"). Ultimately, then—especially for African and Asian Americans—the major barrier to assimilation was whites' prejudiced attitudes rather than the inability or lack of

desire of African and Asian Americans to assimilate. This hypothesis became a major premise of assimilationist theories and led to an emphasis on the study of attitudes.

The "Marginal Man"
Another concept credited to Park is that of the "marginal man"—the person caught between two cultures. According to Park, this marginal person is produced in the process of building civilization, as new peoples are incorporated into one society. Often racially or ethnically mixed, this person assumes the role of the stranger, fitting into neither of the two cultures that produced him or her. Rather, the "marginal man" embodies a new personality type, created by the processes of acculturation that accompany the race relations cycle. He understands both cultures or groups that produced him, but he is neither at home in, nor accepted by, either group.

Impact on Theories of Race Relations
Park's theory of the race relations cycle laid the groundwork for a major trend in sociology: assimilationist theories of race relations, which assume the possibility of a harmonious "melting pot" society in which race and ethnicity are not significant determinants of social status. The melting pot theory influenced many of the sociologists who followed Park, including Louis Wirth and Gunnar Myrdal. These sociologists shared Park's analysis of ethnicity and race, arguing that the assimilation difficulties faced by African Americans constituted an aberration—or, as Myrdal put it in his seminal 1944 study of the same name, an "American dilemma." Even assimilationists who took issue with Parks, such as Milton Gordon—who argued that minorities were not expected to join in the melting pot so much as to meet the demands of "Anglo-conformity"—can trace their intellectual roots to Park. Elements of the race relations cycle theory have been applied to race relations in many areas, including studies of social distance; measurement of racial prejudice and changes in those attitudes over time; studies of cultural differences among those who have not been assimilated; and studies of the extent to which society remains segregated.

Today, Park's theory of the race relations cycle is generally criticized for assuming that assimilation is inevitable. Assumptions implicit in Park's theory remained rooted in later assimilationist theories: an assumption that the United States is an open, meritocratic society; an assumption that discrimination is caused by prejudice; the view that, upon their enslavement, African Americans lost any culture they once had and that they should therefore embrace acculturation; the belief in the inherent superiority (or, at least, desirability) of the dominant culture; the belief that racial inequality is abnormal in what is otherwise an egalitarian society; and

an assumption of the assimilative effects of urbanization and industrialization. Spearheaded by the work of Park assimilationist theories remained predominant until the latter twentieth century, when the Black Power movement and subsequent ethnic movements signaled that racial and ethnic minorities exist who neither embrace the dominant culture nor seek inclusion in it.

Impact on Public Policy
Park's premise that society, to achieve assimilation, must minimize social distance and racial prejudice has been instrumental in the promotion of racial integration in education, housing, and work. For example, Jonathan Kozol, in his book *Savage Inequalities: Children in America's Schools* (1991), detailed the social costs of segregation and promoted the concept that only when members of different races minimize their social distance by early contact with one another, as children in schools, will Americans reach accord through mutual understanding. Such studies helped give rise to the busing of African American children from predominantly black to predominantly white schools during the 1970's. Likewise, public and private universities across North America have adopted policies intended to end racial strife by minimizing racial prejudice through mutual exposure and appreciation. A more controversial policy adopted by some institutions involves punishment for the verbal expression of racial hatred ("hate speech"), critics claiming that such policies impinge on the constitutional protection of free speech.

Numerous studies measuring social distance have polled American citizens on whether they would tolerate the presence of people with different racial backgrounds in their neighborhoods, in their churches, in their schools, and as members of their families. Results indicating that whites have minimized their social distance from people of color are taken as evidence that racial prejudice has declined and that, therefore, the United States is moving toward an assimilated society. A number of sociologists, however, including Joe R. Feagin, have argued that racism is driven more by discrimination, which can be unintentional, than by prejudiced attitudes. Feagin and others question the validity of a focus on racial prejudice as the underlying basis of racial conflict in society.

More negative, even punitive, consequences of a belief in the value of assimilation can be seen in examples in which acculturation—the process by which culturally distinct groups understand, adapt to, and influence each another—was forced on people of color in order to minimize their differences from the dominant white society. For example, many schools for American Indian children in the nineteenth and early twentieth centuries (some run by missionaries, some by the federal government's Bureau of Indian Affairs) aimed to "civilize" the children by removing them from their parents and placing them in boarding schools where teachers worked to eliminate all vestiges of traditional culture. This pattern of forced acculturation is a good example of how government policy toward immigrants and racial minorities both drove, and was driven by, assimilationist assumptions. Park's theory of assimilation, articulated in the wake of such government policies, echoed the status quo in American society, assuming that the dominant Euro-American society is an open society in which racial and ethnic divisions will inevitably be eroded and replaced by a true meritocracy.

Assimilationist assumptions in the educational system have also invested schools with the responsibility of teaching both the English language and the values of citizenship, important tools in the acculturation process. Feagin notes, as evidence of society's emphasis on acculturation, the development of nativist citizen groups that promote "English-only" schooling. These groups insist that all children must learn the language of the land if they wish to participate as full members of society.

Assimilationist scholars have found ready partners in government policymakers as well. In the 1960's, for example, a report issued by Daniel P. Moynihan entitled *Report on the Negro Family: A Case for National Action* cited the "peculiar" structure of many African American families—dominated or headed by a female—as responsible for the failure of blacks to be fully assimilated into American society. This family structure, Moynihan held, promoted values alien to those needed for successful integration into the dominant society. Some scholars followed this report by emphasizing that blacks who have moved into the middle class have done so by virtue of their acculturation to the dominant culture; they claimed that racial prejudice is not the true barrier to assimilation but rather that failure to acculturate is the problem. In the 1990's, such applications of Park's pioneering theory of assimilation were common among those who sought to end what they believed were "preferential" programs for assimilation, such as affirmative action in hiring and in admissions to colleges and universities. *Sharon Elise, adapted by Chris Moose*

Core Resources
Robert Park's *Race and Culture* (Glencoe, Ill.: Free Press, 1950) collects the essays in which Park developed his theory of the race relations cycle. E. Franklin Frazier's *Black Bourgeoisie* (Glencoe, Ill.: Free Press, 1957) is a classic study of the "marginal man" dilemma applied to the black middle class. Perhaps the most famous heir to the Park tradition was Gunnar Myrdal, whose classic *An American Dilemma: The Negro Problem and Modern Democracy* (New York: Harper Brothers, 1944) grappled with the "aberra-

tion" of the African American experience. Robert Blauner, in *Racial Oppression in America* (New York: Harper & Row, 1972), criticizes assimilationist theories and counters their focus on racial prejudice with an analysis of racial privilege as embedded in a system of internal colonialism. Stanford M. Lyman, *The Black American in Sociological Thought* (New York: Putnam, 1972), reveals some of the racial biases in the development of the sociology of race and ethnic relations. Michael Omi and Howard Winant, in *Racial Formation in the United States* (New York: Routledge & Kegan Paul, 1986), examine the major paradigms of race relations—the dominant ethnic model, the class model, and the nation model—followed by their own "racial formation" thesis. Joe R. Feagin, in his textbook *Racial and Ethnic Relations* (5th ed., Englewood Cliffs, N.J.: Prentice-Hall, 1996), offers an introductory survey of race relations theories, analyzing each of the United States' major ethnic and racial groups against the background of competing sociological explanations.

See also: Assimilation theories; Carlisle Indian School; Competition theory and human ecology; Contact and adaptation patterns; Contact hypothesis; English-only and official English movements; Melting pot theory; Pluralism vs. assimilation; Race as a concept; Racial/ethnic relations: theoretical overview.

Race riots of 1866

> **Significance:** Economic and social disparities between the races, along with a continuing military presence, led to violence during Reconstruction.

Racial disturbances in Memphis and New Orleans in 1866 were the result of economic, social, and political issues that troubled the nation during Reconstruction. Given the upheaval in the lives of Southerners after the Civil War, the racial disturbances are hardly surprising. In the simplest terms, one of the major tasks of Reconstruction was to assimilate the more than four million former slaves into U.S. society. A more complex view must consider the problems faced by the newly freed African Americans who had to achieve a new identity in a society that had allowed them no control over their own lives. White Southerners had to live with the economic, social, and political consequences of defeat. The military occupation of the South by federal troops after the Civil War angered Southern whites, who believed in their right to rebuild and rule their own society without interference from the North. The presence of federal troops (many of them African Americans), an armed citizenry, and the psychological difficulty of accepting the end of the world they had known created explosive conditions that erupted into violence.

The Black Codes

The Memphis and New Orleans riots were one result of this upheaval. Soon after the surrender of the Confederate army at Appomattox in April, 1865, legislatures in the South acted to pass a series of black codes. These laws were intended to maintain control over the lives of the newly freed African Americans and, in effect, keep them enslaved. For example, harsh vagrancy laws allowed police to arrest black people without cause and force them to work for white employers. President Abraham Lincoln's Emancipation Proclamation, on January 1, 1863, had freed the slaves in the Confederate states. The United States Congress, having abolished slavery throughout the nation with the Thirteenth Amendment to the Constitution in 1865, founded the Freedmen's Bureau to assist the former slaves and was in the process of enacting, over the strong opposition of President Andrew Johnson, a series of Reconstruction Acts intended to repeal the South's black codes. President Johnson resisted congressional attempts to admit African Americans to full citizenship, but Congress ultimately overrode his veto and took control of the Reconstruction program in the South.

Many former slaves, rejecting the life they had known on the plantation, moved to the cities of the South. Most African Americans were refugees without any economic resources, competing with Irish and German immigrants for scarce jobs in the war-torn South. Southern white Protestants feared both the immigrants and the African Americans as threats to the social order.

Conditions in Memphis were especially volatile in May, 1866. The city was a rowdy river town known for heavy drinking, gambling, prostitution, and fighting. In 1865, the black population of Memphis had increased to between twenty and twenty-five thousand, many of them living in a run-down district near Fort Pickering. The white citizens were alarmed by incendiary newspaper accounts of crime and disorder.

The Memphis police, mostly Irish immigrants, were corrupt and ill-trained and had a record of brutality toward black people. Added to this already explosive mixture was a body of federal troops, four thousand of whom were black soldiers stationed at Fort Pickering waiting to be mustered out of the army. The violence began on April 29, with a street confrontation between black soldiers and white policemen. On May 1, the violence escalated, with fights breaking out between groups of black soldiers and the city police. By May 2, the mob included a number of people from the surrounding countryside as well as white citizens of Memphis. The mob rampaged through the black district, attacking families, raping women, and burning homes. Civil authorities took no steps to curb the disturbance.

After considerable delay, Major General George Stoneman, commanding the federal troops, brought the city under control. The three days of mob violence resulted in the deaths of forty-six African Americans and two white people. An estimated seventy to eighty other people were injured, and some ninety homes of black people, along with several African American churches and schools, were destroyed. Southern newspapers and civic officials blamed the black soldiers for the outbreak. A committee appointed by Congress, however, attributed the disturbances to the hatred of white people for the "colored race."

The New Orleans Riots

Although the Memphis riots were the result of local conditions, the New Orleans disturbance of July 30 was caused by state politics and had national significance. Louisiana governor James Madison Wells, a Union sympathizer who needed to consolidate his power over the Confederates in New Orleans and the state, supported a plan to reassemble the state constitutional convention that had been disbanded in 1864. This convention, supported by Unionists, planned to gain votes by enfranchising African Americans. The city, sympathetic to Confederate politics, was armed, and the corrupt police force had a record of false arrests and mistreatment of free African Americans. The local newspapers, using highly emotional language, incited the fear of white citizens that African Americans would gain political control.

The commander of the federal troops, General Absalom Baird, should have foreseen the impending violence but apparently ignored the problem. When the delegates to the state convention began to assemble on July 30, fighting broke out between the city police and African American marchers supporting the right to vote. Delegates were dragged from the convention hall and assaulted by people in the street and by the police, who joined in the mob violence. The attacks on African Americans were savage; the wounded were dragged to the city jail and beaten, and the bodies of the dead were mistreated. As the violence escalated, fueled by the drunkenness of the mob, African Americans were dragged from their homes and beaten.

The death toll in the one-day riot included 34 African Americans and 3 white people; approximately 136 people were injured. Although General Baird declared martial law, his action was too late. Several observers, including General Philip H. Sheridan, who was called in to restore order, described the mob violence as a "slaughter." As in the case of the Memphis riots, nearly all the dead and injured were African Americans.

Although the Memphis riots were caused by local conditions, the disturbances in New Orleans had state and national political consequences. The Republican Party lost power, paving the way for Democratic control of the state. Precedents for the racial violence that would mark the years of Reconstruction and beyond had been established. *Marjorie Podolsky*

Core Resources
Eric Foner's "The Meaning of Freedom" and "The Making of Radical Reconstruction," in *Reconstruction: America's Unfinished Revolution, 1863-1877* (New York: Harper & Row, 1988), interprets the scholarly history of Reconstruction and combines older views with newer scholarship. John Hope Franklin's *Reconstruction: After the Civil War* (Chicago: University of Chicago Press, 1961) presents a revised view that rejects the carpetbagger stereotype and argues for a more positive representation of African Americans during Reconstruction. John Hope Franklin and Alfred A. Moss, Jr.'s "The Effort to Attain Peace," in *From Slavery to Freedom: A History of African Americans* (7th ed., New York: McGraw-Hill, 1994), is a widely accepted record of the role of African Americans in U.S. history. Leon F. Litwack's "How Free Is Free?" in *Been in the Storm So Long: The Aftermath of Slavery* (New York: Vintage Books, 1980), is based on the accounts of former slaves interviewed by the Federal Writers' Project in the 1930's. George C. Rable's "The Memphis Race Riot" and "New Orleans and the Emergence of Political Violence," in *But There Was No Peace: The Role of Violence in the Politics of Reconstruction* (Athens: University of Georgia Press, 1984), uses contemporary newspaper articles to bring the riots to life and connect the disturbances with similar events in the twentieth century. Kenneth R. Stampp's "The Tragic Legend of Reconstruction," in *The Era of Reconstruction, 1865-1877* (New York: Alfred A. Knopf, 1969), uses research on race from social scientists to counteract previous historians.

See also: Black codes; Civil Rights Acts of 1866-1875; *Civil Rights* cases; Emancipation Proclamation; Fourteenth Amendment; Freedmen's Bureau; Ku Klux Klan; Race riots of 1943; Race riots of the twentieth century; Reconstruction; Thirteenth Amendment.

Race riots of 1943

> **Significance:** Racial tensions peaked as minorities and whites competed for jobs and social services during World War II.

The urban race riots in the summer of 1943 did not occur spontaneously. A pattern of violence throughout the nation, similar to the racial conflicts that occurred during World War I, had been escalating since 1940, as urban areas swelled with workers drawn to wartime industries. The lack of interracial communication, the failure of local, state, and federal agencies to comprehend the severity of the racial environment, challenges against established southern racial traditions, and extreme shortages of housing and social services created frustration, which manifested itself in racial violence.

The Mobile Riots
Tremendous growth in the population of Mobile, Alabama, caused severe problems in housing and city services. These shortages, combined with the competition for jobs, created racial tension. Whites jealously protected what they considered to be white-only, high-paying, skilled jobs. The largest wartime contractor in Mobile was ADDSCO, the Alabama Dry Dock and Shipbuilding Company. ADDSCO, like numerous other industries, employed African Americans only for unskilled or semiskilled positions. Unable to find enough skilled welders and to appease the local National Association for the Advancement of Colored People (NAACP), led by John LeFlore and Burton R. Morley of the War Manpower Commission, ADDSCO agreed to employ African American welders. On May 24, 1943, black welders reported for work on the third shift at the Pinto Island Yard. No racial incidents occurred during the night, but the next morning, after additional black welders reported for work, violence erupted.

Between five hundred and one thousand whites attacked black workers and drove them from the yards. Governor Chauncey Sparks ordered the Alabama State Guard to intervene, and by noon the rioting had ended. Federal troops occupied the shipyards, and local city and county government ordered all bars and liquor stores closed until the tension eased. Mobile police eventually charged three whites with felony assault, intent to murder, and inciting a riot. On June 5, 1943, the Alabama State Guard pulled out and on June 10, 1943, federal troops returned to their base at Brookley Field.

The Zoot-Suit Riots
As emotions in Mobile calmed, racial tensions in Los Angeles exploded. On June 3, 1943, servicemen from area bases began attacking Mexican American youths known as "zoot-suiters" in response to rumors that the youths had assaulted female relatives of military personnel. Servicemen, accompanied by civilians, roamed the streets, sometimes in taxicabs, in search of zoot-suiters. Streetcars and buses were stopped and searched, and

zoot-suiters found in stores and theaters were disrobed and beaten.

In retaliation, gangs of Mexican American adolescents attacked military personnel. Police arrested reported zoot-suit leaders Frank H. Tellez and Luis "the Chief" Verdusco in an effort to stop Mexican American violence against whites. Fighting reached a climax on June 7, 1943, when a mob of more than a thousand servicemen and civilians moved down Main Street in downtown Los Angeles to the African American neighborhood at Twelfth and Central, and then through the Mexican American neighborhood on the east side, looking for zoot-suiters. The Mexican ambassador to the United States lodged a formal complaint with Secretary of State Cordell Hull, and California governor Earl Warren appointed Attorney General Robert Kenny to investigate the riots. While the riots officially ended on June 7, violent incidents continued throughout the city for the rest of the summer.

As rioting in Los Angeles subsided, racial violence returned to the South. Beaumont, Texas, located between Houston and the Louisiana border, had experienced tremendous wartime growth because of its petroleum production facilities and shipbuilding operations. With emotions already frayed from an earlier suspected rape of a white woman by a black ex-convict, the reported rape of a young white woman by a black man on June 15, 1943, set off a violent reaction among white workers at the Pennsylvania Shipyards. In the early evening, approximately two thousand workers marched on downtown Beaumont. Police Chief Ross Dickey convinced the mob not to lynch any black prisoners.

Around midnight, mobs converged on black neighborhoods in north Beaumont and along Forsythe Street. At the Greyhound bus station, about three hundred whites assaulted fifty-two African American army draftees. Whites looted and burned local businesses and assaulted African Americans until the next morning. Killed during the evening's violence were Alex Mouton and John Johnson, African Americans, and Ellis C. Brown, a white man. Local law enforcement tried diligently to stop the rioting. More than two hundred whites and six African Americans were arrested during the rioting. Martial law was declared on June 16 and lifted on June 20. Although calm had been restored to Beaumont, the violence compelled approximately twenty-five hundred blacks to leave soon after the riots.

Detroit and Harlem

One of the worst riots in the summer of 1943 occurred in Detroit. On Sunday, June 20, 1943, more than one hundred thousand Detroiters, a large percentage of them African American, had gone to the Belle Isle Amusement Park. A group of black teenagers led by

Police officers hold back an African American during the June, 1943, race riots in Detroit, Michigan.

Charles "Little Willie" Lyon began attacking whites. A fight broke out between white sailors and young African Americans on the bridge connecting Belle Isle with the city. The fighting spread, and by 11:00 P.M., an estimated five thousand people were fighting on and around the Belle Isle Bridge.

Rumors of atrocities against African Americans circulated in the Paradise Valley ghetto. Black rioters stoned passing cars of whites and destroyed white-owned businesses. By early morning, whites along Woodward Avenue had retaliated by beating African Americans. Mayor Edward J. Jeffries asked Governor Harry F. Kelly to request federal troops, but Kelly hesitated until Monday evening, and federal troops did not arrive until Tuesday morning. As African Americans rioted along the east side of Woodward Avenue, whites continued congregating along Woodward Avenue. Detroit remained under a curfew and martial law for the following week, and federal troops remained for two weeks. After two days of intense rioting, the Detroit riots were over. Authorities reported thirty-four people, mostly African Americans, killed and more than seven hundred injured. Property damage estimates were around two million dollars.

As the situation calmed in Detroit, tensions were mounting in Harlem, New York. On August 1, 1943, in the late afternoon, Robert Bandy, an African American soldier on leave from the army, argued with James Collins, a white policeman, over the arrest of a black woman at the Braddock Hotel on West 126th Street. A fight ensued, and Collins shot Bandy, inflicting a superficial wound. Rumors quickly spread that a black soldier trying to protect his mother had been killed by a white policeman. Crowds of angry African Americans gathered at the Braddock Hotel and the twenty-eighth police precinct, and by midnight, rioting had started.

The rioting centered in Harlem and never directly involved confrontations between blacks and whites. Mayor Fiorello H. La Guardia acted swiftly to confine the violence by using extra police, firefighters, black Office of Civilian Defense volunteers, and National Guardsmen. African American civic leaders such as Walter White worked alongside city officials to calm Harlem residents. The all-night looting and burning of white-owned businesses left Harlem looking like a war zone. By the time peace was restored, after twelve hours of rioting, six African Americans had been killed by police and National Guard troops, and almost two hundred people reported injuries. Property damage was estimated to be as high as five million dollars. The racial violence of the summer of 1943 had ended, but the problems that triggered riots and violence across the nation remained.   *Craig S. Pascoe*

Core Resources

John Morton Blum's *V Was for Victory: Politics and American Culture During World War II* (New York: Harcourt Brace Jovanovich, 1976) examines established segregation and prejudice in the United States during World War II. Dominic J. Capeci, Jr.'s *The Harlem Riot of 1943* (Philadelphia: Temple University Press, 1977) argues that African Americans became disillusioned with social gains that were meager compared with their contributions to the war effort. Alfred McClung Lee's *Race Riot, Detroit 1943* (1943; reprint, New York: Octagon Books, 1968) is a firsthand account of the Detroit riots.

See also: Detroit riot; Los Angeles riots of 1992; Miami riots of 1980; Newark race riots; Race riots of 1866; Race riots of the twentieth century; Watts riot.

Race riots of the twentieth century

> **Significance:** Race riots both threaten the stability of society and, by their very occurrence, call into question the fundamental fairness of society.

Referring to racial violence in the United States as "race riots" is often misleading. Many race riots were actually one-sided white massacres of blacks; this was particularly true of those prior to 1921. Nineteenth century race riots were often called "slave revolts" or "slave insurrections." These slave revolts were most frequent in the areas of the South where blacks constituted at least 40 percent of the population. Fearing that slave revolts in one part of the South would trigger similar revolts throughout the South, slaveholders quelled such rebellions quickly and viciously.

Twentieth century race riots differ from nineteenth century riots in both motive and location. Whereas nineteenth century riots were primarily concerned with maintaining the institution of slavery, twentieth century riots—particularly those in the years before World War II—were often designed to maintain white supremacy over urban blacks. Also, where nineteenth century race riots were almost exclusively a southern phenomenon, twentieth century race riots took place in almost every major urban area of America.

1900-1945

Race riots prior to World War II often followed a consistent pattern. In almost all cases, the riots were initiated by whites against blacks. In only two of the major riots—Harlem, New York, in 1935 and again in 1943—did African Americans initiate the riots. Second, most riots were caused by a white fear of blacks competing for jobs that previously were held by whites. The rapid movement of blacks from the South to the urban industrial areas of the North contributed to this fear. Third, most riots took place during the hot and humid summer months when young people were out of school. Finally, the riots were often fueled by rumors—allegations of police brutality against blacks or allegations of black violence against whites heightened racial tensions.

One of the major race riots during this period occurred in East St. Louis, Illinois, in 1917. An automobile occupied by four whites drove through black areas firing shots. When a similar car was seen, blacks opened fire and killed two occupants, both of whom were police officers. Whites invaded the black community, burning three hundred homes and killing fifty blacks. The summer of 1919 saw twenty riots in communities such as Charleston, South Carolina; Washington, D.C.; Knoxville, Tennessee; and Chicago. The riots of 1919 were so bloody that the period was called the "Red Summer."

Post-World War II Riots

Although post-World War II riots were fueled by rumor and also took place during the summer months, they differed from pre-World War II riots in two important ways. First, a majority of the riots were initiated by blacks, not whites. Second, many of the post-World War II riots were not confined to the black community. In several cases, whites were singled out as victims of black violence.

The race riots of the 1960's threatened to destroy the fabric of American society. The 1964 Harlem riot in New York City and the 1965 Watts riot in Los Angeles were both triggered by police incidents. The Watts riot lasted six days and resulted in thirty-four deaths and four thousand arrests. "Burn, baby, burn" became a battle cry in black ghettos throughout the United States.

The year 1967 brought major riots to Newark, New Jersey, and to Tampa, Cincinnati, Atlanta, and Detroit. Newark's riot was the most severe, resulting in twenty-six deaths and $30 million in property damage. The assassination of Martin Luther King, Jr., on April 4, 1968, triggered racial violence in more than one hundred cities. In response to the urban racial violence, President Lyndon B. Johnson appointed the National Advisory Commission on Civil Disorders, better known as the Kerner Commission. After investigating the causes of the rioting the commission presented a series of recommendations. According to the Kerner Commission, the most important grievances of the black community were police practices, lack of employment opportunities, and inadequate housing. The ominous conclusion of the Kerner Commission was that unless the causes of urban violence were addressed, the United States would continue to become two societies, one black, one white—separate and unequal.

1980's and 1990's

Although there was a lull in race riots during the 1970's, the Miami riots in May of 1980 signaled a renewal of urban racial unrest. On December 17, 1979, a black insurance agent, Arthur McDuffie, was stopped by Miami police officers after a high-speed chase. A fight ensued, and McDuffie was beaten to death. The police officers engaged in a cover-up and reported that McDuffie died as a result of a motorcycle crash. When the cover-up unraveled, five Miami police officers were arrested. Four were charged with manslaughter, and one was charged with tampering with evidence. After deliberating less than three hours, an all-white jury found all defendants not guilty. Within hours of the verdict, the Liberty City section of Miami exploded in violence. Before order was restored three days later, eighteen people were dead, including eight whites who had

the misfortune to be driving through Liberty City when the riot began.

The riot that took place in Los Angeles in May of 1992 was triggered by a similar event. Almost immediately after four white police officers were acquitted of assault in the videotaped beating of Rodney King, a black man, one of the most violent race riots in American history broke out. Before it was over, more than sixty people had died, more than four thousand fires had been set, and Los Angeles had suffered property damage totaling more than a billion dollars.

Although the patterns of racial violence may have altered over the decades, the fact remains that race riots continue to occur. Once a southern phenomenon, they have become a national problem in search of a solution.

Darryl Paulson

Core Resources

See James W. Button, *Black Violence: Political Impact of the 1960's Riots* (Princeton, N.J.: Princeton University Press, 1978); Robert Connery, ed., *Urban Riots* (New York: Vintage Books, 1969); Bruce Porter and Marvin Dunn, *The Miami Riot of 1980* (Lexington, Mass.: Lexington Books, 1984); *Report of the National Advisory Commission on Civil Disorders* (New York: Bantam Books, 1968); and Elliott Rudwick, *Race Riot at East St. Louis* (New York: Atheneum, 1972).

See also: Black Power movement; Civil Rights movement; Commission on Civil Rights; Detroit riot; Kerner Report; King, Rodney, case; Los Angeles riots of 1992; Miami riots of 1980; National Advisory Commission on Civil Disorders; Newark race riots; Race riots of 1866; Race riots of 1943; Watts riot.

A banner, cross, and flowers mark the spot at the corner of Florence and Normandie in Los Angeles where violence first erupted and escalated into the 1992 riots.

Racial and ethnic demographics in Canada

Since the 1970's, Canada has been transformed from a relatively homogeneous to a racially and ethnically diverse nation, primarily through large-scale immigration from virtually all regions of the world. Also, the widespread intermarriage that has occurred over the course of Canadian history has added to the diversity and made it increasingly difficult to delineate ethnic divisions precisely. The Canadian census, seeking to accurately describe people's ethnicity, has given respondents the opportunity to report more than one ethnic origin. Unfortunately, this policy has created a complicated picture of the Canadian population, clouding the very notion of ethnic origin. An additional problem was introduced in the 1996 census: The format of the ethnic origin question was changed, making it easier for people to identify themselves simply as "Canadian" rather than as any specific ethnicity.

Despite these difficulties, 64 percent of Canadians reported a single ethnic origin in 1996, making it possible to spell out in some detail the ethnic configuration of the nation. Canada's population can be divided into three major ethnic groups: the two founding groups (British and French), the non-British/non-French groups, and aboriginal peoples.

Charter Groups

The two founding, or charter, groups constitute the largest components of the Canadian population. In the 1996 census, 11.5 million identified themselves as English, Scottish, Welsh, or Irish in either single or multiple responses. Those giving British Isles-only responses numbered 4.9 million, or 17 percent of the total population. Those identifying themselves as French in ethnic origin accounted for 5.6 million single and multiple responses; 2.7 million identified themselves as French-only in origin (9 percent of the total population). These percentages are understatements of the size of the British and French groups, however, owing to the large number who reported "Canadian" ethnic origins (19 percent), the majority of whom are probably British or French. Moreover, delineating the French Canadian population is better accomplished by querying for language preference, which indicates that 24 percent of Canadians are francophones (primarily French speakers).

Non-British/Non-French Groups

The non-British/non-French groups constitute almost 30 percent of the total Canadian population. These groups represent an extremely diverse spectrum, the largest among them (in descending order) Irish, German, Italian, Ukrainian, Chinese, Dutch, Polish, South Asian (including Indian, Pakistani, Bangladeshi, Sri Lankan, and others from the Indian subcontinent), Jewish (recognized as an ethnic group in the Canadian census), Norwegian, Portuguese, Swedish, Russian, Hungarian, Filipino, American, Spanish, Greek, and Jamaican. These groups are the historic product of Canada's two major periods of immigration: the late nineteenth and early twentieth centuries and the last three decades of the twentieth century. Particularly since the 1970's, the size of these groups as well as their cultural variety has altered Canada's basic ethnic composition.

Aboriginal Peoples

The third major element in the Canadian ethnic mosaic is the native, or aboriginal, groups, who make up about 3 percent of the total population. Among these groups are Native Indians (the "First Nations"), Inuit, and Metis, the latter of mixed racial origins. Those claiming aboriginal ancestry in 1996 numbered 1.1 million. Of these, 867,000 (395,000 single responses) reported Native Indian ancestry, 221,000 Metis (50,000 single responses), and 50,000 Inuit (33,000 single responses).

The 1996 census also asked an identity question of aboriginals. Those identifying themselves as aboriginal people numbered 800,000, of which 554,000 were Native Indian, 210,000 Metis, and 41,000 Inuit. As with other categories, the aboriginal count was somewhat affected by the inclusion of "Canadian" among the possible categories listed on the 1996 census questionnaire.

Visible Minorities

An important racial and ethnic category in Canada is "visible minorities." As defined by the Employment Equity Act, these are people, other than aboriginal peoples, who are "non-Caucasian in race or non-white in color." This essentially refers to all non-European Canadian groups.

The total visible minority population in 1996 was 3.2 million, representing 11.2 percent of the total Canadian population. This increase from 9.4 percent in 1991 and 6.3 percent in 1986 reflects the changing sources of immigration to Canada starting in the 1970's. Whereas prior immigrant waves were mainly European, the most recent immigrants have been primarily Asian and secondarily Caribbean. In 1996, the largest groups among the visible minorities were Chinese (27 percent), South Asians (21 percent), and blacks (18 percent). Most of the blacks in Canada are of Caribbean origin.

Geographical Distribution of Ethnic Groups

The British-origin population of Canada is the most dispersed geographically. Other groups, however, are strongly concentrated in particular provinces and urban

Toronto is home for many of Canada's visible minorities. This supermarket in Little India caters to Asian Indians, Pakistanis, and those from the West Indies.

areas. The French-Canadian population is situated primarily in a single province, Quebec, where about 80 percent reside. The non-British/non-French European groups live primarily in the three largest provinces, Ontario, Quebec, and British Columbia. More specifically, most live in Canada's three largest urban areas: Toronto, Montreal, and Vancouver.

As for visible minorities, almost all live in large urban centers, especially Toronto and Vancouver. Toronto is the epicenter of Canada's visible minorities, who make up one-third of that city's total population. Almost half the South Asian and black populations of Canada live in Toronto, along with about two-fifths of Canada's Chinese, Korean, and Filipino populations. In Vancouver, 31 percent of the total population are visible minorities, most them Chinese or South Asian. Other urban areas with large visible minority populations are Calgary (16 percent), Edmonton (14 percent), Montreal (12 percent), Ottawa-Hull (12 percent), and Winnipeg (11 percent).

About three-quarters of Status Indians (those officially classified as Indians under the Canadian Indian Act) live on reserves established by the government. Metis reside mostly in western Canada, and Inuit have remained relatively isolated geographically in the far North. *Martin N. Marger*

Core Resources

The Canadian census is conducted every five years and constitutes the primary source for statistical information on Canada's racial and ethnic groups. Reports are published by Statistics Canada and many can be found on the Internet. Statistics Canada's Web site can be accessed at www.statcan.ca. A range of demographic issues regarding Canadian racial and ethnic groups is covered in *Ethnic Demography: Canadian Immigrant, Ra-*

cial, and Cultural Variations, edited by Shiva S. Halli, Frank Trovato and Leo Driedger (Ottawa: Carleton University Press, 1997). A general introduction to racial and ethnic relations in Canada can be found in Martin N. Marger's *Race and Ethnic Relations: American and Global Perspectives* (5th ed., Belmont, Calif.: Wadsworth, 1999).

See also: Aboriginal Canadians; African Canadians; Asian Indians in Canada; Chinese Canadians; European immigration to Canada: 1867-present; Francophone; French Canadians; Indian-white relations: Canada; Japanese Canadians; Metis; Multiculturalism in Canada; Reserve system of Canada; Separatist movement in Quebec; Sikhs in Canada; Status Indians; Vietnamese Canadians; Visible minority allophones in Canada.

Racial and ethnic demographics: trends

Significance: The demographic makeup of the United States and Canada have changed over the years, affecting the relations between and relative power and dominance of the various racial and ethnic groups that live in these nations of immigrants.

The United States, Canada, and Australia are the three most important "receiving" countries for immigrants worldwide. The United States and Canada, as a result of their immigration policies, have become two of the world's most ethnically diverse geographical areas. Two centuries ago, the population of these two nations was predominantly of white European heritage, but in the twenty-first century, nonwhites and people whose heritage is not European are expected to become an increasingly large part of their populations. Because the United States and Canada both possess a strong democratic ethos and high standard of living, they are likely to attract many more people, especially oppressed ethnic minorities.

United States

Since 1790, as required by the U.S. Constitution, a census has been conducted every ten years. The initial purpose of the census was to enable the U.S. government to determine an equitable apportionment of tax dollars and the number of representatives each area would send to Congress. During its early history, the census was executed by temporary workers in nonpermanent facilities. It was not until March, 1902, that the government created the Bureau of the Census with a full-time staff and permanent facilities.

A perennial issue for the bureau has been the underreporting of certain subpopulations, including the very young, the poor, immigrants, and nonwhites. The resulting lower numbers have often resulted in those populations having less government representation and, unfortunately, fewer benefits. In the latter part of the twentieth century, the bureau made great efforts to correct these shortcomings by making questionnaires available in Spanish and developing methods for assessing the undocumented immigrant population.

During its first hundred years, the United States had an open immigration policy. It was not until 1882 that Congress passed the Chinese Exclusion Act, which outlawed Chinese immigration for ten years. This anti-Chinese legislation followed thirty years of heavy Chinese immigration during which more than two hundred thousand Chinese came to the United States to escape overpopulation, poverty, and warfare in China.

The history of legal immigration to the United States between 1820 and 1985 exhibits dramatic changes in the regions of the world from which immigrants came. Examination of the table "Regional Background of U.S. Immigrants (1820-1985)" reveals these changes. Most striking is the decline of European immigrants, largely whites, and the significant increase in immigrants from Latin America and Asia, mostly Hispanics and nonwhites. Experts have projected population changes that suggest that by 2080, the U.S. population will consist of 49.8 percent white non-Hispanics, 23.4 percent Hispanics, 14.7 percent blacks, and 12 percent Asians and other persons.

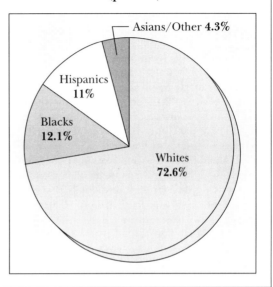

U.S. Population by Ethnicity, 1997
(percent)

Source: Data are calculated from U.S. Bureau of the Census, *Statistical Abstract of the United States, 1997* (117th ed.). Washington, D.C.: U.S. Government Printing Office, 1997.

Canada

Canada, founded by the British and French, had exclusionary laws that discouraged nonwhite, ethnic immigrants, but these laws were relaxed after World War II. The nation's present multicultural population reflects the new immigration policies: Of the almost 29 million people in Canada, as estimated in the 1996 census, about 40 percent are of British ancestry, 27 percent are of French, 20 percent are of other European, and 1.5 percent are of Indian and Inuit ancestry. The remaining population, 11.5 percent, consists of people of African,

Regional Background of U.S. Immigrants, 1820-1985
(percent)

	1820-1860	1861-1899	1900-1920	1921-1960	1961-1970	1971-1980	1981-1985
Northern and western Europe	95	68	41	38	18	7	5
North America	3	7	6	19	12	4	2
Southern and eastern Europe	—	22	44	20	15	11	6
Asia	—	2	4	4	13	35	48
Latin America	—	—	4	18	39	40	35
Other	2	1	1	1	3	3	4

Source: L. F. Bouvier and R. W. Gardner, *Immigration to the U.S.* Washington, D.C.: Population Reference Bureau, 1986.

Asian, and Hispanic origins. Although the number of people with non-European ancestry in Canada's population is expected to increase in the next century, it is anticipated that people of European descent will continue to dominate its culture and seats of political power.

Ancient Peoples of North America

Recent archaeological research suggests that human beings, probably *Homo erectus*, were living in North America as far back as 135,000 years ago. At the time of the first European contact, about 12 million to 15 million Indians and 20,000 Inuit (Eskimos) were living in North America. According to the 1990 U.S. census, about 2 million American Indians and around 81,000 Inuit lived in the United States. In Canada, in 1996, census takers reported fewer than 500,000 aboriginals, that is, people of either Indian or Inuit background. Mistreatment by whites and deadly epidemics account for the great reduction in the Indian population. Better living conditions (partly due to distance from early settlers) explain the increase in the Inuit population.

African Americans

The United States, with about 30 million African Americans, has the third-largest black population in the world (Brazil and Nigeria have larger populations); however, Canada has fewer than 1 million blacks, mostly of West Indian descent. Contrary to popular belief, the first blacks in North America were not slaves. In 1619, twenty black men became indentured servants to wealthy Virginian white men. Unfortunately, most of the other blacks who landed in the United States came as slaves. From the beginning of the American slave trade in the 1600's to the Emancipation Proclamation in 1863, almost 90 percent of all blacks in what is now the United States were slaves. The first U.S. census in 1790 reported 757,000 blacks. By 1800, they numbered 1 million. In the 1860 census, there were about 4,442,000 blacks. The 1990 U.S. census reported almost 30 million blacks, or about 12.1 percent of the total U.S. population of almost 250 million. By 2080, it is projected that blacks will reach around 14.7 percent of the U.S. population. Although blacks have made tremendous progress in the second half of the twentieth century, many serious problems still need to be addressed and solved.

Hispanics

Hispanics were among the earliest nonnative peoples to populate North America. In 1513, Juan Ponce de León discovered Florida, and in 1565, Spaniards settled St. Augustine in present-day Florida. They also colonized Mexico and parts of the American Southwest. As a result, Hispanics have largely been concentrated in the Southwestern states: Texas, New Mexico, Colorado, Arizona,

and California. In the past one hundred years, large Hispanic populations have also developed in New York, New Jersey, Florida, and Illinois. In 1996, Hispanics numbered 28 million, or around 11 percent of the U.S. population. By 2080, this group is estimated to constitute about 23.4 percent of the U.S. population and be the largest ethnic group in the country.

Asians and Arab Americans

The first Asians to arrive in the United States were the Chinese. In 1849, there were only 54 Chinese in the whole nation. The 1990 U.S. census estimated the Chinese American population at 1,645,000. The census counted 815,450 Japanese Americans, some 800,000 Korean Americans, about 815,000 East Indians, and 870,000 Arab Americans. More than two-thirds of the Arab Americans live in ten states and about one-third live in three metropolitan areas: Detroit, Michigan; New York City, and the Los Angeles area. Metropolitan Detroit has the largest Arab American community in the United States.

In the 1880's, Chinese and Japanese immigrants came to Canada to help construct the railroad and work on other industrial projects. They were soon followed by East Indians. Between the early 1900's and World War II, exclusionary laws kept most Asians from immigrating to Canada. However, after the war, Canada relaxed its immigration policies, and many Asians and other ethnic groups came to Canada.

The Future

For the last five hundred years, the United States and Canada have been dominated by white European peoples and cultures. However, in the last fifty years, non-Europeans, nonwhites, Hispanics, and Asians have become the fastest-growing populations in these nations. By 2080, experts predict that more than 50 percent of the U.S. population will be non-European and nonwhite and that the largest ethnic group will be Hispanic. In Canada, although the makeup of the population is changing, it is not likely that the U.S. population patterns will be duplicated. However, the proportion of British, French, and European people in the overall population is projected to fall. In the face of these trends, the power and influence of the dominant white group in the United States and Canada will probably diminish somewhat, and the two nations will continue to be pluralistic and democratic societies that attract refugees and immigrants.

R. M. Frumkin

Core Resources

Some helpful books on the racial and ethnic demographics of the United States include the *Statistical Abstracts of the United States: 1997* (117th ed., Washington,

D.C.: U.S. Bureau of the Census, 1997), L. F. Bouvier and R. W. Gardner's *Immigration to the U.S.* (Washington, D.C.: Population Reference Bureau, 1986), and R. T. Schaefer's *Racial and Ethnic Groups* (4th ed., Glenview, Ill.: Scott, Foresman/Little, Brown Higher Education, 1990). Information on Canadian demographics can be obtained from the government agency Statistics Canada, Statistical Reference Center, in Ottawa, Canada.

See also: Aboriginal Canadians; African Canadians; Censuses, U.S.; Chinese Americans; Chinese Canadians; European immigration to Canada: 1867-present; European immigration to the United States: 1790-1892; European immigration to the United States: 1892-1943; Indian-white relations: Canada; Indian-white relations: United States; Japanese Americans; Japanese Canadians; Latinos in the United States; Racial and ethnic demographics in Canada.

Racial/ethnic relations in Canada

> **Significance:** Many white Canadians are largely unaware of or oblivious to the racial discrimination that exists around them and are reluctant to acknowledge that a race relation problem even exists. Proponents of reform have occasionally encountered a defensive reaction when they have exposed the plight of "visible minorities" (blacks, Chinese, Filipinos, Japanese, Koreans, Latin Americans, Pacific Islanders, South Asians, Southeast Asians, West Asians, and Arabs) struggling for fair and equal treatment in a society that prefers to ignore the problem rather than strive to overcome it.

The extent of discrimination in Canada has varied depending on the region, economic necessity, and the policies of provincial and federal governments. Because the issue of aboriginal Canadians has been dealt with in a separate essay in this encyclopedia, their plight will not be examined in this essay.

Systemic Discrimination

Historically, racism in Canada has not been confined to interactions between white and ethnic minority individuals, although these personal interactions fueled the entire scope of discriminatory treatment, particularly where Asians were concerned. Instead, systemic and institutionalized discrimination has been a marked feature of Canadian history. Systemic discrimination historically involved provincial and federal legislation to keep out visible minority immigrants, to segregate schooling and thereby hinder the upward mobility of African Canadians, to prevent family reunification for Asian male immigrants already in Canada, to disfranchise Asian Canadians and restrict their economic opportunities, to confine Japanese Canadians in detention camps and confiscate their property during World War II, and to deny refuge to Jews fleeing from Nazi persecution in Europe. The discrimination involved almost every level of Canadian government, which produced immigration and refugee determination policies and regulations designed to keep Canada white.

Given a political context that was hostile to the establishment of visible minority communities, it was almost inevitable that some of those individuals who persisted and came to Canada found themselves isolated, marginalized, restricted in employment opportunities, and denied access to adequate housing and education. They were subjected to negative stereotyping, to mockery of cultural differences, and to racial harassment. Ironically, although they were treated as inferior beings, most Asian immigrants exemplified the very values that were highly prized in middle-class white mainstream Canadian society. These immigrants were largely hardworking, thrifty, determined to succeed, family-oriented, and dedicated to their communities and their religious ideals. Because of these core traditions and values, they thrived in spite of the racism, excelling in business, blue-collar work, and later the professions.

Although racism may never be expunged from Canadian society, systemic discrimination has declined. Visible minorities in Canada received an indirect boost from the success of decolonization in Asia and Africa following World War II. As the newly independent states took their place in the United Nations and Commonwealth, it became embarrassing for the Canadian government to continue systemic discrimination at home when it was seeking so avidly to play a leading role as champion of democracy and human rights on the international stage. Canada also needed to trade with these nations and could not afford the reputation of being a racist country. Economic factors facilitated a change of policy. Canada championed international human rights covenants and scrambled to undo discrimination internally to provide an appearance of adhering to its international commitments. The result, in 1967, was a color- and race-neutral points system for immigrants that enabled qualified Asians and Africans to come to Canada. In 1982, Canada officially committed itself to a policy of multiculturalism and included this pledge in the Canadian Charter of Rights and Freedoms. On paper, at least, discrimination was dismantled, and Canadian citizenship, the vote, and all benefits were conferred regardless of race or color.

A Chronology of Race Relations in Canada

Year	Event
1600's	Aboriginals are enslaved in New France.
1608	Black slaves are brought to Canada.
1800's	Chinese workers are imported to build the Canadian Pacific Railway.
1833	Slavery is abolished in Canada.
1849	Segregated schooling is established in Upper Canada (segregated schooling in Ontario ends in 1965).
1858	Gold is discovered in Fraser Valley, British Columbia, prompting Chinese immigration.
1875	British Columbia disfranchises Chinese and Japanese.
1885	$50 head tax is imposed on Chinese immigrants.
1887	Riots erupt in Vancouver against Chinese.
1895	British Columbia denies vote to Asians, effectively barring them from federal vote as well (rescinded 1947-1948).
1897	British Columbia passes Alien Labor Act to prohibit Chinese and Japanese employment on public works projects. Federal government disallows the legislation.
1900	$100 head tax imposed on Chinese immigrants.
1903	$500 head tax levied on Chinese immigrants.
1905	Khalsa Diwan Society establishes Sikh temple in Canada.
1907	Racial violence breaks out against Asians in British Columbia.
1907	Asian immigrants subject to rule requiring $200 in landing money.
1908	To prevent immigration from India, continuous passage rule stipulates that immigrants must arrive in Canada without having stopped elsewhere.
1912	Saskatchewan passes legislation making it an offense for an Asian businessman to hire a white woman.
1914	Sikhs, challenging the continuous passage rule, sail directly to Canada on the *Komagata Maru* but are refused entry anyway.
1919	Landing money requirement for Asians is raised to $250.
1920	Ku Klux Klan established in Canada.
1923	Government develops policy to allow only immigrants from predominantly white Commonwealth countries.
1923	Chinese Immigration Act bars immigrants from China (repealed 1947).
1930	Immigration Act prevents arrival of Asian immigrants.
1931	Japanese Canadian World War I veterans, but not their descendants, gain franchise rights.
1932	Ku Klux Klan gains provincial charter in Alberta.
1939	Japanese Canadian Citizens League pledges support of the Canadian government in the war effort.
1942	Japanese Canadians deprived of personal property and interned in camps during World War II.
1952, 1957	Immigration Acts bar immigrants on basis of nationality, ethnic group, habits, class, customs, unsuitability to climate, and modes of life.
1962	Immigration Act eliminates racial criterion as basis for barring immigration.
1967	Immigration Act establishes a race-neutral points system that focuses on would-be immigrants' qualifications.

1970	Canada ratifies the International Convention on the Elimination of All Forms of Racial Discrimination. Hate propaganda becomes a criminal offense.
1971	Government of Canada makes official its commitment to multiculturalism (Multiculturalism Act is passed in 1988).
1973	United Nations proclaims Decade for Action to Combat Racism and Racial Discrimination.
1976	Burnaby, British Columbia, residents protest against establishment of a Muslim mosque and community center.
1982	Canadian Charter of Rights and Freedoms, a constitutional commitment to uphold multiculturalism, is enacted.
1988	Prime Minister Brian Mulroney's government pays $300 million as compensation to Japanese Canadians who were interned during World War II.
1990's	Chinese Canadian National Council seeks compensation of $1 billion for head taxes imposed on Chinese immigrants between 1885 and 1923.
1998	Canadian Supreme Court endorses practice of quizzing prospective jurors about their racial biases. Saskatchewan is the first province to implement this practice.

Lingering Attitudes

The implementation of these policies and the promulgation of these ideas has however been painfully slow. Visible minorities continue to be underrepresented politically at the municipal, provincial, and federal levels, in the civil service, and in government appointments. By 1998, only eleven hundred visible minority members were employed in the regular military force, which numbered approximately sixty-three thousand. A survey of the military in 1996 found a greater degree of racial intolerance in the armed forces than in the general population, a factor that may have been a disincentive to about eighty-eight thousand visible minority members who could potentially have been recruits. Access to employment, particularly in nontraditional fields and access to housing continue to be serious problems for racial minorities. The plight of visible minority women is even more severe because they suffer both racial and gender-based discrimination.

Because most incidents of racism occur on a personal level, they escape quantification and public notice and remain largely in the realm of anecdotal evidence, discussed among the visible minority communities but not widely known. The unfortunate result of this is that many white Canadians tend to believe that the paper guarantees of racial equality mirror the reality of life for visible minorities. Scholars, lawyers, and community activists who have attempted to present a more accurate picture of the reality of visible minority life in Canada have produced a variety of reactions in the white majority from disbelief to avoidance of the issue to hostility. Those members of visible minorities who have fought against or pointed out racism have been categorized as troublemakers, misfits, and worse. Although this is a generalization, it appears that unlike in the United States, where there has been a lengthy dialogue at many levels on race relations and a clear desire to confront and deal with the issue, in Canada, bringing this topic to the fore is likely to result in the speaker's being considered confrontational, difficult, demanding, and controversial, characteristics that are not perceived as being conducive to the "Canadian way of life."

The pervasiveness of the myths about Canada being a kinder, gentler version of the United States, a society of compromise rather than confrontation, continues to bedevil efforts at reform. Community activists have found that some white Canadians will simply not admit to racial prejudice being a significant factor in their society, preferring instead to search for other motivation for incidents of discrimination against minorities. If the problem does not exist, obviously there is nothing to be concerned about and no necessity for change. The issue does, however, come very uncomfortably to the fore when members of racial minorities are assaulted and murdered. Although sporadic, these racially motivated incidents have involved victims from the elderly to children and, unlike most other acts of discrimination, these murders receive the attention of the Canadian media.

Slavery and the Black Minority

Few Canadians are even aware that aboriginal peoples were enslaved during the seventeenth century and that

African slaves were imported to work in New France, Upper Canada, and other areas in the sixteenth and seventeenth centuries. Upper Canada stopped the importation of slaves in 1793, but slavery was not abolished in Canada until its demise throughout the British Empire in 1833. Although slavery was over, racism, discrimination, and grinding poverty continued to be the lot of African Canadians, who were provided with infertile land for farming, confined to poorly funded segregated schools, denied employment opportunities, and prevented from moving upward in society.

During the American Revolution, the British government in Canada offered freedom and some land to any American slaves who could escape to Canada. However, the former slaves found that in Canada, they were paid lower wages than white workers, given inferior land, and denied the vote or the right to sit on juries. The Civil War in the United States caused many slaves to flee to Canada, but an estimated 75 percent of them eventually returned to the United States.

The Canadian government did not encourage black immigration until the 1950's and 1960's, when the numbers of this visible minority doubled, largely because of immigration from the Caribbean islands.

During the second half of the twentieth century, a number of confrontations took place between Canadian whites and blacks: Individuals at a hockey game in 1973 experienced racially motivated assaults, and a black teen was murdered in a racial incident in Toronto in 1975. Discrimination also took a number of other forms. Blacks were the subject of racial slurs and signs in Nova Scotia, and employment agencies and real estate companies in Ontario were found to be withholding the names of applicants and customers of color from prospective employers and housing vendors. African Canadians were denied service in some Ontario restaurants during the 1950's. Racism also affected accessibility to theaters, hotels, bars, and recreation centers.

Minority Canadians, especially those of African descent, have complained about discriminatory treatment at the hands of police forces. Between the late 1970's and the mid-1990's, about sixteen black people were shot, ten of them fatally, by police in Ontario. Although criminal charges were brought in nine of these cases, none of the officers involved was convicted. In 1988, Ontario police shot four black men and in 1991 shot four civilians. In 1995, the Report of the Commission on Systemic Racism in the Ontario Criminal Justice System revealed the existence of discrimination and a strong perception of different treatment given minorities caught in the criminal justice system. Significantly, the report found that any suggestion of racial bias was negatively and defensively perceived as a commentary on the individual officials involved and on their own decisions and actions.

African Canadians greet each other during the Caribana festival. Immigration of blacks was not encouraged in Canada until the 1950's and 1960's, when many Caribbean blacks entered the nation.

"Indignant denials" were the response to any charges, and the report concluded that "racism is still entrenched in Canadian society."

Sports have provided one venue of escape for a few African Canadians. Their prowess and excellence allowed them to overcome racial barriers. They have represented Canada internationally and have brought much prestige to the country along with a wealth of medals.

Japanese Canadians
Scholar Mitsuru Shimpo divided the Japanese experience in Canada into four parts: the period of free immigration (1877-1907), the period of controlled immigration (1908-1941), the period of deprived civil rights (1942-1948), and the period of restored civil rights (from 1949). Initially, Japanese immigration was perceived as threatening by some elements of white society who feared economic competition. The Japanese settled primarily in British Columbia, where they numbered nearly five thousand by 1901. They worked with great success in a variety of fields, ranging from forestry and mining to fishing and boat and railroad construction. When

head taxes were imposed on Chinese immigrants, officials in British Columbia proposed that the Japanese be similarly treated. The province's attempts to raise the head tax to five hundred dollars in 1898 and 1899 and impose it on Japanese as well as Chinese immigrants were not successful.

In 1875, the provincial government had deprived the Japanese of their franchise, thereby severely restricting the political and economic scope of their lives. They could not vote provincially or federally, hold public office, become school trustees, or be on juries. The legislation also disqualified Canadian-born children of Japanese immigrants. In 1896, the Japanese and Chinese were denied the right to vote in municipal elections in British Columbia. The following year, a provincial Alien Labor Act prohibiting the employment of Japanese and Chinese on public works projects was rejected by the dominion government as was an attempt to bar Chinese and Japanese workers from mining jobs. The provincial government sought in 1900 and 1903 to make knowledge of English or a European language a criterion in order to preclude Japanese and Asian immigrants and workers, but these attempts failed.

Japanese Canadians were supported by extensive lobbying by Japanese consular officials in Canada and by the diplomatic intervention of the Japanese government. Japan was the only major Asian country to have escaped European colonial domination, and its protests against the racist treatment of Japanese Canadians prevented them from receiving the treatment meted to the Chinese in Canada. As Japan was an ally of Britain before and during World War I, restrictions on Japanese immigration to Canada existed but were not implemented very severely. Although Japanese Canadians who volunteered for military service during the Boer War were rejected, several groups of Japanese Canadian soldiers participated in World War I.

Labor shortages in Canada during World War I decreased the hostility to immigrants, but in 1919, British Columbia attempted to curtail the number of fishing licenses issued to Japanese Canadians by about one thousand and agitated against Asian immigration and Asian economic involvement in development of resources such as agriculture, forestry, mining, fishing, and industries. Economic competitiveness and Japanese Canadian financial success were at the heart of the racial animosity and motivated the harassment. Driven from the fisheries, Japanese Canadians in British Columbia turned to farming and by the mid-1930's enjoyed considerable success and again generated enormous hostility for their efforts.

When the Japanese government became the enemy of Canada in World War II, the situation for Japanese Canadians changed dramatically. Although Japanese Ca-

nadians pledged their support for the Allied war effort, they were rebuffed. Three months before the attack on Pearl Harbor, the Royal Canadian Mounted Police undertook the compulsory registration of all Japanese adults in Canada, and Japanese Canadians were required to carry identification cards.

In 1942, the thriving Japanese Canadian community was torn asunder by governmental actions that forced the evacuation of men, women, and children from coastal communities and their internment in detention camps. There was no conclusive evidence of Japanese Canadian collusion or conspiracy with the Japanese government to justify such drastic action against this community. Those taken to the camps included Canadian citizens of Japanese ancestry. Japanese schools were closed, and educational opportunities were drastically curtailed. Japanese-language newspapers were prohibited. Japanese Canadians could not own radios, automobiles, or cameras. Their mail was censored. More than twelve hundred Japanese fishing boats were confiscated. The British Columbia Security Commission oversaw the transfer of thousands of Japanese civilians into detention, the confiscation of their vast property holdings by the Custodian of Alien Property, and the sale of the seized properties. Some researchers suggest that the property seizure demonstrates that the detention of Japanese Canadians was economically and politically motivated rather than a matter of military security. Hardship followed for the Japanese Canadian detainees who were forced to build roads in British Columbia, Alberta, and Ontario and work in sugar-beet production. After World War II ended, about four thousand Japanese Canadians moved to Japan.

For those who remained, the scars of wartime detention, forced labor, and the deprivation of all their personal property meant a very painful adjustment back into society. Racism hindered them in various realms. Lethbridge, Alberta, forbade Japanese Canadians to live in the city until 1952. Gradually, the restrictions were lifted, and Japanese Canadian civil rights restored. In 1988, the Canadian government of Prime Minister Brian Mulroney provided $300 million (Canadian) as compensation to the Japanese Canadian community.

Chinese Canadians

Economic need and the desire for profit facilitated the importation of thousands of Chinese workers, who were desperately needed to perform railroad, mining, and forestry work because of the shortage of white laborers. Between 1881 and 1884, nearly sixteen thousand Chinese men were brought in to build the Canadian Pacific Railway. These men did back-breaking physical labor for lower wages than white workers, lived in miserable conditions, and suffered social isolation. Once the railway was completed, various measures were undertaken to persuade them to leave the country. Family reunification was hindered by the imposition of excessively high head taxes on new immigrants. In contrast, white British immigrants were encouraged to emigrate with travel funding. Chinese Canadians were denied both the provincial (British Columbia) and federal vote in 1895. This effectively denied them employment in any occupation requiring an official license as they were not on a voter's list. Ironically, they continued to pay full taxes. Between 1924 and 1947, Chinese immigration was legislatively halted.

Sir Richard McBride, administrative head of British Columbia, stated in 1914, "To admit Orientals in large numbers would mean in the end the extinction of the white people, and we have always in mind the necessity of keeping this a white man's country." Chinese Canadians were not allowed to obtain Crown land, work on publicly funded projects, or own liquor or logging licenses. In 1923, they lost certain fishing rights. Chinese Canadians were also denied the opportunity to work as teachers, lawyers, and pharmacists and did not receive the vote until 1947.

The Chinese community in Canada during the nineteenth century was overwhelmingly male. An environment of racial prejudice, head taxes on immigrants, and the curtailment of immigration in 1923 prevented Chinese women from joining their husbands in Canada. These factors created a community in 1911 with a male-female ratio of 2,790 to 100. The disruption of family life and long years of forced separation took an enormous toll psychologically and emotionally for thousands of individuals caught in the coil of systemic racism in Canada. Family reunification was allowed following the repeal in 1947 of the Chinese Immigration Act. About twenty-two thousand Chinese immigrants arrived between 1947 and 1962, rectifying the sex imbalance somewhat.

In 1962, the Chinese gained the right of entry as independent immigrants, and between 1968 and 1976, Canada accepted more than ninety-one thousand Chinese immigrants. During the 1980's and early 1990's, Chinese immigration into Canada was actively encouraged by the Canadian government. The scheduled 1997 annexation by China of the British colony of Hong Kong brought a flood of well-to-do, entrepreneurial, highly motivated and skilled businesspeople and professionals to Canada. Their presence set off a financial boom in British Columbia as they built enormous mansions, engaged in development projects, and enthusiastically pursued their vision of the Canadian dream. However, the euphoria was short-lived. The media portrayed their disillusion with the racism, marginalization, and social isolation some of them encountered in Canada, and a

number of them returned to Hong Kong, taking their vast fortunes, their dynamism, and their expertise with them. Hong Kong immigration declined, and this, combined with other factors, caused a serious economic downturn in British Columbia during the late 1990's. However, the same period witnessed a surge in immigration from China. Chinese—the language of about 3 percent of the total population—became Canada's third most-spoken language. In 1998, the United Chinese Community Enrichment Services Society complained about lengthy delays in immigration acceptance of Chinese spouses and attributed this to discriminatory attitudes among Canadian bureaucrats.

The Chinese community in Canada triumphed over tremendous obstacles to become a very significant minority contributing extensively in business, the professions, and numerous other realms. Chinatowns in large Canadian cities draw tourists from around the world. In order to redress past injustices, during the late 1990's, the Chinese Canadian National Council sought the return of the approximately $1 billion (1998 dollar value) paid in head tax by Chinese immigrants between 1885 and 1923.

Immigrants from India

At the beginning of the twentieth century, Asian Indians came to Canada to work on the railroad, in mining, and in construction jobs, which were experiencing a severe labor shortage. However, the presence of a few Indian immigrants in Canada alarmed authorities and propelled the Canadian government to pass an Order in Council in 1908 that immigrants had to reach Canada from the country of their birth by "continuous passage," an almost-impossible feat in those days of relatively primitive traveling systems. The measure was specifically designed to keep out Indians who had no normal means of continuous passage from India to Canada. However, a group of nearly four hundred Sikhs decided to test the Canadian law. They charted a ship, the *Komagata Maru* in 1914 and arrived at Vancouver, having traveled in a "continuous passage." After three months, the passengers were denied entry to Canada, and the ship and its occupants were eventually turned away. The Canadian navy was used to uphold the discriminatory actions of the government.

Indians suffered from many of the debilitating racial restrictions imposed on the Chinese and Japanese. They were also disfranchised and therefore deprived of the opportunity to engage in certain occupations. Those who were employed had to work at far lower wages than their white counterparts and were exploited to provide profit for the development of Canadian resources.

The termination of official racist immigration policies in the 1960's resulted in the arrival of many Indian professionals whose skills in medicine, university-level instruction, engineering, and the law were a valuable contribution to Canadian society. Indians tend to congregate in large urban centers such as Toronto, where their community activities are extensive. Although held in great respect by many Canadians because of their conscientious dedication to their patients, employers, and clients, Indian professionals still report that they encounter prejudice and racism when they venture into nontraditional opportunities.

Undoing History

During the early 1960's, Alabama governor George Wallace commented to a Canadian Broadcasting Company (CBC) interviewer, "You folks are pretty smart. You got your immigration laws fixed so that you don't let anybody come into your country but who you want to let in." This ringing endorsement by a segregationist reveals the extent of the problem then faced by visible minorities in Canada. However, change did come, albeit slowly. In 1967, immigrants were allowed into Canada on the basis of a points system that examined qualifications, language fluency, ability, education, and other factors that were racially neutral. These measures enabled large numbers of immigrants from Asia, Africa, the Caribbean, and Latin America to enter Canada.

If judged by its laws and policies on paper, at the end of the twentieth century, Canada had a strong measure of fairness to minorities and conceivably one of the better legal underpinnings of equal and fair treatment. Unfortunately, it has been less successful in the implementation and practice of these laws and policies. In the 1960's and beyond, the Canadian provinces and federal government established a system that consists of human rights commissions with investigative and adjudicative elements to provide a measure of protection to disadvantaged minorities. Human rights codes exist throughout Canada to prevent racial discrimination and provide remedies. A plethora of legislative documents elucidate various rights, ensuring employment equity and nondiscrimination in the public service, measures against discrimination in housing, fair treatment of suspects in criminal matters, and a host of related areas of concern. However, implementation and enforcement have not kept pace with the legislation. Fostering greater awareness and tolerance in the white community for minority members may be the key to reducing prejudice. Some

Systemic and institutionalized discrimination have largely vanished from the schoolyard. These Toronto children seem unconcerned about their racial and ethnic differences as they watch a man paint numbers on their playground.

visible minority members, instead of waiting for Canadian society to change, are opting to return to their home countries or to migrate to the United States because they perceive that nation as more willing to recognize the problem of race relations and confront it.

Ranee K. L. Panjabi

Core Resources

Race and ethnic relations are examined in Daniel G. Hill and Marvin Schiff's *Human Rights in Canada: A Focus on Racism* (3d ed., Ottawa: Canadian Labour Congress and the Human Rights Research and Education Center, University of Ottawa, 1988); *Racial Minorities in Multicultural Canada* (Toronto: Garamond Press, 1983), edited by Peter S. Li and B. Singh Bolaria, and John Boyko's *Last Steps to Freedom: The Evolution of Canadian Racism* (2d rev. ed., Winnipeg: J. Gordon Shillingford, 1998). Employment issues are examined in Nan Weiner's *Employment Equity: Making It Work* (Toronto: Butterworths, 1993). The judicial system and race is the topic of the *Report of the Commission on Systemic Racism in the Ontario Criminal Justice System: A Community Sumary* (Toronto: The Commission, 1995).

See also: Aboriginal Canadians; African Canadians; Anglophone; Asian Indians in Canada; Charter of Rights and Freedoms; Chinese Canadians; Discrimination: intentional vs. unintentional; Employment in Canada; European immigration to Canada: 1867-present; Francophone; French Canadians; Immigration law: Canada; Japanese Canadians; *Komagata Maru* incident; Metis; Multiculturalism Act; Multiculturalism in Canada; Racial and ethnic demographics in Canada; Sikhs in Canada; Visible minority allophones in Canada.

Racial/ethnic relations: race-class debate

Significance: The race-class debate is the scholarly argument concerning whether racial group membership or socioeconomic status is more significant in determining an individual's life chances. At its heart, this debate also concerns whether race is a fundamental organizing feature of American society or economic stratification is of central importance.

One of the major debates to arise in the field of race relations is referred to as the "race-class debate." It centers on the issue of whether it is the treatment based on the racial group membership of minorities which explains their failure to achieve social mobility, or whether it is only poor racial minorities who face roadblocks in social mobility. Some sociologists think that racism and racial minority status are more important in determining one's life chances than is social class; racial organization, some say, is an independent and fundamental facet of American society. Others view the economic arrangement under capitalism and one's social class to be more significant than race. They view racism as an outgrowth of capitalism and the economic exploitation which, they claim, is an ongoing feature of capitalist society.

Race-Based Theories

Scholars who place significance on racial organization often cite black sociologist and political activist W. E. B. Du Bois, who proclaimed in his 1903 publication, *The Souls of Black Folk*, that "the problem of the twentieth century is the problem of the colorline." This implies that racial categorization is fundamental in American society; hence, issues of poverty and social mobility, along with persistent race discrimination can be traced to the issue of a "colorline" in American society. A major race relations theory supporting such a view is internal colonialism, articulated by Robert Blauner in his *Racial Oppression in America* (1972). Internal colonist theorists view contemporary race relations as growing out of a distinct process of colonialism, which describes the manner in which people of color were incorporated into American society. In this view, the low status of racial group members results from their nations being attacked and conquered, and then from them being defined as inferior, placed in the lowest positions of the society as labor or commodities, and excluded from the means for social mobility (such as education and political participation). In contemporary society, this subordinate status is maintained by the political, economic, and social practices of a powerful white majority that continues to exclude racial minorities from positions of power and privilege and to define them as comparatively inferior.

Another sociological perspective mirroring internal colonial theory's contention that race is central to social organization in U.S. society is articulated in the 1986 book *Racial Formation in the United States*, authored by Michael Omi and Howard Winant. Omi and Winant, following the Du Bois thesis, argue that "[f]rom the very inception of the Republic to the present moment, race has been a profound determinant of one's political rights, one's location in the labor market, and indeed one's sense of 'identity.' " Their "racial formation" argues that class-based theories and colonial or nation-based theories subsume race under other social categories (class or nation). Furthermore, they argue that both mainstream (assimilationist) theories and radical (class and colonial) theories have underestimated the tremendous significance of race in U.S. society.

Class-Based Theories

On the other side of the debate, class-based theories view economic forces as most significant in both determining and understanding race relations. For example, the Marxist sociologist Oliver C. Cox, in his 1970 work *Caste, Class, and Race: A Study in Social Dynamics*, argues that racism is a product of capitalism, which maintains the power of the ruling class by dividing workers from one another on the basis of race. Furthermore, racist ideology justifies the economic exploitation of people of color. Similrly, in the 1981 publication *Racial Inequality: A Political-Economic Analysis*, sociologist Michael Reich argues that workers who allow themselves to be divided by race are victims of "false consciousness" because they would benefit more from uniting and organizing as an economic class (against capitalists). In both views, racism flows from economic exploitation, and it is economic exploitation, not racism, which is the fundamental problem.

Another class-based sociological theory is that of William J. Wilson, presented in his 1978 work, *The Declining Significance of Race*. Wilson argues that, historically, race was more significant in determining where blacks would fall in the United States' stratified society. He says that in contemporary society, however, Americans have achieved racial equality through changes brought about by civil rights legislation, which, he argues, resulted in social mobility for those blacks who are now in the middle and upper classes. According to Wilson, those blacks who remain subordinated in society are in that position primarily because of their membership in the lower class, not because of their race. Wilson, then, stresses class differences among blacks, rather than racial solidarity, as being of greater significance. He bases this conclusion on changes brought about through massive protest and the protective legislation that ensued; he believes that these changes resulted in the broader inclusion of some blacks, who were able to advance economically, and thereby to distance themselves from the ghetto. To Wilson, their poor counterparts, unable to take advantage of those gains because of their low class position, have remained stuck in the inner cities which have only continued to deteriorate.

Policy Implications

The race-class debate has tremendous consequences for public policy, with widely divergent strategies resulting from taking either of these theoretical orientations. Generally, if the race thesis is more influential, policymakers respond by continuing to investigate the extent and manifestations of racism. They also create policies designed to minimize the social differences between racial groups and to break down barriers created by racism. If policymakers are influenced by arguments that economic deprivation, not racism, is responsible for the problems of racial minorities, then racially directed policies (such as affirmative action) lose their mandate for achieving parity between racial groups.

If racism is viewed as the critical issue, the distance between whites and people of color is the focus. Solutions revolve around protective measures to shield racial minorities from white racism. Labor experts and civil rights activists argue that when people have similar levels of educational attainment and work in similar occupations, any remaining inequality may be the product of race discrimination. This remains a powerful argument for both the maintenance and strengthening of civil rights legislation against race discrimination and for protective hiring practices such as affirmative action. The Civil Rights Act of 1964, Voting Rights Act of 1965, and Fair Housing Act of 1968 are examples of legislation designed to promote equal opportunity and end racial discrimination. Furthermore, special educational programs in higher education, such as "remedial" courses and mentoring programs, are designed to target racial minorities, who appear far more likely than their white counterparts to drop out of college.

Despite civil rights legislation, racial minority group members who believe their lives are shaped more by race than by social class may not expect the white majority-dominated government to provide relief against racial barriers. This may lead to the generation of grassroots efforts to redress grievances and to the organization of political protest among fellow racial group members,

regardless of their socioeconomic status.

On the other hand, policymakers who are convinced that the major problems confronting racial minorities afflict only the poor among them may seek one or both of two routes: They may seek to abandon any and all racially designed policies such as affirmative action or school integration; and they may create policies and programs specifically targeted for poor racial minorities. For example, scholars with remarkably differing views, such as William J. Wilson and neoconservative economist Thomas Sowell, have argued that affirmative action programs benefit primarily middle-class blacks and that group no longer faces racial discrimination. Moreover, Wilson highlights the differences between affluent and poor people of color, focusing upon African Americans, to say that class conflict has been heightened between group members and that middle-class African Americans inhabit a vastly different social universe from that of the poor, inner-city African American underclass with which he is primarily concerned. Wilson advocates government intervention for poor people of color, particularly in the devastated inner cities, to assist them in education, job training, and financial assistance. He claims that they suffer from economic dislocation caused by societal changes in the economy. Meanwhile, Sowell argues that inner-city dwellers lack the kind of "human capital," such as motivation, values, skills, and training, that employers are seeking. Sowell also finds that affirmative action policies constitute "reverse" discrimination against whites. This kind of argument formed the rationale for the well-known *Bakke* case (*Regents of the University of California v. Bakke*, 1978), in which the Supreme Court held that a white man, Allan Bakke, had been unfairly blocked from admission to medical school because of his race. Generally, adoption of the class-based thesis results in the advocation of policies that are color-neutral, or racially blind. Policies and programs such as the Equal Opportunity Program in higher education are generally color-blind, targeting all economically disadvantaged students for special advising, mentoring, and tutoring to overcome deficiencies in their secondary education and ensure their successful completion of college.   *Sharon Elise*

Core Resources

Robert Blauner's *Racial Oppression in America* (New York: Harper & Row, 1972) analyzes racism using a colonial model, positing that American society remains divided by race and that the division is by design. James Geschwender's *Racial Stratification in America* (Dubuque, Iowa: Wm. C. Brown, 1978) discusses racial stratification in the work of major sociological theorists and surveys major models in race relations, including assimilationist, colonial, and class models. Andrew Hacker's *Two Nations:*

Black and White, Separate, Hostile, Unequal (New York: Maxwell Macmillan International, 1992) provides detailed evidence for his thesis that race remains critical to the maintenance of the United States as a dual society in which African Americans are subordinated to their white counterparts at every level of society. Michael Omi and Howard Winant's *Racial Formation in the United States* (New York: Routledge & Kegan Paul, 1986) offers a critical assessment of the major race relations theories. William J. Wilson's *The Declining Significance of Race* (Chicago: University of Chicago Press, 1978) surveys major epochs of race relations in American society, detailing the influence of race historically and the contemporary emergence of class stratification among blacks and of an entrenched underclass.

See also: Black middle class/black underclass relations; Class theories of racial/ethnic relations; Marxist models; Racial and ethnic relations: theoretical overview; Racial formation theory; Social mobility and race.

Racial/ethnic relations: theoretical overview

Theories of racial and ethnic relations fall, generally, into three large groups: assimilation theories, power-conflict theories, and pluralistic theories. In the former school, assimilation, the supplanting of minority identity with that of the majority, is seen as both a natural and desired occurrence. Therefore, assimilation theories tend to see homogeneity as one outcome of the contradictions—particularly the social inequality—associated with racially and ethnically heterogeneous societies. Power-conflict theories, on the other hand, emphasize the conflicts among groups as they vie for power within the larger society.

Assimilation/Order Theories

The modern study of racial and ethnic relations can be traced to the early twentieth century with Robert Ezra Park's theory of the race relations cycle, one of the earliest of the assimilationist/order theories of racial and ethnic relations. The race relations cycle theory posits that, through a series of stages, minority groups are assimilated into the majority society.

Park's cycle is straightforward in its delineation of the stages of assimilation. The first stage represents *contact* between minority and majority groups. The particular ways in which groups make contact vary over time and place. Social push/pull factors such as unemployment, religious and political persecution, and war can necessitate large-scale emigration of groups. So, too, annexa-

tion, colonialism, slavery, extermination, and expulsion can initiate involuntary mass movements of peoples. However contact is initially effected, contact itself is followed by *competition* (up to and sometimes including violence) for scarce resources such as land, jobs, housing, services, and so on. *Accommodation*, a condition of relative tolerance in which the knowing of one's place marks the status quo, is the next stage in the cycle/order. The intensity of group competition is dissipated in the form of getting along and the need to end group competition. At last, given the process of gradual acculturation (cultural and behavioral incorporation of the minorities), *assimilation* results in the merging of the minority group into the larger, dominant, or host group. What this process suggests is that the minority groups lose a significant degree of their cultural identity.

In actual heterogeneous societies, any number of factors might inhibit the literal linear progression of the cycle. Doubtless in some societies, assimilation might not occur at all. Nevertheless, the socially ordered character of the race relations cycle does imply the longitudinal assimilation of minorities.

Park's stages were augmented by Milton Gordon's perspective, presented in his influential work *Assimilation in American Life* (1964). Gordon begins at the assimilative stage and adds incremental definitions to the final process of assimilation itself. According to Gordon, assimilation moves through the following stages in the this order: first, *cultural assimilation* (acculturation), whereby cultural/behavioral differences become increasingly minimized; second, *secondary structural assimilation*, in which small group and informal organizations are integrated; third, *primary structural assimilation*, in which larger and more formal social organization are opened to the minority. Miscegenary barriers, if they exist at all, are set aside in the fourth stage, *marital assimilation*, within which racial and/or ethnic intermarriage takes place routinely over time. Of such profound influence are the previous assimilative increments on the psyche of the minority group that, during the fifth stage, *identification assimilation*, the minority group begins to perceive its fundamental identification as that of the majority group. Consequently, the reciprocal attitudes of minority and majority are close enough that hostility and other forms of socially negative residues are essentially destroyed during the sixth stage, *attitude-receptional assimilation*; in the seventh stage *reciprocal behaviors* are subsequently of a positive character, in keeping with attitudes, and hence mutual civility is established. Eighth and finally, the assimilative process is culminated in a kind of *civic assimilation*, or confluence of interest, membership, and harmony. Amalgamation is thus presumed to end racial and ethnic conflict.

Many sociologists of racial and ethnic relations have

been influenced by Gordon's assimilationist theories. However, other theorists recognized some of the innate problems with assuming that full participation in society is the inevitable outgrowth of assimilation. As early as 1915, philosopher and educator Horace Kallen coined the term *cultural pluralism* to acknowledge the rights of different ethnicities to maintain their cultural heritage; in 1963, Nathan Glazer and Daniel P. Moynihan (the future U.S. senator), in *Beyond the Melting Pot*, noted that, despite assimilation, European ethnic groups retained their identification with the home culture beyond the third immigrant generation. Most assimilationist theories had considered different groups of European, or white, peoples immigrating to North America. In 1964, however, Gunnar Myrdal, in *An American Dilemma*, pondered why these assimilation theories had not proved to hold for African Americans, concluding that the "lag in public morals" might make assimilation and enjoyment of full rights impracticable for that group. In his 1978 book *Human Nature, Class, and Ethnicity*, Gordon himself acknowledged that his theory does not adequately address issues of power and conflict.

Other theories have arisen to fill that gap, including the competition theory (for example, Susan Olzak's *The Dynamics of Ethnic Competition and Conflict*, 1992) and the "human ecology" school, which consider that part of the assimilation process concerned with the movement of groups and their competition for resources. Such theories paved the way for the more modern emphasis on power-conflict theories.

Power-Conflict Theories

If assimilation/order theories are designed to endorse the integrative and harmonious prognosis of intergroup relations, power/conflict theories address the issues of group dominance and inequality. Inherent in power-conflict models of race relations is the concept of one group's having power over other groups' identity and, in that sense, their racial or ethnic destiny along all measures of social existence.

Karl Marx can be credited with the popularization of conflict theory. Despite Marx's emphasis on social class as the most important unit of analysis in analyzing social inequality, with race and ethnicity as epiphenominal variables, the adaptation of Marxian class conflict theory to race and ethnic relations is commonplace. The blend of race and ethnicity as ultimately reducible to class oppression in the form of "neo-Marxist" analysis as emphasized by W. E. B. Du Bois ("Is Man Free?," *Scientific Monthly*, May, 1948) and Oliver C. Cox (*Caste, Class, and Race*, 1948).

Closely aligned to the neo-Marxist perspective is the *internal colonial* model (Robert Blauner, *Racial Oppression in America*, 1972), which determines that domestic minority groups and communities are exploited, op-pressed, and otherwise treated differentially in ways very similar to the international, or external, colonial model associated with the heyday of European exploitation of large areas of the non-European world. Unlike most Marxist theories, however, internal colonialism sees racism and class (economic) oppression as two separate, if interrelated, dynamics. Perhaps the most outstanding example of internal colonialism is the system of slavery that arose in colonial America, particularly as Southern farmers came to exploit imported African Americans—a system that persisted into U.S. nationhood and, effectively through Jim Crow laws, beyond Emancipation following the Civil War.

Racial and Ethnic Pluralism

In opposition to both the cycle/order and the power-conflict theories of racial and ethnic relations stand theories of *racial and ethnic pluralism*, very often institutionally suggested by the term *diversity*. Particularly in the United States during the 1960's, for example, the belief that relative social equality was tantamount to the desire of minority groups to become assimilated into the Anglo-American "core culture" was questioned via the various movements to maintain unique racial and ethnic identities while still demanding equal and global opportunity. The American Indian Movement, Black Power, Brown Power, Gay Rights, various white ethnic, Asian American, and feminist dimensions all definitively stipulated that a person's cultural roots should remain intact and sacrosanct. It can be suggested that the desire among racial and ethnic minorities (as well as other types of minorities) to become socially equal to members of the dominant group and to be recipients of equal opportunity is not synonymous with forfeiting an individual's racial or ethnic identity and culture.

Pluralistic models include the idea of *oppositional culture*, or *cultures of resistance*, as partial antidotes to majority domination. Such cultures arise primarily among non-European groups who have not experienced the same degree of full social participation and civil rights afforded through assimilation to white subgroups. Ethnic groups who follow the oppositional culture model tend to be "bicultural," asserting language and cultural traditions that stand in contrast to white Anglo-Protestant traditions: African American Kwanzaa, Latino or Asian American bilingualism, French Canadian bilingualism, and so on. Such cultural resistance or opposition has found ultimate expression in *anticolonialism*, such as Molefi Kete Asante's Afrocentrism, black nationalist movements, pan-Asian movements, and Jewish Zionism.

The resistance to assimilation is both a blessing and a curse in heterogeneous societies. It is a blessing because it holds open the possibility that minority groups do not have to give up a sense of their respective cultural uniqueness and peoplehood in order to fit in and succeed in the mainstream society. It may, on the other hand, be a curse in that the very blessing itself constitutes the seeds for potential intolerance of other groups and hence a rebirth of social inequality and tragedy. The primary difference is that in time only the identities of the victims change, as do the identities of those who would make them victims of racial and ethnic persecution, for they themselves are likely to be descendants of minorities.   *Eugene F. Wong*

Core Resources

Robert Blauner's *Racial Oppression in America* (New York: Harper & Row, 1972) examines inequality in America with a real-world emphasis on understanding the phenomenon. Oliver C. Cox's *Caste, Class, and Race: A Study in Social Dynamics* (New York: Modern Reader Paperbacks, 1948) provides insightful perceptions of social change over time in the urban environment. W. E. B. Du Bois's *Battle for Peace: The Story of My Eighty-third Birthday* (New York: Masses and Mainstream, 1952) is a longitudinal recollection of the author's socio-ideological development. Milton M. Gordon's *Assimilation in American Life: The Role of Race, Religion, and National Origins* (New York: Oxford University Press, 1964) is considered by many in the race relations field to be a groundbreaking attempt to make theoretical sense of the complexities of the American malaise. Karl Marx and Friedrich Engels's *Selected Works in Two Volumes* (Moscow: Foreign Languages Publishing House, 1955) includes some of the seminal works on class conflict and the internationalization of the class struggle.

Robert E. Park's "Human Migration and the Marginal Man," in *American Journal of Sociology* (33, May, 1928), is one of the classic attempts to analyze the dilemma of intergroup conflicts and their social impact. Nathan Glazer and Daniel P. Moynihan's *Beyond the Melting Pot* (Cambridge, Mass.: MIT Press, 1963) is another classic that looks at the polyglot and diverse nature of the American condition. Gunnar Myrdal's *Assimilation in America* (New York: Harper & Row, 1964), although restricted to black-white relations, serves as an early effort to address the issue of social inequality head-on. Mario Barrera's *Race and Class in the Southwest* (Notre Dame: University of Notre Dame Press, 1979) breaks with the traditional emphasis on biracial white-black controversies over race and social class to include persons of other colors and cultures, particularly Latino.

Molefi Kete Asante's *Afrocentricity* (Asmara, Eritrea: Red Sea Press, 1988) provides the reason, if not the convincing logic, to counter an assumed Eurocentricity in historiography. Michael Omi and Howard Winant's *Racial Formation in the United States* (New York: Routledge, 1994) is an attempt to provide historical substance to the biological myth that race is the prime determinant of group destiny. Joe R. Feagin and Clairece Booher Feagin's *Racial and Ethnic Relations* (5th ed., New York: Prentice-Hall, 1996) is a good basic textbook on racial and ethnic concepts that incorporates background information on a number of America's most significant minority groups.

See also: Accommodationism; Afrocentrism; Assimilation: cultural and structural; Assimilation theories; Attitude-receptional assimilation; Behavior-receptional assimilation; Civic assimilation; Colonial model of racism; Competition theory and human ecology; Contact hypothesis; Cultural pluralism; Identification assimilation; Internal colonialism; Marital assimilation; Marxist models; Melting pot theory; Moynihan Report; Oppositional culture; Pluralism vs. assimilation; Progressive inclusion theory of assimilation; Race relations cycle; Resistance, cultures of; Segmented assimilation theory; Social stratification theories; Sociobiology and race; Structural assimilation.

Racial formation theory

Racial formation theory was the outcome of a process of introspection by social scientists who had been frustrated by both academic attempts to explain race and racism and political ideologies that attempted to collapse race into other social categories such as nationality or economic class. The theory was developed principally by sociologists Michael Omi and Howard Winant in their book *Racial Formation in the United States* (1986, 2d ed. 1994).

Racial formation theory avoids two mistakes in analyzing race in the United States. The first mistake is the tendency to view race and races as fixed social or biological facts, which is not plausible. Attempts to develop biological classifications that match social definitions of the races have failed. Different societies have defined race and races very differently, and all definitions have changed over time, often over the course of a single lifetime.

The second mistake attempts to correct for the first but overcompensates. In this view race is wholly illusory, a fictional product of cultural representation. Omi and Winant argued that this perspective, however appealing to those who would rather live in a "color-blind" society, unrealistically suggests the remedy of merely ignoring or eliminating race and races—as if society could simply learn to do without race. The problem with this view is that race is such a fixture of American political, cultural, and economic reality that to pretend it does not exist would be to ignore all of its serious consequences for society, such as racial discrimination and segregation.

Race and racism have in fact been at the core of the American experience since the nation's inception, and Omi and Winant argue that they always will be, although race is impossible to pin down as a fixed concept. The theory handles this contradiction by defining racial formation as the process that both creates the racial categories with which people identify and transforms these categories over time.

By this reasoning, race exists as both social structure and symbolic representation. Historically, the racial projects that seek to allocate various resources one way or another along racial lines are the same movements that create, impose, or change racial definitions. At any one point in time, these categories seem to most participants to be fixed and normal, a sort of common sense of race. However, that static appearance masks a turbulent undercurrent of racial projects. These projects take place at the macro level of society in the struggles of social movements and state policies and at the micro level in the daily social interactions and private battles of identity that all Americans face.

While describing race as a fluid concept reflecting the outcome of centuries of social struggle, racial formation theory defines racism more simply. Racism is a racial project that perpetuates domination based on categories of race. The theory thus allows for the ever-changing nature of race as a social construction while simultaneously establishing criteria for identifying and challenging racism as a problem to be combated.

Philip N. Cohen

See also: "Color-blind" society; Race as a concept; Racism: history of the concept.

Racial hierarchy

A hierarchy is a social system in which power is distributed among different layers with little ambiguity as to who has the power. The more hierarchical a system is, the more the distance between its top and bottom. The racial hierarchy in the United States has been of whites at the top and ethnic minorities at the bottom. However, stratification also exists among the ethnic minorities. A profound historical shift in the role of power in social life and how it is organized has resulted in stratification among ethnic minorities, creating a multifaceted rather than binary racial hierarchy. Much of the shift involves what Howard Winant and Michael Omi refer to as the transition from domination to hegemony. Although the racial hierarchy was overtly clear with white domination before the Civil Rights movement, in modern society, the idea of which race is at the top and which is at the bottom is often not completely clear. As society has become more

complex, racial power has increasingly taken the form of the ability to control events and resources, and people have become more hierarchically organized. Although markers of domination (such as segregation) are no longer visible, other signs (such as geography of race) reinforce racial segregation and hierarchy.

Mary Yu Danico

See also: Racial formation theory; Social stratification theories.

Racial propaganda

> **Significance:** Racial propaganda is the attempt to shape or control other people's opinions or actions using particular ethnic stereotypes, images, or prejudices. It has had a major impact on many significant aspects of civil life and public policy: elections, immigration, criminal justice, civil disorder, welfare, public education, and public health.

Most people associate racial propaganda with racist hate groups, but artists, writers, professionals, scientists, and pseudoscientists have all contributed to racial propagandizing. Propagandists use the media of the day to convey their message. Handbills and pamphlets were popular in the eighteenth and nineteenth centuries. Radio and television provided new forums for propaganda: talk shows, advertisements, news shows, and political campaigns. Cable and the Internet have expanded the opportunities for hate groups and other more marginal racial propagandists to disseminate their messages.

Throughout U.S. history, crime, poverty, disease, and unemployment—the social problems that came with industrialization, urbanization, and the rise and fall of the business cycle—were blamed on immigrants. Americans found it hard to believe that the problems swirling around them could come from their own society or people. They tried to solve these social problems by limiting immigration. These anti-immigrant movements produced propaganda supporting the racial superiority of white "native" Americans and the inferiority of immigrant groups. Handbills, broadsides, and editorial cartoons in the illustrated papers and magazines of the day were common sources of racial propaganda.

Anti-Irish Propaganda

The first major flurry of anti-immigrant propaganda was directed against the Irish, whose mass migration to the United States followed the great potato famine of the 1840's. The poverty and squalor found in Irish American neighborhoods allowed Americans to view the Irish as less than human. Cartoons from the era portray Irish Americans as monkeylike. It is sometimes hard to tell the difference between caricatures of Irish Americans and of African Americans; both were depicted as apelike.

The anti-Irish propaganda was also strongly anti-Catholic. "Papism" was reputed to promote ignorance and discourage any education beyond church teachings. Thomas Nast, the most famous cartoonist of the nineteenth century, is known for his attacks on political corruption, but he also drew many anti-Catholic and anti-Irish cartoons. His most inflammatory image showed schoolchildren being threatened by crocodiles who were really bishops, their miters forming the crocodiles' jaws.

The Know-Nothing Party

The anti-immigrant feelings in the mid-nineteenth century found institutional support in the American Party, known as the Know-Nothing Party for its practice of refusing to answer questions about its platform. The Know-Nothing broadsides and tracts blamed the immigrants for the anti-immigrant riots (and most other problems). Know-Nothings pledged to vote only for

Chinese Americans were depicted as evil creatures eating rats in this piece of anti-Chinese propaganda from the 1800's.

American candidates who supported stopping immigration. The Know-Nothings proved extremely popular with the American public and might have even captured the White House if the Civil War had not distracted attention away from the immigration issue.

Anti-Italian Propaganda

New waves of immigration in the late nineteenth and early twentieth centuries generated new waves of anti-immigrant sentiment. As with the Irish, the poverty and different cultural practices of the Italian, Chinese, and Eastern European Jewish immigrants made them easily identifiable and easy to blame for the social problems other Americans faced.

Italians were portrayed as Mafiosi and anarchists and blamed for both crime and labor troubles. Cartoonists portrayed Italians as shifty-eyed and always armed with knives or guns. Rats were the favored animal used to depict them. The labor troubles of the day were often blamed on the Italians, who had a history of labor and fraternal organizations.

Anti-Asian Propaganda

Chinese immigration in the 1860's quickly triggered Americans' xenophobia. Chinatowns in U.S. cities were feared by liberals and conservatives alike. The culture, language, and religion of the Chinese immigrants were so far from the European roots of Americans that the immigrants were widely feared and despised. Reformer Jacob Riis, known for his sympathy for European immigrants, wrote of the Chinese immigrant in 1890:

> He is by nature as clean as the cat, which he resembles in his traits of cruel cunning and savage fury when aroused. . . . I may be accused of inciting persecution of an unoffending people. Far from it. Granted, that the Chinese are in no sense a desirable element of the population, that they serve no useful purpose here . . . yet to this it is a sufficient answer that they are here, and that, having let them in, we must make the best of it.

Anti-Semitic Propaganda

One does not find much anti-Semitic propaganda before the 1870's, but once Eastern European Jews began immigrating, Jews were the focus of all sorts of stereotypical images and claims. Jews were believed to control pornography and prostitution in the large East Coast cities, and conspiracy theories often placed Jews at the center of plans to corrupt the American way of life. In the early twentieth century, a document called *The Protocols of the Elders of Zion* appeared, claiming to be the Jewish plan for taking over the world. It is unclear who actually produced this book, but it was not the Jews. This book continues to figure in conspiracy theories.

After the horrors of the Holocaust became known following World War II, anti-Semitic propaganda became less visible and less mainstream, although it lived on in the publications of groups such as the Ku Klux Klan. Anti-Semitism was also evident in African American publications and folklore that blamed slavery on Jews and Jewish bankers. In the 1980's, a variety of right-wing populist groups known variously as survivalists, skinheads, neo-Nazis, and militia popularized conspiracy theories in which the State of Israel and "Jewish bankers" were responsible for all of the problems that were facing "white" Americans. Some groups also began to deny that the Holocaust had taken place, saying it was nothing more than Jewish propaganda.

Anti-Latino Propaganda

In the late twentieth century, Latinos became the main group targeted by nativist campaigns to limit immigration. Conservative politicians and talk-radio shows played up the image of illegal aliens who sneak into the United States to take jobs away from Americans and bring in illegal drugs. These propaganda campaigns were used to tighten the border with Mexico, limit Latino immigration, cut off welfare to immigrants (both legal and illegal), and draft English-only legislation designed to make English the official language of the United States.

Anti-African American Propaganda

Anti-African American propaganda has existed since the birth of the nation. Southern states actively promoted the "Sambo" image of ignorant and inferior blacks to justify slavery and white dominance. Alternatively, blacks would be portrayed as savages to justify the brutal treatment and the severe punishments handed out for defying white authority: Nat Turner's rebellion provided ample evidence for propagandists of the danger of treating slaves too leniently. The end of slavery was supported by many northern whites, but ending slavery was not the same as providing equality, and most whites were not in favor of equality. Antiabolitionist propaganda capitalized on the ambivalence that white Americans felt toward the idea of equality for African Americans. The fear of race mixing, for example, was exploited in *Miscegenation: The Theory of the Blending of the Races, Applied to the American White Man and Negro*, an 1860's booklet published by antiabolitionist forces.

The Emancipation Proclamation (1863) and the end of the Civil War (1865) did not end the propagandizing. Reconstruction became the new ideological battleground. Populist politicians and southern Democrats became the leading political propagandists, promoting racial segregation. More violent racial propaganda came from underground organizations such as the Ku Klux

Klan. Jim Crow laws handed southern segregationists a political victory that quieted propagandizing until the Civil Rights movement of the 1950's and 1960's disturbed the status quo and led to a new round of racial propaganda. Hate groups thrived, turning their attention to affirmative action and other programs that attempted to remedy the inequities of earlier eras.

In Times of War

Nations always wage massive propaganda campaigns in times of war, both to generate solidarity at home and support from the international community. In U.S. history, wartime propaganda has often adopted a strongly racial tone. In World War I, newspapers, magazines, military training materials, and government advertising posters featured images of the "Hun," with monocle and spiked helmet; World War II produced images of slant-eyed and buck-teethed Japanese. These images were recycled into "gooks" during the Korean conflict and the Vietnam War. Arab "terrorists" became a popular scapegoat in the 1980's and 1990's, with the Iran hostage crisis and Operation Desert Storm.   *Paul Eisenhauer*

Core Resources

Among the few resources that solely address racial propaganda are Forrest Wood's *Black Scare: The Racist Response to Emancipation and Reconstruction* (Berkeley: University of California Press, 1968) and Noel Ignatiev's *How the Irish Became White* (New York: Routledge, 1995). Racial propaganda is often part of the larger story of ethnicity in the United States, so the best secondary sources are general histories of different ethnic groups. To learn more about racial propaganda, browse through old copies of *Life, Punch, The Judge, Time, The New York Times,* or *Newsweek* to see the cartoons and editorials that depict different ethnic groups in U.S. history.

See also: African American stereotypes; Anti-Catholicism; Anti-Semitism; Asian American stereotypes; Chinese Americans; Eastern European Jews; English-only and official English movements; Epithets and pejorative language; Hate crimes; Hate speech; Holocaust denial; Irish American stereotypes; Irish Americans; Italian Americans; Jewish Americans; Jewish stereotypes; Jokes and humor; Ku Klux Klan; Latino stereotypes; Latinos in the United States; Nativism; Turner's slave insurrection.

"Racial" vs. "ethnic"

The terms "race" and "ethnicity" carry with them wide ranges of connotations, both in everyday social life and in modern scientific usage. In the social sciences, the problem is complicated by the fact that the terms tend to be defined in various ways. In simplest terms, a "racial" group is a population whose similar physical appearance (phenotype) distinguishes it from other populations, suggesting a shared genetic heritage that is judged to reflect membership in a common gene pool (genotype). An "ethnic" group, in contrast, is a population that shares and acts out a common cultural tradition that is transmitted socially from each generation to the next and that distinguishes it from other populations. Although this distinction between inborn racial and acquired ethnic factors is thus grounded, respectively, in biogenetic versus cultural origins and dynamics, a given population may of course be regarded as both racially and ethnically distinguishable from other populations.

What makes these group distinctions meaningful and significant, socially as well as scientifically, is the patterns they assume in the form of racial and ethnic relations. Such patterns of relationship vary considerably from one society to another and, within a given society, from time to time. Therefore, in order to account for the existence of these patterns of relationship, their persistence, or the dynamics as they become relatively more hostile or harmonious, it is necessary to analyze the history of group migration and immigration and to probe for the basis of social-psychological shifts in intergroup attitudes.

Because of the diversity that marks American society, the study of racial and ethnic relations has given rise to a rich literature. Although anthropologists have tended to focus more on the cultural dimensions of ethnically distinct groups, sociologists are inclined to examine the social structural contexts and dynamic processes that are affected by patterns of racial or ethnic relations. For certain analytic purposes, especially those focusing on intergroup tensions, the distinction between racial and ethnic designations recedes into minor significance; for others, including those seeking strategies for resolving such tensions, the distinction assumes greater weight.

When conflict occurs between racial or ethnic groups, inequalities of group access to valued economic or political resources tend to make the distinction between race and ethnicity relatively inconsequential. At issue, typically, are disparities in power, with one group seeking to maximize access while commensurately dispossessing the other group or groups. Such power struggles over scarce resources transcend racial and ethnic distinctions and are better understood as conflicts between dominant and minority groups.

Racial versus ethnic distinctions do assume significance, however, among policies designed to reduce group hostilities. The American melting pot model depicts the lessening of *ethnic* differences through the gradual merging of cultures in an assimilation process; however, erasing *racial* distinctions could result only

from amalgamation, the blending of disparate genetic traits through systematic and long-term racial intermarriage.

Harry H. Bash

See also: Ethnicity and ethnic groups; Race as a concept.

Racism as a "system of advantage"

Defining racism as a system of advantage serves two major purposes: It avoids the typical "blame the victim" approach to racism by focusing on those who are advantaged, rather than disadvantaged, by it, and it posits racism as a system that operates at many levels, beyond just individual prejudice.

One major effect of centuries of racism in the United States is that people of color lag behind whites on many indicators of social status, including earnings, wealth, and housing. For example, government-sponsored housing audits in several major metropolitan areas of the United States revealed that realtors and landlords discriminate against people of color about half the time—every other time they do business (*Housing Discrimination Study*, U.S. Government Printing Office, 1991). Although the effect of this discriminatory behavior on people of color is clear, what is less evident is the advantage that this creates for whites. When an apartment is not rented to a person of color because of racism, that leaves the unit available for a white person. The white tenant benefits from racism, or receives privilege or advantage, even though he or she did not perpetuate the initial discrimination (Beverly Daniel Tatum, *Why Are All the Black Kids Sitting Together in the Cafeteria?*, 1997). Thus, just as people of color are disadvantaged by racism, whites are advantaged by racism, regardless of their individual wishes or preferences. This "white privilege" typically remains an unacknowledged given in a white person's life. Peggy McIntosh ("White Privilege: Unpacking the Invisible Knapsack," in *Peace and Freedom*, July/August, 1989) lists forty-six privileges she "cashes in on" each day by being white—such as "flesh-colored" bandages matching her skin color, not being followed in a store, and seeing members of her "race" widely represented in the media. These privileges exist on an unearned basis, contrary to the myth of meritocracy upon which American society is based.

Further, this privilege is doled out within the context of a system. Although prejudiced individuals (such as a discriminatory landlord) may carry out their preferences on an individual basis to create an advantage in a fairly overt manner, more often than not it is unquestioning compliance with institutional policies that fuels racism as business-as-usual. Tatum likens racism to an airport's moving walkway. Prejudiced individuals run on the conveyor belt, but most whites ride the racist current just by standing there, without thinking about it; they may not move individually, but their very presence on the conveyor belt is what maintains the system. The unsuspecting tenant accepted by a prejudiced landlord would be an example of someone who may be without individual prejudice but who still benefits from a system of advantage. Under this definition of racism, the major solution for racism occurs when whites deliberately refuse their advantage, as in the case of white antiracists or "race traitors" (*Race Traitor*, Noel Ignatiev and John Garvey, 1994). *Eileen O'Brien*

See also: Racism: changing nature of; Racism: history of the concept; Whites.

Racism as an ideology

> **Significance:** Racism can be described as an ideology—a belief that helps to maintain the status quo. More specifically, "racism" refers to the belief that one race is superior to other races in significant ways and that the superior race is entitled, by virtue of its superiority, to dominate other races and to enjoy a larger share of society's wealth and status.

Race, according to almost all scientists, is a socially defined concept rather than a biologically determined reality. "Race" is therefore real only in the sense that certain groups have, for whatever reason, decided to categorize people according to certain aspects (arbitrary and even superficial aspects) of their physical appearance. Terms such as "black" and "white," then, must also be viewed as socially, rather than biologically, meaningful distinctions.

Sociologist Howard Schuman has defined racism as the belief that there are clearly distinguishable human races, that these races differ not only in superficial physical characteristics but also innately in important psychological traits, and that the differences are such that one race (almost always one's own) can be said to be superior to another. According to this view, it follows that the advantages which the superior race enjoys with respect to health care, housing, employment, education, income and wealth, and status and power are attributable to its superiority rather than to discriminatory social structures. Consequently, according to this view, racial inequality is no reason to change any of society's institutionalized ways of doing things; the social structure can

be maintained. Racism is, then, an ideology: a belief that rationalizes the status quo.

"White racism," Schuman says, "is the belief that 'white' people are inherently superior to['black'] people in significant ways, but that the reverse is not true." Prior to the mid-twentieth century, the prevailing form of white racism was the belief that blacks were genetically inferior, especially with respect to intelligence. Since that time the view that blacks are inferior to whites has persisted, but racist whites have changed their minds about the cause of the inferiority. Schuman cites a helpful statistic: In 1942, 42 percent of a national sample of whites said they believed that blacks were as intelligent as whites; by 1956, 78 percent of whites agreed that blacks were as intelligent.

The National Opinion Research Center (NORC) found, in 1991, that 14 percent agreed that blacks were disadvantaged in housing, income, and education because they have less inborn ability. The remaining 86 percent, however, did not all believe that blacks and whites were biologically and psychologically equal and that the differences in housing, income, and education were attributable to discriminatory social structures. Only 40 percent said the differences were attributable "mainly to discrimination." Fifty-five percent said that the difference existed "because most blacks just don't have the motivation or will power to pull themselves up out of poverty." If racism is the belief that one race is superior in significant ways to other races, and if "free will" is considered to be a significant trait (and it is if differences in education and income are attributable to differences in free will) then such a belief is an example of racism. Schuman, analyzing similar data prior to the 1970's, concluded that "the phrase 'white racism' appears wholly appropriate."

Psychologist William Ryan (1976) concurs. The old-fashioned ideology was that blacks were genetically defective. The modern ideology is that they are environmentally defective, that the defects are caused by "the malignant nature of poverty, injustice, slum life, and racial difficulties." Ryan notes that "the stigma, the defect, the fatal difference—though derived in the past from environmental forces—is still located *within* the victim, inside his skin."

The ideology of racism has injured not only those in "nonwhite races" but those in certain white ethnic groups as well. The historian John Higham (*Strangers in the Land: Patterns of American Nativism 1860-1925*, 1955) traced the history of "race thinking" about European immigrants to the United States:

> Several generations of intellectuals took part in transforming the vague and somewhat benign racial concepts of romantic nationalism into doctrines that were precise,

malicious, and plausibly applicable to European immigration. The task was far from simple; at every point, the race-thinkers confronted the liberal and cosmopolitan barriers of Christianity and American democracy.

Challenges to the Ideology

The most direct attack on the ideology of racism has been challenges to the very concept of race. If there are not in fact different "races" of people, then obviously all arguments about the superiority and inferiority of various races are false. Science has challenged the concept of race. The sociologist James W. Vander Zanden (1983) has traced the progress of science's views from the "fixed type school" to the "breeding population school" and ultimately to the "no-race school." The fixed type school held the view that "races are relatively fixed and immutable hereditary groupings that reach back into antiquity." The breeding population school held the view that races start with a common genetic heritage and that geographic and social isolation (breeding barriers), mutation, natural selection, and genetic drift gave rise to "more or less stable, differentiated gene pools among humankind"—populations that differ with respect to the frequency of certain genetic traits. The "no-race school" denies that races, as discrete biological entities, are real.

Race nevertheless remains a social reality. People are socially defined as belonging to different races, and they are treated differently based upon these social definitions. The differences in treatment produce differences in outcomes for the different races, and these different outcomes are then used as evidence to support the ideology of racism. Consequently, the ideology of racism can also be challenged by examining the way any social institution functions. If the institutions of education, health care, religion, the family, the polity, or the economy treats all races equally, then differences among races with respect to that institution might be attributable to racial differences. If those institutions treat people in different races unequally, then these differences in treatment may be sufficient to explain any differences among groups, and any racial explanation would more likely be an expression of the ideology of racism.

History of the Ideology

The ideology that one race is superior to others, particularly with respect to intelligence, has existed for thousands of years. The sociologists Brewton Berry and Henry L. Tischler quote a letter from Cicero, the Roman statesman and orator, to Atticus (c. 100 B.C.E.): "Do not obtain your slaves from Britain because they are so stupid and so utterly incapable of being taught that they are not fit to form a part of the household of Athens." Almost two thousand years later, Count de Gobineau returned the insult, complaining about the Italians, as well as the

Irish and "cross-bred Germans and French" who were immigrating to the United States. They were, in de Gobineau's opinion, "the human flotsam of all ages . . . decadent ethnic varieties."

Just as de Gobineau was not deterred by Cicero's low opinion of northwestern Europeans, so are many of the descendants of those Italians, Irish, Germans, French (and others) not deterred by de Gobineau's opinion from thinking that they constitute a superior race. Consequently, one of these descendants, psychologist R. Meade Bache, in an 1895 study entitled "Reaction Time with Reference to Race," reached the conclusion that whites were intellectually superior to blacks and American Indians, even though whites had the slowest reaction times of the three groups. Bache interpreted the results to mean that whites "were slower because they belonged to a more deliberate and reflective race."

Bache was the first of a long line of so-called scientists who managed to confirm the superiority of their own race. After him came the famous psychologist Robert Yerkes, who developed intelligence tests for World War I recruits and concluded that the tests proved the intellectual inferiority of blacks. Then Carl Brigham used the Yerkes data to prove that more recent European immigrants were genetically intellectually inferior to earlier European immigrants. This ideology of racism has continued to the present day, when many are still convinced that whites are intellectually superior to other races because they average higher scores on IQ tests.

During the last four centuries, prejudices toward blacks have changed, but such prejudices still exist. As scientific research slowly convinces many people that a particular prejudice is factually incorrect, informed people begin to laugh and scorn when it is expressed, and others become ashamed to express it. Yet as that particular prejudice falls into disuse, another is invented, often by respected and influential people, to take its place. This occurs because continuing discrimination requires prejudice to rationalize it. In the future, if racial discrimination continues, so will racism as an ideology.

Donald M. Hayes

Core Resources

Stephen Jay Gould's *The Mismeasure of Man* (New York: W. W. Norton, 1981) challenges the concept of intelligence as a single entity that can be quantified by one number (as an IQ score) that can then be used to rank order according to worthiness—invariably to find that oppressed groups are innately inferior and least worthy. William Ryan's *Blaming the Victim* (rev. ed., New York: Vintage Books, 1976) is an excellent rebuttal of racism as an ideology. James W. Vander Zanden's *American Minority Relations* (4th ed., New York: Alfred A. Knopf, 1983) includes a discussion of the concept of race in chapter 2.

See also: Intelligence and race; Race as a concept; Racism: changing nature of; Racism: history of the concept; "Scientific" racism.

Racism: changing nature of

> **Significance:** Overt racism—such as legal discrimination and open use of derogatory language—largely disappeared in the 1960's and 1970's but racism lingers on in the form of covert racism, often manifest through the use of "code words" and in subtly, even unconsciously, racist attitudes and policies.

Various ethnic groups have experienced racism—both overt and covert—since the colonization of the Americas by European explorers in the 1500's. Although some of the worst forms of discrimination, including slavery, have been abolished, racism still exists in the United States. Recent U.S. history contains numerous examples: During World War II, Japanese Americans were incarcerated in concentration camps, and until the 1950's and 1960's, African Americans were legally segregated from whites in residential areas and public facilities, including schools, buses, and restaurants.

Decline of Overt Racism

Some of the events and legislation that contributed to a climate of reform and the gradual demise of overt racism include the 1954 U.S. Supreme Court decision in *Brown v. the Board of Education,* which legally ended discriminatory "separate but equal" policies for whites and blacks, and Rosa Parks's 1955 refusal to give up her bus seat to a white woman and the subsequent Montgomery bus boycott. The 1963 civil rights marches in Birmingham, Alabama, and the Freedom March on Washington, D.C., where Martin Luther King, Jr., gave his famous "I Have a Dream" speech, helped bring about the passage of the Civil Rights Act of 1964, which prohibited discrimination on the grounds of race or sex. Another important piece of legislation was the Voting Rights Act of 1965, which banned barriers to free exercise of the right to vote and led to a dramatic increase in black voter registration.

In most parts of the United States, using racial epithets and engaging in racist activities is socially unaccept-able, and throughout the nation, denying someone housing, employment, education, or opportunity on the basis of race is illegal; however, racism has not disappeared from American culture. Some examples of overt racism can still be found, such as the 1998 murder of a black hitchhiker, James Byrd, Jr., in Jasper County, Texas. Byrd died after being picked up by three white men, tied to the back of their truck, and dragged. However, for the most part, racism has gone underground, becoming either covert or unconscious.

Covert Racism

Covert, or what has been called inferential, racism is the form of racism that develops in a society that declares itself to be free of racism despite abundant evidence to the contrary. Such racism, according to researcher Stuart Hall, is actually more dangerous and difficult to combat than overt racism simply because it is harder to pinpoint and because it is often expressed unconsciously by "well-meaning liberals" with seemingly antiracist intent.

One way that covert racism operates is by recoding race into what appears to be a nonracial discourse. In this way, race "can be spoken silently, its power can be exerted invisibly," according to John Fiske in *Media Matters* (1994). Some people believe that race was recoded as a discourse on "family values" in Republican politics in the early 1990's. For example, in a May, 1992, address at the Commonwealth Club of California in San Francisco, former vice president Dan Quayle commented on a "poverty of values" in the African American community. More specifically, he attributed the 1992 uprisings in South Central Los Angeles, a predominantly minority area, to a "breakdown of family structure, personal responsibility, and social order." He went on to discuss the formation of a new underclass "dependent on welfare

In 1993, thirty years after Martin Luther King, Jr.'s March on Washington, thousands of people reenacted the historic march to draw attention to the continued existence of racism in the United States.

for very long stretches" and said that "the intergenerational poverty that troubles us so much is predominantly a poverty of values." Many people believe that his statements imply that poverty and welfare problems in the United States are a black problem, not a white problem, and that African Americans do not have the appropriate values (those held by the white majority) to avoid or escape poverty.

Another example of recoding race into a "nonracial" discourse—in this case, law and order—is a campaign advertisement produced in support of Republican George Bush's bid for the U.S. presidency in 1988. The advertisement featured African American and convicted felon Willie Horton, who, upon his release from jail on a "weekend pass" in Massachusetts, raped and stabbed a white woman and stabbed a white man. Designed explicitly to convince people that Michael Dukakis, Bush's opponent and governor of Massachusetts, was soft on crime, the campaign spot played on white Americans' stereotypical view of black men as violent and hypersexual.

A second type of inferential racism, according to Fiske, is denial. This occurs when the racial intent or impact of an action or comment is denied, despite protestations of racism by the offended group or others. For example, the videotaped 1991 beating of African American Rodney King during an arrest by Los Angeles Police Department officers is regarded by many people as a racially motivated incident. However, a white juror in the 1992 trial of four white police officers accused of excessive force in the beating of King, commenting on the not-guilty verdict, said of the prosecution, "They kept trying to bring race into it, but race had nothing to do with it."

Although the denial of racism is a common strategy used by conservatives, Fiske argues that liberals who claim to be nonracist "are more likely to exert a form of nonracist racism unintentionally by marginalizing or silencing any explicit references to the topic." As an example, he cites the white liberal senators who supported Anita Hill's sexual harassment accusations against Clarence Thomas, the black conservative judge appointed by George Bush to the U.S. Supreme Court. In supporting Hill, these senators emphasized her gender and ignored or marginalized her blackness, although many black and white Americans believed that race was a central factor in the culture's prurient fascination with both Thomas's and Hill's sex lives.

A final way in which inferential racism exerts itself is through American culture's assumption that whiteness is the default value, the norm or the "natural" state of being. Whiteness is never examined or dissected, but what is instead open for discussion and debate is blackness or race in general. Therefore, any problems created by racism or relations between races are termed "the race problem"—situations or difficulties occurring within the black community and largely that community's responsibility. What is not addressed is the need for whites to examine their own racist values and practices.

Susan Mackey-Kallis

Core Resources
Books and articles on the changing nature of racism include John Fiske's *Media Matters: Everyday Culture and Political Change* (Minneapolis: University of Minnesota Press, 1994), Ruth Frankenberg's *White Women, Race Matters: The Social Construction of Whiteness* (Minneapolis: University of Minnesota Press, 1993), Toni Morrison's *Playing in the Dark: Whiteness and the Literary Imagination* (New York: Vintage, 1993), and Stuart Hall's "The Whites of Their Eyes: Racist Ideologies and the Media," in *The Media Reader*, edited by Manual Alvarado and John Thompson (London: BFI, 1990).

See also: Discrimination: overt/expressed vs. covert; Horton, Willie, incident; King, Rodney, case; Politics of hate.

Racism: history of the concept

Significance: Racism as a widespread social phenomenon rose in the late fifteenth and early sixteenth centuries as European explorers encountered the indigenous peoples of unknown lands, who looked, spoke, and lived so differently that it was easy to deny their humanity.

The concept of race is an invention of the early modern world. The ancient and medieval worlds did not identify persons by race. Individuals were recognized during these earlier periods in geographic terms. Hence, an African would be called Ethiopian or Egyptian as opposed to being called black or Negro.

Origins
Racial emphasis came into use as a support for imperialism and its accompanying institution of slavery. Although the origin of the word "race" is obscure, experts believe that it began as a loose description of similar groups. This description originally was not restricted to biologically similar people. For example, in 1678, John Bunyan in *Pilgrim's Progress* wrote of a "race of saints."

The first English record of the use of the word "race" was in 1508. In that year, William Dunbar in a poem spoke of "bakbyttaris if sindry racis" (backbiters of sundry races).

It was not until 1684 that the term "race" was used to designate skin color and other distinguishable physical features. It was then used by the Frenchman François

Bernier, who used his experiences as a traveler and physician to employ such an application.

It appears, however, that such classifications did not become commonplace immediately. It was only after science adopted the concept of race as an explanation for human variation that it became a broadly accepted tenet.

Citations of Earlier Prejudices

Some scholars, such as Winthrop Jordan and Joseph Harris, have documented evidence of racial prejudice all the way back to the earliest contact between whites and nonwhites. These actions appear to be based more on geographic differences than on color differences. For example, fantastic fables about Africans circulated among Europeans. Equally preposterous stories about Europeans, however, circulated in the ancient and medieval world among Europeans. Thus, such views seem to be the products of encounters between different peoples in an age that was characterized by superstition and fear of the unknown.

Scientific Racism

The year 1798 has been cited as marking the beginning of scientific racism. This later form of racism was not restricted to skin color alone. It was used to slight Jews and Catholics as well as nonwhite people. In its earliest use, scientific racism was employed mainly as a justification of economic inertia. Thus, it was said that human deprivation could not be relieved through charitable donations. According to the proponents of scientific racism, government volunteer agencies or individuals would simply be throwing money away if they were to invest it in the segment of humanity that was hopelessly and irretrievably at the bottom of the social and economic ladder.

This employment of a pseudoscientific justification for racism was expanded with the introduction of Social Darwinism in the late nineteenth century. Purveyors of this doctrine imported Charles Darwin's theory of evolution from biology and applied it to a social context. Whereas Darwin himself had only theorized about species, the Social Darwinists declared that one race was superior to another because it had evolved further and faster than had the inferior group. A chain of evolutionary progress was created that placed the black race at the bottom and whites of the Nordic pedigree at the summit of humanity. Thus, black people were portrayed as animalistic, subhuman, and therefore incapable of higher thought, while Nordic Europeans were said to be natural leaders.

The use of science to prop up racism has probably been the most pernicious development in the history of racism. When zoology, anatomy, and other fields of scientific study advanced explanations of human differ-ences, they were given serious hearings. Consequently, the layperson accepted the scientist's word as authoritative in spite of its theoretical and unproved claims.

Religious Influences

From the beginning of the European enslavement of Africans, religion was an element in the process. As early as 1442, Pope Eugenia IV granted absolution to Portuguese seamen who, under the direction of Prince Henry the Navigator, took African "souls" and sold them. Within ten years, however, it became unnecessary to ask for absolution, because Pope Nicholas V gave the king of Spain his blessing to enslave "pagans." Christopher Columbus's writings show that he used this same justification for the enslavement of Native Americans. Chapels were included in most of the slave factories, also known as "castles," which were erected along the west coast of Africa. Their presence was indicative of organized Christianity's approval of slavery.

At first, the Spanish provided for enslaved Africans to be manumitted upon their conversion to Christianity, since it was considered wrong for one Christian to hold another Christian in bondage regardless of the bondsman's race. As conversions to Christianity became commonplace among African slaves, however, manumissions became uncommon. By the middle of the seventeenth century, Europeans began to identify black skin with a lifetime of slavery.

The Bible was used to "prove" that blacks were a cursed people. A favorite scriptural citation for this purpose was Noah's curse upon his grandson Canaan because his father Ham had mocked his own father (Genesis 9:20-27). This scripture was given a racial interpretation by the slavocracy's hermeneutists. They declared that Ham was the father of the black race and that Noah's specific condemnation of Canaan should be expanded to include all black people. Thus, religious justification for the enslavement of blacks evolved from the belief that it was immoral for a Christian to enslave another Christian, regardless of race, to the nineteenth century idea that the African was eternally condemned to be a servant of others. By the nineteenth century, proponents of slavery declared that it simply was the natural order for the African to be "a hewer of wood and drawer of water" for the more advanced races. As the "peculiar institution" of slavery became more prevalent, the argument to legitimate it—especially from a religious perspective—became more vindictive toward nonwhite lands.

Cultural Racism

Both slavery and imperialism used cultural arguments to control other races. The doctrine of the "white man's burden" said that Europeans had a moral responsibility to expose deprived nonwhites to the superior culture of the whites. Thus, Africans who were kept on a plantation were thought to benefit from their close association with their masters. It was said that Africans, if left alone, would languish in retrogressive ignorance and backwardness.

This paternalistic view was not unique to American slavery. Both Europe and the United States used the concept of the white man's burden to justify the usurpation of the lands of nonwhite people. In each territory, the indigenous people were characterized as savage and uncivilized. Only exposure to the white man's superior culture would save such people. This attitude of superiority legitimated the takeover of other peoples and lands.

This view reflected the belief that many whites held during the age of imperialism. They saw themselves as God's gift to humanity. Officially, this concept came to be known as Manifest Destiny. The imperialists believed that they had a mission to expand beyond others' borders to uplift those people to the imperialists' level. This attitude was arrogant and discriminatory. Anything of note that had been done by nonwhite people was ignored, while every important aspect of human civilization was always in some way considered a product of white genius. Such a polemical view of culture helped to solidify white supremacy and the existence of racism.

Economic Racism

During slavery, the argument was advanced that the institution was necessary for the benefit of black people. It was declared that they were childlike and incapable of self-support. As long as they remained on the plantation, they had a haven that protected them from want. Slavery's defenders used this argument to portray slavery as advantageous to the slaves. Even after the Civil War, many southern historians continued to use the economic argument to show that slavery was an economic boon to blacks. They pointed to postbellum vagabondage and government dependency among freed slaves as proofs that black people were better off on the plantation, where they were given food, clothing, and shelter.

Those who advanced these "proslavery arguments" failed to acknowledge that it was the years of exploitation and neglect on the plantation that had contributed to the freed slaves' deplorable condition. Also, they never addressed the freed slaves and antebellum free blacks who, in the face of tremendous difficulties, still managed not only to support themselves and their families but also to become entrepreneurs, landowners, and employers, sometimes even of whites.

Even in the twentieth century, economics was used as a defense for racism: South Africa's apartheid policy and business transactions carried on there were justified by American and European corporations. In the wake of an international call for divestiture, these companies argued that their continued operation in South Africa was for the good of the blacks and colored people at the bottom of the economic ladder. Divestiture would deprive these two groups of a livable wage. Therefore, it was prudent for nonwhite people to continue to work for these corporations while the corporations used their influence to effect change.

Social Segregation

After the American Civil War and Reconstruction, Jim Crow laws were instituted throughout the southern United States. These laws segregated society on the basis of race in practically every area of life. Except in menial jobs, blacks could not enter white restaurants, hotels, schools, or any other "whites only" public facility. When they were allowed in the same buildings as whites, African Americans had separate, well-defined places such as balconies or basements to occupy.

Most southern states reinforced their segregation policies with laws that prohibited interracial marriages. Propagandists repeatedly warned that having one drop of Negro blood meant that one was a Negro. To the racist, amalgamation was a deadly sin.

Resulting from such hysteria was a Negrophobia that frequently manifested itself in the worst imaginable forms of brutalization. In the late nineteenth century and the first half of the twentieth century, it was common for African Americans to be lynched at the hands of white gangs without due process of law. The most common offense was the rape, real or imagined, of white women. Frequently, it was the latter. A celebrated case of this sort occurred when fourteen-year-old Emmett Till was murdered in Money, Mississippi, in 1955. Apparently, his only offense was that he called a white woman "baby."

Institutional Racism

With the massive urbanization of African Americans in the United States in the twentieth century and the resulting residential segregation in cities, the stage was set for the emergence of institutional racism. This form of racism was more covert than was individual racism, which was person-to-person, emotional and blunt. Institutional racism resulted in a denial of equal access to goods and services by predominantly black sections of the cities. For example, higher prices and less desirable products were more often found in the predominantly black and Hispanic inner cities than in the white suburbs.

Since this type of discrimination manifested itself through institutions and was not conducted by individuals, many people were simply oblivious to its existence. In addition, because of diminished interracial contact in urban areas, many suburbanites, as a result of ignorance of the ways in which societal institutions discriminate, were prone to blame deplorable living conditions within inner cities on the residents' lack of initiative and concern rather than on institutional biases.

Institutional racism can explain a disproportionate number of nonwhites being unemployed, underemployed, and incarcerated in prisons. Despite affirmative action policies and legal gains during the twentieth century, African Americans and other minorities were excluded and ignored by many institutions, such as employers, lenders, and investment agencies. A prime example is the absence of stockbrokers' and other investment advertisements in African American-oriented media.

New Conflicts

Many African American leaders have argued that it is impossible for black people to be racist. They believe that they can be prejudiced, but not racist, because they lack the power to enforce their prejudice.

While this position has been advanced by the African American left, the white right has charged that group with "reverse" racism. Many conservatives contended that government affirmative action programs and the preferential treatment accorded minorities since the passage of civil rights legislation victimize whites in the same way that nonwhites previously experienced discrimination. Even black neoconservatives have argued that "race preferences" victimize blacks and other people of color by minimizing their achievements.

Efforts to Eradicate Racism

Persons of goodwill have seen the wisdom in freeing humanity of racial bigotry. Although racism has been opposed since its inception, the most celebrated and concentrated efforts began with the modern Civil Rights movement, which began with the bus boycott in Montgomery, Alabama, in 1955. Under the nonviolent leadership of Martin Luther King, Jr., racism was exposed as morally wrong. King's philosophy accentuated the brotherhood of humanity and love for one's neighbor, regardless of race, nationality, or ethnicity.

By developing an integrated coalition and marching peacefully under King's leadership, King's followers erected a workable model of human cooperation that could be emulated throughout the world. Ironically, those who brutalized these nonviolent protesters with police dogs and fire hoses convinced many people throughout the world that racism was an insidious evil that should be stamped out.

As a result, people have become more reluctant to be known as racists. Therefore, racially sensitive issues have become increasingly difficult to discuss openly, and instead such discussions have adopted code words or centered on peripheral issues such as socioeconomic class. Racism continues to flourish, but it has become more covert and institutional than overt and individual.

Randolph Meade Walker

Core Resources

Michael Banton and Jonathan Harwood's *The Race Concept* (New York: Praeger, 1975) is a general discussion of the evolution of the idea of race. Jacques Barzun's *Race: A Study in Superstition* (rev. ed., New York: Harper & Row, 1965) is an interesting refutation of Nazi teachings that addresses the expanded use of race beyond color applications. Allan Chase's *The Legacy of Malthus: The Social Costs of the New Scientific Racism* (New York: Alfred A. Knopf, 1977) is a thorough treatment of scientific racism. Earl Conrad's *The Invention of the Negro* (New York: Paul S. Eriksson, 1967) contends that black Africans did not suffer extreme degradation until the slave trade became big business in the Americas. Winthrop D. Jordan's *White over Black: American Attitudes Toward the Negro, 1550-1812* (New York: W. W. Norton, 1977) contends that racism produced slavery, providing an interesting contrast to Conrad's thesis.

See also: Civil Rights movement; Economics and race; Employment among African Americans; Eurocentrism; Individual racism; Institutional racism; Lynchings; Race as a concept; Proslavery argument; Racism as a "system of advantage"; Racism as an ideology; Racism: changing nature of; "Reverse" racism; "Scientific" racism; Sexual fears and racism; Slavery: history; Social Darwinism and racism; White man's burden; White supremacy groups.

Rainbow Coalition

The Rainbow Coalition, a multicultural effort to unify racial and ethnic groups that have been marginalized in the U.S. political process, was founded in 1983 under the leadership of the Reverend Jesse Jackson.

Historically, racial and ethnic groups in the United States have experienced differing levels of participation in formal political institutions, leading to substantial inequalities in the distribution of political power among various groups. African Americans, for example, were historically excluded from participation in political processes through such legal and extralegal means as poll taxes, intimidation, and gerrymandering.

What political power African Americans did acquire was often symbolic, achieved through appointments of black leaders to high-profile positions. This tradition led to the development of a black elite that accepted the role of junior partner in the process of achieving racial integration. Most of this leadership came from minority group members in nonelected positions and from extrapolitical movements such as strikes, boycotts, and acts of civil disobedience.

In the early 1980's, Jackson organized a united front of liberal integrationists, socialists, trade unionists, feminists, gays, and racial minority constituencies to work together in the 1984 presidential campaign. The Rainbow Coalition platform was based on four premises: that Jackson had a base among the "black masses," that he was an important figure in southern black politics, that the campaign would stimulate registration of black voters, and that Jackson's presidential candidacy would create "coattail" effects that would propel other outsiders into the electoral process. None of these premises was supported by subsequent events.

To appeal to a broad range of voters, Jackson moved the left-leaning Rainbow platform toward the political center for the time of the 1988 presidential campaign. Jackson purged the coalition of its activists by blocking democratic elections of local Rainbow leadership and by placing gag orders on radical dissenters. In 1989, Jackson asserted the right to appoint all coalition leaders at the congressional district rank. In response, thousands of activists left the coalition, and several splinter groups were organized.

In the 1990's, Democratic leaders including Bill Clinton acted to undermine Jackson's leadership role in the African American community, severely diminishing the power of the Rainbow Coalition. Clinton's 1992 presidential victory was followed by the political rise of Ron Brown, one of Jackson's protégés, who had become the chair of the Democratic National Committee and was appointed Secretary of Commerce. Such developments led many members to leave the Rainbow Coalition and to adhere to Clinton's policies.   *Glenn Canyon*

See also: Civil Rights movement.

Rap music

Rap music emerged as a significant form of African American music and political protest in the late 1970's. As a performance-based musical form popular in clubs and at parties, rap was initially associated with hip-hop culture and the break dancing made popular by African American youths on city streets and in urban nightclubs in the early 1980's. Rap represents the latest form of black music that articulates responses to prejudice, institutionalized racism, and oppression. Earlier musical forms that influenced rap include ragtime, jazz, blues, gospel, rock and roll, and reggae.

Although a number of popular rap artists were making music in the 1970's, including Gil Scott-Heron and Grand Master Flash, rap did not become widely popular and visible until the 1980's, when rap songs moved to the top of the musical charts. Rap artists such as N.W.A. (Niggers with Attitude), Public Enemy, Ice-T, Ice Cube, Sister Souljah, Queen Latifah, and 2 Live Crew gained

Rap artist and actor Ice-T rose to fame in the 1980's.

both fame and notoriety for their electric performance styles, their shocking lyrics, and their sometimes outrageous actions.

The rise in popularity of rap during the politically conservative 1980's can be attributed in part to the anger and discontent felt by urban blacks who faced cuts in welfare benefits and programs, the deterioration of inner-city neighborhoods, the loss of job opportunities, and the rise in drug use, crime, and violence. These disfranchised people used rap to express their feelings and viewpoints.

Rappers have been compared to ministers in African American churches who exhort their congregations to see and act in a particular fashion. Rap has also been called the "CNN (Cable News Network) of the black community" because it serves as a source of information on what is happening in black communities. Rap music, for example, often makes reference to and comments on significant cultural and political events such as the 1991 beating of African American Rodney King by four white Los Angeles Police Department officers and the 1992 Los Angeles riot that erupted after the officers were found not guilty of using excessive force.

Rap music, as a musical genre, is known for its intertextuality (references to other rap songs and art forms), its sampling (use of sound bites from radio, television, popular records, and the street), and its styling (use of rhythm, rhyme, and a constant, hard-driving beat). Rap music, however, is as diverse as any musical genre. As such, it is a mistake to generalize about the artists, their purposes, techniques, popularity, and impact. For example, although it is true that some rap music, gangsta rap in particular, has been criticized for glorifying a gangster lifestyle of crime, drugs, and misogyny, other rap artists have been applauded for their empowering messages for and about black youth, black women, and American youth generally.

Susan Mackey-Kallis

See also: African American literature; African American music; African American stereotypes; Motown Records; Soul.

R.A.V. v. City of St. Paul

During the early morning hours of June 21, 1990, "R.A.V."—an unnamed, male seventeen-year-old, self-described as a white supremacist—and several other teenagers burned a makeshift wooden cross on the front lawn of the only African American family in their St. Paul, Minnesota, neighborhood. They were prosecuted for disorderly conduct in juvenile court under the city's "bias-motivated crime ordinance," which prohibited cross burning along with other symbolic displays that "one knows" or should know would arouse "anger, alarm or resentment in others on the basis of race, color, creed, religion, or gender."

The state trial court ruled that this ordinance was unconstitutionally overbroad because it indiscriminately prohibited protected First Amendment speech as well as unprotected activity. The Supreme Court of Minnesota reversed the lower court's decision and upheld the ordinance, which it interpreted to prohibit only unprotected "fighting words," face-to-face insults that are likely to cause the person to whom the words are addressed to attack the speaker physically.

The U.S. Supreme Court ruled unanimously in favor of R.A.V. and invalidated the ordinance, but the justices did not agree in their reasoning. Stating that they found the cross burning reprehensible, Justice Antonin Scalia, writing for the majority, nevertheless concluded that the ordinance was unconstitutional because it criminalized only specified "fighting words" based on the content of the hate message and, consequently, the government was choosing sides. He noted that the ordinance would prohibit a sign that attacked Catholics but would not prohibit a second sign that attacked those who displayed such an anti-Catholic bias.

Four justices concurred in the ruling of unconstitutionality, but Justice Byron White's opinion sharply criticized the majority opinion for going too far to protect racist speech. He reasoned that the ordinance was overbroad because it made it a crime to cause another person offense, hurt feelings, or resentment and because these harms could be caused by protected First Amendment

speech. Justices Harry A. Blackmun and John Paul Stevens also wrote separate opinions complaining that hate speech did not deserve constitutional protection.

The ruling called into question numerous similar state laws designed to protect women and minorities from harassment and discrimination. Some of these individuals and groups may still invoke long-standing federal civil rights statutes, however, which carry severe criminal penalties of fines and imprisonment. In 1993, *R.A.V.*'s significance was called into question by the *Wisconsin v. Mitchell* decision upholding a state statute that increased a sentence for a crime of violence if the defendant targeted the victim because of the victim's race or other specified status.

Thomas E. Baker

See also: Epithets and pejorative language; Hate crimes; Hate speech; *Wisconsin v. Mitchell.*

Reapportionment cases

Significance: This series of U.S. Supreme Court decisions announced from March 26, 1962, to February 17, 1964, required election districts to be determined by population. The reapportionment remedied the gross underrepresentation of racial minorities that had developed in many cities.

Among the many profound changes ushered in by the twentieth century, few have had a more far-reaching effect on U.S. society than urbanization. The United States has not always adjusted to the changes wrought by urbanization. This has been especially true in the area of democratic political representation in the various states. By 1960, there were flagrant examples of malapportionment in the majority of states, both in state legislatures and in delegations to the U.S. House of Representatives. Incumbent state legislatures, dominated by rural elements, had refused to reapportion representation to reflect population shifts accurately; to do so would have strengthened urban areas at the expense of the rural groups in control. Delaware, for example, had not reapportioned its legislature since 1897; Tennessee and Alabama had not done so since 1901. These were only the worst cases. In all but six states, less than 40 percent of the population could elect a majority of the legislature.

State legislatures frequently ignored provisions in their state constitutions that required periodic reapportionment on the basis of the decennial census. Such a situation imperiled the very basis of democracy. Yet the Supreme Court, prior to 1962, had refused to intervene on the grounds that apportionment was a political question and thus outside the jurisdiction of the Court. This dictum had been handed down in the case *Colegrove v. Green* (1946). The resulting malapportionment has been likened to the eighteenth century English "rotten boroughs."

Supreme Court Activism

In 1963, the Court finally abandoned its unwillingness to act on the matter of apportionment and took a strong stand in favor of democratic representation in *Baker v. Carr*, a case challenging the apportionment of the Tennessee state legislature. The Tennessee state constitution called for reapportionment every ten years, although none had taken place since 1901. As a result, urban areas were greatly underrepresented in the legislature, while rural areas were overrepresented. Moore County, with a population of 3,454, elected one legislator, while Shelby County (which includes Memphis), with a population of 627,019, elected only three. The inequities were starkly evident.

The federal district court in Tennessee, in which suit had been filed originally, refused to take action on the basis of the precedent established in *Colegrove v. Green*. When the case was appealed to the Supreme Court, however, that body ruled by a six-to-two margin that the Tennessee case was justiciable and returned it to the lower court for a decision. Political reformers finally had realized their aim: The Court, under Chief Justice Earl Warren, had agreed to deal with the problem of equitable apportionment of representation, although it had made no actual decision on the subject. Justices Felix Frankfurter and John M. Harlan dissented in *Baker v. Carr*, again arguing that apportionment was a political question and therefore not within the Court's jurisdiction.

As a result of *Baker v. Carr*, a spate of litigation and legislation regarding apportionment followed. By the end of 1963, federal suits had been filed in thirty-one states and state suits in nineteen others. During that same period, twenty-six states adopted new legislative apportionment plans. Nevertheless, these plans did not always satisfy political reformers. The plans varied greatly in intent and effect, because the Court had not actually ruled on apportionment and therefore had not established guidelines for the states to follow.

The "One Man, One Vote" Principle

This confusion over the Court's views was partially remedied in March of 1963, when *Gray v. Sanders* struck down Georgia's so-called county unit rule. That rule assigned a certain number of units, or votes, to each county in elections for statewide offices and operated in a manner similar to the federal electoral college. The result of the county unit rule was severe discrimination against voters in the more populous areas. The Court ruled eight to one, Justice Harlan dissenting, that the Georgia system violated the equal protection clause of the Constitution, and Justice William O. Douglas, in writing the majority opinion, used the momentous phrase "one man, one vote." Again, the Court had not ruled directly on the question of apportionment, but it had given a broad hint as to what it expected.

Gray v. Sanders foreshadowed *Wesberry v. Sanders*, a landmark case decided in 1964, in which the Court used the "one man, one vote" principle to void a 1931 Georgia congressional apportionment law. Justice Harlan again dissented, contending that the Court was intruding upon the proper province of Congress. The Court, however, was now clearly committed to guaranteeing equitable apportionment and democratic representation in the United States House of Representatives as well as in state legislatures. Later in 1964, the Court further delineated its standards in six cases involving Alabama, New York, Maryland, Virginia, Delaware, and Colorado.

The cases in Alabama and New York were particularly important because, in addition to rural-urban issues, they also presented strong race issues. As cities such as Birmingham and New York grew after World War I, their most densely populated sections became predominantly African American. Not only was the "one man, one vote" ideal not being met, but racial minorities also were grossly underrepresented. In Alabama, *Reynolds v. Sims* (1964) challenged apportionment policies set up in 1901, when the state constitution was designed to preserve rule by white, conservative Democrats. The New York case of *WMCA v. Lomenzo* received national attention when New York City radio station WMCA decided early in 1961 to begin challenging state apportionment policies outlined in the state constitution of 1894. The Supreme Court ruled in favor of reapportionment in the WMCA case on June 1, 1965; Justice Harlan again dissented.

The effect of these decisions was to create a movement for a remedial constitutional amendment in Congress—a movement that failed, as did a vigorous effort to call a federal constitutional convention to consider apportionment. The Court had served notice that malapportionment would not be tolerated, and in 1967 it reaffirmed its endorsement to the "one man, one vote" principle in *Swan v. Adams*.

Frederick J. Dobney, updated by Geralyn Strecker

Core Resources

Howard Ball's *The Warren Court's Conceptions of Democracy: An Evaluation of the Supreme Court's Apportionment Opinions* (Rutherford, N.J.: Fairleigh Dickinson University Press, 1971) explores the political dynamics within the

Supreme Court and the effects they had on the outcomes of apportionment cases. Richard C. Cortner's *The Apportionment Cases* (Knoxville: University of Tennessee Press, 1970) explores the genesis and impact of the apportionment cases, paying particular attention to *Baker V. Carr* and *Reynolds v. Sims*. Gene Graham's *One Man, One Vote: "Baker v. Carr" and the American Levellers* (Boston: Little, Brown, 1972) follows the *Baker v. Carr* case from its beginnings to its residual impact a decade after the decision. Calvin B. T. Lee's *One Man, One Vote: WMCA and the Struggle for Equal Representation* (New York: Scribner's, 1967) follows *WMCA v. Lomenzo* from the radio station's first decision to fight apportionment in 1961 to the Supreme Court decision on June 1, 1965. Nancy Maveety's *Representation and the Burger Years* (Ann Arbor: University of Michigan Press, 1991) examines the impact of reapportionment after twenty-five years. Timothy G. O'Rourke's *The Impact of Reapportionment* (New Brunswick, N.J.: Transaction Books, 1980) charts the effects of reapportionment on elections in legislative districts in Delaware, Kansas, New Jersey, Oregon, South Dakota, and Tennessee.

See also: *Baker v. Carr; Colegrove v. Green*; Representation: gerrymandering, malapportionment, and reapportionment; *Reynolds v. Sims; Wesberry v. Sanders*.

Reconstruction

> **Significance:** Reconstruction denotes both the period and the process after the Civil War in which the Union attempted to solve the problems, and restore the status, of the southern secessionist states. During this period, formerly enslaved African Americans both enjoyed new freedoms and suffered new atrocities at the hands of segregationists and white supremacists intent on preserving the old racial hierarchy.

Soon after the Civil War commenced in 1861, northern leaders began to debate how the Confederate states should be readmitted to the Union and the many attendant problems to be resolved. For example, how should punishment for secession (withdrawing from the Union) be meted out, and against whom? What human and civil rights should be extended to the approximately four million freed slaves, and how could those rights be protected? In 1863 President Abraham Lincoln announced his plan for Reconstruction, but it was countered a year later by a proposal from Congress which touched off a national debate over who should establish Reconstruction policy.

Status of Blacks

After the Civil War ended on April 9, 1865, the status of blacks quickly became the most critical issue of Reconstruction. In January, 1865, Congress had proposed the Thirteenth Amendment to the U.S. Constitution, which called for the abolition of slavery. By March, Congress had created the Freedmen's Bureau to protect the rights of southern blacks, most of whom had no private homes, money, or formal education because southern laws had relegated slaves to subhuman status. The Freedmen's Bureau obtained jobs and set up hospitals and schools for blacks. In December, 1865, the Thirteenth Amendment was ratified. Most northerners hoped that the United States could be quickly reunited and the rights of blacks protected. Tragically, however, vicious attacks on former slaves increased in 1865 and 1866. Some were accompanied by race riots. Whites murdered about five thousand blacks in the South. By December, 1865, a secret organization called the Ku Klux Klan had been founded in Tennessee. It grew rapidly, spreading terror by murder and intimidation.

Johnson's Plan

After Andrew Johnson became president following Lincoln's assassination in April, 1865, he announced his own Reconstruction plan. It did not offer blacks a role in the process of Reconstruction—a prerogative left to the southern states themselves. During the summer and fall, new state governments were organized under Johnson's plan, but they began passing a series of restrictive laws against blacks called the black codes. These laws did little more than put a new face on the old practices of slavery. As a result, Republicans in Congress, both moderates and radicals, became convinced that President Johnson's plan was a failure and that the rights of both blacks and whites needed greater protection. The radicals also thought that giving blacks the right to vote was the only way to ensure the establishment of southern state governments that would remain loyal to the Union and administer uniform justice.

Civil Rights Legislation

Early in 1866, Congress passed the Civil Rights Act, which guaranteed basic legal rights to former slaves. Though Johnson vetoed the bill because he did not think that the federal government should protect the rights of blacks, Congress overrode the veto, making the 1866 Civil Rights Act the first major law in U.S. history to be passed over the official objection of the president.

In June, 1866, Congress proposed the Fourteenth Amendment to the Constitution, which gave citizenship to blacks and mandated that all federal and state laws apply equally to blacks and whites. Though President Johnson urged the states to reject it (which all the

Confederate states except Tennessee did), the Fourteenth Amendment was finally ratified in 1868. A third Reconstruction amendment to the Constitution, the Fifteenth, was proposed in 1869. Ratified by the states in 1870, this amendment made it illegal to deny any citizen the right to vote because of race.

Reconstruction Governments

In 1867, Congress passed a series of laws called the Reconstruction Acts. These enactments abolished the newly formed state governments and placed every secessionist state (excluding Tennessee) into one of five military districts. Federal troops stationed in each district enforced martial law. By 1870 all southern states had been readmitted to the Union, and new state governments were reestablished.

Southern whites (the majority of whom were Democrats) protested the Reconstruction Acts by refusing to vote in elections which established the new state governments. Thousands of blacks (who were Republicans) did vote, and as a result Republicans won control of every new state administration. Most whites in the South refused to support the Reconstruction governments because they could not accept the idea of former slaves voting and holding elected positions. Many whites turned to violence despite military attempts to halt attacks on blacks. Army troops had little success in preventing the Ku Klux Klan and similar groups from terrorizing people and controlling the outcome of elections.

The Legacy of Reconstruction

As white Democrats began regaining control of state governments in the South during the early 1870's, northerners lost interest in Reconstruction. The 1876 presidential election led to the end of Reconstruction when the Republicans agreed to a compromise with three southern states. Their disputed election returns were resolved in favor of Republican candidate Rutherford B. Hayes in exchange for the complete withdrawal of U.S. troops.

Reconstruction produced mixed results. The Union was restored, some rebuilding of the South did occur, and some blacks did get a taste of basic human and civil rights. In the end, however, most things scarcely changed at all. Many blacks remained enslaved by poverty and lack of education. Most continued to pick cotton on land owned by whites. Some scholars have suggested that the most fundamental flaw of Reconstruction was its failure to redistribute land, which would have provided an economic base to support the newly acquired political rights of black citizens.

The most important indicator of the impact of Reconstruction on American justice is the way blacks were treated after 1877. Ending slavery did not, and could not, end discrimination. The southern states continued to violate the rights of blacks for many decades afterward. It was only in the mid-1950's that black Americans inaugurated the intense struggle for complete legal equality known as the Civil Rights movement. This movement was based on the most significant judicial legacy of the Reconstruction period—the Fourteenth and Fifteenth Amendments to the Constitution. Eventually these amendments were used to establish a national system of protecting equality before the law.   *Andrew C. Skinner*

Core Resources

Of the many books on Reconstruction, two are classics. Eric Foner's *Reconstruction: America's Unfinished Revolution, 1863-1877* (New York: Harper & Row, 1988) is the most comprehensive; an abridged version is available as *A Short History of Reconstruction, 1863-1877* (New York: Harper & Row, 1990). The other classic is James M. McPherson's *Ordeal by Fire: The Civil War and Reconstruction* (New York: Alfred A. Knopf, 1982). Other important works include Leon F. Litwack's *Been in the Storm So Long: The Aftermath of Slavery* (New York: Alfred A. Knopf, 1979); Richard W. Murphy's *The Nation Reunited: War's Aftermath* (Alexandria, Va.: Time-Life Books, 1987), which is copiously illustrated; and Kenneth M. Stampp's *The Era of Reconstruction, 1865-1877* (New York: Alfred A. Knopf, 1965).

See also: Black codes; Civil rights; Civil Rights Acts of 1866-1875; Civil War; Freedmen's Bureau; Jim Crow laws; Ku Klux Klan; Slavery: history.

Red Scare

Significance: In the wake of Russia's Bolshevik Revolution, the United States was struck by a wave of xenophobia and fear of communism that pitted native Americans against both immigrants and resident minorities.

In early 1919, a congressional investigation into German propaganda activities quickly veered into an anti-Bolshevik investigation. During the summer of 1919, race riots in Washington, D.C., and Chicago, Illinois, seemed to confirm the suspicions of many that society was threatened not only by labor organizations and radical political associations, but also by African Americans, who were viewed as especially vulnerable to Bolshevik lures because of the economic, social, and political injustice under which they lived. As early as 1918, the Federal Bureau of Investigation had hired its first official black informant, convinced that radicals had already made significant advances in the African American community. Propaganda, often distributed by white suprema-cists and Ku Klux Klan members, went so far as to suggest that the summer riots were only a prelude to a Red-sponsored race war.

Government Intervention

By the fall of 1919, public clamor for some kind of government action was intense. Attorney General Alexander Palmer responded to the swelling chorus that was demanding the arrest and deportation of the alien radicals who supposedly were instigating subversive events. In August, 1919, Palmer had established the antiradical General Intelligence Division in his department. At its head he had placed young J. Edgar Hoover, who promptly began to assemble an elaborate card index of radical organizations, publications, and leaders. On November 7, Hoover's agents raided the headquarters and branches of a labor society known as the Union of Russian Workers. Throughout the country, state and local officials carried out smaller raids on suspected radicals. Congressmen began to introduce deportation bills; one senator even proposed that radical native-born citizens be expelled to a special penal colony on the island of Guam. On December 21, a group of 249 deportees set sail from New York aboard the old army transport ship *Buford*, informally labeled "the Soviet Ark." In January, 1920, came the last and greatest raids, as the Red Scare crested and finally broke.

Although the public's concern over the intentions of the new Soviet regime can be understood, it is difficult, in retrospect, to comprehend the hysteria that engulfed Americans responding to small groups of poorly organized radicals at home. Social psychologists, however, explain the events of 1919-1920 as follows: People who are fearful of losing an established social and economic position in society may become hostile toward or fearful of those whom they see as threatening that equilibrium. They may be willing to launch a purge to seek to be safe from the "intruder" they see as the threat. Rapid changes in American life, brought about first by industrialization and urbanization and then by World War I, may have left many Americans in such a state of disequilibrium that they could not relieve their anxieties and regain their sense of security without taking some sort of action. The postwar drive for "one hundred percent Americanism" may well have been an attempt to reaffirm traditional beliefs and customs and to enforce conformity by eradicating the "alien" who appeared to be wrecking the traditional society. Deportation was literally a purge.

From the perspective of the present day, the actions that took place during the Red Scare may seem despicable. In 1919, however, a few thousand Bolsheviks had suddenly become the masters of more than a hundred million Russians, murdering the czar and his entire family along with thousands of nonconforming Russians. In the light of such an example, many otherwise fair-minded people in the United States were not inclined to allow a few thousand Bolsheviks to repeat the performance in their country.

Waning of the Red Scare

Whatever the origins of the Red Scare, the raids and deportations sharply diminished after January, 1920. This decline of anxiety is even more difficult to explain than its rise. Perhaps the Red Scare never really ended; amnesty for World War I conscientious objectors and other political prisoners became no easier to obtain under President Warren G. Harding than it had been under Woodrow Wilson. The U.S. Army conducted antiradical training and seminars during the 1920's. The restrictions on immigration grew tighter: In 1924, the National Origins Act, or Immigration Act of 1924, imposed a quota system that drastically checked the flow of aliens into the United States. Throughout the 1920's, neo-patriotic organizations appropriated the nationalistic rhetoric of the Red Scare to attempt to deny pacifist associations, such as the Women's International League for Peace and Freedom, legitimacy as foreign policy interest groups. Antipacifists invested words like "patriotism" and "internationalism" with meanings that linked the peace movement to un-American ideas and activities. These attacks often forced pacifists to moderate their ideas and actions. Other measures, such as loyalty oaths, textbook censorship, and an "American plan" for labor unions, were characteristics of U.S. society in the 1920's.

Nevertheless, the degree of panic after early 1920 was minimal. The very excess of the raids aroused opposition to them and renewed an appreciation for toleration and freedom of expression. Secretary of Labor William B. Wilson, who, in his Immigration Bureau, had never condoned the antiradicals, regained control over them. It is possible that the final withdrawal of U.S. troops from Russia in 1920 and the failure of communist revolutions in Germany and Central Europe brought about a modicum of reassurance. In June, 1920, federal judge George W. Anderson, in the case of *Colver v. Skeffington*, found Justice Department methods to have been brutal and unjust, and its raids sordid and disgraceful. Attorney General Palmer, whose actions had been not entirely unrelated to his thirst for the presidential nomination, failed in his bid at the Democratic National Convention in 1920. Persons of moderation had begun to regain the initiative. *Burl L. Noggle, updated by Christy Jo Snider*

Core Resources

Theodore Draper's *The Roots of American Communism* (New York: Viking Press, 1957) is a detailed examination of the patterns, characteristic themes, and leaders of U.S.

communism during the period from 1919 to 1923. David M. Kennedy's *Over Here: The First World War and American Society* (New York: Oxford University Press, 1980) explores topics of race, gender, and radicalism. Theodore Kornweibel, Jr.'s "Black on Black: The FBI's First Negro Informants and Agents and the Investigation of Black Radicalism During the Red Scare" (*Criminal Justice History* 8, 1987) discusses the hiring of African American operatives by the Federal Bureau of Investigation during and after World War I. Robert K. Murray's *The Red Scare: A Study in the National Hysteria, 1919-1920* (Minneapolis: University of Minnesota Press, 1955) analyzes the events, personalities, and fears encompassed by the Red Scare. Louis F. Post's *The Deportations Delirium of Nineteen-Twenty* (Chicago: Charles H. Kerr, 1923) is an account by the assistant secretary of labor in 1920, one of the few men in the Wilson administration who showed restraint and a concern for due process during the Red Scare.

See also: Immigration Act of 1917; Immigration Act of 1924; Nativism; Rosenberg trial; Russian Americans; Xenophobia, nativism, and eugenics.

Redemption period

Redemption refers to the reestablishment of conservative Democratic political dominance in the post-Reconstruction South. During Reconstruction (1863-1877), northern forces rebuilt the governments in the southern states after the South's defeat in the Civil War. The seeds of redemption were sown in the late 1860's as Union troops began gradually withdrawing from the South and Democrats organized locally to reclaim state legislatures and governorships. By 1877, all eleven states of the old Confederacy were controlled by conservative political interests. The chief political goals of these redeemer Democrats were reduction of government, debt repudiation, expansion of the rights of landlords, encouragement of northern capital investment, and the promotion of white supremacy.

Under redeemer state governments, the paltry advances that African Americans had made under Reconstruction were systematically reversed. Black suffrage was first nullified through electoral fraud and later circumscribed through poll taxes, literacy tests, and "grandfather clauses" that prevented all but a handful of southern blacks from voting. Sharecropping defined economic life for increasing numbers of blacks and poor whites. Violence against African Americans escalated throughout the redemption period; by the 1890's, lynchings of black men had become commonplace in many southern localities. By the turn of the century, Jim Crow legislation inspired by the Supreme Court's *Plessy v. Ferguson* (1896)

decision had given legal sanction to segregation and a racial caste system that would dominate southern society well into the twentieth century.   *Michael H. Burchett*

See also: Jim Crow laws; Lynchings; *Plessy v. Ferguson*; Reconstruction.

Redistricting

> **Significance:** The racial or ethnic makeup of various voting blocs can be a significant consideration when drawing electoral district boundaries. Once established, multi-ethnic districts may also experience intense political competition among different groups.

Redistricting is a procedure that has tremendous significance for the way that the individual votes cast by U.S. citizens are translated into the selection of legislative representatives. Racial and ethnic groups, as well as any number of other groups, may be either concentrated in particular districts or divided among many districts.

The Process
The citizens of the United States are divided into 435 congressional districts, with each district electing one legislator to the U.S. House of Representatives. Each state is allocated a certain number of districts based on its relative population. Every ten years, after the census is completed, the 435 congressional seats are "reapportioned" among the states based on the new population figures.

The states then draw new district boundaries, both to permit an increase or decrease in their allotment of congressional seats and to ensure that all districts include approximately the same number of voters. These objectives derive from prevailing voting rights standards. In *Wesberry v. Sanders* in 1964, the U.S. Supreme Court decreed that congressional representation must be based on the one man, one vote principle; that is, districts must be created "as nearly as practicable" with roughly equal numbers of voters.

Gerrymandering
Simply creating districts with numerically comparable populations does not ensure that the one-person, one-vote principle is observed. With knowledge of certain voting indicators (such as party affiliation), a district can be drawn that is heavily weighted toward a particular political party or group. This practice is known as "gerrymandering." Gerrymandering has a long tradition in U.S. politics, having been observed in reapportionment

efforts since the late eighteenth century. In the latter half of the twentieth century, however, various redistricting plans were rejected for their overt skewing in favor of a particular party. In *Davis v. Bandemer* in 1986, the U.S. Supreme Court held that gerrymandering could be considered a violation of the equal protection clause of the Fourteenth Amendment.

Yet at the same time, gerrymandering based on race or ethnicity (rather than party affiliation) seems to have the support of institutions such as the U.S. Department of Justice and the Supreme Court. Beginning in the 1970's and 1980's, districts intentionally created to include a large percentage of racial minorities officially were seen as an appropriate corrective to address the small number of minority legislators in the U.S. Congress and in various state and local legislatures. In other words, it was assumed that the voting strength of racial and ethnic groups could be increased by concentrating their votes in individual districts. Such a procedure was understood to fulfill the objectives of the 1965 Voting Rights Act and was bolstered by a 1982 amendment to the act that upheld the right of African Americans and Hispanics "to elect representatives of their choice."

This reasoning implies that racial and ethnic groups have unique, shared interests; that those interests can be represented only by a member of the group; that the members of a racial and ethnic group tend to vote in the same way; and that "outsiders" will tend not to vote for a member of the group. If all of these suppositions are true, then dividing a racial group between two districts may indeed dilute the voting strength of the bloc. Yet critics claim this reasoning conflicts with the traditional principles of U.S. liberalism, which place individual interests above group interests, and which hold ascriptive characteristics such as race to be irrelevant to the awarding of political benefits.

Legal Challenges to Majority-Minority Districts

In the 1990's, the notion of "majority-minority" districts came under increasing, powerful attack. Although many leaders of minority groups continued to defend such districts as a necessary mechanism for increasing minority representation, the public mood and the U.S. Supreme Court turned against the idea.

A watershed occurred with the *Shaw v. Reno* decision in 1993. In this case, two predominantly African American districts in North Carolina were at issue. Under pressure from the U.S. Department of Justice, the North Carolina legislature had created the districts in an attempt to ensure that the state, whose population was 22 percent African American, would elect its first black congressional representatives in more than a century. Both districts did indeed elect African Americans in 1992. However, five white voters in one of the districts

sued the state, claiming that they had been effectively disfranchised by the reapportionment plan. The case reached the Supreme Court, whose 5-4 majority decision instructed the lower courts to reconsider the constitutionality of the district lines, which created a "bizarre" shape and had an "uncomfortable resemblance to political apartheid." Although the lower courts again upheld the district (while making findings to satisfy the Supreme Court), *Shaw* opened the door for more legal challenges to majority-minority districts. In the ensuing court and policy battles, minority groups that stood to "lose" districts created expressly for them were pitted against whites. The National Association for the Advancement of Colored People (NAACP), the Southern Christian Leadership Conference, the Congressional Black Caucus, and various other groups associated with minority issues expressed their support of the concept of majority-minority districts. Some claimed the trend would lead to the "ultimate bleaching of the U.S. Congress."

In 1995, the Supreme Court more definitively rejected the notion of race-based districts in *Miller v. Johnson*. In this case, the Court rejected redistricting plans in which "race was the predominant factor motivating the legislature's decision to place a significant number of voters within or without a particular district." *Miller* forced the Georgia legislature to amend its reapportionment plan, and subsequent decisions forced other states to do the same. A number of incumbent minority legislatures found themselves running for reelection in districts that no longer had a high proportion of minority voters. Many minority groups saw this as a reversal in their quest for greater representation. Some even claimed that *Miller* was akin to the 1857 *Scott v. Sandford* decision, which held that blacks "had no rights which the white man was bound to respect." However, many of these incumbent legislators were reelected in their newly white-dominated districts. The relationship between race and redistricting was being rethought once again.   *Steve D. Boilard*

Core Resources

An outline of legal and political developments concerning race and redistricting is provided in David G. Savage's "The Redistricting Tangle," in *State Legislatures* (September, 1995). Mark F. Bernstein offers a strong defense of majority-minority districts in "Racial Gerrymandering," in *The Public Interest* (Winter, 1996). A more optimistic assessment of developments during the 1990's is offered by Carol M. Swain in "Limiting Racial Gerrymandering," in *Current* (January, 1996).

See also: Reapportionment cases; Representation: gerrymandering, malapportionment, and reapportionment; "Reverse" racism; *Shaw v. Reno*.

Redlining

Redlining is a broad term, denoting the discriminatory treatment of people living in certain neighborhoods by mortgage lenders, insurance agencies, and other businesses. In effect, a "red line" is drawn around certain areas on a community map, and these areas are either excluded as potential clients or are subjected to more stringent conditions. Perceptions of redlining have triggered charges of racism by various minority groups.

Redlining arises when business decisions are made not with regard to particular individuals but with regard to particular neighborhoods. Automobile insurance, homeowner's insurance, mortgage insurance, business loans, and other risk-sensitive financial products are often priced based on conditions in a particular neighborhood or region. For example, an insurance policy for a home in a floodplain might reasonably be priced higher than the same home on higher ground because of the increased risk. Similarly, homes, automobiles, and businesses in areas with high levels of crime, fires, and other risks might be treated differently by insurance agencies and lenders. This is the most neutral definition of redlining. In itself, this practice has sometimes been the target of criticism, since it treats people as groups rather than individuals. For example, some people have objected to automobile insurance rates being set on the basis of a person's zip code rather than strictly on the basis of the individual's driving record.

The issue of redlining therefore turns on how people are categorized. Businesses such as insurance underwriting usually require that distinctions be made about different types of policyholders (smokers versus nonsmokers, young versus old, urban versus rural, brick dwelling versus wood-frame dwelling). Various laws and court decisions have established that race (as well as other characteristics) cannot be a basis for such business decisions. However, racial issues emerge when it is suspected that certain criteria (such as a person's neighborhood) are used as surrogates for race.

The issue of race becomes especially relevant when high-risk areas also happen to have high concentrations of minority households and businesses. Because many predominantly minority neighborhoods also happen to be poor, the housing stock can be older and in worse repair than the average. Further, these poorer minority neighborhoods can be more likely to experience problems with gangs, vandalism, and other forms of criminal activity. The racial issues emerge from differing perceptions about the linkage between risk, race, and business practices. The question is whether white mortgage lenders and insurance agents are motivated strictly by a color-blind analysis of risk potential or if they make unfair and unsubstantiated risk assumptions about minority neighborhoods and minority households.

Redlining on the basis of race is prohibited by federal law as well as by many state and local laws. In addition, the 1977 Community Reinvestment Act (CRA) requires financial institutions to serve all segments of the community, irrespective of race, income, and other factors. However, the CRA does not require that all applicants must be afforded the same loan conditions and terms. Instead, lenders may consider risk in issuing loans and policies. The central racial issue with regard to redlining is whether race and ethnicity are considered in evaluating risk.

Steve D. Boilard

See also: Discrimination: racial and ethnic; Housing.

Redress movement

The redress movement sought to secure reparations for Japanese Americans who had been interned during World War II. The movement achieved its objective in the late 1980's.

The concept of reparations, although simple in principle, has been the center of complex policy debates in the United States. The United States has long supported reparations in international contexts: For example, it insisted that Germany pay war reparations after World War II and required Iraq to pay reparations after invading Kuwait in 1990. However, the matter of paying reparations to U.S. citizens for alleged injustices has been more controversial. A number of groups, including veterans allegedly exposed to chemical defoliants in Vietnam and persons allegedly exposed to radiation in atomic tests, have pressed for reparations payments with mixed success.

The issue of reparations can have an adverse impact on racial and ethnic relations when claimants belong to a minority group and particularly when they claim that their alleged injury was sustained because of their race or ethnicity. This is the case with Japanese Americans in the redress movement. During World War II, many Japanese Americans living along the West Coast were required to surrender themselves to relocation camps. Most of their property was confiscated as well. The federal government claimed that Japanese Americans posed a threat to the national security of the United States because they might be inclined to aid and abet the Japanese government or its soldiers. This claim has been the subject of controversy for decades.

Claiming that their civil rights had been violated, groups of survivors of the internment camps subsequently pressed reparations claims against the federal government in court. Although Japanese Americans were somewhat divided on the issue, the National Council for Japanese American Redress vigorously lobbied the U.S. Congress for reparations payments.

The government initially responded that the wartime relocation and internment program was necessary to prevent espionage and sabotage. The government alternatively suggested that Japanese Americans were placed in the relocation camps for their own safety, given that anti-Japanese sentiment was high and Japanese Americans were susceptible to racist assaults. The controversy triggered tension between Japanese Americans and white Americans in the 1970's and 1980's. Japanese Americans, including those who had not been relocated, tended to view the redress movement as a noble effort to redress a gross civil injustice of the past. Many white Americans, particularly veterans, took the view that the decision to relocate Japanese Americans was reasonable given the circumstances, and therefore they viewed any potential reparations payments to be tantamount to an undeserved apology and an insult to American veterans.

Eventually, the U.S. government publicly acknowledged that the relocation and internment program had violated the civil rights of American citizens of Japanese ancestry. The Civil Liberties Act of 1988 authorized payment of twenty thousand dollars to each surviving internee. It should be noted, however, that although the recipients had been interned on the basis of their Japanese ancestry, it was their individual injuries rather than their membership in an oppressed group that determined their eligibility for reparations payments. The settlement of the redress movement therefore is distinct from the kind of reparations sought by African Americans for the experience of slavery. *Steve D. Boilard*

See also: Asian American stereotypes; Civil Liberties Act of 1988; Japanese American internment; Japanese Americans.

Refugee fatigue

More commonly known as "compassion" fatigue, refugee fatigue refers to the reluctance of host countries to extend or expand assistance, asylum, or resettlement to refugees—people, often victims of political persecution, who are fleeing from other nations in an attempt to find asylum in a host nation. Compassion fatigue is more likely to occur when the refugee population begins to become a significant burden on the host community's economic and social infrastructure, or at least when the perception develops that such burdens are growing. Refugees sometimes flee into areas where they can find support among ethnic kinspeople, as often happens in Africa. In Asia, however, the flight of Sino-Vietnamese refugees into the Philippines, Indonesia, Thailand, and Malaysia during the 1970's and 1980's excited substantial xenophobic responses that greatly accelerated perceptions of compassion fatigue in the region.

Such concerns may be allayed somewhat if other countries agree to provide opportunities to resettle in a third country and to finance the costs of temporary haven in the country of first asylum. However, donor country populations and governments often grow tired of accepting resettled refugees and financing large overseas programs. When both host nations and countries of resettlement experience refugee or compassion fatigue simultaneously, pressures grow to eliminate humanitarian aid programs and to repatriate refugees or asylum seekers to their original homelands. In some cases, racial or ethnic biases heighten popular resentment of such humanitarian programs; more often, economics is the central cause of compassion fatigue.

During the 1980's, owing to the civil wars in Central America, large numbers of asylum seekers joined the stream of illegal immigrants or undocumented immigrants from Mexico seeking work and safe haven in the United States. For many Americans, this influx led to fears of uncontrolled immigration and a hardening of attitudes toward those in distress. *Robert F. Gorman*

A Japanese American woman looks over photographs, news clippings, and letters regarding the internment of Japanese Americans during World War II.

See also: Refugees and racial/ethnic relations; Refugees: Canadian policy; Refugees: U.S. policy.

Refugees and racial/ethnic relations

> **Significance:** The controversies attending large refugee flows into the United States have been both a product of and a determinant of U.S. refugee policy. Fears of increased cultural and racial heterogeneity and the perceived international political interests of the United States have affected public policy and practice in this area.

Refugees are viewed by some factions within the white majority population in the United States as being relatively nonaffluent and unwilling to assimilate to American culture. Furthermore, these factions and some well-established minority groups have expressed resentment over the success of the "ethnic enclave" strategy that has created significant local political power and prosperity for more recently arrived groups. In addition, some refugee groups have expressed anger at the perceived discriminatory application of refugee legislation. The result has been an exacerbation of tensions across racial and ethnic lines.

History of U.S. Refugee Policy

In 1951, the United Nations held the Convention Relating to the Status of Refugees, which established the still-accepted definition of a refugee and prohibited "refoulement," that is, forcible repatriation. The United States was instrumental in establishing that to be a refugee, a person must be fleeing personal governmental persecution, not economic deprivation. This definition served U.S. Cold War interests by embarrassing new communist regimes that were generating large refugee populations. However, the United States did not sign the convention, preferring to handle asylum issues through domestic legislation.

Throughout the 1950's, the United States avoided making commitments to refugees that were of little political value to the nation. The ideological focus of U.S. refugee policy that developed throughout the 1950's and 1960's is illustrated by the fact that from the mid-1950's through 1979, only 0.3 percent of refugee admissions were to people from noncommunist countries.

"Political" vs. "Economic" Refugees

U.S. legislation still extends asylum to "political refugees," but those fleeing bad economies are termed "economic migrants" and are deported if they immigrate illegally. Awareness is growing that governmental oppression, economic malaise, and widespread social problems often go hand in hand, making it increasingly difficult to disentangle the reasons that people leave their homelands. Many displaced people are fleeing reigns of terror perpetuated by their governments, ethnic conflicts, civil wars, and systematic and severe economic deprivation, but these people are not technically eligible for asylum. Although it seems clear that unprecedented numbers of forcibly displaced people are inadequately protected, the official recognition of a broader definition of "refugee" is unlikely because of the undeniable economic and perceived social and cultural costs of growing populations of people who have received asylum.

The U.S. government has become increasingly concerned about the dramatically increasing numbers of asylum seekers, especially those who enter the country illegally, outside of established refugee-processing channels. The government's position is understandable, as is that of the illegal entrants. For example, from 1980 to the early 1990's, hundreds of thousands of Salvadorans fled in the face of death squads that had murdered their relatives and associates, and a similar situation existed in Guatemala. Yet, during this period, only fifty-four Sal-

A Cambodian family carries its ration of fish in a refugee camp. The influx into the United States of Vietnamese and Cambodian refugees after the Vietnam War was first warmly received, then criticized as the numbers grew.

vadorans and no Guatemalans were accepted for resettlement in the United States, in spite of the fact that Central American refugee camps could assist only a small fraction of these people. Many of those remaining entered the United States illegally.

Charges of Political and Racial Bias

U.S. refugee policy was openly directed by Cold War considerations until 1980. Although there was some criticism of the United States' refusal to extend asylum to those fleeing the regimes of U.S.-supported authoritarian leaders—the shah of Iran (Muhammad Reza Pahlavi), François "Papa Doc" Duvalier in Haiti, General Augusto Pinochet in Chile, and President Ferdinand Marcos of the Philippines—the flow of refugees was controlled, and a possible domestic political backlash avoided.

The 1980 Refugee Act removed the requirement that refugees be fleeing communist regimes. That year, 800,000 immigrants and refugees entered the United States legally, a number that surpassed the combined total for the rest of the world. Growing sentiment for more restrictive policies emerged. The administration of President Ronald Reagan responded by reducing refugee admissions by two-thirds and heavily favoring those from communist countries, in spite of the new law. The Mariel boatlift (1980) brought 130,000 Cubans to the United States in five months, and the policy of forcibly returning Haitians, Salvadorans, and Guatemalans to brutal governments while admitting less physically threatened refugees from communist countries was soundly criticized in some quarters.

The differential treatment accorded asylum seekers from Haiti and Cuba has generated charges of racial bias. As tens of thousands of desperate Haitians were deported or detained at sea and returned before reaching the United States, the U.S. government welcomed hundreds of thousands of Cubans fleeing Fidel Castro's regime. The Congressional Black Caucus set up a task force to study the issue and, after failing to change the U.S. policy, joined prominent church leaders and the Voluntary Agencies Responsible for Refugees in stating publicly that racism was behind the differential treatment of Haitians and other asylum seekers because of a reluctance on the part of the United States to admit large numbers of black refugees. Even as this controversy raged, the government announced that all Vietnamese and Laotians who reached safe haven would be considered refugees, while those fleeing Haiti were subjected to case-by-case screening and deportation.

President George Bush continued Reagan's policies. After the fall of the government of Jean-Bertrand Aristide in Haiti created an upsurge of "boat people," the Bush administration successfully petitioned the Supreme Court to lift a ban on forced repatriation and intercepted and returned tens of thousands of Haitians. The administration of President Bill Clinton continued this practice and then forced the reinstatement of the Aristide government in an effort to stem the flow of refugees. *Jack Carter*

Core Resources

Gil Loescher and Robert Scanlan discuss U.S. refugee policy from World War II to the mid-1980's in *Calculated Kindness: Refugees and America's Half-Open Door, 1945 to Present* (New York: Free Press, 1986). *Immigration and Ethnicity: The Integration of America's Newest Arrivals*, edited by Barry Edmonston and Jeffrey S. Passel (Washington, D.C.: The Urban Institute Press, 1994), examines assimilation issues and controversies. A set of essays addressing refugee-related problems and policies in Western nations, including the United States and Canada, are contained in *Refugees and the Asylum Dilemma in the West*, edited by Gil Loescher (University Park: Pennsylvania State University Press, 1992). Vernon M. Briggs, Jr., and Stephen Moore discuss the effect of growing restrictionist sentiment on refugee policy in *Still an Open Door? U.S. Immigration Policy and the American Economy* (Washington, D.C.: American University Press, 1994).

See also: Immigration and emigration; Mariel boatlift; Push and pull factors; Refugee fatigue; Refugees: Canadian policy; Refugees: U.S. policy; Repatriation; Sanctuary movement.

Refugees: Canadian policy

In contemporary usage, "refugee" is a term for a person who, because of a natural disaster (such as earthquake or flood) or war or fear of persecution for political, religious, racial, or sexual reasons, flees the homeland in search of refuge in a place of safety. Generally, refugees differ from immigrants in that they do not wish to leave their own country but are forced to do so.

Recognizing that the refugee problem is a universal one, Canada once preferred to provide assistance abroad via a coordinated international effort rather than attempting to accept massive numbers of refugees. The nation also had a long history of unofficial and official opposition to refugees based partly on racial prejudice, partly on fear of adverse economic consequences, and partly on resentment toward pseudo-refugees or would-be immigrants who used fraudulent claims of persecution in order to bypass the lengthy immigration process. However, the Canadian Immigration Act of 1952 accepts convention refugees (people qualifying as refugees according to a 1951 United Nations convention), referring claimants to an elaborate process administered by the

Immigration and Refugee Board (IRB), the largest independent tribunal in Canada, whose chief executive officer, the chairperson, reports to Parliament through the minister of citizenship and immigration.

The IRB has three divisions: the Convention Refugee Determination Division (CRDD), the Immigration Appeal Division (IAD), and the Adjudication Division. The CRDD deals exclusively with claims across Canada, which average about twenty-five thousand per year. Each claim is decided in accordance with the rules of national justice and the Canadian Charter of Rights and Freedoms, and refugee status is decided by reference to the 1951 United Nations Convention Relating to the Status of Refugees (incorporated into Canada's Immigration Act) and the 1967 protocol to the convention. A two-member panel holds nonadversarial hearings, usually in-camera, and claimants have a right to counsel and an interpreter. If successful, a claimant is granted refugee status, which enables the claimant to apply for permanent residence and ultimately Canadian citizenship.

If noneligible, a claimant is ordered deported but has the right to appeal to the Immigration Appeal Division (IAD), which has the powers of a superior court of record. Appeals can be inordinately lengthy and distressing to those already in economic and social misery. IAD hearings are adversarial in nature with appellants having the right to counsel. The minister responsible for the Immigration Act is represented, but proceedings are open to the general public, although measures can be taken to protect confidentiality if there is a serious threat to the life, liberty, or security of any individual.

The Adjudication Division became part of the IRB in 1993 and is staffed by independent officers who determine whether a person will be allowed to enter or remain in Canada under the Immigration Act. In addition, the officers review, on a regular basis, the detention of any person pursuant to the Immigration Act. The inquiries and reviews follow the format of the IAD. Decisions rendered by the three divisions can be reviewed in turn by the federal court of Canada. Moreover, if an automatic postdetention review by immigration officials shows that an appellant would be at significant risk if deported, then the appellant may apply for permanent residence.

Keith Garebian

See also: Immigration law: Canada; Refugees and racial/ethnic relations; Refugees: U.S. policy; Repatriation.

Refugees: U.S. policy

U.S. refugee policy has both overseas and domestic components. The United States provides overseas assistance to the millions of refugees who need support and protection. It also selects a much smaller number of refugees for resettlement to the United States. The United States has been the principal architect of the world's refugee assistance network, which has assisted and protected millions of refugees throughout the world without regard to their ethnic or racial backgrounds since the end of World War II. Persecution of refugees by their home countries is often grounded in ethnic and racial differences, and the nondiscriminatory way in which international assistance reaches refugees of all backgrounds is a tribute to the humanitarian instinct.

In the area of resettlement of refugees to the United States, however, there is a good deal more controversy. Although the United States is the leading country of resettlement for refugees, U.S. law and policy regarding who is accepted for resettlement has led some critics to accuse the U.S. government of racial bias or discrimination. Very few Africans, for example, have been resettled in the United States, although more than 1.5 million Indochinese refugees have been accepted. Refugees from Eastern Europe and more recently from Bosnia have been resettled in large numbers as have Cubans. However, Haitians are rarely accepted, and Central American asylum seekers were rejected in large numbers.

Others counter that U.S. refugee resettlement policy is grounded in the particular definition of refugee status found in U.S. law, and that the political and humanitarian needs of particular groups of refugees, rather than ethnic background or race are the determining factors in who gets accepted for resettlement to the United States. The U.S. government's definition of refugee status, which reflects the post-World War II preoccupation with repressive communist governments, requires that asylum seekers demonstrate a well-founded, individually based fear of persecution by their country of nationality. In Africa and many other parts of the world, whole groups of people flee because of general turmoil and disorder in their countries rather than because of specific acts of persecution aimed at individuals by their government. Moreover, in Africa, most refugees are welcomed in their countries of first asylum, and, having found protection there, do not as a general rule require resettlement to safer countries of asylum.

In Southeast Asia, by contrast, regional governments refused to grant even temporary haven to asylum seekers, until governments such as the United States stepped forward to offer resettlement opportunities. The fact that Vietnamese and Cambodian refugees fled from communist governments opposed by the United States made it easier for the U.S. government to justify accepting such large numbers of them as refugees. Similarly, Cubans fleeing from Fidel Casto's communist regime have been accepted while Haitians fleeing from right-wing dictator-

Cuban refugees arrive in the United States in 1967. U.S. refugee policy has been criticized as racist for welcoming Cubans and not Haitians.

ship and a desperately poor economic situation have been routinely rejected as economic migrants. Supporters of U.S. refugee resettlement policies point out that the principle of family reunification is a major factor in accepting refugees for resettlement. This principle tends to favor ethnic groups who are already present in the United States in greater numbers.   *Robert F. Gorman*

See also: Haitians and Haitian refugees; Immigration and emigration; Refugee fatigue; Refugees and racial/ethnic relations; Refugees: Canadian policy; Repatriation; Sanctuary movement.

Reitman v. Mulkey

In the May 29, 1967, *Reitman v. Mulkey* decision, California's adoption of Proposition 14, which repealed the state's fair housing laws, was struck down by the U.S. Supreme Court.

In 1959 and 1963, California established fair housing laws. These statutes banned racial discrimination in the sale or rental of private housing. In 1964, acting under the initiative process, the California electorate passed Proposition 14. This measure amended the state constitution so as to prohibit the state government from denying the right of any person to sell, lease, or refuse to sell or lease his or her property to another at his or her sole discretion. The fair housing laws were effectively repealed. Mr. and Mrs. Lincoln Mulkey sued Neil Reitman in a state court, claiming that he had refused to rent them an apartment because of their race. They claimed that Proposition 14 was invalid because it violated the equal protection clause of the Fourteenth Amendment. If Proposition 14 was unconstitutional, the fair housing laws would still be in force. The Mulkeys won in the California Supreme Court, and Reitman appealed to the Supreme Court of the United States.

Justice Byron White's opinion for the five-justice majority admitted that mere repeal of an antidiscrimination statute would not be unconstitutional. In this case, however, the California Supreme Court had held that the intent of Proposition 14 was to encourage and authorize private racial discrimination. This encouragement amounted to "state action" that violated the equal protection clause of the Fourteenth Amendment.

The four dissenters in the case agreed on an opinion by Justice John M. Harlan. Harlan argued that California's mere repeal of its fair housing laws did not amount to encouraging and authorizing discrimination. If the repeal were to be seen that way, then a state could never rid itself of a statute whose purpose was to protect a constitutional right, whether of racial equality or some other. Harlan also suggested that opponents of antidiscrimination laws would later be able to argue that such laws not be passed because they would be unrepealable. Indeed, several ballot measures which have reversed or repealed civil rights laws protecting gays and lesbians have been struck down on the basis of *Reitman v. Mulkey*.

Reitman v. Mulkey has not had a major effect on American civil rights law. The Supreme Court has not been disposed to expand the "authorization" and "encouragement" strands of constitutional thought. The principle of "state action"—which is all that the Fourteenth Amendment equal protection rules can reach—has not been further broadened. Nevertheless, the precedent remains, with its suggestion that there is an affirmative federal constitutional duty on state governments to prevent private racial discrimination.   *Robert Jacobs*

See also: Discrimination; Fair Housing Act; Fourteenth Amendment; Housing.

Relative deprivation theory

In studies of revitalization and nativistic social movements, in which there is frequently differential social change between various types of ethnic or social groups, David Aberle (1962) contended that an individual or group may perceive a negative discrepancy between a legitimate expectation and the actual occurrence or fulfillment of that need or desire. Though deprivation is seldom absolute, this sense of disillusionment is often based not only on an awareness of extreme discrepancy between expectations and actual physical needs but also on a person's awareness of being deprived of such things as personal freedom, the right to education, health services, equal employment, and religious freedom and other expressions of social and cultural conditions.

Often groups experiencing relative deprivation compare themselves with specific peer groups, not necessarily to the world at large. Relative deprivation is therefore not an objective state of affairs, for actuality varies given a person's perception or interpretation. In some instances of relative deprivation, the leaders of revitalization movements will emphasize, even dramatize, the disparaging socioeconomic differences that are perceived by the group as compared with the holdings of a more dominant group within the society. Relative deprivation may eventually result in alienation or anomie.

John Alan Ross

See also: Alienation.

Religion-based ethnicities

Significance: Like ethnicity itself, religion is a primary basis of group identity. For this reason, religion has played an important role in the solidarity and consciousness of many different race and ethnic groups. Religion has also played an important role in shaping the response of one group to the movement of another group into its territory, its economy, or its social world.

The United States was founded on the principle of freedom of religion and defined from the arrival of the Pilgrims in New England to the present day as a "nation of immigrants." The history of both the United States and Canada can be viewed as a history of multiple and complex interrelationships among groups with ethnic origins all over the world and representing the diverse religions of the world.

European Protestants and Native Peoples
When Protestant groups fleeing religious discrimination in England and Northern Europe arrived in New England, they were greeted by diverse tribes of native peoples whose religious beliefs and spiritualities were poorly understood and frequently dismissed as "pagan" or "primitive" belief systems. Viewing native religions as grossly inferior to Protestant faiths was an important ingredient in the dehumanization of native peoples that occurred in the removal of Indian peoples from their native lands during the Indian Wars and the push westward to the Pacific coast by the European settlers. This period is well described in Dee Brown's *Bury My Heart at Wounded Knee* (1970). Similarly, the boarding school movement in which the U.S. Bureau of Indian Affairs removed native children from their families and sent them to live in residential schools in which their languages and religions were to be eliminated is a more recent example of the profound and harsh consequences of failing to understand and respect the religious beliefs of a different ethnic group. The Sun Dance movement among Native Americans in the 1920's is an example of an ethnic minority group's attempt to retain a sense of group identity based on religion in the face of attacks on its culture by the white Christian majority group. The Sun Dance movement involved large gatherings of native peoples of many tribes to perform the ritual Sun Dance as a means of returning to native religious roots and reinforcing cultural identity.

The War with Catholic Mexico for the Southwest
When the territorial ambitions of the Protestant "pioneers" turned to the lands owned by Mexico, the second conquest of an existing population occurred. The Catholic Mexicans whose lands became Texas, Arizona, and New Mexico were profoundly affected by this clash of cultures or "chocacultura." The Protestants were more individualistic, more acquisitive, more competitive, less reverent, less familistic, and less respectful of women than the Catholic Mexicans. Roman Catholic Marianism, which gives central place to Mary, mother of Jesus, in Catholic religious thought and practice, tends to elevate the status of women generally and of motherhood specifically. The individualistic culture and society of Western Protestants and their treatment of women had a profoundly disorganizing effect on the close-knit families and communities of the Mexicans.

Catholic and Jewish Immigration from Eastern Europe
The Industrial Revolution and the consequent urbanization of the East and Midwestern United States during the late nineteenth century is another major transformation of American society that was shaped by religion-based ethnic groups and relationships among them. In *The Protestant Ethic and the Spirit of Capitalism* (1920), social theorist Max Weber argues that the Industrial Revolution was in large part the product of the individualism, work ethic, and emphasis on rewards in this world over rewards in heaven that characterized Protestant faiths such as

Calvinism. As the movement from farms to urban manufacturing centers occurred first in Europe and then in the United States, two waves of European immigrants crossed the Atlantic to the United States. First, northern and western European Protestants from England, the Netherlands, Scandinavia, and Germany left under economic pressures and settled in the United States. A second wave of immigrants, Catholics and Jews from southern and eastern Europe, faced far greater discrimination in education and work because of their greater differences in appearance and in religion. These European Catholics and Jews—among them the Irish, Italians, Poles, and Greeks—shaped the development of urban America, providing its industrial labor force, the populations of its first urban ghettos, and the police forces and political machines of the great American cities.

African American Religions and Identity

The clergy of black Christian churches in the South, led by Dr. Martin Luther King, Jr., pastor of Ebenezer Baptist Church in Atlanta, Georgia, formed the backbone of the mass movement for an end to segregation and for the rights of black people to equal education, access to public accommodations, housing, and employment that culminated in the Civil Rights Act of 1964. Black Americans view their struggle for freedom and equal rights as a moral struggle against injustice and bigotry. Using the tactics of nonviolent or passive resistance, King and other civil rights activists staged sit-ins at lunch counters that refused to serve blacks, boycotted buses that discriminated against black passengers, and marched through neighborhoods to protest injustices.

At the same time, the Nation of Islam, led by Elijah Muhammad and Malcolm X, united African Americans in a struggle for economic and political survival and a reassertion of their Muslim origins. (Many of the West Africans brought to the United States as slaves were believed to be Muslims when they were captured.) In the 1960's, many blacks began to reject the family names that originated during slavery and adopt African Muslim names. World heavyweight boxing champion Mohammad Ali (formerly Cassius Clay) is a prominent example of this reassertion of Muslim African roots. In 1996, Muslim leader Louis Farrakhan led a large group of African American men in the Million Man March on Washington, D.C., to seek repentance and renew their commitment to their families and communities.

Another example of a religion-based black identity or consciousness movement is the Rastafarians of Jamaica; in the 1980's their religious concept of "dread" became the namesake for their popular hairstyle known as "dreadlocks." The concept of "dread" and Rastafarian religion in general seeks to connect at a deep level with the awe and power of black racial identity.

The Impact of Asian Religions

Asians who migrated to the United States to build the transcontinental railroad, to provide health care in poor communities, to labor in factories and shops, and to provide leadership in technical fields brought with them the religions of Buddhism and Hinduism and the mind-body meditations and practices that have become part of American culture. From corporate executives who meditate daily to relieve stress to university students who formed the core of the Transcendental Meditation movement of the 1960's to Hollywood film stars who find creative energy through study with Tibetan religious leaders, many Americans have turned to Asian religions to heal their minds and bodies, to learn to relax, to deal with pain, to age more comfortably, or to increase their human potential.

Asian religions are syncretic; that is, they allow for the inclusion or incorporation of elements of other religions without creating conflict, and so these religions and their practices can and do peacefully coexist with other faiths. In addition, Asian cultures are subtle and their social ethics and religious thought stress harmony, balance, and respect for all living beings. These cultural attributes decrease social conflict based on religion.

These Orthodox Jewish boys walk down a New York City street. Religion plays a major role in shaping these children's identities.

Religion and Prejudice

Religion plays a complex and important role in a group's response to other social groups and to social change. Raymond Grew argues that Protestant fundamentalism in the United States arose largely as a means to deal with the stresses and temptations of modern life. In times of rapid change and in social environments in which there are many choices and no clear, universally accepted criteria for making these choices, the individual's first protection against the dangers of modern life is to accept a fundamental core of belief, doctrines, and behaviors from which there can be no deviation or compromise. Among fundamentalist groups, adherence to this core set of beliefs and behaviors becomes both a measure of belonging to the community and a defense against social changes and behaviors that are perceived as threatening and dangerous. This unyielding adherence to core beliefs and doctrines has also been associated with an intolerant attitude toward people whose attitudes, beliefs, and behaviors differ from those of the fundamentalists. Prejudice and even hatred toward other groups can arise in an environment that combines intellectual strictness or closed-mindedness with emotional intensity, as fundamentalist faiths often do.

Although religious intolerance can contribute to racial and ethnic prejudice, religious ethics can also form the basis of an individual's or group's motivation and ability to overcome prejudice. Sallyann McKey notes that "prejudice in its various forms is a vital ethical concern. It affects moral decision making at the personal and social levels." In a similar vein, philosopher Paul Ricoeur stresses the importance of Christian ethical reflection to "recognize, lament, and overcome prejudice."

Religion and Racial and Ethnic Identity

The roots of identity in both ethnicity and religion are deep and profound. Sociologist Edward Shils refers to three bases of social belonging: primordial, sacred, and kinship ties. Both religion and ethnicity have elements of primordial bases of social group belonging, the deepest bases. Psychologist Erik Erikson, philosopher Paul Ricoeur, and Bernard Longeran each deal with the subconscious and preconscious elements of religion. Ritual, argues Erikson, is an individual's and group's way of dealing with the uncomfortable feelings of guilt and shame that form the very basis of moral behavior in a group. Pope John Paul II describes religion as a society's attempt to deal with the question of what it means to be a human being and to try to find the purpose of life. In Martin Marty's words, religion addresses the questions: Who am I? What do I or should I do? To whom do I belong? How shall I act? and Whom shall I trust? Race and ethnic identity also addresses these questions to some extent and in various ways. *Judith R. Mayo*

Core Resources

Religion, Ethnicity, and Self-Identity: Nations in Turmoil, edited by Martin E. Marty and R. Scott Appleby (Hanover, N.H.: University Press of New England, 1997), provides an in-depth analysis of the diverse functions of religion for individuals and groups. Peter C. Phan's *Ethnicity, Nationality, and Religious Experience* (Lanham, Md.: University Press of America, 1995) also offers excellent analyses of the functions of religion in group life, including Paul Ricoeur's "Theory of Narrative." Joseph Owens's *Dread: The Rastafarians of Jamaica* (Kingston, Jamaica: Sangster, 1976) is an interesting exploration of the deep connections between racial and religious identity. J. Milton Yinger's *Religion in the Struggle for Power: A Study in the Sociology of Religion* (Durham, N.C.: Duke University Press, 1946) is one of the first major U.S. sociological studies of religion. Dee Brown's *Bury My Heart at Wounded Knee: An Indian History of the American West* (New York: Holt, Rinehart and Winston, 1970) is a saga describing misunderstanding and dismissiveness toward native peoples and their religious beliefs and practices as well as toward other aspects of their lifestyles.

See also: AME Church; American Indian Religious Freedom Act; Anglo-Protestants; Black church; Christian Identity movement; *Church of the Lukumi Babalu Aye v. Hialeah*; Civil Rights movement; European immigration to the United States: 1790-1892; Ghost Dance religion; Indian-white relations: United States; Jamaican Americans; Judaism; Million Man March; Nation of Islam; Native American Church; Peyote religion.

Relocation of American Indians

> **Significance:** Though the relocation program launched by the U.S. government in the 1950's did not achieve its goal of assimilation, it did contribute to the rapid urbanization of Native Americans.

The 1930's saw a departure in federal Indian policy from the usual goal of assimilating Indians into the mainstream of American society; instead, the Indian New Deal stressed the idea of tribal self-determination. After World War II, however, Congress and the Bureau of Indian Affairs (BIA) began to press for a return to assimilation. In the early 1950's, several assimilationist policies emerged: termination, which sought to "free" Native Americans by dissolving their tribes; the assumption by the states of more legal jurisdiction over Indian

This relocated American Indian family stands in front of its new low-cost home in South Dakota. Sometimes the relocated people were poorly prepared for life in their new surroundings.

Urban Problems

The experience of many participants in the program often ended in frustration. Most reservation Indians were poorly prepared for life in urban America. Coming from cultures that were communal and cooperative, many found it hard to adjust to the impersonal and competitive character of metropolitan life. The BIA often provided little job training and inadequate counseling. Many Indians found that they could obtain only menial or temporary jobs. Too often, those relocating found themselves becoming slum dwellers cut off from family and friends. Alcoholism became a particular problem. The death in 1955 of war hero Ira Hayes, a Pima whose life was shattered by despair and alcoholism after he was relocated to Chicago, brought attention to the problems often faced by the new urban Indians. By 1959, a third of those participating in the program had returned to the reservation.

The BIA attempted to respond to mounting criticism of the program. Relocation officials began to moderate their sales pitches in the later 1950's, and more attention was given to preparing participants prior to departure. The program continued to attract criticism, however, and many Native Americans closely associated it with the widely hated policy of termination. After the latter policy was ended in 1962, relocation continued. During the John F. Kennedy administration, the program's name and focus was changed to one of employment assistance. More attention was paid to job training, and more of an effort was made to place Indians in cities closer to their reservations.

Impact of Relocation

As a program to foster the assimilation of Indians into American society, relocation largely failed to achieve its aim. Yet, in other ways, some of them paradoxical, the program had important influences on Native American life.

The most evident effect of the program was to foster one of the most important Indian demographic trends of the second half of the twentieth century: urbanization. Despite the difficulties they encountered, Indians continued to move to urban areas. In 1940 only about 7 percent of Indians lived in cities; by 1980 almost half did, and by 1990 a majority lived in metropolitan areas. There is some irony in the fact that the majority of Indians who moved

communities; and relocation, which sought to move Indians to large cities. Although at the time termination gained the most attention, relocation proved more persistent and had the more lasting effect.

Planning and Implementation

The BIA began its relocation efforts on a small scale in 1948, with efforts to place Navajos, whose reservation was believed to be overcrowded, in western cities. In 1952, the program was expanded into the national Voluntary Relocation Program. Offices were established on most reservations and in Oklahoma. BIA agents working on a quota system employed a hard-sell approach as they pressured Indians to relocate. Los Angeles, Chicago, and Denver were first designated to receive the new urban dwellers; seven other western and midwestern cities were later added to the list. Indians were sometimes sent to more distant cities on purpose in the hope that distance would lessen tribal ties.

Indians volunteering for the program were given a month to prepare for the transition. When the time came, they were given one-way bus or train tickets, fifty dollars each to cover moving expenses, and modest sums for subsistence. Upon arriving in their new home cities, they received help from local relocation offices in finding housing and employment and a month's financial assistance (forty dollars a week for an individual or couple).

to cities did so on their own and not as program participants, largely because of suspicion of the BIA and the tendency to associate relocation with termination. The relocation program, however, did contribute to this informal migration. More than thirty-five thousand Indians relocated under the program, and the cities to which they moved (the ones with relocation offices) became the main centers of Native American urbanization.

Regardless of whether they were program participants, urban Indians continued to have more than their share of social problems. They also tended to be less tolerant of substandard conditions and more critical of government policies than reservation Indians. It is not surprising that many of the leaders of the more radical Indian movements of the 1960's and 1970's had urban backgrounds. Moreover, urbanization contributed to the growth of pan-Indianism. By bringing together Indians of many different tribal backgrounds, the relocation program encouraged interaction among them and the discovery that they shared many problems. It may be the greatest irony of relocation that this assimilationist program fostered instead a greater sense of Indian separateness and encouraged a more activist and confrontational attitude toward the federal government.

William C. Lowe

Core Resources
The relocation process is discussed in Larry W. Burt's *Tribalism in Crisis: Federal Indian Policy, 1953-61* (Albuquerque: University of New Mexico Press, 1982); Donald L. Fixico's *Termination and Relocation: Federal Policy, 1945-1966* (Albuquerque: University of New Mexico Press, 1986); James S. Olson and Raymond Wilson's *Native Americans in the Twentieth Century* (Provo, Utah: Brigham Young University Press, 1984); Francis Paul Prucha's *The Great Father: The United States Government and the American Indians* (2 vols., Lincoln: University of Nebraska Press, 1984); Alan L. Sorkin's *The Urban American Indian* (Lexington, Mass.: D. C. Heath, 1978); and *The Indian in Urban Society* (Boston: Little, Brown, 1971), edited by Jack O. Weddell and O. Michael Watson.

See also: American Indian demographics; Bureau of Indian Affairs; Indian New Deal; Termination Resolution; Urban Indians.

Repatriation

Repatriation refers to the act of a person returning to his or her country of origin or nationality, either voluntarily or through deportation by a government. Voluntary repatriation is considered a right of individuals. Therefore, under international law, governments are required to permit persons to return to their countries of nationality. At the same time, under international treaties and increasingly under international customary law, governments are to refrain from involuntarily repatriating those persons who have refugee status—that is, persons who are recognized by the host government as being in flight from persecution in their country of origin. However, persons who are not refugees or who are illegal aliens may be repatriated against their will. The key to determining whether a person may be involuntarily repatriated, then, turns on his or her status as a refugee.

The United States government, for example, has treated Haitian asylum seekers as economic migrants rather than as political refugees and therefore has repatriated the vast majority. During the early 1990's in Southeast Asia, boat people who fled Vietnam were screened to determine which were political refugees who would qualify for resettlement to third countries, and which were economic migrants who could be validly repatriated to Vietnam. Controversy inevitably surrounds such status-determination procedures. Protests against screening procedures were raised by resettled Vietnamese communities in the United States, Canada, and other resettlement countries, and for those sent back home against their wishes, the experience was traumatic.

Robert F. Gorman

See also: Refugee fatigue; Refugees and racial/ethnic relations; Refugees: Canadian policy; Refugees: U.S. policy.

Representation: gerrymandering, malapportionment, and reapportionment

As of 1995, the citizens of the United States were divided into 435 congressional districts, with each district electing one representative. Every ten years the congressional seats are "reapportioned" through a process of drawing new districts based on the latest census data. In *Wesberry v. Sanders* in 1964, the Supreme Court decreed that congressional representation must be based on the "one man, one vote" principle; that is, districts must be created "as nearly as practicable" with roughly equal numbers of voters. Reapportionment thus is necessary to account for population shifts over each ten-year period. Malapportionment describes the situation that results when districts are not fairly drawn.

Simply ensuring roughly equal population does not necessarily ensure that the "one man, one vote" principle is observed. With knowledge of the patterns of party affiliation within a region, a district can be drawn which gives an advantage to one particular political party. This practice is known as "gerrymandering," after Massachusetts governor Elbridge Gerry, who oversaw the creation of contorted districts, one of which was said to resemble a salamander. Gerrymandering has a long tradition in American politics, having been observed in reapportionment efforts since the late eighteenth century. Gerrymandered districts ensured continued control by party "machines" and were blamed for various political ills. In *Davis v. Bandemer* (1986), the U.S. Supreme Court held that gerrymandering could be considered a violation of the equal protection clause of the Fourteenth Amendment. To avoid charges of gerrymandering, districts must be reasonably and compactly drawn.

More recently the issue of representation has been subjected to another justice claim. Some see the incongruity between the racial makeup of the population and the racial makeup of elected bodies as evidence that racial voting strength has been "diluted." This reasoning implies that (1) racial and ethnic groups have unique, shared interests, (2) those interests can be represented only by a member of the group, (3) the members of such a group tend to vote in the same way, and (4) outsiders will tend not to vote for a member of the group. If all these suppositions are true, then dividing a racial group between two districts may indeed dilute the voting strength of the bloc. Critics, however, claim that this reasoning conflicts with the traditional principles of American liberalism, which place individual interests above group interests and hold ascriptive characteristics such as race to be irrelevant to the awarding of political benefits.

By the early 1990's some districts, such as supervisorial districts in Los Angeles County, had been designed specifically to include a significant proportion of minority citizens, presumably giving those groups more weight in the outcome of an election. The issue remains controversial, however, with some claiming that this government-sanctioned "racial gerrymandering" amounts to creating districts that isolate minority votes. The U.S. Supreme Court supported that charge by holding racially gerrymandered districts unconstitutional in *Shaw v. Reno* in 1993. The Court's 1995 *Miller v. Johnson* decision reaffirmed the unconstitutionality of districts drawn with race as the dominant factor in their design.

Steve D. Boilard

See also: Discrimination: racial and ethnic; Reapportionment cases; Redistricting; *Shaw v. Reno*; Voting Rights Act of 1965; *Wesberry v. Sanders*.

Republic of New Africa

The Republic of New Africa (RNA) is a revolutionary black nationalist organization that was founded in 1968. Its objectives included territorial separation of African Americans from the dominant white society in the area of the five southern states considered the "Black Belt" (Mississippi, Louisiana, Alabama, Georgia, and South Carolina); cooperative economics and community self-sufficiency (as defined by the Tanzanian principles of "Ujamaa"); and the collection of reparations from the U.S. government in the amount of ten thousand dollars per person to compensate for retrenchment of the Reconstruction promise of "forty acres and a mule" to freed slaves.

The Republic of New Africa formed a government for the "non-self-governing Blacks held captive within the United States." "Consulates" were established in New York, Baltimore, Pittsburgh, Philadelphia, Washington, D.C., and Jackson, Mississippi. The RNA was seen as an internal threat to the security of the United States and targeted for attack by the U.S. federal government.

M. Bahati Kuumba

See also: Black Power movement; National Coalition of Blacks for Reparations in America.

This political cartoon ridicules Massachusetts governor Eldridge Gerry, whose name forms the basis of the term "gerrymandering."

Reservation system of the United States

> **Significance:** As the United States expanded and increasing numbers of white Americans moved westward, the confinement of American Indians to reservations was deemed the most efficient way to separate Indians and whites while allowing whites access to the greatest amount of land.

In colonial times and the earliest years of the United States, there was little thought given to the need for a permanent answer to the competition for land between Europeans and Native Americans. Because there were vast uncharted areas of wilderness to the west, it was generally thought that the Indian population could be pushed westward—eventually, across the Mississippi—whenever problems arose. This was the main policy of the pre-Civil War era, as eastern tribes were "removed" westward, many to land in present-day Oklahoma.

The movement to place all Indians on reservations began in earnest after the Civil War during the presidency of Ulysses S. Grant (1869-1877). The policy came about because of the failure of previous programs and the desire of white Americans to open more western land for white settlement. From the end of the American Revolution to 1830, Indian tribes had been treated as if they were foreign nations within the United States. The federal government sent ambassadors to negotiate treaties with the tribes, and many groups, such as the Cherokee in northern Georgia, had established their own governments and states within the United States. Others had traded territory in the East for land farther west. Trouble began in Georgia after the discovery of gold on Indian land. Eventually, Congress passed a law, supported by Andrew Jackson, offering territory west of the Mississippi River to tribes willing to relinquish their lands in the East. All Indians would have to accept this trade or face forced removal. Several wars and the infamous Trail of Tears, which saw the deaths of thousands of Native Americans, followed the imposition of this removal policy.

Early Reservation Policy

Most of the new Indian lands were in the Plains region—or the "Great American Desert," as whites, who at first believed that it was too hot and dry for farming, called it. In the 1840's, thousands of white settlers began crossing this "desert" on their way to California and Oregon. Travel through Indian Territory could be dangerous and difficult because of Indian attacks, so travelers and settlers called for a safe corridor to be maintained by the army. From this proposal a concentration policy developed, under which Indians would be driven into southern and northern colonies with a wide, safe passageway to the Pacific in the middle. These Indian enclaves, it was said, would be safe from white settlement. In the early 1860's, these Indian lands were closed to all whites except those on official business. In 1869, Congress created a Board of Indian Affairs within the Department of the Interior to control the reservations, and two years later ended the policy of treating Indians as residents of foreign states within the United States. On March 3, 1871, the Indian Appropriation Act declared that tribal affairs would be managed by the U.S. government without consent of the tribes.

Indians were supposed to have enough land on their reservations so that they could continue to hunt, but this idea lasted only briefly as land hunger among white farmers and ranchers after the Civil War led to demands for greatly reducing the size of Indian Territory. If Indians learned to farm rather than hunt, Indian affairs commissioners and congressmen (and most whites) believed,

This Paiute family lives on a reservation in Pyramid Lake, Nevada. Although some reservations have benefited from the sale of mineral rights or other financial developments, many reservations remain quite poor.

more land could be put to productive use, and the natives would give up their "wild" ways and enjoy the fruits of civilization. Indians were given a choice: Either they could relocate, or volunteer armies would be recruited to force them to move. On the reservations, Indians were to get education for their children, rations from the government until they knew how to grow their own crops, and certain other benefits. By 1877, more than 100,000 Indians had received rations on reservations.

Reservation education programs did not work quickly enough to satisfy many in Congress; additionally, some claimed, they cost too much money. Maintaining a large army in the West to keep Indians within their boundaries also proved expensive. The notion that Indians would become farmers proved false. Congress reacted to these problems by reducing rations, which caused terrible suffering and malnutrition among Indians, and by reducing the number of reservations as more tribes were moved into Indian Territory (Oklahoma). The federal government mandated that all Indian males receiving rations would have to work, but since few jobs existed on Indian lands, this policy proved a miserable failure. To improve education and help Indians become more like whites, Congress commanded that all instruction take place in English and that the teaching of Indian religions be banned.

General Allotment Act

In 1887 Congress changed Indian policy by passing the General Allotment Act (Dawes Severalty Act). Designed by Senator Henry Dawes of Massachusetts, who considered himself a friend of the Indians, the new policy provided for an eventual end to the reservation system and the abolition of tribal organizations. In the future, Indians would be treated as individuals, not as members of tribes. Each head of a family would be allotted 160 acres of reservation land, and each adult single person would get 80 acres. The government would keep this land in trust for twenty-five years, and at the end of that period Indians would get title to the land and full citizenship rights. Land on reservations not distributed to Indians would be declared surplus land and could be sold to the highest bidder.

When the bill was passed, there were about 138 million acres of land on reservations. Between 1887 and 1900, Indians had been allotted only 3,285,000 of those acres, while almost 30 million acres were declared surplus and ceded to whites. In addition, of the 32,800 Indian families and individuals getting allotments, fewer than one-third managed to remain on their land for the required twenty-five years to attain full ownership. The program was never applied among the Indians of the Southwest, and these were the tribes most successful in retaining their traditional cultures. In 1891 Indians received the right to lease their lands for agriculture, grazing cattle, and mining. The pressure for leases from cattle ranchers and mining companies was enormous, and hundreds of thousands of acres found their way to white control through leasing provisions that took advantage of Indian poverty. Many reformers and politicians denounced leasing, but only because it made Indians who lived off their leases idle—not because it took advantage of them and made them poor.

Between 1900 and 1921 Congress made it easier for Indians to dispose of their allotments. A 1907 law, for example, gave Indians considered too old, sick, or "incompetent" to work on their land permission to sell their land to whomever they wished. White reservation agents decided questions of competency. Under this program, millions more acres were lost as impoverished Indians sold their property at very low prices just to survive. This policy was speeded up in 1917 under the "New Policy" of Indian Commissioner Cato Sells, who declared that all adults one-half or less Indian were "competent," as were all graduates of Indian schools once they reached twenty-one years of age. Under this policy, more than twenty-one thousand Indians gained control of their lands but then quickly lost them because they could not afford to pay state property taxes or went bankrupt. This policy was reversed in 1921, but Indians faced new problems as the federal government in the 1920's moved to end all responsibility over Indians.

In 1923, John Collier, a white reformer, became executive secretary of the American Indian Defense Association, the major lobby defending Native American interests before Congress. Collier believed Indian civilization, especially Pueblo culture, to be superior in many ways to the materialistic, violent society found in the United States and Europe. For the first time, under Collier's leadership, Indians presented a program to Congress aimed at preserving their traditional values and way of life. Reservations, it was argued, had to be retained to save these old ways but needed economic assistance to survive. Collier's program called for civil liberties for Indians, including religious freedom and tribal self-government.

The "Indian New Deal"

The Great Depression hit Indian reservations, particularly the poorest in South Dakota, Oklahoma, Arizona, and New Mexico, very hard. By 1933, thousands of Indians faced starvation, according to reports from the Emergency Relief Administration. President Franklin D. Roosevelt appointed Collier to lead the Bureau of Indian Affairs and deal with the crisis. Collier, with the president's help, pushed the Indian Reorganization Act through Congress in 1934. This law radically changed Indian-white relations and gave Native Americans control of their lands; it was nicknamed the Indian New Deal. The law ended the allotment system, gave local councils authority to spend relief money, and allowed Indians to practice traditional religions and customs. Congress increased appropriations for reservations from twelve million dollars to an average of forty-eight million dollars while Collier held his post. The commissioner had his critics, mainly advocates of assimilation and western senators and congressmen fearful of Indian self-rule. In 1944, the House Indian Affairs Committee criticized Collier's policy and called for a return to the old idea of making Indians into Americans. The next year Collier resigned, and many of his programs ended.

Policy Since World War II

Creation of the Indian Claims Commission in 1946, which was empowered by Congress to settle all Indian land claims against the government, resulted in victories for some tribes. Between 1946 and 1960 the commission awarded more than 300 million dollars to Indian tribes wrongfully deprived of their lands, but Congress saw this as an excuse to end other assistance to reservations. Some BIA officials foresaw the abolition of the reservation system. In the 1950's relocation became a popular idea. More than sixty thousand Indians were moved to cities such as Denver, Chicago, and Houston. To save money and hasten the end of separate development for Native Americans, Commissioner Dillon S. Meyer took away powers of tribal councils and returned decisions concerning spending to BIA headquarters.

In 1953, Congress terminated federal control over Indians living on reservations in California, Florida, Iowa, New York, and Texas. The states now had criminal and legal jurisdiction over the tribes. Results proved disastrous, especially after removal of federal liquor control laws. Unemployment and poverty increased under the termination program. The BIA tried to resolve the unemployment problem by expanding the relocation program, hoping that jobless Indians would find work in cities, but by 1958 more than half of the relocated workers had returned to the reservations.

In the 1960's, Congress reversed direction yet again and revoked the termination policy. During the federal government's War on Poverty, it increased tribal funds for education, health care, and job training. Expanded federal aid greatly improved living conditions for Indians, and reservation population increased from 367,000 in 1962 to 452,000 in 1968. Life expectancy improved from a dismal 51 years (1940) to 63.5 (1968), not yet up to white American levels but a great improvement nevertheless. In 1975 the Indian Self-Determination and Education Assistance Act gave tribes control over school funds and returned most important economic decision-making powers to locally elected councils. Three years

later Congress established a community college system on reservations in which native languages, religions, and cultures were taught.

The American Indian Religious Freedom Act (1978) protected traditional practices, and the Supreme Court advanced Indian self-determination by authorizing tribal courts to try and punish even non-Indians for violations of the law committed on Indian territory. In a key ruling in 1978, the Court said that tribes could be governed by traditional laws even if they conflicted with state and federal laws. In the 1980's, such ideas of separate development continued to dominate reservation policy, and the Reagan administration followed a policy of "government-to-government relationships" among the states, the federal government, and the tribes. In many ways this "new" policy greatly resembled ideas first enunciated by George Washington in 1794, when Americans also doubted the possibility of assimilation and opted for a policy of pluralism and cultural separation. Although a few reservations have become quite rich because of the lease or sale of mineral rights, most remain very poor. When a Bureau of the Census study of poverty in the United States in the 1980's listed the ten poorest counties in the union, eight of them were on reservations. Cultural self-determination, improved education, and increased financial assistance had not yet improved economic conditions for many Native Americans. Reservations in South Dakota and New Mexico were the poorest; they also had the highest levels of alcoholism, divorce, and drug addiction found anywhere in the United States.   *Leslie V. Tischauser*

Core Resources

Henry E. Fritz's *The Movement for Indian Assimilation, 1860-1890* (Philadelphia: University of Pennsylvania Press, 1963) is comprehensive analysis of government policy in the critical period when assimilation policy was the order of the day. *History of Indian-White Relations*, vol. 4 in *Handbook of North American Indians* (Washington, D.C.: Smithsonian Institution Press, 1988), edited by Wilcomb E. Washburn, contains several useful essays on past and current reservation policy. Washburn's *The Indian in America* (New York: Harper & Row, 1975) is arguably the best one-volume survey of the Indian experience in North America, with many useful insights and comments concerning the reservation system.

See also: Allotment system; American Indian Defense Association; General Allotment Act; Indian Appropriation Act; Indian Claims Commission; Indian New Deal; Indian Reorganization Act; Indian Territory; Indian-white relations: United States; Relocation of American Indians; Reserve system of Canada; Termination Resolution; Trail of Tears; Urban Indians.

Reserve system of Canada

Significance: Until well into the twentieth century, Canada's Indian reserve system assumed that lands not specifically defined "surrendered" to white settlement were for traditional Indian use; reactions to abuses in "surrender" arrangements brought more protective self-government and ownership provisions in the 1990's.

The history of Indian reserves in Canada began at the end of the French and Indian War (1754-1763), when French claims on Canada were abandoned to British imperial control. A British royal proclamation in 1763 forbade governors of both the Canadian and the American colonies from issuing any land grants to colonists unless it was clear that the land in question was not "traditionally occupied" by Indians. This act began the so-called policy of protection, which stipulated that only the Crown held ultimate responsibility for protecting or acquiring traditional Indian lands. Such acquisition, or "surrendering over," was to be with the consent of tribes; what was not "surrendered" to the Crown was presumed to remain Indian property.

Ideal and Reality of Traditional Reserve Policy
When the American Revolution ended in 1783, the influx of Loyalists into Canada caused pressures for colonial land grants to rise. In response, the Crown initiated a series of treaties and purchase agreements, particularly with tribes in Ontario. What was not turned over by sale or treaty agreement would from that date be called Indian "reserves." What appeared to be benevolent recognition of the Indians' traditional lands, however, was not always that generous. In a few extreme cases, such as the Chippewa (Ojibwa) agreement to surrender their Chenail Ecarte and St. Clair lands, only a very small portion was left for exclusive tribal use (in this case, some 23,000 acres out of a total of 2.7 million acres).

For a number of years there was no specific definition of what responsibilities the British might accept with respect to Indian rights within their reserves. This changed by the 1830's, when it became obvious that Indians even farther west were going to be affected by expanding white settlements and that, as their traditional way of life would no longer be possible in areas left as reserves, government assistance would have to be part of the land surrender process. Thus, an agreement concerning the Manitoulin Islands near the north shore of Lake Huron became, in 1836, part of a "new" attitude toward reserves: Indians there were to receive, free from "the encroachments of the whites . . . proper houses . . . and assistance . . . to become civilized and to cultivate land."

At the same time, it became increasingly apparent that the "traditional" reserve system would have to involve higher degrees of Indian dependence on Crown authorities to intercede between them and aggressive settler communities anxious to gain access to the natural resources on Indian land. In 1850, a decade and a half before Canada's federal/provincial arrangement (the Constitutional Act) placed the authority of the Crown across the entire width of the Atlantic, troubles broke out over settler access to minerals in the Lake Superior area. William Robinson was appointed treaty commissioner in order to define how Indian hunting and fishing rights could be preserved while sale and development of mining rights on the same land passed to outside bidders.

With the coming of Canada's independent status after 1867, it became apparent that a specific Indian act would be necessary and somehow should be binding on all provinces of the federal system. Neither the first Canadian Indian Act of 1876 nor later acts, however, provided for the establishment of new reserves. The object of all Canadian Indian acts (into and through the twentieth century) was supposed to be to improve the management and developmental prospects of reserves that already existed. Nevertheless, the traditional but in many ways manipulated concept of what constituted a reserve in Canada continued, for nearly a century, to allow for "surrender" of lands considered to be in excess of tribal needs. Thus, in Quebec Province, some 45,000 choice acres considered Indian reserves in 1851 would be given over to white settlement between 1867 and 1904. The most spectacular case of additional surrenders occurred in Saskatchewan, the source for nearly half of the nearly 785,000 acres of Indian lands taken in the early twentieth century. In addition to formal acts of surrender, amendments in 1895 and 1918 to the Indian Act allowed the superintendent-general of Indian affairs to recognize private leases of reserve land that was not being exploited economically by the tribes.

Perhaps the most striking example of consequences that could come from application of these and other amendments occurred in the 1924 Canada-Ontario Indian Reserve Lands Agreement, which would stand, despite challenges, into the 1990's. The 1924 agreement essentially acknowledged Indian rights to exploit *non*-precious minerals on their land, but provided for separate conditions to govern (external) exploitation of, and revenues from, precious mineral mines in Ontario (and by extension, elsewhere in Canada).

Post-1930 Trends Toward Self-Government on Reserves
The year 1930 was a watershed, for after that year, federal, or Dominion, approval for surrenders would become the exception rather than the rule. In the same

year, the Dominion transferred public land control rights in the Prairie provinces to the provincial governments of Saskatchewan, Alberta, and Manitoba, with the express condition that existing Indian reserves would be maintained unchanged under federal control. The 1930 agreements nevertheless recognized the applicability of the 1924 precious metals "exception" (the Canada-Ontario Reserve Agreement) to any Indian reserves in the Plains provinces.

Rising governmental and public attention to Indian affairs came in the early 1960's, partially in the wake of the government's *Report on Reserve Allotments* (published in 1959) and partly following publication of a major study by Jean Lagasse on native populations in Manitoba. Lagasse's findings brought the beginnings of community development programs on Indian reserve lands, but they remained limited mainly to Manitoba itself. By 1975, a specific scheme for self-management and community government was legislated in the James Bay and Northern Quebec Agreement, but this again had limited geographical scope.

Substantial change in conditions affecting life on reserve lands across Canada would not come until passage of the 1989 Indian Act. A good portion of the local legislative precedents that formed the bases for the 1989 Indian Act can be seen to have been drawn from key decisions ranging from the James Bay and Northern Quebec Agreement through the Municipal Grants Act of 1980 and the much broader 1986 Sechelt Indian Band Self-Government Act. When legislators extended such precedents to define the status of the totality of Canada's Indian population, the government in Ottawa granted for the first time several essential principles of self-government to tribes throughout the country. They now included the right to hold full title to property formerly considered their "reserves" (but ultimately controlled by Dominion authorities) and to dispose of that property legally as they might see fit (through sales, leases, or rentals) through procedures they would determine via the autonomous channels of their own councils.

Byron D. Cannon

Core Resources

The reserve system is explored in Richard H. Bartlett's *Indian Reserves and Aboriginal Lands in Canada* (Saskatoon: University of Saskatchewan, Native Law Center, 1990); James Frideres's *Canada's Indians: Contemporary Conflicts* (Scarborough, Ont.: Prentice Hall of Canada, 1974); the Indian-Eskimo Association of Canada's *Native Rights in Canada* (Calgary: Author, 1970); and Mark Nagler's *Natives Without a Home* (Don Mills, Ont.: Longman, 1975).

See also: Aboriginal Canadians; Fifteen Principles; Indian Act of 1876; Indian Act of 1951; Indian Act of 1989; Indian-white relations: Canada; Proclamation of 1763; Reservation system of the United States.

Resistance, cultures of

Cultures of resistance are forms of alternative or oppositional strategies, direct actions, norms, values, attitudes, behaviors, and agendas that are developed and employed by groups who seek change through noninstitutionalized means. Often, these are groups who feel marginalized from the mainstream and excluded from decision making in major institutions of society. Within political, educational, economic, family, religious, and other institutions, marginalized groups exhibit cultures (as reflected in language, dress, music, hairstyles, and so on) that stand in opposition to the culture of majority groups. Cultures of resistance are inherently political, based upon self-defined standpoint experiences, inextricably embedded in race, gender, and class relations, and serve as sites for struggle. Historically, African Americans, Latinos, Native Americans, Asian Americans, and other racial and ethnic minority groups have engaged in direct action to protest discrimination, prejudice, and alienation. African Americans engaging in sit-ins, boycotts, and marches are expressing a culture of resistance.

Bernice McNair Barnett

See also: Oppositional culture; Rap music.

Restrictive or racial covenants

Restrictive covenants, sometimes called racial covenants, were agreements that barred specific racial, ethnic, and religious minorities from owning or renting certain properties. These "covenants," sometimes contracts but more often clauses placed in deeds by developers, became popular in the early twentieth century with the advent of mass black migration to northern urban areas. Restrictive covenants prevented the integration of many urban and suburban neighborhoods by denying entry to minority groups, encouraging the formation of inner-city ghettos and precipitating shortages of housing available to minorities.

Restrictive covenants proliferated after the U.S. Supreme Court upheld their constitutionality in the case of *Corrigan v. Buckley* (1926). Civil rights attorneys subsequently targeted restrictive covenants as part of their legal strategy, winning a major victory before the Supreme Court in *Shelley v. Kraemer* (1948). The Court ruled in *Shelley* that state courts, by enforcing the covenants, had violated the Fourteenth Amendment by denying minorities equal protection of the law. Yet residential segregation through covenants continued virtually un-abated as few of its victims could afford to challenge these private contracts in court. In 1968, the Supreme Court, in the case of *Jones v. Alfred H. Mayer Company*, outlawed restrictive covenants by upholding the Civil Rights Act of 1968, which banned racial discrimination in the sale or rental of real estate.   *Michael H. Burchett*

See also: Civil Rights Act of 1968; Housing; *Jones v. Alfred H. Mayer Company; Shelley v. Kraemer.*

Retribalization

Retribalization refers to the empowerment of Native American tribal organizations as governmental institu-tions in the United States. During the late nineteenth and early twentieth centuries, the federal government attempted to destroy the authority and independence of tribal organizations. This process was temporarily halted in 1934, when the Indian Reorganization Act granted limited powers of self-rule to tribal governments. Native American communities lacking such institutions were urged to create them along guidelines provided by the federal government. After World War II, the federal government again undermined the authority of the tribes with a policy known as termination, which de-creased the amount of federal assistance available to the tribes, dissolved some tribal governments, and extended the power of state law enforcement agencies over reser-vations in some states. This policy quickly proved to be a failure, and in the early 1970's terminated groups such as the Menominees in Wisconsin were restored to their status as federally recognized tribes. The policy of self-determination implemented during the 1970's encour-aged tribal governments to play a greater role in offering services on the reservations, including welfare programs and law enforcement. However, this process remained incomplete as some tribes met with resistance from some state and federal officials opposed to the renewal of Native American tribes.   *Thomas Clarkin*

See also: Federally recognized tribes; Indian Reorgani-zation Act; Termination Resolution.

"Reverse" racism

"Reverse" racism is a term applied to government-supported programs designed to remedy past injustices caused by racial discrimination. Remedies such as hiring quotas and affirmative action favor one race at the ex-pense of random members of another race to make up for privileges that the second race once enjoyed at the expense of the first. In the simplest terms, such policies have been questioned on the basis of whether two wrongs can make a right. The term "reverse" racism has also been applied to racial consciousness-raising methods among minority groups that use the denigration of the majority racial group as a means of attaining intraracial solidarity. These methods are practiced by minority political and religious figures such as the Nation of Islam's Louis Farrakhan and academics such as Leonard Jeffries, head of the African-American Studies Department of City College of New York, who has told his classes that the lack of melanin in the skin of whites has rendered them inferior to blacks.   *William L. Howard*

See also: Affirmative action; Cress theory; Political cor-rectness; Quotas; Racism: changing nature of.

Reynolds v. Sims

The 1960's witnessed a significant change in the appor-tionment of state legislative and congressional delega-tions. For the first time, the U.S. Supreme Court inter-fered with the apportionment practices of the states. The Court's action was an attempt to rectify what it deemed to be the malapportionment of a great majority of Ameri-can state legislatures and of state delegations to the national House of Representatives

This situation had developed over the years because predominantly rural state legislatures continually ig-nored the population shifts that produced the tremen-dous growth of the country's cities in the twentieth century. In many cases, state legislatures, out of a fear that equitable redistricting would shift the rural-urban balance of power, deliberately ignored the provisions within their own state constitutions for periodic redis-tricting. The result was a constitutional abnormality that was distorting the democratic political process.

In a series of cases brought before the Court in the 1960's, the malapportionment problems were judicially corrected when the Court applied a "one person, one vote" principle. In 1964, a federal district court ordered the state of Alabama to reapportion but nullified two plans that did not apportion the legislative districts solely on the basis of population. The state appealed to the Supreme Court, which held that the equal protection clause of the Fourteenth Amendment requires that the seats in both houses be equally apportioned. The exist-ing apportionment of the Alabama state legislature was struck down when the Court, in an 8-1 majority, applied the one man, one vote principle in the case. Writing for the majority, Chief Justice Earl Warren declared that restrictions on the right to vote "strike at the heart of representative government." The Court, he added, had "clearly established that the fundamental principle of representative government in this country is one of equal representation for equal numbers of people, without regard to race, sex, economic status, or place of residence within the state." The concept of one person, one vote was virtually a pure and intractable rule.

In his dissent, Justice John M. Harlan argued that the decision had the "effect of placing basic aspects of state political systems under the pervasive overlordship of the federal judiciary." This type of "judicial legislation" frightened not only Harlan but a number of conservatives who did not want to see the Supreme Court become more active in producing equal voting rights.

The legacy of this case is clear: In *Reynolds* and several companion cases decided the same day, the Supreme Court determined that it had an obligation to interfere in the apportionment practices of the states in order to guarantee that no person was deprived of the right to vote. By guaranteeing those individual rights, the legislatures as well as the House of Representatives would more properly reflect the genuine complexion of American society.   *Kevin F. Sims*

See also: Reapportionment cases; Redistricting; Representation: gerrymandering, malapportionment, and reapportionment; Voting Rights Act of 1965.

Richmond v. J. A. Croson Company

In 1983, the City Council of Richmond, Virginia, adopted a minority set-aside program for city contracting. Under the plan, 30 percent of all city construction subcontracts were to be granted to (or "set aside" for) minority-owned business enterprises. The J. A. Croson Company, a contracting firm which had been the low bidder on a city project, sued the city when its bid was rejected in favor of a higher bid submitted by a minority-owned firm. Croson's position was that the minority set-aside violated the equal protection clause of the Fourteenth Amendment by establishing a racial classification. Richmond argued that the minority set-aside was valid as an attempt to remedy past discriminations. An earlier case, *Fullilove v. Klutznick* (1980), had approved a similar set-aside program for federal government contracts. The city pointed out that only 0.67 percent of its prime construction contracts had gone to minority firms between 1978 and 1983.

By a vote of 6 to 3 the Supreme Court decided for the Croson Company. The opinion of the Court was written by Justice Sandra Day O'Connor. Justice O'Connor argued that the earlier federal case was not relevant because the federal government has legislative authority to enforce the Fourteenth Amendment. State governments are limited by it. Race-conscious affirmative action programs are valid only where there is a showing of past discrimination by the state government itself. In the case of the Richmond statute, there was no such showing. It was undeniable that there had been discrimination against minority contractors, but that discrimination was by private firms, not by the city itself. While the city has the power to remedy private discriminations, she argued, it may not do so by setting up a quota system which is itself racially biased.

Justice Thurgood Marshall wrote the major dissenting opinion. He argued that the majority's view of the facts was too narrow. The extraordinary disparity between contracts let to minority and nonminority firms showed that there was systematic and pervasive discrimination which could be remedied in practice only by a set-aside or quota program of the kind passed in Richmond. He pointed out, as he had in earlier cases, the irony of a constitutional rule which forbids racial classifications for benign purposes, given the long history of constitutionally permitted racial classifications for discriminatory purposes. Justice Marshall insisted that the court should not scrutinize racial classifications strictly so long as the purpose of the classification is benign. Justices William J. Brennan and Harry A. Blackmun joined Marshall in his dissent.

Richmond v. J. A. Croson Company cast doubt on the future of race-conscious programs designed to remedy past discriminations. At the very least it meant that racial quotas, however well-intentioned, were likely to be held unconstitutional.   *Robert Jacobs*

See also: *Adarand Constructors v. Peña*; Affirmative action; *Bakke* case; *Fullilove v. Klutznick*; Quotas; Set-asides.

Riel Rebellions

> **Significance:** In 1869-1870 and 1885, revolts against the government of Canada led to the dispersal and marginalization of the once-thriving Metis.

Canadian policies that threatened both the Metis and Indian ways of life were at the heart of two separate revolts in Canada's newly acquired prairie region. (Metis people are of mixed Indian and European descent.) In 1869, the Hudson's Bay Company relinquished its claim over Rupert's Land and the Northwest to the recently confederated nation of Canada. Prime Minister John A. Macdonald set out to build a great nation joined from the Atlantic to the Pacific by a rail line. Although the government negotiated treaties that established Indian reserves, it offered the Metis, whom it did not regard as legally Indian, no such consideration. This contributed significantly to the erosion of the Metis economic and social life.

Red River Rebellion, 1869-1870

Preparing to take over the new territories in the fall of 1869, Canada sent survey parties into the Red River region. The Metis of the region had for many years occupied long, narrow farmsteads along the riverbank. Contrary to this practice, the surveyors delineated square township lots. Both fearing the imminent arrival of large numbers of English-speaking Protestants and fearing that their long-established land tenure would be ignored once Canada asserted control over the area, the Metis and a few of the original white settlers declared a provisional government in early November, 1869. Prairie-born but Montreal-educated, Louis Riel, Jr., was elected secretary and, within a few weeks, president of the government of Assiniboia.

The Red River Rebellion actually involved very few military skirmishes. On November 2, 1869, the Metis seized Upper Fort Garry and arrested fifty Canadians including a militant Orangeman named Thomas Scott. Scott escaped from custody twice but was recaptured each time. He was tried, convicted of treason against the Metis government, and executed in March, 1870. Scott's execution became a rallying point in English Canada against the mainly French Catholic Metis. Riel, who was president of Assiniboia at the time, was held responsible. He was forced into exile for much of the next fifteen years.

The Metis of Assiniboia had no intention of remaining independent of Canada and issued a declaration of their desire to join the Confederation of Canada as a new province with full representation in Parliament. According to their declaration, the new province would have both English and French as its official languages, control of public lands would remain with the local legislature, and the citizens would retain the property rights they held prior to entering confederation.

In May, 1870, after several months of negotiation between Ottawa and the Metis, the Canadian Parliament passed the Manitoba Act. While the establishment of the new province should have met many of the Metis' demands, in practice it did not. The province was limited to 100,000 square miles, Parliament rather than the Manitoba Legislature retained control of the public lands, and the conveyance of the Metis' land titles was delayed so long that many Metis sold their rights to land speculators and moved farther west.

Northwest Uprising, 1885

Many of the same economic concerns that caused the 1869-1870 Red River Rebellion fueled the Northwest Uprising of 1885. This second revolt, however, included Cree and Assiniboine Indians as well as the Metis. Ottawa, fearing a general Indian uprising on the prairies, responded with swift military action rather than negotiation.

Faced with the near extinction of the buffalo and once again with the fear of being uprooted by new settlers, the Metis around Batoche on the Saskatchewan River invited Riel to return from exile to argue their claims with Ottawa. Riel, however, had changed greatly in the intervening decade and a half. He had spent several years in insane asylums in Montreal before settling on a farm in Montana. He was obsessed with the idea that it was his divine mission to establish a French Catholic state in the northwest. He viewed the arrival of four Metis emissaries on June 4, 1884, as divine intervention and returned to Canada to fulfill his mission.

Riel spent much of his time drafting petitions to Ottawa outlining the Metis' grievances. Finally, reminiscent of events in 1869, the Metis, led by Riel and Gabriel Dumont, seized the parish church at Batoche and declared a provisional government. The army and the Northwest Mounted Police responded promptly, and the entire revolt was crushed within two months. The Metis and the Indians, however, did inflict casualties. The first skirmish occurred near Duck Lake when the Mounted Police arrived to assert Canadian authority. The Metis, joined by a few Indians, killed ten of the police and forced the remainder to retreat.

The Indians, starving as a result of the loss of the buffalo and then Ottawa's withholding of treaty rations, were encouraged by the Metis victory at Duck Lake. The Cree and Assiniboine were easily persuaded to join the revolt. Several hundred hungry Indians under the leadership of Poundmaker attacked the fort at Battleford, burning the homes and looting the stores. Other Cree, led by Big Bear, killed nine people, including the Indian agent and two priests in what became known as the Frog Lake massacre. Three others were spared by Big Bear.

The Canadian military response was swift. Eight thousand well-armed troops were dispatched to the region, and the revolt was summarily crushed. Among the leaders of the revolt, Dumont escaped to the United States, where he performed for a time with Buffalo Bill Cody's Wild West Show. Big Bear and Poundmaker each received three years in prison. Riel, who used his trial as a forum for his cause, was found guilty of treason and hanged on November 16, 1885. Many of the Metis and Cree fled to Montana. Others dispersed to the north. Fearing additional Indian uprisings, the Canadian government rushed to complete the Canadian Pacific Railroad and promptly began to settle the West.

Richard G. Condon and Pamela R. Stern

Core Resources

The Riel Rebellions are discussed in Hugh A. Dempsey's *Big Bear: The End of Freedom* (Vancouver: Douglas & McIntyre, 1984); Thomas Flanagan's *Riel and the Rebellion: 1885 Reconsidered* (Saskatoon: Western Producer Prairie Books, 1983); J. R. Miller's "The Northwest Rebellion of 1885," in *Skyscrapers Hide the Heavens: A History of Indian-White Relations in Canada* (Toronto: University of Toronto Press, 1989); Donald Purich's *The Metis* (Toronto: James Lorimer, 1988); and George F. G. Stanley's *The Birth of Western Canada: A History of the Riel Rebellions* (2d ed., Toronto: University of Toronto Press, 1960).

See also: Indian-white relations: Canada; Metis; Treaties and agreements with Indians: Canada.

Roldan v. Los Angeles County

In the case of *Roldan v. Los Angeles County* (1933), a California appeals court overturned a 1931 decision by a county clerk to deny a marriage license to Salvador Roldan, a Filipino, and Marjorie Rogers, a white woman. California law, while prohibiting *miscegenation* (the marriage of whites to nonwhites), was unclear as to the racial classification of persons of "Malay" (Filipino) origin, leaving decisions regarding the race of individuals to local officials. The California Court of Appeals ruled in January, 1933, that Filipinos did not fall under the statutory definition of "Mongolian" and thus were permitted under California law to marry whites.

The *Roldan* decision is significant as the first high court ruling on the racial classification of Filipino Americans. Nevertheless, the victory was a short-lived and pyrrhic one, producing a backlash that fueled anti-Asiatic sentiments in the western United States. Anti-Asian American state officials subsequently launched a campaign to restrict intermarriage between whites and Filipinos, culminating in adoption by the California legislature of two amendments to the antimiscegenation statutes classifying Filipinos as nonwhite. The amendments, introduced before the *Roldan* decision by state senator Herbert C. Jones, were signed into law by Governor James Rolph in April, 1933, and became effective the following August, less than seven months after the court's ruling.   *Michael H. Burchett*

See also: Filipino Americans; Interracial and interethnic marriage; Miscegenation laws; *People v. George Hall.*

Roosevelt coalition

The Roosevelt coalition was an electoral bloc that supported the candidacy of President Franklin D. Roosevelt, who won office four times between 1932 and 1944. It consisted of a number of racial and ethnic minority groups that rallied around Roosevelt's New Deal policies. The programs that Roosevelt implemented as part of his New Deal had not only eased the privations of the Great Depression but, to some voters, also seemed to promise economic opportunity and the possibility of a racially just society. The Roosevelt coalition included African American, Jewish, Irish American, Italian American, and Polish American voters.

Maintaining this coalition was a difficult balancing act, particularly after the outbreak of World War II. Roosevelt had to reconcile the demands of Polish Americans and Jewish Americans that U.S. foreign policy engage Nazi Germany (which was persecuting Poles and Jews in Europe) with the isolationist sentiments of the majority of the American public. A. Philip Randolph, president of the Brotherhood of Sleeping Car Porters, threatened to lead a march on Washington, D.C., in 1941 to protest discrimination against African Americans in defense industries and the armed forces. Roosevelt responded by establishing the Fair Employment Practices Committee to address these concerns. The coalition of minority voters and solid Democratic supporters that Roosevelt created laid the foundation for the dominance of the Democratic Party through the middle of the twentieth century.   *Aristide Sechandice*

See also: Brotherhood of Sleeping Car Porters; Desegregation: defense; Employment among African Americans; Fair Employment Practices Committee; Labor movement.

Roots

Roots: The Saga of an American Family, published by Alex Haley in 1976, is one of the most widely read works ever written by an African American. A fictionalized version of actual events, *Roots* details the history of seven generations of an African American family in the United States. Haley began the story by detailing the life of his ancestor, Kunta Kinte, who was sold into slavery and taken to the United States. Haley introduced readers to U.S. history as experienced by African Americans. His work was so compelling that Haley received a Pulitzer Prize for *Roots.* Network television serialized the saga in 1977, and it received tremendous attention and large viewerships. More than 130 million viewers reportedly tuned in to watch the incredible tale, which featured some of the most popular actors of the 1970's. Historians praised the television series, which is now available on video in most school libraries and video stores, for its accurate depictions of U.S. history and eye for detail. Many people

O. J. Simpson (left) and LeVar Burton star in the 1977 television miniseries *Roots*. The very popular miniseries instilled a strong sense of pride in many African Americans.

argue that both the book and the television miniseries had a significant impact on race relations because it introduced many Americans to the severity of the African American experience.   *Donald C. Simmons, Jr.*

See also: African American literature; African Americans and film; Slavery and race relations; Slavery: history.

Rosenberg trial

The Rosenberg espionage case created international debate, pitting national security issues against First Amendment rights, and raised questions about the American justice system's vulnerability to the anticommunist political climate of the Cold War era.

The trial of Julius and Ethel Rosenberg and Morton Sobell, a former classmate of Julius, began on March 6, 1951. The Rosenbergs were accused of being part of a communist-inspired spy ring that supplied atomic research data from the Los Alamos project to the Soviet Union. The trial judge was Irving R. Kaufman, and the chief litigator was assistant prosecutor Roy M. Cohn. Emanuel Bloch acted as the Rosenbergs' defense attorney. David Greenglass, Ethel Rosenberg's brother, appeared as the government's principal witness. The Rosenbergs insisted on their innocence of all charges throughout the trial and refused to answer questions about their political beliefs and activities. After only two weeks of court time, the trial ended with the conviction of all three defendants. Judge Kaufman found Sobell guilty of espionage not directly linked to atomic research and sentenced him to thirty years in prison. He sen-

tenced both the Rosenbergs to death.

After the convictions, the National Committee to Secure Justice in the Rosenberg Case began to question the proceedings openly. They pointed out that the prosecution's case rested completely on unsubstantiated circumstantial evidence and perjured testimony, that there was no documented evidence, and that references had been made throughout the trial to the Rosenbergs' leftist political beliefs.

Upon public discussion of the trial proceedings, many clergy and some leading scientists, including Albert Einstein, joined the movement asking that clemency be granted to the Rosenbergs. The movement continued to gain momentum and became international in scope. The U.S. Supreme Court, meanwhile, refused to hear an official appeal of the case, and appeals for clemency to Presidents Harry S Truman and Dwight D. Eisenhower were unsuccessful.

A stay of execution on a legal point was granted by Justice William O. Douglas but was denied by a vote of the U.S. Supreme Court at large, which reconvened for a special term in order to rule on the case. On June 19, 1953, as thousands of people demonstrated against the executions in cities in the United States and Europe, the Rosenbergs were killed in the electric chair at Sing Sing Prison.

A series of books were written protesting what was perceived as the failure of justice and the misrepresentation of evidence in the case. Most important among them were Walter and Miriam Schneir's 1965 *Invitation to an Inquest* (reissued in 1983) and Michael and Robert Meeropol's 1986 *We Are Your Sons*. Documents released through the Freedom of Information Act have revealed that Greenglass devised false evidence that was used against Ethel Rosenberg in the trial and that the government attempted to use its prosecution of Ethel as a tool to force Julius to confess.

In 1995, the decades-old case took another turn when the government released formerly classified documents consisting of decoded transmissions, some of them fragmentary, between Soviet operatives. These messages show that Julius Rosenberg was indeed a Soviet spy and that Ethel was at least aware of his activities, although they do not confirm her active involvement. Although the coded messages portray Julius as the leader of a spy ring, they do not specifically contain corroboration of the charges that he transmitted high-level atomic secrets. Finally, in spite of the confirmation of Julius Rosenberg's espionage activities, it is clear that false evidence was given by government witnesses at the trial.   *Barbara Bair*

See also: Red Scare; Xenophobia, nativism, and eugenics.

Royal Commission on Aboriginal Peoples

> **Significance:** In April, 1991, the government of Canada, in response to aboriginal leaders' concerns, established the Royal Commission on Aboriginal Peoples to review the role and place of aboriginal people in contemporary Canada. The final report, published in November, 1996, made 440 recommendations in response to problems that have long plagued the relationship between aboriginal peoples, the Canadian government, and Canadian society as a whole.

In April, 1991, the government of Canada set forth a sixteen-point mandate for the seven commissioners (four aboriginal, three nonaboriginal) of the newly constituted Royal Commission on Aboriginal Peoples. Amid much upheaval, uncertainty, and in some cases violence, the commissioners held 178 days of public hearings, conducted public hearings in 96 communities, listened to dozens of expert witnesses and testimony, and engaged in additional research. Acknowledging that the colonial policy of the federal government for the last 150 years had been wrong, the commission attempted to determine the "foundations of a fair and honorable relationship between the aboriginal and nonaboriginal people of Canada." The commissioners sought to examine this relationship as a central facet of Canada's heritage, describe how the relationship became distorted, and examine the terrible consequences for aboriginal people in the loss of lands, power, and self-respect. The commissioners hoped that the report would repair the damaged relationship and provide a new footing for mutual recognition and respect, sharing, and responsibility. Consisting of five volumes of several thousand pages each, the final report provided a comprehensive answer to the guiding question and related questions and problems.

A History of Mistakes
"Aboriginal peoples" refers to organic and cultural entities stemming from the original peoples of North America, not to collections of individuals united by "racial" characteristics. The commissioners traced the relationship of aboriginal and nonaboriginal peoples through

four stages. The first stage was before 1500, when no contact had been made between North American aboriginals and Europeans. The second stage started in the 1500's and was marked by initial mutual curiosity and then increasing trust, trade, exchange of goods, intermarriage, and military and trade alliances that created bonds between and among nations. This stage was crowned by the Royal Proclamation of 1763, which governed the relations between nations on the question of land rights. The third stage began in the 1800's as increasing numbers of Europeans immigrated to Canada. Respect gave way to domination. The new policy of "assimilation" proved, in time, to be a form of cultural genocide. The solution to the problems left by the assimilation policy, the report stated, is in recognizing that "aboriginal peoples are nations." This affirmation is not to say that these peoples are nation-states seeking independence from Canada but rather collectivities with a long, shared history, a right to govern themselves, and a strong desire to do so in partnership with Canada. The fourth stage, the report concluded, was just beginning. The report hoped to assist the process of "renewal and renegotiation" well into the twenty-first century.

The mistakes that characterize the relationship with aboriginal peoples have been serious, often deadly. On average, the life expectancy of aboriginals is lower than that of nonaboriginals, illnesses such as alcoholism and diabetes are more prevalent, families are more often broken or marred by violence, abuse, and criminality, leading to a disproportionately high number of aboriginals in jail, and educational failure and dropout for children is common. The commission argued that these problems had reached the point where aboriginal peoples had become tired of waiting for handouts from governments. It found that these people wanted control over their lives instead of the well-meaning but ruinous paternalism of past Canadian governments. They needed their lands, resources, and self-chosen governments in order to reconstruct social, economic, and political order. They needed time, space, and respect from nonaboriginals to heal their spirits and revitalize their cultures.

Renewing and Restructuring the Relationship
Four principles formed the basis for renewed relationships between aboriginals and nonaboriginals: *recognition* by nonaboriginals of the principle that aboriginals were the original caretakers of the land along with the recognition that nonaboriginals now share, and have a right to, the land; *respect* between peoples for their rights and a resistance to any future forms of domination; *sharing* of benefits in "fair measure"; and *responsibility*, the hallmark of a "mature relationship," which includes accountability for promises made, for behaving honor-

ably, and for the effect of one's actions on the well-being of others. The needs and problems of all groups in their diversity cannot be addressed piecemeal. The renewed relationship entails a fundamental structural component that is centered on reclaiming aboriginal peoples as "nations." These nations, however, are not to be formed by every single aboriginal community in Canada. The commission concluded that the right of self-government cannot reasonably be exercised by small, separate communities, whether First Nations, Inuit, or Metis. It should be exercised by groups of a certain size—groups with a claim to the term "nation." The commission went on to suggest a process for doing this, beginning with a royal proclamation, issued by the monarch as Canada's head of state and guardian of the rights of aboriginal peoples. Such a move would dramatically signal a new day for aboriginal people, setting out the principles, laws, and institutions necessary to turn these into reality. This new royal proclamation would not supplant, but instead support and modernize the Royal Proclamation of 1763, or so-called Aboriginal Peoples' Magna Carta.

The commission recommended that the proclamation contain the following elements: a reaffirmation of Canada's respect for aboriginal peoples as distinct nations; acknowledgment of harmful actions by past governments, which deprived aboriginal peoples of their lands and resources and interfered with family life, spiritual practices, and governance structures; a statement placing the relationship on a footing of respect, recognition, sharing, and mutual responsibility, thus ending the cycle of blame and guilt and freeing aboriginal and nonaboriginal peoples to embrace a shared future; affirmation of the right of aboriginal peoples to fashion their own lives and control their own governments and lands—not as a grant from other Canadian governments but as a right inherent in their status as peoples who have occupied these lands from time immemorial; and acknowledgment that justice and fair play are essential for reconciliation between aboriginal and nonaboriginal peoples and a commitment by Canada to create institutions and processes to strive for justice.

Such a proclamation would be followed by the enactment of companion legislation by the Parliament of Canada. The legislation would create the new laws and institutions needed to implement the "renewed relationship" with a view to providing both the authority and the tools needed for aboriginal peoples to structure their own political, social, and economic future.

Governance and Polity

The most dramatic and sweeping proposal made by the commission was the creation of a parallel parliament for aboriginal peoples. The commission suggested that after the royal proclamation, the Canadian government draft and pass an act that would establish a body to represent aboriginal peoples within federal governing institutions and advise Parliament on matters affecting aboriginal peoples. A constitutional amendment would create a "house of first peoples" that would become part of Parliament along with the House of Commons and the Senate.

Other recommendations included restructuring the federal government to allow the Department of Indian Affairs and Northern Development (DIAND) and the ministerial position that goes with it to be replaced by a senior cabinet position, the "minister for aboriginal relations," and a new "department of aboriginal relations." In addition, the commission recommended establishing a minister and department of Indian and Inuit services to deliver the gradually diminishing services coming from the federal level.

It recommended three models of self-government: *national* government, to be exercised among aboriginal peoples with a strong sense of shared identity and an exclusive territorial base inside which national governments would exercise a wide range of powers and authority; *public* government, in which all residents would participate equally in the functions of government regardless of their heritage; and *community of interest* government, to be exercised primarily in urban centers where aboriginal persons form a minority of the population but nonetheless want a measure of self-government in relation to education, health care, economic development, and protection of culture. The latter would operate effectively within municipal boundaries, with voluntary membership and powers delegated from aboriginal nation governments and/or provincial governments.

Land Rights and Claims

The commission stated that the land claims process is "deeply flawed" and recommended that it be replaced by a fairer and more balanced system in which the federal government does not act as both defender of the Crown's interests and judge and jury on claims. The commission further stated that this process is not open to Metis claims, thereby leaving Metis people without a land and resource base and with no mechanisms for settling grievances. It also categorized as unfair the governmental demands that aboriginals "extinguish" their general land rights in favor of specific terms laid down in claim settlements and recommended a new process that would result in three categories of allocation: lands selected from traditional territories that would belong exclusively to aboriginal nations and be under their sole control; other lands in their traditional territories that would belong jointly to aboriginal and nonaboriginal governments and be the object of shared management arrangements; and land that would belong to and remain under the control of the Crown but to which aboriginal peoples would have special rights, such as a right of access to sacred and historical sites.

In support, the commission recommended establishing regional treaty commissions and an aboriginal lands and treaties tribunal that would facilitate and support treaty negotiations. Also, the commission called on the federal government to allocate to aboriginal nations "all land promised to them in existing treaties," "to return to First Nations all land it has expropriated or bought, then left unused," and "to establish a fund to help aboriginal people purchase land on the open market." The commission recommended one major piece of companion legislation, namely an aboriginal treaties implementation act that would seek to establish a process for "recognized aboriginal nations to renew existing treaties or negotiate new ones." The act would also "set out processes and principles to guide negotiation, include a commitment to implement existing treaties according to their spirit and intent, and . . . renegotiate treaty terms on which there was no meeting of minds when they were originally set down" and would "establish regional treaty commissions to convene and manage the negotiation process, with advice from the aboriginal lands and treaties tribunal on certain issues."

Other Measures Proposed

Other recommendations included measures to overcome epidemic health problems, child abuse, welfare and economic dependency, and related socioeconomic problems, including poor housing and a lack of overall infrastructure in aboriginal communities. In recommending aboriginal control of education, the commission noted that aboriginal peoples are simply asking for no more than what other communities already have—the chance to say what kind of people their children will become. Aboriginal peoples want schools to help children, youth, and adults learn the skills they need to participate fully in the economy, develop as citizens of aboriginal nations, and retain their languages and the traditions necessary for cultural continuity. The commission also recommended that aboriginal peoples be given control over youth and adult education, including education not only in aboriginal culture, customs, and traditions but also that will assist in overcoming the massive problems of unemployment in aboriginal communities.

The report of the Royal Commission on Aboriginal Peoples challenged aboriginal and nonaboriginal relationships. It documented the myriad problems of the past century and offered a considered and considerable number of recommendations for change. However, these recommendations, detailed and numerous though they were, are probably not enough to bring

about change. As the commissioners noted, "It will take an act of national intention—a major, symbolic statement of intent, accompanied by the laws necessary to turn intentions into action." *Gregory Walters*

Core Resources

The final report of the Royal Commission on Aboriginal Peoples consists of five volumes: *Looking Forward, Looking Back*; *Restructuring the Relationship*; *Gathering Strength*; *Perspectives and Realities*; and *Renewal: A Twenty Year Commitment* (Ottawa: Canada Communication Group, 1996). *Governments in Conflict? Provinces and Indian Nations in Canada*, edited by J. Anthony Long and Menno Boldt in association with Leroy Little Bear (Toronto: University of Toronto Press, 1988), addresses aboriginal-provincial relations focusing on self-government, provincial jurisdiction, land claims, and financial responsibility. *The Quest for Justice: Aboriginal Peoples and Aboriginal Rights*, edited by J. Anthony Long and Menno Boldt in association with Leroy Little Bear (Toronto: University of Toronto Press, 1985), presents a broad cross section of tribal, geographic, and organizational perspectives. The authors discuss constitutional questions such as land rights, concerns of Metis, non-Status Indians and Inuit, and historical, legal/constitutional, political, regional, and international rights issues. J. R. Miller's *Sweet Promises: A Reader on Indian-White Relations in Canada* (Toronto: University of Toronto Press, 1991) contains key, previously published articles concerned with regional developments from the days of New France to the present. *Justice for Natives Searching for Common Ground*, edited by Andrea P. Morrison with Irwin Cotler (Montreal: McGill-Queen's University Press, 1997), came together around the Oka crisis between aboriginal people in Quebec and the government. Its thirty-five essays and stories provide helpful discussions on native women and the struggle for justice, self-determination, title and land claims, the Oka crisis, and legal relations and models for change. Bradforse W. Morse's *Aboriginal Peoples and the Law: Indian, Metis and Inuit Rights in Canada* (rev. ed., Ottawa: Carleton University Press, 1989) provides a basic resource for cases and materials on the original inhabitants of Canada.

See also: Aboriginal Canadians; Department of Indian Affairs and Northern Development; Indian Act of 1876; Indian-white relations: Canada; Oka crisis; Status Indians.

Runyon v. McCrary

In this 1976 case, the U.S. Supreme Court broadened the meaning of Title 42, section 1981 of the 1866 Civil Rights Act to outlaw discrimination in all contracts.

Parents of African American children brought suit in federal court against private schools in Virginia that had denied their children admission. Disregarding the defendant schools' argument that a government-imposed obligation to admit black students to their unintegrated student bodies would violate constitutionally protected rights of free association and privacy, the district and appellate courts both ruled in the parents' favor, enjoining the schools from discriminating on the basis of race.

The parents had based their case on a section of the 1866 Civil Rights Act that was still in effect. In 1968, the Supreme Court had held in *Jones v. Alfred H. Mayer Company* that section 1982 of the act prohibited racial discrimination among private parties in housing. In *Runyon*, the Court broadened this holding to imply that section 1981, the act's right-to-contract provision, outlawed all discriminatory contracts, whether involving public or private parties—including one between private schools and the parents of student applicants.

In the wake of *Runyon*, lower federal courts employed section 1981 to outlaw racial discrimination in a wide variety of areas, including banking, security deposit regulations, admissions to amusement parks, insurance, and mortuaries. The breadth of the Court's interpretation in *Runyon* of section 1981 also caused it to overlap with Title VII of the Civil Rights Act of 1964, governing employment contracts. This overlap, together with ongoing concern about the extensiveness of the interpretation of section 1981, caused the Court to consider overruling *Runyon* in *Patterson v. McLean Credit Union* (1989). Instead, *Patterson* severely restricted *Runyon* by declaring that section 1981 did not apply to postcontractual employer discrimination. *Patterson* went so far as to declare that although section 1981 protected the right to enter into employment contracts, it did not extend to future breaches of that contract or to the imposition of discriminatory working conditions. Congress in turn overruled this narrow reading of section 1981 in the Civil Rights Act of 1991, which includes explicit language permitting courts to prohibit employment discrimination that takes place after hiring.

The reason for the Court's about-face with regard to section 1981 can be found in its changing political composition. *Runyon* was decided midway through Chief Justice Warren Burger's tenure, when the Court was dominated by justices who occupied the middle of the political spectrum. In 1986, however, one of two dissenters in *Runyon*, Justice William H. Rehnquist, had succeeded Burger. Rehnquist, who had always been outspoken in his criticism of what he regarded as the Court's excess of liberalism under Chief Justice Earl Warren, dissented in *Runyon* on grounds that the Warren-era *Jones* case had been improperly decided. By 1989, when the Court handed down its decision in *Patterson*, Rehnquist had been joined by enough fellow conservative thinkers to overrule *Runyon*'s interpretation of section 1981 by one vote.

Lisa Paddock

See also: Civil Rights Act of 1991; Civil Rights Acts of 1866-1875; *Jones v. Alfred H. Mayer Company*.

Russian Americans

Significance: Russian Americans have blended well with mainstream American society, many having peasant or industrial backgrounds similar to those of other European immigrants, while others were refugees from the Russian upper class or Jews who did not consider themselves Russian. Some immigrants were, however, suspected of promoting communism or being members of the Russian mafia.

Throughout the late nineteenth and twentieth centuries, large numbers of Russians immigrated in successive waves to the United States and Canada. Many were members of the Russian Orthodox church, and Orthodoxy remains one of the visible hallmarks of Russian immigrant communities. Its rituals and teachings are followed in Russian communities in Alaska, Los Angeles, and Brooklyn's Brighton Beach. Nevertheless, Russian Jews were, and are, numerically the largest group of immigrants, particularly to the United States. However, because Russia was not very accepting of Jews, many of these immigrants were more likely to identify themselves as Jews rather than Russians upon entering the United States and Canada. In addition, because many came from western Russia, the so-called Pale of Settlement to which Russian Jews were restricted, which was once part of Poland-Lithuania, they might equally well have considered themselves Polish or Lithuanian Jews.

The first Russians to reach the shores of North America came as traders, adventurers, and explorers. These hardy fur traders and missionaries settled the Alaskan wilderness when that territory belonged to Russia. The first Russians settled on Kodiak Island, Alaska, in 1784, and converted many natives to the Russian Orthodox religion, which many still practiced in the late twentieth century. However, with the sale of Alaska to the United States in 1867, many of these first settlers returned to Russia.

The First Wave
A huge influx of immigrants from czarist Russia reached North America between 1881 and 1914. Almost half of these were Jews fleeing pogroms and other forms of

Not all immigrants from Russia were Jewish. The choir sings before the congregation at a Russian Baptist church.

The Third Wave

The third major wave of Russian immigration resulted from the massive dislocations of World War II. Germany had at various times occupied much of the Soviet Union, captured many Russians, and made them work in forced labor camps. After the war, many of these people were forcibly returned to the Soviet Union, where they were often accused of collaboration with the enemy. Others, fearing similar oppression, chose to remain in displaced-person camps in Germany and Austria until they were allowed to immigrate to North America. This brought approximately twenty thousand Russian Americans to the shores of North America.

The Fourth Wave

In contrast to earlier emigrations from Russia and the Soviet Union, these immigrants left Russia near the end of the twentieth century without hindrance on the part of the government in power. The impetus for this emigration was in large part agreements between the United States and the Soviet Union allowing Jews to leave Russia, nominally for Israel, but often in fact for the United States. Following their lead, a number of other Russians emigrated as well. This migration caused some social disturbances in the United States because a number of Russian mafia members who were among the newcomers caused major problems for newly arrived immigrants and the population at large.

Gloria Fulton

Core Resources

Paul R. Magocsi's The Russian Americans (New York: Chelsea House Publications, 1987) traces the immigration and settlement of Russians in North America, focusing on historical and economic issues, the people who might be considered Russian Americans, and the extent to which these peoples have become assimilated in North American society. A useful reference book on Russians in the United States is *The Russians in America: A Chronology and Fact Book*, edited by Vladimir Wertsman (Dobbs Ferry, N.Y.: Oceana Publications, 1977). Religious reasons for immigrating are discussed in Susan Wiley Hardwick's *Russian Refuge: Religion, Migration, and Settlement on the North American Pacific Rim* (Chicago: University of Chicago Press, 1993).

See also: Eastern European Jews; Jewish Americans; Soviet Jewish immigrants.

persecution following the 1881 assassination of Czar Alexander III, for which the Jews were blamed. During this period, Jews were allowed to live only in the Pale of Settlement in western Russia, lands taken from Poland during the partitions of Poland a hundred years earlier. Most of these Jews lived in *shtetls*, and many were impoverished. Only about sixty-five thousand ethnic Russians left Russia during this period, most for economic reasons. Others, from the Carpathian area of the Ukraine and the eastern reaches of the Austro-Hungarian Empire, did self-identify as Russians and were adherents of the Orthodox or the Uniate religion.

The Second Wave

The second wave of immigration occurred as a result of events in Russia that made it impossible for many persons, particularly members of the upper classes, to remain there. These events were the Bolshevik Revolution of October 1917 and the Russian Civil War from 1920 to 1922. More than two million people fled the new communist nation, many to the Balkans, Western Europe, and Manchuria. Of these, approximately thirty thousand came to the United States. Among them were former White Russian soldiers (as opposed to the Red Communist armies), aristocrats, clergy, artists, and intellectuals. United in their hatred of the Bolsheviks, many intended to stay only until the Bolsheviks were ousted. Ironically, anticommunist movements in the United States often singled out these extremely anticommunist Russians for oppressive treatment, suspecting that a communist lurked behind every fur hat.

S

Sabotage

Historically, sabotage meant to incite a labor action. More broadly, sabotage refers to any behavior done to ensure the failure of another's efforts. Racial or ethnic sabotage is often clandestine and waged against subordinate groups by dominant groups with the intent to cause harm, act out prejudice, or maintain the dominant group's privilege. Sabotage is a form of covert discrimination that is difficult to document and prove. When used in the workplace, sabotage impedes work efforts and undermines the advancement of subordinate groups, often by making them appear incompetent.

The following examples demonstrate covert sexual and race discrimination through the use of sabotage. In a research study, a female African American postal worker claimed that her white, male coworkers in the post office hid some mail that she was required to deliver. Unknowingly, she finished her daily route and returned to discover the hidden mail. Her manager disciplined her by switching her to a less favorable, high-crime route. Jean Y. Jew, a Chinese American, went to court to fight the false rumors that blocked her advancement as a medical-school professor. Colleagues sabotaged her promotion by claiming that she had had an affair with a former department chair. She won a legal victory in 1991 and was granted full professorship and a monetary settlement from the University of Iowa. Despite her legal victory, she still faced subtle discrimination from peers and graduate students who resisted working with her. Thus, both women endured the personal and economic costs of sabotage.

Rosann Bar

See also: Discrimination: behaviors; Discrimination: overt/expressed vs. covert.

Sacco and Vanzetti trial

Significance: This 1927 trial was a celebrated example of anti-immigrant feeling during a period of heightened nativism.

One of the most famous U.S. trials of the twentieth century, the robbery and murder case against Nicola Sacco and Bartolomeo Vanzetti, generated worldwide protests, strikes, and riots as it focused the international spotlight on the small town of Dedham, Massachusetts.

The Crimes
The two events, which may or may not have been connected, that culminated in the arrest of Sacco and Van-

Bartolomeo Vanzetti (left) and Nicola Sacco arrive at a Massachusetts courthouse in April, 1927.

zetti began on December 24, 1919, payday for the L. Q. White Shoe Company of Bridgewater, Massachusetts. A truck carrying approximately thirty-three thousand dollars in company payroll was unsuccessfully attacked. Pinkerton Agency detectives investigated the incident, and during eyewitness interviews they determined that one of the suspects appeared to be foreign-born, with a dark complexion and mustache, and that he fled in a large vehicle, probably a Hudson. The identified license plate had been stolen a few days earlier in Needham, Massachusetts, as had a Buick touring car. Thus, despite witnesses to the contrary, the detectives concluded that the Buick likely had been used in the robbery. No suspects were arrested, although tips emerged connecting the getaway car to a group of Italian anarchists.

On April 15, 1920, in nearby South Braintree, the payroll for the Slater and Morrill Shoe Factory was being escorted, on foot, from the office to the factory by two security guards, Frederick Parmenter and Alessandro Berardelli. En route, the guards were attacked, robbed, and murdered by two men who escaped in a waiting vehicle. At the inquest, twenty-three eyewitnesses testified that the assailants appeared to be Italian, but few claimed they could positively identify the men.

Recalling the tip about Italian anarchists storing a car in Bridgewater, police chief Michael E. Stewart traced the lead to Feruccio Coacci, an Italian scheduled for deportation. Coacci revealed that the car belonged to his housemate, Mike Boda, a known anarchist, and that it was currently being repaired in a garage in West Bridgewater. A police guard was planted outside the garage to wait for Boda.

Meanwhile, as a result of the prevalent U.S. attitude toward radicals and in the wake of a national roundup and arrest of aliens, Italians Nicola Sacco and Bartolomeo Vanzetti had decided it would be wise to destroy their anarchist literature. The abundance of material required transportation, and they arranged to borrow Boda's vehicle. Although the trap was laid for Boda, Sacco and Vanzetti were arrested as they attempted to claim the car. Neither man had a police record, but both were armed.

Because the men were not informed of the reason for their arrest, they assumed they were being held as anarchists. Although they were read their rights, the language barrier may have obstructed their complete understanding. They were fingerprinted, their weapons confiscated but not tagged, and they were questioned for seven days without being charged. There was no lineup; the two were paraded in front of witnesses who were asked if they were the men involved in the holdup. On May 12, 1920, Vanzetti was charged with attempted murder and robbery at Bridgewater.

The Trials

Vanzetti's trial began on June 22, 1920, in Plymouth, Massachusetts, with Judge Webster Thayer presiding. The initial interviews by the Pinkerton detectives were not admitted, and all witnesses for the defense were of Italian origin. After only five hours of deliberation, the jury found Vanzetti guilty of assault with intent to rob and murder. Six weeks later, he was sentenced to twelve to fifteen years for intent to rob. The attempted murder charge was dropped after it was discovered that one of the jurors had brought his own shell casings for comparison.

In September, 1920, Sacco and Vanzetti were charged with the murder of Alessandro Berardelli and Frederick Parmenter during the South Braintree robbery. Each pleaded not guilty. A committee for their defense raised enough money to hire the radical California attorney Fred Moore, who cited the case as an establishment attempt to victimize the working man.

The trial began on May 31, 1921, in Dedham, Massachusetts, once again under Judge Thayer, who, as the presiding judge in Vanzetti's first trial, should have been disqualified. On June 4, the all-male jury was sworn in, and on June 6, Sacco and Vanzetti were marched, handcuffed, into the courtroom. Throughout the trial, the prosecution presented a bounty of circumstantial evidence: less-than-convincing "eyewitness" testimony; a cap from the scene, alleged to be Vanzetti's, that was too small; expert testimony qualified with "I am inclined to believe"; no positive identification on the getaway car; ballistic evidence that was technical and confusing; and the accusation of "consciousness of guilt," based on the false statements of the two when they thought they were being held for anarchy. Judge Thayer charged the jury to be "true soldiers" who would display the "highest and noblest type of true American citizenship," and he referred to the defendants as "slackers." On July 14, once again after a five-hour deliberation, the jury returned a verdict of guilty of first-degree murder. The standard penalty in Massachusetts at the time was death by electrocution.

Aftermath and Executions

Sacco and Vanzetti remained incarcerated for six years while motions were filed in their behalf. The presiding judge heard all appeals, and each was weighed and denied by Judge Thayer. One motion stated Judge Thayer himself had demonstrated out-of-court prejudice against the two. Despite the growing doubt about the guilt of the men, Thayer remained adamant, and his animosity grew toward Moore. On November 8, the defense committee forced Moore to resign and hired William G. Thompson.

While the legal avenues encountered roadblocks, Sacco was slipped a note from another prisoner, Celestino Madeiros, who confessed to the crime. From the note, Thompson traced a link to the Morelli brothers, an Italian gang in Providence. This group had attacked the shoe factory in the past, and one member of the gang bore a resemblance to Sacco. Based on the new evidence, Thompson filed a motion for retrial, which was denied, and in April of 1927, Sacco and Vanzetti were sentenced to die the week of July 10. Due to the public outcry, the date was moved to August 10, and Vanzetti wrote a plea for clemency to Massachusetts governor Alvan T. Fuller. In the letter, he asked not for pardon but for a complete review of the case.

On June 1, the governor appointed a committee to review the case, but after examining their findings, he denied a new trial. On August 10, Sacco and Vanzetti were readied for execution. Thirty-six minutes before the time set for the execution, the governor issued a postponement, awaiting results of a Supreme Court appeal. On August 19, the U.S. Supreme Court refused to hear the case, citing no authority.

In Europe and South America, mobs rioted and marched on U.S. embassies. In France, Italy, and the United States, workers struck in protest. Five hundred extra policemen, armed with machine guns and tear gas, barricaded the crowd of thousands outside the jail. Just after midnight, on August 23, 1927, Sacco and Vanzetti were executed.   *Joyce Duncan*

Core Resources
Alice Dickinson's *The Sacco-Vanzetti Case* (New York: Franklin Watts, 1972) is an abbreviated overview of the case, including chronology and photos. Herbert Ehrmann's *The Case That Will Not Die: Commonwealth vs. Sacco and Vanzetti* (Boston: Little, Brown, 1969) is a liberally illustrated account by the case's assistant defense attorney from 1926 to 1927. *The Letters of Sacco and Vanzetti* (New York: Octagon Books, 1971), edited by Marion Denman Frankfurter and Gardner Jackson, contains correspondence by both men written from prison, including Vanzetti's letter to the governor. G. L. Joughin and E. M. Morgan's *The Legacy of Sacco and Vanzetti* (New York: Harcourt, Brace, 1948) is an early but masterful analysis of the case.

See also: Criminal justice system; Italian American stereotypes; Red Scare; Rosenberg trial; Xenophobia, nativism, and eugenics.

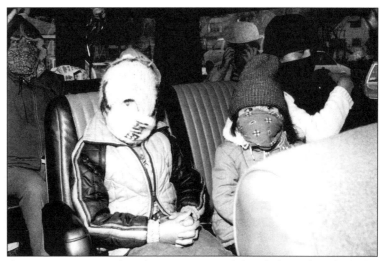

The Sanctuary movement, based in Tucson, Arizona, sheltered refugees from El Salvador in a Presbyterian church in the early 1980's. Other churches followed suit. In 1984, these Guatemalan youngsters and their parents sought sanctuary in Vermont with the help of religious activists.

Sanctuary movement

Following more than a decade of increasingly violent altercations between the Salvadoran government and the poor of El Salvador and attacks against those who supported human rights issues, the Sanctuary movement was born. In the summer of 1981, Southside Presbyterian Church in Tucson, Arizona, under the leadership of Reverend John Fife, opened its doors to several undocumented aliens seeking refuge in the United States. Although Fife and his followers were violating civil law, they felt they were upholding the dignity of all people, regardless of race or station in life. Many of those who fled El Salvador were the victims of internal power struggles based on economics or political views. They feared for their lives but had been denied refugee status and legal entrance to the United States. Those involved in the Sanctuary movement sought to protect Salvadorans who were in danger and to bring their story to the world in an attempt to eradicate injustice.

El Salvador was founded in 1524 by Pedro de Alvarado in the name of Spain. Since that time, those of Spanish descent have held the power, and the native Indian population has dwindled to a small minority. In the 1950's, economic development touched El Salvador; coffee and cotton seeded well-intentioned attempts at modernization. In the 1960's, the United States sought to assist El Salvador with the Alliance for Progress, a program that stressed the need for land reform, free democratic elections, and continued rural development. The program was fiercely opposed by the ruling oligarchy. By the 1970's, fraudulent elections and oppression of the landless had the country in turmoil. When religious workers and clergy spoke up for the poor, many were murdered. In 1980, Catholic archbishop Oscar A. Romero of El Salvador and four churchwomen from the United States were killed.

In the 1980's, the Sanctuary movement began to work in earnest to prevent further bloodshed and to protect those who were in danger because they expressed opposition to government policies. Many were victims because of their ethnic heritage, their station in life, or their religious beliefs. The Sanctuary movement sought to offer them hope and safety. The movement gained the support of parishes and other religious groups and spread across the United States. As the 1990's came to a close, the movement continued to function but in a quieter fashion, offering political and financial support to the oppressed in El Salvador and elsewhere.

Kathleen Schongar

See also: Latinos in the United States; Refugees: U.S. policy.

Sand Creek massacre

> **Significance:** This November 29, 1864, attack on an almost defenseless Indian camp galvanized the Cheyenne and their allies into a war that lasted until 1869.

The Treaty of Fort Laramie (1851) gave the Cheyenne and Arapaho a tract bounded by the North Platte and Arkansas Rivers on the north and south and by the Continental Divide and a line from Dodge City, Kansas, to North Platte, Nebraska, on the west and east. The discovery of gold in 1858 brought many white settlers into this region, however, precipitating a conflict.

Background

Some Cheyenne and Arapaho leaders signed the Treaty of Fort Wise (1861), ceding all lands except a triangle bounded by Sand Creek and the Arkansas River. Efforts to live there were a failure, and many Cheyenne and Arapaho repudiated the treaty.

Governor John Evans tried to negotiate in the fall of 1863, but the Cheyenne and Arapaho refused his overtures. Clashes in the spring of 1864 between the Cheyenne and the First Colorado Cavalry alarmed settlers, who were already uneasy at the transfer of troops east to fight in the Civil War and deeply divided over the question of statehood. Cheyenne and Arapaho raids continued through the summer, prompting the War

Department to approve the muster of a regiment of hundred-day volunteers. By the end of August, 1864, more than a thousand ill-equipped settlers eager for action had joined the new Third Colorado Cavalry.

Preparations

Command of the new troops, as well as those in the First Colorado Cavalry, fell to Colonel John M. Chivington, the commander of the Military District of Colorado. Chivington apparently thought that quick and decisive action was necessary by late summer of 1864. His veterans were ready for a fight, as were his new recruits. He also knew that the latter's enlistments would expire before the end of the year and that his other troops might be sent elsewhere if he did not win a dramatic victory. Finally, Chivington was politically ambitious—those who were pushing for statehood had already elected him to a seat in the United States House of Representatives (and Evans to the Senate) if Colorado were to be admitted.

Concerned with the situation, seven Cheyenne and Arapaho chiefs met with Evans and Chivington in late September, 1864. The pair refused to sign a treaty with the Indian leaders because the latter admitted that they had little control over many warriors. Upon the advice of Evans and Chivington, however, some of the Indians settled on Sand Creek, near Fort Lyon, about nine miles northeast of present-day Chivington. These Cheyenne and Arapaho, led by peace-minded chiefs such as Black Kettle, believed that they would be protected by the federal garrison.

Event

Chivington arrived at Fort Lyon in late November. He could have attacked a Cheyenne and Arapaho camp on Smoky Hill, fifty miles beyond Sand Creek, but that concentration, which was definitely hostile, was much larger and could easily have eluded his troops. Instead, he prepared for an attack on the smaller camp at Sand Creek, despite the protests of some of his officers and others in the federal garrison who insisted that the Indians had been promised safety. The force that Chivington led from Fort Lyon toward Sand Creek included about 250 members of the First Colorado Cavalry, approximately 500 members of the Third Colorado Cavalry, and more than 100 of the federal garrison.

At dawn on November 29, 1864, Chivington's force attacked. There were no more than 500 Indians, most of whom were women and children, sleeping in about one hundred Cheyenne lodges and a few lodges of their allies, the Arapahos. Black Kettle raised a U.S. flag and a white flag over his lodge when the assault began, then fled when it had no effect. Other Indian leaders were killed after trying to persuade the troopers to stop. A few braves tried to establish a defensive position, but their simple weapons were no match for the modern rifles and howitzers of the attackers. Many Indians, including women and children, were shot as they dug shallow pits in the sand for protection.

Nine troopers were killed and thirty-eight were wounded in the attack. Reports on the number of Cheyenne and Arapaho casualties vary, but most agree that several hundred were killed. A large proportion, probably a majority, were women and children. The troopers looted the camp after the assault, and many of them mutilated the Indian bodies that they found. Scalps, fingers, and other body parts were taken to Denver as trophies.

Aftermath

The Third Colorado Cavalry volunteers were greeted as heroes by their neighbors when they left the service in December, 1864, but officials in Washington were more critical. Benjamin F. Wade, chairman of the Senate Committee on the Conduct of the War, ordered an investigation, as did Army Chief of Staff Henry W. Halleck, who first demanded a court-martial but settled for a military investigation after Chivington resigned from the military during January, 1865. These inquiries were disrupted twice by the death of officers who testified against Chivington, and a distinctly hostile reception in Colorado soured congressional investigators, who condemned Chivington.

The scandal interrupted the political careers of some of those involved. Evans was forced to resign. Chivington lost at least one election to an opponent who raised the specter of Sand Creek, and he held only minor offices for the remainder of his life. The affair was also used as a political club by those who blocked Colorado statehood for another decade.

The massacre led to a general uprising among the Plains Indians, including the Cheyenne and Arapaho, and white settlers endured several years of attacks. Cheyenne raids in Colorado continued until the summer of 1869, when the Battle of Summit Springs ended their operations in that area. By that time, many Cheyennes had died, including Black Kettle. He was mistakenly reported as killed at Sand Creek but was actually shot in 1868 by federal troops on the Washita River in the Indian Territory, where he had led his followers in a vain attempt to save them.   *Richard B. McCaslin*

Core Resources

Sources on the Sand Creek massacre include Reginald S. Craig's *The Fighting Parson: The Biography of Colonel John M. Chivington* (Los Angeles: Westernlore Press, 1959); William R. Dunn's *"I Stand by Sand Creek": A Defense of Colonel John M. Chivington and the Third Colorado Cavalry*

(Fort Collins, Colo.: Old Army Press, 1985); Stan Hoig's *The Sand Creek Massacre* (Norman: University of Oklahoma Press, 1961); Duane Schultz's *Month of the Freezing Moon: The Sand Creek Massacre, November 1864* (New York: St. Martin's Press, 1990); and David Svaldi's *Sand Creek and the Rhetoric of Extermination: A Case Study in Indian-White Relations* (Lanham, Md.: University Press of America, 1989).

See also: Indian-white relations: United States; Little Bighorn, Battle of the; Wounded Knee massacre.

Santa Clara Pueblo v. Martinez

The Santa Clara Pueblo (New Mexico) passed an ordinance stating that if a male member of the tribe married a woman who was not a member of the tribe, their children would be eligible for membership in the tribe. However, children born of a woman from the tribe who married a nonmember man were not eligible for enrollment in the tribe.

When the tribe refused to enroll her daughter, Julia Martinez, an enrolled member of the Santa Clara Pueblo married to a Navajo, brought suit against her tribe on behalf of her daughter. Martinez charged that the tribal law violated her daughter's rights to equal protection under the American Indian Civil Rights Act (1968), and further, Martinez contended that the law discriminated against her based on her sex. The tribe argued that its rules for membership were culturally based on a traditional patrilineal system that predated the United States and its laws. The tribe also asserted its sovereign right to determine who is a tribal member without federal government involvement.

In deciding the case in 1978, the U.S. Supreme Court declined to interfere with the tribe's conception of membership. The Court also stressed that the Indian Civil Rights Act did protect the civil rights of individuals from unjust acts of tribal governments, but its overriding purpose was to promote tribal self-government and self-determination rather than impose the dominant society's standards of equal protection. This case deepened the concept of tribal sovereignty and reinforced the sanctity of tribal customs.   *Carole A. Barrett*

See also: American Indian Civil Rights Act; Tribal sovereignty.

Santería

This Afro-Cuban religious "complex" is a cultural retention with origins in the African diaspora to the New

World. The basic tenets, rituals, practices, and associated institutional mechanisms derive from the Yoruba priests and priestesses of the *orishas*, who were slaves at the close of the eighteenth and during the early decades of the nineteenth centuries. Santería, "the way of the saints," is an admixture of Yoruba and other African practices with Roman Catholic traditions developed as a functional adaptation by many Cubans.

The Cuban immigrants who entered the United States after Fidel Castro's successful revolution in their homeland brought these religious practices with them. These rituals enjoy special significance as part of the new immigrants' coping repertoire, enabling them to adjust better to acculturation in the United States. The

Reading tarot cards is a form of Santería divination. Cuban Americans are among the religion's practitioners.

practices of Santería are part of the larger spiritualistic belief system of other black West Indians (Jamaicans, Trinidadians, Haitians, Puerto Ricans, and Guyanese) who immigrated to the United States. As these immigrants begin to live in urban spatial proximity and strive to maintain and regain their African cultural heritage, they and native African Americans have adopted Santería. In cities such as Miami and New York, there are many spiritual adherents. *Aubrey W. Bonnett*

See also: *Church of the Lukumi Babalu Aye v. Hialeah*; Cuban Americans; Haitians and Haitian refugees; Jamaican Americans; Latinos in the United States; Puerto Rico; Religion-based ethnicities; West Indian Americans.

Scandinavian Americans

> **Significance:** Scandinavian Americans are those residents of North America who emigrated from the Scandinavian peninsula, currently occupied by Sweden and Norway.

The earliest European immigrants to the Western Hemisphere are believed to have been Vikings of Scandinavian origin. In 986 C.E., a Norse expedition headed by Bjarni Herjolfsson sighted land thought to have been on the east coast of Canada. It was followed some dozen years later by Leif Eiriksson, who made landing. Norse expeditions attempted to colonize Vinland (Newfoundland) in 1003-1006 and 1007-1008 but ultimately failed

because of infighting and conflicts with the natives. These and subsequent expeditions did not result in permanent settlements on the North American continent. The first documented settlements were Swedish and included a community along the Delaware River in 1638. John Hanson, the first president of the Continental Congress, claimed to be a fourth-generation descendant of immigrants tracing their ties to Swedish royalty. Early Swedish enclaves founded in Delaware (Maryland), Massachusetts, New Jersey, and Pennsylvania still maintain their cultural affiliations.

The Nineteenth Century

In nineteenth century Scandinavia, social and economic conditions were stifling: Primogeniture ensured that only first sons could inherit their families' estates, land foreclosures abounded, and the nobility controlled much of the property and paid few taxes. Cleng Peerson (originally Kleng Peterson Hesthammer), a dissenter persecuted by the Lutheran State Church of Norway, left for the United States in 1821. He became so enamored of the United States that he purchased a sloop, the *Restauration*, and began a career as an immigrant agent.

Peerson and other agents helped bring about a historically unparalleled exodus of citizens from both Sweden and Norway. Approximately 750,000 Norwegians emigrated to North America between 1849 and 1914; the Swedish exodus during this same period totaled approximately 1.2 million, nearly one-fourth of Sweden's population. By 1890, about four hundred Minnesota towns sported Swedish names, and Norwegian-speaking travelers in North Dakota could find more people who spoke their native language than who spoke English.

Seafarers historically, Norwegians founded communities on both coasts, in places such as Massachusetts and the Pacific Northwest. Many also followed Peerson to Texas to bask in the milder climate. Others were attracted to the open lands of the upper Midwest, particularly after the Homestead Act of 1862 allotted 160 acres of newly opened land to anyone who could "prove up" a claim. Some enterprising couples positioned their bedrooms, and even their conjugal beds, exactly on the property line between two allotments in order to qualify for two allotments, or 320 acres.

Religious Influences

Both Swedish and Norwegian immigrants carried with them a religious faith that saturated every aspect of their existence. It shaped their behavior, the cycle of their daily lives, and even their community identities. Both groups came from heavily Lutheran environments, where the mandate of "the Word alone, grace alone, faith alone" translated to immediate personal responsibility to God.

Lutheranism, however, was not always a uniting influence for Scandinavians. Subdivisions within the church, called synods, reflected ethnic affiliations. The Swedish Lutherans supported the Augustana synod, and Norwegian Lutheranism included at least six synods. Some of the Norwegian Lutherans were followers of Hans Neilsen Hauge, a reformer who experienced a call to preach the gospel to Norway while working on his farm. His American followers were pious and hardworking, separating themselves from those whom they regarded as frivolous. Haugeans, for example, abstained from dancing, believing that it facilitated contact between the sexes that was fraught with temptation and spiritual peril.

Swedish Covenant, Methodist, Baptist, Mormon, and a few Roman Catholic denominations also attracted both Swedish and Norwegian immigrants, and each group took their differences seriously. Haugeans, especially, abhorred anything resembling Roman Catholicism, while Catholics regarded Lutherans as spiritual heretics deprived of ritual. Interfaith marriages, when they did occur, alienated entire families; moving to different ethnic or religious communities could result in social isolation. In many instances, an unmarried pregnant woman was not allowed to marry the father of her child if he was not of her religion.

The Swedish and Norwegian pioneers' work ethic was also rooted in their religious orientation. Both groups frowned on complainers; both subscribed to biblical passages reminding the faithful that labor was an opportunity bestowed by God. Sunday Sabbath, however, was observed with diligence—any activity resembling work, even use of scissors or knitting needle, was avoided, and a farmer who worked in his fields on a Sunday invited general disapproval. Sundays were devoted to worship and visiting with neighbors.

Intergroup Relations

Despite the many traits and attitudes they shared, Norwegians and Swedes preserved distance from each other, both socially and theologically. Norwegians tended to view Swedes as somewhat undisciplined, and Swedes typically regarded Norwegians as cold and dour. A cemetery might well have separate sections for each ethnicity; the family of one Norwegian woman, for example, was disappointed that she had to be buried in the Swedish section of a cemetery because she had married a Swedish man.

The Scandinavians' relationships with other immigrant groups were usually civil and often amicable. As long as ethnic boundaries coincided with those of cities and schools, mutual respect prevailed. Sometimes, however, school athletic rivalries became metaphors for national differences, as exemplified by the rivalry between two small towns in southern Minnesota, one predominantly Polish Catholic and the other, Norwegian Lutheran. Rivalries persisted for years, often to the point that character traits were assumed, by each side, to

Norwegian Americans wear traditional clothing for a Norwegian Independence Day parade in New York City.

correlate with place of residence. The two small schools did not consolidate until the latter part of the twentieth century.

The ethnic and national boundaries began to blur in the twentieth century. Within the Lutheran Church, ethnic and synodical mergers began to bring Swedes, Norwegians, Danes, Germans, and Finns together in worship. Automotive mobility brought together groups of people who had never been face to face before. Religious intermarriages were no longer exotic, much less reprehensible.

However, there was one group with whom the Scandinavian Americans did not get along: the Native Americans. The Native Americans in the areas where Scandinavian Americans settled saw no particular advantage in the mainstream society's intruding into theirs. The Scandinavian immigrants, like other settlers, viewed American Indians' lifestyle as anachronistic and in need of "civilizing." They defined civilization in terms of religious conversion, manifested by "whitening" of dress and behavior. A church worker involved in relations between Indian tribes and Scandinavian Americans noted that Norwegians, particularly, were in cultural opposition to the Native Americans. Norwegians were insular, while Native Americans were committed to their communities. Norwegians avoided dependence on others, while to the Native Americans, giving honored both the giver and the recipient. Many of these differences contributed to the cultural separation that persisted through the end of the twentieth century between Scandinavian Americans and American Indians, particularly in towns bordering Indian reservations.

Although Scandinavian Americans initially sought to immerse themselves totally in the mainstream culture, they gradually took steps to preserve their culture. The colleges they built preserved their ethnic and doctrinal definitions, until, following the path of the ethnic small towns, they, too, became more inclusive. Swedish and Norwegian Americans also established museums and hosted festivals and found them to be not only personally but also economically bountiful. Ethnicity, once a stigma, was now a distinction.

Brenda E. Reinertsen Caranicas

See also: European immigration to Canada: 1867-present; European immigration to the United States: 1790-1892; European immigration to the United States: 1892-1943.

"Scientific" racism

For as long as humans have recognized differences between groups of people, there has been racism in the form of cultural prejudice. In the nineteenth century, racism acquired a scientific character, primarily as a result of intellectual developments in Western Europe. The roots of that change lie in the Enlightenment, an intellectual movement of the latter part of the eighteenth century. Rationality, a scientific view of the world, and a penchant for classifying natural phenomena motivated Enlightenment thinkers. They sought to find an order in the human and social world comparable to the order of the physical universe. In many ways, the Enlightenment merely applied the insights of the scientific revolution of the sixteenth century to human affairs.

Just as the Swedish botanist Linnaeus (Carl von Linné) had classified every living species known to him within a system of taxonomy, so Enlightenment thinkers endeavored to specify the full range of human variation with a similar system. The young science of anthropology, the study of humans, provided such a conceptual framework. Johann Friedrich Blumenbach, often regarded as the father of physical anthropology, divided humans into five races. Other anthropologists later condensed his scheme, and the division of humanity into three races—Caucasoid, Negroid, and Mongoloid—became standard.

Biological theory seemed to offer support for this view. Naturalist Charles Darwin's theory of natural selection posited the constant divergent evolution of all species in response to different environmental conditions. Because humans inhabit almost all areas of the world, this process would presumably be most pronounced among humans. The research of Gregor Mendel, the founder of modern genetics, explained differences between variations within a species in terms of gene frequencies, or the frequency of occurrence of genes embodying particular traits found in a population. Gene frequencies are reflected in phenotypes, visible expressions of the traits embodied in genes. Dark or light skin; curly, straight, or kinky hair; and facial bone structure are all examples of phenotype.

After 1850, inspired by evolutionary theory, various writers began scholarly studies of race. Principal among these was Joseph-Arthur de Gobineau, who published his four-volume *Essay on the Inequality of the Human Races* between 1853 and 1855. This work placed human differences into a hierarchy, asserting that "all civilization flows from the White Race." Later, the architects of the European empires that swallowed the globe toward the end of the nineteenth century legitimated the domination of "inferior" races by referring to scientific theories such as Gobineau's.

Since Gobineau's time, science has shown that the concept of biological race is untenable. The supposed direct link between genes and their corresponding phenotypes has been disproven. What appeared to earlier theorists to be racial distinctions were in fact only adaptations to the environment among populations that had been geographically isolated from each other for a long period of time. Because increasingly effective means of transportation have gradually created a global community and have all but ended geographic isolation, genetic traits are now combined in infinite variations, thus hollowing out the concept of race, which suggests a finite number of mutually exclusive categories. Though bankrupt as a scientific concept, race lingers as a cultural construct, and so does racism.   *Aristide Sechandice*

See also: Biosocial theories; Race as a concept; Social Darwinism and race; Sociobiology and race.

Scotch-Irish "race"

The term "Scotch-Irish" refers to a group who migrated to North America and settled the frontier in the eighteenth century. A more modern label is "Scots-Irish."

The Scotch-Irish originated largely from Ulster, the northern counties of Ireland. Scotch-Irish immigration to North America began around 1695 and continued through the early 1800's, the largest wave arriving between 1717 and 1775. These consisted of native Ulster Protestants and Scots who had settled Ulster. Mostly Presbyterian, they brought to the New World a strong Calvinist tradition. Some may originally have been Catholic but adopted Protestantism after arrival, in response to social prohibitions on Catholicism. Desires for land and religious freedom were the primary motives for immigration. Edged out by English settlers for arable land in the low country, the Scotch-Irish traveled the wagon roads that led to the western areas of Virginia and the Carolinas.

The Scotch-Irish developed a reputation for being rugged, devout, and fiercely independent, leaving a stamp on the regions they pioneered. Past experiences created a deep suspicion of authority among the Scotch-Irish. A majority of Scotch-Irish Americans supported the American Revolution and later backed the Confederacy in the Civil War.

Although early Scotch-Irish settlers referred to themselves simply as "Irish," the term "Scotch-Irish" came into use in the nineteenth century, as Protestant Irish disdained identification with a newer group of immigrant Catholic Irish, a visible immigrant community by the late 1800's. As such, the Scotch-Irish are more properly classified as a "subculture" than as a "race."

Gene Redding Wynne, Jr.

See also: Celtic Irish; Irish Americans; Irish Catholic "race."

Scott v. Sandford

> **Significance:** In the March 6, 1857, *Scott v. Sandford* decision, the U.S. Supreme Court ruled that Congress could not limit slavery in the territories, nullifying the Missouri Compromise.

In 1834, Dred Scott, a slave of African descent, was taken by his owner, John Emerson, an army surgeon, to the free state of Illinois and then to Wisconsin Territory, which was free by the provisions of the Missouri Compromise of 1820. Emerson returned to Missouri with Scott in 1838. After Emerson's death in 1846, Scott sued Mrs. Emerson in the Missouri courts for his freedom, on the grounds of his residence in a free state and later in a free territory. Although he won in the lower court, the state supreme court reversed the decision in 1852 and declared that Scott was still a slave because of his voluntary return to Missouri. During this litigation, Mrs. Emerson remarried and, under Missouri law, the administration of her first husband's estate passed to her brother, John F. A. Sanford. (Sanford's name was misspelled when the suit was filed.) Because Sanford was a citizen of New York, Scott's lawyer, acting on the grounds that the litigants were residents of different states, sued for Scott's freedom in the U.S. circuit court in Missouri. The verdict there also went against Scott.

The Supreme Court's Ruling
The case was appealed to the U.S. Supreme Court, where it was argued in February, 1856, and reargued in January, 1857. For a variety of reasons, the Supreme Court justices determined to deal with the controversial questions of African American citizenship and congressional power over slavery in the territories. The Supreme Court announced its decision on March 6, 1857.

Although each of the nine justices issued a separate opinion, a majority of the Supreme Court held that African Americans who were descendants of slaves could not belong to the political community created by the Constitution and enjoy the right of federal citizenship; and that the Missouri Compromise of 1820, forbidding slavery in the part of the Louisiana Purchase territory north of 36°30' north latitude, was unconstitutional. According to the opinion of Chief Justice Roger B. Taney, African Americans were "beings of an inferior order" who "had no rights which the white man was bound to respect." Taney's comments established a perception of African Americans that transcended their status as slaves. In considering the issue of equality, Justice Taney did not limit his assessment of African Americans to those who were slaves, but also included

African Americans who were free. Taney's opinion raises questions about the extent to which this precept of the inferiority of African Americans helped to establish conditions for the future of race relations in the United States.

Although individual states might grant citizenship to African Americans, state action did not give blacks citizenship under the federal Constitution. Therefore, concluded Taney, "Dred Scott was not a citizen of Missouri within the meaning of the Constitution of the United States, and not entitled as such to sue in its courts."

Taney also declared that, since slaves were property, under the Fifth Amendment to the Constitution—which prohibited Congress from taking property without due process of law—Congress had only the power and duty to protect the slaveholders' rights. Therefore, the Missouri Compromise law was unconstitutional. This part of Taney's opinion was unnecessary, an *obiter dictum*, for, having decided that no African American could become a citizen within the meaning of the Constitution, there was no need for the Supreme Court to consider the question of whether Congress could exclude slavery from the territories of the United States.

Reaction

The nation reacted strongly to the Supreme Court's decision. The South was delighted, for a majority of the justices had supported the extreme southern position. All federal territories were now legally opened to slavery, and Congress was obliged to protect the slaveholders' possession of their chattel. The free-soil platform of the Republicans was unconstitutional. The Republicans denounced the decision in the most violent terms, as the product of an incompetent and partisan body. They declared that when they obtained control of the national government, they would change the membership of the Supreme Court and secure reversal of the decision. Northern Democrats, while not attacking the Supreme Court, were discouraged by the decision, for if Congress could not prohibit slavery in any territory, neither could a territorial legislature, a mere creation of Congress. Therefore, popular sovereignty also would cease to be a valid way of deciding whether a federal territory should be slave or free.   *John G. Clark, updated by K. Sue Jewell*

Core Resources

Paul Finkelman's *Dred Scott v. Sandford: A Brief History with Documents* (Boston: Bedford Books, 1997), Don Edward Fehrenbacher's *The Dred Scott Case: Its Significance in American Law and Politics* (New York: Oxford University Press, 1978), and Walter Ehrlich's *They Have No Rights: Dred Scott's Struggle for Freedom* (Westport, Conn.: Greenwood Press, 1979) take a closer look at the famous case. Charles Morrow Wilson's *The Dred Scott Decision* (Phila-

delphia: Auerbach, 1973) combines a biography of Dred Scott with descriptions of the court cases and appeals. Derrick Bell's *Faces at the Bottom of the Well: The Permanence of Racism* (New York: Basic Books, 1992) employs literary models in addressing the issue of how African Americans experience racial injustice in the judicial system in the United States. Bell's *Race, Racism, and American Law* (2d ed., Boston: Little, Brown, 1980), presents a comprehensive analysis of U.S. law that asserts that racial inequality is integrated into the legislative and judicial system in the United States. K. Sue Jewell's *From Mammy to Miss America and Beyond: Cultural Images and the Shaping of U.S. Social Policy* (New York: Routledge, 1993) discusses how institutional policies and practices in the United States contribute to social inequality for African Americans in general, and African American women in particular. *Black Americans and the Supreme Court Since Emancipation: Betrayal or Protection?* (New York: Holt, Rinehart and Winston, 1972), edited by Arnold Paul, explores precedent-setting Supreme Court cases that reveal the Court's failure to ensure equal rights for African Americans.

See also: Civil War; Missouri Compromise; Slavery: history.

Scottsboro trials

> **Significance:** The 1930's trials of nine young African Americans for rape mirrored both entrenched southern bigotry and antiliberal sentiments.

On March 25, 1931, nine African American boys were pulled off a freight train in Scottsboro, Alabama, after an alleged fight with a group of white youths. As the African Americans were being rounded up by sheriff's deputies, two women riders told onlookers that they had been raped by the entire group. Within a month, the boys were tried in Scottsboro, and eight of them were convicted and sentenced to death; the case of the youngest boy, only thirteen years of age, was declared a mistrial. Because of the speed of the convictions, the questionable nature of much of the testimony, and the hostile atmosphere in which the trial had been held, the case soon attracted widespread attention. Both the International Labor Defense (ILD), an arm of the Communist Party, and the National Association for the Advancement of Colored People (NAACP) expressed concern about the possibility of injustice and launched an appeal for a new trial. The boys and their parents chose the ILD to manage their defense.

The Retrials

In *Powell v. Alabama* (1932), the U.S. Supreme Court overruled the convictions and sent the cases back to a lower court. There followed another series of trials in Decatur, Alabama, beginning in March, 1933, and lasting until December. This time, only three of the boys were tried, all of whom received convictions and death sentences, but the Supreme Court sustained an appeal that irregularities in the selection of jurors invalidated the verdicts. The specific irregularity was that the voting rolls showed no African Americans registered to vote in that county, in spite of a large population of qualified African Americans.

In January, 1936, a third group of trials, held in Decatur, resulted in the conviction of Haywood Patterson, who was sentenced to seventy-five years' imprisonment. After more than a year of delay and behind-the-scenes negotiations between Alabama officials and a group of the defendants' supporters, the remaining eight were tried in the summer of 1937. One received the death penalty, three were sentenced to long prison terms, and the four others were released without charges. Although the one death sentence was later commuted to life imprisonment, the five convicted Scottsboro boys were unable to obtain a reversal. One was paroled in 1943, two more in 1946, and a fourth in 1950. The final prisoner escaped from a work gang in 1948 and managed to reach Michigan, from where the governor refused to extradite him. The former defendant quickly found himself in trouble, committing a murder and being sentenced to Michigan's worst prison.

Most observers outside Alabama and an increasingly large number of people within the state came to believe that the defendants were innocent and were, therefore, the victims of southern racial injustice. One of the two women accusers, Ruby Bates, had retracted her testimony by 1934 and admitted that she had lied in her original accusations. The other, a prostitute named Victoria Price, presented testimony so full of contradictions that one of the judges in the 1933 trials, Alabamian James E. Horton, overruled the jury's guilty verdict and declared a mistrial. At least one of the defendants was ruled physically incapable of rape, and a physician testified that a medical examination of Bates and Price, performed shortly after the presumed attack, did not support their claims. Although both women were found to have had recent sexual intercourse, there were no contusions or other injuries that would have matched their stories about brutality at the hands of the nine men. None of this had any appreciable effect on the juries, the prosecutors, or Judge William W. Callahan, who presided after Horton was removed from the case. Even the milder sentences meted out in 1937 resulted as much from a desire to end the unfavorable publicity surrounding the trials as from any reevaluation of the evidence.

Repercussions

Besides serving as a symbol of southern bigotry, the Scottsboro trials attracted attention because of the efforts of the Communist Party to identify the cause of the defendants with their own. Working through the ILD, the Communist Party was one of the first groups to protest the verdicts in the 1931 trials, and it was the only group to offer direct aid at that time. For several years, it engaged in a running battle with the NAACP and an "American Scottsboro Committee" over the right to manage the boys' defense. The effect of these struggles was to unite many Alabamians against all "reds and foreigners" and make it more difficult to revise the verdicts. The chief defense counsel after 1931 was Samuel Leibowitz, a Jewish attorney from New York who became the target of attacks from the prosecutors. Even he, along with Judge Callahan and part of the Alabama press, came to regard the communist support as a liability and sought to dissociate the ILD from the case. In 1935, the NAACP, the American Civil Liberties Union, and the ILD joined to form the Scottsboro Defense Committee (SDC), designed to coordinate support for the defendants and to seek cooperation from moderate Alabamians. Although the ILD played a much smaller

The 1930's trials in Scottsboro, Alabama, of nine African American youths for rape created controversy and questions about the fairness of the American justice system.

role in the case from that point on, there remained enough hostility toward outside interference in Alabama to frustrate the SDC's efforts.

The Scottsboro case mirrored many of the important social currents of the 1930's. While illustrating the extent to which white southerners would go to defend a system of white supremacy, it also marked a change from the not too distant era when the defendants might well have been summarily lynched. The hysterical attitude with which many Alabamians reacted to outside interest in the case underlined a regional insecurity that had been intensified by the unsettled conditions of the Depression. It was common for both men and women to hop onto freight trains, which the nine men had done, as had the two alleged victims. The Scottsboro boys had gotten into a fight with several white men. In Scottsboro and Decatur, race was on trial, not nine boys and men, much to the lasting chagrin of the state of Alabama. In 1976, the Alabama Board of Pardons and Paroles granted Clarence Norris a full pardon.

Courtney B. Ross, updated by John Jacob

Core Resources

Dan T. Carter's *Scottsboro: A Tragedy of the American South,* rev. ed. (Baton Rouge: Louisiana State University Press, 1979) analyzes the trials and treatment of the nine African Americans and discusses the impact of the events on the South. Allan Knight Chalmers's *They Shall Be Free* (Garden City, N.Y.: Doubleday, 1951) is an account of the Scottsboro trials from the perspective of one of the defense attorneys who also argued before the Supreme Court. In Clarence Norris and Sybil D. Washington's *The Last of the Scottsboro Boys* (New York: Putnam, 1979), the last and most literate of the defendants presents his case. Haywood Patterson and Earl Conrad's *Scottsboro Boy* (Garden City, N.Y.: Doubleday, 1950) is the first book to shed personal light on the plight of the nine.

See also: Crime and race/ethnicity; Criminal justice system; Jury nullification; Jury selection; Lynchings; Sacco and Vanzetti trial.

Segmented assimilation theory

Assimilation, the process by which subordinate individuals or groups assume the characteristics of the dominant group, is a nonlinear process and does not occur at simultaneous rates or places for all immigrants. During the early 1900's, the earlier stages of race relations theory, this process appeared simpler and more complete, especially for predominantly northern European immigrants, whose Caucasian roots permitted greater assimilation. The revised conceptualization of segmented assimilation theory suggests or postulates that assimilation, especially for children of "new immigrants" (for example, Cubans, Vietnamese, Dominicans, Haitians, Jamaicans) to North America, is more continuous and slower, or at times fragmented. Faced with continuing racial discrimination, poorly educated parents, inferior schools, and an economy less geared to labor-intensive jobs, these children's assimilation is skewed toward an adversarial culture. Their proximity to marginalized African Americans and Mexican Americans, socialized to conflict with society's norms, affects them negatively and accelerates their second-generation decline.

This process, however, is by no means universal and the children of some groups, including Asian Indians, Koreans, and Chinese, are more closely approximating the dominant group as they excel in educational, economic, and other institutional endeavors.

Aubrey W. Bonnett

See also: Assimilation: cultural and structural; Assimilation theories.

Segregation

> **Significance:** Segregation of minorities in the United States was a negative social and economic practice that kept the country from achieving "liberty, freedom, and equality," promises upon which the nation was founded; the practice consigned millions of people to second-class citizenship.

American segregation was born in the colonial era, when the "majority" practiced de facto segregation. When most blacks were slaves, free blacks suffered de facto segregation in housing and social segregation based on custom and folkways. As the northern colonies abolished slavery, de facto segregation sometimes became de jure separation supported by local ordinances and/or state law.

As long as the South maintained slavery, that institution regulated race relations, and de jure segregation was not needed. In 1865, however, the southern slaves were set free and legal segregation made its appearance. After the Civil War, most southern states passed legislation known as black codes, which resembled the old slave codes. Under the new codes, social segregation was often spelled out. For example, most states moved immediately to segregate public transportation lines. By the end of Reconstruction (1863-1877), race lines had hardened, and social segregation was the rule rather than the exception.

Unsuccessful Challenges

Some African Americans challenged segregationist laws. In 1896, blacks from Louisiana sued a public transportation company (railroad) that operated segregated passenger cars, as stipulated by Louisiana's state laws. Black leaders argued that the state laws and the railroad's actions violated the Thirteenth and Fourteenth Amendments to the Constitution. The case, *Plessy v. Ferguson*, reached the United States Supreme Court, which ruled that segregation was legal as long as "separate but equal" facilities were made available for minorities. A lone dissenter, Justice John M. Harlan, who happened to be a white southerner, rejected the majority opinion, saying that the Constitution should be "color-blind" and that it should not tolerate "classes" among the citizens, who were all equal.

Until the late 1960's, in the South, segregated bathrooms and separate entrances for blacks and whites were common features of public facilities such as this movie theater.

Despite Harlan's dissent, the *Plessy* decision gave absolute legal sanction to a practice that many states, including some in the North, were already practicing by custom and tradition—*Plessy* froze segregation into the highest law of the land. Thereafter, segregationists, especially those in the South, used their legislatures to pass a host of new laws that extended the supposed "separate but equal" doctrine to all areas of life. For example, restaurants, hotels, and theaters became segregated by law, not only by custom. Railroad cars and railroad stations divided the races; hospitals, doctors' offices, and even cemeteries became segregated. Some southern state laws called for segregated prisons, while prisons in other states took criminals from both races but separated them within the facility. At least one state passed a law that forbade a white and a black prisoner to look out the same prison window at the same time. If the prisoners were physically close enough to look out at the same time, they were too close to please segregationists.

As the United States matured during the twentieth century, segregation was extended whenever technology made it seem necessary. For example, in 1915, Oklahoma became the first state in the Union to require segregated public pay telephone booths. When motor cars were first used as a taxi service, taxi companies were segregated—a "white" taxi serving whites only and a "black" taxi serving African Americans only. Public water fountains became segregated, as did public restroom facilities.

Another problem became associated with segregation. Often, there was no separate facility for blacks, who were denied service altogether. For example, as late as the 1960's, President Lyndon B. Johnson's personal maid and butler-handyman experienced difficulty traveling by car from Washington, D.C., back to Johnson's Texas home. There were few if any motels along the way that would rent rooms to African Americans.

Successful Challenges

Eventually, the National Association for the Advancement of Colored People (NAACP) launched new attacks against segregationist laws—especially in circumstances in which no separate facilities existed for African Americans.

For example, in *Gaines v. Missouri* (1938) and *Sweatt v. Painter* (1949; a Texas case), the Supreme Court ruled that blacks could attend white law schools because no separate school was available in state for African Americans. In 1950, in *McLaurin v. Oklahoma*, the NAACP tested the same concept and won another court battle. As *McLaurin* showed, the University of Oklahoma had admitted a black student to its graduate program but then had segregated him on campus. After the Supreme Court ruled that such segregation was unfair and illegal because it denied equal education, Thurgood Marshall of the NAACP became even more determined to challenge segregation. He did so successfully when, in *Brown v. Board of Education* (1954), the Court declared segregated public education illegal.

If segregation was unjust and unconstitutional in education, it seemed clear that it was also unjust in other areas of life. In 1955, under the leadership of Martin Luther King, Jr., and others, a nonviolent protest movement took to the streets and eventually won victories that included new laws such as the Civil Rights Act of 1964 and the Voter Registration Act of 1965. Ultimately, a limited social and economic revolution occurred that condemned segregation and, in part, created a new American society.   *James Smallwood*

Core Resources
Segregation and its consequences are discussed in Bob Blauner's *Racial Oppression in America* (New York: Harper & Row, 1972); Taylor Branch's *Parting the Waters: America in the King Years, 1954-1963* (New York: Simon & Schuster, 1988); Joe R. Feagin and Clairece B. Feagin's *Racial and Ethnic Relations* (5th ed., Englewood Cliffs, N.J.: Prentice-Hall, 1996); James Forman's *The Making of Black Revolutionaries* (2d ed., Washington, D.C.: Open Hand, 1985); Fred Powledge's *Free at Last? The Civil Rights Movement and the People Who Made It* (Boston: Little, Brown, 1991); and Harvard Sitkoff's *The Struggle for Black Equality, 1954-1992* (New York: Hill & Wang, 1993).

See also: Bigotry; Black codes; Integration; *Plessy v. Ferguson*; Racism: history of the concept; Segregation: de facto and de jure; Segregation vs. integration; Slavery: history; *Sweatt v. Painter*.

Segregation: de facto and de jure

When used in reference to American history, *de jure* segregation (separation of races "by law") most often refers to the system of segregation that existed in the South between the 1870's and the mid-1950's. *De facto* segregation (separation "in fact" or in practice) most often refers to the continuation of segregation after legally mandated segregation was declared unconstitutional in 1954. Yet it is somewhat misleading to pigeonhole segregation with such definitions, as both types may exist simultaneously. Moreover, de facto segregation existed before the Jim Crow laws of the late nineteenth century as well as after the end of legal segregation. Both types testify to a refusal to admit various categories of Americans to full membership in American civic culture.

De jure segregation's constitutionality was upheld by the U.S. Supreme Court in *Plessy v. Ferguson* (1896). Only with the Supreme Court's unanimous decision in *Brown v. Board of Education* (1954) did de jure segregation end in the United States. The ruling specifically concerned segregated schools, but it spelled the beginning of the end for all forms of legally mandated segregation. The persistence of de facto segregation in American cities largely results from white outmigration from urban areas to suburbs.   *Malcolm B. Campbell*

See also: Black codes; *Brown v. Board of Education*; Civil Rights movement; Jim Crow laws; *Plessy v. Ferguson*; Segregation vs. integration.

Segregation on the frontier

Significance: Several thousand African Americans moved to the American West in the late nineteenth and early twentieth centuries in an effort to escape the racism that existed in the eastern United States. Once on the frontier, blacks established segregated communities that allowed them to live apart from whites who would discriminate against them.

Most people who have studied the western frontier have concluded that racial discrimination existed there, but that it was different from that found in the former slave states in the southeastern United States. For example, some western territories and states passed statutes requiring segregation of the races in schools and other public facilities, but these laws were not enforced as vigorously as in the South. Incidents of racial violence (such as white mobs lynching African Americans) were less numerous on the frontier than they were east of the Mississippi River.

Still, racism did exist on the frontier, and African Americans sought to avoid it. Even before the Civil War (1861-1865), free blacks established segregated communities in isolated areas of Arkansas, Louisiana, and Texas. After the war, blacks who had been slaves to Native Americans created several all-black towns and agricultural colonies in Indian Territory. Other African Americans availed themselves of the provisions of the Homestead Act (1862), which allowed them to claim a 160-acre parcel of public land on the frontier. Many of these black homesteaders created segregated communities where they could live by their own rules rather than those imposed upon them by white Americans.

All-Black Communities
Several of the all-black settlements were towns in which all of the businesses were owned by African Americans. Others were agricultural colonies whose residents expected to earn their living primarily by farming. In reality, however, the distinction between the two types of communities often became blurred. The farmers needed businesses to supply some of their needs, and the business owners often farmed to make extra money. Consequently, many of the segregated frontier communities were small urban areas surrounded by farms.

Perhaps the most famous all-black frontier settlement

was Nicodemus, Kansas. A few promoters of an all-black settlement chose a spot on the western Kansas prairie to establish Nicodemus. They filed homestead claims and mapped out town lots on part of their land. They then went back East to make speeches and distribute brochures encouraging people to move to the proposed town. The promoters then charged the recruits fees for helping them move to Kansas and for filing their homestead papers.

The Nicodemus settlers established churches, schools, and various social organizations to improve their quality of life. This attempt to create a sense of community was essential in making the colonists feel content in strange surroundings. As the people became friends with their neighbors and worked to help one another succeed, the sense of community began to grow and to become stronger. This sense of community was one of the main reasons that African Americans chose to live in segregated settlements on the frontier. However, while the sense of community was strong in Nicodemus and other all-black frontier colonies, other factors caused most of them to fail.

The frontier environment was such that droughts often led to crop failures, which sometimes caused residents to grow disillusioned and move elsewhere to farm. A second problem was that many of the settlers lacked the capital to obtain enough animals, supplies, and equipment to make farming successful. This, of course, had an adverse effect on the businesses that relied on the farmers' patronage. Many businesses went broke, and African American farmers often had to work for nearby whites in order to eke out a living from the harsh frontier land. Eventually, many inhabitants of all-black communities abandoned their claims and moved into or near towns where whites also lived.

Black Neighborhoods in White Communities

Even in these larger, predominantly white settlements, African Americans usually segregated themselves. Many frontier towns had a neighborhood where African Americans lived and socialized, creating a black community within the larger, white-controlled community. In these situations, African Americans experienced social segregation while participating in an integrated business environment that allowed them to benefit from their more prosperous white neighbors. Some blacks worked as hired hands and domestic servants for white families, and others ran restaurants, hotels, barbershops, laundries, repair shops, and other businesses that catered to customers of all races.

Laws and customs of the late nineteenth and early twentieth centuries dictated that the social contact between blacks and whites be limited. This was true in the American West just as it was in the older eastern sections of the country. However, a relatively low level of prejudice on the western frontier allowed for much business activity between the races. Thus, although African Americans on the western frontier usually lived in segregated communities, their lives were more prosperous and successful when they engaged in commerce with their white neighbors.   *Roger D. Hardaway*

Core Resources
Norman L. Crockett discusses four all-black frontier towns (Nicodemus, Kansas, and Boley, Clearview, and Langston, Oklahoma) in *The Black Towns* (Lawrence: Regents Press of Kansas, 1979). Kenneth Marvin Hamilton examines Nicodemus, Boley, Langston, and Allensworth, California, in *Black Towns and Profit: Promotion and Development in the Trans-Appalachian West, 1877-1915* (Urbana: University of Illinois Press, 1991). Black communities in predominantly white towns are the subject of Thomas C. Cox's *Blacks in Topeka, Kansas, 1865-1915: A Social History* (Baton Rouge: Louisiana State University Press, 1982) and of William L. Lang's "The Nearly Forgotten Blacks on Last Chance Gulch, 1900-1912," in *Pacific Northwest Quarterly* (70, 1979). A general survey of the various types of western black settlements is Roger D. Hardaway's "African American Communities on the Western Frontier," in *Communities in the American West*, edited by Stephen Tchudi (Reno: Nevada Humanities Committee and University of Nevada Press, 1999).

See also: African American cowboys; Ethnic enclaves; Segregation.

Segregation vs. integration

> **Significance:** Segregation is the separation of groups of people, either by law or because of custom or economic disparities. Integration means that all people and groups in a society are considered equal under the law and are allowed to move freely and live without unequal restrictions.

Examples of segregation may be found throughout history, as groups considered inferior or subordinate have been forced to live in specific areas of a city or town. Jews in Europe were forced into separate communities, called ghettos, in the Middle Ages by Christians who believed the Jews were "unclean" and racially inferior. The caste systems in India and Southeast Asia forced persons born into "inferior" castes to live in separate areas of a community. Some people, considered so unclean that merely breathing the same air they breathed would contaminate a higher caste member's body, were forced to live outside the walls surrounding many Indian villages. These "untouchables" suffered miserably, but their status was defined by Hindu religious beliefs, and they could do little to improve their living standards. Though the caste system has been outlawed by the Indian government and all citizens are considered equal in the eyes of the law, beliefs die hard, and Indians considered lower caste are still victims of discrimination and segregation. Other examples of segregation include the apartheid system that existed in South Africa and the Jim Crow system that existed in the southern part of the United States. South Africa officially repudiated its system of separate racial communities in 1992, and, since 1964, discrimination based on race has been illegal in the United States. Yet segregation is still found in both countries. Though legal (or de jure) segregation has largely disappeared, de facto segregation resulting from attitudes and customs, can be found almost everywhere in those two countries.

School Segregation

In 1954, the U.S. Supreme Court outlawed racial segregation in public schools in *Brown v. Board of Education*. Separating children by race, the Court found, created a feeling of inferiority among African American students. Segregation made them feel unwanted by the white majority, and this feeling prevented them from getting an equal educational opportunity. The Court ordered school districts to desegregate "with all deliberate speed." White reaction, however, which turned violent in many southern communities, prevented rapid compliance with the Court's ruling. By 1966, only 15 percent of southern school districts were desegregated. In an effort to push integration forward, the Office of Civil Rights in the Department of Health, Education, and Welfare began to withhold federal money from segregated districts. These financial sanctions encouraged fuller compliance with the *Brown* ruling so that by 1973 almost half of the districts in the South had desegregated. In the North and West, on the other hand, where the government did not threaten to withhold money, almost 70 percent of school districts remained highly segregated.

In 1990, racially integrated schools (defined as those with some black students but with white students in the majority) remained a distant goal. More than 63 percent of African American children attended segregated schools.

Housing Segregation

Housing patterns and neighborhood segregation were the primary reasons for this racial division. Segregation in the American school system has also resulted directly

from the attitudes and actions of white parents who refused to send their children to schools attended by blacks.

Many white Americans, according to studies of public opinion, hold beliefs that help prevent integration. Generally, whites say that they believe in equality for all, but when it comes to action that would make that principle possible, they reject any changes. For example, many white Americans fear that once a few black people move into a neighborhood, more will quickly follow, and the racial change will greatly lower the value of their property. They also fear that crime rates will increase—even if many, or most, of the newcomers are middle class—and that educational quality will decline. White residents flee, and neighborhoods quickly become re-segregated. Unlike most whites, a majority of African Americans (more than 70 percent) in the late 1980's support and say they would choose to live in mixed communities. The ideal neighborhood, according to polls of African Americans, would be 55 percent white and 45 percent black. Whites polled, on the other hand, have said they would probably move if the black population reached more than 20 percent.

White Attitudes

Many white Americans do not believe that racism and racial discrimination are major problems. These whites believe that integration and affirmative action programs have all but ended inequality and that blacks exaggerate the negative effects of inequality on their educational and employment opportunities. Only 26 percent of white Americans in a national poll in the late 1980's thought that African Americans faced any "significant" discrimination in their daily lives. More than twice as many blacks (53 percent) responded that they faced significant amounts of prejudice and discrimination in their day-to-day affairs. Many white Americans believe that African Americans deserve the rejection they receive in American society, believing that it is "their" fault they are economically and socially unequal. If "they" simply worked a little harder, drank less, made a greater effort to find better jobs, and took firmer control of their own lives, this argument goes, they would be accepted as equal by whites. Other surveys of white attitudes, however, show that this belief is not borne out in reality. Many whites want little or no contact with blacks and will, in fact, go to great expense and move considerable distances to maintain racial isolation and separation. This type of de facto segregation is the norm in American society, and it is very difficult to change.

Remedial Efforts

Before the Civil War (1961-1865), slavery was the principal system of maintaining white supremacy in the United

States. The slave system rigidly segregated African Americans into an inferior status; under the laws of most slave states, slaves were not even considered human beings. With the abolition of slavery in the aftermath of the bloodiest war in American history, southern whites constructed a system of legal segregation to maintain white supremacy and keep blacks in an inferior economic and social status. That system of legal segregation, called Jim Crow, in which it was a violation of state law for black and white Americans to attend school or church together, or to eat together, lasted until the 1960's.

Officially the Civil Rights Act of 1964 barred discrimination in education, employment, or housing based on race, religion, ethnicity, or gender. Still, the attitudes of white superiority remained dominant in the minds of most whites, and actual integration in schools, employment, and housing, occurred very slowly, if at all. In the 1980's in Illinois, for example, African Americans composed 18.7 percent of the student population, and 83.2 percent of them attended totally segregated schools. In Mississippi, African Americans totaled 55.5 percent of school enrollments, with 80.3 percent going to segregated classrooms. Such numbers reflect the continuing segregation of American society.

Even within integrated schools some observers find an internal system of student segregation. Black students make up about 16 percent of all public school students in the United States but 40 percent of all pupils considered to be retarded, to have a disability, or to be deficient. Black students are therefore further segregated by "tracking," in which students are separated by scores on standardized tests and according to their "potential." Black students are found in overwhelming numbers in the lowest track. African American children enter school with great disadvantages in socioeconomic backgrounds and cultural opportunities; those two factors, especially the first (which refers to family income), are directly related to doing well in school and on achievement tests. Unless economic opportunities for black families greatly improve, it is likely that the large gap in educational outcomes will not be significantly reduced. Disparities in family income account for most of the differences among white students on these same tests, so it should not be surprising that, given the large income gap between white and black families, with median wealth for black families ($6,837 in 1984) being less than 25 percent of white family wealth ($32,667 in 1984), African Americans would do less well in schools.

Some American communities have achieved a degree of integration, but usually it requires some restrictions and positive actions on the part of local leaders. In one study in the 1980's, it was noted that the number of black residents could not be allowed to become more than 16 to 20 percent of any neighborhood, or whites would begin to move. Citizens interested in integration must take charge of their own communities and not allow real estate interests to take advantage of racial fears through "blockbusting" tactics. Oak Park, Illinois, has shown that a carefully controlled housing market can promote racial integration. It has been shown in this Chicago suburb that white citizens will remain in an integrated community as long as black residents make up less than half of the population. White anxieties about crime are significantly reduced in these circumstances.

In other areas and communities, desegregation of public schools could be accomplished only by an extensive busing program that took students out of their neighborhoods and transported them to integrated school facilities. Although such programs met with mixed success, they did help to jump start school integration during the 1970's. Other ideas, such as freedom-of-choice plans (whereby students can voluntarily attend any school in the district), and so-called "magnet schools," offering special programs for selected students, have done little to reduce segregation.

Leslie V. Tischauser

Core Resources

John Hope Franklin's *The Color Line: Legacy for the Twenty-first Century* (Columbia: University of Missouri Press, 1993) is a series of lectures delivered by an eminent African American historian looking into the past and the future of race relations in the United States. Andrew Hacker's *Two Nations: Black and White, Separate, Hostile, Unequal* (New York: Charles Scribner's Sons, 1992) provides direct statistical evidence from polls bearing witness to the deteriorating state of race relations in the United States. Gunnar Myrdal's *An American Dilemma: The Negro Problem and Modern Democracy* (New York: Harper & Row, 1962), originally published in 1944, is a classic study of race relations in the United States.

See also: *Brown v. Board of Education;* Busing and integration; Caste model; Integration; Jim Crow laws; *Plessy v. Ferguson;* Segregation; Segregation: de facto and de jure; White flight.

Self-determination movements

In its traditional usage, the idea of self-determination refers to the right of a group of people to sovereignty, independence, and self-government. The United States made such a claim in its Declaration of Independence from England. The idea has been incorporated into international treaties such as the covenant of the League of Nations and the charter of the United Nations. Since the end of World War II, more than a hundred countries around the world have achieved sovereign statehood through claims of self-determination, many having been former colonies of European states.

However, there are many more peoples and nationalities around the world than there are nation-states. Some countries, such as those in Africa, may have hundreds of distinct ethnic groups, many of which aspire to national self-determination. This often creates conditions of violence and civil war. Even countries that have relatively long-standing, legitimate governments, such as Canada, face claims regarding self-determination from ethnic groups within their borders. During the 1990's, the Soviet Union broke up into many republics that in turn faced ethnic groups that wanted to break off and form their own states. In the Balkans, claims to national self-determination led to brutal civil war and vicious policies of ethnic cleansing.

The United States is a country of great ethnic diversity, and yet it has not faced any considerable degree of agitation from advocates for ethnic self-determination. There are several reasons for this. First, unlike many other countries, the United States' ethnic minorities are not concentrated into particular geographical areas. Claims for self-determination are almost always associated with the geographic concentration of minority populations—situations such as that in Canada, where French Canadians are concentrated mainly in southern Quebec. Second, the U.S. federal system encourages much political activity at the state and local levels, which diffuses any wider claim to ethnic self-determination against a too-intrusive national government. Third, the U.S. Constitution affords American citizens a high degree of individual rights and civil liberties and fairly responsive democratic political institutions, which minimizes the growth of minority resentment. Finally, Americans generally are members not only of ethnic communities but also of various religious denominations, interest groups, political organizations, and private associations. The great opportunity for multiple, ethnicity-crossing civic associations tends to dilute the drive for ethnic self-determination.

This does not mean that minority groups in the United States lack any sense of their distinctiveness. The multicultural movement of the 1980's and 1990's underscored the ethnic and racial awareness of many American groups, including African Americans, Latinos, Native Americans, and Asian Americans. However, the fact that such ethnic communities are themselves divided along geographical, religious, and political lines has muted their growth into full-fledged self-determination movements. Democratic government offers the hope that any grievances such communities feel can be mediated and addressed through free and open political discussion and action so that revolutionary violence is rendered unnecessary. Ethnic violence sometimes erupts in the most democratic of countries, as it has in the United States from time to time. However, the wider experience of nations suggests that revolution and civil war result where political grievances are ignored or repressed, thereby further stoking fires of resentment that find ultimate expression in full-scale wars of self-determination. *Robert F. Gorman*

See also: Black nationalism; Separatism; Separatist movement in Quebec; Universal Negro Improvement Association.

Self-identification among Asian Americans

Europeans invented the concept of "Asia" to refer to countries east of the Urals and the Bosporus. When immigrants from Asia arrived in the United States, few knew about the culture of other Asians, and they rarely spoke one another's languages. Before 1920, government agencies classified them by specific countries of origin rather than as "Asians." It was the Immigration Act of 1924 that began using the term "Asian" in order to exclude them from further immigration to the United States.

Although offspring of the first generation of Asians in the United States were automatically American citizens, they became bicultural, identifying with their parents' home country while becoming Americanized. Nevertheless, the various Asian American groups did not find opportunities to interact together as "Asians" because they were separated occupationally and residentially.

Within Hawaii, where whites have always been a numerical minority, the term "Asian" is not in common use, even today. Chinese, the first arrivals, were recruited to work in the sugarcane fields but left for entrepreneurial pursuits in the towns soon after their work contracts expired. Japanese, the largest Asian group in the islands, tended to remain on the plantation for two generations because whites generally refused to hire them for any other work; some, however, passed civil service exams and advanced to middle-class status by working for the federal government. Filipinos, who also began as plantation laborers, have been the slowest to rise in status because few have acquired the educational qualifications for white-collar positions. Each group has depended upon itself rather than banding together. Because whites dominate the Republican Party and Japanese have long controlled the Democratic Party,

Chinese Republicans and Filipino Democrats can only be junior partners in ethnic voting coalitions.

On the U.S. mainland, Asians generally suffered undifferentiated discrimination, but Japan's aggression in Asia did much to create disunity with Chinese, Filipinos, Indonesians, Koreans, Malays, and Vietnamese. After World War II, political turmoil in China and Indochina promoted further animosity among Asians, who brought Cambodian-Vietnamese, Chinese-Taiwanese, and other rivalries with them.

An Asian American coalition emerged from two sources. One was the advent of ethnic studies in the 1970's, resulting in Asian studies curricula, film festivals, and museums. The second stimulus for Asian American coalition building came from Japanese Americans, who sought redress from the federal government for Japanese Americans who were unjustly placed into internment camps during World War II. Alone, Japanese Americans carried little weight within the political landscape, but when Japanese Americans gained support from other Asian American groups, they reached critical mass to lobby the U.S. government for an apology that entailed monetary compensation. No other issue, past or present, has served to bring Asian Americans together. *Michael Haas*

See also: Asian American movement; Civil Liberties Act of 1988; Redress movement.

Self-identification among Latinos

Although many Anglo-Americans tend to lump Latinos together as a homogeneous group, the members of this sector of U.S. society distinguish among themselves in a number of different ways. National origin, race, and culture serve to create distinctive subgroups. Some nineteen different countries, as well as the Commonwealth of Puerto Rico, contribute to Latino immigration. Racially the membership includes Amerinds (so-called Indians), Asians, Caucasians, and African Americans. Both race and national origin have contributed to the evolution of distinctive cultural traits among Latinos as well.

The three major Latin American groups found in the United States have their roots in Mexico, Central America, and the Caribbean. The rate of immigration from some South American countries increased in the late twentieth century, but the numerical rate was still quite small statistically. An examination of the three major contributors illustrates the complexity of Latino identities.

Mexican Americans

Self-identification among Mexican immigrants and their descendants born in the United States covers a number of categories. Migration from what is now Mexico into what became the U.S. Southwest began as early as the sixteenth century. There are Latinos in New Mexico today who refer to themselves as Spanish Americans because their ancestors arrived from Mexico when that country did not exist as a nation but was only a colony of the Spanish crown.

Some politically active Mexican Americans regard themselves as a separate cultural and even racial entity, referring to themselves as Chicanos or as La Raza, even though racially they represent a blend of Caucasian and Amerind strains. More recent immigrants still consider themselves Mexican, although that identification tends to fade for some with the passage of time. This is especially true for those more closely fitting the racial stereotype of Anglo-American.

Caribbean Americans

The three islands providing the Caribbean segment of the Latino population are Puerto Rico, Cuba, and Hispaniola. Puerto Ricans are distinct from other Caribbean islanders in that they are U.S. citizens under a federal law (commonly known as the Jones Act) passed in 1917.

Nevertheless, Puerto Ricans did not begin to immigrate to the mainland in significant numbers until the inauguration of inexpensive air fares following World War II. Then they came to escape the lack of economic opportunity on their island. Most were either semiskilled or unskilled. In the 1990's, estimates place the number of Puerto Ricans born on the island or their descendants born on the mainland at the two million mark. These Puerto Ricans reside mostly in the U.S. Northeast. Latino cultural identification remains strong even among those born on the mainland. The term "Nuyoricans" has been used to describe Puerto Ricans making New York their home.

The massive wave of Cuban immigration to the United States began in January, 1959, when Fidel Castro and his followers seized control of the island. Because this initial group contained a large number from Cuba's business and professional elite, they quickly established themselves as an economic and political force in the greater Miami area. The very oldest of the initial wave still consider themselves Cubanos and expect to return to the island once Castro is no longer in power.

The island of Hispaniola is divided between the Latino Dominican Republic and the French- and Creole-speaking country of Haiti. Both countries suffer from severe economic problems, and therefore many in their population seek to emigrate in any manner possible to the United States. Dominicans seeking to enter the

United States illegally have often proceeded through Puerto Rico, where they seek to pass as Puerto Rican citizens. Poor and often ill-trained, they are prepared to accept jobs at the entry level. Like many Puerto Ricans, Dominicans have also settled in the greater New York area in large numbers; there they can blend in easily with the larger Latino population.

Central Americans

The most recent example of mass immigration of Latinos to the United States occurred in the decades of the 1970's, 1980's, and 1990's, when in excess of one million political and economic refugees arrived from Central America, mainly from three countries. These newcomers did not regard themselves as Central Americans but rather as Guatemalans, Salvadorans, and Nicaraguans, for Central America has a history of political divisions since its emergence from Spanish colonialism.

In the late 1990's, the region remained divided with little indication of the possibility of political unification. Among themselves, immigrants from Central America call one another *Guanacos* (Salvadorans), *Catrachos* (Hondurans), *Chapines* (Guatemalans), *Chochos* (Nicaraguans), and *Ticos* (Costa Ricans). When arriving in the United States, they tend to join colonies of their countrymen who have preceded them, many in Southern California.   *Carl Henry Marcoux*

See also: Chicano movement; Cuban Americans; Dominican Americans; Haitians and Haitian refugees; Jones Act of 1917; Latinos in the United States; Puerto Rico; Sanctuary movement.

Self-segregation

The racial integration of American institutions was an important part of the 1960's Civil Rights movement. However, many neighborhoods, schools, and social and religious organizations continued to be segregated even after laws enforcing segregation disappeared. Some observers have maintained that this is largely a result of self-segregation by minority group members, sparking debates over the extent and desirability of self-segregation.

Racial segregation by law, also known as de jure segregation, was common in the United States until the Civil Rights movement. Since the passage of the 1964 Civil Rights Act, the integration of American institutions has been a major goal for many governmental organizations and concerned citizens. However, the end of segregation by law did not produce the end of actual segregation. In their influential book *American Apartheid: Segregation and the Making of the Underclass* (1993), sociologists Douglas

S. Massey and Nancy A. Denton offered evidence that American neighborhoods were becoming more racially segregated over the course of the twentieth century. The National School Boards Association reported in 1989 that a majority of African American schoolchildren were attending racially segregated schools. Even when residential areas and institutions were integrated, many whites and African Americans associated primarily with members of their own racial groups.

Given this continuing racial separation, the issue of self-segregation became a topic of debate on several points. First, observers have disagreed as to what extent continuing segregation was a product of self-segregation rather than of continuing racial discrimination. Second, it is often unclear whether minority group members are more likely than whites to avoid social contacts with outsiders. Third, some commentators have argued that self-segregation is undesirable and destructive for minority group members and for American society in general, while others have held that voluntary segregation can often be beneficial.

In *American Apartheid*, Massey and Denton pointed to residentially segregated neighborhoods as evidence of continuing systematic discrimination in American housing. However, sociologist Orlando Patterson responded that African Americans tended to live in majority black neighborhoods as a matter of choice. Because school districts are based on residential areas, if Patterson is correct, segregated schools, as well as segregated neighborhoods, would be largely a product of voluntary self-segregation.

Some of those who object to the continuing segregation of American society have criticized minority group members for clustering in their own neighborhoods or friendship groups. However, according to a study of college students by University of Michigan scholar Sylvia Hurtado, white students are more likely than African Americans, Mexican Americans, or Asian Americans to voluntarily segregate themselves. Therefore, minority self-segregation may be a response to a real or perceived lack of complete acceptance by whites. When minority members do engage in self-segregation, they often do so in order to overcome disadvantages. In her book *Blacks in College* (1984), for example, Jacqueline Fleming reported that African Americans in majority black colleges showed more academic progress and higher graduation rates than did African Americans in majority white colleges.   *Carl L. Bankston III*

See also: Assimilation: cultural and structural; Black colleges and universities; Hypersegregation; Integration; Positive ethnocentrism; Segregation vs. integration.

Sell-out

"Selling out" is a term that is commonly used to refer to minority group members who are seen as betraying their community and their heritage. Expressing beliefs or engaging in acts that are perceived as detrimental or simply nonsupportive of the community as a whole is considered selling out. Individuals accused of selling out have their racial identities questioned and their membership in their communities threatened. One can be accused of selling out for a variety of economic, political or social reasons. For example, an African American who grew up in an inner-city community but who achieves financial success and moves into an affluent, predominantly white neighborhood might be accused of selling out. A minority group member who marries a white person might also be accused of selling out. On a public level, the term is often applied to political figures such as Supreme Court justice Clarence Thomas, who is African American but who opposes affirmative action, because his political views are seen as in opposition to the best interests of the black community as a whole.

Erica Childs

See also: Assimilation: cultural and structural; Black conservatism; Internalized racism; Interracial and interethnic marriage.

Selma-Montgomery march

During 1964, with civil rights upheavals reaching crisis proportions, leaders in the Southern Christian Leadership Conference (SCLC) realized the urgency of forcing the enactment of a voting rights act to enfranchise southern blacks. The SCLC selected Selma, Alabama, seventy-three miles west of Montgomery, as the place to organize voter registration demonstrations. Early in 1965, Martin Luther King, Jr., announced that the SCLC would lead blacks to the courthouse in Selma to register them to vote. During January, more than two thousand blacks were arrested for trying to register, leading to demonstrations in which blacks and their white supporters, who poured in from across the nation, were also arrested.

King scheduled a march from Selma to Montgomery, culminating in the marchers'

handing Governor George Wallace a petition demanding enfranchisement for blacks. State troopers attacked the marchers, beating them with nightsticks and shocking them with cattle prods. This brutality attracted national attention and led President Lyndon B. Johnson to support the Voting Rights Act of 1965, the passage of which, along with Supreme Court decisions upholding the Twenty-fourth Amendment, which outlawed the poll tax in federal elections, enfranchised southern blacks and changed forever the course of politics in the South.

R. Baird Shuman

See also: Civil Rights movement; Southern Christian Leadership Conference; Voting Rights Act of 1965.

The Reverend Martin Luther King, Jr., leads marchers across the Alabama River bridge in Selma, Alabama, on March 21, 1965, on their way to Montgomery, the state capital.

Seminole Wars

> **Significance:** The Seminole Wars were the most costly wars waged by the United States government against Native Americans. The death of more than fifteen hundred soldiers and an expenditure of more than thirty million dollars failed to achieve the government's policy objectives of Indian removal.

The Seminoles were largely Indians who had separated themselves from the Georgia Creeks to live in Spanish Florida. There they were joined by refugees from other tribes as well as by escaped slaves from the Southeast. In the first half of the nineteenth century, the U.S. government waged a series of wars against these people in an attempt to bring the area on its southern border, and its inhabitants, under its control.

The First War, 1817-1818

In the 1810's, the U.S. Congress was dominated by "hawkish" politicians from the South and the West who wanted to annex territory on the southern border. The first area to be attacked was part of West Florida, where runaway slaves inhabited an abandoned British fort. A group of volunteers from Tennessee, Louisiana, and Mississippi were led by General Andrew Jackson to the fort on a river at a place called Prospect Bluff. The fort on Prospect Bluff was surrounded by free black farmers who numbered about a thousand. The garrison of the fort itself consisted of about three hundred blacks, various renegade Indians, and some Seminole warriors under the leadership of a former slave named Garcon. The U.S. government wanted to destroy this community because of its proximity to Southern plantations and its attraction to runaway slaves. Jackson and his volunteers made an illegal attack on the fort in the summer of 1816, killing almost all of its inhabitants and destroying all the farms in the vicinity. Garcon and some of the Indian chiefs survived the destruction of the fort but were later executed. Most of the farmers lost their property but not their lives.

The First Seminole War began in late 1817 as an effort to regain runaway slaves but quickly became a war of annexation. Soon after the founding of the country, the United States sought to expand its borders. Expansion on the southern border brought the country into conflict with Spain. Slaves had continually sought their freedom in Spanish Florida after escaping from plantations in Georgia and the Carolinas. After many decades of infuriating plantation owners, the runaway slaves were attacked; many were returned by military invasions led by Jackson. Eventually, Florida was annexed to the United States by the Adams-Onís Treaty, which became effective in 1821.

The capture of runaways brought the government into conflict not only with the Spanish, who sought to protect the slaves, but also with the Seminoles, who had befriended them. The blacks and Indians fought three American invasion forces in which they lost their dwellings and most of their possessions. They regrouped, however, forming new villages to which runaways continued to be welcomed.

The Second War, 1835-1842

In the aftermath of the first war and the annexation of Florida, General Jackson was sent there to form a territorial government. When this government was created by Congress in 1822, there were four thousand Indians and eight hundred blacks in Florida. Both groups posed problems for the new region. Florida citizens desired Indian lands, and Georgia slaveowners wanted their runaways returned. After a decade of broken treaties, cash-settlement negotiations, and general friction, another period of fighting ensued.

The second war occurred when the federal government tried to remove the Seminole Indians in Florida to the Indian Territory west of the Mississippi River. At the

This drawing shows General Andrew Jackson and his forces capturing Seminole Indian chiefs during one of the Seminole Wars.

outbreak of the war in 1835, the Seminoles relied on African Americans as interpreters and consultants regarding American culture. Black leaders were active politically and militarily. Neither the Indians nor the blacks, however, could withstand the military power of the United States. Most Indians were moved into the Arkansas Territory, and many blacks were returned to slavery.

The Third War, 1855-1858

This final war resulted because the Second Seminole War had not fully succeeded. Billy Bowlegs, a Seminole leader, continued to attack whites from his headquarters in the Florida Everglades. Government bribes and harassment were of no avail. The black allies of the Seminoles were no longer available, and soon most of the war chiefs were gone; Bowlegs was the last to leave. In a few years another war would occupy the Union. The army was ultimately unable to remove all Seminoles from Florida.   *William H. Green*

Core Resources

The Seminole Wars are examined in Joshua R. Giddings's *The Exiles of Florida: Or, The Crimes Committed by Our Government Against the Maroons Who Fled from South Carolina and Other Slave States, Seeking Protection Under Spanish Laws* (1858; reprint, Gainesville: University of Florida Press, 1964); Daniel F. Littlefield, Jr.'s *Africans and Seminoles: From Removal to Emancipation* (Westport, Conn.: Greenwood Press, 1977); John K. Mahon's *History of the Second Seminole War, 1835-1842* (Gainesville: University of Florida Press, 1967); Virginia Peters Bergman's *The Florida Wars* (Hamden, Conn.: Archon Books, 1979); and James Leitch Wright, Jr.'s *Creeks and Seminoles: The Destruction and Regeneration of the Muscogulge People* (Lincoln: University of Nebraska Press, 1986).

See also: African American-American Indian relations; Indian Removal Act; Indian-white relations: United States.

Separatism

As a conception, separatism may be defined as the goal or policy of a group of people—usually united by ethnic or racial, linguistic, geographical, and/or religious bonds—that wishes to free itself from the rule of a different people and to establish an independent form of self-government or that, lacking the capacity to free itself from the government of an existing state, attempts to establish exclusive or segregated social mechanisms in which to express and to preserve the group's common identity and to insulate the group from wider cultural influences. Full-blown separatism can lead to revolution and civil war. Less extreme versions of separatism can lead to localized violence.

In the United States, white and black separatist movements exist, often in opposition to one another. The militia and survivalist movements reflect a similar mentality. Separatism of these sorts does not appeal to the majority of Americans. Moreover, owing to the distinctive pluralism of American society, the U.S. government tolerates such group expressions as long as they do not threaten public order or safety. Because most Americans are members of many groups with cross-cutting interests, separatist movements have a difficult time winning wider public participation or support.   *Robert F. Gorman*

See also: Black nationalism; Ethnic enclaves; Self-determination movements; Separatist movement in Quebec; White supremacist groups.

This Montreal, Quebec, home displays the fleur-de-lis in support of Quebec separatism.

Separatist movement in Quebec

> **Significance:** The efforts of French-speaking Quebecers to gain independence for their province build a sense of nationalism within Quebec but create a rift between English- and French-speaking Canadians.

In 1960, Canada's Liberal Party, led by Jean Lesage, won a narrow victory in Quebec's provincial election. Once in power, the Liberals initiated a period of considerable reform and unintentionally unleashed nationalist forces that would bring the issue of sovereignty for Quebec to the forefront. For much of the period between 1944 and 1960, this province, where 85 percent of the people spoke French, had been under the control of Maurice Duplessis and his Union Nationale Party. The Duplessis regime was marked by political corruption and ruthless intimidation of opponents. A powerful combination of political bosses, the Roman Catholic Church, and big business successfully suppressed trade unions, radical organizations, and any liberating ideas that challenged the established conservative order. Intellectuals later labeled this era the Great Darkness. Anglo-Canadians and the United States controlled the economy, while most French-speaking Quebecers (Québécois) were relegated to a subservient status within their homeland. While the province became increasingly urban, industrial, and secular, Duplessis still defended the values of a rural, religious, traditional-minded people. In short, Quebec's institutions had become outmoded and no longer conformed to social and economic reality.

Lesage's Reforms

Although Georges-Émile Lapalme was the intellectual inspiration behind the Liberal program, it was the pragmatic and energetic Jean Lesage who, as premier, instituted the reforms that were to transform Quebec completely. His cabinet introduced numerous electoral reforms, which included reducing the voting age from twenty-one to eighteen, attacking political corruption and patronage, and providing for better representation of urban areas, previously dramatically underrepresented. Social welfare programs were created, expanded, and better funded, particularly in the crucial areas of health care and old age pensions. The labor code was modernized; many workers were empowered to form trade unions, bargain collectively, and strike under limited conditions. Quebec's educational system, previously dominated by a rigid Catholicism that emphasized classical education, was completely revamped. The govern-ment created a modern, secular school system and put in motion plans to create a new University of Quebec and a number of regional colleges. This new educational system was now capable of producing the elites needed to run a modern state, well skilled in the fields of science, technology, and business.

In the crucial economic sector, the state became the engine responsible for economic expansion. Under René Lévesque, minister of hydraulic resources, private power companies were nationalized, creating the giant corporation Hydro-Québec, which provided superior service and reasonable rates to the entire province. The government established the Caisse de Dépôt et Placement, which held government pension funds and provided capital to help Quebec industries. Within the growing public sector, the government systematically inserted an increasing number of French-speaking Quebecers into positions of authority. In all its decisions, the government attempted to ensure that jobs, profits, and raw materials stayed within the province to benefit the people of Quebec rather than foreign interests. Their motto was *Maître chez nous* ("masters of our own house").

The Quiet Revolution

The Liberals won reelection easily in 1962 but were upset in the election of 1966; the Union Nationale returned to power, thus ending one of the most dynamic periods in Quebec's history. The Liberal achievement has been labeled the Quiet Revolution, a revolution that was accomplished not by bloody insurrection in the streets, but rather by changes within the confines of government agencies, business offices, and school classrooms. Perhaps the real revolution was a change in values, attitude, and mentality. Quebecers emerged from this period confident, self-assertive, and taking immense pride in their accomplishments. It was inevitable that unleashing such forces would ultimately lead the Québécois to question the constitutional relationship with the rest of Canada, if they were to preserve their French language and unique Québécois culture.

Some, like the radical youth who joined the Front de Libération du Québec, employed violence to achieve Quebec's separation from Canada. The vast majority, like Lévesque, took the democratic path. Lévesque had been a popular leader of the Liberal government, an immensely gifted statesman who was both a crafty politician and a profound thinker. Now freed of government responsibility, he came to the conclusion that Quebec must be sovereign in the political sphere, although he desired to retain a close economic association with the rest of Canada. After the Liberal Party rejected his sovereignist ideas at its 1967 conference, Lévesque quit the party in order to found a new movement. Further galvanizing sovereignist sentiment that year was the visit of the French president, Charles de Gaulle, to Quebec. On July 24, in Montreal, de Gaulle issued his famous cry, *Vive le Québec libre!* (Long live a free Quebec!), thereby suggesting that Quebec's sovereignists had a powerful international ally in France.

There already were two small sovereignist parties on the scene, the Rassemblement pour L'Indépendance Nationale (Union for National Independence, or RIN), a left-wing party, and the Ralliement Nationale (National Rally, or RN), which tended to be conservative. Together, these two parties had won almost 9 percent of the vote in the previous election. In November, 1967, Lévesque founded the Mouvement Souveraineté-Association (MSA), committed to promoting political sovereignty for Quebec and economic association with Canada. The RIN and RN began to discuss the prospect of merger with Lévesque's new movement, and within a year they, in effect, merged with the MSA. The larger Quebec trade unions also showed keen interest in this project.

The year 1968 was decisive. In January, Lévesque published his best-selling book, *Option Québec*, which promoted the idea of sovereignty association. In April, the MSA voted to become a provincial political party. The first convention was held in Quebec City from October 11-14, and delegates adopted the name of Parti Québécois (PQ). The party's program was more radical than its leaders would have preferred, giving the PQ a decided left-of-center orientation on social and economic issues and an even more aggressive stance against the Canadian government than PQ's leaders thought wise. Commentators across Canada were impressed by the quality of the party's debates, and many Anglo-Canadians found Lévesque a fresh and fascinating figure, honest, passionate, and flamboyant.

The new party generated much enthusiasm and grew quickly. It attracted teachers, students, trade unionists, civil servants, liberal priests, and the new business elites. By the following spring, public opinion polls showed that 26 percent of the electorate would vote for the Parti Québécois. The party was particularly successful with Québécois youth. At its second convention in October, 1969, approximately two-thirds of the delegates were less than thirty-five years of age. The party received a further boost when Jacques Parizeau, a highly respected economist, announced his intention to run as a PQ candidate, thereby legitimizing the party's contention that separa-

Three days before the October 30, 1995, vote on the referendum that could end in Quebec's separation from Canada, crowds wave the flags of Canada and Quebec in support of a unified Canada.

tion was economically feasible.

Thus, the 1960's saw the emergence of a new Quebec nationalism that differed sharply from that of the past. The old nationalism was defensive and insular, suspicious of the state and the city, believing that both were the enemy of a simple, religious, agrarian folk. This nationalism had valued traditionalism, Catholicism, and even race. It had sprung from feelings of inferiority and a ferocious desire to preserve the past. The new nationalism of the 1960's was confident and assertive. Liberal, secular, and reformist, it revolved more around language and economics than race or religion. It embraced modernity, recognized the crucial importance of a technological society, and viewed the state as a benevolent partner in creating a just and affluent society. This nationalism was to be a prominent feature of the sovereignist movement in the decades to come.

David C. Lukowitz

Core Resources

Michael Behiels's *Prelude to Quebec's Quiet Revolution: Liberalism Versus Neo-Nationalism 1945-1960* (Montreal: McGill-Queen's University Press, 1985) examines the intellectual origins of the Quiet Revolution and the separatist, or sovereignist, movement. Graham Fraser's *René Lévesque and the Parti Québécois in Power* (Toronto: Macmillan, 1984) offers a penetrating insight into Lévesque's personality and political style. Alain-G. Gagnon and Mary Beth Montcalm's *Quebec Beyond the Quiet Revolution* (Scarborough, Ont.: Nelson Canada, 1990) examines the subsequent impact of the policies, legislation, and trends initiated during the Quiet Revolution.

Gilles Gougeon's *A History of Quebec Nationalism*, translated by Louisa Blair, Robert Chodos, and Jane Obertino (Toronto: James Lorimer, 1994), is a fascinating series of interviews with seven leading Québécois scholars; chapter 3 gives an expert analysis of the 1960's by Richard Desrosiers. John Saywell's *The Rise of the Parti Québécois, 1967-1976* (Toronto: University of Toronto Press, 1977) is arguably the best introductory account of the party's early years. Dale C. Thomson's *Jean Lesage and the Quiet Revolution* (Toronto: Macmillan, 1984) is the definitive work on the subject, ably researched by a respected Canadian scholar.

See also: Bloc Québécois; Charter of the French Language; French Canadians; Meech Lake Accord; October crisis; Official Languages Act; Politics and racial/ethnic relations in Canada.

Sephardic Jewish Americans

Sephardic Jews follow the liturgy and customs developed by Jews in medieval Spain and Portugal as well as Babylonian Jewish traditions in a linguistic blend of Spanish (or Portuguese), Hebrew, and Arabic. Sephardic Jews, an upper class consisting mostly of intellectuals and members of the business elite, have a proud multicultural heritage the combines Islamic and Christian influences. Members have published biblical commentaries, literature, and works on science, philosophy, and legal issues. One of the most influential Sephardic thinkers was the Dutch philosopher Baruch Spinoza.

Sephardic Jews (derived from *sepharad*, a place of exile) were persecuted by Catholics during the Inquisition; they were forced to either become Christian or face expulsion from the Iberian peninsula. Spanish Jews left in 1492 and the Portuguese in 1497. Most Sephardic Jews settled in Holland, Brazil (Recife), Martinique, and various islands in the West Indies, where they prospered as a merchant class.

Sephardic Jews were the first Jewish immigrants to arrive in the North American colonies. Some historians believe that Sephardic Jews accompanied Columbus on his voyage to America in 1492. Other historical records indicate that in 1634, Portuguese Jew Mathias de Sousa arrived in Maryland and established the first American Jewish settlement. Shortly after, another Sephardim, Jacob Barsimson, arrived in the colonies on a Dutch West India Company boat. In the mid-1600's, some Sephardic Jews settled in Rhode Island and Virginia.

In 1654, twenty-three Jewish refugees from Brazil arrived in New Amsterdam. These refugees were not welcomed by the governor, Peter Stuyvesant, whom some historians describe as a bigot and anti-Semitic. The policy of tolerance for Jews, followed in the Dutch American colonists' native land, was applied in the colonies, and the Jews were allowed to remain, but some historians claim that this deference toward the Jews was primarily sparked by the colonists' fear of losing economic benefits in New Amsterdam. The Sephardic Jews in New Amsterdam were not allowed to build a temple or practice their religious beliefs in public; however in 1682, they rented a house for prayer meetings, and in 1730, the first synagogue, Shearith Israel, was built in New Amsterdam.

Gradually, Sephardic Jews succeeded in becoming participants in the political process. They became a dominant force; however, in the first part of the nineteenth century they seemed to lose connection with their Jewish ancestry. Prominent, wealthy Sephardic families moved in the same social circles as Christian families such as the Rockefellers. Intermarriage with Christians led to a weakening of Jewish faith and culture among the Sephardic Jews, who remained prominent society members and set standards of morality, education, and social life. Competition arose between Sephardic and Ashkenazic Jews, who often attended Sephardic synagogues and followed Sephardic ritual. Language was another barrier; the Sephardi spoke Ladino (a mix of medieval Castilian and Hebrew), while the Ashkenazi spoke Yiddish (a mix of German, Eastern European languages, and Hebrew). Nineteenth century American Jews opted to assimilate into the Anglo-Saxon culture, thereby creating their own brand of Judaism. Sephardic Jews were soon outnumbered by Ashkenazi immigrants who began to dominate American Jewish culture.

Maria A. Pacino

See also: Ashkenazic and German Jews; Eastern European Jews; Jewish Americans; Soviet Jewish immigrants.

Set-asides

In the Public Works Employment Act of 1977, Congress legislated a 10 percent set-aside of federal grants awarded by the Department of Commerce to minority-owned businesses, intending to remedy lingering discrimination. White contractors who felt discriminated against brought suit. The U.S. Supreme Court, in *Fullilove v. Klutznick* (1980), upheld the legislation's constitutionality. Concurring justices argued that Congress has a unique role to play in eradicating discrimination; dissenting justices contended that *Fullilove* reinstated race-based preferences and, therefore, was unconstitutional. Subsequently, in *Richmond v. J. A. Croson Company* (1989), the Supreme Court declared a Richmond, Virginia, plan that required primary contractors to subcontract 30 percent of contract dollars to minority contractors a violation of the equal protection clause of the Fourteenth Amendment. All state and local governmental racial classifications, the Court held, must be strictly scrutinized. In *Metro Broadcasting v. Federal Communications Commission* (1990), however, the Supreme Court upheld a policy of the Federal Communications Commission (FCC) to increase broadcast licenses to minority groups, affirming proportional representation as a societal goal, even absent past or present discrimination. At the time, strict scrutiny was not yet applicable to the FCC, a federal agency. Later, in *Adarand Constructors v. Peña* (1995), the Supreme Court declared that a Department of Transportation policy requiring primary contractors to subcontract to certified disadvantaged businesses violated the equal protection component of the Fifth Amendment's due process clause. Following *Adarand*, strict scrutiny of racial classification by any governmental agency necessitates demonstrating a compelling governmental interest.   *Gil Richard Musolf*

See also: *Adarand Constructors v. Peña*; *Fullilove v. Klutznick*; *Richmond v. J. A. Croson Company*.

Settlement houses

Settlement houses originated in 1884 in London with Toynbee Hall. Americans copied this model to develop settlement houses among the poor in the United States. Both countries drew heavily from the cultural values of the Victorian period and from various Christian religious practices in creating these houses. The original goal was for settlement house workers to live among the poor, become neighbors of the poor, and share their cultural values with them, thereby helping poor immigrants to assimilate faster. Workers would then be able to tell others how to work with the poor.

By 1890, settlement houses were developed in Boston, Chicago, and New York, each founded upon differing ideologies. The workers of the settlement houses and their residents were typically white, affluent, well-educated women and men. The settlement houses were located in poor, dilapidated, immigrant neighborhoods and provided the surrounding community with a place to hold meetings, medical and educational services, and instruction in religious philosophy.

Settlement house workers made a distinct division between African Americans and European immigrants. Racism was a blatant and acceptable practice among many Americans at the time, and laws supported segregation of blacks and whites. When settlement workers tried to work with racial and ethnic immigrants, they experienced various difficulties such as in securing funds or in working with these groups of people, mostly because of their own personal biases and inability to meet these groups' needs. Among the various ethnic and racial groups, African Americans were perhaps the least involved with the settlement house movement, especially during their massive migration from southern states to the North.

Those few settlement houses that worked with racial and ethnic groups were developed specifically to serve the needs of a particular group. For example, the True Sunshine Mission was a settlement house developed in 1908 to provide the Chinese with a facility to learn English and skills such as sewing and cooking as well as to serve as a playground for their children. The Elizabeth Russell Settlement house in Tuskegee, Alabama, was formed in 1897 to teach African Americans on the plantations proper hygiene and educate them on skills of sewing, cooking, and gardening. The Little Italy Neighborhood House arose in 1904 in New York to provide lectures in Italian, advocacy, and medical services. Integration of racial and ethnic groups was a rarity. Several settlement houses offered services to racial and ethnic groups, especially African Americans, only when the facilities were not being used by whites.

By 1970, a few hundred settlement houses still existed, but only four had residents. Historians believe the decline in settlement houses stemmed from their failure to change their traditional assimilationist approach and

Most settlement houses dealt with whites rather than blacks. The members of the girls' club in the Chicago Hull House pose with their dolls.

the loss of their major source of funding, the Community Chest, to the United Way. The settlement house movement had good intentions but perpetuated the existence of separate racial and ethnic groups.

Jennifer Lynn Gossett

See also: Assimilation theories; Segregation.

Sexual fears and racism

Significance: The connection between sexual fears and racism has been discussed by historians, sociologists, and novelists, notably historian Lillian Smith and novelist and essayist James Baldwin. This connection is a metaphor for the interplay in American society between sex, race, gender, and power.

The mingling of sex and race has characterized racial relations since Africans were forcibly brought to North America in 1619, throughout the period of slavery, and beyond. This simultaneous hatred of and fascination with black male sexuality in particular, originates in the rape of black women by white men. Social mores of the seventeenth, eighteenth, and nineteenth centuries placed white women on a pedestal, too pure for white men to let lose their sexual passion. Though some sexual contact was necessary for procreation, white men created the myth of lustful, insatiable black women to justify raping them.

The rape of black women was not simply a brutal form of social control and a reaffirmation of white power. The violation also signified for black men their powerlessness to protect their wives, mothers, sisters, and daughters. Nevertheless, the threat of revenge by black men for these atrocities was real for white men. English colonists believed in the supposed hypervirility, promiscuity, and aggression of black men, which psychologists today might see as a projection of their own sexual aggression and guilt. If black women were perceived as by nature lascivious, attitudes about black men were further exaggerated by this fear of retribution.

Lynching and Sexual Fears
The white man's fear of black male sexual aggression manifested itself in the use of lynching as "punishment" and social control. Exact numbers are impossible to verify, but according to historian Lillian Smith in her seminal history of the south, *Killers of the Dream* (1949), approximately 3,148 lynchings took place in the South from 1882 to 1946, and during that time, no member of a lynch mob was given a death sentence or life imprison-

ment, and only 135 people in the United States were convicted of being members of lynch mobs. Although the desire to prevent insurrection is sometimes given as a reason for the lynchings, the most socially compelling "rationale" for the murders was to avenge black men's alleged sexual assaults upon white women.

Castration and Homoeroticism
Castration of black men, though a frequent element of lynching, is often neglected in the scholarly literature. When castration is referenced, as in Winthrop Jordan's *White Over Black* (1968) or in W. J. Cash's *The Mind of the South* (1941), it is usually offered as further evidence of unspeakable cruelty or of white males' feelings of sexual inadequacy in the light of cultural myths of black male sexual prowess.

Novelist and essayist James Baldwin expands the connection between sex and racism in the novel *Another Country* (1960) and the short story "Going to Meet the Man" (1966). In these works, the white sheriff participates in his first lynching, and the castration reads like a sexualized rite of passage: "The man with the knife took the nigger's privates in his hand, one hand, still smiling, as though he were weighing them. . . . Jesse felt his scrotum tighten; and huge, huge, much bigger than his father's flaccid, hairless, the largest thing he had ever seen till then, and the blackest. The white hand stretched them, cradled them, caressed them." An undeniable but often unmentionable aspect of the history of race relations, Baldwin suggests, is an obsession with black male sexuality that is rooted in "a secret desire mingled with fear and guilt."

Chalis Holton

Core Resources
Gerda Lerner's *Black Women in White America: A Documentary History* (New York: Vintage Books, 1972) surveys the literature of protest by black women against lynching, rape as social control, and against the myths of the "bad" black woman. Lerner's text also reprints journalist and activist Ida B. Wells's pamphlet *A Red Record* (1895), which is probably the most well-regarded antilynching document of the nineteenth century. Wells was one of the first to openly protest the habitual rape of black women by white men, and she contradicted the myth that all sexual contact between white women and black men was based on rape. W. J. Cash openly explores the sexual nature of American racism in *The Mind of the South* (New York: Alfred Knopf, 1941), and Lillian Smith's *Killers of the Dream* (New York: W. W. Norton, 1949) is recognized as a seminal history of southern race relations. The early history of racism in the United States and the West Indies and the sexual link are discussed by Winthrop Jordan in *White Over Black: American Attitudes Toward the Negro, 1550-1812* (Durham: University of

North Carolina Press, 1968). James Baldwin is perhaps the only novelist to explore the history of racism and sexual desire so overtly, in both the interracial and homosexual contexts. See Baldwin's *Another Country* (New York: Dell, 1960) and "Going to Meet the Man" (New York: Dell, 1966). Sociologist Calvin Hernton's *Sex and Racism in America* (New York: Grove Press, 1965) is a now classic study of the psychology of racism and the intersecting myths of sex and race.

See also: African American stereotypes; Black "brute" and "buck" stereotypes; Lynchings.

Sharecropping

In the aftermath of the American Civil War (1861-1865), the South faced many difficulties. Its cities, factories, and railroads had been shattered, and its valuable agricultural industry had been turned upside down. Many large planters lost their entire workforce when the Thirteenth Amendment to the U.S. Constitution freed southern slaves. Newly freed slaves, most of whom were farmworkers, had no land to cultivate. Landowners, former slaves, and small farmers negotiated a compromise: sharecropping. The system they created would eventually lead to a steady decline in southern agriculture during the twentieth century.

Deeply in debt after the war, many southern landowners were forced to give up all or fragments of their property to local merchants, banks, and corporations. By the end of Reconstruction (1863-1877), large portions of southern farmland were controlled by absentee landlords who neither lived on nor worked their land but managed it from afar. Southern landowners had a large number of acres to be planted and not enough money to hire farm laborers. At the same time, thousands of African Americans were free from slavery but without the homes, land, or tools they needed to support themselves.

To earn a living, agricultural laborers agreed to become tenants on farmland. Landlords provided tenants with land, a small house, and tools to grow a crop. Tenants worked the land and promised a percentage of their annual crop yield, usually between 20 percent and 50 percent, to the landlord. Landlords frequently arranged credit for tenants with local merchants to help them establish a household and buy seed. Storekeepers and landowners, who sometimes were the same person, placed liens on the farmers' crops to protect their interests. Tenants hoped to yield enough profit from their labor not only to pay off their liens but also to eventually purchase the land they worked.

A bad year or depressed cotton prices could easily leave many farmers in debt at the end of the season.

A sharecropper and his children head home through the pine woods after spending the morning working at a tobacco farm in Grenville, North Carolina, in July, 1939.

Sharecroppers frequently promised an additional percentage of their crop to local merchants to purchase the next year's seed and feed their families through the winter. Year after year, sharecroppers became more indebted. Forced to work until liens were paid, tenants became bound to their land, continually impoverished and with little hope of becoming property owners.

Sharecropping in the South increased steadily in the latter half of the nineteenth century until approximately 75 percent of all southern farmers were sharecroppers. Cotton prices began to drop after the turn of the century and then fell drastically during the Great Depression of the 1930's. These conditions forced thousands of tenants to leave the land and move to northern cities in search of employment. Others were forced to leave when landlords decided farming was no longer profitable. As a result of this loss of labor and increases in technology, sharecropping represented only a small percentage of farming in the South by the end of the twentieth century.

Leslie Stricker

See also: Great Migration; Poverty and race; Reconstruction.

Shaw v. Reno

By calling for close scrutiny of a predominantly black congressional district whose shape it considered "bizarre," the Supreme Court in *Shaw v. Reno* (1993) struck a blow against the practice of drawing district boundaries to create "majority-minority" electoral districts.

After the 1990 census, the state legislature of North Carolina began the task of "reapportionment," or redrawing its electoral districts. Although about 22 percent of the state's population was African American, no blacks had been elected to Congress for almost a century. To remedy this, and ostensibly to meet provisions of the Voting Rights Act, the legislature created two majority-nonwhite districts. In order to avoid disturbing incumbents' districts, the legislature drew one of the two districts largely along an interstate highway, snaking 160 miles through the north-central part of the state. The resulting district was 53 percent black.

Five voters filed suit against the reapportionment plan, objecting that the race-based district violated their right to participate in a nonracial electoral process. The case reached the Supreme Court, whose 5-4 majority instructed the lower courts to reconsider the constitutionality of such a district in light of its "bizarre" shape and its "uncomfortable resemblance to political apartheid." In essence, the majority expressed its concern about the practice of creating districts on the basis of race and of establishing contorted geographical boundaries. The coupling of the two practices presumably could result in districts that patently violated the Constitution's equal protection clause, unless a compelling state interest could be demonstrated.

When the *Shaw* case was subsequently returned to North Carolina, a federal panel upheld the reapportionment plan after finding that the state did indeed have a compelling interest in complying with the Voting Rights Act. Nevertheless, the Supreme Court's *Shaw* decision has been the basis for other important decisions concerning racially defined districts. In 1994, for example, a majority-black district in Louisiana was rejected by a federal district court invoking *Shaw*. The court expressed particular concern that the district was intentionally created on the basis of the voters' race. More significant, in 1995 the U.S. Supreme Court extended *Shaw*'s admonitions about racial reapportionment to argue that voters' rights are violated whenever "race was the predominant factor motivating the legislature's decision to place a significant number of voters within or without a particular district," irrespective of shape.

Shaw served as a watershed in the contest between advocates of racial representation and those who champion a "color-blind" electoral system. It came at a time when various racial issues that had for years remained largely outside sharp political debate—affirmative action, welfare reform, and so forth—had been thrust into the center stage of American political discourse. Although *Shaw* by no means resolved these debates, it helped to delineate the battle lines.   *Steve D. Boilard*

See also: Reapportionment cases; Redistricting; Representation: gerrymandering, malapportionment, and reapportionment; Voting Rights Act of 1965.

Shelley v. Kraemer

In the 1948 *Shelley v. Kraemer* decision, the Supreme Court acknowledged the right of private individuals to make racially restrictive covenants but ruled that state action to enforce such covenants was a violation of the Fourteenth Amendment.

After J. D. Shelley, an African American, purchased a house in a predominantly white neighborhood of St. Louis, Missouri, one of the neighbors, Louis Kraemer, sought and obtained an injunction preventing Shelley from taking possession of the property. Unknown to Shelley, the neighboring landowners had signed a contractual agreement barring owners from selling their property to members of "the Negro or Mongolian race." Supported by the National Association for the Advancement of Colored People (NAACP), Shelley challenged the constitutionality of the contract in state court, but the Missouri Supreme Court upheld its legality. Appealing to the U.S. Supreme Court, Shelley's case was argued by the NAACP's leading counsels, Charles Houston and Thurgood Marshall. President Harry S Truman put the weight of the executive branch in favor of the NAACP's position.

This was not the first time that the issue of residential segregation had appeared before the Court. In *Buchanan v. Warley* (1917), the Court had struck down state statutes that limited the right of property owners to sell property to a person of another race, but in *Corrigan v. Buckley* (1926) the Court upheld the right of individuals to make "private" contracts to maintain segregation. *Corrigan* was based on the establishment principle that the first section of the Fourteenth Amendment inhibited the actions of state governments, not those of individuals.

The Court refused to declare restrictive contracts unconstitutional, but it held 6-0 that the Fourteenth Amendment's equal protection clause prohibited state courts from enforcing the contracts, meaning that the contracts were not enforceable. The decision, written by Chief Justice Fred Vinson, emphasized that one of the basic objectives of the Fourteenth Amendment was to prohibit the states from using race to discriminate "in the enjoyment of property rights." The decision did not directly overturn *Corrigan*, but it interpreted the precedent as involving only the validity of private contracts, not their legal enforcement. In a companion case five years later, *Barrows v. Jackson* (1953), Chief Justice Vinson dissented when the majority used the *Shelley* rationale to block enforcement of restrictive covenants through private damage suits against covenant violators.

Eliminating the last direct method for legally barring African Americans from neighborhoods, *Shelley* was an important early victory in the struggle against state-supported segregation. Civil rights proponents hoped that a logical extension of the case would lead to an abolition of the distinction between private and state action in matters of equal protection, but in later decisions such as *Moose Lodge No. 107 v. Irvis* (1972), the majority of judges were not ready to rule against private conduct that was simply tolerated by the state.

Thomas T. Lewis

See also: *Buchanan v. Warley*; Civil Rights Act of 1968; Civil Rights movement; Fair Housing Act; *Heart of Atlanta Motel v. United States*; *Moose Lodge No. 107 v. Irvis*; Restrictive or racial covenants; Segregation: de facto and de jure.

Sikhs in Canada

Sikhs are a religious community whose origins are in South Asia's Punjab region. Initially, they advocated peace, a casteless society, the oneness of God, and the unifying of Hindus and Muslims. Vicious persecution contributed to their transformation into the *Khalsa*, a soldier-saint brotherhood. They are easily recognizable because they wear turbans over their uncut hair. Throughout their history, Sikhs have been respected for their martial valor, innovativeness, adaptability to diverse situations, and migratory tradition.

The Sikh community in Canada comprised 85 percent of all East Indian immigration to Canada up to 1950. Large-scale Sikh emigration from India first took place under British rule. British authorities respected the Sikhs for their loyalty and martial qualities and encouraged them to serve throughout the British Empire, especially in Asia and Africa. Besides doing labor and business, Sikhs were noticeable in the government administration and military, constituting 20 percent of the Indian army.

Therefore, it is not surprising that Sikhs were part of the Hong Kong military contingent that stopped in Vancouver, Canada, as they were traveling to take part in Queen Victoria's Jubilee celebrations in England. The Sikh soldiers were treated very well and learned of economic opportunities in the Vancouver area, which some returned to pursue. Word spread to Punjab about opportunities in Vancouver, and the migration started. By 1907, the Sikhs made up 98 percent of Canada's East Indian population of five thousand, who were attracted by jobs in the lumber industry, in agriculture, and in the construction of railroads. On January 19, 1908, the first *gurdwara*, or Sikh place of worship, in North America was opened in Vancouver; a second opened in Victoria in 1912 and a third on Vancouver Island in 1918. The Sikhs, however, faced considerable discrimination from British Columbians and became the targets of violence and anti-Asian immigration laws. As a result, some went south to the United States, only to face discrimination and violence there. Some returned to the Punjab; others went elsewhere. By 1941, their numbers had dropped to around fourteen hundred.

When India gained independence in 1947, Canadian policy became more liberal toward East Indians. They were given the right to vote and more were allowed in to study at Canadian universities but not to settle. A 1962 amendment lifted the embargo on immigration from countries outside Europe and the United States. Immigration regulations were completely rewritten in 1967 to remove any racial bias and to establish a point system related to the needs of the Canadian economy.

India had a ready supply of highly skilled and educated people who began to enter Canada under the new

Sikh men gather on a Toronto street. One wears a garment emblazoned with the phrase "Proud to be a Sikh."

regulations. Although the Sikhs no longer dominated the six thousand annual entrants from India, their numbers were significant. Like the other post-1967 immigrants, they quickly entered lucrative employment but did not form areas of concentrated settlement. Except for the Sikh *gurdwaras*, Hindu temples and Muslim mosques scattered throughout Canada, the only recognizable South Asian community in Canada is in Vancouver. The second- and third-generation Sikhs in Vancouver continue to support *gurdwaras* and Sikh associations while participating in civic organizations such as the Rotary Club and local chambers of commerce.

Arthur W. Helweg

See also: Asian Indians in Canada; Asian Indians in the United States; *Komagata Maru* incident; Sikhs in the United States.

Sikhs in the United States

The Sikhs are a religious community whose origins are in South Asia's Punjab region. Their founder, Guru Nanak Dev (1469-1539), advocated peace, a casteless society, the oneness of God, and the unifying of Hindus and Muslims. Vicious persecution contributed to this peaceful community being transformed into the *Khalsa*, a soldier-saint brotherhood who believed it was right to draw the sword for a just cause.

The Sikhs' tenth and last Guru, Gobind Singh (1666-1708), instituted the 5Ks, a term used for the symbols Sikhs wear, uncut hair under a turban being the most noticeable. Throughout their history, Sikhs have been respected for their martial valor, innovativeness, adaptability to diverse situations, and migratory tradition. Sikh communities are found throughout the world.

The initial influx, from 1904 to 1923, consisted primarily of Sikhs who originated in rural Punjab and had agricultural backgrounds but were residing in Canada. They migrated south to escape being targets of violence. Some obtained employment in the lumber trade around Bellingham and Everett, Washington. In 1907, about one thousand Sikhs were expelled from the Pacific Northwest because local laborers believed they were depressing wages. The Sikhs and other Indians moved south to work on the farms in the Sacramento, San Joaquin, and Imperial Valleys in the summer and labored in the California cities of Yuba City, Stockton, and El Centro in the winter. Their numbers probably never exceeded six thousand. Newspapers talked about the "Hindoo invasion" and "turbaned tide."

In 1918, the "Hindoo" conspiracy trials brought adverse publicity to the Sikh and Indian community of California. In 1913, the Ghadr (revolutionary) Party was formed and headquartered in San Francisco with the aim of gaining India's independence from Britain. The defendants in the Hindoo case, active members of the Ghadr Party, were charged with violating U.S. neutrality laws. Much of the evidence and impetus to prosecute came from British agents.

In 1923, immigration from India was effectively halted; legislation prevented South Asians from owning land, becoming citizens, or bringing spouses to the United States. As a result, some Sikhs married Mexican women. The Ghadr Party remained active, but at a reduced level. During the 1930's, many Sikhs returned to India, and the population decreased to less than fifteen hundred. In 1946, the Luce-Celler Bill was passed, giving people of Asian Indian descent the right to become citizens and creating an immigration quota for India.

In 1965, immigration legislation ended the national origins quotas. Immigration to the United States was based on the candidate's ability to meet a set of qualifications. In India, a cadre of highly educated doctors, engineers, and scientists was ready to take advantage of the new laws. The Sikhs who immigrated under the relaxed laws are residentially dispersed in affluent suburbs. They gather in their local *gurdwaras*, or Sikh places of worship, which are part of the landscape of every major city in North America.

Arthur W. Helweg

See also: Asian Indians in Canada; Asian Indians in the United States; Sikhs in Canada.

Sikhs gather at a religious service in a Sikh temple in California.

Simpson, O. J., trial

> **Significance:** The murder trial and acquittal of former football star Orenthal James "O. J." Simpson in 1995 polarized racial attitudes about American criminal justice and police racism. Both before and after the trial, most whites thought Simpson was guilty, and most African Americans thought he was innocent.

On the night of June 12-13, 1994, the slashed and stabbed bodies of Nicole Brown Simpson and her friend Ronald Goldman, both white, were discovered at the Los Angeles condominium of Nicole Simpson. After making a preliminary investigation, police left the crime scene and went to the nearby Brentwood estate of Nicole Simpson's former husband, O. J. Simpson, the African American former football star. Finding blood on the door of a white Ford Bronco parked askew on the street in front of the house, Los Angeles Police Department detective Mark Fuhrman climbed the fence without a warrant, allegedly to protect Simpson from any possible danger, and admitted other detectives to the premises.

Simpson was not at home, but Fuhrman, who had been at the Simpson residence five years earlier to answer a domestic violence complaint, used the opportunity to search for evidence linking Simpson to the murder. A bloody glove he allegedly found behind the guest quarters later became a key factor in the trial.

When Simpson returned from Chicago, where he had flown the evening of the murder, he quickly became the only suspect in the case. After a bizarre low-speed vehicle chase watched by millions on live television, Simpson surrendered to police on June 17. Denied bail, he remained in jail during the lengthy trial. He used his wealth to hire a "dream team" of famous attorneys. Jury selection began in September, 1994, and took most of the fall.

The Trial

What the media dubbed the "trial of the century" began in late January, 1995, under Judge Lance Ito with a heavily sequestered jury of mostly African Americans. Shortly afterward, O. J. Simpson's self-exonerating book *I Want to Tell You* was published, the first of dozens of books about the case. Gavel-to-gavel coverage on Cable News Network (CNN) guaranteed continuous public attention, and the rest of the electronic and print media rapidly followed suit.

Prosecutors Marcia Clark and Christopher Darden began with a case emphasizing the history of domestic violence in the Simpsons' stormy marriage, but they soon shifted to an emphasis on DNA (deoxyribonucleic acid) evidence linking the blood of O. J. Simpson and both victims to physical evidence found at the crime scene and the Brentwood estate. This made Detective Fuhrman a key witness, along with his partner Detective Philip Vannatter. Another key witness from the Los Angeles Police Department was Dennis Fung from the crime lab, who admitted under cross-examination that some of the blood evidence had been processed by a trainee, Andrea Mazzola. The most damaging cross-examination was that of Fuhrman by defense attorney F. Lee Bailey, who scathingly portrayed Fuhrman as a bigoted racist and perjurer who denied his own racist statements and actions despite several witnesses to the contrary. Vannatter was also portrayed as a racist because of his association with Fuhrman and was accused of mishandling blood samples before turning them over to the crime lab.

These and various other defense accusations of police misconduct and conspiracy left sufficient doubts in the minds of jurors, and they acquitted Simpson of both murders after only a brief deliberation on October 3, 1995. The passionate summation by defense attorney Johnnie Cochran made it quite clear to both the jury and the general public that the alleged racism and misbehavior of Fuhrman and the rest of the Los Angeles Police Department were more important elements in the case than either DNA evidence or domestic violence, thus alienating Cochran from Simpson's other principal attorney, Robert Shapiro.

The cast of characters made race an obvious factor in the trial from the very beginning. Simpson, Darden, and Cochran were African Americans, as were nine of the jurors. The detectives, the other attorneys, and both victims were white. Judge Ito was a Japanese American married to a white police captain.

Near the end of the trial, surveys conducted by CBS News found that 64 percent of whites surveyed thought that Simpson was guilty, while 59 percent of African Americans thought that he was not guilty. Only 11 percent of whites surveyed thought Simpson was not guilty, and only 12 percent of African Americans thought he was guilty. Only about one-fourth of each group was undecided, and the disparity of perceptions between the races had actually increased during the trial.

Reactions to the Trial

After the verdict was announced, many African Americans rejoiced and treated the outcome as if it were a conviction of the Los Angeles Police Department on charges of racism and conspiracy to frame Simpson. This response should be viewed in the light of the highly publicized 1991 Los Angeles beating of African American motorist Rodney King by white police officers, four of whom were acquitted of state criminal charges, lead-

O. J. Simpson, flanked by lawyers F. Lee Bailey (left) and Johnnie Cochran, clenches his fists in pleasure when the jury finds him not guilty in the murders of his ex-wife Nicole Brown and her friend Ron Goldman.

ing to massive racially motivated rioting in Los Angeles, but two of whom were later convicted of federal criminal charges.

Meanwhile many white people expressed their dismay at the Simpson acquittal and asserted that a combination of Simpson's money and reverse jury bias had led to a serious miscarriage of justice. These feelings were not greatly diminished sixteen months later when Simpson was held liable for the deaths of the two victims in a civil lawsuit and assessed punitive damages of $25 million, which compares interestingly with the nearly $20 million that the criminal trial cost both sides.

Explanations of the Verdict
Various explanations have been put forward to account for Simpson's acquittal in the criminal trial. They include reasonable doubt, the lack of a specific theory of the crime, jury nullification, and "evidence" of a police conspiracy.

The simplest explanation is that the jurors did not find persuasive evidence of Simpson's guilt and followed the judge's instructions to acquit the defendant if there was not proof beyond a reasonable doubt. Many African Americans hold this view and give the jury credit for a job well done despite the brevity of their deliberations.

A somewhat more complex version of this explanation is that the prosecution never advanced a specific theory of the crime. For example, they asserted throughout the trial that Simpson committed the entire crime by himself despite circumstantial evidence that an unknown accomplice may have been involved before, after,

or during the murders. Some African Americans may have felt that this was condescending or patronizing to the jury and therefore have given jury members credit for realizing that a more complex theory might make better sense of the known facts. Simpson's DNA fairly clearly placed him at the crime scene on the night in question, but to this day, there is no specific scenario for the crime.

Many whites feel that some jury nullification of crucial evidence must have occurred to produce such a speedy acquittal. Very little of the evidence handled by Fuhrman and Vannatter was formally excluded by Judge Ito, and it was left up to the jurors to decide what weight to give each item of evidence. In the belief that evidence obtained through biased procedures by racist police officers ought not to count against the African American defendant, it would be quite conceivable for nullificationist jurors to neglect the entirety of the evidence found at the Brentwood estate and some of the evidence found at the crime scene. Many whites clearly felt that this was exactly what happened, so the jury may have neglected part of its job.

A further twist on this argument is that a police conspiracy was involved and that key pieces of evidence such as a bloody glove and a bloody sock found in the bedroom were planted by overzealous officers to incriminate Simpson. Cochran's very controversial summation encouraged this viewpoint, and many African Americans, including some of the jurors, may have agreed. However, most whites did not agree even if they thought Simpson was not guilty. This was probably the most divisive outcome of the trial, because despite Simpson's acquittal, it tended to reaffirm racially polarized opinions about the extent of previously alleged inequities toward minorities in the U.S. criminal justice system.

Unresolved Questions
The entire jury system was called into question by the Simpson trial. Its cost and its fairness, both to defendants and to victims or their families, are still hotly debated. The fairness of televising criminal trials was also called into question, though the public clearly has an immense appetite for such events. However, only a few people still have any doubts as to the verdict itself, and only a few people have changed their minds. Despite his lost wealth and status, after the trial Simpson still golfed at public courses and professed his love for his former wife, Ni-

cole. In 1999 Simpson's fight for custody of his two children was nearing conclusion.   *Tom Cook*

Core Resources

Tapes from the Cable News Network (CNN) are crucial to a thorough study of the trial. However, more succinct analyses can be found in Vincent Bugliosi's *Outrage: The Five Reasons Why O. J. Simpson Got Away with Murder* (New York: W. W. Norton, 1996), Alan M. Dershowitz's *Reasonable Doubts: The O. J. Simpson Case and the Criminal Justice System* (New York: Simon & Schuster, 1996), Frank Schmalleger's *The Trial of the Century: The People of the State of California vs. Orenthal James Simpson* (Englewood Cliffs, N.J.: Prentice-Hall, 1996).

See also: Crime and race/ethnicity; Criminal justice system; King, Rodney, case; Jury nullification; Los Angeles riots of 1992; Race card.

Sioux War

> **Significance:** The Minnesota Sioux lost their tribal lands to encroaching white settlers in one of the largest mass slaughters in U.S. history.

On August 17, 1862, four Santee Sioux men, returning from a fruitless search for food beyond the boundaries of their southern Minnesota reservation, attacked and killed five white settlers near Acton, in Meeker County. Ordinarily, the culprits would have been surrendered to white authorities, but these were no ordinary times. The Sioux of Minnesota were starving. Long-promised annuities were slow in coming, as usual, and doubts about the ability of a nation divided by civil war to fulfill its obligations to an isolated frontier led traders at the Redwood Agency to refuse to open their warehouses until payment in gold arrived from Washington, D.C. Trader Andrew Myrick had advised the starving population to "go home and eat grass, or their own dung." On August 18, a large war party attacked and looted the Redwood Agency and wiped out most of a military expedition from Fort Snelling. Myrick, among the first to fall, was found with his mouth symbolically stuffed with grass. As politicians argued over payment of annuities in paper money or in gold, the Great Sioux War began.

First Engagements

The Sioux, reluctantly led by Chief Little Crow, their longtime spokesman, were inefficient attackers. Most of the inhabitants of the Redwood Agency escaped to spread the alarm at Fort Ridgely. During the first week,

far more whites were spared than were killed, many taken prisoner by Little Crow and protected from harm in his camp. Attacks on New Ulm and settlers in Brown and Renville Counties convinced the Sioux that success was imminent. Little Crow knew that Fort Ridgely, which protected the Minnesota River Valley, would have to fall. Meanwhile, panic spread across the Midwest, as politicians from Iowa, Wisconsin, Nebraska, and Dakota Territory petitioned the federal government for troops and leadership. Minnesota governor Alexander Ramsey, who had negotiated the fateful 1851 treaties, appointed his old political rival, former governor Henry H. Sibley, to lead the Minnesota Militia against the Sioux. General John Pope, in disgrace because of his defeat at the Second Battle of Bull Run in Virginia, was assigned to head the new Northwest Department. His policy of pursue and confine would dominate American Indian policy in the trans-Mississippi West for years to come. He directed the Minnesota war from St. Paul.

On August 20 and again on August 22, before Sibley reached Fort Ridgely with a motley crew of raw recruits, Little Crow and Chief Mankato attacked. The fort's cannon was used to devastating effect; only three of the fort's defenders were killed, and both attacks were repelled. The Sioux attacked New Ulm the second time on August 23, but again failed. Several other settlements suffered attacks, but the fate of the now demoralized Sioux was sealed.

By the middle of September, Sibley had formed his sixteen hundred troops into a fighting unit and moved north. On September 23, Sibley defeated several hundred warriors under Chief Mankato, who was killed. As most of the combatants slipped away, Sibley rounded up 400 Sioux, conducted trials, and sentenced 306 to death. President Abraham Lincoln reviewed the records and, refusing to "countenance lynching, within the forms of martial law," commuted most of the sentences. On December 28, 1863, 38 Sioux were hanged on a single scaffold at Mankato, the largest mass execution in U.S. history.

Conclusion

The war was not over. Little Crow was murdered near Hutchinson in 1863. The U.S. Army, following General Pope's orders, pursued the Sioux west. Such occasional engagements as the Battle of White Hill, Dakota, in 1863, and the Battle of the Little Bighorn, in Montana Territory in 1876, kept the Sioux moving. The Great Sioux War cost the lives of 413 white civilians, 77 soldiers, and 71 American Indians, counting those 38 hanged at Mankato. There was no treaty, no negotiation to end the war. All Sioux, blanket and farmer, were condemned to lose all but a minuscule piece of their tribal lands in Minnesota, and ultimately, their way of life. The 1890

Wounded Knee massacre, in which U.S. troops killed almost 200 Sioux, was the last battle in the American Indian wars.   *Stephen G. Sylvester*

Core Resources

Gary Clayton Anderson's *Little Crow: Spokesman for the Sioux* (St. Paul: Minnesota Historical Society Press, 1986) is a carefully researched and documented biography of the most important Native American war leader. *Through Dakota Eyes: Narrative Accounts of the Minnesota Indian War of 1862* (St. Paul: Minnesota Historical Press, 1988), edited by Gary Clayton Anderson and Alan R. Wool-worth, contains first-person accounts of the war. Theodore C. Blegen's *Minnesota: A History of the State* (St. Paul: University of Minnesota Press, 1975) contains a chapter on the Sioux War that is solid and balanced. Richard N. Ellis's *General Pope and U.S. Indian Policy* (Albuquerque: University of New Mexico Press, 1970) provides insight into the policy of punishment and containment that grew out of the war. Robert M. Utley's *The Indian Frontier of the American West: 1846-1890* (Albuquerque: University of New Mexico Press, 1984) places the war in the context of Western policy toward the American Indians.

See also: Apache Wars; Bison slaughter; Little Bighorn, Battle of the; Nez Perce exile; Sand Creek massacre; Wounded Knee massacre.

Skinheads

Skinheads are loosely organized groups of white supremacists. Compared with other white supremacist groups, such as the Ku Klux Klan, skinheads tend to be younger, more violent, and more concentrated in urban areas.

Skinheads originated in England in the 1970's. The original skinheads were mostly young, white, working-class men. They were influenced heavily by punk culture as well as neo-Nazi ideals. They listened to "oi" music (a blend of punk and heavy metal), the lyrics of which often glorified Great Britain and denigrated immigrants and minorities. Skinheads shaved their heads and often sported tattoos and insignia with swastikas and other Nazi themes.

The skinhead movement came to the United States in the early 1980's. American skinheads, like their British counterparts, shaved their heads. They wore steel-toed workman's boots, jeans, white T-shirts, red suspenders, and black bomber jackets. They listened to oi music, both British bands such as Skrewdriver and American bands. American oi music was as racist as the British music.

American skinheads adopted the bigoted beliefs of their British forebears. They take a strong stance against Jews, gays and lesbians, immigrants, people of color, and even the homeless. Although the majority of skinheads come from working-class backgrounds, in some areas the members are more affluent.

Skinheads have been actively involved in committing hate crimes throughout North America. In their mildest form, these crimes include graffiti painting and vandalism, often of homes, cemeteries, and places of worship. Skinheads are also known, however, for committing acts of extreme violence. These have included brutal assaults with baseball bats and knives, "stompings" with their workman's boots, and even murders. In 1989, for example, several skinheads in Portland, Oregon, attacked an Ethiopian immigrant, Mulugeta Seraw, and beat him to death, kicking him with their steel-toed boots and hitting him with baseball bats.

Skinhead groups in the United States have been allied with other white supremacist organizations, including the Ku Klux Klan, militia groups, and neo-Nazis, although they are typically more loosely organized than these groups. However, in some cases attempts have been made to organize skinheads; often these attempts have been made by older people with current or former ties to other white supremacist groups. In California, for example, Tom Metzger, a former Klansman, created

In January, 1989, skinheads join the Ku Klux Klan in their annual Pulaski, Tennessee, march in protest of the celebration of Martin Luther King, Jr.'s birthday. African American bystanders mock the skinheads' Nazi salute.

the White Aryan Resistance, which has a hotline and newsletter and has made recruiting efforts in other locations.

By the end of the 1990's, skinhead groups had made wide use of technology and the media to try to spread their views. Some groups maintained sites on the World Wide Web, and others appeared on talk shows and local cable access programs. In response to the actions of skinheads and other white supremacist groups, by the late 1990's most states had enacted special hate-crime laws. These laws target the violent activities of these groups by enhancing the penalties for hate-motivated crimes. It is unclear, however, whether these laws are effective in reducing the criminal behavior of skinheads.

Phyllis B. Gerstenfeld

See also: American Nazi Party; Hate Crime Statistics Act; Hate crimes; Hate speech; Ku Klux Klan; White supremacist groups.

Slave codes

> **Significance:** Slave codes were colonial and state laws dealing with slavery. In Virginia, these codes were used to make slavery an institution; in Ohio, they were used to discourage blacks from moving to the state.

The first colonial laws recognizing and institutionalizing slavery were enacted in Virginia in the mid-seventeenth century. A similar series of Ohio laws denying civil rights to African Americans were enacted to discourage black immigration to that state in the early nineteenth century.

Virginia

In March, 1661, the Virginia General Assembly declared that "all children borne in this country shalbe held bond or free only according to the condition of the mother." Enacted to alleviate confusion about the status of children with English fathers and African mothers, this law was the first in a series of laws recognizing perpetual slavery in Virginia and equating "freedom" with "white" and "enslaved" with "black." This law is especially indicative of the hardening of race relations in mid-seventeenth century Virginia society, as status in the patriarchal society of England traditionally was inherited from the father. By reversing this legal concept, perpetuation of enslavement for blacks was ensured for their children, whether of black or white ancestry.

Despite the extent to which the 1661 law narrowed the options for defining Africans' status, this act did not in itself establish slavery. Africans had two available win-

dows through which they could obtain freedom—conversion to Christianity and manumission (formal emancipation). In 1655, mulatto Elizabeth Key brought a successful suit for her freedom, using as her main argument the fact that she had been baptized. In 1667, a slave named Fernando contended that he ought to be freed because he was a Christian and had lived in England for several years. Not only did the court deny Fernando's appeal, but also that same year the General Assembly took another step toward more clearly defining blacks' status, by declaring "that the conferring of baptisme doth not alter the condition of the person as to his bondage or freedome." Planters felt that if baptism led to freedom, they would be without any assurance that they could retain their slave property. The 1667 law thereby built on the earlier one to define who would be a slave, and was clarified in 1670 and again in 1682, when the Assembly declared that any non-Christian brought into the colony, either by land or by sea, would be a slave for life, even if he or she later converted.

In 1691, colonial leaders provided a negative incentive to masters wishing to free their slaves by declaring that anyone who set free any "negro or mulatto" would be required to pay the costs of transporting the freedmen out of the colony within six months. Although manumissions still occurred and some free blacks managed to remain in the colony, the primary status for African Americans in Virginia was that of chattel.

Although who was to be a slave in Virginia had now been defined, it had yet to be determined precisely what being a slave meant on a daily basis for Africans and their descendants. Between 1661 and 1705, nearly twenty separate laws were passed limiting, defining, and prescribing the rights, status, and treatment of blacks. In general, these laws were designed to protect planters' slave property and to protect the order and stability of white society from an "alien and savage race."

The piecemeal establishment of slavery in these separate laws culminated in 1705 in a comprehensive slave code in Virginia. This code reenacted and strengthened a number of earlier slave laws, added further restrictions and harsher punishments, and permanently drew the color line that placed blacks at the bottom of Virginia society. Whites were prohibited from trading with, having sexual relations with, and marrying blacks. Blacks were forbidden to own Christian servants "except of their own complexion," leave their home plantation without a pass, own a gun or other weapon, or resist whites in any way.

Many of the harsher penalties for slave crimes, for example, the death penalty and maiming, were not carried out nearly as frequently as the laws suggest, because doing so would harm or destroy the master's property. Laws prohibiting slaves from trading or hiring themselves out were disregarded almost routinely. The disadvantage for slaves of this lack of enforcement was that laws prohibiting cruel treatment or defining acceptable levels of correction often were ignored as well. Where abuse was blatant, action against white offenders was taken only reluctantly, and punishments were insignificant and rare. Generally, laws in the economic and political interest of the white planter elite were enforced and respected; laws that restrained planters' pursuits were not.

Ohio and the Northwest Territory

The Northwest Territory was established in 1787 and ultimately became the states of Ohio, Indiana, Michigan, Illinois, and Wisconsin. In 1800, what was to become the state of Ohio separated from the rest of the territory. Two years later, Ohio elected delegates to a constitutional convention in preparation for a statehood petition, which was approved in 1803.

Although the Northwest Ordinance prohibited slavery in that territory, Ohio's constitutional convention debated the issue during its sessions. With the slaveholding states of Virginia on Ohio's eastern boundary and Kentucky on its southern boundary, there was considerable pressure for Ohio to recognize slavery. Many of the immigrants to Ohio came from slave states and saw nothing evil in the system. While many southern Ohioans did not object to slavery, persons in the northern part of the state were more likely to oppose it.

Delegates at the 1802 constitutional convention debated several questions that focused on African Americans. There was no strong feeling for instituting slavery in Ohio; there was, however, strong opinion in favor of limited rights for African Americans. After a major debate over allowing African Americans to vote, it was decided not to delete the word "white" from the qualifications for the franchise. Nevertheless, the African American population grew from five hundred in 1800 to nearly two thousand by 1810. In 1804, the legislature debated and passed the first of the "Black Laws," statutes intended to discourage African Americans from moving into Ohio and to encourage those already there to leave.

A few years later, an even stronger bill to restrict African Americans was presented in the Senate. In its final version, it forbade African Americans from settling in Ohio unless they could present a five-hundred-dollar bond and an affidavit signed by two white men that attested to their good character. Fines for helping a fugitive slave were doubled. Finally, no African American could testify against a white in court.

However restrictive the original Black Laws were, the new law was far worse. African Americans were stripped of legal protection and placed at the mercy of whites. Whites did not need to fear being tried for offenses against African Americans unless there was a white witness who would testify. There is evidence of at least one African American being murdered by whites, with only African American witnesses to the crime. African American witnesses could not provide evidence against a white assailant. Even if a case went to court, it would be heard by an all-white jury before a white judge. African American victims could not testify on their own behalf, because of the restrictions against providing testimony against whites. Because they could not vote, African Americans could neither change nor protest these laws.

While the Black Codes of 1804 and 1807 were enforced only infrequently, they still were the law and were a constant reminder that African Americans in Ohio had only the barest minimum of human and civil rights—and those rights existed only at the whim of white society. The laws fell into disuse and finally were repealed in 1849, long after the abolitionist movement, with its western center located in Oberlin, Ohio, was well under way, and long after the Underground Railroad had opened several stations in Ohio.

Laura A. Croghan and Duncan R. Jamieson

Core Resources

Joseph Boskin's *Into Slavery: Racial Decisions in the Virginia Colony* (Philadelphia: J. B. Lippincott, 1976) provides an account of the evolution of perpetual slavery and a representative selection of relevant primary documents. *In the Matter of Color: Race and the American Legal Process, the Colonial Period* (New York: Oxford University Press, 1978), by A. Leon Higginbotham, Jr., recounts the events culminating in the legal recognition of slavery in the British mainland colonies. Philip J. Schwartz's *Twice Condemned: Slaves and the Criminal Laws of Virginia, 1705-1865* (Baton Rouge: Louisiana State University Press, 1988) uses criminal trial records to examine slave resistance and whites' efforts to control threatening slave behavior. Robert B. Shaw's *A Legal History of Slavery in the United States* (Potsdam, N.Y.: Northern Press, 1991) illustrates the history of slavery in terms of its legislative and judicial background, from settlement through emancipation. Charles Jay Wilson's "The Negro in Early Ohio" (*Ohio Archeological and Historical Quarterly* 39, 1930) is the most complete analysis of Ohio's Black Laws.

See also: Abolition; Black codes; Fugitive slave laws; Missouri Compromise; Slavery: North American beginnings; Underground Railroad.

Slave rebellions

Slave rebellions were attempts by African slaves to resist oppression by the white, slave-owning population of

North America. In the southern United States, where the slave population was the greatest, blacks made up more than half of the population. In order to guarantee their way of life, white southern plantation owners used terror to control their slave populations. Despite the harsh treatment of African Americans, slaves developed a number of methods of resisting their masters' orders. Running away was always a popular alternative to work in the field and was punished through torture or, in repeat cases, amputation of a foot. Slaves also engaged in work slowdowns; slaves would purposely work more slowly or break and lose tools.

The most serious response to slavery, however, was the slave uprising. Despite harsh repression in most slave nations to discourage such occurrences, several slave uprisings occurred in the seventeenth, eighteenth, and early nineteenth centuries. Most slave revolts were unsuccessful and were met by extreme repression by armed whites fearing a takeover by black slaves. There were successful slave uprisings, however. One successful slave revolt, the Haitian Revolution, freed the French colony of Haiti and created the first nation of freed slaves in the Western Hemisphere.   *Jason Pasch*

See also: *Amistad* slave revolt; John Brown's raid; Slavery: history; Turner's slave insurrection.

Slavery and race relations

> **Significance:** The enslavement of people of African ancestry was closely connected to the development of both racial prejudice and racial inequality in the United States. The heritage of slavery prevented African Americans from entering into the mainstream of American life even after slavery was abolished. Debates over responsibility for slavery and the legacy of slavery have complicated relations between African Americans and whites.

One of the theoretical points debated by historians is whether Europeans and Euro-Americans imposed slavery on people from Africa because they viewed Africans as inferior or whether racism came into existence as a justification for slavery. Some historians have suggested that as Europeans expanded their control over much of the world, they came into contact with many who were unlike themselves in appearance and in culture. Ethnocentrism, the tendency to see one's own group as the standard by which all others are to be judged, may have led Europeans to see the people of Asia and Africa as inferior to themselves. Thus, people from China, as well as people from Africa, were brought to the Americas as forced labor at various times.

Historians such as George Frederickson, however, have maintained that racism was a consequence rather than a cause of slavery. From this point of view, the growth of plantation economies in North and South America encouraged the importation of slave labor because these economies required large numbers of workers. Native Americans did not make good slaves because they were in their homeland and could easily escape.

Slave owners needed to justify holding other humans in bondage, according to this theory, so they argued that their slaves were childlike and needed the protection of their masters. Thus, the influential apologist for slavery Henry Hughes argued in his *Treatise on Sociology* (1854) that the simple slaves as well as the masters benefited from the arrangement.

To some extent, the relationship between slavery and racism is similar to the ancient question of whether the chicken or the egg came first. The European enslavement of Africans was probably encouraged by feelings of European superiority. Once slavery became established, though, it was necessary to justify it, and the American descendants of Europeans could comfort themselves with claims that their slaves were inferior beings.

Many of the stereotypes of African Americans developed during slavery continued to flourish well into the twentieth century. The racism of slavery outlived slavery itself; films, radio programs, and books before the Civil Rights era often portrayed black Americans as childlike, comic, servile, or dangerously unable to control themselves. The sociologist Stanford M. Lyman has observed that popular American films ranging from *Birth of a Nation* (1915) to *Gone with the Wind* (1939) drew on the racial images of slavery to portray "good" blacks as humorous, loyal, obedient family servants and "bad" blacks as rebellious and violent.

Consequences of Master-Slave Relations

Economist Raymond S. Franklin has noted that one of the debates regarding consequences of master-slave relations concerns whether slaves and their descendants were in some way damaged by being owned and controlled. A number of historians, including Kenneth Stampp, Stanley Elkins, and William Styron, have held that being slaves left psychological scars on the slaves and damaged social institutions that slaves passed on to free black Americans. Along these lines, in 1966, Daniel Patrick Moynihan published a controversial report on the black family, in which he maintained that the experience of slavery contributed to the weakness of the black family. More recently, Harvard sociologist Orlando Patterson has claimed that the slave status undermined the roles of husband and father for black men and reinforced the central role of women in families.

A freed slave reaches his arms out toward his emancipator, Abraham Lincoln. Many of the master-slave relationships survived emancipation, sometimes taking the form of landowner-sharecropper or master-servant.

1860, on the eve of the Civil War, 94 percent of the people of African ancestry in the United States were concentrated in the slave-owning states of the South. This percentage did decline notably in the years following World War I, and the descendants of slaves did move to other regions over the course of the twentieth century. Nevertheless, at the end of the century, the geographical legacy of slavery was still evident; the 1990 U.S. census showed a majority of the American black population residing in the South.

In many areas of the South, working as sharecroppers or low-paid wage laborers during the years following slavery, African Americans continued to do much the same sort of agricultural labor that they had performed as slaves. In order to maintain white domination, in regions with large black populations, southern whites sought to replace slavery with segregation, which placed blacks in a separate and disadvantaged position. This kept African Americans dependent on whites and subservient to whites in a manner that was similar in many ways to the old master-slave relationship. These patterns may have even survived the years following the Civil Rights movement. As recently as the 1990's, sociologist Ruth Kornfield, looking at a rural community in Tennessee, found that patron-client relationships between white employers and black employees continued to mirror master-slave relationships.

The continuing concentration of African Americans in the South was one of the reasons that early actions of the Civil Rights movement concentrated primarily on this region. Despite the stubborn survival of many old patterns of racial inequality in this region, numbers have given African Americans in this part of the country some measure of power. In 1993, two-thirds of the black-elected officials in the United States were from the southern states. Furthermore, the major southern cities of Atlanta, Georgia; New Orleans, Louisiana; Birmingham, Alabama; and Richmond, Virginia, all had black mayors.

The Legacy of Slavery and Urbanization

Although the South did not cease to be home to the largest proportion of African Americans, the group did shift from being heavily rural to being heavily urban. Over the course of the twentieth century, the agricultural jobs that black Americans continued to perform after slavery became increasingly unavailable as farms mechanized. In the years following World War II, African Americans moved to cities. They tended to settle in central urban areas because the U.S. government built housing projects reserved for the poor in these urban areas, and the heritage of slavery and of the system of segregation that had emerged from slavery left African Americans disproportionately poor. During the same

Franklin observes that some historians and social thinkers have argued that the master-slave relationship actually strengthened many black social institutions by promoting the need to resist slavery. Historian Herbert Gutman, for example, offered evidence that slavery had actually strengthened black families. The historian Eric Foner has traced the origins of the black church, a central institution in African American history, to the religious activities of slaves who organized themselves into churches after emancipation.

Geographical Consequences of Slavery

Slaves were heavily concentrated in the southern part of the United States. Even after the end of slavery, African Americans continued to be a southern population. In years, whites were moving from cities to suburbs. Racism, an ideology with roots in America's centuries of slavery, contributed to the unwillingness of homeowners, real estate companies, and mortgage lenders to allow blacks to move into homes in the suburbs.

As a result of the movement of whites to suburbs and African Americans to cities, the two groups came to live in separate places. Although schools and other public facilities ceased to be legally segregated after the 1960's, many urban neighborhoods and schools contained virtually no whites. This not only limited contact between members of the different races, but it also separated African Americans from the jobs and opportunities that became much more abundant in the suburbs. Further,

even after it became easier for middle-class blacks to move into suburban neighborhoods, the poorest were left isolated in inner cities.

Questions of Responsibility

Professor and social commentator Shelby Steele has observed that the question of innocence is central to race relations in the United States. Many African Americans maintain that they are innocent victims of the aftermath of slavery. The problem of race relations, from this perspective, is one of achieving equality of condition for people who suffer disadvantages as a group through no fault of their own.

White Americans also frequently put forward claims of innocence. They maintain that white people alive at the end of the twentieth century, well more than a century after the end of slavery, cannot be held responsible for the legacy of slavery. Therefore, programs such as affirmative action that aim at increasing African Americans' share of positions in employment and education seek to benefit the descendants of slaves at the expense of whites who are innocent of responsibility for slavery. In discussing issues of historical responsibility, whites will often become defensive, and any assertions of black disadvantage will sometimes be seen by whites as moral accusations.

Reparations

The issue of reparations is one of the most controversial consequences of the thorny ethical issue of historical responsibility. The term "reparations" refers to compensation paid by one nation or group of people to another for damages or losses. The United States government, for example, has made some payments to Japanese Americans for violating their civil rights by imprisoning them during World War II.

Advocates of reparation payments for African Americans, such as the scholar Manning Marable, have argued that slavery was a massive denial of civil rights to this group. These advocates point out that slave labor built up much of the nation's wealth, allowing it to industrialize and therefore making it possible for the United

African Americans Living in the Former Slave States of the South, 1860-1990

(as percentage of all African Americans)

Year	Percentage
1860	94.2
1870	92.1
1880	91.8
1890	91.0
1900	89.9
1910	89.0
1920	79.4
1930	73.6
1940	77.0
1950	68.0
1960	60.3
1970	53.0
1980	53.0
1990	52.8

Percentage

Source: U.S. Census of Population and Housing, 1860-1990.

States to achieve its current level of development. They point out that the descendants of slaves continue to suffer damages from slavery because African Americans have lower incomes, on average, than other Americans and tend to hold much less of the country's wealth.

Opponents of reparations maintain that while slavery is a historical source of contemporary disadvantages of African Americans, reparations would attempt to right a past injustice by penalizing present-day whites. Further, if reparations were paid to all African Americans, some rich African Americans would be receiving tax money taken from middle-class or even poor whites. Finally, opponents of reparations suggest that payments of this sort would be enormously unpopular politically and might increase racial hatred and conflict.

Carl L. Bankston III

Core Resources

George M. Frederickson's *White Supremacy: A Comparative Study in American and South African History* (New York: Oxford University Press, 1981) is a classic work on the development of racism and racial exploitation. The second chapter of Raymond S. Franklin's *Shadows of Race and Class* (Minneapolis: University of Minnesota Press, 1991) gives an excellent summary of major debates regarding the legacy of slavery. Ira Berlin's *Many Thousands Gone: The First Two Centuries of Slavery in North America* (Cambridge, Mass.: Belknap Press, 1998) is a comprehensive study of the history of American slavery and of how slavery shaped racial identities. Edward Ball considers the impact of slavery both on his own family of former slave owners and on the descendants of his family's slaves in *Slaves in the Family* (New York: Farrar, Straus & Giroux, 1998). The last work looks not only at the lingering resentment and suspicion toward local whites of the descendants of the slaves but also at the feelings of ill-defined guilt and defensiveness among the descendants of the slave owners. Clarence J. Munford gives arguments for the payment of reparations for slavery to African Americans in *Race and Reparations: A Black Perspective for the Twenty-first Century* (Trenton, N.J.: Africa World Press, 1996). On the other hand, Dinesh D'Souza's highly controversial book *The End of Racism: Principles for a Multiracial Society* (New York: Free Press, 1995) claims that whites bear no responsibility at all for contemporary racial inequality. D'Souza also denies that the history of slavery gives African Americans any moral claims as a group.

See also: African American stereotypes; Black conservatism; Great Migration; Moynihan Report; National Coalition of Blacks for Reparations in America; Slavery and the justice system; Slavery: history; Slavery: North American beginnings; White flight.

Slavery and the justice system

> **Significance:** Slavery defined the legal treatment of African Americans for two and one-half centuries, and the crusade against slavery gave rise to modern concepts of citizenship and civil rights.

The first African laborers in the English colonies of North America arrived in Virginia in 1619. By the 1770's, slaves made up one-fifth of the population of the English colonies. At this time, slave labor was used in every colony, including those in the North. Only in the South, however, did slavery dominate economic life. Slaves were used primarily to grow staple crops such as tobacco and rice for exportation to Europe and the Caribbean.

Slavery and the Territories

As Americans moved westward, the issue of whether slavery should expand into the new territories became increasingly important. Americans realized that new western states would determine the balance of political power between North and South. Congress initially divided the new territories between North and South. In the Northwest Ordinance (1787), Congress banned slavery in the lands north of the Ohio River while implicitly accepting slavery south of the Ohio. In regard to the Louisiana Purchase, the Missouri Compromise of 1820 banned slavery north of the line 36° 30′ latitude while allowing slavery to exist south of the line.

The Missouri Compromise resolved the issue of slavery in the territories until the Mexican-American War of 1846-1848 added new western lands to the United States. Subsequently, four positions emerged regarding the issue. Many northerners favored the Wilmot Proviso, a proposal to ban slavery in the territories. Other Americans favored popular sovereignty, which would allow the people of the territories to decide the issue for themselves. Some Americans favored extending the Missouri Compromise line to the Pacific coast. Many southerners believed the federal government should protect slavery in the territories.

In the 1850's, the popular sovereignty approach gained ascendancy. The Compromise of 1850 applied popular sovereignty to California, New Mexico, and Utah. The Kansas-Nebraska Act (1854) repealed the old Missouri Compromise boundary and enacted popular sovereignty for the Louisiana Purchase. The Kansas-Nebraska Act created such great controversy that the existing political alignment was shattered. Opponents of the act created a new antislavery political party, the Republican Party, while supporters of the act reconstructed the Democratic Party as a proslavery party.

Disagreements regarding slavery-related issues and sectional competition for political power led ultimately to the outbreak of the Civil War in 1861. During the war, northern military officials increasingly believed that freeing the South's slaves would severely injure the Confederacy. President Abraham Lincoln issued the Emancipation Proclamation in 1863, proclaiming that the Union Army would henceforth liberate the Confederacy's slaves. In 1865, the Thirteenth Amendment to the U.S. Constitution freed all remaining slaves belonging to American citizens.

Slavery and the U.S. Constitution

Slavery significantly influenced the writing of the U.S. Constitution. The Constitutional Convention of 1787 nearly broke up because of disagreements regarding sectional issues. Ultimately the sectional impasse was resolved with the Compromise of 1787. Direct taxes and representation in the House of Representatives were to be apportioned according to the three-fifths rule: All free people and three-fifths of the slaves were to be counted in determining a state's tax burden and congressional representation. Congress could prohibit the importation of slaves into the United States after the lapse of twenty years. States were prohibited from freeing fugitive slaves, and slaveholders were given the right to cross state boundaries to recapture fugitives. Congress was prevented from taxing exports so that slavery would not be injured by excessive taxes on the products of slave labor. Finally, to ensure that the compromise would not be abrogated, the clauses regarding the international slave trade and the three-fifths rule were declared by the Constitution to be unamendable.

As the Civil War approached, Americans debated the significance of these actions. What was the relationship between the U.S. Constitution and slavery? Before 1860, most Americans believed that the Constitution did not establish a federal right to own slaves. Slavery was thought to exist as a result of state laws, and the federal government was thought to have few constitutional powers regarding slavery. Northerners and southerners disagreed regarding the practical application of this idea. Southerners believed the federal government was increasingly intruding into matters related to slavery. They called for an end to federal interference with slavery. Northerners argued that the federal government had been indirectly providing protection to slavery for years. They called for the withdrawal of this protection.

In the 1840's and 1850's, militants on both sides developed new constitutional theories regarding slavery. Some southerners claimed that there was a federal right to own slaves, established in the fugitive slave clause and the privileges and immunities clause of the U.S. Constitution. The federal government, they said, must protect the right of citizens to own slaves in the territories. Some southern extremists argued that the federal right to own slaves was so comprehensive that even northern states could not outlaw slavery within their own boundaries. Ironically, the branch of the abolitionist movement led by William Lloyd Garrison agreed with this argument, claiming that the Constitution protected slavery and arguing that northern states should abandon this corrupt document by withdrawing from the Union.

Another branch of the abolitionist movement, led by Gerrit Smith and William Goodell, argued to the contrary that the Constitution was best read as an antislavery document. They claimed that citizenship was based on residence in the United States and that slaves therefore were citizens. The privileges and immunities clause of the Constitution, they claimed, prevented both the states and the federal government from giving unequal treatment to citizens. The due process clause of the Fifth Amendment prevented citizens from losing their liberty without due process of law. Slavery violated these principles, and judges therefore ought to declare slavery unconstitutional. While this interpretation of the Constitution seemed extreme and utopian at the time, after the Civil War, the abolitionists' constitutional ideas were incorporated into the Fourteenth Amendment.

Fugitive Slave Laws

One of the most significant controversies regarding slavery involved fugitive slave laws. In 1793, Congress adopted legislation to enforce the fugitive slave clause of the U.S. Constitution. The Fugitive Slave Act of 1793 allowed slaveholders to obtain warrants from either state or federal courts for the rendition of fugitive slaves. In the 1820's and 1830's, several states passed personal liberty laws to prevent state officials from assisting in the recapture process. In *Prigg v. Pennsylvania* (1842), the U.S. Supreme Court upheld the constitutionality of personal liberty laws by ruling that the enforcement of fugitive slave laws rested entirely in the hands of the federal government.

Without the assistance of state officials, slaveholders found that it was difficult to recapture their slaves. Southerners clamored for federal assistance. Congress responded by passing a new Fugitive Slave Act as a part of the Compromise of 1850. A new group of federal officials was created for the sole purpose of assisting slaveholders recapture slaves. State officials were forbidden to resist the rendition of fugitives. Even ordinary citizens could be compelled to serve in posses for the purpose of capturing fugitives. To prevent blacks who were seized as fugitives from challenging their seizure, their legal rights, including the right of *habeas corpus*, were abolished.

The Fugitive Slave Act of 1850 was met with strong opposition in the North. Hundreds of fugitives, and even some free blacks, migrated to Canada to avoid seizure under the new law. Many northern communities formed vigilance committees to assist fugitives, and in a few cases northern mobs tried to rescue fugitives from the hands of government officials.

One rescue in 1854 led to a conflict between Wisconsin and the federal government. This case is notable because Wisconsin, a northern state, used states' rights arguments to challenge federal authority, a ploy normally used by southerners to defend slavery. Sherman M. Booth, an abolitionist, was arrested by federal marshals for participating in the rescue of a fugitive slave. The Wisconsin State Supreme Court twice issued writs of *habeas corpus* to free Booth from federal imprisonment and declared the federal Fugitive Slave Act to be unconstitutional. The U.S. Supreme Court in *Ableman v. Booth* (1859) reasserted the primacy of federal over state law and the right of the federal government to enforce its own laws through its own courts. The Wisconsin court accepted this decision, now believing that it did not help the antislavery cause to promote the idea of states' rights and nullification of federal law.

Legal Treatment of Slaves

African laborers occupied an ambiguous status in the American colonies before 1660 because English law did not recognize the status of slavery. Some Africans were held as slaves; others were held as indentured servants, persons whose term of labor expired after several years. Indentured servants enjoyed certain additional legal protections since, unlike slaves, their physical bodies were not owned by their masters. After 1660, Virginia and Maryland constructed elaborate slave codes to establish the legal status of slavery. For the next two centuries, the vast majority of blacks in America were slaves.

In making and enforcing slave codes, Americans recognized slaves as both people and property. As property, slaves generally had few legal rights as independent beings. Slaves could not own property, enter into contracts, sue or be sued, or marry legally. Slaves had no freedom of movement. Masters could sell their slaves without restriction, and there was no legal protection for slave families against forced separation through sale. The status of slave children was inherited from their mothers, a departure from the traditional common-law doctrine that children inherited the status of their fathers.

In some ways, the masters' property rights in slaves were limited by compelling public interest. Most southern states made it difficult for masters to free their slaves on the theory that free blacks were a nuisance to society. Most southern states also tried to prevent slaves from becoming a threat to society. State laws often required slaves to carry passes when traveling away from their masters' homes. Laws in several states prohibited slaves from living alone without the supervision of whites. In all but two states, it was illegal for anyone to teach slaves to read or write. Some states banned the use of alcohol and firearms by slaves; others outlawed trading and gambling by slaves. Although these laws were primarily a burden to the slave population, they also restricted the manner in which masters could manage and use their property.

Southern law codes occasionally recognized slaves as people as well as property. By the mid-nineteenth century, most states provided slaves with a minimal degree of protection against physical assaults by whites, although these laws were generally poorly enforced. All states outlawed the murder and harsh treatment of slaves. Although masters were occasionally put on trial for murder of their slaves, evidence suggests that most homicidal masters either received light sentences or were not punished. Laws protecting slaves against other forms of inhumane treatment (such as excessive beatings or starvation diets) were almost never enforced. In practice, masters could beat or starve their slaves with impunity. Battery of slaves by strangers was illegal and was often punished by southern courts. Rape of slaves by whites, however, was not illegal. Masters had the full legal right to rape their own slaves, although masters could charge other whites with criminal trespass for an act of rape without the master's permission.

Under the law, blacks were assumed to be slaves unless they could prove otherwise, meaning that free blacks were forced always to carry legal documents certifying their freedom. Many actions, including the use of alcohol and firearms, were illegal for slaves but not for whites. Penalties for crimes were generally more severe for slaves than for whites. For slaves, capital crimes—those for which death was the penalty—included not only murder but also manslaughter, rape, arson, insurrection, and robbery. Even attempted murders, insurrections, and rapes were subject to the death penalty.

Despite the harshness of the law, actual executions of slaves were rare because even slave criminals were valuable property. State laws generally required governments to pay compensation to the masters of executed slaves. The fact that the labor of slaves was valuable meant that, in all states except Louisiana, imprisonment was rarely used as punishment for slave criminals. Instead, most penalties involved physical punishments such as whipping, branding, or ear-cropping, punishments which were rarely used against whites after the early nineteenth century. While southern courts did not give blacks and whites equal treatment, the courts made some effort to be fair to slaves, probably because of the influence of wealthy slaveholders with an economic interest in the acquittal of their property. The proportion of slaves among those people accused of crime was about equal to the proportion of slaves in the population. Slaves appear to have been convicted at nearly the same rate as whites. Southern law codes also reflected the slaveholders' interests. Many states required that slaves have access to counsel and protected them against self-incrimination and double jeopardy. Slaves, however, could not testify in court against whites, meaning that it was nearly impossible to prosecute crimes against slaves when blacks were the only available witnesses. *Harold D. Tallant*

Core Resources

The most readable and comprehensive survey of slavery and the law is Harold M. Hyman and William M. Wiecek's *Equal Justice Under Law: Constitutional Development, 1835-1875* (New York: Harper & Row, 1982). Alan Watson's *Slave Law in the Americas* (Athens: University of Georgia Press, 1989) offers a succinct comparison of the law of slavery in several Western Hemisphere societies. Mark V. Tushnet's *The American Law of Slavery, 1810-1860: Considerations of Humanity and Interest* (Princeton, N.J.: Princeton University Press, 1981) discusses the tension within American law regarding the slaves' dual role as both property and people. The best survey of the legal treatment of slaves is Philip J. Schwarz's *Twice Condemned: Slaves and the Criminal Laws of Virginia, 1705-1865* (Baton Rouge: Louisiana State University Press, 1988).

See also: Abolition; Emancipation Proclamation; Free-Soil Party; Fugitive slave laws; Kansas-Nebraska Act; Missouri Compromise; Reconstruction; *Scott v. Sandford*; Slave codes.

Slavery: history

> **Significance:** Slavery has historically constituted a significant denial of human rights and, as practiced in the United States, laid the foundations for conflict between whites and blacks for generations to come.

Slavery is one of the oldest institutions of human society. Slavery was present in the earliest human civilizations, those of ancient Mesopotamia and Egypt, and continued to exist in several parts of the world through the late twentieth century.

Definitions

Despite the near universality of slavery, there is no consensus regarding what distinctive practices constitute slavery. In Western society, a slave typically was a person who was owned as property by another person and forced to perform labor for the owner. This definition, however, breaks down when applied to non-Western forms of slavery. In some African societies, slaves were not owned as property by an individual but were thought of as belonging to a kinship group. The slave could be sold, but so too could nonslave members of the kinship group. In certain African societies, slaves were exempted from labor and were used solely to bring honor to the master by demonstrating his absolute power over another person.

The sociologist Orlando Patterson suggested that slavery is best understood as an institution designed to increase the power of the master or the ruling group. Slaves can fulfill this role by laboring to make the master rich, but they can also do so by bringing honor to the master. One of the defining, universal characteristics of slavery is that the slave ceases to exist as a socially meaningful person. The slave relates to society only through the master. Slavery includes many mechanisms to remove the slave from membership in any groups, such as the family, through which the slave might derive an independent sense of identity. By placing the master in a dominant position over another individual, slavery is believed to increase the honor and power of the master. The slave's status is permanent and it is typically passed down to the slave's children.

History

The use of slavery was widespread in the ancient world, especially in Greece and Italy. During the classical ages of Greek and Roman society, slaves constituted about one-third of the population. Following the collapse of the Roman Empire in Western Europe during the fifth and sixth centuries, declining economic conditions destroyed the profitability of slavery and provided employers with large numbers of impoverished peasants who could be employed more cheaply than slaves. Over the next seven hundred years, slavery slowly gave way to serfdom. Although serfs, like slaves, were unfree laborers, serfs generally had more legal rights and a higher social standing than slaves.

Familiarity with the institution of slavery did not, however, disappear in Western Europe. A trickle of slaves from Eastern Europe and even from Africa continued to flow into England, France, and Germany. Western Europeans retained their familiarity with large-scale slave systems through contacts with southern Italy, Spain, and Portugal, and with the Byzantine Empire and the Muslim world, where slavery flourished. Western Europeans also inherited from their Roman forebears the corpus of Roman law, with its elaborate slave code. During the later Middle Ages, Europeans who were familiar with Muslim sugar plantations in the Near East sought to begin sugar production with slave labor on the islands of the Mediterranean.

Thus, as Western Europe entered the age of exploration and colonization, Europeans had an intimate knowledge of slavery and a ready-made code of laws to govern slaves. During the sixteenth century, as European nations sought to establish silver mines and sugar plantations in their new colonies in the Western Hemisphere, heavy labor demands led to efforts to enslave Native Americans. This supply of laborers was inadequate because of the rapid decline of the Indian population following the introduction of European diseases into the Western Hemisphere. The Spanish and Portuguese then turned to Africa, the next most readily available source of slave laborers. Between 1500 and 1900, European slave traders imported 9.7 million African laborers into the Western Hemisphere. Every European colony eventually used slave labor, which became the principal form of labor in the Western Hemisphere. Because the wealth of several modern nations was created by slave labor, some contemporary African Americans have claimed the right to receive reparations payments from nations such as the United States, which continue to enjoy the wealth accumulated originally by the use of slave laborers.

Slavery and Race

The large-scale use of African slaves by European masters raised new moral issues regarding race. There is no necessary connection between slavery and race. A massive survey by Orlando Patterson of slave societies throughout history found that in three-quarters of slave societies, masters and slaves were of the same race. Slavery in the Western Hemisphere was unusual in human history because slaves were drawn almost exclusively from the black race.

In most colonies of the Western Hemisphere, the use of African slaves was accompanied by the rise of racism, which some scholars claim was a new, unprecedented

African slaves work in rice cultivation near Savannah, Georgia, in the nineteenth century.

phenomenon caused by slavery. Scholars seeking to understand contemporary race relations in the United States have been intrigued by the rise of prejudice in new slave societies. Did Europeans enslave Africans merely because they needed slaves and Africa was the most accessible source of slaves? If so, then prejudice probably originated as a learned association between race and subservience. Modern prejudice might be broken down through integration and affirmative action programs aimed at helping whites to witness the success of blacks in positions of authority. Did Europeans enslave Africans because the Europeans saw Africans as inferior persons ideally suited for slavery? If so, then contemporary racism is a deeply rooted cultural phenomenon that is not likely to disappear for generations to come. African Americans will receive justice only if the government establishes permanent compensatory programs aimed at equalizing power between the races.

Historical research has not resolved these issues. Sixteenth century Europeans apparently did view Africans as inferior beings, even before the colonization of the Western Hemisphere. These racial antipathies were minor, however, in comparison to modern racism. Emancipated slaves in recently settled colonies experienced little racial discrimination. The experience of slavery apparently increased the European settlers' sense of racial superiority over Africans.

After the slave systems of the Western Hemisphere became fully developed, racial arguments became the foundation of the proslavery argument. Supporters of slavery claimed that persons of African descent were so degraded and inferior to whites that it would be dangerous for society to release the slaves from the control of a master. In the United States, some proslavery theorists pushed the racial argument to extreme levels. In explaining the contradiction between slavery and the American ideal that all persons should be free, writers such as Josiah Nott and Samuel Cartwright claimed that blacks were not fully human and, therefore, did not deserve all the rights belonging to humanity.

A minority of proslavery writers rejected the racial argument and the effort to reconcile slavery and American egalitarian ideals. Writers such as George Fitzhugh claimed that all societies were organized hierarchically by classes and that slavery was the most benevolent system for organizing an unequal class structure. Slavery bound together masters and slaves through a system of mutual rights and obligations. Unlike the "wage slaves" of industrial society, chattel slaves had certain access to food, clothing, shelter, and medical care, all because the master's ownership of the slaves' bodies made him diligent in caring for his property. Slavery was depicted by some proslavery theorists as the ideal condition for the white working class.

The Antislavery Movement

From the dawning of human history until the middle of the eighteenth century, few persons appear to have questioned the morality of slavery as an institution. Although some persons had earlier raised moral objections to certain features of slavery, almost no one appears to have questioned the overall morality of slavery as a system before the middle of the eighteenth century. Around 1750, however, an antislavery movement began to appear in Britain, France, and America.

The sudden rise of antislavery opinion appears to be related to the rise of a humanitarian ethos during the Enlightenment that encouraged people to consider the welfare of humans beyond their kin groups. The rise of the antislavery movement was also related to the growing popularity of new forms of evangelical and pietistic religious sects such as the Baptists, Methodists, and Quakers, which tended to view slaveholding as sinful materialism and slaves as persons worthy of God's love. The rise of the antislavery movement was encouraged by the American and French Revolutions, whose democratic political philosophies promoted a belief in the equality of individuals. The rise of antislavery opinion also coincided in time with the rise of industrial capitalism. The historian Eric Williams argued in *Capitalism and Slavery* (1944) that the economic and class interests of industrial capitalists rather than the moral scruples of humanitarians gave rise to the antislavery movement.

Antislavery activism initially focused on the abolition of the Atlantic slave trade. Reformers succeeded in prompting Britain and the United States to abolish the slave trade in 1807. Other nations followed this lead over the next half century until the Atlantic slave trade was virtually eliminated.

The campaign to abolish the slave trade achieved early success because it joined together moral concerns and self-interest. Many persons in the late eighteenth and early nineteenth centuries were prepared to accept the end of the slave trade while opposing the end of slavery itself. Even slaveholders were angered by the living conditions endured by slaves on crowded, disease-infested slave ships. Some masters, in fact, attempted to justify their ownership of slaves by claiming that the conditions on their plantations were more humane than the conditions on slave-trading ships or in allegedly primitive Africa. Some slaveholders supported the abolition of the slave trade because they realized that limiting the supply of new slaves from Africa would increase the value of the existing slave population. Finally, many persons believed that it was wrong for slave traders to deny liberty to freeborn Africans, but that it was not wrong for slave masters to exercise control over persons who were born into the status of slavery. Indeed, supporters of slavery argued that the well-being of society required masters to exercise control over persons who had no preparation for freedom and might be a threat to society if emancipated.

The campaign to eradicate slavery itself was more difficult and was accompanied by significant political upheavals and, in the case of Haiti and the United States, revolution and warfare. British reformers such as William Wilberforce, Thomas Clarkson, and Granville Sharp made, perhaps, the most significant contributions to the organization of a worldwide antislavery movement. In 1823, British activists formed the London Antislavery Committee, soon to be renamed the British and Foreign Antislavery Society. The society spearheaded a successful campaign to abolish slavery in the British Empire and, eventually, worldwide. It remained in existence in the 1990's. Known by the name Antislavery International, the society had the distinction of being the world's oldest human rights organization. Antislavery reformers were also active in the United States. From the 1830's through the 1860's, abolitionists such as William Lloyd Garrison, Wendell Phillips, and Frederick Douglass sought to arouse the moral anger of Americans against slavery. More effective, however, were politicians such as Abraham Lincoln, Charles Sumner, and Salmon P. Chase, whose antislavery message was a mixture of idealism, self-interest, and expedience.

Emancipation of Slaves

Beginning in the late eighteenth century and accelerating through the nineteenth century, slavery was abolished throughout the Western Hemisphere. This was followed in the late nineteenth and twentieth centuries by the legal abolition of slavery in Africa and Asia.

In evaluating the success of abolition in any society, it is necessary to distinguish between legal and de facto emancipation. Changing the legal status of a slave to that of a free person is not the same thing as freeing the slave from the control of a master. Legal emancipation often has little impact on persons held as slaves if governments fail to enforce the abolition of slavery. For example, Britain in the nineteenth century outlawed slavery in its colonies in India, the Gold Coast, Kenya, and Zanzibar. Yet, fearing a disruption of economic production in these colonies, the British government simply abstained from enforcing its own abolition laws until pressure from reformers put an end to slavery. A similar situation existed in Mauritania, where slavery was prohibited by law three separate times, in 1905, 1960, and 1980, yet the government of Mauritania enacted no penalties against masters who kept slaves in violation of the emancipation law, and the government waged no campaign to inform the slaves of their freedom. As a result, journalists and investigators for the International Labor Organisation found slavery still flourishing in Mauritania in the 1990's.

Dates of Legal Emancipation in the United States

State	Year
Alabama	1863-1865
Arkansas	1863-1865
California	1850
Connecticut	1784
Delaware	1865
Florida	1863-1865
Georgia	1863-1865
Illinois	1787
Indiana	1787
Iowa	1820
Kansas	1861
Kentucky	1865
Louisiana	1864
Maine	1783
Maryland	1864
Massachusetts	1783
Michigan	1787
Minnesota	1858
Mississippi	1863-1865
Missouri	1865
New Hampshire	1783
New Jersey	1804
New York	1799
North Carolina	1863-1865
Ohio	1787
Oklahoma	1866
Oregon	1846
Pennsylvania	1780
Rhode Island	1784
South Carolina	1863-1865
Tennessee	1865
Texas	1863-1865
Vermont	1777
Virginia	1863-1865
Washington, D.C.	1862
West Virginia	1863
Western Territories	1862
Wisconsin	1787

Even in societies that vigorously enforced their acts of abolition, legal emancipation was usually followed by a period of transition in which former slaves were held in a state resembling that of slavery. The Abolition of Slavery Act of 1833, which outlawed slavery in most colonies of the British Empire, provided that slaves would serve as apprentices to their former masters for a period of four to six years. In the American South after the Civil War, former slaves were subject for a time to black codes that greatly reduced the freedom of movement of African Americans and required them to work on the plantations of former slave masters. After the Civil Rights Act of 1866 and the Fourteenth Amendment outlawed such practices, southerners created the sharecropping and crop-lien systems, which allowed planters to control the labor of many blacks through a form of debt bondage.

The efforts of former masters to control the labor of former slaves were a part of a larger effort by postemancipation societies to determine what rights freedpeople should exercise. In the United States, for instance, emancipation raised many questions regarding the general rights of citizens, the answers to which often remained elusive more than a century after the abolition of slavery. Should freedpeople be considered citizens with basic rights equal to other citizens? How far should equality of citizenship rights extend? Should equality of rights be kept at a minimum level, perhaps limited to freedom of movement, the right to own property, and the right to make contracts and enforce them in a court of law? Should citizenship rights be extended to the political realm, with guarantees of the right to vote, serve on juries, and hold political office? Should citizenship rights be extended to the social realm, with the protection for the right to live wherever one wanted, to use public spaces without discrimination, and to marry persons of another race?

Antislavery and Imperialism

Ironically, the international effort to abolish slavery raised troubling new moral issues. During the last quarter of the nineteenth century, in the name of suppressing the African slave trade at its source, Britain and other European nations demanded of African rulers certain police powers within African kingdoms. The Europeans also organized new African industries to encourage the shift from the slave trade to the "legitimate trade" in other commodities. In this manner, the humanitarian impulse of antislavery combined with less humane motives to produce the New Imperialism of the 1880's through the 1910's. During this thirty-year period, nearly all of Africa fell under European domination. Time and again, the campaign to suppress the slave trade became a cloak for the imperialist ambitions of the European powers. It is worth remembering that the two international conferences in which the European powers agreed to carve up Africa among themselves, the Berlin Conference of 1884-1885 and the Brussels Conference of 1889-1890, both devised significant agreements for ending the African slave trade.

Slavery in the Contemporary World

In the twentieth century, most Westerners believed slavery to be nothing more than a memory of the past. Major international treaties such as the Slavery Convention of the League of Nations (1926), the Universal Declaration on Human Rights (1948), and the United Nations (U.N.) Supplementary Convention on the Abolition of Slavery (1956) seemed to indicate the emergence of an international consensus that slavery in all its forms should be eradicated. In reality, throughout the twentieth century, new forms of slavery continued to appear. The U.N. Supplementary Convention defined debt bondage, serfdom, bridewealth (bride price), and child labor as modern forms of slavery. Many persons considered the use of compulsory labor by authoritarian regimes such as those of Nazi Germany and the Soviet Union to be a form of slavery.

International cooperation toward ending slavery in the twentieth century sometimes faltered because of Cold War rivalries. Communist states were often hostile to the antislavery work of the United Nations because Westerners sought to define the compulsory labor systems in several communist states as a form of slavery. The Soviets, likewise, charged that the wage system of capitalist countries constituted a type of slavery, since the wage system compelled people to work in jobs they did not like out of fear of starvation.

On the eve of the twenty-first century, investigations by international human rights organizations and by journalists found that millions of people still served as slaves in Haiti, the Dominican Republic, Brazil, Peru, Sudan, South Africa, Mauritania, Kuwait, Pakistan, India, Bangladesh, Thailand, and China. Even in countries such as the United States, where slavery had long been actively suppressed by the government, isolated cases of the enslavement of workers occasionally came to light with regard to migrant farmworkers and illegal aliens.

Harold D. Tallant

Core Resources

The Antislavery Debate: Capitalism and Abolitionism as a Problem in Historical Interpretation (Berkeley: University of California Press, 1992), edited by Thomas Bender, is a collection of essays that debate the question of whether the rise of industrial capitalism caused the emergence of the antislavery movement. David Brion Davis's *The Problem of Slavery in the Age of Revolution, 1770-1823* (Ithaca, N.Y.: Cornell University Press, 1975) is a Pulitzer Prizewinning study of the intellectual background of the rise of the antislavery movement. Davis's *Slavery and Human Progress* (New York: Oxford University Press, 1984) is an excellent introduction to many of the ethical issues regarding slavery organized around a discussion of changing concepts of progress. Moses I. Finley's *Ancient Slavery and Modern Ideology* (New York: Viking Press, 1980) is a study of the moral, intellectual, and social foundations of slavery by the leading expert on ancient slavery. Eric Foner's *Nothing But Freedom: Emancipation and Its Legacy* (Baton Rouge: Louisiana State University

Press, 1983) is a brief but thought-provoking study of the problems associated with emancipation in several countries. Orlando Patterson's *Slavery and Social Death: A Comparative Study* (Cambridge, Mass.: Harvard University Press, 1982), the most important study of slavery in its various forms, is based on a massive survey of slave societies on all continents from the beginning of history. William D. Phillips's *Slavery from Roman Times to the Early Transatlantic Trade* (Minneapolis: University of Minnesota Press, 1985) is a highly readable historical survey of the transition from ancient slavery to modern slavery.

See also: Abolition; Civil rights; Emancipation Proclamation; Racism: history of the concept; Slavery and race relations; Slavery: North American beginnings.

Slavery: North American beginnings

> **Significance:** The establishment of institutionalized slavery in the British colonies of North America would have untold consequences for the history of the continent.

In August of 1619, a Dutch warship carrying "20 and odd" Africans landed at Point Comfort, Virginia. These Africans, the first to arrive in the British colonies, were probably put to work not as slaves but as servants. Neither the laws of the mother country nor the charter of the colony established the institution of slavery, although the system was developing in the British West Indies at the same time and was almost one hundred years old in the Spanish and Portuguese colonies. To be sure, African servants were discriminated against early on—their terms of service were usually longer than those of white servants, and they were the object of certain prohibitions that were not imposed on white servants—but in the early seventeenth century, at least some black servants, like their white counterparts, gained their freedom and even acquired some property. Anthony Johnson, who labored on Richard Bennett's Virginia plantation for almost twenty years after he arrived in Virginia in 1621, imported five servants in his first decade of freedom, receiving 250 acres on their headrights. Another former servant, Richard Johnson, obtained one hundred acres for importing two white servants in 1654. These two men were part of the small class of free blacks that existed in Virginia throughout the colonial period.

Such cases as the two Johnsons were rare by midcentury. As early as the 1640's, some African Americans were in servitude for life, and their numbers increased throughout the decade. In 1640, for example, in a court decision involving three runaway servants, the two who were white were sentenced to an additional four years of service, while the other, an African named John Punch, was ordered to serve his master "for the time of his natural Life." In the 1650's, some African servants were being sold for life, and the bills of sale indicated that their offspring would inherit slave status. Thus, slavery developed according to custom before it was legally established in Virginia.

Slave Codes

Not until 1661 was chattel slavery recognized by statute in Virginia, and then only indirectly. The House of Burgesses passed a law declaring that children followed the status of their mothers, thereby rendering the system of slavery self-perpetuating. In 1667, the Virginia Assembly strengthened the system by declaring that in the case of children that were slaves by birth "the conferring of baptisme doth not alter the condition of a person as to his bondage or freedome; that divers masters, freed from this doubt, may more carefully endeavor the propagation of christianity." Until this time, Americans had justified enslavement of Africans on the grounds that they were "heathen" and had recognized conversion as a way to freedom. This act closed the last avenue to freedom, apart from formal emancipation, available to African American slaves. In 1705, Virginia established a comprehensive slave code that completed the gradual process by which most African Americans were reduced to the

This drawing depicts African slaves arriving on the shores of the New World. Although the first Africans transported to the colonies were servants, not slaves, slavery established itself in the colonies during the 1600's.

status of chattel. Slaves could not bear arms or own property, nor could they leave the plantation without written permission from the master. Capital punishment was provided for murder and rape; lesser crimes were punished by maiming, whipping, or branding. Special courts were established for the trials of slaves, who were barred from serving as witnesses, except in the cases in which slaves were being tried for capital offenses.

In the other British colonies, the pattern was similar to that of Virginia. African racial slavery existed early in both Maryland and the Carolinas. Georgia attempted to exclude slavery at the time of settlement, but yielding to the protests of the colonists and the pressure of South Carolinians, the trustees repealed the prohibition in 1750. The Dutch brought slavery to the Middle Colonies early in the seventeenth century. The advent of British rule in 1664 proved to be a stimulus to the system in New York and New Jersey; but in Pennsylvania and Delaware, the religious objections of the Quakers delayed its growth somewhat and postponed legal recognition of slavery until the early eighteenth century. In seventeenth century New England, the status of Africans was ambiguous, as it was in Virginia. There were slaves in Massachusetts as early as 1638, possibly before, although slavery was not recognized by statute until 1641, which was the first enactment legalizing slavery anywhere in the British colonies. New England became heavily involved in the African slave trade, particularly after the monopoly of the Royal African Company was revoked in 1698. Like Virginia, all the colonies enacted slave codes in the late seventeenth century or early eighteenth century, although the New England codes were less harsh than those of the Middle or Southern Colonies. In all the colonies, a small class of free blacks developed alongside the institution of slavery, despite the fact that formal emancipation was restricted.

Slavery grew slowly in the first half of the seventeenth century. In 1625, there were twenty-three Africans in Virginia, most of whom probably were servants, not slaves. By midcentury, a decade before the statutory recognition of slavery, the black population was only three hundred, or 2 percent of the overall population of fifteen thousand. In 1708, there were twelve thousand African Americans and sixty-eight thousand whites. In a little more than fifty years, the black population had jumped from 2 percent to 15 percent of the total Virginia population. In the Carolinas, blacks initially made up 30 percent of the population, but within one generation outnumbered whites, making South Carolina the only mainland colony characterized by a black majority. In New England, blacks numbered only about one thousand out of a total population of ninety thousand. The eighteenth century would see the rapid development of the system of African racial slavery, particularly in the

Southern colonies, where it became an integral part of the emerging plantation economy.

Anne C. Loveland, *updated by Laura A. Croghan*

Core Resources

Slavery's North Amercian beginnings are examined in David Brion Davis's *The Problem of Slavery in Western Culture* (Ithaca, N.Y.: Cornell University Press, 1966); Lorenzo J. Greene's *The Negro in Colonial New England, 1620-1776* (New York: Columbia University Press, 1942); Winthrop D. Jordan's *White over Black: American Attitudes Toward the Negro, 1550-1812* (New York: W. W. Norton, 1968); Edmund S. Morgan's *American Slavery, American Freedom: The Ordeal of Colonial Virginia* (New York: W. W. Norton, 1975); and Peter B. Wood's *Black Majority: Negroes in Colonial South Carolina from 1670 Through the Stono Rebellion* (New York: Alfred A. Knopf, 1974).

See also: Slave codes; Slavery: history.

Smith v. Allwright

> **Significance:** In *Smith v. Allwright*, the U.S. Supreme Court in 1944 ruled that disfranchisement of African Americans in state primary elections was unconstitutional.

In 1923, the Texas legislature sought to disfranchise African American voters in the state by passing a resolution that "in no event shall a Negro be eligible to participate in a Democratic primary. . . ." Since the 1890's, in Texas as in all other southern states, nomination in the Democratic primary was tantamount to election; therefore, while African Americans would be permitted to vote in the general election, they would have no meaningful role in the political process.

The NAACP's Challenges

Almost immediately after the Texas legislature barred African Americans from participating in the Democratic primary, the National Association for the Advancement of Colored People (NAACP) secured a plaintiff, Dr. L. A. Nixon, to test the constitutionality of the legislative act. In *Nixon v. Herndon* (1927), the U.S. Supreme Court, in an opinion written by Justice Oliver Wendell Holmes, Jr., held that the Texas statute violated the equal protection clause of the Fourteenth Amendment to the U.S. Constitution by discriminating against African Americans on the basis of race. He also ruled, however, that it was unnecessary to strike down the white primary as a denial of suffrage "on account of race[or] color" repugnant to the Fifteenth Amendment.

The Texas legislature reacted defiantly to the Supreme Court decision. On June 7, 1927, the legislature passed a new resolution granting to the state executive committees of every political party the authority to establish the qualifications of their members and to determine who was qualified to vote or otherwise participate in the party. In turn, the Democratic Party State Executive Committee limited participation in its primary to white voters in Texas.

Once again Nixon filed suit, this time against James Condon, the election officer who refused to give him a ballot in the 1928 Democratic primary. In *Nixon v. Condon* (1932), the Supreme Court struck down this new Texas statute as a violation of the equal protection clause.

The Democratic Party State Executive Committee immediately rescinded its resolution prohibiting African Americans from voting in its primary, but the state party convention voted to limit participation in its deliberations to whites. In July, 1934, Richard Randolph Grovey in Houston, Texas, was refused a ballot to vote in the Democratic primary. On April 1, 1935, in *Grovey v. Townsend*, Justice Owen J. Roberts ruled that the Democratic Party was a private organization, and that its primary, although held under state law, was a party matter paid for by the Democrats. Since Roberts could find no state action in the process by which Democrats nominated their candidates, there was, he said, no violation of the Fourteenth Amendment. Because the Democratic Party was a private organization, it was free to establish membership qualifications, and there was not sufficient state involvement to invoke the guarantees of the Fourteenth Amendment.

In 1941, however, in *United States v. Classic*, a case that ostensibly had nothing to do with African Americans or the white primary, the Supreme Court held for the first time that the right to vote was protected in a primary as well as in the general election, "where the state law has made the primary an integral part of the process of choice or where in fact the primary effectively controls the choice."

United States v. Classic dealt with a Louisiana primary in which there had been fraudulent returns, but otherwise there was no way to distinguish the Texas primary from the one held in the neighboring southern state. In Texas, as in Louisiana, in 1941 as in 1923, Democratic Party nomination in its primary was a virtual guarantee of election, and the general election was a mere formality.

The *Smith* Case

The NAACP was back in action. Lonnie Smith, a Houston dentist and NAACP member, sued a Texas election official for five thousand dollars for refusing to give him a ballot to vote in the 1940 Democratic congressional primaries. The NAACP's legal counsel, Thurgood Marshall, and William Hastie, dean of the Howard Law School, brought *Smith v. Allwright* to the United States Supreme Court.

In April, 1944, mindful of southern sensibilities but intent upon overruling the nine-year-old precedent in *Grovey*, the Court chose Stanley Reed, a Democrat from Kentucky, to write its opinion. Justice Reed's opinion made it clear that the Court, except for Justice Roberts (the author of the *Grovey* decision), had concluded that the primary was an integral part of a general election, particularly in the southern states. The *Classic* decision, wrote Justice Reed, raised the issue of whether excluding African Americans from participation in the Democratic Party primary in Texas violated the Fifteenth Amendment. The answer was in the affirmative, and *Grovey v. Townsend* was expressly overruled.

The long litigative battle against the Texas white primary seemed to be over—but it was not. In Fort Bend County, Texas, the Jaybird Democratic Party, organized after the Civil War, held primaries closed to African American voters; its candidates consistently won county offices. In spite of *Smith v. Allwright*, the Jaybirds refused to open their primary to African Americans, arguing that they did not operate under state law or use state officers or funds. Nevertheless, in *Terry v. Adams* (1953), the Supreme Court held that the Jaybird primary violated the Fifteenth Amendment, because it controlled the electoral process in Fort Bend County.

It took twenty-one years for the United States Supreme Court to rule that the Texas white primary violated the right to vote guaranteed by the Fifteenth Amendment. It would take another twenty-one years before the Voting Rights Act of 1965 finally secured the ballot for African Americans in the South. In the interim, the fall of the white primary had the practical effect of increasing African American registrants in the southern states from approximately 250,000 in 1940 to 775,000 seven years later. African Americans were still intimidated and defrauded of their suffrage rights, but *Smith v. Allwright* was an important landmark on the road to uninhibited enfranchisement. It also was a symbol that the Supreme Court would examine the reality behind the subterfuge and act to protect African Americans in the enjoyment of their civil rights.   *David L. Sterling*

Core Resources

John D. Fassett's *New Deal Justice: The Life of Stanley Reed of Kentucky* (New York: Vantage Press, 1994) is a biography of the conservative Democratic justice who wrote the majority opinion in *Smith v. Allwright*. Darlene Clark Hine's *Black Victory: The Rise and Fall of the White Primary in Texas* (Millwood, N.Y.: KTO Press, 1979) is an examination of the background of the white primary and the struggle to bring about its demise. Steven F. Lawson's *Black Ballots: Voting Rights in the South, 1944-1969* (New York: Columbia University Press, 1976) traces the development of African American enfranchisement from *Smith v. Allwright* to the Voting Rights Act of 1965 and its aftermath. Includes a chapter on the white primary.

See also: Disfranchisement laws in Mississippi; Fourteenth Amendment; *Grovey v. Townsend*; *Nixon v. Herndon*; Voting Rights Act of 1965.

Social Darwinism and racism

Charles Darwin's evolutionary theory stimulated thought about the implications of biology for human society. His theory incorporated the notion of natural selection, that some species are better adapted to their environment than others and therefore are more likely to thrive in the competition for limited resources.

Later thinkers sought to apply Darwin's theory of biological evolution to the social world. Social Darwinists asserted that human groups are locked in a competition just like the competition between species for survival. They contended that races and peoples are like organisms: Some are more fit for survival than others. Hence, Social Darwinists considered conquest, imperialism, and domination of one race by another to be consistent with the laws of nature. Darwin disavowed the Social Darwinists' extension of his theory. He was a humanist who believed that human beings are qualitatively distinct from other animals in their capacity for charitable works and compassion, a characteristic that positively counteracts natural selection. Still, the implications of Darwin's thought, which fit with the racist assumptions of European societies, acquired a dynamic of their own.

To Social Darwinists, the conquest of African and Asian peoples in the late nineteenth century by European empires proved the superiority of the white "race." White Europeans had supposedly reached the pinnacle of evolution, while other races remained at a more primitive stage of development. In particular, Social Darwinists portrayed Africans as childlike and appraised their mental abilities as rudimentary. They regarded Africans as close cousins of the ape rather than fully human. In the United States, this attitude justified the enslavement of Africans. Champions of slavery pointed to the civilizing influence of captivity, claiming that slaves would regress to a barbaric state if released.

It should be noted that Social Darwinists focused on other factors besides race. They characterized the poor, even of their own race or nationality, as relatively less equipped for survival than the prosperous middle and upper classes. Wealth itself suggested the fitness of the wealthy, and Social Darwinists held welfare programs and charity to be an interference with the natural law that had decreed the demise of the destitute in the interests of the race. Social Darwinist principles also became associated with the imperialist struggle between the so-called advanced nations. According to the ethos prevailing among European states in the late nineteenth century, the state that was most successful in subjugating other peoples around the world and crowding out its imperial rivals had the greatest claim to survival. In this sense, Africans suffered both directly as a consequence of the racist content of Social Darwinism and indirectly because of the resulting contest between European states over control of the African continent. Though Social Darwinism has all but disappeared as an ideology, the debate over such issues as genetic determinants of intelligence demonstrates that its legacy lives on.

Aristide Sechandice

See also: Biosocial theories; Intelligence and race; Intelligence testing; Race as a concept; Sociobiology and race.

Social identity theory

> **Significance:** Social identity theory examines the relationship between group membership and self-esteem. It has provided insights into intergroup conflict, ethnocentrism, cultural affirmation, and self-hatred, predicting both individual and group responses to an unfavorable self-concept.

Social identity theory maintains that all individuals are motivated to achieve and maintain a positive self-concept. A person's self-concept derives from two principal sources: personal identity and social identity. Personal identity includes one's individual traits, achievements, and qualities. Social identity includes the group affiliations that are recognized as being part of the self, such as one's image of oneself as a Protestant, a blue-collar worker, or a conservative. Some individuals emphasize the personal aspects in their quest for a favorable self-image, while others emphasize their social identities. Social identity theory focuses on the latter. It attempts to explain when and how individuals transform their group affiliations to secure a favorable self-concept.

Psychologist Henri Tajfel introduced social identity theory in 1978. The theory maintains that a person's social identity emerges from the natural process of social categorization. People categorize, or classify, themselves and other people by many criteria, including occupation, religious affiliation, political orientation, ethnicity, economic class, and gender. An individual automatically identifies with some categories and rejects others. This creates a distinction between "in-groups," with which one identifies, and "out-groups," with which one does not identify. A person who identifies himself or herself as a Democrat, for example, would consider other Democrats members of the in-group and would view Republicans as members of the out-group. Individuals inevitably compare their groups with other groups; the goal of the comparisons is to establish the superiority of one's own group, or the group's "positive distinctiveness," on some level, such as affluence, cultural heritage, or spirituality. If the comparison shows that the individual's group memberships are positive and valuable, the social identities become an important part of the self. If, however, one's group appears inferior, one's self-image acquires "negative distinctiveness." The individual is then motivated to acquire a more satisfactory selfconcept.

Enhancing the Self-Concept

Tajfel and John Turner proposed three strategies that can be used to enhance one's self-concept: "exit," "pass," and "voice." The first two strategies represent attempts to validate the self. Both involve rejecting or distancing oneself from the devalued group to improve identity; both presume that social mobility exists. Exit involves simply leaving the group. This response is possible only within flexible social systems that permit individual mobility. Although individuals cannot usually shed affiliations such as race or gender, they can openly discard other affiliations, such as "Buick owner" or "public school advocate." If dissatisfied with an automobile, one trades it in for another; if unhappy with the public school system, one may exit and move one's children into a private school. Pass, a more private response, occurs when individuals with unfavorable group memberships are not recognized as belonging to that group. A Jew may pass as a Gentile, for example, or a fair-skinned black person may pass as a Caucasian. Typically in such cases, the objective features that link the individual to the devalued group are absent or unnoticeable.

Voice, the final strategy for identity improvement, is a collective response: Group members act together to alter the group's image and elevate its social value. Also called the "social change" approach, it is common in rigid social systems in which individual movement away from the disparaged group is impossible. It also occurs when psychological forces such as cultural and personal values bind the individual to the group. Members of such physically identifiable groups as women, blacks, or Asians might adopt the social change strategy, for example, as might such cultural or religious group members as Irish Catholics or Orthodox Jews.

Voice is a complex response. Simply recognizing that social mobility is blocked for members of one's own group is insufficient to prompt social change activity.

Two additional perceptions of the overall social structure are important: its stability and its legitimacy. Stability is concerned with how fixed or secure the social hierarchy seems. Theoretically, no group is completely secure in its relative superiority; even groups that historically have been considered superior must work to maintain their favored position. If members of a denigrated group believe that alternatives to the current social hierarchy are possible, they are encouraged to reassess their own value. Legitimacy, in contrast, involves the bases for a group's negative distinctiveness. If a group believes that its social inferiority is attributable to illegitimate causes such as discrimination in hiring practices or educational opportunities, group members will be more likely to challenge their inferior position.

Voice challenges to negative distinctiveness take two general forms: social creativity and direct competition. Social creativity involves altering or redefining the elements of comparison. The group's social positions and resources, however, need not be altered. In one approach, a group may simply limit the groups with which it compares itself, focusing on groups that are similar. A group of factory workers may choose to compare itself with warehouse workers or postal employees rather than with a group of advertising executives. This approach increases the chances that the outcome of the comparison will be favorable to one's own group. The group might also identify a new area of comparison, such as bilingual fluency, in its effort to enhance group distinctiveness.

Finally, the group might recast some of its denigrated attributes so that its value is reassessed. A new appreciation for group history and culture often emerges from this process. The Civil Rights movement, an important force for social change in the 1960's, caused such a recasting to occur. In the context of that movement, the label "Negro" was replaced by "black," which was recast by African Americans to symbolize group pride. Under the slogan "Black is beautiful," the natural look became more valued than the traditional Euro-American model. African Americans were less likely to lighten or straighten their hair or use makeup to make their skin appear lighter.

Direct competition, in contrast, involves altering the group's social position. It is often an institutional response; consequently, it encourages competition among groups. Displaced groups target institutions and policies, demanding resources in an effort to empower the group politically and economically. In the 1960's, for example, black students demonstrated for curricular changes at colleges and universities. They demanded greater relevance in existing courses and the development of black studies programs to highlight the group's social and political contributions. In the 1970's, the women's movement demanded economic and political changes, including equal pay for equal work, and greater individual rights for women, such as abortion rights and institutionalized child care.

In-Group Bias

Social identity theory has been used to explain several intergroup processes. Among these are the phenomenon known as in-group bias (observed in laboratory experiments) and the actions of some subordinate groups to challenge their relative inferiority through collective (voice) approaches. The response of African Americans in the 1950's and 1960's to negative perceptions of their group illustrates the latter process.

In-group bias is the tendency to favor one's own group over other groups. In laboratory experiments, young subjects have been put in groups according to simple and fairly arbitrary criteria, such as the type of artwork they preferred. The goal was to establish a "minimal group situation": an artificial social order in which subjects could be easily differentiated but which was free of any already existing conflicts. Once categorized, subjects were asked to perform one of several tasks, such as distributing money, assigning points, evaluating the different groups, or interpreting group members' behavior. In all the tasks, subjects repeatedly showed a preference for their own groups. They gave to in-group members significantly more points and money than they gave to out-group members despite a lack of previous interaction among the subjects. When describing in-group members, they attributed altruistic behavior to the persons' innate virtuous and admirable qualities rather than to outside causes. When describing out-group members, however, they reversed the pattern, attributing altruistic behavior to situational factors and hostile behavior to personal character. Thus, even without any history of competition, ideological differences, or hostility over scarce resources, subjects consistently demonstrate a preference for their in-group.

Social identity theory predicts this pattern. The powerful need to achieve a positive self-image motivates a person to establish the value of his or her group memberships. Since groups strongly contribute to an individual's self-image, the individual works to enhance the group's image. Group successes are, by extension, the individual's successes. Daily life offers many examples of group allegiance, ranging from identification with one's country to support of one's hometown baseball team. Experiments in social identity suggest that ethnocentrism, the belief in the superiority of one's own ethnic group, serves important psychological needs.

Working for Change

Social identity theory also explains why some subordinate groups challenge their relative inferiority through rebellion or social change while others do not. The theory predicts that individuals who are objectively bound to negatively distinct groups by gender or skin color, for example, will have fewer options for self-enhancement. Because they are driven by the powerful need to obtain a worthy self-image, however, they are unlikely to engage in self-hatred by accepting the denigrated image imposed on them by others. Instead, they will engage in some form of voice, the collective approach to image improvement.

Black Self-Images

Psychologists studying social identity do not directly explore the historical background of a group's negative self-image. Rather, they perform laboratory experiments and field studies designed to determine individuals' actual perceptions of groups, how individuals identify groups, and whether they see them as having a positive or negative image. Social psychologists also attempt to measure the changes that occur in group self-image over time; they can then infer that social or political movements have affected that image. Studies involving African American children for whom the essential identifying element is a physical one, race, provide an example.

In the landmark 1954 Supreme Court decision *Brown v. Board of Education*, which mandated school desegregation, social scientists presented evidence that educational segregation produced feelings of inferiority in black children. Support was drawn in part from a 1947 study by Kenneth and Mamie Clark, in which they compared the preferences of black and white children between the ages of three and seven for dolls with either dark or fair skin tones. Approximately 60 percent of the black children said that the fair-skinned doll was the "nicer" doll, the "nicer color" doll, or the doll they "preferred to play with." The dark-skinned doll, by contrast, "looked bad." Based on a combination of this negative self-image and the fact that African Americans are objectively bound to their group by their race, social identity theory would predict collective action for social change.

The Civil Rights movement embodied that collective, or voice, activity, and it offered blacks a new context within which to evaluate black identity. Results from studies performed in the 1970's suggest that, indeed, there was a significant rise in black self-esteem during that period. A replication of the Clarks' study by other researchers showed a clear preference for the dark-skinned doll among black children. Later analyses of comparable doll studies showed that such preferences for one's own group were most common among young subjects from areas with large black populations and active black pride movements.

A positive self-image may also emerge when social and cultural themes and historical events are reinterpreted within a group. A group's cultural image may be emphasized; its music, art, and language then become valued. To continue using the African American example, in the twentieth century, black music—work songs and spirituals—which once had been the music of the oppressed evolved into a music that communicated ethnic identity in a new way. Blues and jazz became a focus of group pride; jazz, in particular, become renowned worldwide. The acceptance of jazz as a valuable art form by people of many races and nationalities illustrates another frequent outcome of activity for generating a positive self-concept: It often initiates a response from the larger society that improves the group's relative position in that society.

Jaclyn Rodriguez

Core Resources

Differentiation Between Social Groups: Studies in the Social Psychology of Intergroup Relations (London: Academic Press, 1978), edited by Henri Tajfel, presents the work of the team of European social psychologists that conceptualized and formalized social identity theory. Tajfel's *Human Groups and Social Categories* (Cambridge, England: Cambridge University Press, 1981) is an easy-to-read account of Tajfel's conceptualization of intergroup conflict. Tajfel and John Turner's "The Social Identity Theory of Intergroup Behavior," in *Social Psychology of Intergroup Relations*, edited by Stephen Worchel and William G. Austin (2d ed., Chicago: Nelson-Hall, 1986) is an excellent summary of social identity theory. Turner's *Rediscovering the Social Group: A Self-Categorization Theory* (New York: Basil Blackwell, 1987) provides the reader with a valuable backdrop for understanding many of Tajfel's predictions in a readable blend of theoretical and empirical work.

See also: Black Is Beautiful movement; Black Power movement; Ethnocentrism; Internalized racism; Passing; Positive ethnocentrism; Prejudice: effects; Psychological theories of intergroup relations; Social perception of others.

Social mobility and race

Significance: One measure of equal opportunity within a society is the ability of its members to move from one social stratum to the next higher, a task complicated by the addition of racial or ethnic factors.

Social mobility is the movement of individuals and groups from one stratum to another in society. The processes of social mobility are rendered much more complex if those individuals are members of minority groups. If class is defined as a stratified system of structured inequality, where those in different strata have unequal access to wealth, power, and social prestige, then the degree of upward social mobility becomes the critical measure of a society's approaching (or not approaching) the goal of equality of opportunity. It follows that barriers to upward mobility will depend not only on economic forces (class) but also on such sociocultural forces as color, religion, national origin, language, and regional subculture (race/ethnicity). Sociologists debate endlessly about how the two kinds of inequality bear mutually on each other.

Conditions Affecting Social Mobility
In economic terms, technologically more advanced urban-industrial and postindustrial societies provide a better platform for the reduction of inequality and for increasing mobility than preindustrial, agrarian-commercial societies, including the so-called developing countries of the Third World. Politically, relatively democratic societies characterized by free elections and by majority rule with minority rights are more likely to reduce inequality and stimulate mobility of both class and race than authoritarian or totalitarian governmental systems. In any given society, it is expected that racial and ethnic mobility will take place within a class structure on a continuum from relatively open to relatively closed. However, the power of groups to dominate other groups on the basis of color or culture is so great that the overlay of race on class can be the decisive and most important problem confronting the entire society.

Patterns of Mobility
An examination of a series of strategic case studies reveals the consistencies and contradictions in mobility patterns around the world. In rapidly developing Brazil, for example, contrary to the myth of racial egalitarianism, there is considerable racial discrimination, but fundamentally, the striking pace of social mobility is driven by the economics of class. In South Africa, under racial apartheid, the entire economic-political system was for whites only. This produced a "separate and unequal" racial caste structure with incredibly restricted class mobility for black Africans and only slightly less restricted mobility for mixed "coloreds." With apartheid demolished and a black-majority government in power, it still may be decades before increased black mobility can result in partially closing the white-black "racial gap" in household income, education, and housing.

Much depends on societal receptivity to sociocultural change—even in the short term—such that the dominant group in power is compelled to yield to pressure to develop a more open society in terms of both class and

A Korean American grandmother cries as she carries her granddaughter past a burned Koreatown shopping center after the 1992 Los Angeles riots. Because of what they perceived as the financial success and social mobility of the Korean immigrants relative to African Americans in Los Angeles, some angry rioters looted and burned Korean-owned businesses.

race. Historically, Great Britain has been a virtually homogeneous urban-industrial democratic society with quite tight class stratification; class was all, mobility limited. In the years after World War II, Britain became more heterogeneous in race and ethnicity as a result of the immigration of thousands of Afro-Caribbeans, Indians, and Pakistanis. Their rate of mobility has been impeded by considerable racial discrimination, and subsequently, immigration has been curtailed. However, the Asian communities have been able to solidify their position in the lower-middle and middle class, with the Afro-Caribbeans following the same route, though more slowly, from a largely working-class base.

The United States
In the United States, surveying the great historical immigration saga of white European immigrants—from

the arrival of the Irish Catholics in the mid-nineteenth century to the entry of millions of newcomers from eastern and southern Europe, including large numbers of Jews—it is clear that successive generations of immigrants have, on the whole, achieved a significant degree of upward social mobility. For the newer immigrants, primarily from Latin America, the Caribbean, and Southeast Asia, the variation by group in rate of mobility is greater, in particular where the racial overlay on immigrant status is at play.

All these groups, with the exception of the Japanese Americans and Jewish Americans, remained heavily working class in the 1990's, and some still had higher than average proportions below the poverty line. Generally, however, they appeared to be making their way into the middle class, though they will be underrepresented there for some time. The mobility is taking place in a climate more receptive to pluralism and retention of ethnic subcultures in a multicultural society than it was during the nineteenth or early twentieth centuries.

People of Color
However, for African Americans and some Hispanic groups, especially Mexican Americans and Puerto Ricans (who are not immigrants but migrants from the Commonwealth), and above all, for Native Americans, the white European ethnic-generational-mobility pattern does not hold.

In a sense, the enlarged and vigorous black middle class represents a successful racial version of the Jews' ethnic mobility transition, but this view neglects, or at least minimizes, what in the African American case constitutes the force of the color overlay on class. Without doubt, social mobility for black Americans has increased, with consequent narrowing of the racial gap in family income, education, and housing. However, the rate of change has slowed and at times has become static. In the central cities, among the near poor and the poor, termed the "black underclass" by sociologist William Julius Wilson, the path of social mobility is blocked. Theirs is a static condition rooted in a historic and enduring racism but increasingly the consequence of structural changes in an industrial and postindustrial system that drastically constricts job opportunities for blacks in a changing market economy.

Within any single society, racial and ethnic discrimination constitutes a basic blockage to social mobility. Minorities are singled out for differential and unequal treatment, their status based on a categorical definition of "inferiority" or "the wrong color." If they are already overrepresented in the lower reaches of the class structure, color reinforces class. In the Deep South in the United States, for example, "poor whites" were higher than "poor blacks" in the status hierarchy. Even when minority status is built into a more solidly anchored lower-middle-class and middle-class position, the buffer of class protection can erode under pressure of bigotry, emanating from both above and below, suddenly increasing in intensity in times of economic and political crisis. The ethnic Chinese in Malaysia, the Philippines, and Indonesia are made more vulnerable during times of crisis. Similarly, when economic stress occurs, the Korean American merchant communities in Los Angeles and New York become the targets of racism by members of the black working-class neighborhood.

Beyond psychological explanations for these barriers to social mobility—such as stereotyping, prejudice, racial/ethnic hatred—the essential theoretical key to the nearly universal racial/ethnic constrictions on social mobility lies in the imbalance of power that enables the dominant group to define, subordinate, and exploit the racial/ethnic minorities at the institutional level. Researcher Norbert Elias has framed this concept of power imbalance as a relation between "the established" and "the outsiders" and has applied the framework to British class structure, the survival of caste in village India, and the position of the Japanese Burakumin, a group physically indistinguishable from other Japanese but marginalized and discriminated against because of their historical role and position in society.

In societies ranging from agrarian to postindustrial, from democratic to authoritarian and totalitarian, from those with relatively open to those with relatively closed class structures, an overarching challenge is that of the struggle against inequality whose central index is the degree of social mobility across the lines of both class and race/ethnicity.   *Richard Robbins*

See also: Black middle class/black underclass relations; Caste model; Class theories of racial/ethnic relations; "Classless" society; Social stratification theories.

Social perception of others

Significance: Social perception deals with how people think about and make sense of other people: how they form impressions, draw conclusions, and try to explain other people's behavior.

Social perception deals with two general classes of cognitive-perceptual processes through which people process, organize, and recall information about others. Those that deal with how people form impressions of other people's personalities (called person perception) form the first class. The second class includes those processes that deal with how people use this information to draw conclusions about other people's motivations, intentions, and emotions in order to explain and predict their behavior (called attribution processes). The importance of social perception in social psychology is revealed in the fact that one's impressions and judgments about others, whether accurate or not, can have profound effects on one's own and others' behavior.

Causal Attribution

People are naturally motivated to understand and predict the behavior of those around them. Being able to predict and understand the social world gives people a sense of mastery and control over their environment. Psychologists who study social perception have shown that people try to make sense of their social worlds by determining whether other people's behavior is produced by disposition, by some internal quality or trait unique to a person, or by something in the situation or environment. The process of making such determinations, which is called causal attribution, was developed by social psychologists Fritz Heider, Edward Jones, Keith Davis, and Harold Kelley in the late 1950's and early 1960's.

According to these attribution theorists, when one decides that a person's behavior reflects a disposition (when, for example, one decides that a person is friendly because he acted friendly), one has made an internal or dispositional attribution. In contrast, when one decides that a person's behavior was caused by something in the situation—he acted in a friendly way to make someone like him—one has made an external or situational attribution. The attributions one makes for others' behaviors carry considerable influence in the impressions one forms of them and in how one will behave toward them in the future.

Unfortunately, people's impressions and attributions are not always accurate. For example, in many situations, people seem to be inclined to believe that other people's behavior is caused by dispositional factors. At the same time, they believe that their own behavior is the product of situational causes. This tendency has been called the actor-observer bias. Moreover, when people try to explain the causes of other people's behavior, especially behavior that is clearly and obviously caused by situational factors (factors such as a coin flip, a dice roll, or some other situational inducement), they tend to underestimate situational influences and overestimate the role of dispositional causes. This tendency is referred to as correspondence bias or the fundamental attribution error. In other words, people prefer to explain other people's behavior in terms of their traits or personalities rather than in terms of situational factors, even when situational factors actually caused the behavior.

Heuristics

In addition to these biases, social psychologists have examined other ways in which people's impressions of others and inferences about the causes of their behavior can be inaccurate or biased. In their work, for example, psychologists Daniel Kahneman and Amos Tversky have described a number of simple but efficient thinking strategies, or "rules of thumb," called heuristics. The availability heuristic is the tendency to explain behaviors on the basis of causes that are easily or quickly brought to mind. Similarly, the representativeness heuristic is the tendency to believe that a person who possesses characteristics that are associated with a social group probably belongs to that group. Although heuristics make social thinking more efficient and yield reasonable results most of the time, they can sometimes lead to significant judgment errors.

Schemata

Bias can also arise in social perception in a number of other ways. Because of the enormous amount of social information that they must process at any given moment, people have developed various ways of organizing, categorizing, and simplifying this information and the expectations they have about various people, objects, and events. These organizational structures are called schemata. For example, schemata that organize information about people's membership in different categories or groups are called stereotypes or prototypes. Schemata that organize information about how traits go together in forming a person's personality are called implicit personality theories (IPTs). Although schemata, like heuristics, help make social thinking more efficient and yield reasonable results most of the time, they can also sometimes lead to significant judgment errors, such as prejudice and discrimination.

Finally, social perception can be influenced by a variety of factors of which people are unaware but which can exert tremendous influence on their thinking. Social psychologist Solomon Asch was the first to describe the primacy effect in impression formation. The primacy effect is the tendency for things that are seen or received first to have a greater impact on one's thinking than things that come later. Many other things in the environment can prime one, or make one "ready," to see, interpret, or remember things that one might not otherwise have seen, thought about, or remembered. Priming occurs when something in the environment makes certain things easier to bring to mind.

During the 1970's and 1980's, social psychologists made numerous alterations and extensions of the existing theories of attribution and impression formation to keep pace with the field's growing emphasis on mental (cognitive) and emotional (affective) processes. These changes focused primarily on incorporating work from cognitive psychology on memory processes, the use of schemata, and the interplay of emotion, motivation, and cognition.

Biases and Social Problems

Social psychologists have argued that many social problems have their roots in social perception processes. Because social perception biases can sometimes result in inaccurate perceptions, misunderstandings, conflict between people and groups, and other negative consequences, social psychologists have spent much time and effort trying to understand these perception biases. Their hope is that by understanding such biases they will be able to suggest solutions for them. For example, in a number of experiments, social psychologists have attempted to understand the social perception processes that may lead to stereotyping, which can result in prejudice and discrimination.

One explanation for why stereotypes are so hard to change once they have been formed is the self-fulfilling prophecy. Self-fulfilling prophecies occur when one has possibly inaccurate beliefs about others (such as stereotypes) and acts on those beliefs, bringing about the conditions necessary to make those beliefs come true. In other words, when one expects something to be true about another person (especially negative things), one frequently looks for and finds what one expects to see. At other times, one actually brings out the negative (or positive) qualities one expects to be present. In a classic 1968 study by social psychologists Robert Rosenthal and Lenore Jacobson, for example, children whose teachers expected them to show a delayed but substantial increase in their intelligence (on the basis of a fictitious intelligence test) actually scored higher on a legitimate intelligence quotient (IQ) test administered at the end of the school year. Presumably, the teachers' expectations of those students caused them to treat those students in ways that actually helped them perform better. Similarly, social psychologists Rebecca Curtis and Kim Miller have shown that when people think someone they meet likes them, they act in ways that lead that person to like them. If, however, people think a person dislikes them, they act in ways that actually make that person dislike them.

The behaviors that produce self-fulfilling prophecies can be subtle. For example, in 1974, social psychologists Carl Word, Mark Zanna, and Joel Cooper demonstrated that the subtle behaviors of interviewers during job interviews can make applicants believe that they performed either poorly or very well. These feelings, in turn, can lead to actual good or poor performance on the part of the applicants. What was most striking about this study, however, was that the factor that led to the subtle negative or positive behaviors was the interviewers'

stereotypes of the applicants' racial group membership. Black applicants received little eye contact from interviewers and were not engaged in conversation; the behaviors displayed by interviewers in the presence of white applicants were exactly the opposite. Not surprisingly, black applicants were seen as less qualified and were less likely to be hired. Clearly, subtle behaviors produced by racial stereotypes can have major consequences for the targets of those stereotypes.

The relevance of social perception processes to everyday life is not restricted to stereotyping, although stereotyping is indeed an important concern. In academic settings, for example, situational factors can lead teachers to form impressions of students that have little bearing on their actual abilities. Social psychologist Edward Jones and his colleagues have examined the way in which primacy effects operate in academic settings. Two groups of subjects saw a student perform on a test. One group saw the student start out strong and then begin to do poorly. The other group saw the student start out poorly and then begin to improve. For both groups, the student's performance on the test was identical, and the student received the same score. The group that saw the student start out strong and then falter thought the student was brighter than the student who started out poorly and then improved. Clearly, first impressions matter.

Finally, research on the correspondence bias makes it clear that one must be very careful when trying to understand what people are like. In many situations, the demands of people's occupations or their family roles force them to do things with which they may not actually agree. Substantial research has shown that observers will probably think these persons have personalities that are consistent with their behaviors. Lawyers, who must defend people who may have broken the law, debaters, who must argue convincingly for or against a particular point of view, and actors, who must play parts that they did not write, are all vulnerable to being judged on the basis of their behavior. Lawyers may not actually believe that their clients are innocent, but must defend them as though they do. Debaters often argue for positions with which they do not agree. Actors play roles that do not match their personalities. Unless one is particularly sensitive to the fact that, when they are doing their jobs, these persons' behaviors do not reveal anything about their true personalities, one may actually (and incorrectly) believe that they do.

John H. Fleming

Core Resources

J. Richard Eiser's *Social Judgment* (Pacific Grove, Calif.: Brooks/Cole, 1991) presents a detailed and broad overview of topics in social judgment, including categorization, the effects of emotion on judgment, causal attribution, and other issues. Fritz Heider's *The Psychology of Interpersonal Relations* (New York: John Wiley & Sons, 1958) is a classic text that presents Heider's attribution and balance theories as well as a number of ideas that were to influence the field for more than twenty years. Robert Rosenthal and Lenore Jacobson, in *Pygmalion in the Classroom* (New York: Holt, Rinehart and Winston, 1968), demonstrated the self-fulfilling prophecy at work in the classroom. Edward Ellsworth Jones's *Interpersonal Perception* (New York: W. H. Freeman, 1990) presents a detailed overview and review of topics including impression formation, emotion perception, causal attribution, and attributional biases. Kelly G. Shaver's *An Introduction to Attribution Processes* (Cambridge, Mass.: Winthrop, 1975; reprint, Hillsdale, N.J.: Lawrence Erlbaum, 1983) is a good primer of basic theoretical and conceptual issues.

See also: Discrimination: behaviors; "Other" theory; Prejudice and stereotyping; Prejudice: effects; Psychological theories of intergroup relations; Psychology of racism; Social identity theory; Stereotyping and the self-fulfilling prophecy.

Social rearticulation

The concept of social rearticulation has a complex intellectual history which originates in classical political economy, moves through Italian intellectual Antonio Gramsci, and in the late twentieth century found voice in the work of sociologists Michael Omi and Howard Winant (*Racial Formation in the United States*, 2d ed., 1994). According to Omi and Winant, social rearticulation is the "discursive reorganization or reinterpretation of ideological themes and interests already present in the subjects' consciousness, such that these elements obtain new meanings or coherence." In practice, social rearticulation involves the dual process of disorganizing "dominant ideologies"—the values of the dominant group—and constructing "oppositional cultures"—cultures that are different from the dominant culture but that reflect or react to the society around them. Dominant ideologies can be reorganized in various ways. However, in order to be termed social rearticulation, the process must involve the imparting of new knowledge to established traditions and norms, and the recombination of preexisting meanings with new conceptions of social identities. Examples of preexisting systems and beliefs being reformulated can be found not only in social movements but also in popular and intellectual discourse. Therefore, social rearticulation is quintessentially a political process, a way of destabilizing, reorganizing, and initiating civil and state reform. As a social

construct, its trajectory is complex, uneven, and marked by considerable instability and tension. However, as a way to break away from cultural and political predecessors, social rearticulation is an important sociohistorical process in which racial and social categories are created, inhabited, and transformed. *Antwi A. A. Akom*

See also: Oppositional culture; Racial formation theory; Resistance, cultures of.

Social stratification theories

Significance: All societies divide people into various social strata or hierarchies based on one or more characteristics such as race, gender, age, or social class. The concept of social stratification, derived from geology, refers to this structured inequality. Generally, stratification takes the form of either a class system or caste system. Although a class system is more open to upward social mobility than a caste system, both systems severely and systematically restrict people's access to such valued social resources as wealth, education, power, and prestige.

Social stratification theories are attempts to explain why stratification occurs and how it is maintained. They fall into four broad categories: biologically based theories, conflict theories, functionalist theories, and cultural theories.

Biologically Based Theories

Prominent among biologically based theories is Social Darwinism. Grounded in Charles Darwin's theory of evolution, Social Darwinism erroneously applied the concept of natural selection, the key evolutionary mechanism, to the variation in human societies and cultures. Although Darwin believed that human beings belong to a single species because of a common ancestry, he theorized that races constitute various subspecies within the human species. The Social Darwinists, reflecting the nineteenth century European prejudices toward those they had colonized or enslaved, interpreted this to mean that races were unequal in their evolutionary advancement and that white Europeans represented the apex of human evolution.

British sociologist Herbert Spencer, who used the phrases "struggle for existence" and "survival of the fittest" to provide a general philosophical framework within which to understand Darwin's theory, believed that human groups and nations were involved in a relentless struggle for survival, pushing aside, out, and under the unfit groups and nations while continuously improving the species. William Graham Sumner, an American sociologist who wrote at the beginning of the twentieth century, also held Social Darwinist views.

Historically, belief in evolutionary explanations for social stratification has led to overt subjugation, exclusion, or genocide of ethnic and racial minorities. Racist ideologies emerge to legitimize continued oppression. When overt forms of oppression disappear, resistance to changes in the existing social structure persists.

For example, Ernst Haeckel, a nineteenth century German thinker, seized upon Darwin's theory to propagate the myth of the superiority of the Aryan race. He believed that the Nordic "race" with what he saw as its distinct physical and mental characteristics—blond hair, blue eyes, great physical strength, superior intelligence, and bravery—had the natural right to rule the "inferior" races. Haeckel's ideas quickly became popular in nineteenth century Germany and were eventually used as an ideological prop by the Nazis.

A more recent extension of Social Darwinism is sociobiology, systematically presented by American biologist E. O. Wilson in his classic work *Sociobiology: A New Synthesis* (1975). Sociobiologists reject the charge of supporting a racist ideology; however, they assert that values, culture, and behavioral patterns are grounded in biology, which leads to the conclusion that social stratification is a function of genetics.

Theories that link race and intelligence to explain the class structure of a society also have their early beginnings in the nineteenth century Social Darwinism and eugenics movement. Francis Galton, one of the founders of the eugenics movement, believed that superior races with superior intelligence naturally ended up on top of the social hierarchy. A modern statement of this position is found in *The Bell Curve: Intelligence and Class Structure in American Life* (1994), by Richard Herrnstein and Charles Murray. Such theories resurface from time to time, despite the fact that human genetic material (de-

Representative Social Stratification Theorists and Their Positions

Theorist	Main Work	Theoretical Perspective	Summary of Ideas
Herbert Spencer	*Principles of Psychology*	Social Darwinism	Stratification is a function of competition for survival.
Karl Marx	*Kapital*	Conflict theory	Capitalism produces two social classes: workers and proletariats.
Emile Durkheim	*Division of Labor in Society*	Functionalism	Stratification is a function of job specialization.
Gunnar Myrdal	*The Challenge of World Poverty*	Cultural theory	Poverty is a function of cultural defects.
Max Weber	"Class, Status, and Party"	Social Darwinism	Class, status, and power define stratification.
E. O. Wilson	*Sociobiology: A New Synthesis*	Social Darwinism	Social stratification is biologically grounded.
T. Bottomore	*Elites and Society*	Conflict theory	The power elite consisting of economic, military, and political elites maintain the class system to their advantage.
Ralf Dahrendorf	*Class and Class Conflict in Industrial Society*	Conflict theory	Social classes are maintained by the authority structure of contemporary societies.
Kingsley Davis and Wilbert Moore	"Some Principles of Stratification"	Functionalism	Stratification systems result from meritocracy.
Richard Herrnstein and Charles Murray	*The Bell Curve: Intelligence and Class Structure in American Life*	Social Darwinism/ Genetic determinism	Social stratification is a function of IQ, which is genetically determined.
Oscar Lewis	"Five Families: Mexican Case Studies in the Culture of Poverty"	Culture of poverty	The underclass is characterized by a culture with distinct traits.

oxyribonucleic acid, or DNA) is nearly identical across all human ethnicities and races.

Conflict Theories

The classical conflict theory is found in the writings of the nineteenth century economist and political philosopher Karl Marx, who held that the capitalist social structure creates two classes of people: the bourgeoisie, who own the means of production, and the proletariat, who work for the bourgeoisie. The capitalist system of production is designed to maximize profit or surplus value for the bourgeoisie by paying the proletariat the lowest possible wages for their labors. The more the workers produce, the more the capitalists benefit, progressively impoverishing and alienating the former while empowering the latter.

The Marxist tradition has never enjoyed much vitality and favor in American society. However, modified class conflict theories have always found some level of acceptance in the United States. Ralf Dahrendorf, for example, has shown that the authority structure of contemporary advanced societies, while successful in preventing violent revolutions, is still grounded in class conflicts. Gerhard Lenski, utilizing Marxist ideas and functionalist insights, has made historical comparative analyses of the formation of class structures based on power, prestige, and wealth. His hypothesis, however, that greater democratization will result in greater economic equality has not been borne out by historical experiences.

Functionalist Theories

Functionalists compare society to a machine or an organism whose efficiency depends upon the proper coordination of its diverse parts. If some phenomenon is universally and persistently found in a society, such as poverty or crime, functionalists conclude that it must serve a positive function for the entire society. The originator of functionalism in sociology was the French theorist Émile Durkheim.

The principles of a functionalist explanation are found in one of his early works, *The Division of Labor in Society* (1893), in which he analyzed the transition of simple societies to more complex, modern societies. Key to this transition, he argued, was the social division of labor, or the proliferation of specialized social roles. Consequently, complex societies, which he called organic societies, are characterized by interdependence. Although this is a positive development, it is also accompanied by many social pathologies including anomie or alienation. What needs correction is not the proliferation of specializations resulting in social stratification, but the social pathologies it creates.

After World War II, theorists such as Kingsley Davis, Wilbert Moore, Talcott Parsons, and Robert Merton popularized functionalism. With the United States' postwar ascendance to superpower status, functionalism, which supports the status quo, quickly spread.

The four major components of a social system identified by Parsons are economy, polity, society, and the fiduciary system, which includes religion. Contemporary functionalists argue that changes to the social structure must be gradual and only to the extent that is necessary to maintain the system's equilibrium among these four components. Existing divisions of labor among social classes and racial and ethnic groups are reaffirmed as beneficial to the system. Davis and Moore's contention that the existing stratification system is the result of most suitable groups or individuals filling important positions in the social system is still widely accepted. Functionalists fear that insistence on equality will harm the system by making it unable to choose the most qualified individuals to fill highly valued social positions.

Cultural Theories

Cultural theorists believe that social groups and nations occupy varying positions in the social hierarchy based on their cultural ideas and value systems. German social theorist Max Weber proposed a cultural theory to demonstrate the power of ideas to influence people's material condition. Weber did not deny the advantage that certain groups had already gained by their economic positions. However, he stressed that values have social and economic consequences. Weber's classic work, *Protestant Ethic and the Spirit of Capitalism* (1920), is an attempt to demonstrate this thesis.

Weber contended that such Puritan values as hard work, asceticism, frugality, and deferred gratification have contributed to the development of what he called "the spirit of capitalism." These cultural values, originally articulated and promoted by religious reformers, have eventually become ingrained in the Protestant ethic that underpins the capitalist enterprise. Financial success, in other words, is a function of the values by which one lives.

Those who share similar values and lifestyles join together to form status groups and discriminate against those who have dissimilar values. Friends and associates are chosen on the basis of a level of comfort based on shared values. Members of the same status groups tend to intermarry, reside in the same neighborhood, choose similar occupations, belong to the same or similar organizations and associations, and enjoy similar forms of entertainment. Based on these considerations, Weber identified three distinct dimensions of stratification: class, status, and power.

Referring to the racial conflicts in the United States, Weber observed that the antipathy between whites and blacks is not natural but political. Whites made interracial sex a taboo and a crime only after the abolition of slavery. When former slaves demanded equal civil rights they were perceived by the whites as a threat to their competitive advantage. Even the slightest admixture of black ancestry was made a bar to their admission to the status hierarchy of the whites.

Once a group is marked out to be despised, denigrated, and held in contempt, not only their physical characteristics but also their customs, lifestyles, and values are despised and rejected. Over the course of time, a minority group's exclusion from the dominant population results in the widening of the cultural gap, leading to further isolation and hostility. Culture, historical experiences, and physical characteristics thus become interlinked, strengthening the basis of stratification.

Culture of Poverty Thesis

Weber's contention that the Protestant ethic, which is the spirit of capitalism, underlies the success of this system has generated much debate on the cultural basis of poverty and stratification. Anthropologist Oscar Lewis contends that poverty is one of the numerous traits—he identified fifty-five—of what he called the "culture of poverty." In his view, although poverty is an essential trait of this culture, poverty alone does not account for it. The culture that generates poverty is a "total system" of ideology and psychological attitudes, including marginality, helplessness, dependency, lack of future orientation, and indulgence of impulses.

The culture of poverty thesis has found wide-ranging acceptance among economists and policymakers such as Gunnar Myrdal, John R. Commons, and Booker T. Washington to explain the economic status of African Americans. Myrdal attributed the economic situation of blacks to their "low standards of efficiency, reliability, ambition, and morals." Conservative thinkers, relying on a cultural explanation, oppose social programs meant to improve the conditions of the poor as ineffective in overcoming chronic poverty. They blame poverty and inequality on a variety of cultural factors, including single motherhood, illegitimacy, teen pregnancy, laziness, the ingratitude of immigrants, rap music, and the drug culture.

Rational Choice Theory

Weber maintained that rationalization—choosing the most efficient means to optimize benefits while minimizing costs—is the dominant trend in contemporary societies. Later theorists have seized on Weber's rational action model to analyze the social status of individuals as the outcome of a series of choices that they make under the constraints of available resources. They assert that even choices that later turn out to be bad are rational at the time they are made. Applying this theory to race and ethnic relations, rational choice theorists

argue that individuals align themselves with their own racial and ethnic groups to maximize their chances of success, creating in-groups and out-groups. The outcome of the resulting competition among different groups is the creation of the various social strata.

Impact on Social Policy

While some of these theories serve to legitimize existing inequalities, others offer grounds for critiquing them. Biological theories of stratification have had a profound impact on U.S. social policy toward minorities. During the late nineteenth and early twentieth centuries, the United States restricted immigration from non-English-speaking countries and denied equal educational opportunities to African Americans in the belief that these racial and ethnic groups lacked the genetic capacity to become successful in American society. The culture of poverty thesis is often evoked by conservative politicians to criticize social programs. Most social ills that disproportionately affect the underclass—drug addiction, illegitimacy, teen pregnancy, welfare dependency, unemployment, poverty, and crime—have been blamed on the culture of poverty. Liberal politicians have used diluted versions of conflict theory to pass laws and programs, such as civil rights legislation and affirmative action programs, in an attempt to reverse the ill effects of past oppression of minority groups.

Mathew J. Kanjirathinkal

Core Resources

The theory of class conflict is a general theme in the writings of Karl Marx. The works particularly relevant to social stratification are *Capital: A Critique of Political Economy* (New York: Random House, 1906), *The Grudnrisse*, edited by David McLellan (New York: Harper Torchbooks, 1971), and *The German Ideology* (New York: International Publishers, 1965). Talcott Parsons's elaboration of the functionalist view is found in *The Structure of Social Action* (New York: Free Press, 1937) and *The Social System* (New York: Free Press, 1951). In his 1968 essay, "The Distribution of Power in American Society," in *C. Wright Mills and the Power Elite*, edited by William Domhoff and Hoyt B. Ballard (Boston: Beacon Press, 1968), Parsons acknowledges the need to incorporate some aspects of the conflict perspective into functionalism to explain social stratification. The essay "Some Principles of Social Stratification," by Kingsley Davis and Wilbert Moore, in *American Sociological Review* (10, 1945) is a succinct and clear statement of the functionalist position on stratification. Max Weber's classic work that shows the relationship between cultural factors and economic change is *The Protestant Ethic and the Spirit of Capitalism*, translated by Talcott Parsons (London: G. Allen & Unwin, 1930).

A focused analysis of the notion of social class is

contained in Weber's *From Max Weber: Essays in Sociology*, edited and translated by Hans Gerth and C. Wright Mills (New York: Oxford University Press, 1946). George Gilder, in *Wealth and Poverty* (New York: Basic Books, 1981), offers theoretical support for the conservative fiscal policies of the 1980's by asserting that the rich are rich because of their superior abilities. Charles Murray's work *Losing Ground: American Social Policy, 1950-1980* (New York: Basic Books, 1984) is frequently cited by conservative thinkers to critique social programs that were instituted to help the poor. Richard Herrnstein and Charles Murray, in their well-known work, *The Bell Curve: Intelligence and Class Structure in American Life* (New York: Free Press, 1994), argue that the poor are poor because of their low mental ability, as shown by average IQ scores. *Inequality by Design: Cracking the Bell Curve Myth* (Princeton, N.J., Princeton University Press, 1996), by Calude S. Fisher et al., offers a rebuttal to Hernnstein and Murray's contention that social stratification is a function of inherited intelligence. Harold R. Kerbo's textbook, *Social Stratification and Inequality* (New York: McGraw-Hill, 1996), provides an overview of the theories and dimensions of social stratification in the United States.

See also: Aryan "race"; Assimilation theories; Biosocial theories; Caste model; Class theories of racial/ethnic relations; Culture of poverty; Intelligence and race; Marxist models; Nordic "race"; Racial/ethnic relations: theoretical overview; Social Darwinism and racism; Sociobiology and race.

Socialization and reference groups

> **Significance:** The concept of reference groups helps to explain the dynamics underlying intergroup behavior. Among the effects of reliance on reference groups can be an ethnocentric outlook on life that leads to social conflict.

Since its inception many decades ago, the concept of reference groups has found a number of applications in the social sciences because of its ability to illuminate certain motives underlying human action. Among the more important of these applications has been its use in the race relations field to help explain the dynamics underlying prejudice and discrimination. Because these phenomena are such deeply rooted and persistent problems, much effort has been applied to understanding their genesis. Sociologist Tamotsu Shibutani, in 1955, carefully discussed some of the implications inherent in

the concept of reference groups. He argued that one can find at least three such implications. First, reference groups may be seen as standards which actors use to gauge their definition of particular situations; that is, individuals, in attempting to interpret unfamiliar situations, often emulate groups whose orientation they find influential. Individuals ask themselves, "What would x do in these circumstances?" Second, reference groups may be viewed as groups in which an actor desires to participate. Third, reference groups are groups whose viewpoint constitutes an actor's frame of reference. This implication, though similar to the first, differs in an important way: It implies a continuous socialization into the culture of the reference group, whereas the former does not. In the former usage, the idea is that at crucial moments, the individual will turn to his or her understanding of the reference group for guidance. In the latter, this orientation is more or less permanent, since the individual is constantly submerged in the norms and values of the reference group. It would not occur to the person that any other course of action is possible. Shibutani argues that the third meaning of reference groups is most important because of its association with culture and socialization.

Reference Groups in Pluralistic Societies

Seen from the point of view of culture, reference groups are an outcome of the process of socialization. In this process, the norms and values of particular groups are inculcated into individuals such that they become their own. They reflexively act and feel as do others in their particular group. The group's frame of reference becomes one's own. The individual is able to anticipate the attitudes and feelings of others in the group because the individual is like them.

Racial and ethnic groups are among the most important of the groups into which individuals are socialized, since they often generate intense in-group loyalty, and, hence, conflict. As reference groups, they are especially important in plural societies with their multiplicity of racial and ethnic groups. In such societies, the desire for social advancement can heighten racial and ethnic consciousness. Consequently, it becomes relatively more difficult to resolve conflicting group interests, since in-group members are unable (or unwilling) to take the viewpoint of others in competing racial or ethnic groups. The respective frames of reference are often too far apart to allow a rapprochement.

Paradoxically, pluralistic societies can also undermine the particularistic leanings that lead to racial and ethnic conflict. By definition, these groups are not the only ones that exist in plural societies; there are many others. Significantly, some of these—such as occupational groups, classes, and religious groups—cross-cut racial and ethnic groups. Since individuals can belong to numerous groups at the same time, they might find that they have conflicting reference groups. The norms and values predominating in one group might conflict with those in another. For example, a racially conscious individual might harbor negative sentiments toward members of another race; however, he might also belong to a religious group which teaches that such feelings are wrong. Similarly, an individual might dislike members of a competing ethnic group but might find herself working closely with members of that ethnic group. As psychologist Gordon Allport has shown, close cooperation of this sort tends to undermine negative racial and ethnic sentiments. The task of reference group theory in circumstances such as those just noted is to predict which set of affiliations will win out in the

These students at Our Lady of Perpetual Help High School in Brooklyn, New York, follow the school's dress code: plain blouses and pleated skirts. Uniforms are a visible marker that help set apart an individual's reference group and increase an individual's sense of belonging.

end. According to Shibutani, this might depend on such factors as the individual's commitment to the respective groups or the depth of the interpersonal relationships that have developed in the groups. The expectation is that the reference group to which the individual is most deeply committed will be relatively more influential in guiding behavior.

Some sociologists say that reference groups are crucial to individuals in modern pluralistic societies such as the United States because they provide a frame of reference through which individuals make sense of the world. It is virtually impossible to imagine the nonexistence of reference groups, since they are the natural outgrowth of the process of socialization. Through this process, individuals assume that the norms and values of the groups into which they have been socialized are standard for all groups. Reference group formation, therefore, is inherently ethnocentric. Pluralism, however, can offset this ethnocentrism by providing individuals with the opportunity to belong to competing reference groups.

Conflict in Pluralistic Societies

The concept of reference groups is useful for explaining conflict in plural societies. One example of this is the situation to be found in former colonies. In many such societies, there exists a pattern of ethnic stratification in which, as the colonial rulers give up power, indigenous elites approximating them in culture (and sometimes in color) rise up to take their place. At the same time, the groups that traditionally resided at the bottom of colo-

nial society remain subordinated. Thus, the end of colonialism, far from radically restructuring these societies, tends to maintain the status quo; indigenous elites, like the colonial masters before them, tend to despise the groups that reside at the bottom of the society. The concept of reference groups provides a clue as to how this pattern might be explained.

The former British colonies of the West Indies provide an example. Traditionally, these territories have exhibited a tripartite social structure quite unlike the sharp racial dichotomy to be found in the United States. Whereas Americans, relying on the "one-drop rule," have tended to classify individuals with even remote black ancestry as "black," the West Indian countries have recognized three distinct social strata: a tiny white (and largely foreign) elite residing at the top of the society, a middle stratum made up of mixed-race individuals, and a large group of blacks (who constitute the bulk of the population) residing at the bottom of the society. Social status varied from top to bottom according to color and occupation. As was the case in the United States, "blackness" was denigrated and blacks were discriminated against. There was a crucial difference, however, since mixed-race individuals (who would be considered "black" in the United States) were recognized as constituting a distinct social category. Also, as historian Douglas Hall has shown, the idea existed that upward mobility could partially offset the stigma of black skin. Thus, the concept arose that "money whitens." This meant, essentially, that as upwardly mobile blacks adopted British culture more fully, they became increasingly "acceptable" to the British elite. This elite, therefore, constituted a reference group for the whole society. Their viewpoint, through socialization, became the prism through which blacks—mixed and unmixed—viewed the world. Writers such as Diane Austin and Gordon Lewis have shown that the family and the education system are the two most important institutions for transmitting British culture. They argue, further, that the effectiveness of this transmission can be seen in the fact that West Indians overvalue educational credentials and "proper behavior" (such as forms of speech), and they evince deep class consciousness.

In the postcolonial period (formally inaugurated with Jamaica's independence in 1962), the British presence declined, but British culture remained very influential. As they withdrew from the region, the mulattoes, Syrians, and Jews who bore the closest physical resemblance to the British gradually occupied the elite position formerly occupied by the British. One aspect of this ethnic succession was the wholesale adoption of the antiblack stereotypes that had formerly been held by the British. The new elite's thorough inculcation into British culture meant that few other reference groups could rise to challenge the traditional way of viewing the world. Thus, the actual withdrawal of the British from the islands had little effect on racial attitudes. British culture acted as a conservative force to perpetuate existing inequalities even after the physical removal of the original British reference group. One could say, therefore, that race relations in the West Indies (and a number of other former colonies) cannot be understood without grasping the historical importance of reference groups.

In a similar vein, psychologist Jeff Howard and physician Ray Hammond have argued that the concept is useful in explaining underachievement among African Americans in the educational system. They argue that this problem stems from blacks' fear of competing intellectually because of stereotypes of black inferiority that have been broadcast by the majority group. For Howard and Hammond, the majority group is a reference group which establishes certain criteria for what will be defined as "success" and which undermines the confidence of African Americans by sowing doubt about the capabilities of African Americans. The majority group is able to do this because, by definition, majority groups exercise political, social, and cultural dominance in the societies in which they exist. Minority groups, on the other hand, are subordinated and face an uphill fight in getting their point of view to prevail.

If one bears in mind Shibutani's discussion of reference groups, one can see that writers use the term in different ways. For example, Shibutani wishes to confine the term to groups that provide an automatic frame of reference to individuals because of socialization. The analysis of West Indian racial attitudes, however, implies that reference groups serve as standards for making judgments, are groups which others aspire to join, and provide a frame of reference for upwardly mobile West Indians. Thus, in the West Indian context, the concept of reference groups embraces the full complement of meanings outlined by Shibutani. On the other hand, as used by Howard and Hammond, the term implies only the idea of groups that provide standards of judgment—in this case, intellectual. Therefore, one always needs to examine the context in which the term is used to determine its full meaning.

Belonging to multiple groups—for example, being a black immigrant from Africa and working as an engineer—can lead to the problem of deciding which identity will take precedence: the racial identity that stems from being black in America, the ethnic identity that stems from having an African background, or the class identity that stems from occupation and education? How an individual resolves such conflicts might well revolve around which reference group he or she views as being most salient. Living in a plural society also increases the number of encounters that individuals have with members of different groups. These encounters are potentially anxiety-producing, since cultures vary widely. Quite likely, an individual's response will be strongly affected by salient reference groups. For example, immigrants to the United States sometimes adopt negative stereotypes of groups already living here, even though they have previously had little experience with these groups. This prejudice can be explained by viewing it as a learned response deriving from native groups which the immigrants view as reference groups.   *Milton D. Vickerman*

Core Resources

For more on the work of Tomatsu Shibutani, see his *Society and Personality* (Englewood Cliffs, N.J.: Prentice-Hall, 1961) and *Ethnic Stratification* (New York: Macmillan, 1965). Gordon W. Allport's *The Nature of Prejudice* (Cambridge, Mass.: Addison-Wesley, 1954) is a classic overview of prejudice and discrimination. Diane J. Austin's *Urban Life in Kingston, Jamaica: The Culture and Class Ideology of Two Neighborhoods* (New York: Gordon and Breach Science Publishers, 1984) compares two neighborhoods in Kingston, Jamaica, in an attempt to analyze differences in middle-class and working-class culture. Robert K. Merton and A. Katt's "Contributions to the Theory of Reference Group Behavior," in *Studies in the Scope and Method of "The American Soldier,"* edited by Robert K. Merton and Paul F. Lazarsfeld (Glencoe, Ill.: Free Press, 1950), extends the concept of reference groups to include groups that others aspire to join and groups that shape the perceptual field of others.

See also: Options for ethnic identity; Prejudice: effects; Psychological theories of intergroup relations; Social identity theory; Social perception of others; West Indian Americans.

Society of American Indians

On October 12, 1911, more than fifty Native American delegates met in Columbus, Ohio, at the founding conference of the Society of American Indians (SAI). The date, Columbus Day, was significant: This gathering marked a reclaiming of indigenous voices, a rediscovering of native pride.

The "father" of this organization was a non-Native American sociologist from Ohio State University, Fayette A. McKenzie. Six months prior to the October conference, McKenzie had met with Dr. Charles Eastman (Sioux), Dr. Carlos Montezuma (Apache), attorney Thomas L. Sloan (Omaha), Laura Cornelius (Oneida), and Henry Standing Bear (Sioux). Coming from different backgrounds, these educated professionals united to form a native-run association. Already assimilated into the dominant society, they sought to retain their Native American identity. Calling themselves the American Indian Association, the group rallied around pan-Indian reforms, especially in the educational arena.

At the October convention, the historical, legal, and cultural bonds connecting all natives were emphasized. The delegates drafted a constitution that advocated native advancement, true historical presentation, native citizenship, and legal assistance. To assert that this was a native movement and not a "white-run" organization, delegates changed the name to the Society of American Indians. National meetings were to be held annually, and Washington, D.C., was designated as the society's headquarters.

The SAI's publication, the *Quarterly Journal*, was first issued on April 15, 1913. The masthead was framed with the society's emblem, the American eagle on one side and a lighted torch on the other. Below this was the SAI's motto: "The honor of the race and the good of the country shall be paramount."

The journal's editor, Arthur C. Parker (Seneca), was the SAI's most intellectual influence. With his anthropological background, Parker sought to design the SAI after Tecumseh's historical visions. Parker ardently fought for educational reforms, for an American Indian Day, and for visible Native American role models.

As a peacekeeper, Parker often tempered the rising factionalism in the SAI. In 1913 the SAI was at its membership height with more than two hundred active (native) members and more than four hundred associate (non-native) members. Friction in the following years sharply eroded membership numbers, however; lacking resources for assisting tribes with legal aid and for affecting the structure of the Bureau of Indian Affairs (BIA), members began to air their frustrations internally. Conflicts involved arguments over the abolition of the BIA, the denouncement of peyote religion, and the responsibility of individual tribal complaints. The SAI officially rejected peyote religion, but no consensus was reached on the BIA question, an issue that eventually splintered the SAI.

A change in focus was attempted by renaming the society's publication *The American Indian Magazine*. One of its editors, Gertrude Simmons Bonnin, a Yankton Sioux, became involved in the SAI by opening an educational center among the Utes. Even with Bonnin's strong contributions, however, the SAI's status remained precarious.

In the early 1920's, a sense of despair clouded the SAI's visions. Pan-Indian unification attempts had failed, BIA abolition was hopeless, political clout was slight (many members were not franchised), and individual interests were detracting from pantribal ones. On June 2, 1924, the Indian Citizenship Act was signed, marking the success of one of the SAI's hardest fought battles. By this time, however, the group was almost completely defunct, and symbolically, this date marks the end of the SAI.

Tanya M. Backinger

See also: American Indian activism; Indian Citizenship Act; Pan-Indianism; Peyote religion.

Sociobiology and race

Sociobiology is the study of the biological basis of social behavior. Sociobiologists attempt to trace the origins of behavior to biological strategies for maximizing the survival and proliferation of genes. Biological determinants of group-level associative and discriminating behaviors, including racial segregation, are among the variety of topics addressed by sociobiological theories.

Sociobiology emerged from earlier biosocial theories and ethnological principles largely because of the work of Edward O. Wilson of Harvard University in the 1970's. As a scientific discipline, sociobiology resides at the intersection of biology, sociology, and psychology, where practitioners are concerned with the biological underpinnings of human social behavior. Sociobiologists contend that social behavior can be explained, and ultimately predicted, by a thorough understanding of the interactions between the genetic composition of an organism and environmental constraints. Critics of sociobiology, notably Richard C. Lewontin of Harvard University, argue against the oversimplification of human behavior and the fatal error of explaining racial and cultural stereotypes according to biological measurements. Instead, he and other critics say, socioeconomic inequalities and differences in environmental quality are responsible for perpetuating social characteristics commonly found among racial aggregates.

Sociobiology is among several theories that have been proposed to explain variations in human culture and behavior on the basis of innate biological characteristics. At the core of these so-called biosocial theories is the inevitable challenge of resolving the complex interactions between nature and nurture, or in modern terminology, between genetic and environmental determinism. Early biosocial theories concerned with racial differences included phrenology, the pseudoscience of measuring cranial dimensions as a way of predicting racial identity and behavior. The reemergence of interest in the intelligence quotient (IQ) measurement is based on biosocial theories of innate and racially determined differences in cognitive abilities essential for succeeding in a technologically driven society. At the extreme end of genetic determinism in the continuum of behavioral gene-environment interactions reside the discredited tenets of eugenics. Eugenicists advocate the purification of the human genetic stock by curbing the reproduction of inferior genotypes, which tend to be disproportionately identified among racial minority groups.

At the other end of the gene-environment continuum, staunch environmentalists declare that human racial identities are based entirely on social and cultural prejudices lacking any basis in biological parameters. Indeed modern genetic measurements show that molecular differences that exist within socially defined racial groups are typically larger than differences between these groups. Therefore, all biosocial theories about racial characteristics and behavior are fundamentally flawed because there is no credible biological definition of race.

Scholars primarily concerned with ranking human races in terms of inferiority or superiority have used sociobiology theories erroneously to support their controversial points of view. Speculations about poorly characterized molecular determinants of racial differences in innate intelligence, violent behavior, and sexual characteristics have retarded scientific progress toward understanding the diversity of human cultural and behavioral characteristics. Ultimately, scientific understanding of race relations may not depend at all on measurable biological determinants, but sociobiology offers one way to appreciate human diversity. *Oladele A. Ogunseitan*

See also: Ability testing; Biosocial theories; Intelligence testing; Race as a concept; "Scientific" racism; Social Darwinism and racism; Xenophobia, nativism, and eugenics.

Somatic norm theory

H. Hoetink, a Dutch sociologist, developed a somatic norm theory of race relations in his 1973 book, *Slavery and Race Relations in the Americas: Comparative Notes on Their Nature and Nexus*. A somatic norm is an image of perfect beauty that every racial or ethnic group has developed over time. According to Hoetink, Chinese people (for example) have an image of beauty that is quite different from that of Africans, Native Americans, or Pygmies. This image of beauty affects every interaction between people of different racial and ethnic groups. For example, Africans will always show a preference to live with, marry, and associate with others who correspond to their conception of beauty. In multiracial societies, under this theory, little contact is expected among people from groups with different visions of beauty. Thus, somatic norms tend to preserve the separation that exists between individuals of different skin color or ethnic background. To associate with other, less beautiful people violates the sense of perfection that individuals are taught to appreciate from the very beginning of their lives. These images of beauty are not easily changed. Hence, racism is part of every social system.

Leslie V. Tischauser

See also: Race as a concept; Racism: history of the concept.

Soul

For African Americans the term "soul" is positively associated with anything "authentically black." The term "soul" came to be applied especially to the culture—slang, humor, religion, food—of lower-class African Americans in the urban ghettos. The idea of soul was also related to the black nationalism that emerged from the Civil Rights movement in the 1960's. Black nationalists urged African Americans to take pride in black culture. Sociologist Ulf Hannerz, writing in 1970, observed that soul was a kind of folk conception of African American national character.

Some music scholars and critics use the term "soul music" to refer to all African American popular music produced in the 1960's and early 1970's. Most critics, however, use the term more precisely to refer to a particular genre of African American music that combined gospel-derived vocals with rhythm and blues. These vocals, described by critics as grainy, gritty, hoarse, or rasping, led critics to see this music as more authentically black than, for example, the African American music being produced at Motown Records, which deliberately smoothed out its vocals to appeal to white audiences.

Soul recording artists included Otis Redding, Sam and Dave, and Aretha Franklin.   *Donald M. Whaley*

See also: Black nationalism; Motown Records; Rap music.

Southern Christian Leadership Conference

> **Significance:** The SCLC was one of the major organizations instrumental in the Civil Rights movement in the American South in the 1950's and 1960's.

The Southern Christian Leadership Conference originated in a bus boycott organized in 1955 to protest segregation in Montgomery, Alabama. Martin Luther King, Jr., a young minister, led the Montgomery Improvement Association, which spearheaded the boycott. His leadership marked the emergence of African American ministers as organizers in the Civil Rights movement. King and other black ministers became increasingly involved in the Civil Rights movement.

The SCLC was formed in December, 1957, as a result of this church-led protest movement and others that had occurred in southern communities. The SCLC was distinctly different from the National Association for the Advancement of Colored People (NAACP, established in 1909), long the premiere organization involved in the struggle for the rights of African Americans. In contrast to the NAACP, the SCLC was confined to the South. It did not have individual memberships, in part so that it would not be seen as competing with the NAACP. Instead, it was an umbrella organization bringing together local affiliates in a loose alliance. Each affiliate paid the SCLC a fee of twenty-five dollars, in return receiving a certificate of affiliation signed by King. Each affiliate had the right to send five delegates to the group's annual meeting. Most affiliates were composed of African American ministers and their churches. At least two-thirds of the thirty-three members of the governing board were ministers, primarily Baptist. Northern activists, including Bayard Rustin and Stanley Levison, assisted the SCLC in solving problems of organizational cohesion, financial stability, and political direction. The SCLC, however, is identified primarily with King as its leader.

Methods

The approach used by the SCLC was a combination of grassroots activism and political strategy. Its major campaigns concentrated on the use of nonviolent direct action techniques such as marches, demonstrations, boycotts, and civil disobedience to protest segregation and discrimination. Politically, the SCLC worked within the system to change laws.

The organization's initial project, in 1958, was a voter registration drive in the South. As the 1960's began, other groups began launching protest movements of various types. In 1960, African American students launched sit-in demonstrations at lunch counters to protest segregation, and in 1961, the Congress of Racial Equality initiated Freedom Rides on interstate buses. These protests served as training in the use of nonviolent protest methods. In 1961, the SCLC became involved in mass nonviolent demonstrations against segregation in Albany, Georgia, learning how to mobilize the African American community in the process. Although the Albany campaign failed, the SCLC learned the importance of having a strong local base, a clear chain of command, and a coherent strategy. In 1963, the SCLC was successful in desegregating facilities in Birmingham, Alabama. Publicity from that movement, including televised coverage of police officers beating black demonstrators, was

Southern Christian Leadership Conference leader Martin Luther King, Jr., (left of man in white hat) participates in a rally in Montgomery, Alabama, in March, 1965.

a major impetus to passage of the Civil Rights Act of 1964. In 1965, the SCLC was involved in a voting rights campaign in Selma, Alabama. This led directly to passage of the Voting Rights Act of 1965, one of the major achievements of the Civil Rights movement.

After 1965, the SCLC began to look beyond the South. A 1966 attempt to end housing segregation in Chicago failed, in part because the SCLC lacked a base outside the South. King and the SCLC also began to focus on problems of poverty following urban riots in 1964. This effort culminated in the Poor People's Campaign. King was assassinated on April 4, 1968, when he went to Memphis, Tennessee, to support striking sanitation workers as part of his Poor People's Campaign. The campaign continued, and the planned march to Washington, D.C., took place under the leadership of the Reverend Ralph Abernathy. The SCLC held demonstrations in the nation's capital in May and June of 1968.

Following King's death, Abernathy became president of the SCLC. The SCLC subsequently declined in importance. Abernathy lacked King's leadership abilities, and following the major achievements of the 1960's, support for the Civil Rights movement as a whole diminished. In the 1970's, the SCLC faded as an effective force in achieving social and economic progress for African American and poor people. In 1973, Abernathy announced his resignation as president of the SCLC.

Assessment

In 1986, King's birthday was made a national holiday in recognition of his civil rights work. King is the leader most clearly identified with the Civil Rights movement. Passage of the Voting Rights Act of 1965 was one of the notable achievements of the SCLC. That act resulted in an increase in African American voter registration from 2 million to approximately 3.8 million in ten years. This in turn led to a large increase in the numbers of African American elected officials and other elected officials responsive to the needs of the African American community. Although that community continued to face problems, the efforts of the SCLC aided black Americans in securing equal rights within the American system of justice. The SCLC later concentrated its efforts on issues involving African American families and voter registration in the South.   *William V. Moore*

Core Resources

Numerous books document the contributions of King and various civil rights groups. Among them are Taylor Branch's *Parting the Waters: America in the King Years, 1954-63* (New York: Simon & Schuster, 1988); Adam Fairclough's *To Redeem the Soul of America: The Southern Christian Leadership Conference and Martin Luther King, Jr.* (Athens: University of Georgia Press, 1987); David J.

Garrow's *Bearing the Cross: Martin Luther King, Jr., and the Southern Christian Leadership Conference* (New York: William Morrow, 1986); Stephen B. Oates's *Let the Trumpet Sound: The Life of Martin Luther King, Jr.* (New York: Harper & Row, 1982); and Robert Weisbrot's *Freedom Bound: A History of America's Civil Rights Movement* (New York: W. W. Norton, 1990).

See also: Children in the Civil Rights movement; Civil Rights Act of 1964; Civil Rights movement; Congress of Racial Equality; Freedom Riders; Greensboro sit-ins; King, Martin Luther, Jr., assasination; Little Rock school desegregation; National Association for the Advancement of Colored People; Segregation: de facto and de jure; Selma-Montgomery march; Student Nonviolent Coordinating Committee; Voting Rights Act of 1965.

Southern Conference for Human Welfare

A small group of southern liberals founded the Southern Conference for Human Welfare (SCHW) in 1938 in response to the *Report on Economic Conditions of the South* (1938), a devastating critique of the region's prospects and leadership. The report was commonly known as the Mellett Report after Lowell Mellett, director of the National Emergency Council, a group of educators, businesspeople, bankers, farmers, and others from the South who prepared the report in response to a request by President Franklin D. Roosevelt. The president was trying to garner southern support for his second New Deal and needed to demonstrate an understanding of the area's problems. The SCHW remained a small group until the end of World War II, when it spearheaded a widespread reform movement. The SCHW viewed race discrimination as an economic and political problem rather than a social one. Its members advocated strong labor unions, an end to rule by Bourbons (extremely conservative southerners), and the abolition of the poll tax and other disfranchisement laws. By the end of 1946, it had more than ten thousand members. Paid workers lobbied the U.S. Congress and conducted conferences throughout the South. An offshoot, the Southern Conference Education Fund, continued to work for civil rights for black southerners.

The SCHW met its demise in a disastrous attempt to mount a third-party presidential campaign in 1948. Backing Henry Wallace's Progressive Party, the SCHW staged several integrated tours through southern cities. However, as the Cold War heated up, the SCHW became suspect. Although the House Committee on Un-American Activities failed to uncover a single communist in the organization, it tainted the organization with charges of disloyalty. In November, 1948, the SCHW's board of representatives voted to suspend operations.

Robert E. McFarland

See also: Civil rights movement; Labor movement; Roosevelt coalition.

Southwest Voter Registration Education Project

The Southwest Voter Registration Education Project was established in 1974 at San Antonio, Texas, by Willy Velásquez. Its principal goal was the mobilization of Mexican American communities by means of voter registration and participation in elections. The organization was created by young Mexican Americans who had been active in the Chicano movement in the 1960's, an effort to strengthen ethnic pride and build self-determination among Mexican Americans. The young activists' desire to lash out at the established order occurred at a time of international student unrest and idealism. A new concern for civil rights and a desire to fight poverty were encouraged and fostered by the New Frontier goals of the John F. Kennedy era, the Cuban Revolution of Fidel Castro, and the rise of black power in the African American community. Mexican American organizers would no longer tolerate segregated schools, bans on interracial marriages, and the indifference of established politicians.

In Texas, Mexican American activists in the 1960's were led by José Ángel Gutiérrez, who rapidly set the tone by engaging in confrontations with the white power structure. He led a walkout at the high school in Crystal City, Texas, where students demanded changes in policies regarding cheerleaders and the selection of homecoming queens, policies normally controlled by a largely white faculty even though the school was 85 percent Mexican American. Gutiérrez and Mario Compean then set up the Mexican American Youth Organization in San Antonio to empower neighborhoods largely on the basis of volunteer work. Although Mexican Americans constituted 70 percent to 90 percent of the inhabitants of south Texas, no one had ever organized them successfully. Because Mexican Americans had never been part of the political process and most had fewer than three years of primary education and earned about two thousand dollars per year, traditional politicians ignored them. The techniques employed by Gutiérrez and his followers were aggressive boycotts, verbal confrontations with police and school officials, and strident accusations where injustices occurred. Velásquez and other leaders of the Southwest Voter Registration Education Project emerged from this group of activists.

The young activists in the Southwest Voter Registration Education Project established their own goals and identity, publishing analyses of Mexican American voting potential and trends. Gradually, the project gave legitimacy to working for change "within the system." People who supported the project began to believe that things were getting better. A similar organization, the Midwestern Voter Registration Education Project, became powerful in Chicago. With the help of the Voting Rights Act amendments in 1975 and 1982, the Southwest Voter Registration Education Project played a key role in doubling the number of Mexican Americans registered to vote from 1976 to 1985. Despite uncertain funding, it also helped elect Mexican Americans to public office. The group brought hundreds of legal suits challenging reapportioning and at-large voting practices that whites used to dilute Mexican American electoral strength. By 1991, of an estimated four thousand elected Mexican American officials, approximately half were in Texas, in large measure because of the efforts of the Southwest Voter Registration Education Project.

Douglas W. Richmond

See also: Chicano movement.

Soviet Jewish immigrants

When the Bolsheviks assumed power in Russia in 1917, they promised to end the periodic pogroms (massacres) and frequent discrimination that Russian Jews had experienced under the czars. However, the Soviet government soon engaged in widespread, though perhaps less overt, forms of discrimination and persecution against the country's Jewish population. In addition, because the Soviet Union's official communist ideology included a commitment to atheism, Jews, along with other religious groups, were essentially barred from practicing their religion. Houses of worship were closed or destroyed, and religious leaders were imprisoned.

During the era of détente in the 1970's, the Soviet government permitted a significant increase in Jewish emigration. This was partly caused by the passage in the U.S. Congress of the Jackson-Vanik amendment, which tied American-Soviet trade to an increase in the Soviet Union's Jewish emigration permits. Although many Soviet Jews emigrated to Israel, a large portion of these emigrants eventually settled in the United States. Jewish American groups had lobbied the federal government both to pressure the Soviet government to release Jews and to permit more Soviet Jews to settle in the United States.

Although the immigration campaign was highly successful, Soviet Jewish immigrants did not always integrate with the American Jewish community as well as had been hoped. The immigrants were frequently more secular, having grown up in an officially atheistic state. They also tended to be poor and eager to make use of resources made available by American Jewish groups. Politically, many Soviet Jewish immigrants were more conservative than the mainstream American Jewish groups. Also, many of the immigrants did not speak English. A number of American Jewish leaders expressed disappointment about their inability to incorporate and assimilate the new immigrants.

A second wave of Soviet Jewish emigration took place in the late 1980's and early 1990's, when Soviet leader Mikhail Gorbachev liberalized his country's emigration laws. The collapse of the Soviet Union in 1991 in particular created a renewed impetus for Soviet Jews (and others) to leave their country. Many Soviet Jews were attracted to the United States by concerted campaigns by Jewish American groups. The number of Jewish immigrants from the former Soviet Union increased from about 200 in 1986 to a peak of 185,000 in 1990. A total of more than 700,000 Soviet Jews immigrated to the United States between 1987 and 1997.

The fact that many Soviet Jewish immigrants do not look, speak, or behave like mainstream American Jews has underscored an important principle of racial and ethnic relations. Frequently, cultural and societal differences—rather than purely racial, ethnic, or religious differences—have led to friction between groups. Similarly, the mere sharing of ethnic or racial backgrounds does not ensure intergroup harmony.   *Steve D. Boilard*

See also: Eastern European Jews; Jewish Americans; Religion-based ethnicities; Russian Americans.

Split labor market theory

Sociologist Edna Bonacich's split labor market theory suggests that the underlying causes of racial and ethnic antagonism are economic competition and class relations, not racial or cultural differences. Split labor markets develop when labor costs diverge for two or more groups of comparably skilled workers. Labor costs are a function of wages and the expenses associated with workers' recruitment, training, benefits, and propensity to unionize. Labor costs diverge when a particular racial or ethnic group systematically experiences economic and political disadvantages. If they are financially desperate and politically weak, minority workers may be subject to exploitation and may have to accept lower wages, longer hours, and undesirable working conditions. As a re-

sponse to their vulnerability, members of minority groups often migrate to take advantage of better opportunities in developing areas. Labor migration facilitates intergroup contact and threatens higher-cost majority workers with displacement. Regional differences in wages and living standards can exacerbate unequal labor costs. In addition, if migrants have a short-term orientation to employment, they may resist the labor unions of the existing workforce.

According to the theory, split labor markets infuse class conflict with racial or ethnic antagonism because employers will hire minority workers whenever their lower labor costs increase the efficiency of capitalist production. Majority workers, in turn, can respond to a split labor market in three ways. First, they can attempt to exclude the minority group from the labor market. Scholar Terry Boswell has argued that the Chinese exclusion movement of the 1870's and 1880's resulted from the political mobilization of white workers who were threatened by Chinese immigration. Second, majority workers can attempt to institutionalize a caste system that relegates the minority group to less desirable jobs. Bonacich suggests that as blacks migrated out of the South during the 1930's, many labor unions attempted to reduce racial job competition by confining black workers to unskilled positions. Both exclusion movements and caste systems foster racism, nativism, and racial or ethnic violence. Finally, majority workers can attempt to equalize labor costs: They can lobby the government to impose or enforce equal employment standards or they can pursue comprehensive union organizing. This strategy undercuts the potential for minority strike breaking and related conflict. Bonacich has argued that the New Deal legislation of the 1930's helped to equalize labor costs and encouraged U.S. labor unions to incorporate black workers.

Split labor market theory differs from neo-Marxist perspectives that attribute racial and ethnic conflict to the divide-and-conquer tactics of capitalists. Instead, racial and ethnic antagonism results from dynamics internal to the working class. Although employers may benefit, they do not actively cultivate racial or ethnic conflict. The theory also differs from dual and segmented labor market approaches, which explain racial and ethnic inequality in terms of groups' concentration in core and peripheral labor markets. In a dual or segmented labor market, human capital differences prevent majority and minority workers from competing directly for the same jobs. In contrast, the split labor market perspective focuses on the consequences of job competition between different racial or ethnic groups.   *Cliff Brown*

See also: Economics of race; Labor movement; Marxist models; Racial/ethnic relations: race-class debate.

Sports

> **Significance:** Although sports are often prized by fans and participants alike as a refuge from mundane concerns, the sporting world has long provided a highly public forum for the debate and resolution of social issues. Matters of race and ethnicity have long been among the most contentious of these.

The rise of organized sports in the mid- to late nineteenth century coincided with the drawing of the "color line" and the institution of formalized, legally sanctioned modes of discrimination in virtually all walks of American life. In sports as in most other contexts, the most virulent discrimination has typically been directed against African Americans. Although relations between whites, Latinos, Native Americans, Jews, and other ethnic minorities would often be strained, both on the playing fields and in the stands, such tensions historically have been relatively minor in comparison to the intense feelings aroused by the participation of black athletes. As one baseball historian has remarked, "With the breaking of the color barrier, other ethnic identities ceased to have much meaning. . . . where the Blacks were, everybody else was just White"—a statement that encapsulates the history of race relations not only in baseball but also in most other American sports. By the latter half of the twentieth century, the integration of most sports was an accomplished fact, but other issues of race and ethnicity continued to swirl around the world of sports.

Baseball and Discrimination in Team Sports

Baseball, the most popular and most widely played team sport of nineteenth century America, was also the first major sport to attain a secure organizational footing in North America, and in many respects, it long set the pattern for other American sports. In the early years of organized baseball, a certain degree of racial freedom prevailed on American playing fields; although African Americans, Native Americans, and other ethnic minorities did not commonly compete with white players, neither was their participation formally barred. All-black teams occasionally played all-white squads, and African Americans, Latinos, and Native Americans competed with whites in front of racially mixed audiences in the earliest professional leagues.

By the waning years of the nineteenth century, however, such tolerance was becoming increasingly rare. As white America grappled with the changed legal and social status of blacks in the post-Civil War period, segregated facilities and institutions were established in virtually all walks of American life. In 1896, the U.S. Supreme Court gave its blessing to such arrangements by endorsing the "separate but equal" doctrine in the landmark case *Plessy v. Ferguson*. Segregationists had their way in organized baseball as well, and by the century's close, blacks had been effectively excluded from the sport's highest levels by means of an unwritten but nevertheless effective agreement among team owners and managers. (Sole responsibility for adoption of the ban is often assigned to Adrian "Cap" Anson, a star player and manager and a vocal proponent of segregation. Such an assessment, however, oversimplifies the reality; although Anson was one of the game's leading figures, he was only one among many who worked to exclude blacks from the sport. African Americans were being systematically separated from whites in education, housing, and virtually every other arena, and the segregation of the country's most popular spectator sport was virtually inevitable.)

No such restrictions, however, were placed on the participation of Native Americans and light-skinned Latinos in organized baseball. Louis "Jud" Castro, for example, an infielder from Colombia, played in the inaugural season of the American League in 1902, and such Native Americans as Jim Thorpe and Albert "Chief" Bender had successful major league careers in the first decades of the twentieth century. As a consequence, white managers and owners made occasional attempts to pass off talented African American players as "Indians" or "Cubans"; legendary manager John McGraw, for example, tried unsuccessfully to play infielder Charlie Grant under the allegedly Cherokee name Charlie Tokohamo. Although white teams would sometimes play exhibitions against black teams, and although players of all races competed together in Latin America, the color line had been firmly drawn. For more than half a century, no openly African American players were permitted in the white professional leagues. Moreover, although light-skinned Latinos and Native Americans were not barred from the white leagues, they commonly experienced the same slights and racist treatments accorded ethnic minorities in all facets of American life—a fact perhaps reflected by the patronizing nicknames given even to star players; the nickname "Chief," for example, was routinely applied to Native American players, while Jewish players were often nicknamed "Moe." In addition to Bender and Thorpe, Native American pioneers included John "Chief" Meyers, a star catcher for the New York Giants; the most successful Latino player of the early century was Adolpho "Dolf" Luque, a Cuban American pitcher also nicknamed "the Pride of Havana." (In the early part of the century, when many Americans were first- or second-generation European immigrants, ethnic identification was strong even among white players, and the achievements of athletes of Irish, Italian,

German, Polish, or Jewish ancestry were celebrated by their respective communities to an extent unknown to later generations. Nicknames that called attention to a player's ethnicity were common; German American superstar Honus Wagner, for example, was known as "the Flying Dutchman.")

Barred from the white leagues, African American professionals competed against one another in the Negro Leagues, a loose association of teams that flourished in the first half of the twentieth century. Negro League stars such as Oscar Charleston, Josh Gibson, Satchel Paige, and Buck Leonard were widely regarded as the equals of the best white players, but they were allowed to compete against them only in exhibitions, barnstorming tours, and foreign leagues.

In 1946, however, in a move that would have repercussions well beyond baseball or sports in general, baseball's color line was broken by Brooklyn Dodgers executive Branch Rickey, who signed Jackie Robinson, a rising star in the Negro Leagues, to a minor league contract. Robinson reached the majors the following season. Though he endured taunts and harassment both on and off the field, he quickly attained stardom (among Robinson's notable supporters was Hank Greenberg, a Jewish superstar who had long crusaded against anti-Semitism). Robinson's on-field success was matched by the remarkable dignity and restraint with which he bore the torrents of abuse directed at him, and his shining example deprived baseball's powers of any further excuse for continuing to segregate the sport. A flood of talented black players entered the white leagues, and every major league team was integrated by 1958. As a consequence, the Negro Leagues, deprived of their reason for existing, soon shriveled and disappeared.

Football, Basketball, and Integration

When the color line was drawn in baseball, football was in its infancy, and professional structures did not exist. In the early years of the sport's evolution, however, a number of black players excelled at the collegiate level, often while playing for such all-black schools as Howard and Tuskegee Universities. Several black players, moreover, attained collegiate stardom at predominantly white schools; William Henry Lewis was named an All-American in 1892 and 1893 while playing for Amherst, and Paul Robeson starred for Rutgers before becoming famous as a singer and actor. When the first professional leagues were formed in the 1920's, moreover, no color line existed, and Robeson, Brown University graduate Frederick Douglass "Fritz" Pollard, and University of Iowa product Fred "Duke" Slater, among others, were among the best of the early professionals. In the early 1930's, however, professional football followed baseball's lead and excluded black players. Notable early players of other ethnic backgrounds included Jewish stars Sid Luckman and Bennie Friedman and the multitalented Native American Thorpe, whose football achievements surpassed his baseball success.

At the same time that Robinson was integrating baseball to great publicity, the established National Football League (NFL) had to fend off a challenge from the upstart All-America Football Conference, which signed a number of black players in an effort to compete with the older league. Faced with these twin pressures, the NFL owners rescinded their ban on black players. As in baseball, African Americans soon came to play important roles on every professional team.

Basketball, like football, was slow to develop viable professional structures. As in football, therefore, the collegiate level of play was the highest level widely available; although black teams were generally unable to play white opponents, basketball flourished at black colleges. Before the formation of solid professional leagues, traveling professional teams played all comers; among the most successful of these teams were the all-black Harlem Renaissance (or "Rens") and the Harlem Globetrotters. Both teams enjoyed success against white competition; in order, in part, to deflect hostility from white crowds, the Globetrotters learned to supplement their play with minstrel-like antics, and the team eventually evolved into an entertainment vehicle rather than a competitive unit. Jewish players and teams were also important to the rise of the sport, and such stars as Moe Goldman, Red Holtzman, and Eddie Gottlieb endured anti-Semitic taunts from opposing teams and crowds while helping to establish the basis for the first successful professional leagues.

Prior to 1950, blacks were excluded from the National Basketball Association (NBA) and its predecessor organizations. That year, three African Americans were signed by NBA teams; within two decades, African American players would come to dominate the sport. Segregation at the college level would persist for decades, as a number of southern schools refused to use black players or to play against integrated teams. In 1966, in a game sometimes referred to as "the *Brown v. Board of Education* of college basketball," an all-black Texas Western team defeated all-white, heavily favored Kentucky for the national collegiate championship.

Individual and Olympic Sports

Sports based on individual excellence rather than on team play have historically proven somewhat less amenable to overt racism than structured team and league sports; in addition, international competitions such as the Olympic Games have been relatively unaffected by parochial color lines. Nevertheless, issues of race have repeatedly reared their heads in international and indi-

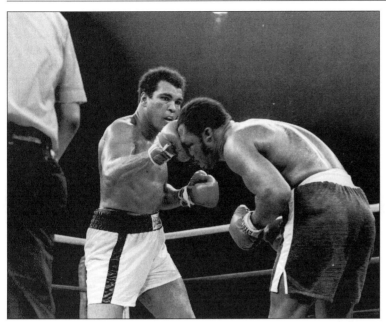

Muhammad Ali (left) punches Joe Frazier in a title bout in Manila, Philippines, in 1975. White boxing champions of the early twentieth century sometimes refused to box against African Americans.

vidual sports. White boxing champions of the nineteenth and early twentieth centuries often refused to fight black competitors, and the 1908 capture of the world heavyweight championship by Jack Johnson, a flamboyant African American who flouted convention by consorting with white women, led to a prolonged search for a "Great White Hope" who could humble Johnson (who was concurrently persecuted by police).

In contrast, the midcentury heavyweight champion Joe Louis was applauded by many whites for his humility; when successors such as the irrepressible Muhammad Ali refused to defer to white sensibilities, racial alarms again were sounded. Among his many celebrated and controversial actions, Ali in 1964 became the first of many prominent black athletes to change his birth name (Cassius Clay) to a name reflecting his African heritage.

Among other individual sports, the "elitist" games of tennis and golf have proven least amenable to widescale integration. In part, this state of affairs has reflected economic realities, as relatively few minority competitors have been able to afford the club memberships and private instruction that most successful players require. Yet the intractability of racist sentiment has played an undeniable part in limiting minority success in both sports. Tennis stars of the 1950's and 1960's such as the Latino legend Pancho Gonzales and the African Americans Althea Gibson and Arthur Ashe often had to battle for permission to compete at race-restricted tourna-

ments and clubs as did leading black golfers such as Lee Elder and Calvin Peete. Even after the resounding successes of golfing sensation Tiger Woods brought legions of new minority fans and players to the sport in the mid-1990's, country clubs across the United States—including some at which leading tournaments were held—refused to admit minority members.

International competitions such as the Olympic Games have traditionally been more open to minority participation. George Poage in 1904 became the first African American Olympic medalist, and Thorpe, generally acclaimed the world's greatest athlete, won two gold medals at the 1912 Games. In 1936, the African American track star Jesse Owens won four gold medals at the Berlin Olympics to the chagrin of the Nazi hosts who hoped to use the Games to demonstrate Aryan supremacy. In 1968, many of the United States' top black athletes refused to participate in the Games, and two, sprinters John Carlos and Tommie Smith, engendered a worldwide controversy by giving a "black power salute" and refusing to acknowledge the U.S. national anthem while receiving their medals (they were subsequently stripped of their medals and removed from the Olympic team).

Other Controversies

As the integration of most sports at the playing level became an accomplished fact, questions of race and ethnicity in the sports world came increasingly to focus on other issues. Perhaps the most persistent of these was the fact that although minorities had made vital contributions as athletes in every major sport, only a handful had risen to fill managerial, administrative, and executive positions. In 1987, a furor erupted when Los Angeles Dodgers executive Al Campanis—who, ironically, had been a teammate and longtime friend of Jackie Robinson—told a television interviewer that blacks were underrepresented in front-office sports jobs because they "lack the necessities" to fill such positions. Although many commentators dismissed Campanis's remarks as the confused, out-of-context ramblings of a tired old man, the incident touched off a round of recriminations and investigations. Yet though baseball and other sports appointed panels to study the situation, more than a decade later, minorities had yet to achieve more than token representation in the power structures of most

American sports. A similar reception greeted golfer Fuzzy Zoeller's indiscreet 1997 remarks that Tiger Woods, who is partly of African American heritage, might have a preference for stereotypically "black" foods such as watermelon and fried chicken. These and other such incidents served as ongoing reminders that racial and ethnic divisions persist in the world of sports to the same extent as they do elsewhere in American society.

Glenn Canyon

Core Resources

Arthur Ashe's *A Hard Road to Glory: A History of the African American Athlete Since 1946* (New York: Warner Books, 1988) is a thorough overview of the black legacy to American sport; two companion volumes carry the discussion back to the earliest days of American history. Sociologist Harry Edwards, who was hired by major league baseball as a consultant in the wake of the Campanis incident, has written numerous thought-provoking analyses of race and sports; his groundbreaking *The Sociology of Sport* (1973) remains useful. *The Bill James Historical Baseball Abstract* (rev. ed., New York: Villard Books, 1988) is a fascinating miscellany with many insightful comments of the history of race relations in the "national pastime." Robert Peterson's *Only the Ball Was White* (Englewood Cliffs, N.J.: Prentice-Hall, 1970) was the first and is still among the best of the many histories of the Negro Leagues.

See also: African American stereotypes; Baseball; Segregation: de facto and de jure.

Standardized testing and IQ testing controversies

> **Significance:** Standardized tests, including intelligence tests, are widely used and, many argue, misused in modern society. Controversies surround the uses to which test results are put and whether intelligence tests truly measure intelligence.

Testing is an integral part of education. Most persons who have been educated formally have participated in some aspect of testing as a means of evaluating their performance. The results of standardized testing can have profound effects on people's lives, as such tests help determine who passes from one grade to the next, who is admitted to special programs, who enters college, who receives scholarships, who is accepted into graduate school, and who is promoted on the job.

Types of Tests

There are several kinds of standardized tests, including intelligence tests, aptitude tests, and achievement tests. Intelligence tests measure analytical and general thinking skills. Aptitude tests measure mental functioning in various subjects or areas. Achievement tests are used to measure skills and information taught in the average American classroom. Testing is a multimillion-dollar industry in the United States, with group intelligence tests being used primarily in business and in schools.

Standardized tests are usually used nationally. They are administered under uniform conditions and are scored according to uniform procedures. Most often group administered, they include such tests as the California Achievement Test (CAT), Scholastic Aptitude Test (SAT), Comprehensive Test of Basic Skills (CTBS), Metropolitan Achievement Test (MAT), Standard Achievement Test (SAT), Iowa Test of Basic Skills (ITBS), Graduate Record Examination (GRE), National Teachers' Examination (NTE), Law School Admissions Test (LSAT), and Dental Aptitude Test (DAT). One of the most popular and frequently used aptitude tests is the Scholastic Aptitude Test. The SAT comprises a verbal section to measure reading comprehension and vocabulary and a mathematical section to measure quantitative abilities closely related to college work. This test is used as a common national standard for evaluating students.

The purpose of tests such as the SAT and others listed above is to determine "achievement," how much a person has gained or learned in a given content area or span of time, or "aptitude," which is a measure meant to predict performance. Thus, standardized achievement tests provide information about students' academic gains, whereas standardized aptitude tests attempt to provide information about a person's potential performance in certain academic pursuits or endeavors.

Intelligence Tests

Intelligence tests are standardized tests used to determine a person's ability to acquire and use knowledge for solving problems and adapting to the world. Standard intelligence tests include the Wechsler Preschool and Primary Scale of Intelligence (WPPSI), Wechsler Adult Intelligence Scale-Revised (WAIS-R), Wechsler Intelligence Scale for Children, third edition (WISC-III), and the Stanford-Binet Intelligence Scale.

The most famous and probably most frequently used of these standardized intelligence tests are the Stanford-Binet test and the Wechsler series. The Stanford-Binet Intelligence Scale consists of a variety of mental tasks arranged by age level. The person's mental age and intelligence quotient (IQ) are determined by the summing of credits for the successful completion of tasks at each level. Test performance is expressed by a single score, which represents a highly verbal measure of general mental ability. The Wechsler intelligence tests are organized by subtest as opposed to age level. Each test contains a Verbal Scale, composed of five or six subtests, and a Performance Scale, which is composed of five subtests.

The dimensions of intelligence that may be measured on a standardized intelligence test include verbal, reasoning, spatial, memory, and quantitative abilities. Thus the information provided by intelligence tests includes a person's abilities in vocabulary memory, mathematical ability, and visual and spatial skills. Intelligence test scores predict future academic behavior and job success in the workplace and have been found to correlate with many other variables.

Controversies and Biases

At least three controversies surround the use of standardized tests, particularly standardized intelligence tests: the controversy concerning reliability and validity; the controversy about possible bias in the tests that affects the performance of minorities; and the controversy over how the tests are used. Reliability in testing refers to the extent to which a test is consistent in measuring what it measures. Validity refers to the extent to which a test measures what it is supposed to measure. Those who do not support the use of standardized tests point out that testing may not adequately portray how much students know.

The fact that minority groups, such as African Americans, American Indians, and Latinos, tend to perform relatively poorly on standardized tests has been a cause for serious concern. Charges have been made that the tests are biased in favor of students from middle-class backgrounds, most of whom are white. Considerable research has examined this problem, and much of it has found ways in which such tests contain subtle bias (almost certainly unintended, at least by the late twentieth century) against ethnic minorities and against females. The makers of standardized tests have taken a variety of approaches to charges of bias; they have both denied that such bias exists and redoubled efforts to create tests that do not contain bias. It is a difficult challenge: Creating a test that does not contain some cultural assumptions (ranging from assumed background knowledge to language use to expected thought patterns) is virtually impossible. The hope is that most assumptions that are discriminatory against particular groups can be eliminated.

A third controversy surrounding standardized testing focuses on the uses to which test results are put. SAT scores, for example, are often tremendously important in colleges' decisions concerning which students to admit. If the tests are indeed biased, then the use of their results in this way actually constitutes an act of discrimination. Standardized tests have also been used to determine people's access to advanced placement programs, scholarship and other financial aid programs, jobs, and job promotions. The denial to minority students of programs that could benefit them increases their risk of falling victim to truancy, dropping out of school, alcohol or drug abuse, or street crime.

Development

Intelligence tests were the first standardized tests developed, and early tests were far from objective. In the nineteenth and early twentieth centuries, intelligence tests (first developed in Europe) were often used to justify the "survival of the fittest," and tests and their interpretations were demonstrably skewed toward proving that white Europeans were mentally the fittest. Cultural bias was rampant. The situation has improved dramatically, but the fact that controversy swirls around standardized tests indicates that there is still a long way to go. Among the cultural factors that have been studied with regard to test results are family influences and the role of race or ethnicity.

Standardized testing controversies should be understood as being related to the influence of the family in American society. Research has shown that there is considerable variation from family to family both within and between different races and socioeconomic statuses. There are many events in the family that affect intellectual functioning. Many of these events are social, but they also include viral infections, unrecognized head injuries, and forms of nutritional deprivation based on individual inabilities to metabolize otherwise normal quantities of specific nutrients; all these elements influence intellectual ability and thus performance on standardized tests.

Deficiencies in the mother's womb or disadvantageous configurations in families may severely depress IQ scores, according to Miles B. Storfer in *Intelligence and Giftedness* (1990). For example, black women tend to become mothers at earlier ages than white women and tend to have more closely spaced births. Their children's IQ scores are likely to be affected adversely. Research continues on parental treatment, biological differences, and socioeconomic differences as influences occurring within the context of the family that might affect a person's standardized test and intelligence test performance.

The IQ scores of Americans rose steadily and rapidly during the twentieth century. Generally, African Americans, Hispanics, and American Indians score about one standard deviation below Anglo-Americans and Asian Americans, while Jews outperform all other groups on standardized measures of intelligence. According to

Storfer, research indicates that the IQ gap that has existed between blacks and whites is decreasing. He argues that efforts to improve the health and early education of lower and lower-middle classes have caused the reduction in the size of this gap.   *Debra A. King-Johnson*

Core Resources
Paul Kline's *Intelligence: The Psychometric View* (New York: Routledge, 1991) summarizes research studies that focus on the nature of intelligence and related human abilities. Miles B. Storfer's "The Black/White IQ Disparity: Myth and Reality," in *Intelligence and Giftedness* (San Francisco: Jossey-Bass, 1990), argues that claims of the genetic inferiority of blacks have been countered by gains in the IQ scores of African Americans and that the gap in IQ scores of blacks and whites can be addressed through improvements in health and early education. Anita E. Woolfolk's *Educational Psychology* (Needham Heights, Mass.: Allyn & Bacon, 1993) discusses socioeconomic differences, race and ethnicity, bilingual education, and gender differences, all of which are pertinent to the topic of standardized and intelligence testing.

See also: Ability testing; College admissions; College entrance examinations; Education and African Americans; Education and racial/ethnic relations; Intelligence and race; Intelligence testing.

Standing Bear v. Crook

In 1865, the Ponca, a small tribe, were guaranteed a ninety-six-thousand-acre reservation along the Missouri River in northern Nebraska. Three years later, the United States gave the entire Ponca Reservation to the Sioux without consulting the Poncas. The government's solution was to remove the Poncas to Indian Territory (Oklahoma). Despite Ponca protests, in 1879 federal troops escorted the whole tribe south to Indian Territory.

Hardships caused by the journey and the radical change in climate caused many deaths among the Ponca. The people longed to return to their homeland, and in January, 1879, one chief, Standing Bear, set out for home with a small group of followers. After the people reached Nebraska, federal troops arrested the runaways in order to return them to Indian Territory.

The plight of Standing Bear captured national attention, and prominent lawyers in Omaha drew up a writ of *habeas corpus* to prevent the people's return to Indian Territory. On April 30, 1879, when the matter came before the United States district court in Omaha, Judge Elmer S. Dundy ruled "an Indian is a 'person' within the meaning of the laws of the United States" and deter-

mined that Standing Bear and his followers had been illegally detained by the federal government. The Ponca affair got national attention and inspired the formation of organizations to fight for Indian rights.

Carole A. Barrett

See also: American Indian activism; American Indian civil rights; Indian Territory; Reservation system of the United States.

Status Indians

Also known as treaty Indians, Status Indians belong to a First Nation that has a signed treaty with the Canadian government and are legally recognized as such under the Indian Act. The term "Indian" describes all native people in Canada who are not Inuit or Metis. All three, Indians, Inuit, and Metis, are collectively recognized as "aboriginal" under the Constitution Act of 1982. (Many Indians prefer to be known as "First Nations" or "aboriginals.")

The 1876 Indian Act recognizes that there are three legal definitions for Indians in Canada: status, nonstatus (those who are not registered as Indians under the Indian Act), and treaty Indians (virtually identical with status). In total, more than 600,000 Canadians have identified themselves as aboriginal people; they constitute 3.6 percent of the country's total population, and 4.4 percent of Canada's total population has some aboriginal ancestry. There are 608 aboriginal communities, representing fifty-two nations or cultural groups with more than fifty languages.

Relations between aboriginal and nonaboriginal peoples in Canada have frequently been difficult and discriminatory, as the history of the Indian Act makes clear. It was not until 1960 that Indians in Canada could vote in federal elections. Before then, many other rights were similarly nonexistent or arbitrarily withdrawn; for example, Indians lost their status as Indians if they left the reserve and moved elsewhere in the country or they married a non-Indian. Relations between aboriginals and nonaboriginals, especially with the federal government, were typically conducted in what has come to be viewed as a paternalistic and colonial fashion. Many past problems and injustices were addressed in the June, 1985, legislation commonly known as Bill C-31, an Act to Amend the Indian Act. This legislation sought to end discrimination, restore status to those who had lost it, and give First Nations the right of control over their own membership.

Gregory Walters

See also: Aboriginal Canadians; Indian-white relations: Canada; Royal Commission on Aboriginal Peoples.

Stereotype

A stereotype is a generalized belief about the characteristics of a group of people. Stereotypes are a natural outgrowth of people's psychological need to simplify and organize the information that they encounter in their lives. In order to meet these needs, people put information into categories; stereotypes are categories of people.

Stereotypes can be beneficial or harmful depending on the truthfulness of the information they contain and the purposes for which they are used. To say that teachers should know more about the subject they are teaching than their students presents stereotypes of students and teachers. These stereotypes are certainly useful, for example, in determining whether to hire a sixth-grade teacher. Furthermore, the promotion of cultural diversity assumes that there are some categorical differences among people of various cultural groups, otherwise people would just talk about individual diversity.

Stereotyping is harmful when negative impressions create and/or reinforce prejudice and discrimination against people. These negative impressions are often based on false information and are frequently exaggerated in order to justify hateful thoughts and hurtful actions. Furthermore, stereotypes tend to be resistant to change ("stereotype" originally referred to a printing plate). People focus more on information that confirms rather than contradicts stereotypical images, perpetuating destructive attitudes.   *Paul J. Chara, Jr.*

See also: African American stereotypes; American Indian stereotypes; Anglo-Protestant stereotypes; Asian American stereotypes; Irish American stereotypes; Italian American stereotypes; Jewish stereotypes; Latino stereotypes; Prejudice and stereotyping; Socialization and reference groups; Stereotyping and the self-fulfilling prophecy.

Stereotyping and the self-fulfilling prophecy

> **Significance:** Stereotyping is a mental process in which generalized beliefs about a group are assigned to all members of that group. When people are confronted with society's stereotyped views of how they are expected to behave, they may actually begin to behave that way; this phenomenon is known as a self-fulfilling prophecy.

Stereotyping is a particular form of social typing involving rigidly held beliefs that are frequently based on incomplete or erroneous information. Stereotyping involves generalizing the identifying characteristics of groups (such as Latinos, blacks, women, homosexuals, or obese people) and applying those generalizations to individual members of the group. Common examples of stereotyping include such widespread notions, held at various points in time, that Italian people are passionate, Irish people fight and drink, women are very emotional, and obese people are jolly.

A central problem with stereotyping is that it involves overgeneralizing: A stereotype is unfairly and rigidly applied to individuals on the basis of identification with a group regardless of whether the individual (or even the group as a whole) actually fits that stereotype.

Schemata

A stereotype can be seen as a form of schema—a mental map or program that helps a person make sense of his or her environment. Schemata help the brain organize and simplify information about people, things, and situations so that people can recognize them readily. The use of schemata is crucial in mental development; children develop schemata as required to think and become familiar with the world. For example, when a young child sees a bird, a parent will tell the child, "That is a birdie," and may explain that birdies hop, fly, and go "tweet-tweet." The child then assumes that all birdies have these characteristics. As the child matures, he or she learns that not all birds have all these characteristics, so the initial schema is amended to encompass new examples.

The process of schema development usually serves humans well, but sometimes it causes problems when people overgeneralize or erroneously assign specific characteristics to all members of the conceptual group. Often a prototypical schema is developed that contains a single, well-defined model describing all members of a group even though there is great variability among group members. When this occurs in stereotyping the attributes or behaviors of other human beings, it can cause a number of problems. One problematic aspect of stereotyping is that stereotypes are most likely to develop when people have strong feelings for or against some identifiable group, and particularly when they have a compelling need to view that group as inferior or threatening. Stereotypes, once formed, are often difficult (if not impossible) to change. Stereotypes are frequently drawn from a small number of people from a larger group, and such a small sample can often be misleading. The choice that one group makes as to what constitutes the defining characteristics of another group is likely to be self-serving more than grounded in objective reality.

Stereotyping and Prejudice

Stereotyping, therefore, is related to prejudice. It involves expectations placed on members of a particular group because of a preconceived, generalized idea of that group. Like other forms of prejudice, it frequently (but not always) serves the function of making one group feel superior to another. Stereotypes permeate societal views in myriad ways. There are gender stereotypes, for example, such as the concept that men are competitive, logical, and ambitious, whereas women are sensitive, quiet, and nurturing. Mentally ill people are often stereotypically thought of as dangerous to others, when this is rarely the case. People with disabilities are often automatically seen as unable to participate fully in society. Everyone has stereotypes embedded in his or her consciousness. The crucial thing is to be aware that they exist and to attempt not to let them prejudicially influence one's attitudes and behaviors toward others.

Stereotypes pervade the media, and various "watchdog" groups are quick to protest when members of their group are portrayed as offensive stereotypes. The snack-food company Frito-Lay once used a cartoon character called the Frito Bandito to sell its chips on television until publicized protests from Mexican Americans forced the company to abandon it. Another stereotypical image, seen regularly in television dramas and films in the 1980's, was the "disturbed" Vietnam War veteran. Films and television programs have traditionally presented stereotypical characters precisely because they automatically fit into viewers' existing stereotype schemata, allowing instant emotional reactions on the part of viewers. The negative side of this is that the tremendous power of film and television is used (intentionally or unintentionally) to reinforce stereotypes.

Self-Fulfilling Prophecies

All stereotypes contain the essential ingredients for creating self-fulfilling prophecies. The central aspect of the self-fulfilling prophecy is the stereotypical expectations held regarding the members of a particular group; in fact, the word "prophecy" here essentially means expectations. Expectations of a person's behavior based on his or her membership in some group (such as an ethnic or gender category) can be either positive or negative. One common gender stereotype is that boys are better at math than girls are. The self-fulfilling prophecy that may occur (and, experts say, has in fact occurred) because of this belief develops because parents and teachers (often unconsciously) encourage boys to excel in math more than they encourage girls. Boys receive more careful instruction and are subtly told that it is appropriate for them to be good at math; therefore, they do indeed begin to excel. In a self-fulfilling prophecy, a stereotypical trait that was originally overgeneralized and invalid becomes "true" because of the expectations and behavior of others toward the person or group at whom the stereotype is directed.

Expectations and Behavior

To a considerable degree, human belief drives human behavior. Any belief about other people (whether correct or erroneous, positive or negative), if strongly held and clearly expressed, can have an effect on the behavior of others. Stereotypes about out-groups have certainly existed since evolution first granted humans the ability to form and express them. The term "stereotype" itself derives from the printing technology of the early nineteenth century; it originally referred to a plate made from a printing surface, and it eventually came to mean any rigidly held or clichéd image or idea.

The scientific study of stereotypes and the effects of expectations (or prophecies of behavior), however, is a phenomenon of the second half of the twentieth century. In the largest sense, it may be seen as an outgrowth of the interest in understanding racism and prejudice that developed after World War II. In the late 1940's, the horrifying realization that the Nazis had systematically put to death more than six million people on the basis of their religion (Jews) or ethnicity (other groups, including Gypsies, were also marked for execution) led social scientists to believe that there was an overwhelming and immediate need to uncover the causes of such hatred and prejudice and to ensure that such an event could never occur again.

A study of teacher expectations by Robert Rosenthal and Lenore Jacobson is considered a classic sociological experiment. Their findings, published as *Pygmalion in the Classroom: Teacher Expectation and Pupils' Intellectual Development* (1968), spawned considerable interest in the area of stereotyping and self-fulfilling prophecies. Also in 1968, sociologist Robert K. Merton, in his edited volume *Contemporary Social Problems*, provided a concise definition of the self-fulfilling prophecy: a "*false* definition of the situation evoking a new behavior which makes the originally false conception sound true." Considerable research on stereotypes and self-fulfilling prophecies appeared in the 1970's.

If the dominant group in a society believes that a particular out-group is violent or wanting in some way, society may communicate its expectations for the out-group in a number of ways—it may simply deny the group progress and sharing of resources (typically blaming the group for its own dilemma), or it may go so far as to segregate the group socially or confine it physically. Expectations communicated by word or action can eventually lead to tremendous frustration that may erupt in violence. Because the likelihood of altering the expectation-behavior relationship is small, the most reasonable goal for social scientists is to harness the power of human belief and find ways to motivate people to adapt the power for beneficial purposes. This could, ideally, lead to improved child rearing within the family, improved results from the education system, and better relations between cultures. There is much for society to gain. On the other side of the coin, however, it is unlikely that humankind will ever completely eliminate those conditions that tend to promote prejudice and stereotypical thinking, so intergroup strife is virtually certain to continue.

Core Resources
Elliot Aronson's *The Social Animal* (3d ed., San Francisco: W. H. Freeman, 1980) details the causes of prejudice, the nature of stereotypes, and their self-fulfilling nature. Harris M. Cooper and Thomas L. Good's *Pygmalion Grows Up: Studies in the Expectation Communication Process* (New York: Longman, 1983) is a thorough assessment of research pertaining to the effects of teachers' expectations for students on student behavior and school performance. The classic study of the self-fulfilling prophecy in the classroom was presented by Robert Rosenthal and Lenore Jacobson in *Pygmalion in the Classroom* (New York: Holt, Rinehart and Winston, 1968). Susan T. Fiske and Shelley E. Taylor's *Social Cognition* (Reading, Mass.: Addison-Wesley, 1984) includes significant sections on schema formation, stereotype development, belief persistence, and the self-fulfilling prophecy. Raymond W. Mack's *Race, Class, and Power* (2d ed., New York: American Book Company, 1968), is a compilation of essays providing comprehensive sociological treatment of topics including minorities, race, social structure, prejudice, discrimination, and stereotyping. Robert A. Rothman's *Inequality and Stratification: Class, Color, and Gender* (2d ed., Englewood Cliffs, N.J.: Prentice-Hall, 1993), discusses stereotyping, the historical roots of certain stereotypes, and the perpetuation of stereotypes through such mechanisms as humor.

See also: Naïveté explanation of racism; Prejudice and stereotyping; Social perception of others; Socialization and reference groups; Stereotype.

Structural assimilation

Structural assimilation is a term coined by sociologist Milton Gordon to refer to an incoming or minority group's impact on, or infiltration into, the social structures of the established host group. It occurs at two distinct levels. At the structural level, it entails increasing access by members of minority ethnic groups to power and privilege within the society's major institutions, including the economy, the polity, and education. Jobs, housing, schooling, and other key arenas of life are progressively acquired without regard for people's ethnic affiliation. At the interpersonal level, it involves increasing interaction among members of different ethnic groups within personal networks—clubs, neighborhoods, friendship circles, and ultimately, marriage. People interact closely without regard for one another's ethnic identity.

Structural assimilation is not a fixed condition but is a process experienced by minority ethnic groups over several generations. Moreover, it is a variable that can range from a minimal degree to virtually complete absorption into the larger society. Euro-Americans, regardless of specific ethnic origin, enjoy relatively equal access to jobs, political authority, and other important life opportunities and increasingly interact with the dominant group in informal settings. This indicates a high level of structural assimilation. African Americans, in contrast, have achieved a much lower degree of integration in the economy, polity, and education, and generally have not entered into intimate relations with members of the dominant group to as significant an extent as have Euro-Americans. African Americans' level of structural assimilation, then, is considerably lower.   *Martin N. Marger*

See also: Anglo-conformity; Assimilation: cultural and structural; Assimilation theories; Behavior-receptional assimilation; Civic assimilation; Identification assimilation; Marital assimilation.

Structural racism

Scholars, along with the general public, historically have viewed racism as consisting of individual behaviors or institutional policies that intentionally discriminate against minority groups. Sociologist Fred Pincus, in his article "From Individual to Structural Discrimination," in *Race and Ethnic Conflict: Connecting Views on Prejudice, Discrimination, and Ethnoviolence*, edited by Fred L. Pincus and Howard J. Ehrlich (Boulder, Colo.: Westview, 1994), introduced the concept of structural racism, which was designed to broaden the understanding of racism by focusing on effect rather than intent. Structural racism is defined as institutional policies conceived by the dominant group as race-neutral but that have harmful effects on minority groups. Examples might include college entrance requirements organized primarily around standardized test scores, on which minority groups historically have scored lower than the dominant group; or business layoff systems organized around seniority in a society where minority groups historically have been hired last. If these example policies were instituted, minority groups would be considerably underrepresented in colleges and in the labor force. These policies, intended to be nondiscriminatory, would have negative effects on minority groups. Structural racism is less visible than individual or institutional racism, making it harder to address. The effects, though, perpetuate the subordination of minority groups to the dominant group. *Cheryl D. Childers*

See also: College admissions; College entrance examinations; Individual racism; Institutional racism; Racism: history of the concept.

Student Nonviolent Coordinating Committee

The insistence of four African American students from the North Carolina Agricultural and Technical College that they be served at a Woolworth's lunch counter in Greensboro, North Carolina, in February of 1960 sparked the student sit-ins of the 1960's. The students' sit-in at the Woolworth's lunch counter precipitated similar protests in more than sixty-five cities. The need to coordinate what began as spontaneous and haphazard events resulted in the establishment of the Student Nonviolent Coordinating Committee (SNCC).

SNCC was founded in April of 1960 by a group of southern African American students, many of whom participated in the sit-ins. They were assisted by long-time civil rights leader Josephine Baker, who insisted that the new student organization pursue its own path. SNCC concentrated its efforts in the South, as its leadership determined that the more immediate problems of racial discrimination and the denial of constitutional rights were occurring there. SNCC spent most of its early years, especially in 1964 and 1965, attempting to register African Americans to vote. The voter registration campaign that SNCC and the Congress of Racial Equality (CORE) carried out, along with the passage of the 1965 Voting Rights Act, proved to have a tremendous impact on southern politics, especially within the Democratic Party.

Despite its various successes, SNCC appeared to be an organization that was in constant turmoil. It was continually struggling over which direction it should take as an incipient social justice organization. SNCC's uncertainty was reflected in the group's frequent changes in leadership. James Farmer, a former Chicago teacher and the first executive secretary of SNCC, attempted to mold it into a highly structured and formal organization. He was replaced by John Lewis, who was committed to nonviolent integrated struggle. In 1966 Lewis was replaced by Stokely Carmichael (Kwame Toure), who advocated total black membership and would later initiate the move toward "black power." SNCC officially adopted "black power" as its slogan at its 1966 convention. Under Carmichael, SNCC decided to stop using integrated teams of field-workers. He took the position that if whites really wanted to help, then they should organize whites in their communities. By 1969 Carmichael had been replaced by H. Rap Brown, who was perceived to be even more militant and changed the group's name to the Student National Coordinating Committee.

SNCC's new philosophy alienated whites, but more important, it put SNCC (along with CORE) at odds with the more traditional civil rights organizations, especially the National Association for the Advancement of Colored People (NAACP) and the Southern Christian Leadership Conference (SCLC). While its new philosophy was embraced by many young African Americans, it moved SNCC further from what many perceived to be the paradigm of the civil rights struggle. Consequently, much of the group's financial support dried up, and the young people who were committed to nonviolent integrated struggle slowly deserted its ranks. By 1970, SNCC had ceased to exist.

Charles C. Jackson

In January, 1967, Stokely Carmichael (center, pointing), head of the Student Nonviolent Coordinating Committee, joins others in protesting the denial of a congressional seat to Adam Clayton Powell.

See also: Black Panther Party; Black Power movement; Civil Rights movement; Congress of Racial Equality;

Freedom Riders; Greensboro sit-ins; National Association for the Advancement of Colored People; Southern Christian Leadership Conference.

Subordinate group

The identification of subordinate groups is based on socially determined systems of structured inequality. These systems of societal stratification influence the control that members of different groups have over their lives, the power they wield, and their access to valued resources. Subordinate groups, sometimes called minority groups, are not determined by numerical size but by the fact that they do not share proportionately in societal wealth, educational attainment, good employment, adequate housing, and other socially valued resources. This stratification system is created and maintained through the actions of dominant groups who benefit from this unequal relationship. The important characteristics or traits that define membership in a subordinate group vary across time and place but are determined by the dominant group. Ethnic subordinate groups are singled out for their cultural differences from the dominant group's cultural norms. Racial subordinate groups are distinguished by some perceived physical difference from the dominant group. The tactics used by dominant groups to ensure their advantaged societal position include ideological rationalizations for inequality and discrimination based on prejudices as well as repressive actions ranging from segregation to extermination.

Todd J. Schroer

See also: Dominant group; Social stratification theories.

Summit Meeting of National Negro Leaders

After five years in office and repeated requests from civil rights activists for an audience, U.S. president Dwight D. Eisenhower held a "summit meeting" in June, 1958, with four African American leaders: Dr. Martin Luther King, Jr.; A. Philip Randolph; Roy Wilkins of the National Association for the Advancement of Colored People; and Lester B. Granger of the National Urban League. The purpose of the summit was to address strategies for dealing with the approaching wave of school integration and to express concerns over the reluctance of the Eisenhower administration to support civil rights and enforce court orders mandating desegregated public schools; yet the significance of the summit lay in the fact that it was Eisenhower's first such meeting with black leaders.

The meeting itself was by all accounts brief and uneventful. The leaders presented Eisenhower with a carefully worded statement calling for increased federal visibility and involvement in advancing civil rights causes and tactfully criticized the president for his previous statement urging them to "be patient" about civil rights. Eisenhower promised the leaders that he would take their statement under consideration but responded evasively to their requests for a national conference on civil rights. The 1958 summit would be the only White House conference of black leaders during the Eisenhower administration; subsequent requests for additional meetings were denied.

Michael H. Burchett

See also: Civil Rights movement.

Supreme Court and ethnic representation

A broadening of the ethnic base of the United States Supreme Court began with the appointment of Louis Dembitz Brandeis to the Court in 1916 by President Woodrow Wilson. Brandeis was Jewish, a Boston public interest attorney whose defense of the labor movement and reform legislation made him prominent. He had revolutionized legal practice by using economic and sociological facts in his brief in *Muller v. Oregon* (1908), a famous Supreme Court case. The principal architect of President Wilson's economic program, he was the first Jew appointed to the Court. Anti-Semitism was prevalent in the United States at that time, and considerable opposition arose to Brandeis's confirmation.

Some members of the bar opposed Brandeis on the pretext that he had engaged in improper practices as a private attorney. President Wilson stood by Brandeis, and after stormy hearings at which the charges against Brandeis were discredited, the Senate approved his appointment. Brandeis began service on June 5, 1916, and served the Court with distinction until old age forced him to retire in 1939. Another Jew, Benjamin Cardozo, was appointed to the Court by President Herbert Hoover in 1932. Cardozo died in 1939 and was replaced by Felix Frankfurter, also Jewish. In this way began the tradition of there being a "Jewish seat" on the Court. Frankfurter, who retired in 1962, was replaced by Arthur Goldberg, also Jewish. In the closing years of the twentieth century, there were two Jewish members of the Court, Ruth Bader Ginsburg and Stephen Breyer.

The first African American to sit on the Supreme Court was Thurgood Marshall. From 1930 to 1933, Marshall attended Howard University's law school, then the only black law school in the country. Howard attracted

Thurgood Marshall, pictured here in 1970, was the first African American to be appointed to the U.S. Supreme Court. He served on the Court from 1967 to 1991.

a great many young black men who wished to participate in the civil rights struggle. After graduation, Marshall affiliated himself with the efforts of the National Association for the Advancement of Colored People Legal Defense and Educational Fund and became an extremely successful civil rights lawyer. His work as an advocate reached its peak with his successful argument in *Brown v. Board of Education* (1954), the case that struck down racial segregation in schools and eventually in all public institutions. Marshall was appointed to the U.S. Court of Appeals for the Second Circuit by President John F. Kennedy in 1961 and, after a brief stint as solicitor-general of the United States, was nominated to the Supreme Court by President Lyndon B. Johnson in 1967. He was the ninety-sixth person to be appointed to the Court and the first African American. Racism was diminishing at the time, and Marshall's nomination met with no significant opposition in the Senate.

Marshall served on the Court until 1991, and after his retirement, President George Bush nominated another African American, Clarence Thomas, to replace him. The nomination became fiercely controversial when Thomas was charged with sexual harassment by Anita Hill, an African American law professor who had been one of Thomas's colleagues. After sensational public hearings, Thomas's nomination was confirmed in a close vote, and he took his seat on the court in 1992.

Robert Jacobs

See also: Criminal justice system; Jewish Americans; Thomas/Hill hearings.

Swann v. Charlotte-Mecklenburg Board of Education

In the 1971 *Swann v. Charlotte-Mecklenburg Board of Education* decision, the U.S. Supreme Court determined that lower courts may properly order local school boards to use extensive school busing to desegregate urban schools.

By the end of the 1960's, a significant percentage of southern school boards had desegregated their schools. The primary exception to this trend was urban schools. Many urban schools by the end of the 1960's were still segregated because of significant residential segregation. In 1968, in *Green v. County School Board of New Kent County*, the Supreme Court ruled that school boards had an "affirmative duty" to take all necessary actions to integrate schools. The question after the *Green* decision was what type of affirmative action must an urban school board faced with considerable residential segregation take in order to integrate its schools.

In the late 1960's, a group of black parents, with the assistance of the National Association for the Advancement of Colored People Legal Defense and Educational Fund, filed a lawsuit seeking to force the school board in Charlotte, North Carolina, to implement an extensive school busing plan to integrate its schools. Prior to the litigation, children in the Charlotte-Mecklenburg school system were assigned to schools on the basis of their residence. As a result, many schools remained all-white or all-black because of the city's residential segregation.

In February of 1970, federal district court judge James McMillan ordered the Charlotte-Mecklenburg Board of Education to adopt an extensive busing plan that would integrate every school in the school system. McMillan's busing plan sparked a firestorm of opposition, with politicians throughout the state and nation, including President Richard M. Nixon, criticizing his action. In June, 1970, the U.S. Supreme Court decided to review the case to decide whether urban school boards were required to engage in extensive school busing to overcome residential segregation. It was understood throughout the country that the *Swann* case would settle the issue of whether school boards would be obliged to engage in school busing to integrate their schools.

In April, 1971, the U.S. Supreme Court unanimously held that school busing was an appropriate method for eliminating segregated schools and that Judge McMillan had acted properly in ordering the Charlotte-Mecklenburg School Board to engage in extensive busing. The Court did say that not every majority black school had to be eliminated in order to satisfy constitutional demands, but it did strongly affirm the legitimacy of busing as a means of integrating urban schools.

In the wake of the *Swann* decision, lower court judges throughout the South ordered urban school boards to adopt school busing plans. In the meantime, members of Congress sought passage of both legislation and constitutional amendments restricting the application of the *Swann* decision. Efforts to amend the Constitution failed, and the legislation that Congress enacted did not significantly inhibit the ability of courts to require school busing. As a result of the *Swann* decision, most urban school systems eventually adopted pupil-assignment plans involving school busing.   *Davison M. Douglas*

See also: *Brown v. Board of Education*; Busing and integration; *Green v. County School Board of New Kent County*; *Milliken v. Bradley*; Segregation: de facto and de jure.

Sweatt v. Painter

Plessy v. Ferguson (1896) established the "separate but equal" doctrine that provided the legal justification for segregation. Civil rights organizations, including the National Association for the Advancement of Colored People (NAACP), although opposed to "separate but equal," decided to use the courts in an attempt to make sure that the "equal" part of the "separate but equal" doctrine was being enforced. In a series of cases running from 1936 to the *Sweatt* decision in 1950, the NAACP attacked the lack of law schools and graduate programs for blacks throughout the South.

If no professional schools existed, clearly the "separate but equal" doctrine was not being met. When African Americans started seeking admission to professional schools throughout the South, many states established "overnight" law schools and professional schools in order to comply with *Plessy*. These schools were certainly separate, but were they equal? Herman Sweatt, a Houston, Texas, postal worker, applied for admission to the University of Texas Law School in 1946. He was denied admission on the grounds that Texas had just created a law school for blacks. To avoid integration, Texas had rented a few rooms in Houston and hired two black lawyers as its faculty.

Sweatt refused to attend the "black law school," saying that it was inferior and he would be deprived of the "equal protection of the law." A unanimous Supreme Court sided with Sweatt, whose case was argued by Thurgood Marshall of the NAACP. Even if the facilities at the two Texas schools were equal, the Court concluded that inequality might exist with respect to other factors "which make for greatness in a law school." Such factors include the reputation of the faculty and administration and the prestige of the alumni. "It is difficult to believe," said Chief Justice Fred M. Vinson, Jr., "that one who had a free choice between these law schools would consider the question close."

The Court ordered that Sweatt be admitted to the University of Texas Law School. The *Sweatt* case marked the first time the Supreme Court found a black professional school to be unequal in quality. Although the Court refused to reexamine *Plessy v. Ferguson*, the decision in *Sweatt* paved the way for the NAACP to launch a direct assault in overturning *Plessy* in *Brown v. Board of Education* only four years later.   *Darryl Paulson*

See also: *Brown v. Board of Education*; Civil Rights movement; National Association for the Advancement of Colored People; *Plessy v. Ferguson*.

Symbolic interactionism

> **Significance:** Symbolic interactionism is the perspective that mind and self are not innate parts of the human body but are created in the social process of interaction among people in intimate, personal communication with one another.

The symbolic interactionist perspective in social psychology is usually traced to the works of social philosopher George Herbert Mead, whose students at the University of Chicago organized and published his lectures and notes in *Mind, Self, and Society* (1934) after his death in 1931. One of these students, Herbert Blumer, is responsible for originating the term "symbolic interactionism."

Seven Basic Propositions
In their book *Symbolic Interaction: A Reader in Social Psychology* (3d ed., 1978), social psychologists Jerome Manis and Bernard Meltzer describe seven basic propositions that summarize the main features of modern symbolic interactionism. The first proposition, and the central idea in symbolic interactionism, is that distinctively human behavior and interaction are carried on through the medium of symbols and their meanings. Human beings do not typically respond directly to stimuli; instead, they assign meanings to the stimuli and act on the

basis of these meanings. The meanings of the stimuli are socially derived through interaction with others rather than being inherent in the stimuli themselves or idiosyncratically assigned by the individual.

The second aspect of symbolic interactionism is that human beings become capable of distinctively human conduct only through association with other human beings. By "distinctively human conduct," Mead and his colleagues meant the ability to imagine how other people feel in given situations, the ability to use symbols, and the ability to behave toward oneself as toward others, which is essential in creating the concept of "self." This proposition expands the previously existing view of socialization from the individual's social learning of culture, statuses, and roles, to the symbolic interactionist conception of socialization as comprising humanization, enculturation, and personality formation.

Third, human society consists of people in interaction; therefore, the features of society are maintained and changed by the actions of individuals. Symbolic interactionists recognize that the organization of any society is a framework within which social action takes place.

This idea sets the stage for the fourth proposition, which is that human beings are active in shaping their own behavior. Symbolic interactionists believe that humans have the ability to select and interpret stimuli and the ability to interact with themselves by thinking; therefore, humans are capable of forming new meanings and new lines of action. Symbolic interactionists believe that humans can modify these influences and in so doing create and change their own behavior.

The fifth proposition is that consciousness, or thinking, involves interaction with oneself. Symbolic interactionists believe that when one thinks, one necessarily carries on an internal conversation. This conversation involves two components of the self: the "I," that part of the individual that is impulsive, spontaneous, and unsocialized by society, and the "Me," which is the social self. The Me is that object that arises in interaction and the one that the individual communicates toward, directs, judges, identifies, and analyzes in interaction with others. This proposition is crucial to understanding symbolic interactionism, for it is only through the use of socially derived symbols in intrapersonal activity that the individual can perform such uniquely human functions as abstract and reflective thinking.

The sixth proposition states that human beings construct their behavior in the course of its execution. Symbolic interactionists believe that the individual is not necessarily a product of past events and experience, although he or she is influenced by them.

The seventh proposition states the chief methodological implication of symbolic interactionism. This proposition states that an understanding of human conduct requires study of the individual's covert behavior as well as overt behavior. Symbolic interactionists believe that human beings act on the basis of their interpretations or meanings; therefore, it becomes essential to understand the individual's meanings in order to understand and explain their conduct. Consequently, the use of procedures allowing sympathetic introspection is part of the methodology of most symbolic interactionists.

Racism and Symbolic Interaction

Sociologist Joel M. Charon presents a symbolic interactionist explanation of racial conflict in his book *Symbolic Interactionism: An Introduction, an Interpretation, an Integration* (1992). According to Charon, people who interact with one another form society. They take one another into account; they communicate, role-take, and cooperate. They share an understanding of reality, and they develop a set of rules to live by. The development of society through cooperative symbolic interaction will, by its very nature, cut off interaction with those outside that interaction. This is the basis for racial problems in society. When interaction creates separate societies, as it has in the United States, each will develop its own culture, and individuals will be governed by different sets of rules and will share a different perspective. Without continuous interaction between the societies, members of each will fail to communicate and to understand the other, and role-taking between them will be minimized. If one of the separate societies has more political power than the other, its members will be able to define the other as having a culture that is unacceptable and even threatening to the dominant society. Through interaction, people in the dominant society develop a perspective that is useful for their understanding of reality. Included in this perspective is their definition of those in the other society and the reasons for their differences, as well as a justification for the inequality that exists between the dominant society and the other society. Through this definition of those who are different, one society develops a justification for taking land from, enslaving, discriminating against, or segregating the other society.

Where interaction is segregated, and all people are therefore unable to develop a shared culture, the others will continue to be seen as different; these differences will be exaggerated and condemned. To the extent that people see their own culture as right and true, others who are different will be perceived and defined as threats. This perception of the other makes destructive actions against them appear justifiable. Destructive action against others also seems justifiable if they can be made into objects instead of people. When people do not regularly interact, communicate, and cooperate with others, it is easy to see others as objects instead of people.

This viewpoint not only encourages destructive action but also works against efforts to help the other. Finally, without interaction, no shared culture is likely to develop, and the conflict is likely to continue. In the symbolic interactionist view, social problems such as racism and racial conflict can be understood through focusing on interaction, cooperation, communication, culture, and definition.   *Karen Anding Fontenot*

Core Resources

George Herbert Mead's *Mind, Self, and Society* (Chicago: University of Chicago Press, 1934) is a well-organized and readable treatment of Mead's ideas concerning social behaviorism, the mind, the self, and society. In *Symbolic Interactionism: Perspective and Method* (Englewood Cliffs, N.J.: Prentice-Hall, 1969), Herbert Blumer, a student of Mead's at the University of Chicago, integrates Mead's ideas with those of John Dewey, William James, Charles Peirce, William Thomas, and Charles Horton Cooley. Other books on symbolic interaction include Joel M. Charon's *Symbolic Interactionism: An Introduction, an Interpretation, an Integration* (4th ed., Englewood Cliffs, N.J.: Prentice-Hall, 1992), Norman Denzin's *Symbolic Interactionism and Cultural Studies* (Cambridge, Mass.: Blackwell, 1992), and *Symbolic Interaction: A Reader in Social Psychology* (3d ed., Boston: Allyn & Bacon, 1978), edited by Jerome Manis and Bernard Meltzer.

See also: Racism: history of the concept; Segregation vs. integration; Self-segregation.

Symbolic racism

The concept of modern, or symbolic, racism was created by social psychologists in the early 1980's in response to the fact that the form of white Americans' racism toward blacks had changed since the early years of research into prejudice.

When scientists first began studying racism in the 1930's, not only did most white Americans have prejudiced beliefs about blacks but also most of them were quite candid in their expression of those beliefs. Researchers would typically give people a checklist of attributes and stereotypes and ask people to indicate those traits that they felt were characteristics of blacks. The majority of white respondents chose much more negative traits for blacks than they did for whites. Whites would also express rejection of integration in schools, neighborhoods, and the workplace.

By the 1970's, however, researchers found that these old methods of measuring racism no longer worked very well. Overt bigotry was no longer considered socially acceptable, and whites were no longer willing to indicate such obviously biased views. They ascribed fewer negative stereotypes to blacks and supported integration. However, racism clearly had not disappeared. Whites were still reluctant to vote for black political candidates, and they continued to oppose such policies as affirmative action. Researchers such as John McConahay, David Sears, Lawrence Bobo, John Dovidio, and Samuel Gaertner called this new form "symbolic" or "modern" racism.

Symbolic racists assert that racism is bad, and they reject most of the old-fashioned stereotypes. They believe in equal opportunities. However, they believe that discrimination no longer exists and that blacks are demanding and receiving unfair benefits at the expense of whites.

People who are high in symbolic racism will often respond to certain "code words" that have come to *symbolize* blacks in the United States (hence the term "symbolic" racism). Examples of these code words are "affirmative action," "crime," and "welfare." According to the researchers, these individuals still harbor anti-black feelings, although they are often not consciously aware of them. These feelings conflict with their beliefs in equality, resulting in ambivalence and conflict. Furthermore, because prejudice is not generally socially acceptable, these people must cloak their feelings in a manner that can be explained by factors other than prejudice, such as fear of crime.

To measure symbolic racism, McConahay created the Modern Racism Scale. The items in this scale attempt to determine the degree to which respondents believe that African Americans have pushed too hard and received more than they deserve. Some have criticized that the scale really measures some other factor, such as political conservatism, rather than racism. However, scores on the Modern Racism Scale have been found to correlate with attitudes toward busing, feeling toward African Americans, voting decisions, and race-based hiring decisions.

Those who study symbolic racism have acknowledged that the form racism takes in the United States is likely to continue to change, and the methods of measuring racism will have to change accordingly. It is unlikely, however, that bigotry and racism will disappear altogether.   *Phyllis B. Gerstenfeld*

See also: Bigotry; "Color-blind" society; Politics of hate; Racism: changing nature of; "Reverse" racism.

Syncretism

In anthropology and sociology, "syncretism" means combining elements from different cultures to make something new. For example, Christmas as celebrated in

Europe and North America combines ideas from Egypt and the Near East—monotheism, the birth of an infant who will grow up to be the savior—with winter solstice observances from northern Europe—Yule log, candles, holly, and the date itself. Examples in racial and ethnic relations are legion. Plains Indian cultures combined Native American ideas with Spanish horses and horse culture. Jazz combines European instruments, notation, and musical ideas with some instruments, vocal practices, and musical ideas from West Africa to form a sound that is uniquely American. Inuit (Eskimo) silk screens combine Inuit artistic ideas with Euro-American print-making techniques.

Syncretism has another use in racial and ethnic rela-tions: to combat naïve notions of ethnocentrism and racial superiority. Many people believe that racist attitudes would largely disappear if Americans understood that their culture is not a "white" product but derives from many cultures and that the current global dominance of European and North American societies and cultural ideas does not imply that whites are or have been smarter. European cultural ideas derived from many sources—China, India, Arabia, Africa, and the Americas. The resulting innovations were syncretic and historic, not genetic, outcomes.

James W. Loewen

See also: Ethnocentrism; Multiculturalism; Racism: history of the concept.

T

Taiwanese Americans

The Immigration and Nationality Act of 1965 brought a surge of Asian immigration to the United States. From 1965 to 1980, many Taiwanese who came to the United States as graduate students decided to remain as immigrants because the economic opportunities were better in America than in Taiwan. Many of these immigrants settled in ethnic communities such as Flushing and Queens in New York and Monterey Park in California. The Taiwanese immigrants felt comfortable in these communities because within them they could speak their native language and interact with other Taiwanese immigrants.

In 1981, when Congress set a yearly quota of twenty thousand Taiwanese immigrants, the characteristics of those arriving changed. The new immigrants typically had not studied in the United States and were less likely to speak English. The concentration of non-English-speaking immigrants in certain areas such as Monterey Park caused a backlash, spawning efforts to have English declared the official language in states such as California in the mid- and late-1980's.

By the end of the twentieth century, more than 250,000 Taiwanese Americans lived in the United States. Of this group, 20 percent were born in the United States and 40 percent were naturalized citizens. The median age of this group was about thirty-five, and with a college graduation rate of 60 percent, a member of this group was much more likely to have completed higher education than was the average American. Eight percent of this group held doctoral degrees, and 48 percent were employed in managerial or professional positions. Taiwanese Americans tended to be very prosperous with average incomes higher than the national median; 71 percent of them owned their own homes.

Throughout the history of Taiwanese immigration, organizations devoted to the social, economic, and political welfare of Taiwanese Americans have existed across the United States. Part of their social and cultural purpose has been to maintain Taiwanese cultural traditions among the immigrants and their descendants and to familiarize other Americans with those traditions. Therefore, many Taiwanese American organizations have introduced their communities to such cultural practices as eating moon cakes to celebrate the autumn festival, celebrating the Lunar New Year, and preparing rice dumplings for the Dragonboat Festival.

Taiwanese American organizations have also attempted to exert political influence in both the United States and Taiwan. In the United States, they have attempted to affect U.S. foreign policy toward China and Taiwan. They have organized demonstrations to protest overseas incidents that have affected Taiwan and have lobbied members of Congress to support Taiwan's efforts to remain free of China. Through political activities designed to affect their homeland, Taiwanese Americans have helped to create a more democratic Taiwan by helping to elect prodemocracy members to the Kuomintang (parliament) and by supporting the prodemocracy candidate in the 1996 presidential elections.

Annita Marie Ward

See also: Chinese Americans; Immigration and Nationality Act of 1965.

Talented Tenth

"Talented Tenth" is a term coined in 1903 by black scholar and activist W. E. B. Du Bois to denote a black intellectual elite that he hoped would provide the leadership necessary to facilitate the advancement of black Americans. Du Bois, who in 1895 became the first African American to receive a doctoral degree from Harvard, drew upon a tradition of northern-based black intellectualism predating the Civil War to promote the development of a classically trained vanguard of "leaders, thinkers, and artists" to educate and uplift oppressed, lower-class blacks. Du Bois's Talented Tenth proposal was largely a response to accommodationists such as Booker T. Washington, who emphasized vocational education as a means for blacks to establish themselves economically and socially in a manner nonthreatening to whites.

Originally a follower of Washington, Du Bois began to dissent from accommodationist policy when Washington's emphasis on industrial education and his influence with northern philanthropists drew resources away from southern liberal arts colleges such as Atlanta University, where Du Bois was a professor of sociology. Although Du Bois's scathing criticisms of accommodationism echoed those of other "radical" black leaders such as Monroe Trotter (who denounced Washington as a race traitor), Du Bois's call for a Talented Tenth was essentially an elitist variation of the doctrine of self-help and racial solidarity that was at the core of accommodationism. Like Washington, Du Bois advocated education as a means of strengthening black communities by alleviating social pathologies brought on by generations of oppression and cultural alienation. While recognizing the necessity of vocational training for young blacks, Du Bois insisted that the true aim of education was "not to make men carpenters (but) to make carpenters men" by imbuing them with a sense of culture and an elevated awareness of their place in the world. To accomplish this, Du Bois argued, it would be necessary to maintain a small number of quality black liberal-arts institutions dedicated to developing and motivating liberally educated black teachers and professionals.

W. E. B. Du Bois coined the term "Talented Tenth" to describe the group of black intellectual elites who he hoped would provide leadership in the struggle for advancement of African Americans.

The idea of a Talented Tenth of black leadership is significant not only as the essence of Du Bois's racial policy but also as a reflection of the changing spirit of black activism in early twentieth century America. By combining elements of accommodationism with strains of postbellum agitation, Du Bois advanced a new synthesis of black protest thought that exerted considerable influence upon the early Civil Rights movement; at the heart of this synthesis was his advocacy of leadership by the Talented Tenth. The Niagara Movement, organized by Du Bois in 1905, consisted mainly of upper- and middle-class black intellectuals from northern states and emphasized agitation as a means of protest. In 1909, key members of the Niagara Movement, including Du Bois, joined forces with progressive upper- and middle-class whites to establish the National Association for the Advancement of Colored People (NAACP), whose strategy of legalism and direct action relied heavily upon the leadership of attorneys and academics. Despite the success of this strategy of legalism and the prominent leadership of scholars such as Martin Luther King, Jr., enthusiasm for the idea of a Talented Tenth waned through the twentieth century as the focus of the Civil Rights movement shifted from the interests of a biracial elite to those of a predominantly black working class.

Michael H. Burchett

See also: Accommodationism; Black colleges and universities; Civil Rights movement; National Association for the Advancement of Colored People; Niagara Movement.

Technology: impact on American Indians

Technology has always been an agent of change. Typically, "technology" refers to the application of an idea to a particular problem. For precontact Native Americans, tools were often as simple as specially shaped stones, bones, and wood. With these materials, hand axes, scrapers, hammers, chisels, files, grinders, and knives were made. As the tools were improved, so were the crafts that they helped make. By the 1500's, Native Americans were using their tools to design and build complex equipment that helped to make their lives easier. They were perfecting stone arrow and spear points and shafts for maximum penetration; they were experimenting with improved nets and weirs, and were developing highly efficient traps and snares; they were inventing new ways to prepare foods, including stone ovens and nonmetallic containers that could contain and store hot liquids; they were developing airtight and waterproof baskets; and they were becoming increasingly aware of how best to protect themselves from the elements using a combination of natural fibers and leather.

After 1500, Native American technology changed rapidly. The primary catalysts for these changes were the Europeans, who, having discovered the "new world," were now enduring danger and hardship to explore it and claim it as their own. As they encountered Native Americans, they sought to "civilize" them by encouraging them in more or less hostile ways to abandon their natural developmental process and to adopt a way of living, technologically speaking, that was hundreds of years in the Native American's future. After contact, Native American technological changes were not so much developmental as they were adoptive.

As trade began between the Europeans and the natives, stone knives and axes gave way to the metal knives and axes that were more easily handled and that could hold a sharper edge better. Iron and steel tools, such as chisels and plows, became highly desirable among the tribes, especially among those that were quickly adopting European ways of life.

While early European guns were inferior to bows and arrows for both hunting and warfare, their foreignness, complexity, and loudness impressed Native Americans. Oral and written accounts of how natives used guns suggest that, prior to the development of a reliable repeating rifle, natives used guns as symbols of their wealth, rather than as weapons; it required many supplies to trade for a single firearm, and more still to get the lead and black powder to fire it. Frontier journals indicate that a skilled archer could powerfully and accurately shoot at least ten arrows in the time it took an early rifler to shoot once, reload, and fire again.

The development of railroads and commercial waterways also changed the ways of Native Americans, especially since both of these transportational technologies helped bring in more invaders. Eventually, Native Americans learned to distrust the European Americans, who with increasing frequency broke treaties and invaded their lands with large machines.

In the nineteenth and twentieth centuries, the technologies that govern natural resources became particularly important for Native Americans. For more than a century, Native Americans have fought for the right to exploit the natural resources that exist on their lands but that are being appropriated by European American technologies such as dams, artificially made canals, oil drilling, strip mining, and timbering. Using legal and political power, contemporary Native Americans are slowly regaining some of the rights over the oil under their land, the ores in their mountains, and the waters that flow through their land.   *Kenneth S. McAllister*

See also: American Indian agriculture; Indian-white relations: United States.

Tecumseh's Rebellion

Soon after the conclusion of the Treaty of Fort Greenville in 1795, frontiersmen, land speculators, and settlers surged into the newly opened lands and beyond into Indian country, thereby exacerbating tensions with the tribes. As pressure mounted for further expansion beyond the line delimited under the terms of the Treaty of Fort Greenville, the governor of the new Indiana Territory, William Henry Harrison, inaugurated a policy designed to acquire additional territory from the Indians incrementally. Hence, between 1802 and 1809, Harrison and Governor William Hull of the Michigan Territory concluded a series of treaties under the terms of which a significant portion of the area between the Great Lakes, the Ohio River, and the Mississippi River was opened for settlement. As the white settlers pressed against the Indians from the south and east, the tribes north of the Ohio Valley were simultaneously pressed from the west by the expansive Chippewa and Sioux in the upper Mississippi region. Hence, under vice-like pressure from several directions, the tribes increasingly concluded that they would have to coordinate their policies and be prepared to fight or perish.

Tecumseh and his brother, the Shawnee Prophet (Tenskwatawa), emerged determined to preserve the identity and territorial integrity of the tribes and their lands in the region between the Great Lakes and the Ohio River Valley. Tecumseh maintained that the Americans had been successful in depriving the Indians of their lands because the tribes had consistently failed to stand unified against external encroachments. Hence, he argued that the tribes must create a meaningful confederation and agree not to cede additional lands to the United States without the concurrence of all the tribes in the union. Only in this way could the tribes negotiate with the Americans from a position of strength. Moreover, Tecumseh and his brother called upon the Indians to purge themselves of corrupting influences, such as alcohol, and return to traditional ways. In 1808, as momentum gathered behind Tecumseh and his new confederation, he and his brother founded Prophetstown, located near the confluence of Tippecanoe Creek and the Wabash River. The Indian leaders hoped that Prophetstown would serve as a center of the confederation movement and that from it Tecumseh and his brother could influence the policies of the tribes throughout the region bounded by the Great Lakes, the Mississippi River, and the Ohio Valley. In addition, in 1808, Tecumseh visited the British at Fort Malden, across the U.S.-Canadian border near Detroit. The British assured Tecumseh of their full support of the tribes' combined efforts to form a confederation and to resist further American encroachments upon their lands. The British authorities, however, urged the Indian leaders not to be the ones to initiate hostilities along the frontier.

As a result of continued efforts by American authorities to detach additional Indian lands (culminating in the Treaty of Fort Wayne in 1809), American intransigence concerning the implementation of the various treaties negotiated since the Treaty of Fort Greenville, and, finally, continued encroachment by American frontiersmen into Indian territory, hostilities again erupted along the frontier in 1810. Both Tecumseh and the British attempted to ameliorate the crisis, but radical elements among the tribes pressed for more aggressive military action against the Americans.

During the summer of 1811, Tecumseh traveled south of the Ohio River in an effort to enlist the support of the Creek, Cherokee, and Choctaw tribes. The Creek expressed support for Tecumseh, but Cherokee and Choctaw leaders were reluctant to take actions that might provoke open warfare with the United States government.

With Tecumseh absent from his center of power north of the Ohio, Harrison decided to avail himself of the opportunity and attack the geographic heart of the confederation movement—Prophetstown. By November 6, 1811, Harrison's force had moved to a position less than a mile from Prophetstown. The following day, on November 7, as Harrison had hoped, the Indians, unrestrained because of Tecumseh's absence, attacked the American force and were severely defeated amid heavy fighting. Following this costly victory at the Battle of Tippecanoe, Harrison's force destroyed Prophetstown before returning to their base of operations at Vincennes.

Following the Tippecanoe Campaign, the frontier war continued; eventually it was submerged in the context of the greater struggle between the United States and Great Britain in the War of 1812. Tecumseh was killed at the Battle of the Thames on October 5, 1813. In many respects, the death of this great Indian leader marked the end of the last real hope of effective Indian resistance to American settlement east of the Mississippi and the extinction of the traditional Indian culture in the eastern portion of the United States.

Howard M. Hensel

See also: Indian-white relations: United States; Northwest Ordinance; Treaties and agreements with Indians: United States.

Termination Resolution

Significance: By the Termination Resolution of August, 1953, Congress ended its policy of special treatment of American Indians.

Termination was viewed by its advocates as freeing American Indians from special laws and regulations, making them equal to other citizens, and by opponents as precipitously withdrawing federal responsibility and programs. The term used for the federal policy came to be applied to the people themselves: terminated tribes. Termination actions included repealing laws setting American Indians apart, ending Bureau of Indian Affairs (BIA) services by transferring them to other federal agencies or to the states, and terminating recognition of the sovereign status of specific tribes.

The Origins of Termination Policy
Termination, many have observed, did not deviate from the norm of federal policy. Its emphasis on breaking up American Indian land holdings is often compared to the General Allotment Act of 1887 (the Dawes Severalty Act). The latter required the allocation of a certain number of acres to each person and, during its forty-seven years in force, reduced tribal lands by nearly ninety-one million acres.

In public debate, opponents of termination argued that the United States had a special obligation to American Indians because they had been conquered and deprived of their accustomed way of life. All people in the United States, opponents said, have the right to be different and to live in the groupings they prefer. Any changes in federal supervision of American Indians should be implemented slowly and with the involvement of the affected tribes; rather than dissolving tribal communities, federal policy should continue meeting tribes' special needs until those needs no longer exist. Opponents also pointed to American Indian culture, tribal lands, and tribal government—their form of community—as their source of strength.

Advocates of termination asserted that all U.S. citizens should be similar, and there should be no communities with special legal rights. Dissolving separate American Indian communities would expedite the integration of these people into the mainstream. American Indians, according to Senator Arthur V. Wakens, would be freed from wardship or federal restrictions and would become self-reliant, with no diminution of their tribal culture. Wakens saw termination as liberation of American Indians and compared it to the Emancipation Proclamation. Non-natives objected to the Indian Reorganization Act

(IRA) of 1934, the prior federal policy, and were swayed toward termination by several arguments: American Indian communal property ownership and their form of government resembled communism; the IRA's promotion of American Indian traditions amounted to condoning heathenism; developers wanted tribal lands made available; and Congress perceived that the resignation of Indian Commissioner John Collier (the IRA's chief advocate) and severe BIA budget cuts had diminished its effectiveness, necessitating a stepped-up program of assimilation.

After Collier's resignation, Senator William Langer asked Acting Commissioner William Zimmerman for a formula for evaluating tribal readiness for termination. On February 8, 1947, Zimmerman presented, in a congressional hearing, three categories of tribes—those who could be terminated immediately, those who could function with little federal supervision within ten years, and those who needed more than ten years to prepare. He discussed the four criteria used in his lists and presented three specimen termination bills. This testimony was embraced by termination supporters and, Zimmerman believed, frequently misquoted.

In 1950, Dillon Myer, a staunch advocate of immediate termination, became Commissioner of Indian Affairs. Although he claimed to be streamlining the BIA, it seemed to some that he was moving to dissolve both the bureau and all IRA programs. Myer was asked to write a legislative proposal for expeditious termination of federal supervision of American Indians. The result was House Concurrent Resolution 108 (August 1, 1953), which passed with little debate. The resolution directed Congress to make American Indians subject to the same laws, privileges, and responsibilities as other citizens; to end their wardship status; and to free specific tribes from federal control as soon as possible. Once the named tribes were terminated, the BIA offices serving them would be abolished.

PL 83-280 (August 15, 1953) also advanced termination. It transferred to the states, without tribal consent, jurisdiction over civil and criminal offenses on reservations in California, Minnesota, Nebraska, Oregon, and Wisconsin. It provided that, by legislative action, any other state could assume similar jurisdiction.

A rush of termination bills was introduced in 1954. As problems with the termination process became known and the membership of congressional committees changed (after 1956), legislation slowed. These acts caused several changes: Tribal lands were either appraised or put under a corporation's management; the federal government no longer protected the land for the tribe; state legislative and judicial authority replaced tribal government; tribe members no longer received a state tax exemption; and tribes lost the benefits of special federal health, education, and other social programs.

Fifteen termination acts were passed between 1954 and 1962, affecting 110 tribes or bands in eight states: the Menominee, Klamath, Western Oregon (61 tribes and bands), Alabama-Coushatta, Mixed-Blood Ute, Southern Paiute, Lower Lake Rancheria, Wyandotte, Peoria, Ottawa, Coyote Valley Ranch, California Rancheria (37 rancherias), Catawba, and Ponca.

The Menominee Litigation
Termination of the Menominee of Wisconsin received the most attention. The tribe was specifically targeted in House Concurrent Resolution 108, and their termination act was passed on June 17, 1954. They appeared to be the healthiest tribe economically, as a result of their lumbering and forestry operations, but were not as ready for termination as they seemed. In 1951, the Menominee won a fifteen-year legal battle against the federal government, awarding them $8.5 million in damages for mismanagement of their tribal forest. They could not obtain the award, however, until Congress passed an act appropriating it. The tribe asked that part of the money be released—amounting to $1,500 per capita. Senator Wakens' Subcommittee on Indian Affairs told the tribe that if they could manage $1,500 per person, they were ready for freedom from federal wardship. Termination, he suggested, was inevitable, and the tribe would not receive the money unless they moved to accept a termination amendment to the per-capita payment bill. The election was not a true tribal referendum, as only 174 members voted; many of these later said that they had not understood what they were voting for.

Final termination of the Menominee did not go into effect until 1961. The tribe had to decide how to set up municipalities, establish a tax system, provide law and order, and sell their tribal assets. There were complications concerning the payment of estimated taxes on Menominee forests. Federal officials saw the tribe's reluctance as procrastination. State agencies could provide only limited assistance, because the tribe was still under federal control.

As a result of these experiences and others, both American Indians and non-Indians became critical of termination. BIA expenditures spiraled in the late 1950's. Many terminated tribe members felt uncomfortable living in the mainstream and often were not accepted socially by non-Indians. Relocated Indians often suffered poverty in the cities and often became dependent on social programs. Some terminated tribes later applied for federal recognition. During its short span (the last act was passed in 1962), termination affected 13,263 of a total population of 400,000, or 3 percent of the federally recognized American Indians. The acts withdrew 1,365,801 acres of trust land, or 3 percent of the approximately 43,000,000 acres held in 1953. The end of federal endorsement of the termination policy was seen in 1969, when President Richard M. Nixon, in a message to Congress, called for promotion of self-determination and the strengthening of American Indian autonomy without threatening community.

Glenn Ellen Starr

Core Resources

Donald L. Fixico's *Termination and Relocation: Federal Indian Policy, 1945-1960* (Albuquerque: University of New Mexico Press, 1986) provides a detailed discussion of termination and other issues from World War II through 1981. Francis Paul Prucha's *The Great Father: The United States Government and the American Indian*, vol. 2 (Lincoln: University of Nebraska Press, 1984) provides a succinct, balanced account of the aims of termination; its articulation in Congress, the popular press, and American Indian publications; congressional and federal actions to bring it about; and its impact. Michael C. Walch's "Terminating the Indian Termination Policy" (*Stanford Law Review* 35, July, 1983) is a well-documented survey of the rise of termination, its effects, and the impact of the fact that Congress did not repeal the termination acts.

See also: Allotment system; American Indian Civil Rights Act; General Allotment Act; Indian Gaming Regulatory Act; Indian Reorganization Act.

Teutonic "race"

First referred to by the ancient Romans in the fourth century B.C.E., the Teutons were an ancient German tribe dwelling in Jutland (the area occupied by present-day Denmark). They moved to Gaul (France) in 105 B.C.E. and disappeared from history several years later when they were defeated by the Roman general Marius. The term "Teutonic" was resurrected in the 1190's to describe a crusading order of German knights who proceeded to sell their services to the North German states to expand control into Slavic Russia and the Baltic.

Neither the tribe nor the knights conform to anything like a race. However, during the rampant racial romanticism of the second half of the nineteenth century, "Teutonic" was frequently used to classify Northern Europeans (Germans, Scandinavians, Dutch, and English). For example, William Z. Ripley in *Races of Europe* (1899) divided western Europeans into Teutonic, Alpine, and Mediterranean peoples. Like the other proponents of Teutonism, he believed in the inherent superiority of the Germanic peoples. Germans in particular liked the term "Teutonic" because it defined a special

destiny against the Slavic people, an important aspect of Pan-Germanic imperial aims. However, for modern scholars the Teutonic "race" is merely a fiction created by racial mythology.

Irwin Halfond

See also: Nordic "race"; Race as a concept; White "race."

Third World strike

The Third World strike led to the establishment of ethnic studies at San Francisco State College and the University of California, Berkeley, in the late 1960's. Against the background of the Civil Rights movement and protests against the war in Vietnam, student activists at San Francisco State College demanded greater educational access for minorities, involvement in community issues, formation of an ethnic studies curriculum, and the hiring of more minority faculty members. In a multiethnic coalition called the Third World Liberation Front, African American, Mexican American, Filipino American, Asian American, and other students joined together to present their requests to the university administration and faculty. Not having received what they considered a satisfactory response, they started a strike on November 6, 1968, that lasted for five months; it became the longest student strike in U.S. history. At the nearby University of California, Berkeley, a Third World Liberation Front strike was also initiated in January, 1969. The strikes led to the creation of a school of ethnic studies at San Francisco and a department of ethnic studies at Berkeley. Similar concerns led to the development of ethnic studies programs at other colleges and universities.

Franklin Ng

See also: Ethnic studies programs.

Thirteenth Amendment

> **Significance:** The first of the Civil War Amendments states that "neither slavery nor involuntary servitude . . . shall exist within the United States."

The Thirteenth Amendment (1865) was one of three amendments known as the Civil War Amendments. The combined purpose of these three amendments was to free the slaves and promote their participation in their country. The Thirteenth Amendment states, in full, "1. Neither slavery nor involuntary servitude, except as a punishment for crime whereof the party shall have been duly convicted, shall exist within the United States, or any place subject to its jurisdiction. 2. Congress shall have power to enforce this article by appropriate legislation."

One of the battles surrounding the Thirteenth Amendment in particular, and all the Civil War Amendments in general, concerned the interpretation of the Tenth Amendment. The Tenth Amendment stated that no federal legislation could detract from the power of state government. Those who opposed the Thirteenth Amendment claimed that the right to allow slavery was not specifically denied in the Constitution and therefore fell within the authority of the state.

With the passage of this amendment, the long fight to abolish slavery was over. The amendment was ratified on December 6, 1865, and officially announced on December 18, 1865. For some abolitionists, such as William Lloyd Garrison, the battle had been won: Slavery was ended. Others saw the Thirteenth Amendment as only a beginning.

Frederick Douglass did not have the same high hopes held by Garrison. Douglass believed that slavery would not be abolished until the former slaves acquired the right to vote. The passage of the Civil Rights Act of 1866 did not provide this right. It was not until the passage of the Fourteenth Amendment, in 1868, that citizenship and the rights thereof were guaranteed to "all persons born or naturalized in the United States." Finally, in 1870, with the passage of the Fifteenth Amendment, former slaves were expressly given the right to vote. Within weeks, the first African American in the U.S. Senate, Hiram R. Revels, took his seat.

Sharon L. Larson

Core Resources

John Hope Franklin's *From Slavery to Freedom: A History of Negro Americans* (3d ed., New York: Alfred A. Knopf, 1967) details the changes undergone by African Americans during the movement toward abolition and after they achieved citizenship. J. C. Furnas's *The Road to Harpers Ferry* (London: Faber & Faber, 1961) contains an enlightening discussion of the problems created or observed in the abolitionist movement. Robert Dale Owen's *The Wrong of Slavery, the Right of Emancipation, and the Future of the African Race in the United States* (Philadelphia: J. B. Lippincott, 1864) collects writings on the issue of slavery in the United States from an abolitionist of the slave era. *1791 to 1991: The Bill of Rights and Beyond* (Washington, D.C.: Commission on the Bicentennial of the U.S. Constitution, 1991) discusses the abolitionist movement and passage of the Civil War Amendments in relation to each other.

See also: Abolition; Civil Rights Acts of 1866-1875; Civil War; Fifteenth Amendment; Fourteenth Amendment; Lincoln-Douglas debates.

Thomas/Hill hearings

U.S. president George Bush's decision to nominate Clarence Thomas, an African American and former head of the Equal Employment Opportunity Commission (EEOC), to fill Thurgood Marshall's seat on the U.S. Supreme Court was immediately controversial because Thomas was a conservative who was opposed to affirmative action and because he was meant to fill the seat left open by the justice who was most closely identified with the Civil Rights movement and who was the first African American on the Supreme Court. Members of the civil rights community and of the broader Left accused Bush of cynically using Thomas as a token black man in order to advance an agenda that was hostile to racial minorities. At the same time, other prominent African Americans, including author and poet Maya Angelou, argued in favor of Thomas's nomination for the associate justice post because of the supposed importance of having an African American on the Court. African Americans and the nation as a whole were already divided in their assessment of Thomas's nomination well before allegations surfaced that Thomas had sexually harassed a black woman named Anita Hill while he was her supervisor at the EEOC.

When word of Hill's allegations reached the media, the congressional confirmation hearings that normally accompany such presidential appointments became a national media spectacle. More than 27 million households tuned in on October 11, 1991, to the first day of the portion of Thomas's confirmation hearings that were meant to examine Hill's allegations and became known as the Thomas/Hill hearings. Some commentators argued that the hearings constituted a watershed in terms of the mass media's representation of African Americans, a rare opportunity to allow the American public to see African American professionals articulately discuss their lives. Others claimed that there was really very little that was new because public interrogations of African American sexuality had been integral to American racial politics from the nation's inception. Thomas himself hit upon this idea forcefully when he claimed that he was the victim of "a high-tech lynching." Thomas's lynching metaphor was perhaps the most rhetorically powerful moment of the hearings, as it served to direct attention away from Hill's allegations and toward the possibility that Thomas was the victim of racism. Although Thomas's charge succeeded in galvanizing support from some sectors of the black community, it alienated other African Americans, who noted that no black man was ever lynched at the behest of a black woman. One of the most important long-term effects of the Thomas/Hill hearings may well be that they rendered the very notion of a monolithic "black commu-

The appointment of Clarence Thomas (left) to the Supreme Court ran into trouble when Anita Hill (right) accused him of sexual harassment.

nity" obsolete, as a mass audience was exposed to struggles within that community.

Thomas was confirmed as an associate justice on October 13, 1991, and in the years since the hearings, he and Hill have become iconic figures on the American cultural landscape. Hill has become an important feminist symbol, and women's outrage at her treatment during the hearings has been widely seen as a contributing factor to a series of women's electoral victories in 1992, which has been dubbed "the year of the woman." The most far-reaching consequence of the hearings, however, may well be the appointment of one of the most conservative Supreme Court justices in recent memory. Thomas's judicial decisions will have impact for years to come. *Jonathan Markovitz*

See also: African American stereotypes; Lynchings; Race card.

Three-fifths compromise

The Constitutional Convention in 1787 adopted the three-fifths compromise, whereby five slaves were counted as three people for purposes of taxation and representation. The idea originated as part of a 1783 congressional plan to base taxation on population. Congress rejected the three-fifths idea, but delegate James Wilson of Pennsylvania resurrected it as an amendment to the Virginia plan at the Constitutional Convention.

The Wilson amendment provoked heated debate over the counting of slaves. Most northern delegates regarded slaves as property and not deserving representation, while southern delegates insisted that blacks be counted equally with whites for purposes of representation. Northern delegates wanted slaves counted for taxation, while southern delegates disagreed.

Delegates also debated whether the Congress or a census every ten years should determine the apportionment of representatives in the national legislature. Several northern delegates wanted Congress to control apportionment because the West was developing rapidly. They considered the three-fifths idea pro-South and opposed its adoption. Southern delegates, meanwhile, threatened to reject the three-fifths idea if Congress controlled representation. Northern delegates eventually agreed to accept a census every ten years and count slaves as people rather than property, demonstrating the numerical strength of the proslavery interests. Until the Civil War, therefore, slaves were counted as three-fifths of nonslaves for purposes of taxation and representation. *David L. Porter*

See also: Censuses, U.S.; Constitutional racism; Representation: gerrymandering, malapportionment, and reapportionment.

Tibetans in North America

After the 1950 Chinese invasion of Tibet, the governments of Tibet and China, in May, 1951, agreed that China would have control of Tibet and that the Dalai Lama would be the political leader of Tibet while the Panchen Lama would be the spiritual leader. In 1959, after an uprising in Tibet, the Dalai Lama and about 100,000 of his followers left Tibet to live in India. The Panchen Lama remained in China, but in 1964, he was removed from power by the Chinese government. The next year, Tibet was made an autonomous region of China; however, by 1966, the Chinese government had control of Tibetan newspapers, radio, and television. The Chinese refused to accept the Panchen Lama's successor, chosen by the Dalai Lama and the Tibetan priesthood, and substituted their own candidate for the position.

In the 1990's, a small number of the Dalai Lama's followers moved to the United States, and by 1999, Tibetans were living in thirty-four states. These Tibetans brought the situation in their homeland to the attention of Americans in the hope that the United States would use its political influence to get the Chinese to recognize the autonomy of Tibet and the authority of the Dalai Lama and the members of the Lama priesthood.

Throughout the United States, various groups such as the Students for a Free Tibet worked to make Americans aware of Tibetan culture and of its problems, presenting statistics on the numbers of Tibetans believed to have been killed by the Chinese and the number of monasteries that were reputedly destroyed. These Tibetans claimed that China had denied them freedom of religion by not allowing Tibetans to choose their own successor to the Panchen Lama or even to hang pictures of the Dalai Lama. As evidence of human rights violations, they related an incident involving Ngavong Choephel, who, in July, 1995, after going to Tibet as a Fulbright scholar to make a film on Tibetan arts, was arrested by the Chinese, charged with being a U.S. spy, and sentenced to eighteen years in prison. These groups noted that self-determination, a universal right named in the United Nations Declaration of Human Rights, was not available to Tibetans.

In 1997, the American Episcopal Church passed a resolution urging talks between China and the Dalai Lama. July 6, the birthday of the Dalai Lama, was recognized as World Tibet Day with an interfaith call for freedom of worship for Tibetans. Festivals were held across the United States; popular rock groups such as Pearl Jam participated in a concert in Washington, D.C., in support of negotiations for a free Tibet. President Bill Clinton and Vice President Al Gore met with the Dalai Lama, and in 1997, Clinton announced the creation of a post for Tibetan Affairs in the State Department. The Tibetan campaign to raise American awareness had become so successful that many Americans plastered "Free Tibet" stickers on their automobile bumpers in support of the cause.

Two pro-Tibetan movies were released by Hollywood in 1997, *Seven Years in Tibet*, starring Brad Pitt, and *Kundun*, a biography of the Dalai Lama, directed by Martin Scorsese. *Kundun* was released even though the Chinese government threatened economic reprisals against the Disney Corporation, which was responsible for the film. Both movies heightened Americans' sympathies toward Tibet. During the opening week of *Seven Years in Tibet*, the International Campaign for Tibet handed out 150,000 action kits, explaining how moviegoers could help free Tibet.   *Annita Marie Ward*

See also: Chinese Americans.

Tibetans protest the control of Tibet by China outside the United Nations headquarters in New York City.

Tokenism

Tokenism is a form of discrimination whereby minorities (such as members of racial and ethnic groups and women) fill roles usually reserved for dominant group members, especially white men. Tokenism can occur in all sorts of settings, including schools, government agencies, and private industry.

In bureaucratic and/or corporate settings, where pressure toward conformity is strong, the inclusion of a small number of "different" individuals is a common practice. Faced with legal and social pressures, tokenism in these settings gives the illusion that white male employers are addressing the issue of discrimination without really challenging the existing balance of power.

Tokenism can have myriad effects on people who fill these roles, including high visibility, increased pressure to perform, and loneliness resulting from their status as outsiders. Tokens also have difficulty advancing because they are often barred from access to the formal and informal networking that is essential for movement up the hierarchy. Studies involving African Americans in corporations have found that token blacks are often placed in staff positions where they either have little power or are restricted to servicing other minorities. Restricted opportunities often lead to high turnover, and pressures to overachieve may result in burnout.

Eleanor A. LaPointe

See also: Desegregation: public schools; Discrimination: behaviors; Glass ceiling; Quotas.

Tolerance

Tolerance is defined, from both a psychological and a sociological perspective, as the ability to look at issues from multiple perspectives, show empathy for other persons' points of view, and be open-minded toward and accepting of cultural and other forms of diversity. An individual's level of tolerance is influenced by family, religious, and community values. People with ultraconservative political and religious viewpoints usually show low levels of tolerance toward cultural diversity. Very liberal individuals also tend to be intolerant of opposing ideas. Thus, tolerance tends to be associated with political and religious ideological extremes.

Swiss psychologist Jean Piaget first identified stages of human development, and Lawrence Kohlberg wrote about stages of moral development. After researching human development, James Banks advanced the theory that as individuals develop and socialize, they go through stages of ethnicity. These stages are ethnic and psychological captivity (negative beliefs about one's identity and low self-esteem), ethnic encapsulation (ethnic isolation and voluntary separatism), ethnic identity clarification (acceptance of ethnic self-identity, a prerequisite for beginning to understand other cultures), bi-ethnicity (a healthy sense of self-identity and an ability to function in two cultures), multiethnicity (the ability to function within several ethnic environments), and finally, the highest stage, globalism and global competency. Individuals who have reached the highest stage are tolerant; they become comfortably reflective in relationships with those who are culturally different. They have the knowledge and skills for effective and meaningful cross-cultural communication.

Social theories of acculturation also have ramifications for tolerance. Acculturation, or adaptation to a culture, can take the form of assimilation or cultural pluralism. Assimilation theories such as the melting pot theory and Anglo-conformity assume that individuals will gradually become like the dominant group of white Anglo-Saxon Protestants. Under cultural pluralism, which is described using a salad bowl metaphor, individuals still identify with their primary culture and language but function and communicate effectively within the society as a whole. Typically, cultural pluralism promotes biculturalism and bilingualism and functional multiculturalism and interculturalism. Therefore, cultural pluralism tends to promote tolerance whereas assimilation views diversity as something that will gradually be eliminated.

Other concepts related to tolerance include xenophobia, ethnocentrism, and cultural relativism. Xenophobics display ignorance and fear toward those who are culturally different and adopt separatist and segregationist attitudes rather than attitudes of tolerance. Ethnocentrics believe that their own culture is superior and preferred over any other culture. They use their own cultural lenses to judge other groups; extreme ethnocentric views lead to stereotyping, prejudice, and discrimination.

Maria A. Pacino

See also: Anglo-conformity; Assimilation: cultural and structural; Assimilation theories; Cultural pluralism; Pluralism vs. assimilation.

Trail of Broken Treaties

During the summer of 1972, Hank Adams (a leader of "fish-ins" in the state of Washington) and Dennis Banks met with other Indian activists in Denver to plan a "Trail of Broken Treaties" caravan. Their hope was to marshal thousands of protesters across the nation to march on Washington, D.C., to dramatize the issue of American Indian self-determination. The group issued its Twenty

Points, a document that sought to revive tribal sovereignty.

The Twenty Points advocated the repeal of the 1871 federal statute that ended the treaty-making era, the restoration of treaty-making status to tribes, the establishment of a commission to review past treaty violations, the resubmission of unratified treaties to the Senate, the governance of all Indians by treaty relations, the formal recognition of more reservations, and the elimination of state jurisdiction over American Indian affairs.

Armed with its demands, the Trail of Broken Treaties caravan moved on to Washington, D.C. Upon arriving on November 3, 1972, days before the presidential election, the protesters learned that there was not enough lodging, so they elected to stay in the Bureau of Indian Affairs (BIA) building for several hours until security guards tried to remove them forcibly. At that point, events turned violent. The protesters seized the building for six days and asserted their demands that tribal sovereignty be restored and immunity be granted to all protesters. Files were seized, and damage was done to the BIA building. American Indian Movement (AIM) leaders claimed that federal agents had infiltrated the movement and had done most of the damage. On November 8, 1972, federal officials offered immunity and transportation home to the protesters. The offer was accepted, and the crisis was resolved for the moment. A few months later, the same issues arose at the occupation of Wounded Knee. In 1976, AIM and other native groups coordinated another nationwide caravan, the Trail of Self-Determination. *Bruce E. Johansen*

See also: American Indian activism; American Indian Movement; Fish-ins; Pine Ridge shootout; Wounded Knee occupation.

Trail of Tears

Significance: Conducted under the authority of the U.S. government, this event brought to a tragic end the traditional life of the five major tribes in the southeastern part of the nation.

The Indian Removal Act, passed by Congress in 1830, set the stage for the eviction of the southeastern tribes from their ancestral lands and their removal to Indian Territory. These tribes had few defenders as they sought to resist removal. Their efforts were further complicated by their own failure to unite for their common defense.

Choctaw

Problems for the Choctaw of southeastern Mississippi began in 1805. By the Treaty of Mount Dexter, the Choctaw were forced to cede 4 million acres of land in exchange for the cancellation of debts at government trading posts. The debts had been encouraged by the government for that desired effect.

In 1820, the Treaty of Doak's Stand approved the exchange of 5 million more acres for 13 million acres in Arkansas and the Indian Territory (present-day Oklahoma). White settlers were already occupying parts of that land, however, and the Choctaw refused to move. In 1829, the state of Mississippi abolished the government of the Choctaw and extended Mississippi law over Choctaw territory. The Treaty of Dancing Rabbit Creek in 1830 gave all remaining Choctaw land to Mississippi. Although a provision of the treaty stipulated that any Choctaw who desired to stay in Mississippi could do so, only token compliance with that provision was allowed.

In December of 1830, the Choctaw began emigrating to the Indian Territory, many dying along the way. By 1832, only about six thousand of twenty-three thousand Choctaw were left in Mississippi, most of whom migrated over the next twenty years.

Creek

The Choctaw experience inspired the twenty-three thousand Creek, in eastern Alabama, to resist removal bitterly. After years of abuse, however, the Creek finally signed the Treaty of Washington in March, 1832, ceding their land to the United States. Numerous promises made by the government in that treaty were soon ignored. Conditions eventually became intolerable for the Creek, and they had no choice but to begin their trip to the West. In 1834 and 1835, small parties of Creek made the journey.

In May of 1836, bands of Creek launched reprisal raids against white settlements, resulting in an order for the army to remove them forcibly. By July, more than two thousand were on their way to the Indian Territory. Ironically, about the same time, several hundred Creek men were forced into service against their Seminole cousins in Florida. By May of 1837, the removal was in full operation. By 1838 it was complete.

Chickasaw

The most uneventful removal was that of the five thousand Chickasaw from northern Mississippi. The process was initiated by the Treaty of Pontotoc Creek in October, 1832, which ceded their land to the United States. Actual removal followed the Treaty of Doaksville in January, 1837, when suitable land was secured in the Indian Territory and travel arrangements were made. The majority of the Chickasaw moved west in 1837, but small groups emigrated as late as 1850.

Unlike most other tribes, the Chickasaw were able to take many possessions with them, and very few died en route. Their major difficulties were horse thieves and substandard food. After their relatively smooth removal, however, the Chickasaw faced great hardships in the Indian Territory. The most serious were attacks by hostile tribes, a smallpox epidemic, and the failure of the government to supply promised food.

Cherokee

The Cherokee, who fought the most determined legal battle to avoid removal, best illustrate the Trail of Tears. In 1830, almost sixteen thousand Cherokee remained on 7 million acres, mostly in north Georgia.

Events leading to Cherokee removal began with the Georgia Compact of 1802. In 1828, after gold was discovered on Cherokee land, Georgia incorporated a large portion of the Cherokee nation and nullified Cherokee laws. As squatters invaded Cherokee territory, Principal Chief John Ross took the Cherokees' case to federal court. In 1832, a surprise decision by Chief Justice John Marshall favored the Cherokees, but President Andrew Jackson refused to enforce that decision.

In December of 1835, a minority of Cherokee leaders signed the New Echota Treaty, declaring that all Cherokee would move west within two years. Protesting this agreement, Ross and the majority refused to emigrate.

The forced removal began with the roundup of Cherokee families in June, 1838. This was followed by "the trail where they cried" (Trail of Tears) to the Indian Territory. The Cherokee were moved west partly by water, but mostly by land. The difficult journey left four thousand unmarked graves along the way. About a thousand Cherokee escaped the removal by fleeing into the southern Appalachian Mountains.

Seminole

The Seminole are descendants of the Creek who had moved to Florida in the eighteenth century. By the nineteenth century, their population in the swamps of central Florida had increased to more than six thousand and included a large number of African Americans, both escaped slaves and free blacks. Soon after the United States acquired Florida from Spain in 1819, efforts to remove the Seminole were initiated. The motives for the removal were to stop Seminole raids against white settlements and to cut off the escape route for runaway slaves from the southern states.

The Treaty of Payne's Landing, signed in 1832 by an unauthorized group of Seminole, declared that all Seminole would give up their land. Resistance, led by Osceola, resulted in the Second Seminole War in 1835. As Seminole were captured, they were sent to the Indian Territory. The war had ended by 1842, and the remaining Seminole slowly migrated west. By 1856, except for a large group in the inaccessible Everglades, the Seminole had been forced out of Florida.

Forced removal exacted a heavy toll from the southeastern tribes. In addition to the incalculable lives lost on the journey, there were tremendous hardships faced as the survivors had to adapt to a new environment that could not support their traditional lifeways.

Glenn L. Swygart

After the passage of the Indian Removal Act of 1830, thousands of Creek, Choctaw, and Cherokee were forced to march to Indian Territory, resulting in many deaths. Their journey, dubbed the Trail of Tears, was depicted in 1942 by Robert Lindneux.

Core Resources

Useful sources include Arthur H. De Rosier's *The Removal of the Choctaw Indians* (Knoxville: University Press of Tennessee, 1970); John Ehle's *The Trail of Tears: The Rise and Fall of the Cherokee Nation* (New York: Doubleday, 1988); Grant Foreman's *Indian Removal* (Norman: University of Oklahoma Press, 1932); Arrell Gibson's *The Chickasaws* (Norman: University of Oklahoma Press, 1971); and Charles Hudson's *The Southeastern Indians* (Knoxville: University of Tennessee Press, 1976).

See also: Indian Removal Act; Indian Territory; Indian-white relations: United States; Seminole Wars.

Transnationalism and ethnonationalism

Transnationalism and ethnonationalism are terms linked to ideologies promoting the unity of peoples of similar culture, ethnicity, or history in a manner that transcends national political boundaries. Transnationalism often overlooks some differences in ethnicity and places emphasis on other factors, such as religion, and is thus not always ethnocentric. Ethnonationalism is almost always transnational in nature.

Examples of transnational and ethnonational movements can be seen around the globe, including in the Middle East. There are also elements of such ideologies in the Balkan states. Zionism was an expression of transnationalism for the Jewish people that led to the foundation of the state of Israel. In many cases, ethnic enclaves in the late twentieth century have sought some form of recognition, home rule, or sovereignty.

In North America, distinct forms of transnationalism and ethnonationalism have emerged. The movement among French Canadians for some type of separatist homeland is one example. However, it is in the United States that a variety of expressions of ethnonationalism have occurred. The most important of these is known as black nationalism.

Black nationalist movements have a long, eclectic history in the United States. Some movements have advocated forms of separatism, while others have called for emigration. The most transnational of all are those suggesting the unity, in whatever form, of all people of African descent. All types of black nationalism share the belief that African Americans are burdened with a subordinate, almost colonial role in relation to whites and that racial solidarity is the only possible solution.

Black nationalism of the emigrational variety dates back to the founding of the nation of Liberia in West Africa in the early nineteenth century. Although Liberia did become home to many freed African American slaves, the emigrationalist movement's main proponents came later, including such figures as Martin Delaney and Marcus Garvey. The crux of their movement was for blacks to go "back to Africa," a phrase that became the name of the movement. Response among African Americans was mixed, and actual emigration was extremely limited.

Religious nationalism has played a role. A variety of movements suggest that, through religious unity, blacks can achieve independence from broader American cultural and political life. The Nation of Islam and the National Committee of Black Churchmen are noteworthy examples of this type of thought. Such movements are often viewed as extremist or unrealistic.

The most radical of all black ethnonationalist move-

ments are those that advocate the creation of separate, all-black states in North America, with clearly demarcated borders and sovereignty. That form of movement shares some ideological links with what was known in the 1960's as revolutionary nationalism. This ideology maintained that liberation for blacks would come only with the overthrow of the entire U.S. system.

More popular black ethnonationalist movements are those that seek to maintain and celebrate African cultural and ethnic unity. Some of these cultural ethnonationalists also maintain the need for some type of separation. Whatever the form of American black ethnonationalism or transnationalism, they are all unusual forms of nationalism with no easily definable link to a specific geographical center, yet bound by a recognizable dissatisfaction with certain aspects of American life.

Gene Redding Wynne, Jr.

See also: American Colonization Society; Black nationalism; Cultural citizenship; Nation of Islam; Pan-Africanism; Republic of New Africa; Separatist movement in Quebec; Zionism.

Transracial adoption

Significance: Transracial adoption is the adoption of a child of a race that differs from that of the adoptive parent or parents. In the United States, it has usually taken the form of white parents adopting minority-race children who were in foster care, group homes, or institutions. The debate over transracial adoption asks whether such adoptions are in the best interest of the children and whether race should be a factor in determining where children are placed.

Finding loving homes for children who need parents is the goal of adoption. In the United States, child placement specialists long believed that matching parent and child as closely as possible was in the best interest of the child. Therefore, adoption law allowed greater consideration of race than was usually allowed under U.S. law. Transracial adoption was considered only after all efforts at same-race adoption were exhausted. Between 8 percent and 10 percent of all U.S. adoptions since the 1940's, including international adoptions, were transracial. White children adopted by parents of other races made up less than 2 percent of all adoptions.

History
Transracial and international adoption began in the United States in the 1940's, when thousands of children

were left parentless because of World War II. In the 1950's and 1960's, the number of transracial adoptions grew sharply, driven by an increase in the number of children in foster homes and institutions and a shortage of minority homes in which to place children. In the 1960's and 1970's, the pool of healthy white infants available for adoption shrank because of the declining birthrate, the availability of abortions, and a drop in stigma for unwed mothers. As more and more nonwhite babies began to be placed with white adoptive parents, people began to question whether transracial adoptions were in the best interest of the children.

A debate arose over whether quality parenting was enough or whether minority children should be adopted only by minority couples (particularly whether black children should be adopted by white couples). Those critical of transracial adoptions say that minority children who grow up with white parents are likely to be unfamiliar with minority culture, and therefore may suffer an identity crisis and be ill-prepared to deal with discrimination. They also say that outplacement of minority children is a form of cultural genocide in that it cuts the children off from their cultural heritage. However, proponents of such adoptions point to empirical studies that have shown that transracial adoptees can grow up adjusted and comfortable with their racial identity and with their adopted families and cultures.

In 1967, the U.S. Supreme Court in *Loving v. Virginia* struck down laws prohibiting interracial marriage. After the ruling, state laws prohibiting transracial adoption were either repealed by state legislatures or held unconstitutional. The decision meant that race could be considered a relevant factor in adoption but could not be the sole consideration.

Beginning in 1972, however, transracial adoptions were drastically curtailed in favor of racial matching. Opposition to transracial adoption by the National Association of Black Social Workers (NABSW) triggered the change. The opposition developed just when the Black Power movement was becoming influential in the United States. By 1987, thirty-five states had laws prohibiting the adoption of black children by white families.

The NABSW opposed placing black or biracial children in white homes for any reason. It argued that transracial adoption was contrary to the black or biracial child's best interest. Its reasoning was that black and biracial children need black parents to develop a positive personal and racial identity and skills for coping with a racist society. The organization also argued that transracial adoption threatened black people with cultural genocide. Under pressure from the NABSW, adoption agencies usually matched black children with black parents and discouraged placement with white parents.

Over the years, many Native American children had been adopted transracially. In 1978, the Indian Child Welfare Act was passed to prevent the decimation of Indian tribes and the breakdown of Indian families and culture. The law made it almost impossible for non-Native American families to adopt Native American children or care for them as foster parents. Keeping Native American families and tribes together and in their native cultures was the purpose of the law.

In the 1990's, institutional barriers to transracial adoption began to be dismantled through federal legislation, including the Multiethnic Placement Act of 1994, the Adoption Promotion and Stability Act of 1995, and the Personal Responsibility and Work Opportunity Reconciliation Act of 1996. These laws made it illegal to prohibit adoption solely on the basis of race.

Impact on Public Policy

Thousands of children who need loving and capable parents are waiting in foster homes, group homes, and other institutions. U.S. law prohibits the use of race as the sole basis for an adoption decision, but race can be considered as one factor in determining the best interest of the child. In practice, transracial adoption is allowed only when same-race parents cannot be found for children waiting for homes.

The challenge for adoption agencies and legislators is to encourage adoption and to eliminate barriers to finding parents for children who are waiting for good homes. Among the solutions that have been considered are subsidies for foster parents who adopt a child in their care and recruitment drives designed to encourage nonwhites to adopt children. While the debate over transracial adoption continues, both sides agree: Adoption by good parents is in the best interest of children.

Fred Buchstein

Core Resources

Adopting and Advocating for the Special Needs Child: A Guide for Parents and Professionals (Westport, Conn.: Bergin & Garvey, 1997), by L. Anne Babb and Rita Laws, provides an excellent introduction to transracial adoption. To learn about transracial adoption from the perspective of the people involved, see *Transracial Adoption: Children and Parents Speak* (New York: Franklin Watts, 1992), by Constance Pohl and Kathy Harris. Lucille J. Grow and Deborah Shapiro's *Black Children, White Parents: A Study of Transracial Adoption* (New York: Child Welfare League of America, 1974) and *Transracial Adoption Today: Views of Adoptive Parents and Social Workers* (New York: Child Welfare League of America, 1975) are both in-depth studies of transracial adoption. Rita J. Simon, Howard Altstein, and Marygold S. Melli's *The Case for Transracial Adoption* (Washington, D.C.: American University Press, 1994) presents the proponents' view; and Dorothy

Roberts's *Killing the Black Body: Race, Reproduction, and the Meaning of Liberty* (New York: Pantheon Books, 1997) states the opposition's view.

See also: Biracialism; Black Power movement; Ethnicity and ethnic groups; Genocide: cultural; Interracial and interethnic marriage; Miscegenation laws.

Treaties and agreements with Indians: Canada

> **Significance:** The character of treaties between the Canadian government and Canada's Indian peoples has varied as Indians have lost and partially regained power.

The capture of Quebec from the French in the Seven Years' War in 1760 allowed Britain to consolidate its holdings in North America. In order to establish colonial governments in the newly obtained Quebec and Florida, King George III issued what has become known as the Royal Proclamation of 1763. A provision of the proclamation reserved for the Indians all lands to the west of Upper Canada and provided a mechanism for the Crown to purchase these and other lands from the Indians. Since the French had never recognized aboriginal title in their colonies, however, Quebec and those portions of the Maritimes captured from the French were exempted from this provision of the proclamation.

The early Indian treaties reflected the strong military position of the Indians, and the stated purpose of most treaties was simply peace and friendship. The Indians were important in military rivalries, first between the French and the British and later between the British and the Americans. There were relatively few Europeans compared with Indians, so land cessions were relatively small and were accomplished with onetime payments (usually in the form of trade goods).

After 1812, the Indians were no longer militarily significant, and the character of treaties changed. In recognition of their weaker position, Indians began to make greater demands for relinquishing their lands. European needs for agricultural lands increased at the same time as a result of increased emigration from Europe. In an effort to save money, the Europeans began the practice of issuing annuities rather than onetime payments. In 1817, a land cession treaty was signed with the Saulteaux and Cree to permit the establishment of the Red River Colony of Thomas Douglas, Earl of Selkirk. This was the first treaty which entirely ceded native title to lands west of Upper Canada.

In 1850, Special Commissioner W. B. Robinson concluded two treaties with the Ojibwa living along the northern shores of Lakes Huron and Superior. Known as the Robinson-Huron and Robinson-Superior Treaties, they were signed after the Ojibwa requested that the Europeans purchase the land before mining it. These two treaties set the precedent of permitting Indians to continue hunting and fishing on their ceded territory.

The Situation at Confederation

Canada was created as a nation in 1867 with the confederation of Nova Scotia, New Brunswick, Quebec, and Ottawa into the Dominion of Canada. The British North America Act, which created Canada, charged the Dominion with discharging the Crown's duties toward the Indians. In 1870, much of the remainder of present-day Canada was transferred from the Hudson's Bay Company to the new nation. This transfer illustrates a paradox in the history of relations between natives and whites in Canada. Although the Royal Proclamation of 1763 preserved native title to this transferred territory and established the Crown as the only legitimate purchaser of Indian lands, the sale of Rupert's Land by the Hudson's Bay Company indicated disregard of aboriginal title. Furthermore, in order to facilitate white settlement in the new territory and to connect, via railroad, the settlements in eastern Canada with the colony of British Columbia, the Crown moved to extinguish any remaining native title to that region. Seven treaties, covering much of present-day Canada, were concluded between 1871 and 1877. The provisions of the treaties varied only slightly and were similar to the two Robinson treaties.

The Numbered Treaties

Treaties 1 and 2, negotiated in 1871, were virtually identical and covered lands held by the Swampy Cree and Chippewa (Ojibwa) in southern Manitoba and southeastern Saskatchewan. In exchange for relinquishing title to 52,400 square miles, the Cree and Chippewa were promised 160 acres of reserved land for each family of five, a school, farm implements, a gift of three dollars for each person, and an annuity of three dollars per person. Chiefs and headmen were awarded additional payments. The area covered by Treaty 1 included the Red River farmsteads of the Metis.

With the signing of Treaty 3, known also as the North-West Angle Treaty, in 1873 by the Saulteaux, the initial payment was raised to twelve dollars and the annuity was increased to five dollars per person. Larger reserves (one square mile per family) were also granted, as well as the continued rights to hunt and fish on unoccupied lands. This provision to allow traditional subsistence activities on the ceded territories appears in the remainder of the numbered treaties. As the prairie provinces were established, however, most of the Crown's lands were transferred to the provinces. Increasingly, the courts have ruled that native Canadians are subject to provincial game laws.

Treaty 4, signed in 1874 by the Saulteaux and Cree, encompasses southern Saskatchewan and small portions of Alberta and Manitoba. Treaty 5 was made in 1875 with the Saulteaux and Cree of central Manitoba and extended to northern Manitoba in 1908. The Blackfeet, Blood, Piegan, Sarcee (Sarsi), and Assiniboine tribes of southern Alberta agreed to Treaty 7 in 1877.

Treaty 6 was made in 1876 with Poundmaker's and Crowfoot's Plains and Wood Cree bands in central Alberta and Saskatchewan; however, the bands led by Big Bear refused to sign until 1884 and succeeded in obtaining somewhat greater concessions. The failure of the government to meet the obligations to which it agreed in the treaty are among the factors that contributed to the Riel Rebellion of 1885. Treaty 6 is interesting also in that it is the only one of the numbered treaties that mentions medical care for Indians. It provides that the Indian agent on each reserve maintain a "medicine chest" for the benefit of the Indians. It is likely that medical care was verbally promised during negotiation for other treaties but was not written into the final documents.

Twenty-two years passed between the signing of Treaty 7 and the next set of treaty negotiations. The last four numbered treaties were made in order to make way for northern resource development rather than to permit white settlement. Treaty 8, signed in 1899 with the Beaver, Cree, and Chipewyan, covers portions of Saskatchewan, Alberta, the Northwest Territories, and British Columbia. It is the only treaty covering the Indians of British Columbia. Several small treaties had been negotiated between coastal tribes of British Columbia and the Hudson's Bay Company in the 1850's, but because the Hudson's Bay Company had no authority to negotiate for the Crown, these treaties were not considered valid. After British Columbia entered Confederation in 1871, an attempt was made to have that province negotiate treaties; other than granting several small reserves, the province refused to acknowledge aboriginal title.

Ontario joined with the federal government in the making of Treaty 9 with the Ojibwa and Cree of north central Ontario in 1905 and 1929. The Cree and other Indian groups ceded their remaining territory in northern Saskatchewan with Treaty 10 in 1906.

Treaty 11 was signed in 1922 with the Dene (Slave, Dogrib, Loucheux, and Hare) Indians who occupy the Mackenzie River region between the sixtieth parallel and the Arctic coast. The impetus for this treaty was the discovery of oil a year earlier at Norman Wells.

The numbered treaties presumably settled all land claims based on aboriginal title for Indians living in the prairie and western subarctic regions, but several court cases have thrown that issue into question. In one of the most important of these cases, *Re Paulette et al. and the Registrar of Titles* (1974), the court held that the Indians covered by Treaties 8 and 11 had not, in fact, extinguished their aboriginal titles to the land.

Modern Land Claims Agreements

Canada The court decisions, coupled with the politicization of Native Canadians, led the federal government to rethink its position on the issue of aboriginal title. The government's desire to develop the natural and mineral resources in its northernmost territories created the conditions necessary for comprehensive land claims settlements. Between 1975 and 1992, five major land claims agreements were concluded. Varying levels of progress were made on several others.

The first of these modern land claims agreements, known as the James Bay and Northern Quebec Agreement, was signed in 1975 by Inuit and Cree of northern and northwestern Quebec, the federal government, and the Province of Quebec. The agreement cleared the way for Quebec to begin hydroelectric development in James Bay. The Northeastern Quebec Agreement, concluded in 1978 with the Naskapi, was for the same purpose.

The James Bay and Northern Quebec Agreement provided $225 million, divided proportionally between the Inuit and the Cree for the lands (excluding mineral rights) in the immediate vicinities of their communities. The natives were allowed to retain exclusive hunting and fishing rights over a much larger area; however, the flooding caused by the hydroelectric development has caused major disruptions of wildlife.

The Inuit chose to form public municipal-type village governments with powers over zoning, taxation, public health, housing, and education. The Cree made their communities into reserves. Representatives of both groups serve on environmental and economic development boards meant to monitor the development of the region.

National native organizations have been highly critical of the James Bay land claims agreements largely because of the clauses that extinguish aboriginal rights. Because the term "aboriginal rights" was not defined, future understandings of its scope have also been negotiated away. In addition, the vague language of the agreement has allowed both the Quebec and federal governments to shirk their obligations.

Far more generous than the James Bay Agreements are the two land claims settlements achieved by the Inuit of the Northwest Territories. The Inuvialuit Final Agreement, which was signed in June, 1984, settled the claim of the twenty-five hundred Inuit living between the Yukon border and central Victoria Island. Under the agreement, the Inuvialuit (or western Inuit) retained title to 91,000 square kilometers but mineral rights to only one-seventh of that land. The Inuvialuit surrendered land covering 344,000 square kilometers. In exchange for the land cessions the Inuvialuit received $152 million to be paid over a thirteen-year period. In an arrangement similar to that established by the Alaska Native Claims Settlement Act, the money has been paid to the Inuvialuit Regional Corporation, which was chartered to invest the proceeds and to manage the land retained by the Inuvialuit. In contrast to the provisions of the numbered treaties, all income earned by the Inuvialuit Regional Corporation from either its lands or investments is subject to taxation.

The Eastern Arctic Claim was negotiated between the federal government and the Tungavik Federation of Natives. Signed in 1992, it settled the claim of seventeen thousand Inuit living in the area of the Northwest Territories between Coppermine and Baffin Island. The claim established Inuit title to 352,000 square kilometers (9.9 percent of the total land and offshore area), making the Eastern Arctic Inuit the single largest landholder in Canada. Unlike other land claims agreements, the Eastern Arctic Agreement includes offshore areas, which continue to be vital food sources. In exchange for relinquishing claim to the remaining territory, the Inuit are to receive $580 million as well as resource royalties earned from their lands. Perhaps the most substantial concession made by the federal government was to allow the Inuit to govern themselves through the formation of a new territory to be known as Nunavut.

Negotiations between the governments of Newfoundland and Canada and the thirty-five hundred Inuit of Labrador have proceeded slowly since 1978. In 1988, agreements in principle were signed between the federal government and the Yukon Council of Indians and with the Dene-Metis Association of the Mackenzie River region. Neither agreement was concluded. At their annual meeting in July, 1990, the Dene Assembly failed to ratify the accord because of divisions within the organization over the "extinguishment" of the still undefined aboriginal rights. After the failure of the Dene-Metis Land Claims Agreement, the federal government agreed to settle the claim on a region-by-region basis. The communities situated along the lower Mackenzie River signed the Gwich'in Final Agreement a year later. The agreement provides resource royalties and $75 million cash in exchange for relinquishing aboriginal rights and title to most of the region. The Gwich'in (Delta area) natives retained title to slightly more than 21,000 square kilometers. They also retained the subsurface mineral rights to about one-fourth of that land. As with the Eastern Arctic Agreement, the Gwich'in Final Agreement established a framework for self-government. *Pamela R. Stern*

Core Resources

Mark O. Dickerson's *Whose North? Political Change, Political Development, and Self-Government in the Northwest Territories* (Vancouver: U.B.C. Press, 1992) discusses the contemporary political issues facing the Dene, Metis, Inuit, and non-native residents of northern Canada. *Aboriginal Peoples and the Law: Indian, Metis, and Inuit Rights in Canada* (Ottawa: Carleton University Press, 1985), edited by Bradford W. Morse, contains a thorough discussion of all aspects of Canadian law (including treaties) as they apply to native peoples. Donald J. Purich's *The Inuit and Their Land: The Story of Nunavut* (Toronto: James Lorimer, 1992) contains a thorough discussion of each of the Inuit land claims agreements, paying special attention to the Eastern Arctic Agreement and the preparations for native self-government in the proposed New Nunavut Territory.

See also: Alaska Native Brotherhood and Alaska Native Claims Settlement; Fifteen Principles; Indian-white relations: Canada; Reserve system of Canada; Riel Rebellions; White Paper of Canada.

Treaties and agreements with Indians: United States

Significance: Native Americans generally look upon their treaties as permanent and inviolate compacts between two sovereign nations. European Americans, in contrast, have tended to consider the treaties to be temporary arrangements subject to alteration and renegotiation. This difference in perspective has been a source of much misunderstanding and bitterness.

Following the American Revolution, the U.S. government continued the European tradition of treating Indian tribes as independent foreign nations, which meant negotiating formal treaties for establishing peace, exchanging land, and recognizing mutual obligations. The government also negotiated agreements or accords, which were less formal and usually dealt with fewer issues. In 1871, Congress passed the Indian Appropriation Act, stating that the American Indians no longer belonged to their own sovereign nations, and treaty making ended. The existing treaties remained valid, unless explicitly abrogated or changed by a law of Congress. Until the twentieth century, the U.S. government often did not look upon Indian treaties as important commitments. Since World War II, however, Native Americans have become increasingly effective in using the federal courts to obtain broad interpretations of treaty rights.

Nature of the Treaties

The U.S. Constitution authorizes the president to negotiate treaties with foreign nations, and these treaties become legally binding after approval by a two-thirds vote in the Senate. Because they are recognized as part of the "supreme law of the land," treaties have the same legal standing as laws passed by Congress. The concept of "supreme law" also means that treaty rights are a matter of federal jurisdiction, and that state governments must follow legal decisions made in federal courts. This is significant, because state governments, reflecting local opinion, often oppose treaty provisions such as the right to hunt and fish off reservation lands.

From 1787 until 1871, the U.S. government negotiated about 800 formal treaties with various Native American tribes and bands, and the Senate ratified some 367 of these into law. The Secretary of War was responsible for negotiating treaties until 1849, when the Office of Indian Affairs was transferred to the Department of the Interior. In 1871, the Indian Appropriation Act, which declared that tribes were not independent nations, ended the practice of contracting by treaty, but the act left the existing treaties in place unless explicitly modified by Congress. Thereafter, the U.S. government continued to enter into agreements with the tribes, but Congress increasingly directed Indian policy by statute. Although Congress passed a statute recognizing all Indians as citizens in 1924, the tribes retained attributes of sovereignty necessary to negotiate agreements and assert treaty rights.

Except for the early period, the U.S. government was generally in a position of dominance when it negotiated treaties with Native American tribes. Following armed conflicts, the government tended to be especially harsh in its demands. Even in the best of conditions, the treaties were written in English, and the Indians frequently did not clearly understand what was written. Basic assumptions, such as the very idea of land ownership, were often foreign to Native American cultures. In addition, the government frequently chose to negotiate with cooperative individuals who were not recognized as legitimate negotiators by tribal majorities. In some cases, as with the Cherokee treaty of removal in 1835, the Senate ratified treaties that had been repudiated by the American Indians.

Indian treaties are especially important for the determination of land claims. About 230 of the treaties included a delineation of boundaries based on a cession of land from the tribe to the U.S. government, with reserved lands (called reservations) for the use of the tribe. Many of the treaties also recognized the retention of hunting and fishing rights in the ceded territories. The treaties usually stated that the tribe would acknowledge the authority of the United States, and the U.S. government promised to provide food and services for the tribe. The treaties generally were silent or unclear concerning whether various provisions were to be permanent or temporary.

Interpretations of Treaties

Because treaties are legal documents, the U.S. Supreme Court has the final authority in determining their meanings. When the language of a treaty is clear, it is applied as written. Because the language is often very unclear, however, the Supreme Court has gradually developed "rules of construction" for resolving disputes. As compensation for the disadvantages of the tribes during the treaty-making process, ambiguities are normally resolved in favor of the Indian perspective, and federal courts attempt to interpret the language as it would have been reasonably understood by the tribal leaders responsible for the negotiations.

In the 1960's and 1970's, for example, some of the most controversial interpretations have involved the meanings of treaties in regard to the rights of Native Americans to fish and hunt with traditional methods in the lands ceded to the government. The treaties tended to use vague language such as "at the pleasure of the president," but Indian negotiators were frequently led to believe that hunting-fishing rights would continue as long as the Indians were peaceful. Since 1968, federal courts have ruled again and again that these rights remain valid unless they have been clearly and explicitly abrogated by an act of Congress. In a major case in 1974, a U.S. District Court of Washington State ruled that Indian tribes had the right to one-half of the salmon harvest, and in subsequent years, there were similar rulings in several states, including Wisconsin and Minnesota. Many non-Indian sports fishers and hunters bitterly resented these decisions, resulting in anti-Indian demonstrations and even threats of violence.

Abrogation of Treaties

If there is an inconsistency between the terms of a treaty and a congressional statute, the more recent of the two is legally binding. Based on this principle, the Supreme Court in *Lone Wolf v. Hitchcock* (1903) reaffirmed that Congress has the full authority to abrogate or modify any treaty. The Endangered Species Act of 1973, for instance, overruled those treaties that included the right to hunt eagles on reservations. If Congress wishes to make changes in a treaty, however, this intent must be clear and explicit in a statute. If there is any doubt about the meaning of a statute, the Supreme Court interprets it in ways that uphold relevant treaties.

Milestones in American Indian Treaties

Year	Event	Impact
1787	Northwest Ordinance	Declares that the United States will purchase Indian lands based on consent and good faith.
1832	*Worcester v. Georgia*	Recognizes that tribes are "domestic dependent nations" immune from state laws.
1871	Indian Appropriations Act	Ends treaty making with Indian tribes.
1887	Dawes Act	Authorizes agreements to replace tribal land titles in exchange for individual holdings.
1934	Indian Reorganization Act	Restores tribal self-determination on the reservations.
1954	Termination Act	Ends the federal relationship with numerous tribes but soon is considered a failure.
1968	*Menominee Tribe v. United States*	Recognizes that treaty provisions remain valid unless explicitly abrogated.
1972	Trail of Broken Treaties	American Indian Movement calls for a restoration of treaty making.

In contrast to treaties made with foreign countries, treaties with Native Americans often establish property rights. The Fifth Amendment guarantees that there be "just compensation" for any property that is "taken" for public use. The power of Congress to abrogate treaties, therefore, does not release it from the duty of providing fair payment for any taking of land or other property. Frequently in the past, of course, the federal government did take property without compensation. In 1946, Congress passed the Indian Claims Commission Act to allow tribes to seek indemnities for their lost property.

During the 1950's, powerful members of Congress wanted to put an end to Indian treaties. Their long-term goal was to promote assimilation, which they argued would produce greater opportunities and equality. As a first step, they pursued "termination" of the political relationship existing between the federal government and the tribes. Based on the termination law of 1954, numerous small tribes lost most of their claims to sovereignty and many of their treaty privileges. In *Menominee Tribe v. United States* (1968), however, the Supreme Court ruled that Indians retained those treaty rights that were not explicitly mentioned in the termination law, including the right to hunt and fish. President Richard M. Nixon repudiated the termination policy in 1970, and gradually most tribes regained their pre-termination status.

In 1972, the Trail of Broken Treaties protest called for the recognition of greater tribal sovereignty and the return of the treaty-making process. Although the protest did not obtain its announced goals, the resulting publicity appeared to produce a greater public respect for the treaties. By that date, the termination policy found relatively few supporters, and a firm majority of Congress appeared to accept the idea that respect for treaty rights, as interpreted by the courts, is a question of national honor.

Thomas T. Lewis

Core Resources

Chapter 6 of William Canby's *American Indian Law* (St. Paul: West, 1983) gives a concise and useful legal analysis of the treaties. John Wunder, in *"Retained by the People": A History of the American Indians and the Bill of Rights* (New York: Oxford, 1994), provides a broad historical account from the Indian point of view, with an excellent bibliography. An older but still useful account is in Wilcomb Washburn's *Red Man's Land/White Man's Law* (New York: Charles Scribner's Sons, 1971). Vine Deloria, Jr., has written and edited many interesting books from a strong Native American perspective, including *American Indian Policy in the Twentieth Century* (Norman: University of Oklahoma Press, 1985). From another perspective, Francis Prucha's scholarly works, including *American Indian Treaties: The History of a Political Anomaly* (San Jose: University of California Press, 1995), view U.S. policy as one of failed paternalism. For the topic of termination, see Larry Burt's *Tribalism in Crisis: Federal Indian Policy* (Albuquerque: University of New Mexico Press, 1982). Ronald Satz's *Indian Treaty Rights* (Madison, Wis.: Wisconsin Academy, 1991) provides a fascinating pro-Indian account of the fishing-rights controversy in Wisconsin and elsewhere. Charles Kappler has produced an edition of most of the actual treaties in *Indian Treaties, 1778-1883* (New York: Interland, 1972).

See also: American Indian civil rights; American Indians in the justice system; *Cherokee Nation v. Georgia* and *Worcester v. Georgia*; Indian Appropriation Act; Indian Citizenship Act; Indian Claims Commission; *Lone Wolf v. Hitchcock*; Trail of Broken Treaties; Tribal sovereignty.

Tribal councils

At one time each native North American tribe ruled with a form of government unique to its culture but usually based on a consensus process. As the tribes were conquered, they were deprived of their sovereignty and subjected to the rule of the U.S. government through the agents of the Bureau of Indian Affairs (BIA). In 1871, Congress ended treaty making with the tribes, and the relationship of the government to the tribes became one of guardian to ward.

In 1934, Congress passed the Indian Reorganization Act (IRA), which has been the subject of heated debate ever since. Under the provisions of this act, any tribe, or the people of any reservation, could organize themselves as a business corporation, adopt a constitution and bylaws, and exercise certain forms of self-government.

Because the IRA did not recognize existing traditional forms of government, such as those provided by spiritual leaders and elders, many people boycotted the process of voting in these IRA-sanctioned governments. As a result, only a minority of tribal members voted to establish the tribal councils, which are structured after European American and hierarchical models.

The matters with which these councils could deal were strictly limited, and decisions and actions were subject to the approval of the BIA. In fact, the reservation superintendent, an agent of the secretary of interior, had full control over the property and financial affairs of the tribe and could veto anything the council did. Because of this, tribal councils were often labeled puppet governments of the BIA.

Various attempts have been made by tribal members to address this situation. In 1944, tribal leaders formed a pan-Indian organization called the National Congress of American Indians (NCAI). In 1961, several hundred native activists issued a "Declaration of Indian Purpose," which called for, among other things, the government's recognition of the rights of tribes. As tribes continue to assert their sovereignty, power has moved from the BIA to the individual tribal councils, which represent the needs of the people.   *Lucy Ganje*

See also: Indian Reorganization Act; National Congress of American Indians; Pan-Indianism; Tribal sovereignty.

Tribal courts

Prior to European contact, all American Indian tribes and bands had institutional mechanisms for settling disputes. The mechanisms varied from Eskimo song duels and Yurok mediation to Cheyenne and Pueblo councils. Under U.S. law, tribal governments have the right to retain or modify adjudication procedures unless Congress limits that right.

For example, in the nineteenth century the Cherokee legal system went through a series of changes from a clan- and council-based system to a system based on an Anglo-American model. In the late nineteenth century Congress expanded federal court jurisdiction in Cherokee territory and finally passed the Curtis Act (1898), which abolished Cherokee tribal courts.

Pueblo adjudicatory systems have been influenced by Spanish and U.S. institutions and policies but were never abolished by federal edict and continue to develop. For example, many Keresan pueblos have a council which decides cases. Many disputes are settled before a partial council or single official acting as a mediator. Important cases are decided by the full council; the presiding officer may act as both prosecutor and a judge. Litigants may be advised by kinsmen or ceremonial group members. In a modification of this system, Laguna Pueblo has a full-time judge while retaining the council as an appellate court.

In the mid-nineteenth century a number of tribes were confined to reservations, creating new problems of social order. In 1883 the Department of the Interior established Courts of Indian Offenses. The judges, tribal members appointed by reservation superintendents, enforced administrative rules established by the Department of the Interior. The superintendent had appellate power over the judges' decisions. In 1888, Congress implicitly recognized the legitimacy of these courts by appropriating funds for judges' salaries.

By 1900, Courts of Indian Offenses had been established on about two-thirds of the reservations. These courts were even established in some pueblos, where they competed with indigenous legal systems. Courts of Indian Offenses have an enduring legacy as a model for the procedures and codes of many contemporary tribal judicial systems.

In 1935, substantive law administered by the Courts of Indian Offenses was revised. Moreover, the Indian Reorganization Act (1934) made it easier for tribes to establish court systems less dominated by the Interior Department. Insufficient tribal economic growth slowed replacement of the Courts of Indian Offenses. By 1992, however, only twenty-two remained. By contrast, there were more than 150 tribal courts.

Tribal courts vary in size, procedure, and other matters. The Navajo nation, for example, now has an independent judicial branch which processed more than eighty-five thousand cases in 1992. There are seven judicial districts and fourteen district court judges. The practice of law before these courts is regulated. Appeals may be taken to the high court. Appellate decisions of note are published. In addition, there are local "peacemaker" courts with 227 peacemakers who act generally as mediators.   *Eric Henderson*

See also: American Indians in the justice system; Indian offenses; Reservation system of the United States; Tribal sovereignty.

Tribal sovereignty

> **Significance:** The rights and obligations of American Indians according to U.S. law have been shaped by the concept of domestic sovereignty, which differs radically from traditional European conceptions of sovereignty.

The European concept of sovereignty, evolving over many centuries, found a unique expression in American constitutional law. This American system of sovereignty came to intermesh in a novel way with the special status of domestic sovereignty which was recognized as adhering in American Indian nations.

European Concept
In the Middle Ages, the concept of sovereignty was attenuated and confused by the intricacies of feudalism and the independent claims of papal legislative authority. With the end of the High Middle Ages and the coming of the Renaissance, European legal and political philosophers such as Niccolò Machiavelli, Marsilius of Padua, and Thomas Hobbes rediscovered the ancient concept that sovereignty is at once illimitable and indivisible. Sovereignty can place limits upon itself, but only so long as it wishes to enforce those limits upon itself.

In the English system, for example, the King-/Queen-in-Parliament is legally omnipotent, and no rights granted in the English Bill of Rights, in the Magna Carta, or in any other document can stand against an act passed by Parliament and signed by the monarch. In addition to the illimitability and indivisibility of sovereignty, the European notion of sovereignty necessitated a monopoly of authority by one sovereignty over a given territory.

By the eighteenth century, the European conception of sovereignty had become dogma. British Tories "refuted" the demands of the American colonies for greater self-government under Parliament with the maxim that one cannot have an *imperium in imperio*—a sovereignty within a sovereignty.

In the aftermath of the American Revolution, the framers of the U.S. Constitution elaborated an intricate system of checks and balances within the national government and a scheme of federalism with reserved powers to states and reserved rights to individual citizens. Although this constitutional order preserved an unlimited and undivided extraordinary sovereignty in the amendment process, its ordinary sovereignty was both limited and divided. Within this system, the problem which Indian nationhood presented was addressed by crafting a unique type of sovereignty—a domestic, dependent sovereignty—for the tribal nations.

Indian Domestic Sovereignty
In the American constitutional order, the domestic sovereignty of the Indian nations bears certain similarities and certain dissimilarities to the sovereignty of the states within the Union. The Constitution specifically recognized the existence of the Indian nations, permitting the courts to view Indian sovereignty as a residual sovereignty which the Constitution was recognizing rather than creating.

In *Johnson and Graham's Lessee v. William McIntosh* (1823, known as *Johnson v. McIntosh*), the Supreme Court under Chief Justice John Marshall recognized the residual Indian sovereignty: "[D]iscovery gave an exclusive right to extinguish the Indian title of occupancy, either by purchase or by conquest; and gave also a right to such a degree of sovereignty, as the circumstances of the people would allow them to exercise." The inherent limits of this sovereignty were made clear, however: "[T]he Indian inhabitants are to be considered merely as occupants, to be protected, indeed, while in peace, in possession of their lands, but to be deemed incapable of transferring the absolute title to others." Furthermore, in his famous opinion in *Cherokee Nation v. Georgia* (1831), Marshall rejected utterly the notion that the Indian nations constitute foreign nations, holding rather that they were "domestic dependent nations."

Until 1871, agreements with the Indians took the forms of treaties. Treaties, however, provided little security to the Indian nations, for a later act of Congress can invalidate part or all of any treaty, as was made clear in the *Cherokee Tobacco* case (*Boudinot v. United States*, 1870). The lands over which Indian tribes exercise a domestic sovereignty, furthermore, remain under the superseding sovereignty of the United States.

After the 1870's
From the 1880's onward, a seesaw effect was produced by court decisions that recognized serious and far-ranging implications inherent in Indian sovereignty and

At this May, 1996, rally in Buffalo, New York, a group of American Indians protests the state's plan to collect sales tax on gasoline and cigarettes sold on reservations to non-Indians. Sovereignty issues have been the source of many conflicts between the federal government and Indian tribes.

by legislative enactments and subsequent court decisions restricting those implications and even moving toward eliminating such sovereignty totally.

In *Ex parte Crow Dog* (1883), the Supreme Court freed the Brule Sioux chief Crow Dog, who had been sentenced to death by a federal district court for the murder of Spotted Tail on Indian territory. Federal law, the Court held, does not automatically apply to Indian lands unless so extended by Congress. Two years later the Major Crimes Act (1885), upheld by the Court in *United States v. Kagama* (1886), sought to overcome the problem posed by *Ex parte Crow Dog* by placing several categories of serious crimes on Indian land under the jurisdiction of the federal courts.

In the General Allotment Act (or Dawes Severalty Act, 1887), Congress moved to eliminate all Indian sovereignty eventually by transforming Indian tribal land into land held individually as ordinary, privately owned U.S. land; Indians were to receive U.S. citizenship. The Curtis Act (1898) went on to attempt to impose that which Congress had attempted to achieve by negotiation under the auspices of the Dawes Act, and in *Stephens v. Cherokee Nation* (1899), the court upheld the Curtis Act. In *Lone Wolf v. Hitchcock* (1903), furthermore, the court recognized a plenary power to reside in Congress concerning Indian relations.

Eventually, after much destructive interference with Indian sovereignty, Congress relented and attempted to reverse direction with the Indian Reorganization Act (also known as the Wheeler-Howard Act, 1934), which undid much of the Dawes Act and actively encouraged tribal organizations.

In a further shift of position by the federal government in the 1950's, Indian sovereignty again came under assault. By Public Law 280 (1953), Congress extended state criminal jurisdiction to Indian territory, and in 1954, under the so-called termination policy, Congress provided for the withdrawal of federal jurisdiction from the Menominee Indian tribe and for their holding of land as an ordinary association or corporation. (Nearly twenty years later, in a full swing of policy, the termination of the Menominee tribe was reversed by the Menominee Restoration Act.)

In *Native American Church v. Navajo Tribal Council* (1959), the U.S. Court of Appeals held that the First Amendment did not bind tribal councils, although in *Colliflower v. Garland* (1965), the U.S. Court of Appeals held that a federal court had the authority to issue a writ of *habeas corpus* to determine the validity of the detention of a person by a tribal court.

The American Indian Civil Rights Act of 1968 applied the Bill of Rights to the relations of Indians to their tribal governments and required the consent of tribes to the imposition of state jurisdiction over Indian territory. That law represented an elaborate compromise regarding Indian sovereignty. Extending the Bill of Rights to individual Indians in their relations with Indian tribal authorities involves a serious interference with Indian sovereignty, although one that is arguably to the benefit of individual Indians. This interference was balanced by undoing the interference of Public Law 280 through making any application of state law the free choice of the tribal government.

In *Oliphant v. Suquamish Indian Tribe* (1978), the Supreme Court upheld the claim of Mark Oliphant, a non-Indian residing on a reservation who was charged with a crime, not to be subject to the tribal courts. Indians protested what they saw as a reduction of their sovereignty, but the decision was in line with prior precedent and practice.

The inherent sovereignty of Indian nations was upheld in *United States v. Wheeler* (1978), in which a claim of double jeopardy was rejected because one of the trials involved had been under the separate sovereignty of an Indian nation. Again, in *Santa Clara Pueblo v. Martinez* (1978), the federal courts held that in the Civil Rights Act of 1968, Congress had provided *habeas corpus* petitions as the sole remedy, with all other suits against the tribe prevented by its sovereign immunity.

The concept of domestic sovereignty has served as the basis for the legal relations of tribal nations with the U.S. government since the adoption of the Constitution, but the plenary power of Congress over that sovereignty has led to a history of shifts between attempts to maintain conditions suitable for the preservation of the unique Indian cultures to periods of forced assimilation with a concomitant attempt to destroy domestic sovereignty and its implications.   *Patrick M. O'Neil*

Core Resources

Tribal sovereignty is discussed in *Documents of United States Indian Policy* (2d ed., Lincoln: University of Nebraska Press, 1990), edited by Francis Paul Prucha; Petra T. Shattuck and Jill Norgren's *Partial Justice: Federal Indian Law in a Liberal Constitutional System* (New York: Berg, 1991); Lyman S. Tyler's *A History of Indian Policy* (Washington, D.C.: Government Printing Office, 1973); Charles F. Wilkinson's *American Indians, Time, and the Law: Native Societies in a Modern Constitutional Democracy* (New Haven, Conn.: Yale University Press, 1987); and Robert A. Williams, Jr.'s *The American Indian in Western Legal Thought: The Discourses of Conquest* (New York: Oxford University Press, 1990).

See also: American Indian Civil Rights Act; *Cherokee Nation v. Georgia* and *Worcester v. Georgia*; Cherokee Tobacco case; *Colliflower v. Garland*; *Ex parte Crow Dog*; General Allotment Act; Indian Reorganization Act; Indian-white relations: United States; *Lone Wolf v. Hitchcock*; *Native American Church v. Navajo Tribal Council*; *Oliphant v. Suquamish Indian Tribe*; Public Law 280; *Santa Clara Pueblo v. Martinez*.

Tribalism

Tribalism is a defining characteristic of American Indian societies. Stress is placed on the concept of the oneness and distinctiveness of ancestry, kinship, language, and culture shared by a group of people. This can be illustrated by the custom of Indian tribes naming themselves "the people" or "the real people," highlighting their uniqueness and the distinctive characteristics that set them off, even from other Native American groups.

Tribalism emphasizes group good, which means that an individual's responsibility to the community is always more important than any individual's rights or privileges. In tribal societies, achieving and maintaining harmony within the group is an overriding concern. In order to achieve harmony, virtues such as respect and generosity are stressed. As a tribal ethic, generosity means sharing all that a person has or possesses with others who are in need. The goal of an individual is not to accumulate items but to provide for others by distributing acquired goods. In this way, the welfare of the group is preserved.

Tribalism, with its stress on group good, is often in opposition to basic principles in American society that stress individual rights and freedoms, and as a result, tribal groups are often at odds with federal legislation and policies. For example, many tribes view the American Indian Civil Rights Act (1968) as an abridgment of tribal rights and obligations because it emphasizes individual rights and freedoms.   *Carole A. Barrett*

See also: American Indian Civil Rights Act; Indian-white relations: United States; Tribal sovereignty.

Triple oppression

Modern societies such as the United States are composed of many subgroups, occupying various racial, ethnic, gender, and social class positions. Members of these groups often have less access to resources such as wealth, power, and prestige than do members of the dominant society. The notion of "triple oppression" applies when a person simultaneously occupies three oppressed groups at once. The term was coined by sociologist Denise A. Segura and promulgated in "Chicanas and Triple Oppression in the Labor Force" (*Chicana Voices: Intersections of Class, Race, and Gender*, edited by Teresa Cordova et al., 1986).

Using the context of work as an example, Segura described how race, class, and gender all play roles in determining occupational attainment and earnings. In general, in countries with capitalist economic systems, poor people do not have the economic and educational resources necessary for business ownership, and their access to well-paying, upwardly mobile jobs is more limited than that of their middle-class and wealth-owning counterparts. In addition, occupational sex segregation limits the job options of women of all races, ethnicities, and classes. Finally, nonwhite men and women routinely encounter race-based discrimination despite the existence of laws designed to ensure equal opportunities.

Taken together, then, those who experience triple oppression are nonwhite (that is, African American, Latina, Asian American, Native American) working-class women, who because of the triple status are inhibited from socioeconomic advancement. In their daily lives the effects of class, race, and gender are both interactive and cumulative in nature.   *Eleanor A. LaPointe*

See also: Discrimination: racial and ethnic; Economics and race; Gendered racism; Women and racism.

Turner's slave insurrection

> **Significance:** The 1831 slave revolt led by Nat Turner sent fear through the southern white community and prompted legislation prohibiting the assembly, education, and movement of plantation slaves.

Although neither the first attempted slave rebellion nor the last during the more than two centuries of African American slavery, Nat Turner's assault against the whites in southeastern Virginia marked the only time a group of black slaves banded together to strike successfully against their white masters.

Background

Turner, as far as is known, spent his entire life as a slave in his native Southampton County, where he had been born on October 2, 1800, on the plantation of Benjamin Turner. His mother was probably a native African, who taught him at an early age to believe that he possessed supernatural powers. He was both a mystic and oriented toward religion. In addition to possessing those traits, he could read, and historians have surmised that he learned this skill from the Turner family. Nat became a Christian through the instruction of his grandmother, Bridget, and mostly read the Bible. Perhaps because of his knowledge of the Bible, he became a Baptist preacher. Because of his mysticism, his ability to read, and his activities as a minister, Turner gained considerable influence over his fellow slaves.

Samuel Turner, Benjamin's son, inherited Nat during times of economic depression in Virginia. A newly hired overseer drove the slaves to work harder, and as a consequence, Nat ran away. Although Nat eluded capture for thirty days, he turned himself in to his owner. His return went unpunished, but in the days that followed, Nat saw that his own freedom could not be realized without his people's freedom.

Nat married a slave named Cherry in the early 1820's, and they had three children. Cherry would later conceal coded maps and lists that Turner used in his revolt, which experts have never been able to decode. When Samuel Turner died in 1922, Nat's family was broken up and sold to different families. Nat went to a neighboring farm owner, Thomas Moore. He was sold again to Joseph Travis in 1831.

Nat Turner thought of himself as an instrument of God. Between 1825 and 1830, Turner gained respect as a traveling neighborhood preacher. He became deeply religious, fasting and praying in solitude. In his own mind he had been ordained—like the prophets of old—to perform a special mission. He professed that God communicated with him through voices and signs in the heavens. On May 12, 1828, Turner heard a "great noise" and saw "white spirits" and "black spirits" battling.

The Revolt

In February, 1831, a certain blueness in the atmosphere—a solar eclipse—persuaded him that God was announcing that the time had come for the slaves to attack their white masters. Turner communicated this message to his band of followers; the rebellion ensued on August 21, when Turner and seven fellow slaves murdered the Travis family. Within twenty-four hours after the rebellion began, the band of rebels numbered seventy-five slaves. In the next two days, an additional fifty-one whites were killed. No evidence exists to indicate that Turner's movement was a part of any larger scheme. One slave, Nat Turner, used the power at his command to attempt to break his shackles and those of his followers.

Turner directed his attack toward the county seat, Jerusalem, and the weapons in its armory; he never made it. The white community responded promptly, and with an overpowering force of armed owners and militia, it routed the poorly armed slaves during the second day of the rebellion. Although he eluded capture for six weeks, Turner and all the rebels were either killed or captured and executed. Hundreds of other nonparticipating and innocent slaves were slain as a result of fright in the white community. Turner's court-appointed attorney, Thomas Gray, recorded Turner's "confessions" on November 1, and on November 11, 1831, Turner was hanged. Gray later remarked on Turner's intelligence and knowledge of military tactics.

Effects

Although Turner's revolt took place in a relatively isolated section of Virginia, the uprising caused the entire South to tremble. Many white southerners called for more stringent laws regulating slaves' behavior, such as making it a crime to teach a slave to read or write. Turner's revolt coincided with the blossoming of the abolition movement in the North, for the rebellion occurred in the same year that William Lloyd Garrison began his unremitting assault on the South's "peculiar institution." Although no one has been able to demonstrate that abolitionist activity had any influence at all on Turner, white southerners were horrified at the seeming coincidence. They described abolitionists as persons who wanted not only to end slavery but also to sponsor a massacre of southern whites. The white South stood as one against any outside interference with its system.

Although white people throughout the South looked anew at slavery, in no place did they look more closely than in Virginia. During the legislative session of 1831-

1832, there occurred the most thorough public discussion of slavery in southern history prior to 1861. Only four months after Turner's revolt, the legislature appointed a committee to recommend to the state a course of action in dealing with slavery.

Those Virginians opposed to slavery made their case. They argued that slavery was a prime cause of Virginia's economic backwardness; that it injured white manners and morals; and that, as witnessed by Turner's revolt, it was basically dangerous. While they did talk about abolition as benefiting the slaves, they primarily maintained that white Virginians would reap the greatest rewards, for the African Americans, after a gradual and possibly compensated emancipation, would be removed from the state. These abolitionists, most of whom were from western Virginia (modern West Virginia), an area of few slaves, could not agree on a specific plan to accomplish their purpose. Slavery's defenders countered by boasting of Virginia's economic well-being and the good treatment and contentment of the slaves. Referring to the well-established belief in the sanctity of private property, they denied that the legislature had any right to meddle with slave property.

The Virginia legislature decided not to tamper with slavery. It rebuffed those who wanted to put Virginia on the road to emancipation. After these debates, white southerners no longer seriously considered any alternative to slavery. In the aftermath of Turner's revolt and Virginia's debate, the South erected a massive defense of its peculiar institution. That defense permeated southern politics, religion, literature, and science. Nat Turner's revolt—the only successful slave uprising in the South—heralded and confirmed the total southern commitment to black slavery. However, Turner left a profound legacy: Slaves would fight for their freedom. Turner's rebellion has inspired black activists since, including Marcus Garvey and Malcolm X.

William J. Cooper, Jr., updated by
Marilyn Elizabeth Perry

Core Resources

Terry Bisson's *Nat Turner* (Los Angeles: Melrose Square, 1988) is an easy-to-read account of Nat Turner's life and motivations. Thomas R. Gray's *The Confessions of Nat Turner: The Leader of the Late Insurrection in Southampton, Va.* (1831; reprint, Miami: Mnemosyne, 1969) contains Turner's own account of his revolt, as given to an official of the court that tried him. William Styron's *Confessions of Nat Turner* (New York: Random House, 1967) is a controversial novel that aimed to show an understanding of Turner's revolt and the institution of slavery but was sharply attacked by African American intellectuals. Henry Irving Tragle's *The Southampton Slave Revolt of 1831: A Compilation of Source Material* (Amherst: University of Massachusetts Press, 1971) reprints primary source material: newspaper accounts, trial records, and other documents written at the time of the revolt.

See also: Abolition; *Amistad* slave revolt; John Brown's raid; *Liberator, The*; Slave rebellions.

Tuskegee Airmen

African Americans made noteworthy gains during World War II, particularly in the Air Force. Despite opposition from southern legislators, African American recruits began training at Tuskegee, Alabama. Challenged by substandard training conditions, discrimination, and segregation, the Tuskegee Airmen responded with resolve and discipline. Between 1942 and 1946, 996 African Americans received their silver wings at Tuskegee Army Air Field. Some 450 of these pilots flew with the 99th Fighter Squadron and later, the 332d Fighter Group. They became known as the "red tails" for the scarlet

Staff Sgt. Leonard D. Nelson teaches a group of African Americans at the U.S. Army Flying School for Negro Cadets in Tuskegee, Alabama. The Tuskegee airmen distinguished themselves in battle during World War II.

coloring on the tail and nose of their P-51B Mustang aircraft. After their baptism of fire in North Africa, the Tuskegee Airmen moved into Italy.

Their commanding officer was Colonel Benjamin O. Davis, Jr. Particularly notable is a daring strafing mission that Davis led in Austria. Despite intense group fire, Davis and his squadron destroyed or damaged thirty-five locomotives, six of which are credited to Davis. At about this time, another pilot in the 332d destroyed a German destroyer single-handedly with machine guns. The Tuskegee Airmen were the first U.S. pilots to down a German jet. The 332d achieved lasting fame when it assumed escort duties for U.S. bombers striking deep into Germany. The 332d established a record for never losing a single bomber in approximately two hundred missions, a truly extraordinary accomplishment. The group's heroics in the air and dignity on the ground won them many medals and broke the color barriers of the U.S. military. By the end of World War II, one out of sixteen aviators in the U.S. Army Air Force was an African American.　　　　　　　　　　　　*Douglas W. Richmond*

See also: Military and racial/ethnic relations; Military desegregation.

Tuskegee experiment

The Tuskegee syphilis experiment was a study conducted in Tuskegee, Alabama, by the U.S. Public Health Service between 1932 and 1972 on four hundred African American men who had syphilis. During the experiment, scientists charted the course of the disease in the men, all of whom had contracted the disease before their participation in the study. None of the men received treatment for his condition. At least 254 men died as a result of the disease or complications stemming from it. None of the subjects knew that he was simply being observed over the course of his illness as part of an experiment on the effects of syphilis on African American men. Instead, the men were told that they were receiving medical treatment.

It has been argued that the Tuskegee experiment was motivated by the assumption that blacks were more susceptible than whites to syphilis, and therefore the Public Health Service was interested in studying whether this was the case and, if so, why. One critic of the study, Martin Levine, goes so far as to argue that the origins of the experiment lay in a stereotypical view of black sexuality: "It was widely believed[among whites] that black racial inferiority made them a notoriously syphilis-soaked race! Their smaller brains lacked mechanisms for controlling sexual desire, causing them to be highly promiscuous. They matured earlier and consequently

were sexually active; and the black man's enormous penis, with its long foreskin, was prone to venereal infections. These physiological differences meant the disease must affect the races differently," (quoted by John Fiske in *Media Matters*, University of Minnesota Press, 1994).

Other critics of this medical study point to it as evidence of the U.S. government's complicity in institutionalized racism against blacks. Comments such as those by John Heller, the director of the Department of Venereal Diseases at the Public Health Service from 1943 to 1948, are often cited as evidence of this racism. Heller, for example, is quoted as saying of the men in the Tuskegee study that their "status did not warrant ethical debate. They were subjects, not patients: clinical material, not sick people" (according to John Jones in *Bad Blood: The Tuskegee Syphilis Experiment—A Tragedy of Race and Medicine*, Free Press, 1984).

For many African Americans, the Tuskegee study has come to represent verifiable evidence that institutionalized racism still exists in the United States. The study is also often cited to support possibly less verifiable claims of such racism. In the early 1990's, the Tuskegee study was often cited as supporting evidence for the AIDS conspiracy theory, which posited that the U.S. government manufactured the AIDS virus and intentionally infected blacks in Africa through immunization programs in order to commit genocide. In the mid-1990's, a widespread rumor in the African American community involved the idea that the company that made Snapple, a popular brand of bottled beverages, was owned by the Ku Klux Klan. On April 19, 1996, ABC's news magazine, *20/20*, aired a segment, narrated by journalist John Stossel, that investigated this claim. Stossel interviewed a number of people from various African American communities, many of whom believed this and other rumors, such as the U.S. government's manufacturing of the AIDS virus, and cited the Tuskegee experiment as evidence that such institutional racism has existed in the past in the United States and still exists today.　　　　　　　*Susan Mackey-Kallis*

See also: African American stereotypes; AIDS conspiracy theory; Health care and racial/ethnic relations; Racism: history of the concept.

Twice migrants

Migration is the physical movement of people within a social system. Sociologists have studied migration through the examination of emigration and immigration—what pushes people to leave their homeland (emigrate) and what pulls people to enter a new culture and country (immigrate). In the latter part of the twentieth century, more complex approaches to migration have emerged as a result of the growing diasporic population of workers. For example, international demands for labor and the shift of capital across national boundaries have increased the rate of multiple migration. Scholar Parminder Bhachu examined a group of Asians of Sikh origin who first migrated to East Africa and then to the United Kingdom. In Africa, this group formed settled communities and shared past experiences as Asians of Sikh origin but also developed a strong East African identity, which was later reproduced in the United Kingdom. Thus, this Asian group created ties in more than one nation or culture through multiple migration. An increasing number of people migrate not just once or twice but even three times to various countries. Multiple migration is not a new phenomenon; however, it has become more common among migrant workers from Third World countries. *Mary Yu Danico*

See also: Immigration and emigration; Push and pull factors; Transnationalism and ethnonationalism.

Tydings-McDuffie Act

On March 24, 1934, President Franklin D. Roosevelt signed into law the Philippines Commonwealth Independence Act, popularly known as the Tydings-McDuffie Act. The law promised independence to the Philippines by 1944, following a ten-year transition period of "commonwealth status." During that time, the islands were to be governed by their own national legislature and executive branches; policy-making power, however, would continue to remain in the United States. This commonwealth system was in place when the Philippines were invaded and occupied by the Japanese in 1942, an event that delayed Philippine independence for two years, until 1946.

Under the structure authorized by the Tydings-McDuffie Act, the goal of true Philippine independence was increasingly circumvented. In the name of independence, American control of the Philippines continued. American suzerainty was magnified by a commonwealth political system that furthered American economic interests at the expense of the islands' competing in the world market. In the end, the Philippines became increasingly dependent on American economic interests. Commonwealth status destroyed that which the Philippines needed in order to compete economically on a global scale: revenue from the export of duty-free goods to the United States. Without trade revenues, the Philippines became increasingly dependent on the United States for loans and investment, made with the understanding that U.S. interests came first. As the Philippine treasury emptied, the commonwealth thus became more indebted to its patron, the United States. The implementation of the Tydings-McDuffie Act both initiated and reinforced this condition.

Thomas J. Edward Walker, Cynthia Gwynne Yaudes, and Ruby L. Stoner

See also: Filipino Americans; Philippine Insurrection.

U

Underclass theories

In his 1968 book *The Unheavenly City*, Edward Banfield bluntly stated that much of what appears to African Americans to be race prejudice is actually class prejudice and that much of what whites interpret as black behavior is actually lower-class behavior. According to Banfield, "lower-class" behavior might involve a large number of specific activities, but their common element was a strong fixation on the immediate present and a very low awareness of and concern for the more distant future. This particular time awareness was manifested in negative attitudes toward schooling and career development, indulgence in alcohol and drug abuse, sexual promiscuity with little concern for pregnancy or disease, eagerness to find "action" in violence, vandalism, and crime, and rejection of "respectable" standards of dress, personal grooming, and speech.

Because personality and behavior patterns are linked to social class, young people tend to adopt these patterns from their family members and from others who appear to be part of their reference group. Clearly lower-class lifestyles, defined in this manner, produce people who have a high probability of living in poverty—indeed, "culture of poverty" is usually identified with the same types of lifestyle and personality.

In his 1994 book *Prescription for Failure*, Byron M. Roth developed these themes still further. Strongly influenced by black economist Thomas Sowell, Roth argued that "most of the problems blacks face in America today are directly attributable to patterns of behavior that have become common in black underclass communities . . . : welfare dependency, crime, illegitimacy, and educational failure, all of which seriously undercut black economic and social advancement, and in addition serve to undermine efforts to facilitate racial integration." Such examples of lower-class behavior are found in all racial and ethnic groups, with the same predictable consequences. To attribute the economic difficulties of African Americans, Native Americans, or Latinos to white racism is, in Roth's view, inaccurate and unfair. Roth contended that even if racism suddenly disappeared, the life of most African Americans would not improve measurably until the "debilitating conditions of life in the underclass" were remedied. On the other hand, if lower-class behaviors—crime, illegitimacy, educational failure—could be halted, Roth believed that African Americans would experience real social and economic growth despite white racism.

Roth notes that much of the disparity between the incomes of blacks and whites arises from factors other than prejudice. Median family income for blacks failed to rise relative to whites over the period 1967 to 1990. However, vastly more of the black families were headed by women and had only one wage earner. For black families headed by married couples, the average income increased from 68 percent of white income in 1967 to 84 percent in 1990. The ratio was even higher for black married-couple families under age forty-four.

Like political scientist Charles Murray, Roth argues that blaming the economic problems of the black underclass on "white racism" has led to public policies regarding education, crime, and welfare that have actually aggravated the problems. He also states that the members of the black underclass themselves have been encouraged to develop defeatist and self-destructive attitudes toward their own situation. *Paul B. Trescott*

See also: Class theories of racial/ethnic relations; Culture of poverty; Poverty and race; Racial/ethnic relations: race-class debate.

Underground Railroad

> **Significance:** The Underground Railroad was a loose network of secret routes by which fugitive slaves made their way from the southern slave states north to freedom, often as far as Canada. Parts of the Underground Railroad may have been in place as early as 1786.

By 1850, southern slave owners were claiming enormous loss of slave property to the Underground Railroad, although many believe these claims were exaggerated. It is impossible to know how many slaves made their way to freedom—estimates range from sixty thousand to a hundred thousand between 1800 and 1865.

Many slaves reached freedom without the aid of the Underground Railroad, and many, especially those in the Deep South, did not flee north but went instead to Mexico or found refuge with the Seminole, Cherokee, or other Native American tribes. However, the majority of fugitive slaves escaped from the border states and fled north. Usually, the most dangerous leg of their journey was reaching a station on the underground line; once there, conductors would pass them from site to site toward safety.

It was almost impossible for a runaway slave to reach freedom successfully without assistance. Most slaves had little or no knowledge of geography and fled with only vague notions of where they were headed; most left with no money and few provisions and had to risk asking strangers along the way for food, shelter, and protection from pursuers. For the most part, persons helping runaways performed impulsive acts of compassion and did not consider themselves to be part of a resistance group. In parts of the country, however, the numbers of fugitives coming through were so great that predetermined escape routes, safe houses, and plans of action were organized. In time, some Underground Railroad lines were highly organized, and at least some routes existed in most of the states between the South and Canada.

The two most frequent escape corridors were from Kentucky and Virginia into Ohio and from there north, and up the Eastern Seaboard through New England. Ohio especially was crisscrossed with routes of escape, as were western Pennsylvania and New York, eastern Indiana, and northwestern Illinois. The Middle Atlantic states and New England also had many well-established routes; lines existed west of Ohio and even, to some degree, in the South. After passage of the Fugitive Slave Law of 1850, organized aid to runaways grew, as the threats to free African Americans as well as fugitive slaves increased and more antislavery sympathizers felt the moral obligation to risk civil disobedience.

Organization

No one knows when or how the name Underground Railroad began, although legend has it that it was coined after a frustrated slavecatcher swore that the fugitives he was pursuing had disappeared as thoroughly and suddenly as if they had found an underground road. As knowledge of the existence of escape routes spread, so did the railroad terminology, with words such as "conductors," "stations," "stationkeepers," and "lines."

Conductors often used inventive means to transport fugitives safely from station to station. Many were hidden under goods or in secret compartments in wagons. A few, such as Henry "Box" Brown, were actually boxed and shipped by train or boat. At least once, slaves were hidden in carriages forming a fake funeral procession. There were so many routing options along some lines that tracing was difficult. Barns, thickets, attics, spare rooms, woodsheds, smokehouses, and cellars were used as stations. Fugitives often were disguised: A hoe could make a runaway look like a hired-out day laborer; fine clothes could disguise a runaway field hand as a servant of gentlefolk; cross-dressing could keep fugitives from matching descriptions on handbills. Mulattoes could sometimes pass as whites. Perhaps the most famous escape effected through disguise was that of husband and wife William and Ellen Craft, who, with Ellen disguised as a white Southern gentleman and William as her valet, made it from Georgia to Philadelphia, where the Underground Railroad then transported them to safety. Once at a station, fugitives were given shelter, food, clothing, and sometimes money, as well as help in reaching the next stop.

Quakers—mostly of the Hicksite sect—played a large and early role in maintaining the Underground Railroad; in 1797, George Washington complained of Quakers helping one of his slaves escape. Other sects, such as Covenanters and Wesleyan Methodists, also contributed a number of agents. Particular locations, such as Oberlin College in Ohio, became important centers of activity. Women as well as men played active roles, especially in

This house near Manassas, Virginia, was a stop on the Underground Railroad.

providing food and clothing to fugitives, and women often organized auxiliaries to support the more visible vigilance and abolitionist committees.

The role played by white antislavery sympathizers, although important, has tended to be overemphasized. In southern states, fellow slaves usually were the source of food and a hiding place for escapees. In border states, free blacks provided the most important help to fugitives, both in all-black settlements and in cities where black abolitionists worked alongside their white counterparts. Many African American churches and vigilance committees extended protection, support, and help in relocation to fugitives who reached the free states.

Whites rarely took the initiative to go south and effect escapes, but a number of former slaves returned to help friends and family flee. The most famous conductor to recruit escapees was the remarkable Harriet Tubman. Having herself escaped from slavery, she made some nineteen daring and successful trips into southern states to bring out groups of slaves, despite the forty-thousand-dollar bounty on her head. She is credited with personally leading more than three hundred slaves to safety, never losing anyone in her charge, and earned the title "the Moses of her people."

The period of greatest activity for the Underground Railroad was from 1850 to 1860. Among the most active white stationkeepers was Levi Coffin: In thirty-five years of activism in Indiana and Ohio, Coffin helped three thousand fugitive slaves on their way north. Quaker Thomas Garrett of Wilmington, Delaware, aided several thousand fugitives over a forty-year period; he lost all of his property to court fines as a result but refused to cease his work.

Important black members of the Underground Railroad included the Reverend William H. Mitchell of Ohio, who in twelve years provided temporary shelter for thirteen hundred fleeing slaves; Robert Purvis of Philadelphia, Pennsylvania; William Whipper of Columbia, Pennsylvania; Henry Highland Garnet of New York; Lewis Hayden of Boston, Massachusetts; Frederick Douglass of Rochester, New York; and William Wells Brown of Buffalo, New York.

However, most of those who hid, fed, transported, and otherwise aided fugitive slaves have remained anonymous. Likewise, records about the fugitives themselves are scarce. Following the Civil War, several prominent activists published memoirs about their Underground Railroad activities that included accounts of some of the slaves they aided. Black stationkeeper William Still of Philadelphia kept notes on almost seven hundred fugitives he helped, providing valuable statistics. His records indicate that 80 percent of runaways were male and that significant numbers of house servants as well as field hands fled. However, the names and profiles of the vast majority of the thousands of men, women, and children who braved the hazards of flight in desperate bids for freedom remain unknown. *Grace McEntee*

Core Resources

Henrietta Buckmaster's *Let My People Go: The Story of the Underground Railroad and the Growth of the Abolition Movement* (Boston: Beacon Press, 1941) discusses the Underground Railroad within the broader context of the growth of antislavery sentiment. Levi Coffin's *Reminiscences of Levi Coffin* (New York: Arno Press, 1968) is an important primary source; this work reprints his third edition of 1898. Larry Gara's *The Liberty Line: The Legend of the Underground Railroad* (Lexington: University of Kentucky Press, 1961) counters popular notions that exaggerate the role of white abolitionists and underplay blacks' contributions in helping fugitive slaves. Wilbur H. Siebert's *The Underground Railroad from Slavery to Freedom* (1898; reprint, New York: Arno Press, 1968) is a landmark history of much value. William Still's *The Underground Railroad* (1872; reprint, Chicago: Johnson, 1972) is a vast collection of narratives and sketches, focusing on the fugitives' stories.

See also: Abolition; Antislavery laws of 1777 and 1807; Fugitive slave laws; Slavery: history.

Undocumented worker/migrant

"Undocumented" refers to an individual who has entered the United States or another country illegally, that is, without the proper visa, passport, or other type of legal documentation, to obtain employment. The term is commonly applied to Mexican and Central American workers in the United States. Undocumented workers have formed the largest immigrant workforce since World War II.

Historically, undocumented workers were referred to as "wetbacks," a reference to the notion that Mexican immigrants illegally cross the U.S.-Mexico border by swimming the Rio Grande (known on the Mexican side of the border as the Río Bravo), which runs along part of the Texas border. Although some illegal immigrants wade across the river, in reality few, if any, swim across, since the river is seldom deep enough to necessitate swimming. Not only was the term "wetback" an inaccurate descriptor for most individuals who entered the country illegally; it soon came to have derogatory and discriminatory connotations when it was applied to all Mexicans and even to native-born U.S. citizens of Mexican or any other Latin American descent who were living in the United States.

A migrant worker stands outside his makeshift home near Salinas, California, in 1991. The term "undocumented worker" is a more neutral word that is sometimes used instead of "illegal alien."

The term "undocumented worker" is less politically charged than "wetback" or "illegal alien" and is a much more accurate and neutral descriptor of the individuals who come to the United States in search of work without legal papers.   *Celestino Fernández*

See also: Epithets and pejorative language; Hate speech; Illegal aliens; Latinos in the United States; Operation Wetback.

United Farm Workers

Using a social justice platform, the United Farm Workers union won collective bargaining rights for previously unorganized Filipino and Latino agricultural workers and helped create the Latino civil rights movement. César Chávez, Dolores Huerta, and others formed the National Farm Workers Association, the precursor to the United Farm Workers (UFW) union, in 1962. The founders emerged from the Community Service Organization (CSO), a Mexican American self-help association based in Los Angeles.

Like the Civil Rights movement, the UFW received much support from students and church members who saw agricultural workers' call for better wages, higher standards in working and sanitary conditions, and union recognition as moral and social justice issues. In the 1960's, a majority of U.S. farmworkers were Mexican or Mexican American. Unlike other occupations, agricultural work was not covered under the auspices of the National Labor Relations Act (Wagner Act) and thus was not protected under the aegis of the National Labor Relations Board. Major unions were not interested in organizing migratory Hispanic workers. The UFW was developed in response to this lack of legal protection or union advocacy. Its approach was based on a platform of philosophical tactics developed by Chávez, who was a student of the nonviolent teachings of Mahatma (Mohandas) Gandhi and Martin Luther King, Jr. In addition to strikes and picketing, the UFW used fasting, mass consumer boycotts, and peaceful demonstration to publicize their cause and exert pressure on growers.

In 1965, the UFW joined the Delano Grape Strike against major California grape growers. Chávez sent letters and telegrams to the growers, offering to negotiate contracts setting minimum pay rates and specifying several other conditions of work, and organized the first of a series of national boycotts of grapes and wine. A three-hundred-mile march from Delano, California, to the state capital of Sacramento began in 1966 and ended with a rally at the state's capitol building on Easter Sunday. The march was patterned after the Freedom March from Selma to Montgomery, Alabama, only a few years before. The march combined the penitence and pilgrimage traditions of Mexican and Filipino culture and Catholic religion with the political purposes of the union. The boycott received wide public support from coast to coast, and union victory in the grape fields came in 1970 with contracts signed with major table grape growers. Organizing then shifted to lettuce fields, with a major boycott campaign focused on iceberg lettuce.

The early 1970's were characterized by backlashes against the UFW, but by 1974 there was a resurgence of strength, and new contracts were signed with growers. Renewed pressure resulted in the passage of the Agricultural Labor Relations Act (1975), the first law that recognized the collective bargaining rights of farmworkers. The UFW's effectiveness declined in the 1980's as anti-union and anti-immigrant sentiment increased under federal and state Republican administrations, undercutting the UFW's organizing power, and the Agricultural Labor Relations Board worked in the interests of growers.

Although overall membership declined in the 1990's and Chávez's charismatic leadership was lost with his death in 1993, the UFW continued to represent workers, lead boycotts, and lobby legislatures and Congress. The Citizenship Participation Day Department, the political wing of the UFW, continued to provide testimony and conduct public education programs about immigration laws, environmental issues surrounding the use of pesticides, and the health concerns of migrant workers.

Barbara Bair

See also: Chicano movement; Labor movement; Latinos in the United States; Selma-Montgomery march.

United Jewish Appeal

The United Jewish Appeal (UJA) is an American organization whose purpose is to raise funds and to unite and support Jewish communities around the world. The UJA was formally born in 1939, resulting from a union of the United Palestine Appeal, the American Jewish Joint Distribution Committee, and the National Refugee Service. At first, the groups did not trust one another, and the Council of Jewish Federations served as mediator. *A History of the United Jewish Appeal 1939-1982* (1982), by Marc Lee Raphael, states that the catalyst for its formation occurred in Germany on November 10, 1938, *Kristallnacht*, when Germans rioted against Jews and many Jewish businesses were vandalized. Despite the atrocities of the Holocaust, American Jews remained fragmented. It was the Six-Day War in 1967, a triumphant victory for the Israelis, that served to solidify the organization's credibility and reliability.

In *Living UJA History* (1997), Irving Bernstein states that Henry Montor, the UJA's first executive vice president, established a union of disparate groups to support the organization. His initiatives strengthened the participation not only of religious Jews but also of less religious Jews, Christians, and women. Most of this work is carried on by local federations. A large percentage of the funds raised are donated to hospitals, clinics, community centers, universities, and museums. *Jonathan Kahane*

See also: American Jewish Committee; American Jewish Congress; Jewish Americans.

United Negro College Fund

Under the direction of Frederick D. Patterson, president of Tuskegee Institute, the United Negro College Fund (UNCF) was established on April 25, 1944, with twenty-seven member colleges and a combined enrollment of fourteen thousand students. The goal was to become one of the world's leading education assistance organizations. With a few exceptions, most UNCF member institutions had been founded by religious societies from the North after the Civil War and before the turn of the century. Located principally in the Southeast and in eastern Texas, these institutions operate with a variety of organizational structures and program offerings.

Since its inception, UNCF has grown to become the United States' oldest and most successful African American higher-education assistance organization. In 1998, UNCF provided support for a consortium of forty-one private, accredited four-year black colleges and universities. UNCF raises operating money for its member schools so that they can maintain the highest academic standards and prepare their students for demanding professions and careers. Although these institutions constitute only about 3 percent of all colleges and universities in the United States, they graduate more than one-quarter of all African Americans who earn the baccalaureate degree and nearly 40 percent of African Americans who later earn a doctoral degree. These graduates help build a stronger nation as community leaders and educators and in numerous other vocations.

Alvin K. Benson

See also: Black colleges and universities; Education and African Americans.

United States Commission on Civil Rights

Significance: The reports and studies of the Commission on Civil Rights have been an important factor in the passage of major civil rights legislation.

The U.S. Commission on Civil Rights was created in 1957 by Congress as part of the Civil Rights Act of 1957. It consisted of six members, appointed by the president and approved by Congress. The original purpose of the agency was to monitor civil rights (particularly violations of voting rights in the South), issue reports, and then disband, but Congress has continuously renewed its mandate. The Commission on Civil Rights (abbreviated as CRC, for Civil Rights Commission) was created in the wake of the 1954 Supreme Court decision in *Brown v. Board of Education.* In this case, the Court decided that separate facilities for black and white students in public education were unconstitutional. A year later, in *Brown II,* the Court ruled that schools must integrate with "all deliberate speed." No specific timetable was given, however, for fear of further alienating southern whites.

The CRC helped lay the foundation for the civil rights legislation of the 1960's. The commission's mandate involved investigating voting rights violations, collecting and studying voting data related to denials of equal protection under the law, and appraising federal laws and policies as they related to equal protection. In addition to creating the CRC, the 1957 Civil Rights Act made the civil rights component in the Justice Department a division, and empowered the U.S. attorney general to initiate civil court proceedings to enforce voting rights. The 1957 statute gave the attorney general the power to intervene only on a case-by-case basis, which was tedious, as there were thousands of cases of voting rights violations.

Civil Rights Legislation

During Dwight D. Eisenhower's administration, the Commission on Civil Rights investigated voting rights violations in eight southern states and found no fewer than a hundred counties using discriminatory measures against African Americans. The Civil Rights Act of 1960 was passed as a result of the CRC's 1959 report. Although the CRC had recommended that Congress pass legislation authorizing federal registrars in obstructionist districts, the act only provided court-appointed referees to oversee and resolve alleged voting rights abuses. Continuing studies by the CRC would assist in more powerful legislation in 1964 and 1965.

The 1964 Civil Rights Act was instrumental in the desegregation of public facilities in a still-segregated South. Based on ongoing concerns and studies by the CRC in education, voting, and employment, and influenced by the intensifying Civil Rights movement and the March on Washington in 1963, the 1964 act forbade racial discrimination in public facilities, voting registration procedures, and employment. The act empowered the attorney general to intervene and take civil action in cases of racial discrimination in public accommodations. It also cut federal funds to school districts that discriminated and created the Equal Employment Opportunity Commission to oversee discrimination complaints in the workplace.

The 1965 Voting Rights Act is the most powerful legislation in the area of suffrage, and it eliminated virtually all remaining loopholes. The act effectively took the process of voter registration out of the hands of states and localities, providing federal machinery for this process. The legislation also forbade literacy tests in most instances. In addition, a preclearance mechanism (often called Section 5) was put in place that required political districts to submit proposed changes in elections or districts to the federal government for approval. A "clean record" provision was instituted, allowing political districts to be removed from coverage of the preclearance provision if no discrimination or voting irregularities have been found for the previous ten years.

The CRC has played a vital role in the extension of the 1965 Voting Rights Act and thus in continued suf-frage among African Americans in the Deep South. One of the most controversial areas of the act, the preclearance provision, was challenged by southerners. Testimony by the CRC revealed that southern states, and particularly Mississippi, were seeking to subvert the intent of the act and dilute the black vote and black political victories. Legislatures did this by racial gerrymandering of political districts, going to at-large systems of municipal elections, developing multimember districts, and consolidating black and white counties. The CRC was instrumental in the extension of Section 5 and the drafting of other provisions of the 1970 Voting Rights Act. Reports by the commission would play an important role in the 1975 and 1982 extensions of the act as well.

Challenges and Impact

A major challenge to the commission came in the early 1980's, after it issued a 1981 statement entitled *Affirmative Action in the 1980's*, which advocated quotas to ensure the hiring of minorities. President Ronald Reagan strongly opposed the recommendations and removed three of the CRC's commissioners, appointing more conservative commissioners. A lawsuit ensued, and in 1983 Reagan was ordered by the courts to reinstate the commissioners he had fired. Also in 1983, the commission was reorganized by a compromise congressional act (Reagan had vowed to veto an act routinely renewing the commission) to consist of eight members chosen by the president and Congress. The commission was criticized from many quarters in the 1980's, partly for appearing to succumb to various political pressures, and many of its leaders, including Clarence Pendleton, were controversial. In the early 1990's, it began to resume the more active role it had played in the past.

Originally intended as a watchdog agency, the Commission on Civil Rights has been essential as a bipartisan fact-finding body and a resource for both Congress and the president in developing legislation. While its early charge was in the area of voting rights, it has conducted numerous studies and provided congressional testimony in education, housing, racial segregation, employment discrimination, and denial of civil rights on the basis of race, creed, color, religion, national origin, sex, age, or disability.   *Mfanya D. Tryman*

Core Resources

Among the best sources for information on the CRC are Gerald David Jaynes and Robin M. Williams, Jr., eds., *A Common Destiny: Blacks and American Society* (Washington, D.C.: National Academy Press, 1989); Theodore Eisenberg's article "Civil Rights Commission," in *Civil Rights and Equality: Selections from the Encyclopedia of the American Constitution* (New York: Macmillan, 1989); Frank R. Parker, *Black Votes Count* (Chapel Hill: University of North

Carolina Press, 1990); Steven F. Lawson, *Running for Freedom* (New York: McGraw-Hill, 1991); Hugh Davis Graham, *Civil Rights and the Presidency* (New York: Oxford University Press, 1992); Charles S. Bullock III and Charles M. Lamb, *Implementation of Civil Rights Policy* (Monterey, Calif.: Brooks/Cole, 1984); and Gertrude Ezorsky, *Racism and Justice* (Ithaca, N.Y.: Cornell University Press, 1991).

See also: *Brown v. Board of Education*; Civil Rights Act of 1957; Civil Rights Act of 1960; Civil Rights Act of 1964; Civil Rights Act of 1968; Civil Rights Act of 1991; Civil Rights Acts of 1866-1875; Civil Rights movement; Voting Rights Act of 1965.

United States v. Bhagat Singh Thind

In 1870, there were only 586 people of Asian Indian origin in United States. Between 1898 and 1914, however, 6,000 Asian Indians entered the United States, mostly settling on the Pacific coast. Anti-Asian feeling was on the rise; Asians were denied citizenship and the rights afforded whites.

Bhagat Singh Thind, a Sikh from South Asia's Punjab, had entered the United States in 1913, served in the U.S. armed forces in World War I, and was determined to obtain his lawful rights. He filed a case rightly claiming Aryan ancestry (both Germans and North Indians trace their ancestry to the Aryans, a group that originated in Central Europe), arguing that he was therefore white and eligible for citizenship. The case went to the U.S. Supreme Court, which in 1923 ruled against him, stating that "the words of the statute are to be interpreted in accordance with the understanding of the common man from whose vocabulary they were taken." In other words, Bhagat Singh Thind was an Asian in spite of his racial origins.   *Arthur W. Helweg*

See also: Aryan "race"; Asian Indians in the United States; Sikhs in the United States.

United States v. Cruikshank

In 1875, William Cruikshank and two others were convicted in a federal court of participating in the lynching of two African Americans. The 1870 Reconstruction statute under which they were convicted was broadly written to make it unlawful to interfere with most rights of citizens. The constitutional authority claimed for this federal statute was the Fourteenth Amendment. Cruikshank and his codefendants, who were charged with interfering with the right and privilege "peaceably to assemble," argued that the Fourteenth Amendment does not authorize the federal government to establish so broad a criminal statute because the amendment was written to limit state governments, not private persons.

In 1876, the U.S. Supreme Court, in an opinion written by Chief Justice Morrison R. Waite, unanimously agreed with Cruikshank. The Fourteenth Amendment, which establishes citizenship and then says, "No State shall make or enforce any law which shall abridge the privileges or immunities of citizens of the United States," applies in the first instance to state, not private, action. Private action such as the lynching in which Cruikshank participated may be punished by the federal government only if it can be shown that the intent was to deprive a specific constitutional right—and even then the indictment must specify the intent very narrowly. The decision effectively sanctioned the lynchings of African Americans for the next few decades.   *Robert Jacobs*

See also: Dyer antilynching bill; Lynchings; Sexual fears and racism.

United States v. Kagama

American Indian "Pactah Billy" Kagama was charged with murdering another Indian on the Hoopa Valley Reservation in California in 1885. Indian tribes were regarded as a separate people within the United States having the power to regulate their own social relations within reservations.

Kagama challenged the Indian Appropriation Act of March 3, 1885, which gave jurisdiction to U.S. federal courts for several specific crimes, including murder, committed by Native Americans on another Native American within an Indian reservation created by the U.S. government and set apart for use by an Indian tribe.

On May 10, 1886, the U.S. Supreme Court declared the act constitutional and reaffirmed that Native American tribes were not to be considered sovereign in the same way as nations or states but to be viewed as largely helpless communities dependent upon the U.S. government for their food, protection, and constitutional political rights.   *Steve J. Mazurana*

See also: American Indians in the justice system; Tribal courts; Tribal sovereignty.

United States v. Reese

United States v. Reese (1876) marked the first major test of voting rights under the Fifteenth Amendment, which had been passed in 1870 and stated that the right to vote "shall not be denied or abridged by the United States or by any State on account of race, color, or previous condition of servitude." A Kentucky voting official was indicted for refusing to let an African American, who had offered to pay his poll tax, vote in a municipal election. The U.S. Supreme Court, by an 8-1 margin, declared unconstitutional the Enforcement Act of 1870, the law on which the indictment was based. The Enforcement Act provided penalties for obstructing or hindering persons from voting in an election. In the majority decision delivered by Chief Justice Morison R. Waite, the Supreme Court ruled that the U.S. Congress had overreached its powers by seeking to punish the denial of voting rights on any grounds and could only legislate against discrimination based on race.

According to the U.S. Supreme Court, the Fifteenth Amendment did not confer the right of suffrage on anyone but merely prohibited the United States from excluding a person from voting because of race, color, or previous condition of servitude. The ruling made it constitutionally possible for southern states to deny the right to vote on any grounds except race, thus allowing the use of poll taxes, literacy tests, good character tests, understanding clauses, and other devices to disfranchise African Americans.   *David L. Porter*

See also: Disfranchisement laws in Mississippi; Fifteenth Amendment; Literacy tests; Poll tax.

United States v. Washington

United States v. Washington is commonly referred to as the Boldt decision after the judge who decided it in federal district court. In a series of treaties negotiated between 1854 and 1855, various Washington and Oregon tribes ceded nearly sixty-four million acres of land but retained the right to continue to fish in accustomed areas. The states of Washington and Oregon eventually sought to regulate Indians' rights to fish in off-reservation areas. In response, some Indian people staged fish-ins in the 1960's to assert their treaty rights. Finally, the state of Washington used its regulatory powers to limit Indian fishing, and in 1970, thirteen tribes sued the state in federal court.

After extensive study, Federal District Judge George Boldt ruled in 1974 that Indians had rights to fish at off-reservation sites because this right had been reserved in the treaties. The court understood the treaties involved a grant from the tribes to the United States, and in return, the tribes obtained rights for its members and heirs. The ruling also stated that United States citizens and tribal people had the right to share equally in the

salmon catch, and both were directed by the court to develop plans to protect and replenish the salmon population.

This decision caused widespread opposition among state officials, sports fishers, and others, and Indian people complained of harassment and continued problems with exercising their fishing rights. On appeal from the state of Washington, the U.S. Supreme Court reviewed the case in 1979 and essentially upheld Boldt's ruling.   *Carole A. Barrett*

See also: American Indian activism; Fish-ins; Treaties and agreements with Indians: United States; Water rights.

United Steelworkers of America v. Weber

In the 1979 *United Steelworkers of America v. Weber* decision, the U.S. Supreme Court ruled that an employer could establish voluntary programs of racial preference, including quotas, in order to eliminate manifest racial imbalance, even without evidence that the employer was guilty of discrimination.

Title VII of the Civil Rights Act of 1964 made it illegal "to discriminate against any individual because of his race, color, religion, sex, or national origin." Within a few years, federal agencies began to use "racial imbalance" as *prima facie* evidence of invidious discrimination, and they encouraged employers to use numerical goals, timetables, and sometimes quotas to promote minority participation in areas of employment where they had been traditionally underrepresented. The Kaiser Corporation's plant in Gramercy, Louisiana, found that while African Americans made up 39 percent of the local workforce, they occupied less than 2 percent of the craft positions in the plant. Fearing that this imbalance might jeopardize government contracts, the corporation and the labor union agreed to a "voluntary" affirmative action plan that included a special training program for craft positions. Admission to the training program was based on seniority, except that half the positions were reserved for African Americans even if they had less seniority.

Brian Weber, a white employee with five years of experience, was disappointed when he was not admitted into the program while two black employees with less seniority did gain admission. He sued both the company and the union with the argument that he was a victim of discrimination in violation of the 1964 Civil Rights Act. After Weber prevailed in both the district court and the court of appeals, the union petitioned the U.S. Supreme Court to review the judgments.

The Court's Decision

The Court voted 5 to 2 to reverse the lower courts' decision and to uphold the affirmative action program at the Gramercy plant. Writing for the majority, Justice William J. Brennan looked to the spirit rather than the literal wording of Title VII. Since the purpose of the law was to advance employment opportunities for members of racial minorities, he reasoned that the law did not prohibit preferences as a means of integrating minorities into the mainstream of American society. The program, moreover, did not "unnecessarily trammel" the interests of Weber; it was only a "temporary measure," to end when a target was reached. Further, it had the limited goal of ending "a manifest racial imbalance." Finally, Brennan noted that if the Court had "misperceived" the intent of Congress, the decision could be corrected easily by legislative action.

In a strongly worded dissent, Justice William H. Rehnquist proclaimed that "no racial discrimination in employment is permissible under Title VII." Noting the explicit wording of the law, he also quoted extensively from the congressional debates to show that the framers of Title VII envisioned a law allowing no preference based on race or gender.

The *Weber* decision was one of the Court's most controversial cases to deal with the question of "reverse discrimination." Supporters of race-conscious remedies for past societal discrimination were delighted that the Court did not apply the strict scrutiny test to an affirmative action program that involved racial preference and quotas. In later cases the justices would continue to be divided over the issue of *Weber*; they would tend to alternate between approving and disapproving affirmative action programs.   *Thomas T. Lewis*

See also: Affirmative action; *Bakke* case; Civil Rights Act of 1964; *Fullilove v. Klutznick*; Quotas; "Reverse" racism; *Richmond v. J. A. Croson Company*; Set-asides.

Universal Negro Improvement Association

Significance: The Universal Negro Improvement Association, an organization dedicated to supporting African American racial pride, did much to advance the growth of black nationalism.

In March, 1916, a young black Jamaican, Marcus Mosiah Garvey, arrived in New York City. He had come to the United States in the hope of securing financial help for the Universal Negro Improvement Association (UNIA), which he had founded in Jamaica two years earlier. After delivering his first public speech in Harlem in May, Garvey began a long speaking tour that took him through thirty-eight states. In May, 1917, he returned to Harlem and—with the help of his secretary and future wife, Amy Ashwood—organized the first American chapter of the UNIA. Though hardly noticed at the time, the establishment of this organization was a significant first step in the growth of black nationalism in the United States. Within a few years, the UNIA would claim millions of members and hundreds of branches throughout the United States, the Caribbean region, and Africa, and Garvey would be one of the most famous black people in the world.

The Beginnings of the UNIA

Garvey was born in St. Ann's Bay, Jamaica, in 1887. He claimed to be of pure African descent. His father was a descendant of the maroons, or Jamaican slaves, who successfully revolted against their British masters in 1739. During his early years, Garvey gradually became aware that his color was considered by some in his society to be a badge of inferiority. Jamaica, unlike the United States, placed the mulatto in a higher caste as a buffer against the unlettered black masses. This reality caused a sense of racial isolation and yet pride to grow in the young black man. By his twentieth birthday, Garvey had started a program to change the lives of black Jamaicans. While working as a foreman in a printing shop in 1907, he joined a labor strike as a leader. The strike, quickly broken by the shop owners, caused Garvey to lose faith in reform through labor unions. In 1910, he started publishing a newspaper, *Garvey's Watchman*, and helped form a political organization, the National Club. These efforts, which were not particularly fruitful, gave impetus to Garvey's visit to Central America where he was able to observe the wretched conditions of black people in Costa Rica and Panama.

Garvey's travels led him to London, the center of the British Empire. There the young man met Dusé Mohamed Ali, an Egyptian scholar, who increased the young Jamaican's knowledge and awareness of Africa. During his stay in England, Garvey also became acquainted with the plight of African Americans through reading Booker T. Washington's *Up from Slavery*. Washington's autobiography raised questions in Garvey's mind: "I asked, where is the black man's Government? Where is his King and his Kingdom? Where is his President, his country and his ambassador, his army, his navy, his men of big affairs? I could not find them, and then I declared, I will help to make them."

Returning to Jamaica in 1914, Garvey created a self-help organization for black people to which he gave the imposing title, the Universal Negro Improvement and Conservation Association and African Communities League. This new organization, renamed the Universal Negro Improvement Association, based its philosophy on the need to unite "all people of Negro or African parentage." The goals of the UNIA were to increase racial pride, to aid black people throughout the world, and "to establish a central nation for the race." Garvey, elected the first president of UNIA, realized that black people would have to achieve these goals without assistance from white people. This self-help concept, similar to the philosophy (but not the practice) of Booker T. Washington, led Garvey to propose a black trade school in Kingston, Jamaica, similar to Washington's Tuskegee Institute. The idea did not attract wide support and Garvey was temporarily frustrated.

In 1915, Garvey decided to come to the United States in order to seek aid for his Jamaica-based organization. Although he had corresponded with Washington, the black leader had died before Garvey arrived in the United States in 1916. Garvey went directly to Harlem, which in the early twentieth century was becoming a center of black culture

The lives of African Americans were rapidly changing in the first two decades of the twentieth century. Metropolitan areas in the North were experiencing mass migrations of African Americans from the South. In New York City, for example, the black population increased from 91,709 in 1910 to 152,467 in 1920. African Americans were attracted by the promise of jobs and by the possibility of escaping the rigid system of segregation in the South.

African Americans found, however, that they could not escape racism simply by moving. Northern whites also believed in the racial inferiority of African Americans and opposed black competitors for their jobs. The new immigrants, like their foreign-born counterparts, were crowded into the northern ghettos without proper housing or the possibility of escape. Racial violence broke out in several northern cities. The North proved not to be a utopia for African Americans.

These harsh realities aided Garvey in establishing the UNIA in New York. The population of Harlem was not attracted to the accommodationist philosophy of Washington or the middle-class goals of the National Association for the Advancement of Colored People. Indeed, urban African Americans were wary of all prophets, even Garvey; but the young Jamaican was able to obtain support from the Jamaican immigrants in Harlem, who felt isolated, and he established a branch of UNIA there in 1917. At first, the organization encountered difficulties. Local politicians tried to gain control of it, and Garvey had to fight to save its autonomy. The original branch of the UNIA was dissolved, and a charter was obtained from the state of New York which prevented other groups from using the organization's name. By 1918, under Garvey's exciting leadership, the New York chapter of the UNIA boasted 3,500 members. By 1919, Garvey optimistically claimed 2 million members for his organization throughout the world and 200,000 subscribers for his weekly newspaper, *The Negro World.*

The Black Star Line and the Collapse of the UNIA

In an effort to promote the economic welfare of blacks under the auspices of the UNIA, Garvey established in 1919 two joint stock companies—the Black Star Line, an international commercial shipping company, and the Negro Factories Corporation, which was to "build and operate factories . . . to manufacture every marketable commodity." Stock in these companies was sold only to black investors. The Black Star Line was to establish commerce with Africa and transport willing emigrants "back to Africa." Although both companies were financial failures, they gave many black people a feeling of dignity. As a result of his promotional efforts in behalf of the Black Star Line, the federal government, prodded by rival black leaders, had Garvey indicted for fraudulent use of the mails in 1922. He was tried, found guilty, and sent to prison in 1923. Although his second wife, Amy Jacques-Garvey, worked to hold the UNIA together, it declined rapidly. In 1927, Garvey was released from prison and deported as an undesirable alien. He returned to Jamaica and then went to London and Paris and tried to resurrect the UNIA, but with little success. He died in poverty in London in 1940. Although a bad businessman, Garvey was a master propagandist and popular leader who made a major contribution to race consciousness among African Americans.

John C. Gardner, updated by R. Kent Rasmussen

Core Resources

E. David Cronon's *Black Moses: The Story of Marcus Garvey and the Universal Negro Improvement Association* (Madison: University of Wisconsin Press, 1955) remains the best introduction to Garvey's life. Marcus Garvey's *Philosophy and Opinions of Marcus Garvey,* edited by Amy Jacques-Garvey, with new introduction by Robert A. Hill (New York: Atheneum, 1992), is a classic collection of Garvey's speeches and writings assembled by his wife. *The Marcus Garvey and Universal Negro Improvement Association Papers* (9 vols., Berkeley: University of California Press, 1983-1996), edited by Robert A. Hill et al., is the most extensive collection of original documents by and about Garvey and his movement.

See also: Black nationalism; Jamaican Americans; National Association for the Advancement of Colored People; Niagara Movement.

Urban Indians

Significance: More than half of the U.S. Native American population resides in a metropolitan area for most or all of the year; in many cities, urban Indians go unnoticed by other ethnic groups.

The term "urban Indians" is problematic for most non-Native Americans. Whether thinking of Native Americans brings forth positive, negative, or neutral images, most non-natives do not imagine natives as members of an urban, technological society, and this lack of urban image has led to a blindness regarding the presence and needs of Native Americans in the cities. Identification of the urban Native American has therefore been one of the central problems surrounding government policy making regarding American Indians since the early 1960's.

Relocation and Migration

All members of a federally recognized tribe in the United States, according to the U.S. Constitution, are due certain benefits and services, by right of their heritage. This unique legal relationship with the U.S. government was never meant to end once an individual moved to a metropolitan area, but in effect that is what has happened. In the mid-1950's, the Bureau of Indian Affairs (BIA), in accord with Congress, began the Voluntary Relocation Program. BIA officers on each reservation were instructed to "sell" the idea of city living to likely candidates. Individuals, and sometimes families, were given a one-way ticket to the chosen city, where housing and employment awaited, all arranged by the BIA. Subsistence money was guaranteed for six weeks, after which these newest immigrants were on their own.

Most Indians who arrived in the city under the relocation program left as soon as they got a good look at their new way of life. Many of the jobs were unskilled, and Native Americans found they were able to afford only the worst housing available in the city. Under these conditions, transition to city dwelling was, for many, impossible. Yet the BIA did not recognize the shortcomings of its multimillion-dollar program and continued to re-

locate as many Native Americans as possible. Noticing that many of their clients were returning to their reservations, the BIA began relocating people as far away from their reservations as could be managed, to make it as difficult as possible to return. Part of the plan was to terminate the reservations eventually. The Voluntary Relocation Program was a failure according to its own goals. This program was based on the prejudiced notion that Native American culture and lifeways would, and should, disappear. The BIA and the U.S. Congress of the 1950's counted on America's cities to speed that process.

Most Native Americans presently living in urban areas did not arrive through the relocation program but migrated independently, usually looking for employment, and settled near relatives or friends from their reservation or hometown. Many are permanent residents, but an approximately equal number are transient—relocating within the city, going from city to city, or spending part of the year in the city and part on the reservation. There is no known "typical" pattern of migration; tribal nations, families, and individuals differ according to their needs. A family may live in the city during the winter so the children can stay in school, then leave for the

Metropolitan Statistical Areas with Largest Native American Populations, 1990	
Metropolitan Statistical Area	*Population*
*Los Angeles-Anaheim-Riverside, CA	85,004
Tulsa, OK	48,116
Oklahoma City, OK	45,623
*New York-Northern New Jersey-Long Island, NY-NJ-CT	44,437
*San Francisco-Oakland-San Jose, CA	39,255
Phoenix, AZ	37,708
*Seattle-Tacoma, WA	29,643
Minneapolis-St. Paul, MN-WI	23,621
Tucson, AZ	20,231
San Diego, CA	19,564
*Dallas-Fort Worth, TX	18,608
*Detroit-Ann Arbor, MI	17,731
Sacramento, CA	16,650
Albuquerque, NM	16,201
*Chicago-Gary-Lake County, IL-IN-WI	15,098
*Denver-Boulder, CO	13,600
*Portland-Vancouver, OR-WA	13,034
*Philadelphia-Wilmington-Trenton, PA-NJ-DE-MD	10,962
Washington, DC-MD-VA	10,685
*Houston-Galveston-Brazoria, TX	10,677

* Indicates a combined metropolitan statistical area (CMSA).

Source: U.S. Bureau of the Census, *Census of Population and Housing, 1990: Summary Tape on CD-ROM.* Washington, D.C.: U.S. Government Printing Office, 1991.

reservation in the summer. Construction workers are often busy in the cities during the warm months and leave in the winter. The powwow season and harvests also draw many urban Native Americans back to the reservations. The frequent moving to and from the reservation and within the city is one factor in the urban Native American's invisibility or elusiveness.

Urban Indian Identity

Another factor until recently has been the reluctance of urban Indians to identify themselves as Native Americans to non-Native Americans in the city. The urban Native Americans' attempts to remain unidentified, coupled with the tremendous mobility of individuals and families, have made it impossible in past years for the U.S. census to come close to an accurate count in the cities. In the 1990 U.S. census, however, there was a huge increase in people identifying themselves as Native Americans, Eskimos, and Aleuts. As the increase cannot be completely explained by actual population growth, there is much speculation regarding what has made so many more Native Americans willing to be identified. Some cynical observers insist that the motive must be monetary: to obtain funds and services that are due Native Americans under the law. One thing that scholars studying Native American culture have learned over the decades, however, is that Native Americans usually cannot be coaxed to take a particular course of action because of the promise of money. Most Native Americans living in cities do not receive federal funds or services of any kind, because they distrust Indian or non-Indian agencies and to seek survival strategies among one another.

Native Americans have arrived in cities all over the United States for many reasons; work opportunities and education are the most commonly cited. Some cities, such as Chicago, operate high-quality schools for Native American children as further insurance against their losing precious traditions and ways of thinking.

Gambling as Urban Legacy

One clear consequence of Native Americans' learning to deal with the bureaucratic state has been the success stories of Indian nations using the existing laws to repair damages done to their nations, such as bringing an economic base to their reservation. One example comes from the small Pequot Nation in Ledyard, Connecticut. In response to a 1988 ruling holding that federal law allows recognized Indian tribes to have gambling on reservations if the state in which they live allows some sort of gambling off the reservation, the Pequots set up a large gambling center, the Foxwoods Resort and Casino.

The gambling question affects reservations all over the country; from California to New Jersey, Native Americans are debating the serious question of what effects the presence of casinos would have on their reservations. Many are now in operation. Although most reservation casinos are not located in large metropolitan areas, gambling brings some aspects of the city (in concentrated doses) to the reservation. Although various forms of gambling have existed traditionally among many Native American nations, the dangers and problems that seem to surround non-Native American casino centers worry many people. Many of the same questions that have concerned native peoples for generations—about the quality of life left for their people—continue to worry them, whether they be on an impoverished reservation, in a large city, or on a reservation that has made casino gambling the economic base of its people's lives. It is clear, however, that the revenues benefit Indian and non-Indian alike.

It is impossible to predict accurately what the long-term effects of such changes will be, but it is likely that current and future generations of Native Americans will be able to draw upon the resilience typical of Indian peoples. They will remain strong and independent as a group while balancing the need to protect their traditions with the need to accept, even embrace, change.

Roberta Fiske-Rusciano

Core Resources

Urban Indians are discussed in Jeanne Guillemin's *Urban Renegades* (New York: Columbia University Press, 1975); Nancy Lurie's "The Contemporary American Indian Scene," in *North American Indians in Historical Perspective*, edited by Eleanor Burke Leacock and Nancy Lurie (New York: Random House, 1971); and Watt Spade and Willard Walker's "Relocation," in *The Way: An Anthology of American Indian Life*, edited by Shirley Hill Witt and Stan Steiner (New York: Alfred A. Knopf, 1972).

See also: American Indian activism; Gambling; Relocation of American Indians; Termination resolution.

Urban underclass and the rural poor

Significance: "Urban underclass" has come to refer to a segment of the population that resides in urban or central-city areas and experiences high and persistent poverty, social isolation, anomie, and a sense of hopelessness. The "rural poor" consist of poverty-stricken persons living in small or sparsely populated communities.

The use of the terms "urban underclass" and "rural poor" is controversial, and there seems to be no consensus regarding how best to define them. It is estimated that 33 million poor people lived in the United States in 1990. Journalist Ken Auletta, in *The Underclass* (1983), estimated the number of American underclass to be anywhere from 2 to 18 million, while Joel A. Devine and James D. Wright, in *The Greatest of Evils: Urban Poverty and the American Underclass* (1993), cited figures of 3 million to 3.5 million. The number of rural poor in the United States was more than 9 million. These dramatically different figures and discrepancies in the totals reflect continued debate surrounding the definitions of both rural and urban poverty.

Urban Underclass

A number of subgroups are more likely to be among the urban underclass than others, including children, the elderly, women, nonwhites, and members of female-headed households. Of these, racial affiliation is perhaps the most noted in research. Sociologist William J. Wilson points out that underclass neighborhoods "are populated almost exclusively by the most disadvantaged segments of the black urban community." This has not changed significantly since anthropologist Gunnar Myrdal wrote in 1962: "The largest and still most handicapped minority group in America is that of the Negroes."

Increased crime and deviant behavior are two of the most disturbing characteristics of the urban underclass. The entrenched hopelessness found on inner-city streets provides little motivation for members of the underclass to adhere to the norms and values of mainstream society. Consequently, drug dealing, use of drugs and alcohol, prostitution, theft, and other forms of crime are prevalent among members of the urban underclass.

Rural Underclass

As defined by the U.S. Bureau of the Census, "rural" generally applies to settlements with concentrated populations of less than 2,500. Demographic studies show that the rural poor are concentrated heavily in the southern region of the United States. For example, the 1987 rural poverty rate in the South was 21.2 percent, 7.6 percent higher than that of the rest of the country. Moreover, in excess of half the rural poor in the United States lived in the South in 1987.

The majority of the rural poor are white. This is not to say that rural blacks, Hispanics, and American Indians do not experience high poverty rates. Statistics show that these subgroups have poverty rates of 44 percent, 35 percent, and at least 35 percent, respectively. These figures represent poverty rates several times higher than those of their white counterparts. Those suffering from persistent rural poverty are more likely to be elderly, black, female, or members of a female-headed household.

There are a number of reasons that many members of the rural population are unable to work. Most noteworthy is the fact that many are children too young to work. Illness and disability are additional reasons that many of the rural poor are not among the workforce. Overriding all this, a large percentage of the rural poor are simply unable to find work because of factory closings or manufacturing cutbacks.

Urban-Rural Comparisons

On the surface it might appear that the only difference between the urban underclass and the rural poor is their geographic location and concentration of population. A closer look at the population subgroups (such as elderly, female-headed households, and nonwhites) reveals that this is not the case. In 1987, for example, the rural elderly had a higher poverty rate than the urban elderly. Also, a significantly smaller number of impoverished rural families live in female-headed households than in urban areas.

It appears that behavior is the key to distinguishing the urban underclass from the rural poor. In his provocative book *The Truly Disadvantaged: The Inner City, the Underclass, and Public Policy* (1987), Wilson maintains that "there is a heterogeneous grouping of inner-city families and individuals whose behavior contrasts sharply with that of mainstream America." The anomie or normlessness displayed among the urban underclass manifests itself through high rates of out-of-wedlock births, welfare, unemployment or underemployment, low educational attainment, drug and alcohol abuse, and crime.

According to numerous studies, the rural poor exhibit attitudes toward work that are different from the attitudes of the urban underclass. For example, U.S. census data from 1973 and 1987 indicate that the percentage of rural poor who worked was a full 10 percent higher than the working urban poor.

Economics and the Poor

From the end of World War II until the late 1960's, the United States experienced an economic boom. There was little urban poverty, and rural poverty declined as a result of migration to cities. During this period of general prosperity, the eyes of the country turned to the less fortunate. When President Lyndon B. Johnson declared unconditional War on Poverty in 1964, the federal government established an official poverty line and assistance programs. Not all elements of the poor population were helped by federal programs; the focus was mainly on the Appalachia area and poor children and mothers.

Sociological research on poverty increased in the 1960's and flourished until the mid-1970's.

Following national economic restructuring beginning in 1979, rural areas experienced economic growth; manufacturers built factories and brought new jobs to small towns. Prices for farm products increased, domestic energy industries expanded, and retirees began moving to rural areas. As Duncan notes, however, this "rural turnaround" was short-lived. Rural poverty began to rise again, mainly because the national economy was hit hard by high inflation, recessions, low wages, unemployment, and slow job growth—the results of international competition, factory closings, and layoffs.

The formation of the urban underclass from the 1960's to the 1990's is generally attributed to the mass exodus of the middle- and working-class residents from cities to the suburbs, and to the simultaneous decline in semiskilled and unskilled employment opportunities in the inner cities. In the early 1980's, many middle-class African Americans left the urban areas to take advantage of educational and employment opportunities in the suburbs.

With the absence of middle-class families and their incomes came a substantial decrease in the tax base available to support public schools and other government-run programs. The quality of education declined and urban youths found opportunities slipping even further out of reach and thus became caught in the poverty trap. The departure of the middle class eventually destroyed other stabilizing social institutions, including black churches and local businesses.

During President Ronald Reagan's administration in the 1980's, the situation worsened. Republican constituents were not, in general, poor or black, but rather middle- and working-class people who were tired of their tax dollars supporting the welfare state. This attitude led to the further neglect of the inner-city poor, which brought with it an increase in underclass violence. Incidents such as the Los Angeles riots in 1992 are evidence of the dysfunctional behavior and anomie characteristic of the underclass.

Liesel A. Miller

Core Resources

Joel A. Devine and James D. Wright's *The Greatest of Evils: Urban Poverty and the American Underclass* (New York: Aldine de Gruyter, 1993) is a thorough study, at the same time nontechnical and interesting. *Rural Poverty in America*, edited by Cynthia M. Duncan (New York: Auburn House, 1992), contends that rural poverty is different from urban poverty and that social, economic, and political barriers keep the rural poor economically disadvantaged. David T. Ellwood's *Poor Support: Poverty in the American Family* (New York: Basic Books, 1988) suggests specific steps to eradicate poverty in logical yet general terms. Michael Harrington's *The New American Poverty* (New York: Penguin Books, 1985) provides readers with a provocative and insightful look at the social and political roots of poverty. Christopher Jencks's *Rethinking Social Policy: Race, Poverty, and the Underclass* (Cambridge, Mass.: Harvard University Press, 1992) deals with affirmative action, intergenerational poverty, urban ghettos, and the size and extent of the urban underclass, making recommendations for welfare reform. *The Urban Underclass*, edited by Christopher Jencks and Paul E. Peterson (Washington, D.C.: Brookings Institution, 1991), provides case studies with solid data, tables, and charts.

See also: Economics and race; Poverty and race; Underclass theories; White flight.

Vietnamese Americans

Significance: Many Vietnamese refugees fled their homeland after the fall of Saigon at the end of the Vietnam War in 1975. Although the rapid influx of Vietnamese immigrants into various North American communities caused some racial and ethnic tension with the majority culture, Vietnamese Americans have built a strong support system for themselves, thus easing their adjustment into American life.

Since 1975, many people from Vietnam have found their way to North America. Unlike many other ethnic groups who immigrated to the Untied States, the Vietnamese were technically not immigrants but refugees. As a result of the Vietnam War, which ravaged their nation in the 1960's and early 1970's, many Vietnamese were displaced. In addition, those Vietnamese who fought with the Americans against the North Vietnamese communists found themselves in danger after the U.S. withdrawal in 1974. In the weeks before the South Vietnamese capital of Saigon fell on April 30, 1975, the United States helped evacuate about 100,000 Vietnamese. This group, the first wave of Vietnamese refugees, were mostly well-educated city dwellers.

After the takeover of South Vietnam by the North, many more refugees left Vietnam for the United States. This group, known popularly as "boat people," were mainly rural peasants or ethnic Chinese. Less well educated and less exposed to Western culture, the people in the second wave had more problems adjusting to life in the United States.

Demographics

By 1998, the population of Vietnamese Americans had reached one million. This population, however, was not a homogeneous group but contained several distinct ethnic communities. In addition to many ethnic Chinese, other minority groups fled communist persecution immediately after the war, including the Montagnards, the Cham, the Khmer, and the Hmong. A third group of refugees included the Amerasians, children of U.S. military personnel and their Vietnamese mates. Called *bui doi* (dust of life), the Amerasians were subjected to racial discrimination, harassment, imprisonment, and even death under the communists. Many became homeless and lived on the streets. More than 68,000 Amerasians settled in the United States under a special program. Various issues involving intergroup relations arose as these very different people found themselves in close contact with each other in the Vietnamese American community.

Intergroup Relationships

The first waves of Vietnamese immigrants met with some hostility from Americans. A 1975 Gallup Poll revealed that many Americans did not want Vietnamese refugees settling in the United States because Americans feared job losses. In response to this concern, the United States government developed the Refugee Dispersion Policy. Sponsors for Vietnamese refugees were sought from all over the country, and the immigrants were settled in various communities, often separated by great distances from their families. Although this policy made it easier to resettle the refugees, it did not take into account the high value the Vietnamese place on family connections. Consequently, after the initial resettlement, many Vietnamese moved closer to family members and other Vietnamese. Over time, such movement led to the growth of a number of Vietnamese American communities within larger urban areas such as Westminster, California, and Versailles, Louisiana.

One of the earliest examples of tension between the growing Vietnamese American communities and an established American community occurred along the Gulf Coast of Texas, Louisiana, and Mississippi during the early 1980's. There, Vietnamese American shrimpers competed with established American shrimpers for an ever-decreasing shrimp catch. Language barriers, different customs, and differences in fishing techniques stood in the way of harmony between the shrimpers. Through programs offered by the U.S. Coast Guard (among other agencies), the two groups learned more about each other and were able to sort through most of their differences.

Perhaps the most tragic moment of intergroup hostility occurred in January, 1989, when an American man opened fire with an assault weapon on a group of Cambodian American and Vietnamese American children at play in a schoolyard in Stockton, California, killing five children and shocking both the Vietnamese American and other American communities. As a result, the two groups pulled together to establish a scholarship foundation and to work toward mutual understanding.

The Vietnamese community also experiences conflict within itself. Differing socioeconomic classes, education levels, and religious affiliations all affect the way that Vietnamese Americans interact with each other. In addition, young, unaffiliated, male adolescent Vietnamese Americans have formed gangs that tend to prey on other Vietnamese Americans.

Although such examples of racial and ethnic disharmony exist, there are many positive examples illustrating the success of Vietnamese Americans in their new homeland. By establishing self-help groups such as mutual assistance associations and the Vietnamese American Association, the Vietnamese American community has provided strong support for its members. As Paul James Rutledge points out in *The Vietnamese Experience in America* (1992), Vietnamese Americans have maintained "cultural integrity" while adapting to the culture of the United States.

Diane Andrews Henningfeld

This Vietnamese American woman enjoys a meal featuring dishes from her native land. Vietnamese immigration to the United States increased sharply in the mid-1970's.

Core Resources

Perhaps the best study of Vietnamese American resettlement is Paul James Rutledge's *The Vietnamese Experience in America* (Bloomington: Indiana University Press, 1992). Thomas Bass has written an important account of the lives of Amerasians in the United States, *Vietnamerica: The War Comes Home* (New York: Soho Press, 1996). Nazli Kibria studies Vietnamese families and their adjustment to life in the United States in *Family Tightrope: The Changing Lives of Vietnamese Americans* (Princeton, N.J.: Princeton University Press, 1993). Nathan Caplan, Marcella H. Choy, and John K. Whitmore have written a widely cited study about the second generation of Vietnamese Americans, *Children of the Boat People: A Study of Educational Success* (Ann Arbor: University of Michigan Press, 1991). An early article detailing problems among Vietnamese fishermen and their American counterparts is Harvey Arden's "Troubled Odyssey of Vietnamese Fishermen," *National Geographic* (September, 1981). *The Dream Shattered: Vietnamese Gangs in America* (Boston: Northeastern

University Press, 1996), by Patrick Du Phuoc Long with Laura Ricard, offers an account of young Vietnamese Americans involved in crime.

See also: Amerasian Homecoming Act of 1987; Cambodian Americans; Hmong Americans; Orderly Departure Program; Refugees and racial/ethnic relations; Refugees: U.S. policy; Vietnamese Canadians.

Vietnamese Canadians

Significance: Vietnamese immigrants to Canada have managed to preserve their own ethnic character through various waves of immigration and without becoming an economic, social, or cultural burden to their host country.

The fall of the South Vietnamese capital of Saigon into North Vietnamese Communist hands on April 30, 1975, forced more than 150,000 Vietnamese nationals out of their home country. At first, the number of departures from South Vietnam was low (less than 10,000 per year) because the Vietnamese people were attempting to adapt to a new regime that proclaimed a gradual transition to socialism. However, once heavy taxes were imposed on peasants and private businesses were abolished (with factories and firms nationalized), there was widespread economic and social discontent. An estimated 160,000 left Vietnam in 1975, heading for Australasia, North America, and Western Europe; 65,000 arrived in Canada, thereby boosting the Vietnamese population in that country to more than 80,000. Before 1975, only a few thousand Vietnamese were in Canada, with the largest numbers in Montreal (800-1,000) and Toronto (500). Most refugees settled in Quebec, partly because many of them felt closer to the French than to the English because of the French colonization of Vietnam in the 1940's. In Montreal alone, approximately 4,000 Vietnamese formed a nucleus within a small area of the city.

Vietnamese restaurants, like this one in Montreal, are a common sight in Canada's cities. The number of Vietnamese in Canada increased dramatically after the fall of Saigon in 1975.

Between 1976 and 1980, after war with Cambodia and China, Vietnam's social life became extremely militarized, prompting a further mass exodus. About 580,000 people left their homeland and about 150,000 others, desperate to escape oppression, became "boat people," taking to the sea in small vessels, often drowning or being murdered by pirates. Survivors were herded into transit camps in Malaysia, Thailand, Hong Kong, or the Philippines, where they waited for an opportunity to go to a welcoming host country. Canadian refugee policy made it possible to offer humanitarian relief, despite some racist opposition, and this was subsequently expanded into a family reunification and sponsorship program, leading to identifiable Vietnamese communities across the country.

Social, Cultural, and Religious Life

Most of the Vietnamese refugees who came to Canada worked hard, often at two or three jobs. The often less well educated boat people usually found work as laborers, but many of the men and the younger women became university students and professionals. Many of the older married women did not work outside the home, instead taking care of all the household chores and duties. The second generation of Vietnamese Canadians, born in the new homeland and the beneficiaries of their parents' hard work, are less disciplined, and their elders fear that North American values and habits will have a negative influence on them.

Vietnamese value the family highly and have a strong code of behavior that decrees respect for elders, including older siblings. Marriage does not exempt an individual from filial duties; traditionally, a young couple must live with the husband's parents and grandparents before setting up their own household. This patrilineal extended-family system fosters mutual help. Such a system is grounded in a Confucian tradition where relations between a ruler and his people are analogous to those linking the husband with his wife and children. It is common practice for exiled or expatriate Vietnamese to send money to relatives and keep in continuous contact with them through the mail.

This inward-looking lifestyle (directed toward the family and other Vietnamese in the community) contributes to the preservation of ethnic identity. Even as far as cultural consumption is concerned, Vietnamese tend to read Vietnamese magazines and newspapers published in Canada, the United States, and other countries to which they dispersed. Many read magazines that are organs of official organizations, such as the Canadian Vietnamese Foundation and the General Union of Vietnamese in Canada. Books, magazines, newspapers, and taped music and shows are generally produced by their own people.

The three main religions are Confucianism, Taoism, and Mahayana Buddhism, although there are some cases of religious syncretism, as when a Catholic married to a Buddhist addresses prayers to both Buddhist deities and Christian saints. Moreover, many families practice ancestor worship, although they consider this less a religion and more a way to consolidate the family. The dead (exiled from the earth) share their exile with their progeny, maintaining a close union with the living.

Ethnic Assertion

Vietnamese Canadians realize that Canada is their permanent home. However, they do not wish to assimilate completely. Instead, they assert their own identity through their language (which, with rare exceptions, is the exclusive medium of communication among them), and an insistence on maintaining the family network and its particular code of behavior. Their resistance to acculturation is manifest in their heritage language classes, publications, radio programs, and public performances at Tet, the lunar new year, all of which foster community cohesion. Vietnamese are willing to become part of the Canadian social milieu provided they are not melted down into an indistinguishable mass.   *Keith Garebian*

Core Resources

In 1983, the Council on Southeast Asia Studies launched *The Vietnam Forum,* a semi-annual review of Vietnamese culture as part of the Yale Southeast Asian Refugee Project. Perhaps because of the United States' involvement in the Vietnamese Civil War, there is much more information on Vietnamese Americans than on Vietnamese Canadians, but a major Canadian study is *Exile in a Cold Land: A Vietnamese Community in Canada,* by Louis-Jacques Dorais, Lise Pilon Le, and Nguyen Huy, no. 6 in the Lac-Viet Series (New Haven, Conn.: Yale Center for International and Area Studies, 1987). Originally written in French and focusing only on Vietnamese in Quebec City, this study was undertaken with the cooperation of the Vietnamese community and is a useful exploration, within a conceptual and theoretical framework, of the historical and cultural background of Vietnam and of the foundation of an ethnic community. It contains a sociological profile, and it follows the diaspora from the homeland to transit camps and resettlement in Quebec City. Its insights into Vietnamese history and culture have a wide application beyond the specifics of Quebec.

See also: Orderly Departure Program; Refugees and racial/ethnic relations; Refugees: U.S. policy; Vietnamese Americans.

Visible minority allophones in Canada

> **Significance:** A nation composed largely of immigrants, Canada originally consisted of three founding peoples, the aboriginals, the English, and the French. However, immigration has made Canada a multicultural society with a growing population of visible minorities: blacks, Chinese, Filipinos, Japanese, Koreans, Latin Americans, other Pacific Islanders, South Asians, Southeast Asians, West Asians, and Arabs.

Canada, founded by the aboriginals, the English, and the French, has recognized the languages of two of these groups via a bilingual policy that makes French and English the nation's official languages. However, in reality Canada is not a bicultural or even tricultural nation but a multicultural, multiethnic, and multilingual community composed of people from every part of the globe who have immigrated to Canada over the years in search of political freedom, human rights, a better economic life, and a chance to live in a democratic society.

Although the United Nations has rated Canada as the most desirable country in the world in which to live, serious problems of adjustment and assimilation remain in a nation that at times seems to consist of people who have more differences than commonalities. The constant tension between English and French Canada is fueled by the incessant threat of French separation. Governmental attempts to placate French-speaking Quebecers, even to the extent of constitutional renewal to declare Quebec a distinct society, have generated feelings of resentment among other Canadians, who feel that too much energy and too many financial resources are diverted to appeasing Quebec rather than addressing the needs of multicultural Canadian society. The challenge to the Canadian government is to adjust the requirements of competing groups with diverse agendas. Canada suffers from an acute need for its citizens to develop a sense of personal and national identity in a rapidly changing demographic situation.

Important Statistics

In Canada, there are three linguistic groups: anglophones, whose main language is English; francophones, whose dominant language is French; and allophones, whose mother tongue is something other than French or English. In 1996, nearly five million Canadians spoke a language other than English or French, an increase of more than 15 percent since 1991. Allophones represented nearly 17 percent of the Canadian population in 1996, up from 13 percent in 1971. The number of allophones has increased dramatically because of immigration to Canada, particularly from areas of the world where neither English nor French is a first language. Canada's third (unofficial) language is Chinese, spoken by nearly 3 percent of the population. In contrast, in 1996, 60 percent of Canadians were anglophones, and 24 percent were francophones.

Between 1991 and 1996, Canada accepted more than one million immigrants, 80 percent of them allophones, mainly from Asia, the Caribbean, and the Middle East. Immigrants have been settling mostly in Canada's largest cities, specifically Toronto, Montreal, and Vancouver, which boast thriving ethnic communities, some having Chinatowns and Little Indias complete with specialty restaurants, gift shops, ethnic food stores, and active community associations. There is a vibrant ethnic press in Canada, and allophones can enjoy television programs in their native language across the nation.

Visible Minorities

The allophone presence in Canada is most noticeable with respect to that segment of the group that is officially categorized as being the "visible minority." On the basis of census data, the government of Canada has officially defined and named the following visible minority groups: blacks, Chinese, Filipinos, Japanese, Koreans, Latin Americans, other Pacific Islanders, South Asians, Southeast Asians, West Asians, and Arabs. Visible minority members consist of those born in Canada (29 percent of the visible minority population in 1996), long-term residents, and recent arrivals. In 1996, about two-thirds of the visible minority population were immigrants and more than three million people (more than 11 percent of the Canadian population) defined themselves as visible minority members. In 1996, Statistics Canada estimated that by 2016, one in five Canadians would be a member of a visible minority and this group would include slightly more than six million adults.

It is the visible minorities who experience most of the problems in assimilation and who encounter discrimination in housing, employment opportunities, treatment at educational institutions, and various realms of Canadian society. They tend to congregate in urban areas because the ethnic communities in cities provide the support they need to sustain their social, psychological, and emotional needs. In 1996, about 94 percent of visible minorities lived in a metropolitan area, with Toronto being home to 42 percent of the visible minority Canadian population. Members of visible minorities can, however, be found in all parts of Canada. Where they are a very small minority, they can suffer from social isolation and relative marginalization. The largest sector of the visible minority population is Chinese, in 1996 representing nearly 1 million people, both long-term residents and a large group of immigrants who arrived during the 1980's and 1990's before Hong Kong (a British colony) was annexed by China in 1997. The Chinese population of Canada is projected to reach 2 million by 2016, at which point it might constitute 5 percent of the total population. In 1996, 671,000 South Asians made up more than 2 percent of Canada's population, and 574,000 people were categorized and defined as blacks by the government. The number of African Canadians is projected to reach 1.3 million by 2016, making them the second-largest visible minority group in Canada. The Chinese, blacks, and South Asians constitute two-thirds of the visible minority population. The other third, slightly more than 1 million people, are Filipinos, Southeast Asians, other Pacific Islanders, Latin Americans, Japanese, Koreans, Arabs, and West Asians.

Visible minorities are seriously underrepresented in Canada's public service positions, both federally and provincially, and in government appointments. The selection of an African Canadian to the Senate in 1998 was significant enough to occasion some public attention. Only a handful of visible minority members sit in Parliament and in provincial legislatures, although the interest of some ethnic groups in changing the social environment via political involvement grew during the 1990's. The Canadian political establishment largely ignores the concerns of visible minorities.

Normally, Canada's national media, newspapers, and television pro-

Shoppers cross a street in East Chinatown, Toronto. Chinese Canadians are one of the largest allophone groups.

vide little or no coverage of visible minority concerns or issues, except when a sensational murder or crime occurs or when there is dissension within an ethnic community. This has occasioned an oft-quoted phrase that has circulated through these communities: "We are Canada's invisible visible minorities."

Visible Minorities and Education

Statistics Canada has found that members of visible minorities tend to be better educated than the general Canadian population and to have a high rate of university education. However, even university graduates in this group were found in 1991 to be more concentrated in clerical and manual labor employment with less likely to occupy professional and management positions than the general population.

Attainment of a university degree among visible minority men varied from a low of 9 percent among Pacific Islanders to a high of 36 percent among Koreans. Among visible minority women obtaining a university degree, the 1991 statistics demonstrated a low of 9 percent among Pacific Islanders and Latin Americans to a high of 25 percent for Filipinos.

Visible Minorities in the Workforce

In part because of the challenges posed to normal upward mobility by the social discrimination prevalent in Canada, visible minority Canadians have stressed the virtues of acquiring a good education, hard work, thrift, family life, and community activity, and a number of them have succeeded notably in professions such as law, medicine, and university teaching. They have also fared well in business endeavors and have contributed extensively to the economies of provinces such as British Columbia. However, the 1991 census established that the unemployment rate for visible minorities was higher (13 percent) than that for other adults (10 percent).

The racial limitations placed on their personal fulfilment of the Canadian dream have frustrated many of the most dynamic of the visible minority members to the extent that in the 1980's and 1990's, many of these talented individuals have been leaving Canada and returning to their country of origin, taking with them their financial capital, their business know-how, and their vibrant energy to the economic detriment of Canada. Although the evidence is anecdotal rather than statistical, it appears that many immigrants have returned on a temporary or permanent basis to Hong Kong (even after it became part of China in 1997), India, Pakistan, Taiwan, and South Korea. More significant is the trend for visible minorities to migrate both temporarily and permanently from Canada to the United States, largely because of a widely held perception among them that the United States offers more opportunity, fewer racial

barriers, and more of a chance to progress simply on the basis of personal ability and hard work. Most detrimental to the Canadian economy is the outflow of highly educated medical and informational technology professionals from these ethnic minorities. The out-migration of physicians has already left some small, remote communities in Canada without medical personnel.

Immigration

Although immigration policy has varied over the years, certain trends indicate the growth of the visible minority population in Canada and the decline in immigration from Europe. In 1981, 67 percent of immigrants living in Canada were from Europe. The figure dropped to 62 percent in 1986 and to 54 percent in 1991. In contrast, the immigrant population from Asia and the Middle East stood at 14 percent in 1981, rose to 18 percent in 1986, and climbed to 25 percent in 1991.

Globalization has encouraged an accelerated pitch of movement among populations since the end of World War II. Immigrants have been drawn to Canada for economic reasons and the desire to live in an environment that provides democratic freedoms and human rights. Significantly, two places of birth that were among the top ten with respect to immigrants arriving between 1981 and 1991 were Hong Kong and mainland China. A high proportion of immigrants become Canadian citizens, a qualification provided after three years of residence. In 1991, 81 percent of eligible immigrants in Canada had obtained citizenship.

Perceptions of the Role of Visible Minorities

Visible minority Canadians elicit a variety of reactions from the rest of the population. The emotions range from tolerant acceptance to outright fear and hatred. Where visible minorities form a significant element of the population as in Toronto, their numerical presence creates a vibrant interracial dynamic, most evident in cultural pursuits and an internationalization of everyday life via the presence of ethnic stores, markets, and restaurants and, most important, daily interaction between people of all races and colors. Although color blindness in terms of race is nowhere near established in Canada, in certain large cities an awareness of diversity does exist.

However, in small-town Canada and in the more remote provinces, where the visible minority members are few and confined to particular areas of employment such as the medical and teaching professions, the value of diversity tends not to be appreciated or recognized. These regions are apt to be self-absorbed politically, fragile economically, and more reluctant to be adventurous in forging social connections with racially different people. Members of visible minority groups, whether in these parts of Canada temporarily or permanently, complain about their systemic exclusion from work opportunities, especially in new fields of endeavor, and the social isolation they feel. They often voice the pain of realizing that no matter how integrated they feel themselves to be, they, for the most part, continue to be outsiders looking at Canadian mainstream society. Some young visible minority Canadians, particularly teenagers, who by language and accent are fully integrated into the mainstream, are still singled out as different and not socially accepted by their peers because of their race. In response, most visible minority members flee to the large urban areas such as Toronto and Vancouver, which are far more accommodating of diversity.

Some Canadian politicians and bureaucrats, particularly those in small communities, deny and fiercely resist any suggestion that discrimination exists. Their refusal to confront and deal with the problem contrasts sharply with the racial awareness and interracial dialogue and discussion that permeate every level of life in the United States (including the media) and to an extent in the United Kingdom. The Canadian avoidance of the racial aspects of a number of issues has acted to intensify the antagonism, exacerbate the mutual hostility, and widen the chasm between groups.

Although part of the fastest-growing group in Canada, visible minority members may on occasion still be faced with a very stark and sharply defined choice: Live a restricted life within the allowable racial parameters or leave the country. Those white people and visible minority members who opt to resist racism and open up minds to the value of diversity—and there are many such trailblazers across the country—will face controversy, conflict, and ostracism until more Canadians become aware of the lingering discrimination.   *Ranee K. L. Panjabi*

Core Resources
Information on the visible minorities of Canada can be found in Statistics Canada's periodicals, *Statistics Canada Daily* and *Canadian Social Trends* (1993-1998), Sanjeev S. Anand's "Expressions of Racial Hatred and Racism in Canada: An Historical Perspective," in *The Canadian Bar Review* (77, March-June, 1998), and Yasmeen Abu-Laban and Daiva Stasiulis's "Ethnic Pluralism Under Siege: Popular and Partisan Opposition to Multiculturalism," in *Canadian Public Policy* (18, no. 4, December, 1992).

See also: Aboriginal Canadians; African Canadians; Anglophone; Arab Canadians; Asian Indians in Canada; Assimilation theories; Bilingualism in Canada; Chinese Canadians; Employment in Canada; Francophone; French Canadians; Immigration law: Canada; Japanese Canadians; Multiculturalism in Canada; Racial and ethnic demographics in Canada; Racial/ethnic relations in Canada; Vietnamese Canadians.

Voting Rights Act of 1965

This legislation essentially abolished a number of practices that had been used at various times to disqualify African American voters, primarily in the South, including literacy, education, and character tests. It authorized the U.S. attorney general to send federal examiners into areas where voter discrimination was suspected; in effect, it allowed federal voting registrars to supersede state ones. Affected jurisdictions could be free from federal scrutiny once they showed that they had not employed discriminatory practices for five years from the time of initial federal intervention. Yet perhaps the most sweeping part of the act was its "preclearance requirements," which applied to areas with low voter registration or participation: They required that any reapportionment plans or proposed changes in electoral requirements be approved by the Justice Department before they could take effect. The act also included a finding that poll taxes were preventing blacks from voting in state elections, spurring the Supreme Court to hold that poll taxes were illegal in 1966 (poll taxes in federal elections had been abolished in 1964).

The act was amended in 1970, 1975, and 1982. The 1970 amendment prohibited literacy tests throughout the country until 1975. The 1975 amendment maintained the provisions of the 1970 amendment, suspending literacy tests indefinitely, after failing to enlist enough supporters to apply the Voting Rights Act to language minorities as well as racial minorities. The 1982 amendment, effective for twenty-five years, directed the federal courts to examine the effect, in addition to the intent, of practices that discriminated against black voting opportunities. This amendment was passed as a result of a 1980 Supreme Court decision (*City of Mobile v. Bolden*) stating that civil rights litigants had to prove that municipalities intended to discriminate against blacks by adopting particular voting procedures.

Passage of the act resulted in a dramatic increase in African American voter registration. By the end of the 1960's, more than 60 percent of blacks in the Deep South were registered. This increase in black voter registration also meant that significant numbers of African Americans were elected to office, although primarily at the local, county, and state levels. The act has proved to be a landmark piece of legislation in ensuring that all American citizens can exercise their constitutionally guaranteed right to vote, a fundamental precept of American citizenship and justice.   *Craig M. Eckert*

See also: Civil Rights Act of 1964; Grandfather clauses; Literacy tests; Poll tax; Representation: gerrymandering, malapportionment, and reapportionment.

Voting rights of aboriginals: Canada

> **Significance:** The special rights granted to Native Canadians by treaties and by the various Indian Acts of Parliament were long given as reasons to deny the ballot and other citizenship rights to Canada's native population.

The history of native voting rights in Canada is linked to government attempts to use the Indian Acts and other forms of coercion to assimilate Native Canadians into white society. These attempts were unsuccessful; most Canadian natives remained disenfranchised until 1960. Prior to confederation in 1867, there had been some isolated instances in which Indians in Ontario, Quebec, and British Columbia voted, but because of restrictive voter qualifications, Indians were, by and large, barred from the polls. After confederation, Indians were prevented from voting both by statute and by requirements of residence or property ownership.

The Indian Acts, the British North America Act, and various treaties established clear distinctions between natives and non-natives, providing both benefits to and restrictions on natives. The treaties obligated the government to pay annuities to all Indians. One of the most valued benefits of the Indian Acts was exemption from taxation for any Indian living on a reserve. This exemption prevented the complete loss of Indian lands through forfeiture, but it also prevented Indians from obtaining full citizenship rights in Canada.

The Indian Acts provided a mechanism for Indians to become Canadian citizens: enfranchisement. Indians who were deemed to be of good moral character, who could read and write French or English, and who were free of debt could apply for enfranchisement. Choosing to become enfranchised, however, meant giving up all the benefits of Indian status, including the right to live on reserve land, annuity payments, and exemption from taxation. It was in the interest of the government to enfranchise as many Indians as possible, and enfranchisement was a stated goal of the Indian Acts. Few Indians, however, opted for enfranchisement. Between 1867 and 1920, only 102 individuals did so. A 1920 amendment to the Indian Act made it possible for the superintendent general for Indian affairs to enfranchise people involuntarily, and activists were sometimes threatened with the stripping of their Indian status. One noted example of this is the case of Frederick Ogilvie Loft, who founded the League of Indians of Canada in 1918. Loft lobbied for Indian civil rights, including Indian control of band funds and the right to vote. In an

effort to silence him, the Department of Indian Affairs informed Loft that it was considering his enfranchisement. The League of Indians ultimately floundered, but not before the involuntary enfranchisement provisions of the Indian Act were repealed when the Liberals assumed control of Parliament in 1921.

The Elected Councils

At the same time that natives were barred from voting in provincial and federal elections, they were forced to elect band councils and chiefs. Claiming to provide Indians with modern institutions of local government, Parliament passed the Enfranchisement Act of 1869. The act forbade traditional methods of leadership selection and imposed municipal-type councils on Indian bands. As in non-native elections of this time, this limited franchise was extended only to men. For the members of the Six Nations, whose leaders were traditionally chosen by women, this was a supreme violation of their sovereign rights. Many bands resisted Ottawa's interference in local politics and continued to choose leaders by traditional methods or to elect the traditional leaders. The statute was relaxed in 1880 to make elected band councils voluntary, but passage of the Indian Advancement Act in 1884 made them mandatory once again. The 1884 act also permitted the superintendent general or his agent to depose any chief or council member deemed unfit to serve. Thus, although Indians were required to elect leaders, they were often denied the leaders that they had chosen.

The Franchise Act of 1885

For the first eighteen years after confederation there were no federal election laws in Canada. Voter eligibility was determined by provincial statutes, which barred Indians from the polls on either racial or class grounds. The Conservative government of Prime Minister John A. Macdonald introduced the Franchise Act in 1885, which established the first federal criteria for the franchise. Careful to preserve the rights of the wealthy, Macdonald's legislation established strict property ownership guidelines for voters. Looking for likely Conservative voters, Macdonald extended the franchise to Indian men living on reserves in Eastern Canada if they possessed and occupied a distinct tract of land valued in excess of $150. It appears that many eligible Indians feared that this was merely a scheme to deprive them of their exemption from taxation and thus dispossess them of their land. Macdonald responded that they need have no such fear. Voting privileges for Indians were short-lived, however; the Liberals, led by Wilfrid Laurier, gained power in 1896 and repealed the Franchise Act. No separate federal franchise was reestablished until 1920. Indians living on reserves were barred from voting.

Since 1917

Large numbers of Indians enlisted in the Canadian armed forces during World War I. In recognition of their service, Indian veterans were granted the vote in 1917 along with all other members of the armed forces and non-Indian women who had male relatives in the armed forces. The franchise was extended to all white women the following year.

In 1920, while specifically excluding Indians living on reserves, the federal government granted the franchise to Metis. There were no major changes in native Canadian access to the polls until after World War II. The wives of Indian veterans were granted the vote in 1948. In 1950, Indians who waived their immunity from taxation were permitted to vote. That same year, the Inuit were granted the franchise on the grounds that they were not deemed wards of the state, nor were they exempt from taxation. It was not until 1960 that all native Canadians, regardless of status or residence, were permitted to vote in federal elections.

The ten provinces and two territories of Canada varied considerably with regard to native voting rights. British Columbia granted the franchise to native residents in 1949. Newfoundland permitted Indians and Inuit to vote when it entered the confederation that same year. Manitoba granted the vote to Indians in 1952, followed by Ontario in 1954. The franchise was extended to the Indians of Saskatchewan and the Northwest Territories in 1960 and to those in Prince Edward Island and in New Brunswick three years later. Quebec withheld voting privileges from Indians until 1969. Although there were never any specific proscriptions against Indian enfranchisement in Nova Scotia or the Yukon Territory, requirements of residency or property effectively kept Indians from the polls until the middle of the century.

Pamela R. Stern

Core Resources

Aboriginal voting rights are discussed in John Garner's *The Franchise and Politics in British North America, 1755-1867* (Ottawa: University of Toronto Press, 1969); Vic Satzewich and Terry Wotherspoon's *First Nations: Race, Class, and Gender Relations* (Scarborough, Ont.: Nelson Canada, 1993); E. Brian Titley's *A Narrow Vision: Duncan Campbell Scott and the Administration of Indian Affairs in Canada* (Vancouver: University of British Columbia Press, 1986); and Norman Ward's *The Canadian House of Commons, Representation* (Toronto: University of Toronto Press, 1950).

See also: Department of Indian Affairs and Northern Development; Indian Act of 1876; Indian Act of 1951; Indian Act of 1989; Indian-white relations: Canada; Reserve system of Canada; Treaties and agreements with Indians: Canada; Voting rights of American Indians: United States.

Voting rights of American Indians: United States

> **Significance:** The related issues of Indian citizenship and suffrage mirror the larger views of the U.S. government and the American public regarding the status of Indians in society.

In the early years of the United States, American Indians were viewed as sovereign or semi-sovereign peoples. The primary means of dealing with them was through treaties. This Indian "sovereignty" was a legal fiction whose result was that courts avoided treating Indian land claims like vested property rights. Such rights would have afforded the tribes, and possibly individual Indians, stronger legal claims. The first United States treaty with an Indian tribe was concluded in 1778, ten years before the Constitution came into operation. More than six hundred others were to follow.

Questions of Indian citizenship or voting rights did not arise in this early legal context, especially since the Constitution gives the power to decide who is eligible to vote to state governments. The states decide who can vote, subject of course to any federal constitutional requirements. It was not until the passage of the Fourteenth and Fifteenth Amendments just after the Civil War that Indian suffrage could have been considered at all.

Amendments and Legislation

The Fourteenth Amendment, ratified in 1868, defines "[a]ll persons born or naturalized in the United States and subject to the jurisdiction thereof" as citizens of the United States and of the state in which they reside. The Fifteenth Amendment, ratified in 1870, forbids the states to deny any one the right to vote on account of race or color. At first glance, these amendments appear to settle the question of Indian citizenship and voting, but the continuing fiction of Indian sovereignty was used to undermine the citizenship rights of Indians who had not clearly left their tribes or reservations. It was argued that they were not "subject to the jurisdiction" of the United States and thus did not fall within the terms of the Fourteenth Amendment. The result was that Indians who remained in "Indian country" and who did not dissociate themselves from their tribes continued to be ineligible to vote. This disfranchisement continued throughout the years of the "allotment and assimilation" movement. Under the allotment plan, Indians could receive grants of land for their personal use, presumably for farming. Once the land had been worked for twenty-five years, title would vest in the individual owner and he or she then became a full citizen of the state and eligible to vote, at least in the formal sense. The plan failed, largely because the majority of Indians did not care to become farmers. Most Indians remained ineligible to vote.

By the beginning of the twentieth century, Congress began to look for other solutions to the continued poverty and disorganization of the Indian tribes. In 1919, Congress passed an act which conferred citizenship on those Indians who had served in the armed forces during World War I. In 1924, the Indian Citizenship Act granted full citizenship to all Indians who had been born in the United States, regardless of tribal affiliation or reservation treaty status.

Obstacles to Voting

Thus, in theory, all Indians were eligible to vote from 1924 on. In practice, however, many of the same barriers to voting that were used against potential black voters were raised for prospective Indian voters. Grandfather clauses, poll taxes, and discriminatory literacy tests were all used. Prospective Indian voters also had to meet state government standards about severance of tribal relations; Indians who adhered to their tribes were not viewed as "civilized" persons and were therefore ineligible to vote. Opponents of Indian suffrage also argued that because the state had no power over Indian conduct on the reservation, the Indians were not "true" residents of the state. In some states, Indians had to meet the claim that as wards of the federal government they were in a state of guardianship and hence legally incompetent to vote. Indeed, Arizona's Supreme Court maintained this position beginning in 1928 and did not reverse itself until 1948. Since then, however, all legal barriers to Indian suffrage have either been repealed or struck down by the courts.

In areas of heavy Indian population, political estab-lishments still occasionally attempt to devise new ways of perpetuating white political control. Contemporary strategies can be subtler than the old. Redistricting so as to "dilute" the Indian vote is one such strategy. Today the major problems that formerly frustrated the Indian desire to vote have been solved. Both the federal government and the states have come to respect the principle of nondiscrimination in voting.

Voting Rights Act, 1965

The Voting Rights Act of 1965 has been particularly effective in the expansion of voting rights for minorities. In this law, Congress provided for federal voting registrars who can be sent into states and regions where fewer than 50 percent of the eligible voting population is registered and where a voting device like a literacy test has been used. In 1975, the act was expanded to require states to provide bilingual ballots and voting information in twenty-four states where Spanish, Asian, Indian, and Alaskan dialects and languages are spoken by large numbers of voters. Thus, the language barrier that discouraged many non-English-speaking minority group members has been largely eradicated.   *Robert Jacobs*

Core Resources

Felix S. Cohen's *Handbook of Federal Indian Law* (Washington, D.C.: Government Printing Office, 1942) is the first and most important treatise on federal treaties and statutes dealing with Indians, written by a brilliant government lawyer. Vine Deloria, Jr., and Clifford M. Lytle's *American Indians, American Justice* (Austin: University of Texas Press, 1983) is an excellent introduction to Indian law in historical perspective. Monroe E. Price and Robert N. Clinton's *Law and the American Indian: Readings, Notes, and Cases* (2d ed., Charlottesville, Va.: Michie, 1983), discusses the far-reaching changes in Indian law, including the area of voting rights, of the 1960's and 1970's.

See also: Allotment system; American Indian civil rights; American Indian Civil Rights Act; Indian Citizenship Act; Reservation system of the United States; Voting rights of aboriginals: Canada.

W

War Brides Act

> **Significance:** The War Brides Act relaxed immigration regulations to allow foreign-born spouses and children of U.S. military personnel to settle in the United States.

Between 1939 and 1946, more than sixteen million U.S. servicemen, primarily single and between eighteen and thirty years of age, were deployed to war theaters in foreign lands. Although the U.S. government discouraged servicemen from marrying at all—believing the single soldier, without distractions, would be of more value to the war effort—one million marriages to foreign nationals occurred during and shortly after the war. Aware of the potential for these liaisons, the U.S. War Department had issued a regulation requiring personnel on duty in any foreign country or possession of the United States to notify their commanding officer of any intention to marry at least two months in advance. Enacted in June, 1942, the regulation demanded strict adherence, and the waiting period was waived rarely, with a possible exception for the pregnancy of the bride-to-be. Usually, permission to marry was granted; however, certain couples, for example U.S.-German, U.S.-Japanese, and those of different races, either encountered longer waiting periods or were denied permission completely.

Passage of the Act

Many of those couples who had been granted permission and had married were separated for two to three years. In October, 1945, the Married Women's Association picketed for transport to allow their families to reunite. Evidently, the three thousand members' voices were heard; on December 28, 1945, the Seventy-ninth Congress passed an act to expedite the admission to the United States of alien spouses and alien minor children of U.S. citizens who had served in or were honorably discharged from the armed forces during World War II. These spouses had to meet the criteria for admission under the current immigration laws, including a thorough medical examination, and the application had to be filed within three years of the date of the act.

The War Bride Ships

Following passage of the War Brides Act, thirty vessels, primarily hospital ships and army troopships, were selected to transport the women, children, and a few men ("male war brides") to the United States. Even the *Queen Elizabeth* and the *Queen Mary* were recruited for the task, because of their capacity to carry large groups of people. Transportation requests were prioritized by the military as follows: dependents of personnel above the fourth enlisted grade, dependents of personnel already placed on orders to the United States, wives of prisoners of war, wives of men wounded in action, and wives of men hospitalized in the United States. At the bottom of the priority pool were fiancées and spouses in interracial marriages.

Before debarking, the spouse (usually a woman) had to present her passport and visa, her sworn affidavit from her husband that he could and would support her upon arrival, two copies of her birth certificate, two copies of any police record she might have, any military discharge papers she might have, and a railroad ticket to her destination from New York. The families who saw them off knew they might never see their children and grandchildren again.

The American Red Cross was officially requested by the War Department to function as a clearinghouse for the brides, and many Red Cross volunteers served as "trainers" for the women in how to become American wives. Since many did not speak English, the Red Cross also offered classes to aid in practical communication skills.

On January 26, 1946, the first war bride ship, the SS *Argentina*, left Southampton, England, with 452 brides, 173 children, and 1 groom on board. Lauded as the "Pilgrim Mothers" voyage or the "Diaper Run," the voyage was highly publicized. Many of the brides, upon arriving in the United States on February 4, were greeted by the U.S. press.

In Germany and Japan, permission to marry had not easily been attained and often was not granted at all. The ban on marriage to Germans was lifted on December 11, 1946, with twenty-five hundred applications submitted by the end of the year; in Japan, the ban lingered much longer.

During the first months of occupation during the war, approximately one-half million U.S. soldiers had been stationed in or near Yokohama. Many young women, fearing for their lives, hid from these "barbarians," but since the U.S. military was often the only source of employment, the women were forced to venture out. The country was in a cultural flux, resulting from economic deprivation, matriarchal predominance and female enfranchisement, and the abjuration of divinity by Emperor Hirohito. As the U.S. soldiers and Japanese women worked together, romantic relationships often developed, and because official permission to marry could not be obtained, many such couples were wed in secret in traditional Japanese ceremonies.

Although as many as one hundred thousand Japanese brides were deserted, others sought immigration to the United States. However, one proviso of the War Brides Act was that émigrés could not be excluded under any other provision of immigration law. The Oriental Exclusion Act of 1924 was still in place, and although Public Law 199 had overridden the act to allow Chinese immigration, the Japanese were still excluded. Many were not allowed admission to the United States until July, 1947, when President Harry Truman signed the Soldier Brides Act, a thirty-day reprieve on race inadmissibility.

Life in America

In many cases, life for the war brides in the United States was not what they had expected. Many were treated poorly by isolationists who placed personal blame on all foreigners for U.S. involvement in the war, and many had to tolerate the scorn of former sweethearts who had had been jilted because of them. Because of the influx of soldiers returning to the civilian population, available housing and jobs were limited. Often the brides found themselves in the middle of a family-run farm, with some as sharecroppers. Frequently, when adjustment to civilian life was difficult for the former military man, he would rejoin his outfit, leaving the bride behind with his family—strangers who were sometimes hostile to the foreigner in their midst. Many of the marriages made in haste soured just as quickly through homesickness, promises unkept, or abuse. War brides who were unhappy or abused often stayed in their marriages, however, from fear of losing their children or of being deported.

Marriage did not confer automatic citizenship on foreign brides. They were required to pass exams to be naturalized, and many were still incapable of communicating in any but their native tongue. Public assistance was unavailable for these women.

Within one year of the mass exodus from Europe and Asia, one out of three of the war marriages had ended in divorce, and it was predicted that by 1950, the statistics would be two out of three. This prediction proved incorrect, however. Many of the war brides not only preserved their marriages but also became valuable members of their communities and contributors to American culture. In April, 1985, several hundred of these women, men, and children journeyed to Long Beach, California, for a reunion, appropriately held aboard the dry-docked *Queen Mary*.   *Joyce Duncan*

Core Resources

Joyce Hibbert's *The War Brides* (Toronto: PMA Books, 1978) discusses the mobilization and acclimation of war brides. Elfrieda Berthiaume Shukert and Barbara Smith Scibetta's *War Brides of World War II* (Novato, Calif.: Presidio Press, 1988), the definitive work on the topic, includes interviews with war brides.

See also: Cable Act; Chinese Exclusion Act; Immigrant women; Immigration Act of 1924; Immigration and emigration; Interracial and interethnic marriage; Women and racism.

Wards Cove Packing Company v. Atonio

Five salmon canneries, owned by Wards Cove Packing Company and Castle & Cooke, recruited seasonal labor for the peak of the fishing season at remote areas in Alaska. Unskilled cannery workers were recruited from Alaska natives in the region and through the Seattle local of the International Longshoreman's and Warehouseman's Union; two-thirds of these employees were either Alaska natives or Filipino Americans, including Frank Atonio and twenty-one other plaintiffs. Higher-paid on-site noncannery support staff, including accountants, boat captains, chefs, electricians, engineers, managers, and physicians, were recruited from company offices in Oregon and Washington, largely by word of mouth; some 85 percent of these employees were white. For all employees, the companies provided race-segregated eating and sleeping facilities.

Plaintiff cannery workers, who believed that they were qualified to hold support staff positions but were never selected for these higher-paying jobs, filed suit in 1974 against the companies under Title VII of the Civil Rights Act of 1964. Their argument was based on statistics that showed ethnic differences in the two classes of workers, cannery versus noncannery. In addition to evidence of segregated company housing, they asserted disparate treatment and adverse impact arguments regarding criteria and procedures used to screen them out. Among these criteria, they claimed that there were preferences for relatives of existing employees (nepotism), rehire preferences, English language requirements, failure to promote from within, and a general lack of objective screening and selection criteria. The procedures to which they objected were separate hiring channels and word-of-mouth recruitment rather than open postings of job opportunities.

Justice Byron White delivered the opinion of a divided Court (the vote was 5-4). According to the majority, the comparison between ethnic groups in the two types of jobs was irrelevant because they were drawn from different labor market pools. The Court then went beyond the case to assert that a statistical difference between ethnic groups does not give *prima facie* evidence of discrimination under Title VII unless intent to discriminate is proved. To provide that proof, plaintiffs must show that specific criteria, even vague and subjective criteria, statistically account for the difference. Moreover, an employer may defend criteria that have been proved to account for the difference if they are "reasoned."

The decision had a deleterious impact on efforts to redress employment discrimination, as it reversed the broad language of *Griggs v. Duke Power Company* (1971) by requiring proof of intent, by allowing the use of separate hiring channels, and by no longer insisting that employers must prove that biased hiring criteria are absolutely essential for job performance. Congress responded by passing the Civil Rights Act of 1991, which codified the original *Griggs* ruling into law. *Michael Haas*

See also: Civil Rights Act of 1964; Civil Rights Act of 1991; Discrimination: racial and ethnic; *Griggs v. Duke Power Company*; *Washington v. Davis*.

Washington v. Davis

African American members of the Washington, D.C., Metropolitan Police Department, as well as unsuccessful applicants to the department, sued the department, claiming that its hiring and promotion policies were racially discriminatory. In particular, they cited a written test that a disproportionately high number of blacks failed. The district court found for the police department, but the appellate court, relying on the Supreme Court precedent of *Griggs v. Duke Power Company* (1971), reversed that decision, finding the disparate impact of the test to be evidence of employment discrimination. When *Washington v. Davis* came before the Supreme Court, however, Justice Byron White's opinion for the Court stated unequivocally that evidence of discriminatory purpose must be present for such tests to be found unconstitutional. The lower appellate court was reversed.

Griggs had been a landmark employment discrimination case which made disparate impact the test for employment discrimination under Title VII of the 1964 Civil Rights Act. In *Washington*, however, the plaintiffs were claiming that the police department's employment practices violated their right to equal protection under the due process clause of the Fifth Amendment. The standards for determining discrimination proscribed under Title VII were not, said the Court, the same as those applied to a claim of unconstitutional racial discrimination, which requires some evidence of intent to discriminate. Here, the Court found, the personnel test at issue was neutral on its face; in addition, it was rationally related to a legitimate purpose: improving employees' communications skills.

The Court indicated that intent to discriminate could be inferred from a totality of circumstances, including disparate impact, but it declined to spell out a more precise test for unconstitutional employment discrimination. In fact, the majority opinion confused the issue. As Justice John Paul Stevens indicates in his concurring opinion, disparate impact and discriminatory purpose are often indistinguishable. When disparate impact becomes proof of discriminatory purpose, the two standards are conflated. Furthermore, by augmenting the consequences of past discrimination, employment policies not intended to be discriminatory can produce results identical to those resulting from conspicuously discriminatory ones.

The test for what constitutes evidence of discriminatory intent was left indeterminate until the Supreme Court strengthened it in *Personnel Administrator of Massachusetts v. Feeney* (1979) to the advantage of employers. In *Feeney*, the Court held that even if discriminatory results of a prospective statute are foreseeable at the time it is passed by the legislature, it is only unconstitutional if these results constitute the reason for passage. The consequences for subsequent civil rights litigants pressing discrimination suits against state employers were profound. *Lisa Paddock*

See also: Civil Rights Act of 1964; Disparate impact theory; *Griggs v. Duke Power Company*; *Wards Cove Packing Company v. Atonio*.

WASP

WASP is an acronym for white, Anglo-Saxon Protestant, which refers to members of the predominant British ethnic group whose legal, cultural, and religious traditions have been most influential in structuring what has become "mainstream" American life. Since the colonial era when Puritan New England enacted the first series of "blue laws" to regulate behavior on Sunday and promote the Puritan religious ethos, members of this group have maintained control of most positions of political, economic, social, and religious power and prominence, enabling them to exercise an influence on national life far in excess of their eventual numbers. Most presidents of the United States have been white, Anglo-Saxon Protestants, and members of this group are the chief executives of most large corporations and financial institutions and many of the most powerful members of Congress. This group's preferred cultural media—from classical music to opera to symphonic music—define American high culture just as pervasively as the group's religious edifices—from the National Cathedral to the countless Main Street churches with Christopher Wren steeples—define the center of American religious life. Although most Americans are not members of this group, WASPs' influence is so pervasive in U.S. society that the sociologist C. Wright Mills coined the phrase "power elite" to describe their transcendent power.   *Sheldon Hanft*

See also: Anglo-conformity; Anglo-Protestant stereotypes; Anglo-Protestants; Anglo-Saxon; Power elite.

Water rights

As European American settlers moved farther and farther west across the continent, Native Americans lost most of their rights to the water they had once used

A Hupa Indian fisherman in northwestern California holds his catch. American Indians began to assert their water rights in the 1970's.

freely. It was not until the twentieth century—and primarily the last two decades of the century—that courts began to recognize Indian rights to the water lying underneath or flowing through their lands. Water is among the most precious of resources in many parts of the United States, notably the Southwest. In 1907, a case known as the Winters decision first recognized the reserved water rights of reservations.

In the 1970's, the protection of water rights began to gain recognition as one of the most important issues faced by American Indian tribes. Debate began to rage, and cases were taken to court, regarding crucial questions of whether a state or a tribe owned various water supplies. In addition to the issue of ownership are questions concerning the uses to which water can be put and regulation of access to water. In 1973, the National Water Commission (created by Congress) criticized the government's failure to protect Indian water rights adequately. A number of cases in 1983 affected water rights. For example, the Supreme Court, in *Nevada v. United States*, upheld the allocation of water rights to the Pyramid Lake Reservation in Nevada. On the other hand, the Court denied five tribes a requested larger allocation of Colorado River water (*Arizona v. California*), and it ruled in *Arizona v. San Carlos Apache Tribe* that state courts have the authority to decide cases involving Indian water rights (tribes were attempting to establish that only federal courts should have jurisdiction over these matters). In 1989, Secretary of the Interior Manuel Lujan announced that the Working Group on Indian Water Settlements, which would report to the Water Policy Council, would establish principles for guiding settlements and would assist in negotiations with tribes.
          Dorothy Zeisler-Vralsted

See also: Fish-ins; Indian-white relations: United States.

Watts riot

Significance: The outbreak of racial violence on August 11, 1965, shattered the summer calm of Los Angeles, California, and eroded the elation felt by many people when President Lyndon B. Johnson had signed the 1965 Voting Rights Act into law only five days earlier. Official investigations confirmed that the causes of the upheaval were deeply rooted in the conditions of ghetto life in the sprawling metropolis. In less immediate terms, however, the upsurge of anarchistic energy stemmed from the existence of intolerable tensions in relations between whites and blacks within U.S. society.

The Watts area of Los Angeles in 1965 provided a perfect setting for racial conflict. The neighborhood had long been the center of African American life in the city. As a result, Watts offered its inhabitants full exposure to the hazards of ghetto existence. More than 30 percent of the workforce was unemployed. Approximately 14 percent of the population was functionally illiterate. The black residents of Watts faced serious barriers in their pursuit of better housing, more remunerative jobs, and improved education. Separated from white society, Watts was a storehouse of combustible material on the southeast side of Los Angeles.

Beginnings

A minor clash between police and African American residents caused the explosion that ripped through Watts. Along the edge of the ghetto, on the night of August 11, a California Highway Patrol officer arrested two young African Americans for reckless driving. While the officer administered a sobriety test, a hostile crowd gathered. The confrontation led to more arrests. Finally, the police departed amid a hail of rocks thrown by irate blacks. Rumors of police brutality spread through Watts. In the hours before midnight, a full-scale riot developed. Automobiles traveling through the ghetto were pelted with rocks and bottles. Police moved back into the area at 11:00 P.M., but flurries of violence continued throughout the night.

After a day filled with tension, the rioters returned to the streets on the night of August 12. Commercial buildings were set ablaze, and firemen who responded to the alarms were greeted with rocks and gunfire. California state officials received reports that estimated the number of rioters at eight thousand. The police were unable to prevent widespread burning and looting.

The upheaval reached its climax on the night of August 13. Crowds of angry African Americans surged through Watts. Arsonists began the systematic destruction of whole city blocks in the ghetto. Police and firemen faced added peril from snipers who took up positions in the ruins. At its height, the riot encompassed an area of more than fifty blocks.

Reaction

In the early hours of August 14, law enforcement officers began to regain control of the streets. At the request of city officials, National Guard troops joined the Los Angeles Police Department in battling the rioters. Ultimately, nearly fourteen thousand members of the National Guard entered the fray. Burning and looting continued sporadically, but the presence of fully armed soldiers in large numbers gradually restored quiet to the riot-torn area. A dusk-to-dawn curfew went into effect on Saturday night, August 14. Three days later the curfew was lifted, and most of the National Guard troops left the city. Amid the rubble, the people of Watts returned to their everyday concerns. The six days of rioting had wreaked widespread destruction on the African American neighborhood. Thirty-four deaths were reported, and police made more than three thousand arrests. Property damage reached the forty-million-dollar mark, as 288 businesses and private buildings and 14 public buildings were damaged and/or looted, and 1 public and 207 private buildings were destroyed.

Yet the most significant harm caused by the riot was beyond specific assessment. In the realm of race relations, the outbreak of violence exacerbated tensions between blacks and whites throughout the United States. Watts became the first chapter in a history of race riots that included upheavals in Detroit, Michigan, and Newark, New Jersey, in 1967, and Washington, D.C., in 1968. Faced with repeated outbreaks of violence, the Civil Rights movement, with its emphasis on civil disobedience and

National Guardsmen patrol the Watts area of Los Angeles during the riots in August, 1965.

interracial cooperation, suffered a significant setback in the short run. Beginning with the explosion at Watts, U.S. race relations entered a new, more ominous phase.

The riot did not, however, mean the end of nonviolent direct action or the total reversal of the multiracial cooperation that had brought important legal victories for desegregation in the United States. The history of civil rights reform after 1965 was marked by a growing realization that the socioeconomic conditions in which African Americans, Mexican Americans, and other minorities lived could not be ignored in the quest for social justice and personal fulfillment for all U.S. citizens. The last major effort by civil rights leader Dr. Martin Luther King, Jr.—who visited Watts at the time of the rioting and asked the insurgents to change their motto from "Burn, baby, burn" to "Build, baby, build"—was a Poor People's Campaign that was implemented two months after his assassination on April 4, 1968.

John G. Clark, updated by Thomas R. Peake

Core Resources
The Governor's Commission on the Los Angeles Riots' *Violence in the City: An End or a Beginning?* (Los Angeles: Author, 1965) focuses on the details and location of damage, with useful maps. Thomas R. Peake's *Keeping the Dream Alive: A History of the Southern Christian Leadership Conference from King to the Nineteen-Eighties* (New York: Peter Lang, 1987) includes extensive material on the urban riots and post-1965 efforts to deal with social problems in big-city ghettos. David O. Sears and John B. McConahay's *The Politics of Violence: The New Urban Blacks and the Watts Riot* (Boston: Houghton Mifflin, 1973) reviews the history of the crisis, the views and actions of urban blacks, and official reactions. The Watts Writers' Workshop's *From the Ashes: Voices of Watts*, edited and with an introduction by Budd Schulberg (New York: New American Library, 1967), contains writings by residents of Watts during the time of the 1965 riots and their aftermath, showing their frustrations as well as their hopes for better answers to social, personal, and economic problems.

See also: Detroit riot; Los Angeles riots of 1992; Miami riots of 1980; Newark race riots; Race riots of the twentieth century.

Weber v. Kaiser Aluminum and Chemical Corporation

Brian Weber, a white worker, challenged a voluntary affirmative action plan created by the United Steelworkers of America Union and the Kaiser Corporation. A quota of 50 percent of new skilled craft trainees were to be African American until the percentage of African Americans in a Louisiana plant equaled the percentage of blacks in the local labor force. Lower federal courts judged that this affirmative action plan violated Title VII of the Civil Rights Act of 1964, which prohibits racial discrimination in employment of people such as Weber.

On June 27, 1979, the U.S. Supreme Court reversed the lower court decisions and ruled that Congress did not intend to prohibit all voluntary, race-conscious affirmative action plans designed to break down patterns of racial segregation. This decision opened employment opportunities historically closed to African Americans.

Steve J. Mazurana

See also: Affirmative action; Civil Rights Act of 1965; Employment among African Americans.

"Welfare queen" stereotype

The politically charged "welfare queen" stereotype stems from a story told by President Ronald Reagan in the 1980's to symbolize abuse of the welfare system (which includes several federal programs, such as Aid to Families with Dependent Children, that provided food and services to poor Americans) and garner support for his plan to cut income taxes by dismantling entitlement programs. In this story, he depicted a fictional woman who drove to the welfare office in her Cadillac to pick up aid checks under several aliases, then spent the money on luxuries. This depiction was linked to another common image of welfare abuse, in which uneducated, urban, typically African American women bore children to increase their check amounts rather than work. Like other stereotypes, these images were based on the perceived negative behavior of a few individuals and generalized to a large, diverse group. Most studies found that aid recipients with these attributes constituted a small minority (for example, most families on welfare were not African Americans). However, these powerful stereotypes helped sway public opinion against welfare programs and reinforced some people's anti-African American attitudes. In the years following Reagan's presidency, "welfare queen" entered the lexicon as a label for any public or private enterprise that used an excess of federal aid.

Carlota Ocampo

See also: African American stereotypes; Aid to Families with Dependent Children; Entitlement programs; Welfare reform: impact on racial/ethnic relations; Welfare stereotypes; Welfare's impact on racial/ethnic relations.

Welfare reform: impact on racial/ethnic relations

> **Significance:** Certain racial groups—notably African Americans—receive a disproportionate level of welfare benefits. Attempts to modify the welfare system therefore trigger the issue of race.

Any attempt to alter the distribution of government assistance inevitably encounters intense lobbying by groups who stand to gain and lose benefits. Welfare reform is a case in point. Both recipients of welfare benefits and the taxpayers who fund welfare programs have strong economic interests in how the program is run. In addition, the matter of welfare reform is connected to deeper racial issues. Because a disproportionate number of certain racial groups receive welfare benefits, efforts to reduce welfare spending are sometimes viewed as racially motivated.

Calls for Welfare Reform

The U.S. welfare system was created in the 1930's during the Great Depression. It was greatly expanded in the 1960's under President Lyndon B. Johnson's Great Society program. Although elements of the system have been altered almost continuously, calls for thorough reform reached a crescendo in the 1980's. These calls were spurred by two factors: First, mounting government debt and increasing hostility to taxes created a political environment that encouraged a reduction in social spending. Second, a consensus began to form that after two decades, the War on Poverty initiated by Johnson had largely failed. In fact, by some measures, poverty had increased even with expanded welfare spending.

The issue of welfare reform had for years been largely associated with the Republican Party. President Ronald Reagan, a Republican, promoted some efforts to reduce welfare spending and tighten eligibility criteria, but the Democrat-controlled Congress was hostile to any serious reduction in welfare benefits. Liberals called the Republican proposals mean-spirited and selfish. More to the point, many minority leaders charged that welfare reform proposals were racist. Although by far whites constituted the largest racial group receiving welfare benefits, a much larger proportion, or percentage, of African Americans (up to 30 percent) received welfare benefits, compared with about 10 percent of Americans overall.

Welfare reform thus became a racially charged topic, with minority groups and African American leaders charging that "welfare" had become a code word for "black," and thus welfare reform was an insidious form of attack against African Americans. In such an environment, only the most incremental welfare reform proposals could make it through the legislative process. Meanwhile, pressure continued to mount from white and other nonblack groups who were becoming frustrated with the inability of the government to address the ineffectiveness of the welfare system. This frustration was dubbed "donor fatigue," whereby many taxpayers despaired that the Great Society programs of the 1960's could ever significantly reduce the problems they were designed to eradicate.

The Republican "Revolution"

It was in this environment that the Republican Party won a majority in both houses of Congress in 1994. After decades as the minority party, the Republicans sought to tap in to the rising conservative mood of the electorate and reverse long-standing programs they derided as too liberal. Welfare was one of these. President Bill Clinton, a Democrat, quickly agreed to work with the Republicans to "end welfare as we know it"—itself an indicator of how potent the public mood was gauged to be. Clinton was criticized by members of his own party for allegedly capitulating to the conservative mood, but the prevailing political environment made defense of the status quo a fatal stance in most districts.

In the next few years, a monumental welfare reform bill was created in Congress. The bill, formally titled the Personal Responsibility and Work Opportunity Reconciliation Act, passed in Congress and was signed by President Clinton in 1996. The act had a number of provisions that were racially controversial. One of these denied welfare benefits to immigrants who entered the country after August 22, 1996 (although these immigrants could later receive benefits upon securing U.S. citizenship). Noncitizens living in the country before this deadline would also be ineligible for benefits, unless they had worked in the United States for at least ten years. Latino and Hispanic leaders were especially opposed to this provision, since by far the largest number of noncitizen immigrants were from Mexico and Central American countries. Although he signed the bill, Clinton promised to fight to "fix" the welfare reform law at a later time. The immigrant provision was removed as part of the following year's budget bill.

The much more important provision of the 1996 welfare reform law terminated the government's Aid to Families with Dependent Children (AFDC) program and converted its funding into grants for state programs. The states would have considerable flexibility in implementing their programs, but several nationwide standards would be imposed. Among these were the limitation of two consecutive years for receiving assistance, a lifetime maximum of five years, and the requirement that persons receiving this aid be actively looking for work, going to school, or performing public work.

Evaluation

Although it would be years before the success of the individual state programs could be evaluated, many immediately weighed in with their assessments of the landmark reform. As regards racial and ethnic relations, groups promoting the interests of African Americans and Latinos tended to be critical of the reforms, although the United States population in general tended to support the reforms. Disagreements focused on two major issues: First, since the reforms required welfare recipients to make a quick transition to the workforce, did the nation's economic system provide opportunities for all, regardless of race and ethnicity, to earn a living wage? Second, was some form of welfare system necessary to help more people of color join the economic mainstream of society?

In general, the welfare reform of 1996 is premised on the belief that welfare should be a form of temporary assistance rather than a long-term way of life. Opponents argue that although that sentiment may be laudable, the existing economic system makes the goal of self-sufficiency unrealistic for some people. Some argue that the legacy of past racial discrimination, and perhaps even continuing discrimination, make economic self-sufficiency impossible for certain groups, at least within the parameters of the reforms.

Proponents of welfare reform counter that poverty is due to economic rather than racial factors. They further argue that the welfare system of the 1960's and 1970's created disincentives in the areas of work, education, and personal responsibility. The 1996 welfare reform attempts to create a new incentive structure that encourages work and facilitates training and education.

At the end of the twentieth century, it was unlikely that racial issues connected with welfare reform would disappear until there were no significant differences in wealth and work between different racial and ethnic groups, and it remained unclear whether the 1996 welfare reform bill or the programs being implemented at the state level would achieve that goal.   *Steve D. Boilard*

Core Resources

A detailed analysis of racial factors in white people's attitudes about welfare is available in Martin Gilens's "'Race Coding' and White Opposition to Welfare," in *American Political Science Review* (September, 1996). More extensive, though more dated, analysis is available in Fay Lomax Cook and Edith J. Barrett's *Support for the American Welfare State: The Views of Congress and the Public* (1992). The Public Broadcasting Service (PBS) has produced a ninety-minute documentary entitled *Ending Welfare as We Know It*, which examines how six women on welfare strive to cope with the new welfare system. The documentary was first aired in June, 1998. The Urban Institute also has examined the effects of the 1996 welfare reform program and has published its findings in "One Year After Federal Welfare Reform: A Description of State Temporary Assistance for Needy Families (TANF) Decisions as of October, 1997" (May, 1998). The report is available through the institute's Internet site (http://new federalism.urban.org/html/1year.html). A more positive evaluation is offered by Daniel Casse in "Why Welfare Reform Is Working," in *Commentary* (104, no. 3, September, 1997).

See also: Conservatives and racial/ethnic relations; Economics and race; Employment among African Americans; Employment among Latinos; Racial/ethnic relations: race-class debate; "Welfare queen" stereotype; Welfare stereotypes; Welfare's impact on racial/ethnic relations.

A woman sits on the steps of her home with her children and the family dog. Because a disproportionate number of African Americans and other minorities receive welfare, attempts to reform the system affect race relations.

Welfare stereotypes

Stereotypes refer to generalizations that are not based in fact, and welfare stereotypes usually refer to mistaken beliefs about the most common types of people receiving welfare. For example, many people have perpetuated a myth that the typical poor person is black or brown and that "welfare queens," young, single black women having more babies to increase the size of their welfare checks, are largely responsible for increases in welfare costs. Furthermore, the welfare recipient often is stereotyped as someone who will not accept a minimum-wage job or as an illegal immigrant whose welfare costs contribute to excessive taxation.

In reality, more than one-third of the poor are children under sixteen, and about half of all income received by the poor is from wages. More than 1.5 million family heads work full-time but have wages below the poverty line. Moreover, even though a disproportionate share of black women are on welfare, more non-Hispanic white men and women than nonwhite people are below the poverty level, and less than half of all single mothers receive welfare. The average welfare family has 2.2 children, and two-thirds receive welfare for less than three years. Furthermore, illegal immigrants are not entitled to welfare.

People and Families in Poverty by Selected Characteristics, 1995

	Numbers in Thousands	Percent of Group
People		
Total	36,425	13.8
White	24,423	11.2
Not of Hispanic origin	16,267	8.5
Black	9,872	29.0
Asian and Pacific Islander	1,411	14.0
Hispanic origin	8,574	30.0
Families		
Total	7,532	10.8
White	4,994	8.5
White, not Hispanic	3,384	6.4
Black	2,127	26.4
Asian and Pacific Islander	264	12.4
Hispanic origin	1,695	27.0
Type of Family		
Married couple	2,982	5.6
White	2,443	5.1
Black	314	8.5
Hispanic origin	803	18.9
Female householder	4,057	32.4
White	2,200	26.6
Black	1,701	45.1
Hispanic origin	792	49.4

Source: Data are from U.S. Bureau of the Census, *Current Population Survey.* Washington, D.C.: U.S. Government Printing Office, 1995.

Welfare stereotypes have been used to reinforce racist beliefs and assumptions that the poor are to blame for their own condition and, therefore, are not deserving of any type of publicly funded assistance. Some who deny that the economy and discrimination create unequal opportunities have used welfare stereotypes to find scapegoats for societal problems. Yet studies such as those reported by M. J. Bane in *Fighting Poverty: What Works and What Doesn't* (edited by S. H. Danziger and D. H. Weinberg, 1986) and E. A. Segal in "Welfare Reform and the Myth of the Marketplace" (in *Journal of Poverty*, 1, 1997) show that major factors explaining poverty include insufficient jobs, low wages, inadequate education, and lack of affordable daycare and other support services. Moreover, because of a history of discrimination, disproportionate shares of nonwhites are disadvantaged by low levels of educational attainment,

poor health, and discrimination in hiring, promotion, and housing. This helps explain why about one-third of African Americans, Hispanics, and Native Americans are below the poverty line.

Welfare stereotypes also refer to other types of mistaken generalizations. One frequently held opinion is that government funding for the poor makes up a large portion of the national budget. Therefore, when the nation experiences economic problems, some people criticize welfare expenditures. Yet in 1996, less than 15 percent of the federal budget went to all low-income social assistance programs, including education and training. According to the Population Reference Bureau in its 1996 report, 43 percent of the federal budget went to "other types of social assistance, such as Social Security and Medicare, which mainly go to middle-class Americans, not the poor." Some argue that tax breaks for the wealthy constitute a much more expensive form of government spending that people overlook in common welfare stereotypes.   *Grace Maria Marvin*

See also: "Welfare queen" stereotype; Welfare reform: impact on racial/ethnic relations; Welfare's impact on racial/ethnic relations.

Welfare's impact on racial/ethnic relations

> **Significance:** The availability and adequacy of welfare programs affect the economic well-being of many racial and ethnic minorities, a larger proportion of whom live in poverty than do whites. Therefore, efforts to reform welfare often have an impact on racial/ethnic relations in America.

National-level welfare programs, such as Temporary Assistance for Needy Families (TANF), the food stamp program, and Supplemental Security Income (SSI), provide a minimum level of income to the most economically disadvantaged members in society. Many states and local governments also provide welfare programs such as General Assistance, which provide a variety of services and functions.

Federal Welfare Programs

Temporary Assistance for Needy Families (TANF) originated in the Social Security Act of 1935 as Aid to Dependent Children and became Aid to Families with Dependent Children (AFDC) in the 1960's. The food stamp program began in 1970, and 1974 saw the start of Supplemental Security Income (SSI), which incorporated the adult categories of public assistance programs (Aid to the Aged, Aid to the Blind, and Aid to the Disabled) that originated in the Social Security Act of 1935. Initially, the two cash assistance programs, TANF/AFDC and SSI, were intended to provide minimal support to those poor considered to be outside the wage labor pool, while the food stamp program, which makes use of vouchers, was designed primarily to increase the food-purchasing power of eligible low-income households. Welfare programs are income- or means-tested for eligibility. Monthly TANF/AFDC payments have historically been lower than those of SSI, reflecting the prevailing norms that the value of public assistance should not

Total Income as Percentage of Poverty Level, 1992

	Less than 50%	Less than 100%	Less than 150%	Less than 200%	200% or greater
Non-Hispanic White					
Transfer income	28.0	17.9	9.0	4.8	0.2
Food stamps	31.6	13.5	5.8	2.8	0.0
Earnings	32.9	46.0	56.6	65.4	82.4
Other income	7.5	22.6	28.6	27.0	17.4
Average income (dollars)	$4,957	$8,731	$12,133	$15,935	$55,769
Non-Hispanic Black					
Transfer income	40.2	31.8	20.6	14.1	0.7
Food stamps	39.8	22.6	13.0	8.6	0.1
Earnings	11.2	29.5	47.6	58.5	89.1
Other income	8.8	16.1	18.7	18.8	10.1
Average income (dollars)	$7,254	$10,475	$12,859	$15,707	$46,183
Hispanic					
Transfer income	39.2	23.3	12.6	8.8	1.0
Food stamps	32.8	14.8	7.8	5.2	0.1
Earnings	21.4	48.4	66.2	73.1	88.9
Other income	6.6	13.5	13.5	12.8	10.4
Average income (dollars)	$7,236	$10,970	$14,511	$17,157	$46,749

Source: Adapted from U.S. Department of Health and Human Services, *Indicators of Welfare Dependence Annual Report to Congress.* Washington, D.C.: Government Printing Office, 1997.

exceed the wages of low-income workers and that poor mothers should be encouraged to rely on the fathers of their children or their own work effort for income.

Impact and Use of Means-Tested Assistance Programs
The table "Total Income as Percentage of Poverty Level, 1992" shows the differential impact of TANF/AFDC, SSI, and food stamps on economic well-being. Reflecting average income among recipients, the two cash transfer programs, TANF/AFDC and SSI, accounted for the highest percentages of total income for non-Hispanic blacks, followed closely by Hispanics. The greatest proportional differences occurred among those with the lowest incomes. Food stamps also accounted for the highest percentages of total income for non-Hispanic blacks among all income groups. The proportional contribution of food stamps to total income among Hispanics, however, was much closer to that of non-Hispanic whites than to non-Hispanic blacks. Hence, non-Hispanic blacks and Hispanics are more dependent than non-Hispanic whites on cash transfer programs for their economic well-being, and non-Hispanic blacks are also more dependent on the food stamp program than either non-Hispanic whites or Hispanics.

As the table "People Moving On and Off Means-Tested Assistance from 1992 to 1993" shows, the use of and exits from TANF/AFDC, SSI, and the food stamp program also vary by race and ethnicity. Non-Hispanic blacks and Hispanics were about five times more likely to move onto the lower benefit TANF/AFDC rolls and only twice as likely to move onto the higher benefit SSI rolls than non-Hispanic whites. Hispanics were nearly four times as likely to move into the food stamp program than non-Hispanic whites. In addition, non-Hispanic whites were more likely to exit each of these means-tested programs than either non-Hispanic blacks or Hispanics. In general, the longer recipients received benefits, the more likely they were to move into one of these means-tested programs and the less likely they were to exit from them. Given the greater likelihood of living in poor or low-income households and the greater impact of means-tested assistance programs on the economic well-being of non-Hispanic blacks and other racial/ethnic groups (such as Puerto Ricans and Mexicans among Latinos/Hispanics and Cambodians, Laotians, and Vietnamese among Asians) than on non-Hispanic whites, changes in the availability and adequacy of benefits brought about by the welfare reform legislation passed in 1996 most adversely affected members of these groups.

Welfare Reform and Its Impact on Racial/Ethnic Relations
In part responding to social and demographic changes, the Congress of the United States passed and President Bill Clinton signed the Personal Responsibility and Work Opportunity Reconciliation Act of 1996. Between the 1970's and 1990's, an increasing proportion of welfare benefits had gone to young, single mothers. Trends in out-of-wedlock births were such that in 1993, white illegitimacy rates approached 24 percent, while those for black mothers was 69 percent. By the early 1990's, immigrant welfare participation was, on average, nearly 2 percentage points higher than that of native-born Americans, while some Latino/Hispanic and Asian immigrant groups, notably Cubans, Laotians, and Cambodians, had more than twice the welfare participation rates of American-born blacks. Many whites had come

People Moving On and Off Means-Tested Assistance from 1992 to 1993
(percent)

	Percentage of Recipients Moving Off Assistance			Percent of the Total Population Moving Onto Assistance		
	TANF/AFDC to Non-TANF/AFDC	FS to Non-FS	SSI to Non-SSI	Non-TANF/AFDC to TANF/AFDC	Non-FS to FS	Non-SSI to SSI
All People	17.7	16.0	8.9	1.0	2.1	0.3
Non-Hispanic white	21.8	21.3	11.0	0.6	1.5	0.3
Non-Hispanic black	13.0	10.2	6.4	3.0	4.9	0.6
Hispanic	19.8	13.9	4.7	2.7	5.3	0.6

Source: Adapted from U.S. Department of Health and Human Services, *Indicators of Welfare Dependence Annual Report to Congress.* Washington, D.C.: Government Printing Office, 1997.

to see welfare recipients as the undeserving poor, and public assistance not as deserved support for the needy but as handouts for malingerers. As reported in the *Congressional Quarterly Weekly Reports*, many black and ethnic congressional leaders, among others, objected to this welfare reform effort, with little success.

With the creation of TANF, the 1996 act ended the entitlement nature of AFDC, capping the annual amount of federal money available to the states and setting a five-year maximum on the number of years recipients could receive cash assistance from the federal government. States were permitted to decrease the time limit. To be eligible for continued federal funds, states were required to take measures ensuring that increasing percentages of TANF/AFDC beneficiaries were involved in work-related activities. Because of their disproportionately high participation in TANF/AFDC, poor non-Hispanic black, Latino/Hispanic, and Asian women and their children were thought to be most adversely affected by the legislation, which probably forced mothers to seek low-wage, dead-end jobs or otherwise make ends meet without federal cash assistance. The 1996 act also barred legal immigrants, many of whom were from Mexico, from receiving food stamps, SSI, and other federally funded medical and social services for the first five years they were in the country. Most controversial was the enforcement of these provisions retroactively, that is, by applying them to legal immigrants who were already in the United States at the time of passage in August, 1996. An estimated 1.5 million legal immigrants, mostly Latino/Hispanic women and children, faced the possibility of losing welfare and health benefits.   *Richard K. Caputo*

Core Resources
Increased racial tensions associated with the politics of welfare reform are addressed in Richard K. Caputo's *Welfare and Freedom American Style II: The Role of the Federal Government, 1941-1980* (Lanham, Md.: University Press of America, 1994), Charles Noble's *Welfare as We Knew It: A Political History of the American Welfare State* (New York: Oxford University Press, 1997), and Jill Quadagno's *The Color of Welfare: How Racism Undermined the War on Poverty* (New York: Oxford University Press, 1994). Ethnicity and entitlements are discussed in Peter Brimelow's *Alien Nation* (New York: Random House, 1995) and Robert Suro's *Strangers Among Us* (New York: Alfred A. Knopf, 1998). The Urban League's Web site, which follows social policy legislation bearing on race relations, can be found on the Internet at www.urban.org.

See also: Aid to Families with Dependent Children; Entitlement programs; Poverty and race; Welfare reform: impact on racial/ethnic relations.

West Indian Americans

> **Significance:** The success of black West Indian Americans has drawn the attention of sociologists and other scholars and created some conflict with other African Americans.

Black West Indian immigrants and their descendants, a small group among the African American population, have achieved considerable economic, educational, and political success in the United States relative to native African Americans. Notable conservatives such as economist Thomas Sowell of Stanford's Hoover Institution and author Dinesh D'Souza contend that this group's relative success in part demonstrates the error in attributing the economic and social plight of some African Americans exclusively to racism. The group's exceptionalism has also been noted by sociologists such as Stephen Steinberg in *The Ethnic Myth: Race, Ethnicity, and Class in America* (1981) and Reynolds Farley and Walter Allen in *The Color Line and the Quality of Life in America* (1989).

The portrayal of exceptionalism is only part of this group's profile. Structural shifts in the U.S. economy mean that segments of this community will face severe sociopsychological adjustments to migration, coupled with constricted assimilation to American society. Pressures against full assimilation are greater for lower-class West Indians. Typically, middle- and upper-class professionals alternate between a more inclusive West Indian American or particularistic African American identity, and the lower/working class chooses a more ethnically focused, West Indian identity.

West Indian Americans are immigrants from the former British West Indian Islands, Belize and Guyana, and their U.S.-born descendants. Most of the West Indian immigrants arrived in the United States in the late nineteenth and early twentieth centuries. In 1924, restrictive immigration legislation effectively halted immigration from the islands. Most of the immigrants settled in the Northeast, creating urban ethnic communities in Miami, Boston, Newark (New Jersey), Hartford (Connecticut), and New York City; they settled in Brooklyn and formed ethnic enclaves in East Flatbush, Flatbush, Crown Heights, Canarsie, and Midwood districts.

West Indian Exceptionalism
Generally, West Indian immigrants have been perceived as models of achievement for their frugality, emphasis on education, and ownership of homes and small businesses. Economist Sowell argued that the group's successes, including those of famous members such as General Colin Powell, derived from a distinctive cultural

One of the better-known West Indian Americans was Jamaican Marcus Garvey, a black nationalist leader and founder of the Universal Negro Improvement Association.

capital source and an aggressive migrant ideology, legacies of their native lands. Home ownership and economic entrepreneurship were financed partly by using a cultural source of capital, an association called *susu* (known in West Africa as *esusu*), that first reached the West Indian societies during slavery. A *susu* facilitates savings, small-scale capital formation, and micro lending. These traditional associations have been incorporated into mainstream financial organizations such as credit unions and mortgage and commercial banks as they adapt to serve the needs of West Indian Americans.

Demographer Albert Murphy, in a report for Medgar Evers College's Caribbean Research Center in New York, found that in 1990, 29.1 percent of West Indian Americans had a bachelor's degree or higher degree, compared with the U.S. average of 20.3 percent. In addition, their median household income in 1989 was $28,000, compared with $19,750 for African Americans overall and $31,435 for whites.

Political and Social Incorporation

Early immigrants such as Pan-Africanists Edward Blyden and Marcus Garvey and poet activist Claude McKay were among the first West Indian Americans to become well-known and well-respected figures. Other famous West Indian Americans are former U.S. representative Shirley Chisholm; Franklin Thomas, former head of the Ford Foundation; federal judge Constance Baker Motley; Nobel laureate Derek Walcott; and world-renowned actor Sidney Poitier. Activist Stokely Carmichael, Deputy U.S. Attorney General Eric Holder, and Earl Graves, businessman and publisher of *Black Enterprise*, have made impressive efforts on behalf of African Americans.

From the 1930's to the 1960's, West Indian American politicians were elected with the help of the African American vote; many of the West Indians, believing their stay in the United States to be temporary, did not become citizens and were ineligible to vote. In the 1970's, this trend changed, and two congressional districts in New York with heavy concentrations of West Indians became represented by African Americans. However, West Indians Americans, becoming increasingly dissatisfied with African American representation, have been fielding their own candidates in state and local elections in New York, Connecticut, and New Jersey. These efforts have been aided by the fact that since 1993, when legislation less favorable to the immigrant population was passed, West Indian Americans have been acquiring U.S. citizenship in greater numbers. This trend in resurgent ethnic political awareness suggests that West Indian Americans may succeed in electing a member of their group to office.

Differential Assimilation

At the beginning of the twentieth century, West Indian Americans and African Americans held negative stereotypes of each other and rarely interacted socially. In the 1930's, 1940's, and 1950's, the children of some West Indian immigrants downplayed their ethnicity and attempted to integrate into the African American community, but both groups' images of each other changed slowly. Powell, in his autobiography, *My American Journey* (1995), recalls his African American father-in-law's reaction when he proposed marriage to his daughter Alma: "All my life I've tried to stay away from those damn West Indians and now my daughter's going to marry one!"

The late 1960's, with its emphasis on racial solidarity and group identity, eroded much of the conflict between African Americans and West Indian Americans and supplanted it with black nationalist sentiments and identity. In the 1990's, many West Indian Americans are caught in an identity crisis, unsure of whether they should be West Indians with a strong ethnic orientation, African Americans with a focus on their racial identity, or "West Indian Americans" with a more hybrid identity. Class pressures play influential roles in this identity dilemma. Lower- and working-class West Indian Americans have strong affiliations with their ethnicity and its cultural symbols, using the ethnic community as a "structural shield" in their coping repertoire. However, a growing segment of West Indian American professionals regard themselves as West Indian Americans because this identity unites the more desirable choices by eliminating obstacles to their ultimate assimilation as Americans. In addition, this community is not monolithic, and class divisions segment the group as well as influence its responses to racism and other societal challenges.

Aubrey W. Bonnett

Core Resources

Ira De Augustine Reid's *The Negro Immigrant, His Background, Characteristics, and Social Adjustment, 1899-1937* (New York: Columbia University Press, 1939) is a classic study of the early pioneers. Other excellent sources are Aubrey W. Bonnett's *Institutional Adaptation of West Indian Immigrants to America* (Washington, D.C.: University Press of America, 1982), Philip Kasinitz's *Caribbean New York: Black Immigrants and the Politics of Race* (Ithaca, N.Y.: Cornell University Press, 1992), Ransford W. Palmer's *Pilgrims from the Sun: West Indian Migration to America* (New York: Twayne Publishers, 1995), Irma Watkins-Owens's *Blood Relations: Caribbean Immigrants and the Harlem Community, 1900-1930* (Bloomington: Indiana University Press, 1996), and Calvin Holder's "The Rise of the West Indian Politicians in New York City," in *Afro-Americans in New York Life and History* (4, 1980).

See also: African American stereotypes; Afro-Caribbeans.

West Indian uprisings

> **Significance:** In the late fifteenth and early sixteenth centuries, Spanish policy of co-opting native West Indians ultimately resulted in rebellion.

The island of Hispaniola (today, the two independent states of Haiti and the Dominican Republic) was the key site of the first New World landing by Christopher Columbus in 1492. Historians have not only Columbus's own account of contacts with the native inhabitants of the Caribbean islands but also a number of descriptions by other explorers and missionaries who soon came to the first outposts in the Western Hemisphere. These accounts tended from the outset to distinguish two West Indian subgroups: Caribs and Arawaks. This conventional dualistic view gradually was reworked as ethnohistorians came to reserve the ethnolinguistic term "Arawak" for mainland populations, using the term "Taino" to refer to island groupings, including the native population of Hispaniola. The westernmost Tainos on Cuba and Jamaica appear to have been the most peaceful, both in their relations with other Taino groupings and in their reaction to the first Spaniards. Ciguayan and Borinquen Tainos of Hispaniola and Puerto Rico had a pre-Columbian tradition of warring, mainly against aggressive raids from groupings now known archaeologically as Island Caribs (from the Lesser Antilles, mainly Guadeloupe). They were, however, relatively receptive in the first ten years after 1492 to trying to adapt to Spanish colonial presence.

First Clashes

It was among the eastern Tainos on the Virgin Islands that the Spaniards encountered the first signs of open hostility to their presence. After clashes with otherwise unidentifiable natives on St. Croix, whom Columbus called Caribs, a number of negative observations began to enter Spanish accounts, including presumed acts of cannibalism and enslavement of women captives (later identified as a ceremonial bride-capture tradition).

These early violent encounters with eastern Tainos stemmed more from the natives' fear of strangers than from a considered reaction against Spanish plans for colonization. However, by the time Columbus became Hispaniola's first governor, a policy had been defined that called for direct methods of colonial control, including the *encomienda* system. The latter involved forced attachment of native laborers to Spanish colonial economic ventures, both in agriculture and in mining. By 1495, when the first West Indian revolt against the Spaniards broke out, the long-term movement of all of Hispaniola's Tainos toward extinction had entered its first stage.

Historians have noted that the native population of Hispaniola declined most dramatically by the first decade of the sixteenth century, mainly because of a lack of immunological resistance to diseases brought by the Spaniards. Scores of thousands died from infectious diseases, others from the overwork and undernourishment associated with the notorious *encomienda* system. A surprising number, however, fell victim to violent repression of resistance movements led by their tribal chiefs.

Between 1495 and 1500, there were at least two armed uprisings against Spanish control. Each of these (that of Caonabo, in 1495, and that of Guarionex, in 1498) was headed by a native tribal head, or *cacique*, who had been able to retain his leadership (in Caonabo's case, as head of a chiefdom west and south of the island's central mountains; in Guarionex's case, local leadership in Magua, near the gold fields north of the mountains) by at first agreeing to cooperate with the main lines of Spanish colonial policy, including the *encomienda*. Especially after the appointment of Governor Nicolás de Ovando in 1502, however, the situation became worse, and Spanish excesses were bound to cause an escalation of violence.

A final royal note to Ovando, dated in September, 1501, authorized Spaniards to take natives into labor service "in order to get gold and do . . . other labors that we order to have done," probably presuming that reasonable wages would be paid for work carried out. In fact, this was the beginning of forced labor that reduced many natives to the status of slaves.

The excessive actions of Ovando against any sign of the *caciques'* discontent with Spanish control set a pattern of violent conflict that took a high toll, especially among the native leadership. Much of the discontent after 1502 came from the sudden dramatic increase in the numbers of Spaniards on Hispaniola. Ovando had arrived with a contingent of about twenty-five hundred persons, including not only soldiers, missionaries (among them the later famous author of the *History of the Indies*, Father Bartolomé de Las Casas), and administrators, but also private settlers, more than tripling the Spanish population of the previous decade. This increased settler population was certain to demand more native forced labor under the *encomienda* system.

The village chiefdom of Higüey, on the eastern tip of Hispaniola, was the first site of what became major clashes between Spanish troops and what seemed to be rebelling elements of the local population. Governor Ovando's decision in 1502 to kill seven hundred Higüey Indians who had reacted violently to the killing of one of their chiefs by a Spanish dog was followed a year later by a wholesale massacre, in the western province of Xaragua (the former territory of Caonabo, the 1495 rebel leader), of some eighty district chiefs. In the 1503 massacre, Caonabo's widow, Anacaona, assembled the chiefs to meet Ovando's party. While the Spanish murdered the subchieftains brutally in a mass slaughter, Ovando's "respect" for Anacaona compelled him to end her life by hanging. The future conquistador of Cuba, Diego Velásquez, at that time Ovando's deputy commander, followed up the massacre by systematic conquest of the entire western half of Hispaniola.

Later Struggles
From 1503 forward, it became obvious that no previously offered Spanish promises to recognize the local ruling authority of *caciques* in any part of Hispaniola would hold. In 1504, some local chieftains, such as Agüeybana in the Higüey region, began trying to organize serious resistance forces before the Spanish dared to carry out added systematic removals or massacres of the remaining *caciques*. Despite the fact that Agüeybana's revolt was joined by diverse tribal elements, including groups the Spanish called Caribs, from the Lesser Antilles (more

likely Eastern Tainos, not the traditional island Carib enemies of Hispaniola's shores), it was brutally repressed. Agüeybana's execution impelled any remaining potential leaders to leave Hispaniola, or at least to take refuge in the more remote eastern Taino region.

Five years after the bloody events in the western region of Xaragua, and shortly after the failure of Agüeybana's abortive efforts in the east, Chief Guarocuya, Anacaona's nephew, tried in 1509 to go into hiding in the island's mountain region of Baonuco. When local troops condemned this act as rebellion, the commanding authorities hunted him down and killed him. More out of fear than in active resistance, the neighboring provinces of Guahaba and Hanyguayaba rebelled, and immediately suffered violent repression by the hand of Diego Velásquez.

With such harsh actions, the short and uneasy period of cooperation between the Spanish and the native West Indians was over. As the native population died off under the overwhelming odds of disease, the process of importing African slave laborers began. They became the ancestors of most of today's West Indian population—the inevitable consequence of this breakdown of the *encomienda* system.

Byron D. Cannon

Core Resources
Peter Hulme's *Colonial Encounters: Europe and the Native Caribbean, 1492-1797* (New York: Methuen, 1986) focuses on literary and anthropological approaches to understanding the psychological distances separating the colonial and colonized populations of the Caribbean. *Earliest Hispanic/Native American Interactions in the Caribbean*, edited by William F. Keegan (New York: Garland, 1991), studies Spanish and native Indian institutions, including methods of agriculture and local administration, before and during the Ovando governorate. Bartolomé de Las Casas's *History of the Indies*, edited and translated by Andrée Collard (New York: Harper & Row, 1971), is a partial translation of the massive work (three volumes in the Spanish edition) of the Spanish missionary who, after coming to Hispaniola with Governor Ovando, turned critical of Ovando's repressive policies. Irving Rouse's *The Tainos: Rise and Decline of the People Who Greeted Columbus* (New Haven, Conn.: Yale University Press, 1992) contains the most extensive coverage of the distant past of the native West Indian population, with a concluding chapter on their short history of contacts with Europeans. S. Lyman Tyler's *Two Worlds: The Indian Encounter with the European, 1492-1509* (Salt Lake City: University of Utah Press, 1988) provides the most concise history of the circumstances of West Indian revolts and repression.

See also: Columbus's voyages; West Indian Americans.

White Aryan Brotherhood

The White Aryan Brotherhood, usually identified as an affiliate or offshoot of the Aryan Nation, was organized in California's San Quentin prison in 1967, some years before the Aryan Nation's foundation under the Reverend Richard Butler. Many of the Brotherhood's first members had belonged to an earlier gang variously known as the Bluebirds, the Diamond Tooth Gang, and the Nazi Gang. Initially, the Brotherhood formed to protect its membership against African American and Hispanic groups such as La Nuestra and the Black Guerrillas. The gang's real or imagined development from an Irish-German ancestry is reflected in its official tattoo, which consists of a shamrock, the letters AB, and three sixes.

Exclusively white, the Brotherhood initially adhered to the primary tenets of most groups later associated with the Aryan Nation, including white supremacy and a neo-Nazi ideology. Its membership is still strictly drawn on racial lines, although its heavy involvement in drug trafficking and extortion sometimes requires temporary alliances with nonwhite gangs or individuals.

Brotherhood members remain bound for life in accordance with a "blood-in-blood-out" code. As a rite of initiation, called "making your bones," each member must kill someone marked for death by the group. Because membership requires the unanimous approval of all local members, some inmates who have made their bones and embraced the Brotherhood's ideals have been denied membership but maintain a very close relationship with the group. Members who are released from prison remain committed to the organization and are expected to advance its agenda.

The Brotherhood's association with the Aryan Nation began in the late 1970's, when that group started a prison outreach program designed to maintain the allegiance of its own imprisoned members as well as benefit from the prison drug trade. In 1987, the Aryan Nation began circulating *The Way*, an underground prison newsletter that helped the Brotherhood spread, recruit new members, and establish a communications network, of vital importance in maintaining the Brotherhood's structure and chain of command. Major policy decisions and targeted murders are approved by a "commission" that communicates its rulings through correspondence from outside members and in attorney interviews and social visits.

Because increasing numbers of Aryan Brotherhood members have been paroled, the outreach effort of the Aryan Nation has had a reciprocal impact on both organizations. It has helped the Brotherhood spread from prison to prison all across the United States, from California to New England. However, unlike many of the affiliates of the Aryan Nation, the imprisoned Brotherhood members engage in no paramilitary activities, having neither the resources nor freedom to do so. In fact, over the years, the group has modified its neo-Nazi credo. It now concentrates on its special identity, sustained by Irish and Viking ancestral myths and symbols. Its main business is drug trafficking, not the sort of antigovernment activities associated with many other splinter groups of the Aryan Nation. Most of the violence associated with the gang during the 1980's and 1990's reflected an internal power struggle, resulting in the death or isolation of many of the earliest members of the gang. Nevertheless, its potential for racial violence remains very strong.   *John W. Fiero*

See also: Aryan Nation; White supremacist groups.

White church

The "white church," a composite of many denominations with predominantly white congregations, has a mixed history in terms of race relations in the United States. Although the most vocal white voices raised in opposition to racism came from the church, those who supported slavery, segregation, and white supremacist politics also came from white Christian congregations.

Herbert Aptheker (*Antiracism in the United States*, 1992) notes that religion was by far the greatest influence on white antiracism. The earliest white statements against slavery came from the pulpit, with Quaker, Methodist, Baptist, and Unitarian ministers being most frequently represented in the abolitionist movement, seeing it as God's work to fight for emancipation. Yet rarely did an entire white denomination take an antislavery stance. Only the Society of Friends, or Quakers—whose homes were a crucial part of the Underground Railroad—successfully barred all slaveholders from their ranks, but even they had problems integrating their own congregations. Most other white Protestant denominations experienced schisms on the issue of slavery. Each had its outspoken abolitionists who saw slavery as an egregious sin, and each had its loyal slaveowners unwilling to make concessions. Both sides cited the Bible for support—abolitionists relied on the Golden Rule and Christ's teachings, while proslavery clergy cited Leviticus, letters from Paul, and Noah's curse on Ham, according to H. Shelton Smith (*In His Image, But . . .*, 1972).

Once the abolition of slavery became a reality, the white South's response was a system of apartheid known as Jim Crow, and religious institutions were no exception. Religious texts such as *The Negro a Beast* and *God the Original Segregationist* fueled the racist fire in mainstream white churches, and the Ku Klux Klan proclaimed itself a Christian group. It was strength mobilized in the black churches that established the Civil Rights movement in the 1950's, and white denominations such as Presbyterians, Congregationalists, and Episcopalians subsequently desegregated their congregations and supported the struggle, according to Joseph Hough, Jr. (*Black Power and White Protestants*, 1968). Still, it was not until 1963 that predominantly white churches, represented by the National Council of Churches (NCC), gave full support (including financial support) to direct-action efforts. The NCC included Protestant as well as Catholic and Jewish representatives and helped make the 1960's the most active decade in terms of white church involvement with antiracist efforts. However, this marriage had dwindled by 1969 when James Forman read his *Black Manifesto* to the NCC, demanding $500 million of white money for reparations for African Americans and citing white churches and Jewish synagogues as some of the primary agents of black oppression, according to James Findlay, Jr. (*Church People in the Struggle*, 1993).

White supremacist Tom Metzger relaxes during his bid for a seat in Congress in 1980. White groups such as the Christian Identity movement backed his candidacy.

Although in the 1990's some of the most vigorous institutional antiracism efforts came from primarily white churches such as the Unitarians, groups such as the Christian Identity movement backed white supremacist politicians including Tom Metzger and David Duke. The "white church" encompasses both the most committed antiracists and the staunchest white supremacists.

Eileen O'Brien

See also: Abolition; Black church; Christian Identity movement; Civil Rights movement; Ku Klux Klan; National Coalition of Blacks for Reparations in America; Segregation; Slavery: history; Underground Railroad; White supremacist groups.

White ethnics

White ethnics, or Southern European Americans, have immigrated from or are the descendants of immigrants from countries such as Italy, Poland, Russia, Czechoslovakia, Hungary, Yugoslavia, and Austria. Southern Europeans arrived in the United States in large numbers between 1800 and 1920. Many of the immigrants were peasants and unskilled laborers. These immigrants settled in the cities and were often employed in entry-level jobs in plants and factories. Many Southern Europeans and their descendants remained in this labor sector well into the twentieth century.

Immigrants from Southern Europe faced prejudice upon their arrival to the United States. Protestantism was the dominant religion in the United States, and many people feared that the increase in Catholic immigrants from Southern Europe would negatively affect the Protestant mores of the country. Immigration from this area was sharply reduced with the passage of the National Origins Act in 1924 but increased again in 1965 when restrictive immigration policy ended with the passage of the Immigration and Nationality Act of 1965.

Many Southern European Americans live in New England, the Mid-Atlantic States, and the Midwest. Indicators of status such as educational attainment, occupational level, and income show that Southern Europeans as a group have reached parity with the Anglo-Protestant population and generally have surpassed non-European groups. In general, Southern European Americans are highly assimilated, and their ethnicity is displayed primarily in symbolic ways.

Amy J. Orr

See also: Anglo-Protestants; European immigration to the United States: 1790-1892; European immigration to the United States; 1892-1943; German Americans; Irish Americans; Italian Americans; Polish Americans; Russian Americans.

White flight

The term "white flight" refers to any pattern of white residents relocating from urban to suburban areas. The motivation for this movement to the suburbs lies in the presumed association of inner cities with high crime rates, high taxes, and urban decay. White flight began to occur in many major cities immediately after World War II and had a number of negative consequences. Besides decreasing the population of the city in favor of the suburbs, it diminished the tax base of the cities, creating a cycle of urban decline. The more affluent inhabitants, with sufficient money to relocate and the greatest capacity to pay taxes, exited the city, rendering municipal governments susceptible to fiscal crises. Recognizing this threat to their stability, municipalities have tried to lure more prosperous suburbanites back into the city by renovating urban neighborhoods, a process called gentrification. This has generally not been very successful.

White flight continues to occur and increases the degree of racial segregation, leaving behind urban districts populated by a preponderance of poor and minority residents. Many suburban dwellers commute into the city to work, leaving again at the end of the business day. Because of the value that American society places on freedom of mobility, white flight is a complex and somewhat intractable racial, economic, and political problem.

Aristide Sechandice

See also: Black flight; Racial and ethnic demographics in Canada; Racial and ethnic demographics: trends.

White man's burden

In 1898, the year of the Spanish-American War, the famous British writer Rudyard Kipling, known as one of the foremost defenders of imperialism, called on Americans to join in the task of extending European law and culture to remoter regions of the earth. In one of his poems, he urged the New World to "Take up the White Man's burden—/Send forth the best ye breed—/Go bind your sons to exile/ To serve your captives' need."

Kipling's poem shocked many, but to expansionists it was apposite. The United States, by dint of the short war with Spain, suddenly found itself a naval and colonial power. What was to be done with Cuba, Guam, Puerto Rico, and the Philippines, all of which had suddenly fallen into American hands? Influenced in part by the views articulated in Kipling's poem, President William McKinley decided to maintain control of the territories ceded by Spain, at least temporarily. In the late 1990's, more than one hundred years later, Guam and Puerto Rico remain U.S. territories.

Kipling's poem—whose real theme was the moral responsibility of the conqueror—has been taken as an expression of racism. The famous phrase "white man's burden" has come to signify the hypocrisy and ethnocentrism of the colonial period. *Robert Jacobs*

See also: Ethnocentrism; Racism: history of the concept.

White Paper of 1969

By the late 1960's, it had long been recognized that Native Canadians had failed to share socially and economically in the general prosperity that followed World War II. They were frequently the victims of discrimination and lacked access to the economic, educational, medical, and social benefits available to the majority of Canadians. These issues were frequently lumped together in the popular media and by government bureaucrats as the "Indian problem." The White Paper of 1969 was a policy statement and plan issued by Prime Minister Pierre Trudeau to resolve the problem.

Running on the campaign slogan "The Just Society," Trudeau led the Liberal Party to victory in the Canadian national elections in June of 1968. The slogan signified a social consciousness that had been growing among the Canadian populace throughout the 1960's. The White Paper was part of a general attempt by Trudeau and his ministers, following that election, to review and reorder all Canadian social and economic policy.

Trudeau and his followers firmly believed that the special status granted to natives by the Indian Act was at least partly to blame for the discrimination against them. According to the White Paper

> The separate legal status of Indians and the policies which have flowed from it have kept the Indian people apart from and behind other Canadians. . . . The treatment resulting from their different status has been often worse, sometimes equal and occasionally better than that accorded to their fellow citizens. What matters is that it has been different.

The White Paper recommended the repeal of the Indian Act, the dissolution of the Indian Division of the Department of Indian Affairs and Northern Development (DIAND), and the transfer to the provinces of all responsibility for the delivery of social services to natives.

In order to gain native approval of its proposals, the government facilitated and funded the formation of a variety of native political organizations. The most prominent of these was the National Indian Brotherhood, which later became the Assembly of First Nations. Much to the surprise of the Trudeau government, these native political organizations were nearly unanimous in their rejection of the White Paper proposal. Their objections were many but hinged primarily on the failure of the Trudeau government to recognize native claims of aboriginal rights and sovereignty. These, they believed, would require the acceptance of long-ignored treaty obligations and the settlement of land claims.

Faced with such outspoken and vocal opposition, the Trudeau government withdrew the White Paper in 1970 but continued in various other says to disavow the notion of distinct rights for natives and other cultural minorities. It was later to acknowledge a measure of "existing aboriginal and treaty rights" via the 1982 Constitution Act. Subsequent governments, while implementing some of the White Paper proposals (specifically the transfer of responsibility for social services to the provinces), have also negotiated land claims and aboriginal rights agreements with a number of native political entities.
Pamela R. Stern

See also: Declaration of First Nations; Indian Act of 1876; Indian Act of 1951; Indian Act of 1989; Indian-white relations: Canada; Tribal sovereignty.

White "race"

The notion of a white "race" is an invention of the eighteenth and nineteenth centuries and can be traced to the racial classification system of Swedish botanist Linnaeus (Carl von Linné) and other scientists writing during this period. German professor of medicine Johann Friedrich Blumenbach, in 1795, based his definition of race on subjective physical beauty, according to biologist Stephen Jay Gould's article, "The Geometer of Race." Linnaeus, Blumenbach, and American scientist Samuel George Morton all contributed to the definition of a white "race."

In 1758, Linnaeus divided the human species into four groups based on geographical locations. They included Americanus, Europaeus, Asiaticus, and Afer (American, European, Asian, and African). He then proceeded to describe each group through specifying color, humor, and posture respectively. In the case of the Europeans, he noted that they were white (color), sanguine (humor), and muscular (posture). Linneaus's classification system was consistent with the classical taxonomic theories during this time and did not suggest any hierarchal ranking.

Blumenbach, a student of Linneaus, decided to modify his teacher's classification scheme. Gould notes that Blumenbach wrote, "I have followed Linneaus in the number but have defined my varieties by other bounda-

American scientist Samuel George Morton used the cranial capacity of human skulls to rank races.

ries." Blumenbach had visited Mount Caucasus, the mountain range between Russia and Georgia, and found the people there to be exceptionally beautiful. He decided that they represented the ideal racial group and placed them at the top of his revised classification scheme. According to Gould

> Blumenbach then presented all human variety on two lines of successive departure from this Caucasian ideal, ending in the two most degenerate (least attractive, not least morally unworthy or mentally obtuse) forms of humanity—Asians on one side, and Africans on the other. . . .

Blumenbach invented a fifth category, Malay, as an intermediary between Europeans and Africans. Unlike Linneaus's system, which was unranked, Blumenbach's was hierarchical and assigned worth to the races.

Morton, an American scientist, joined the race debate by ranking the cranial capacity of human skulls to support hierarchal racial rankings. Initially, Gould notes in *The Mismeasure of Man* (revised and expanded, 1996), Morton estimated the size of the cranial cavity by filling it with sifted white mustard seeds, but this did not produce reliable results so he switched to one-eighth-inch diameter lead shot. His experiment supported the hierarchal racial classification devised by Blumenbach: Caucasians had the largest cranial capacity and Negroes the smallest. Gould, in his book, reexamined Morton's work but did not find any significant differences among the racial groups. At the genetic level, all members of the various races are nearly identical. *Mary R. Holley*

See also: Caucasian; Genetic basis for race; Race as a concept; "Scientific" racism; White ethnics; Whites.

White supremacist groups

> **Significance:** White supremacist groups fluctuate in number and kind, banding and disbanding, but they all share a belief in the superiority of white, Christian European Americans.

Since the end of the Civil War (1861-1865), the United States has been home to a variety of white supremacist groups. Although these groups vary a great deal in membership demographics and behaviors, they all share the belief that Christians of northern and western European ancestry are superior to other people. These groups are sometimes difficult to delineate because many of the groups are interrelated or share leadership and tend to appear and disappear frequently. However, it is possible to identify several major organizations that have had significant impact in the United States.

Ku Klux Klan

The oldest organized white supremacist group in the United States is the Ku Klux Klan (KKK). It was created by several Confederate veterans, headed by Nathan Bedford Forrest, in 1866. Its name came from the Greek word *kuklos*, meaning "circle." The original Klan members engaged in acts of ter-rorism that were meant to keep the newly freed slaves from claiming their rightful places in society. The group's white costumes and pointed white masks were intended to hide the identities of the Klan members while simultaneously provoking more fear in their victims. Within a few years, however, the Klan was disbanded, in part because of internal strife.

The Klan was resurrected in 1915. For the next several years, it experienced its peak popularity, with membership in the millions, including many prominent people. It preached the inferiority of blacks, Jews, and other minorities, and Klan members were responsible for several hundred lynchings. This era in general was one of high xenophobia and anti-immigrant feeling in the United States, and the Klan promised to protect the "American" values that nativists held dear.

After the 1920's, the Klan's popularity tended to surge and wane periodically, but it never approached the large membership it once had. By the end of the twentieth century, it was a small, fragmented organization located primarily in the southern states and rural areas and crippled by several multimillion-dollar lawsuits.

Neo-Nazis

The American neo-Nazi movement began shortly after World War II. Adherents of this movement espouse the views of German Nazi leader Adolf Hitler, who believed in the superiority of the Aryan "race." Although neo-Nazis share many beliefs with the Klan, they are particularly vocal in their hatred of Jews.

There have been a number of loosely allied neo-Nazi groups in the United States. The most influential of

A member of the Knights of the Ku Klux Klan raises his hand in a salute. The Ku Klux Klan is one of the best-known white supremacist groups.

these were the American Nazi Party, the National Alliance, the American Front, Aryan Nation, and the Order. Although neo-Nazi membership has never reached the great numbers that the Klan once boasted, some neo-Nazi groups have been as renowned for their violence as the Klan. Unlike the Klan, neo-Nazi groups have tended to be active in urban areas and in Western states.

Perhaps the most well-known of the these neo-Nazi groups is the skinheads—less an organization than a movement. The skinhead movement began in England in the 1970's among disaffected working-class youth and was loosely related to the punk movement. It came to the United States in the early 1980's, where it attracted young, working-class people who felt pessimistic about their future and, perhaps, were looking for someone to blame. Skinheads got their name from their proclivity for shaving their heads. They created an entire subculture, which involved certain clothing (red suspenders and Doc Marten boots), music ("oi" music, which combines elements of punk, ska, and speed metal and is often overtly racist), and behaviors (beer drinking and violence).

Most skinhead groups are only loosely organized. However, some attempts have been made to unite them and inspire them to further acts of aggression. The most noticeable of these was Tom Metzger's White Aryan Resistance, the youth-oriented arm of which is known as the Aryan Youth Movement. Metzger sent representatives to forge alliances with skinhead groups. After one of these alliances resulted in the brutal murder of an Ethiopian man in Oregon, the slain man's family successfully sued Metzger for $12.5 million. However, Metzger continued his activities, which included running a telephone hotline and a Web site.

Militias

By the 1990's, the most visible and fastest-growing white supremacist groups were the militias. The militia movement actually began in the early 1980's, during the farm crisis, when some people who lost their farms blamed government policies. They were joined by some who lost their jobs during the recession of the late 1980's. Although not all militia groups are white supremacist, many are. They believe that the U.S. government is run as part of a Jewish conspiracy, and that this conspiracy, as well as the increasing number of people of color in the United States, is threatening the future of white people.

Militia groups have tended to be located in the western and midwestern states. Members of these groups reject the authority of the federal and state governments, insisting that the only legitimate power lies at the county level. Many of them engage in tax protests and have set up their own so-called common-law courts, in which they have "convicted" government officials. Some groups, such as the Republic of Texas, have claimed to secede from the United States. Some militia groups have also engaged in violence.

Militia groups believe that government oppression will increase until a revolution occurs, during which white "patriots" will be able to secure their freedom. Paramilitary and survivalist training is common among these groups. They are often inspired by *The Turner Diaries* (1978), by William Pierce writing as Andrew Macdonald, a fictionalized account of the revolution that these groups believe is imminent.

Christian Identity Movement

The Church of Jesus Christ Christian, or the Christian Identity Church, is a religious sect that has ties to many white supremacist groups. It teaches that Aryans are the chosen people, Jews are the spawn of Satan, and people of color are "mud people." Another belief is that a race war is coming, and during this war, all but the Aryan "race" will be exterminated. Although Christianity plays a part in many white supremacist groups, not all white supremacists belong to the Christian Identity movement.

Phyllis B. Gerstenfeld

See also: American Nazi Party; Anti-Semitism; Aryan Nation; Aryan "race"; Christian Identity movement; Ku Klux Klan; Lynchings; Nazism; Red Scare; Skinheads; White Aryan Brotherhood.

Whites

Whites, also called Caucasians or European Americans, are a category of people who share similar physical characteristics, such as relatively white skin. Like the designation "black," however, "white"designates a broad and various (not monolithic) group of people. They are members of a "race" only to the extent that they share a few superficial physical traits and a few European cultural traits—race being more of a sociopolitical-cultural-religious category than a genetic one. Moreover, because of the wide variety of ethnicities identified as "white" and extensive intermarriage among these ethnicities, the different physical and cultural attributes of the various white ethnicities are widely dispersed in North America. Still, in North America, race is a powerful concept with a basis in social, if not genetic, perceptions and realities, and therefore with consequences for members of the society at large.

Although some ethnic groups in North America have maintained their historical customs and traditions, most white Americans have assimilated into the dominant culture, retaining little or no connection to their Irish,

German, Polish, Italian, Scandinavian, Slavic, or other ethnic heritages. Although the loss of most cultural norms was a painful historical process, it is now largely forgotten by most whites. Whereas ethnic conflicts among white subgroups were rampant during the nineteenth and early twentieth centuries, when waves of non-white migration aggravated and threatened resident white power elites, today most whites identify as Americans only, rather than as members of a particular racial or ethnic group. For example, when asked to check a box identifying themselves as members of a particular group on governmental, educational, and employment forms, they do tend to check the appropriate box (which reads simply "white"). Whites also identify racially through segregated living spaces, such as housing, schools, and religion. Two notable exceptions include Hispanics—many of whom have identified as "white," thereby causing the U.S. Census to define this group as a nonracial category that can include many races—and French Canadians, particularly those who are proponents of the separatist (or sovereignist) movement in Canada.

With these exceptions, power and privilege are accorded to members of the dominant white culture upon birth, whereas members of nondominant cultures must achieve them if possible. Thus membership in the "white race" automatically improves life for whites, even though the notion of race is a social, not a biological construct, and has nothing to do with innate abilities or worth.

Eleanor A. Hubbard

See also: Caucasian; Ethnic heritage revival; Ethnicity and ethnic groups; Euro-American; Latinos in the United States; Race as a concept; White ethnics; White "race."

Wilson-Willie debate

The debate between William J. Wilson and Charles V. Willie concerns a central issue in race relations: Is racial inequality primarily a product of historical forces or is it maintained by continuing racism and discrimination?

In the summer of 1977, Wilson, then a professor of sociology at the University of Chicago, reported to a meeting of the Sociological Research Association that social class had become more important than race in determining the access of African Americans to economic resources and political power. The following year, this claim became the basis of Wilson's book, *The Declining Significance of Race* (1978). Wilson maintained that racial discrimination had, historically, limited the life chances of African Americans. Under slavery and the Jim Crow system, African Americans had been legally excluded from many areas of American life. The discrimination continued as the United States became increasingly industrialized. By the 1970's, though, official discrimination had been outlawed by civil rights legislation, and unofficial discrimination had decreased greatly. However, according to Wilson, African Americans continued to experience much greater rates of poverty than whites because historical discrimination had left African Americans with fewer job skills and lower levels of education than whites.

An excerpt from Wilson's book was published in the July/August, 1978, issue of the periodical *Society*. The periodical also published a response from Harvard sociologist Charles Vert Willie, who maintained that the significance of race in American society was not declining but "inclining." Willie argued, on the basis of statistics, that African Americans suffered systematic disadvantages in income and employment, in access to education, and in housing. These disadvantages, according to Willie, could be maintained only by continuing discrimination. Further, Willie suggested that as school desegregation and affirmative action programs brought African Americans into closer contact with whites, race became more—rather than less—important in determining black identities. Middle-class African Americans, who were under pressure to constantly prove themselves, had become obsessed with race, in Willie's view.

Responding to Willie's criticism, Wilson cited evidence that African Americans were achieving higher levels of education than ever before. He argued that the black-white gap in income was steadily decreasing among the well-educated and well-trained. He granted that some of those in the black middle class might feel psychological pressure but suggested that this was an entirely different matter from having their life chances limited by racial discrimination.

The Wilson-Willie debate continued in publications throughout the 1980's. It is a central issue in race relations, one that has been compared to the famous debate between Booker T. Washington and W. E. B. Du Bois in the early twentieth century regarding how to overcome the heritage of slavery. To the extent that social class is the basis of racial inequality, the problem requires class-based solutions such as job training for all poor, black or white. To the extent that discrimination is the basis, tough laws protecting minorities and affirmative action programs may be the best types of solutions.

Carl L. Bankston III

See also: Accommodationism; Affirmative action; Black middle class/black underclass relations; Caste model; Conservatives and racial/ethnic relations; Discrimination: racial and ethnic; Racial/ethnic relations: race-class debate; Underclass theories.

Wisconsin v. Mitchell

Following a showing of the 1988 film *Mississippi Burning*, several African American men and boys congregated at an apartment complex to talk about the film. After a discussion of a scene in the film in which a young African American boy is beaten by a white man, the accused, Todd Mitchell, asked those who joined him outside if they were ready to go after a white man.

Walking on the opposite side of the street and saying nothing, fourteen-year-old Gregory Riddick approached the complex. Mitchell selected three individuals from the group to go after Riddick. The victim was beaten, and his tennis shoes were stolen.

In a Kenosha, Wisconsin, trial court, Mitchell was convicted as a party to the crime of aggravated battery. By Wisconsin law, this crime carried a maximum prison sentence of two years. Mitchell's sentence was extended to four years, however, under a state statute commonly known as the "hate crimes" statute. This statute provided for sentence extensions if it could be determined that the victim was selected because of his or her race, religion, color, disability, sexual orientation, national origin, or ancestry.

Mitchell appealed his conviction and the extended sentence. His conviction was upheld by the court of appeals, but the Supreme Court of Wisconsin reversed the decision of the appellate court. Wisconsin's Supreme Court held that the "hate crimes" statute violated the defendant's First Amendment protection for freedom of speech because it was unconstitutionally overbroad and punished only what the state legislature found to be offensive. Moreover, the state Supreme Court believed that this statute would have a "chilling effect" on a citizen's freedom of speech; that is, a citizen would fear reprisal for actions that might follow the utterance of prejudiced or biased speech.

The U.S. Supreme Court reversed the state court's decision. Chief Justice William H. Rehnquist wrote the opinion in this unanimous decision. The Court held that Mitchell's First Amendment rights to free speech had not been violated.

The Court pointed out that the statute was not aimed at speech but at conduct, which is not protected by the First Amendment. The Court also addressed the concern about the "chilling effect" of the statute, finding that such would not be the case and that the state Supreme Court's hypothesis was far too speculative to be entertained. This decision indicates that the Supreme Court appears ready to uphold legislation designed to enhance punishment for criminal acts based on bigotry and bias without making bigoted or biased speech itself a crime.

Donna Addkison Simmons

See also: Hate crimes; *R.A.V. v. City of St. Paul.*

Women and racism

> **Significance:** As both an evaluation of human beings utilizing pseudoscientific criterion and a constructed system of social oppression, racism has been an external and an internal influence on the history of women and women's issues.

Native American Women

At the beginning of the European colonization of North America, European men encountered quite different societies from Europe in the Americas. Women participated in most tribes as political leaders, religious leaders, warriors, agricultural and horticultural practitioners, and in other roles designated by European patriarchy as male. Many American Indian nations were matrilineal; for example, in the League of the Iroquois, final political decisions rested with female consent. Throughout North America, the many tribes differed in their degree of female authority, but comparison of American Indian society with European society as the basis of gender would designate American Indian culture as nonpatriarchal. It is most significant that indigenous peoples included women in the center of religious and supernatural authority, unlike male-centered Christianity.

These contrasts produced immediate and sustained conflicts. Europeans, especially European men, observed American Indian women as "beasts of burden" and "slaves" to lazy men who, except for hunting and warring ventures, were indolent, nonproductive creatures. As Sara Evans points out in *Born for Liberty: A History of Women in America* (1989), European missionaries were determined to convert heathens to Christianity, in the process establishing the primacy of the male deity and male supremacy in heaven or Christian earth, replacing female authority by patriarchy in all aspects of American Indian culture. American Indians resisted this imposition fiercely but with limited success. In the late twentieth century, however, American Indian nations began reclaiming their traditional nonpatriarchy.

African American Women

The experience of African American women initially was framed and defined by the institution of slavery. The brutality and death inflicted on millions of Africans in the slave trade were exacerbated for African and then African American women by the sexual control and violence enacted by Europeans and white American slave owners. Many scholars have described the conditions of life for African American women in slavery as essentially no different from those for African American men, the punishments and sanctions exacted just as severe, along with the family responsibilities within the controls established by slave owners. Slave women were also subjected to intense, volatile, and negative attitudes and acts by white women in slave-owning families. Although clearly aware of the sexual violation by white male slave owners, these southern white women were also distinctly privileged by their racial identity.

In the post-Emancipation nineteenth century and well into the twentieth century, a dual location in the family/community and labor force produced two results. Jacqueline Jones demonstrates in *Labor of Love, Labor of Sorrow: Black Women, Work, and the Family, from Slavery to the Present* (1985) that the activities of African American women in the home and community centered on a positive locus of family feeling, a refuge from external white racism, whereas their presence in the labor market reinforced the subordinate racial and gender status in the United States. Again, as in the era of slavery, the racial and economic superiority of white females depended upon their control over African American women. Although it is clear that white men provided the economic resources for such economic leverage, it is also significant that racism precluded any effective bonding or formation of a biracial sisterhood. The image and stereotype of the domestic servant as an African American woman became common among women in both the South and the North.

The historical burden of slavery and years of working as servants make it hard for some African American women to succeed in the business world. In 1961, a group of African American students was escorted from the Jackson Public Library after they entered the whites-only main building.

Latinas

The history of racism and Latinos poses a similar but a distinct experience. As indigenous people, Latinas also experienced a comprehensive imposition of Spanish-European religion and culture; as with other European nations, racial consciousness (although not so labeled) dominated social classification. Incorporating a foreign religion with indigenous spirituality and coping with European patriarchy and racial stratification posed several dilemmas that were severely exacerbated by what some have called the invasion and theft of Mexican land by the United States in 1848. The subsequent dispossession of Mexican land, which affected all classes in remaining support systems, forced Mexican Latinos into agricultural work.

United States immigration policies, unofficial or official from the late nineteenth century, eventually encouraged Mexican women to join their spouses in the United States, with many becoming part of the domestic workforce in the Southwest. By the mid-twentieth century, they had expanded into other areas of the marketplace, but Latinas remained in the lowest economic strata and subject to essentially unchanged ethnic or racial discrimination. Puerto Rican women experienced the historical invasion of their island, severe population reduction (as suffered by most indigenous peoples throughout the hemisphere), colonization by the United States, and, for many, subsequent migration to the mainland. The ethnic origins (African, indigenous, and Spanish) of Puerto Rican people engendered a severe racism from Eurocentric or European-origin people on the mainland.

Asian American Women

Asian American women were a limited part of the nineteenth century Asian immigration, both by Chinese and Japanese design and by United States immigration policy. Although control broke down in the late nineteenth and early twentieth centuries, the racial antipathy remained. The Asian female experience was characterized by particularly intense oppression by white labor opposition, the patriarchy of Eurocentric American society, and "normal" racial antagonism. The racially based con-

A Korean American woman and her children wave flags during a parade in New York City. Asian American women, like all minority women, face both racial and gender discrimination when they work outside the home.

centration camp internment of Japanese Americans by the United States government during World War II was a particularly onerous (and distinctive) event for this group, especially for Japanese American women. Ironically, this event was also one of the first comprehensive opportunities for Asian American women of Japanese origin to be outside of their traditional Japanese family context.

Racism and Feminism

The issue of racism within the women's movement and as a component of feminist theory was and is quite problematic. Although the participation of white women in the abolitionist movement of the 1830's, 1840's, and 1850's was instrumental in developing a comprehensive perception and analysis of women's rights, and then organized action on its behalf, the content and context of its meaning was exclusive of women of color. As Angela Davis describes in *Women, Race, and Class* (1981), the racism underlying the subsequent woman suffrage movement became evident in the outcome of the struggle for the Fifteenth Amendment, which granted black male, not female, suffrage. The response by major lead-

ers such as Elizabeth Cady Stanton and Susan B. Anthony indicated their naïveté about white racism as a system of control; some critics have called their language vehemently racist.

This reaction characterizes the overall tendency of the women's movement to define the universal struggle of women in Eurocentric, middle-class terms with both conscious and unself-conscious marginalization of women of color. White middle- and upper-class women often employed women of color as domestic servants, undermining the concept of sisterhood. In the context of white supremacist patriarchy, racial location (that is, being white) established the dominant societal authority of white women over nonwhite men and women. The acceptance of the European racial value system prevailed among white women.

Elizabeth Spelman, the author of *Inessential Woman: Problems of Exclusion in Feminist Thought* (1985), is one of the few important feminist scholars to depict and analyze the marginalization of women of color, which had previously been ignored. Spelman's indictment is particularly eloquent as it calls upon the work of feminists of color. As most feminists of color concluded quite early in the second wave of the women's movement in the 1960's and 1970's, the centering of gender was not adequate to explain the influence of race and racism; that approach or perspective ignored the complicity by white women in sustaining racism. Bell Hooks insists that the "location" of women of color cannot be understood by a singular concept of gender; she is also quite emphatic that neither can the concept of race by a privileged explanation. Paula Giddings, the author of *When and Where I Enter . . . . : The Impact of Black Women on Race and Sex in America* (1984), underscores the intersection of race and gender that separates the experience of women of color from that of both white women and men of color. White feminist Nancie Caraway, in *Segregated Sisterhood: Racism and Politics of American Feminism* (1991), is very critical of the consistent exclusion by white feminist scholars of critiques by feminists of color.

Feminists of color describe a goal of political solidarity that would bridge the chasm in the women's movement created by racism. It is a chasm initially constructed by European racism and white supremacy as imposed by male white supremacy. Hooks and Sleeter, however, further locate a strength of racism in the blindness of most white women and feminists to the rewards granted them through complicity in white racism, whether it is unconscious or not. They and others have concluded that feminism rooted in the singular presentation of gender in regard to women's history and contemporary condition is quite problematic. The recognition of a matrix or intersection of race with gender is fundamental to a comprehensive feminism.   *Carl Allsup*

Core Resources

Paula Gunn Allen's *The Sacred Hoop: Recovering the Feminine in American Indian Traditions* (Boston: Beacon Press, 1986) presents a general analysis of traditional American Indian society as nonpatriarchal and a model for European-origin feminist development. Nancie Caraway's *Segregated Sisterhood: Racism and Politics of American Feminism* (Knoxville: University of Tennessee Press, 1991) is an overview of the disregard by white women feminists of the experience of women of color and the theoretical analysis of feminists of color. Angela Davis's *Women, Race, and Class* (New York: Vintage Books, 1981) offers a concise analysis of racism and class division within the historical women's movement. Bell Hooks's *Feminist Theory: From Margin to Center* (Boston: South End Press, 1984) analyzes the complex relationship of the oppressor and the oppressed by examining race, gender, and class in feminist theory. Elizabeth Spelman's *Inessential Woman: Problems of Exclusion in Feminist Thought* (Boston: Beacon Press, 1988) is one of the most incisive presentations of exclusionary practices in the development of feminist theory.

See also: African American women; American Indian women; Asian American women; Cable Act; Ethnic identities of women; Latinas; Triple oppression; War Brides Act; Women of color.

Women of All Red Nations

The South Dakota organization Women of All Red Nations (WARN) was formed in 1978 for the purpose of achieving autonomy for Native Americans, whatever their tribal affiliation.

Many issues of importance to Native Americans fall within the focus of WARN activities. Health care, in particular women's health matters and the misuse of sterilization practices on Indian women, is the group's main concern. Other problems that WARN addresses include children's foster care, adoption, political imprisonment, and juvenile justice. Inequities resulting from abuses of energy-resources development on Indian-owned land is another concern.

Since WARN is a grassroots organization, its efforts also include community education. Its focus is on self-reliance, whether it be for the individual or the local group affiliation. WARN also encourages Native American women to seek positions of leadership, both in and out of governments. WARN issues publications regarding health problems of Native American women and conducts an annual conference. *Ruffin Stirling*

See also: American Indian activism; American Indian women; Women of color.

Women of color

Significance: As a reaction to the second wave of the American women's movement, which was initially led by middle-class white women, many women of color sought to emphasize the diversity of race in feminism, as well as of class, gender, and sexuality.

"Women of color" as a name for a representative coalition has only been in use since the late 1960's. From that time, women of color groups, such as the Combahee River Collective and the Women of Color Association, have challenged race and class blindness in the women's movement and sexist practices in male-centered anti-racist groups. The descriptive term "woman of color," however, has been in use at least since the nineteenth century. The *Oxford English Dictionary* records the use of "women of color" in Sir Charles Lyell's *Second Visit to the United States of North America* (1849). The more inclusive term "people of color" has been used at least since the eighteenth century, initially in reference to people of African descent.

In the United States, women of color typically include four racial/ethnic groups—African Americans, Asian Americans, American Indians, and Latinas—defined by discriminatory racial laws in which the racial universe is demarcated by the five "color" categories of black, yellow, red, brown, and white. Although "women of color" can be used as a purely descriptive term, this label, in the context of feminism, is typically applied to women of color coalitions. As an organized group, women of color are products of the Civil Rights and women's movements, highlighting the complexity of the intersecting issues of both race/ethnicity and gender.

Oppression and Identity

Although constituting a diverse group, women of color are united by two major issues: a history of oppression and exclusion and a shared desire to combat racist and sexist domination. Members of each of these racially defined minorities have faced a history of oppression: American Indians were massacred, African Americans were enslaved, Mexican Americans suffered under colonialization, and Asian Americans were systematically excluded by immigration laws. Nevertheless, as scholars have noted, these racial and color categories are ambiguous and problematic. What about individuals who are multiracial? What about those nationalities or ethnic and cultural groups—such as Arabs and South Asians—that do not fit neatly into any of these categories? Despite the ambiguity of their name and the diversity of their numbers, women of color activists perceive themselves as a coalition committed to challenging oppressive dominant ideologies. For them, the term carries social and political significance.

Although many groups arising from the modern Civil Rights movement—such as the Black Power movement, La Raza, the American Indian Movement (AIM), and the Asian American Political Alliance—have emphasized cultural nationalism, even separatism, women of color have found unity in the very issue of diversity. Initially, women of color activists such as the Combahee River Collective (composed of black feminists) and Asian Women United worked to help fight against social discrimination within the specific context of their own racial and ethnic groups, but these organizations also recognized their ties with other women of color.

Influence and Commitments

In the late 1960's and early 1970's, women of color groups formed as a reaction against the second wave of the women's movement, which had been led by such white women as Betty Friedan and Gloria Steinem and which had emphasized the needs of the middle-class (generally white) homemaker. As the women's movement sought to challenge the white man as a universal norm, the women of color groups sought to dislodge any myth that the white, middle-class woman represented all women. Recognizing the multiple inequities in their society, women of color challenged white feminists to rethink the relationship among race, gender, class, and sexuality. For them, gender is one factor in a complex system of socially structured oppression. Aware of the discrimination faced by men of color, women of color try to avoid privileging gender over race. At the same time, however, recognizing that as a group they often find themselves at the bottom of the socioeconomic ladder, women of color also vigorously attack the gender inequities found in patriarchal societies.

Early on, women of color activists, often working in both women's and nationalist liberation movements, acknowledged their multiple commitments and the ways in which these commitments affected their identity. Women such as Audre Lorde, Bell Hooks, Gloria Anzaldúa, and Cherríe Moraga believed that discussions of their identity should not exclude their diverse experiences. Acknowledging their hybrid existence, some women of color constructed theories that accounted for the multiplicity of their identity. Anzaldúa's *Borderlands: The New Mestiza-La Frontera* (1987) offers a key reading of this theory of multiplicity, which the author calls a borderland or *mestiza* consciousness. Her new *mestiza* finds that she straddles two or more cultures. Rather than demanding that women of color choose one identity, Anzaldúa understands that she can affirm her multiple "differences." For Anzaldúa, the border-

land/*frontera* provides a space that accommodates multiple discourses of race/ethnicity, class, gender, and sexuality.

While women of color may find this multiplicity liberating, it can also cause fragmentation. In fact, their very strength— their diversity—can be the point that divides women of color. In order to further specific political goals, these individuals may need to form other coalitional groups, highlighting different aspects of their multiple identities.

As women of color gain a greater voice, an increasing number are engaging in coalition projects. In 1980, a group predominantly composed of African American women and led by such activists as Barbara Smith organized the Kitchen Table: Women of Color Press, a publishing company for women of color. In 1981, Anzaldúa and Moraga edited *This Bridge Called My Back: Writings by Radical Women of Color*, a groundbreaking anthology that signaled a shift in feminist studies. During the 1980's and 1990's, growing interest in women of color was demonstrated by the creation of the Women of Color Association, the organization of an annual Women of Color Conference, and the publication of works by and about women of color.

As women of color in the United States create bridges between women from different ethnic and racial groups, they are also encouraging ties with Third World women. In the 1970's and 1980's, the United Nations World Conferences on Women brought together women from both Third World and First World countries. Encouraging women to consider the impact of a global feminism, the conferences further solidified the commitment of American women of color groups to become instruments for global social change for all oppressed peoples.

Sandra K. Stanley

Core Resources

The experiences of women of color are variously discussed in Gloria Anzaldúa's *Borderlands: The New Mestiza-La Frontera* (San Francisco: Spinsters/Aunt Lute, 1987); *The Woman That I Am: The Literature and Culture of Contemporary Women of Color* (New York: St. Martin's Press, 1994), edited by D. Soyini Madison; *This Bridge Called My Back: Writings by Radical Women of Color* (2d ed., New York: Kitchen Table: Women of Color Press, 1983), edited by Cherríe Moraga and Gloria Anzaldúa; and *Women of Color in U.S. Society* (Philadelphia: Temple University Press, 1994), edited by Maxine Baca Zinn and Bonnie Thornton Dill.

See also: African American women; American Indian women; Asian American women; Ethnic identities of women; Latinas; People of color; Triple oppression; Women and racism.

Wong Kim Ark v. United States

> **Significance:** The U.S. Supreme Court held that children born in the United States, even to temporary sojourners, are subject to U.S. jurisdiction regardless of race or nationality.

Wong Kim Ark was born in San Francisco in 1873. His parents were Chinese subjects permanently domiciled in the United States. In modern terminology, they would have been called "resident aliens." They had been in business in San Francisco and were neither employees nor diplomatic agents of the government of China. In 1890, they returned to China after many years in the United States. Wong also went to China in 1890, but he returned to the United States the same year and was readmitted to the country on the grounds that he was a U.S. citizen. In 1894, he again went to China for a temporary visit but was denied readmission to the United States on his return in August, 1895. The government's position was that under the Chinese Exclusion Act of 1882, a Chinese born to alien parents who had not renounced his previous nationality was not "born or naturalized in the United States" within the meaning of the citizenship clause of the Fourteenth Amendment. If the government's position was correct, Wong was not a citizen of the United States and was not entitled to readmission to the country. Wong brought a *habeas corpus* action against the government in the District Court for the Northern District of California. That court's judgment in favor of Wong was appealed to the U.S. Supreme Court by the government.

The Decision

Justice Horace Gray wrote the Supreme Court's opinion for a 6-to-2 majority. Gray's argument begins with the assumption that the citizenship clause of the Fourteenth Amendment has to be read in the context of preexisting law. The Court's opinion begins with a long review of citizenship practices and legal customs. The U.S. tradition had been to distinguish between "natural-born" and naturalized citizens. This distinction came from English common law. In England, for hundreds of years prior to the American Revolution, all persons born within the king's realms except the children of diplomats and alien enemies were said to have been born under the king's protection and were natural-born subjects. This rule was applied or extended equally to the children of alien parents. Moreover, the same rule was in force in all the English colonies in North America prior to the revolution, and was continued (except with regard to slaves) under the jurisdiction of the United States when it

became independent. The first American law concerning naturalization was passed in the First Congress. It, and its successor acts, passed in 1802, assumed the citizenship of all free persons born within the borders of the United States. It was not until the passage of the Chinese Exclusion Act that any U.S. law had sought to alter the rule regarding natural-born citizens.

On the European continent, however, the law of citizenship was different. Most other European countries had adopted the citizenship rules of ancient Roman law. Under the Roman civil law, a child takes the nationality of his or her parents. Indeed, when *Wong Kim Ark v. United States* reached the Supreme Court, the government argued that the European practice had become the true rule of international law as it was recognized by the great majority of the countries of the world.

This was the historical and legal context for the Fourteenth Amendment's language "All persons *born* or naturalized in the United States. . . ." According to Justice Gray, the purpose of the Fourteenth Amendment was to extend the rule providing citizenship for natural-born persons to the freed slaves and their children. The amendment did not establish a congressional power to alter the constitutional grant of citizenship. Gray's opinion reviews many of the Court's prior opinions upholding the principle. The Chinese Exclusion Act, passed after the passage of the Fourteenth Amendment, could not affect the amendment's meaning, according to the majority, and therefore did not affect the established rule of natural-born citizenship. The grant of constitutional power to Congress to "establish a uniform rule of naturalization" did not validate the Chinese Exclusion Act. Wong, as a natural-born citizen, had no need of being naturalized. The Court held that "Every person born in the United States and subject to the jurisdiction thereof, becomes at once a citizen of the United States, and needs no naturalization." Moreover, the majority held that Congress's power of naturalization is "a power to confer citizenship, not to take it away." In other words, Congress had the power to establish uniform rules for naturalization but could not alter the plain-language and common-law meaning of the Fourteenth Amendment's citizenship clause.

Dissents

The dissenting justices saw the case differently. Chief Justice Melville Fuller wrote an extensive dissent in which Justice John Marshall Harlan joined. In their view, the common-law rule sprang from the feudal relationship between the British crown and children born within the realm. American law was not bound to follow the common-law rule because there were differences between "citizens" and "subjects." In a republic such as the United States, citizenship was a status created by and conferred by the civil law. Because nothing in U.S. law had explicitly endorsed the common-law principle of citizenship, the Fourteenth Amendment did not have to be read so as to include it. Fuller argued that Congress is free to pass statutes that define and interpret the citizenship clause of the Fourteenth Amendment. In the dissenters' view, then, the Chinese Exclusion Act could constitutionally limit the reach of the phrase "born or naturalized in the United States and subject to the jurisdiction thereof." Under this interpretation, Wong would not have been a citizen, and his exclusion would have been constitutional. The Court's decision in this case was important because it stripped the government of the power to deny the citizenship of persons born in the United States of alien parents.   *Robert Jacobs*

Core Resources

Sucheng Chan's *Entry Denied: Exclusion and the Chinese Community in America, 1882-1943* (Philadelphia: Temple University Press, 1991) contains a good discussion of the effects and technical aspects of the Chinese Exclusion Acts. Roderick Duncan McKenzie's *Oriental Exclusion: The Effect of American Immigration Laws, Regulations, and Judicial Decisions upon the Chinese and Japanese on the American Pacific Coast, 1885-1940* (New York: J. S. Ozer, 1971) discusses the human aspect of the Chinese exclusion laws. Sherwin White's *The Roman Citizenship* (London: Oxford University Press, 1973) is a complete discussion of the origin of Roman citizenship, the means of acquiring it, and its duties, responsibilities, and privileges.

See also: Chinese Americans; Chinese Exclusion Act; Fourteenth Amendment.

Work ethic

The modern notion of a work ethic is closely approximated by psychologist David McClelland's concept of an "achievement motive" (*The Achieving Society*, 1961). According to this concept, some children grow up with a strong desire to achieve and find psychological fulfillment in achievement entirely aside from material rewards (such as school grades or cash payments). Such people are more likely than most to become entrepreneurs and inventors, and they are much less likely to develop lifestyles predisposed toward poverty.

The classic theory of the work ethic was developed by the German sociologist Max Weber. Weber's *Protestant Ethic and the Spirit of Capitalism* (published in German in1904 and in English translation in 1930) argued that the teachings of theologians Martin Luther and John Calvin shaped the idea of work as a calling, as a religiously favored activity. McClelland links these ideas with

his own by arguing that child-raising practices among Protestants favored children's learning to read and write, and that such concerns helped form achievement-oriented personalities. The American economist Thorstein Veblen argued for the existence of an "instinct of workmanship" (the title of his 1914 book). In contrast to the individualistic McClelland, Veblen stressed the influence of the social environment on people's attitudes toward work and money making.

It is the social environment, especially as an influence on children, that links the subject of the work ethic to the issues of racial and ethnic studies. Race and ethnicity can be important elements in children's environment, viewed as a powerful influence shaping their personalities and values. Many people view the work ethic as a "good thing"—certainly most parents and schoolteachers see it that way. A review of stereotypes relating to racial and ethnic groups quickly reveals the importance of their supposed attitudes toward work and personal achievement. African Americans and Hispanics have been accused of being lazy and indifferent to career goals, of having negative attitudes toward schooling, and being willing to tolerate squalid living conditions—all, in the eyes of many who still hold these stereotypes, symptoms of lack of a work ethic on the job, in school, and in the home. At the other extreme, Chinese, Japanese, and Jewish Americans are often stereotyped as overachievers who create unfair competitive conditions for others. In truth, each of these groups contains a wide variety of personality and attitude types. Moreover, recent adult immigrants (and perhaps especially illegal immigrants) tend to manifest a high commitment to the work ethic, regardless of their ethnic and racial identifications.

Many people attach a moral stigma to persons who do not demonstrate a commitment to the work ethic. The availability of the U.S. public school system and an economic environment in the 1990's in which jobs were abundant and unemployment remarkably low caused many Americans to believe that able-bodied adults who live in poverty have only themselves to blame for their poverty. Such important issues as welfare reform and educational reform have been closely related to the work ethic. Efforts to integrate former welfare recipients into the workplace have demonstrated widespread personality aspects and educational influences in their earlier years that have often mitigated against a work ethic. Those who have spent most of their lives on welfare tend to develop self-defeating attitudes such as lowered expectations of their success in the job market—a factor compounded by the concomitant lack of skills and job experience. Contoversy continues over how to ameliorate this situation, with "workfare" advocates arguing for strict limitations or welfare benefits and "safety net" advocates pointing both to the time required to train people for jobs that will provide a living wage and to the frequent lack of available jobs. *Paul B. Trescott*

See also: African American stereotypes; Asian American stereotypes; Jewish stereotypes; Latino stereotypes; "Welfare queen" stereotype; Welfare reform: impact on racial/ethnic relations; Welfare stereotypes; Welfare's impact on racial/ethnic relations.

Wounded Knee massacre

> **Significance:** The December 29, 1890, killing of hundreds of Sioux ended the Indian wars.

In the post-Civil War decades, the United States began an expansion in both land and industry that for speed and scope was unprecedented. Westward migration, in particular, was peaking. Between 1870 and 1890, settlement of the West—the area between the Mississippi and the Pacific Ocean—rose from seven million to almost seventeen million. This expansion brought exploitation of land and mineral resources, in turn increasing demands for a final, complete removal of tribes "in the way" of progress. Through treaties (new or revised) and by military force, tribes were forced onto reservations.

By the mid-1880's, there were some 180 reservations, containing approximately 240,000 American Indians. Among the last to be confined were the Sioux, who fought fiercely to keep their freedom. Nevertheless, a treaty in 1889 created six small reservations in the Dakotas: Pine Ridge, Rosebud, Cheyenne River, Crow Creek, Lower Brule, and Standing Rock. Crop failures in the summers of 1889 and 1890, plus an epidemic of sickness, brought bitterness and poverty to the Sioux, who were ripe for any vision promising them relief.

The Ghost Dance

In Nevada, a messiah appeared, raising hopes of an Indian revival through creation of a happy new world. Wovoka, a Paiute, had lived with a white family in his youth and from them learned about the life and teachings of Jesus. Upon returning to his people, Wovoka preached a hybrid religion, a mix of Christianity and old Indian beliefs.

Wovoka taught that by participating in a particular dance, the Ghost Dance, and by living harmonious, virtuous lives, Indians could bring into existence a paradise, one in which the buffalo would return and in which there would be no sickness. In 1890, delegates from many tribes traveled to visit Wovoka, several Sioux among them. Prominent were Chief Kicking Bear and his brother-in-law, Short Bull; enamored of the Ghost Dance, they brought the new religion to Rosebud, Pine Ridge, and Standing Rock.

Although the Ghost Dance was performed peacefully by most tribes, among the Sioux it became a rallying cry against the whites. Kicking Bear and Short Bull argued that their people had to assist the Great Spirit in regaining their freedom. A holy shirt was invented, a "ghost shirt" painted with sacred, magic symbols. It was believed that not even bullets could harm a person wearing such a shirt.

The Ghost Dance dominated life on Sioux reservations, greatly disturbing the government agents. There was little or no understanding of the ritual's meaning, and agitated agents and military officers were alarmed at what they perceived to be war preparations. At Pine Ridge, Indian agent Daniel F. Royer, newly arrived in October, 1890, panicked as the people refused his orders to stop dancing. He appealed for soldiers to restore law and order.

Death of Sitting Bull

At Standing Rock in December, 1890, the army attempted to arrest Sitting Bull, a Sioux holy man and staunch champion of traditional ways, thinking that he

The U.S. military buries the dead after the massacre at Wounded Knee, South Dakota, in 1890. Hundreds of Sioux died in the battle.

was behind the Ghost Dance frenzy. Sitting Bull was killed during the attempted arrest, and his death increased tension between Indians and soldiers. Hundreds of Sioux fled Standing Rock, many seeking refuge with Chief Red Cloud at Pine Ridge or with Chief Big Foot (also known as Spotted Elk) at Cheyenne River. Both chiefs were traditionalists, though Big Foot had been earliest in accepting the Ghost Dance. Trying to preserve peace, Red Cloud invited Big Foot and his band to Pine Ridge, a move heartily desired by the army and the Indian Bureau as well.

Big Foot led his people toward Pine Ridge, setting out on December 23, 1890. Their movements were tracked by the army, fearful of treachery. On December 28, only 20 miles from Pine Ridge, a squadron of the Seventh Cavalry, Custer's former command, intercepted the band. Big Foot, ill with pneumonia, persuaded Major Samuel M. Whitside, in command, that he and his people would come peacefully. That night Indians and soldiers camped together beside Wounded Knee Creek. Accounts list 350 Indians, 230 of them women and children, while the Seventh Cavalry counted 500 men.

The Massacre

Colonel James W. Forsyth took command on December 29, his men surrounding the Indian camp. Hotchkiss guns were posted overlooking the camp. Forsyth ordered Big Foot and other leaders to confer with him. He announced that the Indians would be disarmed, and soldiers began entering the tipis, searching for weapons. Yellow Bird, a medicine man, urged resistance, assuring his people that they could not be harmed while wearing their ghost shirts. Black Coyote, said by some Indian witnesses to be deaf, refused to surrender his Winchester rifle; in the ensuing struggle, the gun went off. Both sides began firing, and indiscriminate killing followed. Most of the Indians were unarmed.

Firing fifty rounds a minute, the Hotchkiss guns devastated the Indian camp. Women and children were slaughtered along with the men, few escaping. The fighting lasted less than an hour (or an hour, depending on sources), but Big Foot and more than half of his people were dead. The army's losses were twenty-five killed and thirty-nine wounded. Surviving Indians were loaded into wagons and taken to Pine Ridge, where some were admitted to the military hospital while most, for lack of space, were housed on the floor of an Episcopal church.

Nationwide, reaction to the Wounded Knee massacre was split: Some people praised the soldiers, others condemned them. In actuality, neither side seems to have plotted the battle or to have been able to foretell the tragedy. Mutual fear and suspicion were among the underlying causes of the event.

Sioux holy man Black Elk was at Pine Ridge when the massacre occurred. After the fighting ended, he went to Wounded Knee. When he saw the many corpses, he recognized in them the "killing of a dream." It was the end of Indian armed resistance to the United States as well as the end of the Ghost Dance and its promise of a new world.

S. Carol Berg

Core Resources

The Wounded Knee incident is reviewed in Alan Axelrod's *Chronicle of the Indian Wars: From Colonial Times to Wounded Knee* (New York: Prentice Hall, 1993); Dee A. Brown's *Bury My Heart at Wounded Knee* (New York: Bantam Books, 1972); Francis Paul Prucha's *The Great Father: The United States Government and the American Indian* (Lincoln: University of Nebraska Press, 1984); and Rex A. Smith's *Moon of Popping Trees* (New York: Thomas Y. Crowell, 1975).

See also: General Allotment Act; Ghost Dance religion; Indian-white relations: United States; Reservation system of the United States; Wounded Knee occupation.

Wounded Knee occupation

The 1973 confrontation involving factions of the Teton Sioux people and European American elements of the Bureau of Indian Affairs (BIA), United States marshals, and the Federal Bureau of Investigation (FBI) on the

American Indian Movement leader Dennis Banks (left) burns a federal government offer in protest as Russell Means looks on during the occupation of Wounded Knee, South Dakota, in 1973.

Pine Ridge Reservation in South Dakota reached a stand-off at Wounded Knee.

The elected tribal government at Pine Ridge was headed by Richard Wilson. He was challenged by the traditionalist faction of the tribe led by individuals such as Gerald One Feather. A faction of younger people organized themselves as a chapter of the American Indian Movement (AIM). This was AIM's first reservation-based effort of any scale. AIM had begun as an urban Indian organization in Minneapolis, and it had served as a significant element in the takeover of the BIA headquarters in Washington, D.C., in the fall of 1972.

The difficulties reached a climax at Wounded Knee, the site of the massacre of Oglala Lakota people in 1890 by the United States cavalry. The people within the Wounded Knee area were armed. They were surrounded by United States marshals, and then both groups were surrounded by the reservation BIA police, an arm of the elected tribal government. Fools Crow, the ceremonial chief of the Teton Sioux, started to talk with representatives of the traditionalists and AIM factions, as well as with the federal authorities, when, with-out warning, shots were exchanged. Military overflights added to the considerable confusion, and many were injured or killed.

Fools Crow oversaw the process that brought about negotiations, and leaders of the elected tribal government were excluded from the process. An agreement was signed that ended the siege and addressed some of the problems of unemployment, hunger, and poor living conditions on Pine Ridge Reservation. For example, it was estimated that the United States government was spending approximately $30,000 per capita on the reservation, but people were still living in tarpaper shacks, children did not have enough to eat, and the unemployment rate was higher then 60 percent. The Wounded Knee occupation gave the Pine Ridge Lakota Sioux people a national forum for their grievances.

Howard Meredith

See also: Alcatraz Island occupation; American Indian activism; American Indian Movement; Indian-white relations: United States; Pine Ridge shootout; Wounded Knee massacre.

X

Xenophobia, nativism, and eugenics

> **Significance:** Eugenics refers to the theory that the human race can be improved through controlled or selective breeding. Xenophobia and nativism both gave birth to the eugenics movement and influenced theories about which human characteristics are desirable or undesirable.

Members of premodern (traditional) societies often exhibit distrust and fear of any persons not immediately known to them. Social scientists call this unreasoning and seemingly instinctual fear of strangers "xenophobia." Xenophobia manifests itself in modern societies among members of subcultures, religious sects, ethnic groups, and political movements. Because people of similar beliefs and cultural backgrounds often tend to associate largely with one another, they develop little understanding of people with different beliefs and cultural backgrounds. As a result, in a pluralistic society such as the United States, xenophobia develops between Jews and Christians, between African Americans and European Americans, and between the members of many other groups that have limited interaction with people with backgrounds different from theirs.

Often xenophobia leads directly to ethnocentrism, a conviction that one's own group and its culture are superior to all other groups and their cultures. Xenophobia and ethnocentrism form essential elements of "nativism." Sociologists include nativist movements as part of a larger category called "revitalization movements." Revitalization movements usually occur within societies or groups that have suffered stress and whose cultures have suffered disorganization. Such movements aim to better the lives of their members, often at the expense of the members of other groups. Modern examples include the African American separatist movement in the United States, the Nazi movement in Germany during the period between the world wars, the Branch Davidian religious sect of the late twentieth century, the Indian Ghost Dance movement in the western United States during the last quarter of the nineteenth century, and many others. Several nativist movements, fueled by xenophobia, have actively advocated the use of eugenics to revitalize their own culture by eliminating foreign traits from their memberships.

Eugenics

Eugenics is a branch of science that deals with the improvement of the hereditary qualities of human beings through controlled or selective breeding. Eugenicists argue that many undesirable human characteristics (for example, inherited diseases such as hemophilia and Down syndrome) can be eliminated through careful genetic screening of couples planning to marry. Moderate eugenicists advocate the creation of a central data bank of genetic records for entire populations. A person contemplating marriage would be able to investigate the genetic endowment of his or her chosen partner to ascertain whether that person had a genetic weakness.

More radical eugenicists argue that governments should take a direct hand in racial improvement by passing laws forbidding genetically flawed individuals from reproducing. Others hold that genetically flawed individuals should be medically sterilized. Eugenicists justify their positions on economic and scientific grounds: They maintain that the human race cannot spare scarce resources to tend to those born with genetic handicaps and that people must somehow compensate for the retrogressive evolutionary effects of modern technology.

According to many eugenicists, the cost of keeping genetic defectives alive through the use of modern medical technology will eventually bankrupt world society. These eugenicists also believe that if genetically unsound men and women are allowed to breed uncontrollably, all of humanity will eventually inherit their debilitating characteristics. Before the rise of modern industrial society and the development of medical science, genetically defective individuals rarely lived long enough to reproduce, which controlled their negative influences on the human gene pool. Today, society not only expends increasingly scarce medical care on these people but also allows them to perpetuate and to spread their genes. The only way to reverse this retrogressive evolution, say the eugenicists, is to control or prevent the reproduction of that part of the world's population that carries dysfunctional genes.

The debate concerning eugenics has taken on a greater urgency with the recent strides that have been made in genetic engineering, particularly cloning. This new technology may make possible not only the medical elimination of genetic defects but also the "engineering" of desirable characteristics. It is apparently possible that genetic engineers may in a few decades be able to increase the intelligence of future generations (or decrease it). They may also be able to ensure that progeny will be tall (or short) or fair complected (or dark), to determine their hair color, and even to determine their sex. For some people, these possibilities presage a brilliant future. For others, they conjure up frightening images of an Orwellian nightmare. In either case, ethical questions are profound and complex.

Consequences

The instances in which governments or societies have implemented eugenics principles have not inspired confidence that eugenics goals will ever be achieved. They have not only failed to eliminate undesirable characteristics in the populations on which they were tested but also, in virtually every instance, have resulted in abuses that are indefensible in any moral court. Those who have controlled eugenics programs have been influenced in the passage and implementation of eugenic laws by xenophobia, nativism, and outright racism, rather than by sound scientific principles.

The leading spokesperson for the eugenics movement in the United States for many years was Charles B. Davenport. Davenport taught zoology and biology at Harvard University and the University of Chicago in the late nineteenth and early twentieth centuries. Like many scientists of his era, Davenport assumed that each "race" had its own characteristics.

Davenport led a grassroots nativist movement in the United States that eventually succeeded in passing eugenics laws at both the national and state levels. The Immigration Act passed by large majorities in both houses of the U.S. Congress in 1924 governed who could immigrate to the United States from abroad. Its language made immigration from northern Europe relatively easy, while residents of Africa and Asia found themselves virtually excluded. As several of its supporters (including future president Calvin Coolidge) acknowledged, the Immigration Act was designed to prevent the decline of the "Nordic" race by limiting the influx of members of "inferior" races.

Scientists in Germany, especially anthropologists and psychiatrists, began advocating eugenics legislation before the beginning of the twentieth century. Eugenics

seemed to offer scientific validation for the racial theories of Adolf Hitler and other Nazi leaders (theories based not on scientific evidence but on xenophobia and nativism).

Shortly after the outbreak of World War II, German doctors and directors of medical institutions—apparently authorized by Hitler—began the so-called euthanasia program. In mental institutions, hospitals, and institutions for the chronically ill, doctors began to kill (by neglect, by lethal injection, and by poisonous gas) those persons judged to be "useless eaters." Although it was supposedly terminated after 1941, the program resulted in the deaths of many thousands of people. Some of the personnel involved in the euthanasia program formed the nucleus of the units that carried out the legalized murder of enormous numbers of people in Nazi concentration camps in Poland from 1942 to 1945. Most of the victims were members of races deemed "inferior" by Nazi ideologists: Jews, Gypsies, and Slavs. It is little wonder that many people are fearful of the policies advocated by contemporary eugenicists.

Beginning in the 1930's, the affinity between Nazi racial theories and eugenics caused most biological and medical scientists around the world to renounce eugenics policies and experiments. The information about the concentration camps that became known at the many war-crimes trials held after 1945 seemed to have dealt a death blow to eugenicist dreams of a perfected human race. By the mid-1950's, eugenics societies around the world were seemingly bereft of members and influence. Nevertheless, an increasing number of physicians began to recognize the many possible benefits of continued genetic research.

By the 1970's, genetic researchers had shown conclusively that some ethnic and racial groups were especially susceptible to certain genetic disorders. African Americans are particularly prone to the single-gene disorder called sickle-cell anemia, Ashkenazic Jews to Tay-Sachs disease, and Americans whose ancestors came from the Mediterranean area to Cooley's anemia. The new eugenics/genetics societies in the United States led a movement that resulted in the National Genetic Diseases Act, which funded research into the detection and treatment of genetic disorders. A number of states extended their postnatal screening programs to include many single-gene disorders. Doctors developed a medical procedure known as amniocentesis, which allowed them to identify genetic and chromosomal disorders during the early stages of pregnancy. If an unborn fetus was identified as genetically flawed, parents could elect abortion.

In the 1970's, eugenicists also turned their attention to the population explosion. They found increasing cause for alarm because most of the human population increase was occurring in the Third World (Africa, Asia, and Latin America) and among the bottom socioeconomic strata of industrialized nations. Fearing for the quality of the human gene pool, many eugenics groups began to advocate and finance "family planning" programs in the Third World and among domestic socially disadvantaged populations. These new programs clearly indicate that the nativism and xenophobia that influenced earlier generations of eugenicists are still operative. *Paul Madden*

Core Resources
Charles Benedict Davenport's *Heredity in Relation to Eugenics* (New York: Holt, 1911) is valuable in understanding the arguments of early eugenicists. Loren R. Graham's *Between Science and Values* (New York: Columbia University Press, 1981) is a thoughtful and provocative exploration of the moral and ethical issues raised by genetic engineering; Graham is critical of the old eugenics and of the xenophobia and ethnocentrism upon which it was based. John Higham's *Strangers in the Land: Patterns of American Nativism, 1860-1925* (New York: Atheneum, 1963) shows how nativism was given a measure of scientific legitimacy by the eugenics movement. Daniel J. Kevles's *In the Name of Eugenics: Genetics and the Uses of Human Heredity* (New York: Alfred A. Knopf, 1985) clearly demonstrates the influence of nativism, xenophobia, and outright racism on the leading eugenicists. Benno Muller-Hill's *Murderous Science: Elimination by Scientific Selection of Jews, Gypsies, and Others, Germany 1933-1945*, translated by George R. Fraser (Oxford, England: Oxford University Press, 1988), establishes the relationship between the eugenics movement in Germany and both the euthanasia program and the mass murder in concentration camps.

See also: Ethnic cleansing; Ethnocide; Genetic basis for race; Holocaust; Immigration and emigration; Miscegenation laws; Nativism; "Scientific" racism.

Y

Yellow peril campaign

> **Significance:** The *San Francisco Bulletin*'s "yellow peril" campaign against Japanese immigrants strengthened anti-Asian feeling in the United States.

In 1889, the editor of the *San Francisco Bulletin* began a series of editorials attacking Japanese immigrants and making a case that they were dangerous to white American workers and to American culture. On May 4, 1892, he wrote, "It is now some three years ago that the *Bulletin* first called attention to the influx of Japanese into this state, and stated that in time their immigration threatened to rival that of the Chinese, with dire disaster to laboring interests in California." The *San Francisco Bulletin*'s yellow peril campaign helped strengthen the growing anti-Japanese fervor in California. The campaign was not only against Japanese laborers, who they claimed threatened "real" American workers, but also against their perceived threat to American culture. Met with hostility, prejudice, and discrimination, Japanese in many urban areas settled into ethnic enclaves known as Little Tokyos, where they could feel safe and comfortable among fellow compatriots and secure employment.

Effects

On June 14, 1893, the San Francisco Board of Education passed a resolution requiring that all Japanese students must attend the already segregated Chinese school instead of the regular public schools. Because of Japanese protests, the resolution was rescinded; however, it marked the beginning of legal discrimination against the Japanese in California. In 1894, a treaty between the United States and Japan allowed citizens open immigration, but both governments were given powers to limit excessive immigration. In 1900, because of American protests, Japan began a voluntary program to limit Japanese emigration to the United States.

The Alaska gold rush of 1897-1899 attracted a great number of white laborers, and when the Northern Pacific and Great Northern Railroads worked to build a connecting line from Tacoma and Seattle to the East,

extra laborers were needed. The companies turned to Japanese immigrants as workers. Some of these laborers came from Japan and Hawaii. The rapid influx of Japanese laborers created further anti-Asian sentiments and hostility. With the 1882 Chinese Exclusion Act up for renewal in 1902, the anti-Japanese sentiment occurred in the overall context of a growing anti-Asian movement, especially among labor unions and various political groups. In April of 1900, the San Francisco Building Trades Council passed a resolution to support the renewal of the Chinese Exclusion Act and to add the Japanese to this act to "secure this Coast against any further Japanese immigration, and thus forever settle the mooted Mongolian labor problem." The county Republican Party lobbied extensively to get the national Republican Party to adopt a Japanese exclusion plank in their national platform. San Francisco mayor James Phelan and California governor Henry Gage joined the calls for Japanese to be included in the renewal of the Exclusion Act. However, when the exclusion law was extended in 1902, Japanese people were not included.

After the 1905 defeat of Russia by Japan in the Russo-Japanese War, a growing fear of Japanese power led to further agitation and political tactics to limit Japanese immigration and influence in America. Whereas Chinese were hated and despised by various politicians, labor leaders, and some regular citizens, Japanese were feared. In 1905, the *San Francisco Chronicle* launched another anti-Japanese campaign, emphasizing the dangers of future immigration. Later, the San Francisco Labor Council, at the urging of Dr. A. E. Ross and with the support of San Francisco mayor Eugene Schmitz, launched boycotts against Japanese merchants and white merchants who employed Japanese workers. Later that year, sixty-seven labor organizations formed the Asiatic Exclusion League (sometimes called the Japanese and Korean Exclusion League), and the American Federation of Labor passed a resolution that the provisions of the Chinese Exclusion Act be extended to include Japanese and Koreans.

In 1906, anti-Asian sentiments continued to grow. San Francisco was struck by a major earthquake in April, and civil unrest increased. Japanese persons and businesses were attacked and looted. On October 11, 1906, the San

In 1889, the editor of the *San Francisco Bulletin* initiated an anti-Japanese immigrant campaign, terming the immigrants a "yellow peril." Despite this type of discrimination, many Japanese immigrants managed to establish themselves in the United States, including this couple, the proprietors of a watch shop in Sacramento in about 1910.

war these sentiments resurfaced. The 1917 and 1924 Immigration Acts barred Asian laborers from the United States. In California, a campaign to pass the 1920 Alien Land Act attracted the support of the American Legion and the Native Sons and Daughters of the Golden West.

In an effort to avoid widespread prejudice and discrimination, the Japanese American Citizens League (JACL), founded in 1930 and consisting of second-generation Japanese Americans (Nisei), sought to follow a path of economic success through individual efforts, the cultivation of friendship and understanding between themselves and other Americans, and assimilation into American culture. During the 1930's and 1940's, Nisei were urged by JACL leaders to prove their worth as patriotic Americans by contributing to the economic and social welfare of the United States and to the social life of the nation by living with other citizens in a common community. Their efforts would find a new obstacle in 1941, however, when President Franklin D. Roosevelt issued Executive Order 8802 allowing internment of Japanese Americans in segregated camps.

Gregory A. Levitt

Francisco School Board ordered that all Japanese, Korean, and Chinese students attend a segregated "Oriental school." (This regulation was later changed to include only older students and those with limited English proficiency.) Japan protested that the school board's action violated the U.S.-Japan treaty of 1894, bringing the San Francisco situation into international focus.

The Gentlemen's Agreement

To assuage Japan, President Theodore Roosevelt arranged with the school board to rescind its order in exchange for federal action to limit immigration from Japan. In the ensuing U.S.-Japan "Gentlemen's Agreement," Japan promised not to issue passports to laborers planning to settle in the United States and recognized U.S. rights to refuse Japanese immigrants entry into the United States. In an executive order issued on March 14, 1907, Roosevelt implemented an amendment to the Immigration Act of 1907, which allowed the United States to bar entry of any immigrant whose passport was not issued for direct entry into the United States and whose immigration was judged to threaten domestic labor conditions.

Subsequent California legislation, the Heney-Webb bill or Alien Land Act of 1913, attempted to limit Asian interests within the state by prohibiting Asians from owning property. Although anti-Japanese sentiments lessened during World War I after Japan joined the Allies in the war against Germany, almost immediately following the

Core Resources

Yamato Ichihashi's *The American Immigration Collection: Japanese in the United States* (1932; reprint, New York: Arno Press, 1969) provides a thorough description of Japanese immigration to the United States, with an excellent chapter on anti-Japanese agitation. Carey McWilliams's *Prejudice: Japanese-Americans, Symbol of Racial Intolerance* (Boston: Little, Brown, 1944) is a dated but excellent account of anti-Japanese American prejudice and discrimination up to World War II. Ronald Takaki's *Strangers from a Different Shore: A History of Asian Americans* (Boston: Little, Brown, 1989) is an overview of the broader picture of Asian immigration and settlement in the United States. Robert A. Wilson and Bill Hosokawa's *East to America: A History of the Japanese in the United States* (New York: William Morrow, 1980) is an excellent account of Japanese immigration and settlement in the United States.

See also: Alien land laws; Gentlemen's Agreement; Immigration and emigration; Japanese American internment; Japanese Americans.

Yellow Power

Yellow Power was a political movement of the late 1970's and 1980's that was inspired by the Black Power movement. It was based on the idea that people of color—in this case, primarily Asians—could join together to gain political and economic strength. People who identified themselves as "yellow" were to collectively vote for candidates who supported issues important to the group. If yellow people gained a political voice, economic power would follow.

In general, the idea of yellow power was not successful. Although organizers of the Yellow Power movement sought the membership of Hispanics, one of the largest ethnic groups in the United States, members of the Hispanic group refused to identify themselves as "yellow," preferring to think of themselves as "white." Furthermore, Asian Americans, who are recognized as members of the "yellow" race, have, throughout American history, sought to have other races see them as individual cultural groups—as Japanese Americans, Chinese Americans, and so on. Historic antagonism between several Asian nations created an additional obstacle to Asian American coalition. Therefore, these disparate Asian American groups found it difficult to unite merely on the basis of skin tone to support particular political issues or to vote for particular political candidates.

The Black Power movement was much more successful than the Yellow Power movement because its members were united not only through the color of their skin but also through a common cultural heritage. The people who advocated Yellow Power failed to understand that there were significant cultural divisions between the various peoples who could be identified as having yellow skin. The cultural differences made political coalitions difficult, if not impossible. Later, more successful attempts to build an Asian American movement tried to take into consideration these differences.

Annita Marie Ward

See also: Asian American movement; Black Power movement.

Young Lords

The Young Lords was a Puerto Rican revolutionary organization formed to fight racial, cultural, and language discrimination and economic exploitation. It established chapters in several U.S. cities in the early 1970's.

The first Young Lords Organization (YLO) was formed in Chicago and worked with local Black Panthers and a white revolutionary group in a so-called Rainbow Coalition. A group of young Puerto Ricans in New York City read an article about the Chicago YLO in the June 7, 1969, issue of the Black Panther newspaper, and a month later obtained permission to start their own chapter. In addition to Puerto Ricans, the membership included Dominican Americans, African Americans, Cuban Americans, and Latinos. The group's admiration for the Black Panther Party can be seen in its thirteen-point political program, paramilitary style, and the brown berets that members wore. In May, 1970, the East Coast YLO became the Young Lords Party and published a bilingual newspaper, *Palante* (literally "forward in struggle"). Chapters formed in Hoboken, Newark, and Jersey City, New Jersey; Bridgeport and New Haven, Connecticut; Boston, Massachusetts; and Philadelphia, Pennsylvania.

New York City's chapter was the most active, with early actions focused on improving living conditions in the barrio. When a church refused to give them space to run a free breakfast program, the Young Lords occupied it for eleven days. When neighborhood cleanups were met with hostility from the sanitation department, the Young Lords turned them into "garbage protests" in which the streets of East Harlem were blockaded with trash until the city picked it up. Later, the Young Lords used direct action to improve community health care by hijacking a medical truck to service the community, starting drug treatment programs, and occupying a hospital in the South Bronx to demand better services. Support of Puerto Rican independence and prison struggles were other major areas of activity.

In January, 1970, the police escort members of the Young Lords, a predominantly Puerto Rican activist group, from an East Harlem church in New York City where they had staged a ten-day sit-in.

The Young Lords gave voice to an increasing militancy in the Latino community. Internal debates about sexism and homophobia resulted in advances for women and gays within the organization and also served to educate the community about the dangers of "machismo." In part by embracing an Afro-Indio-Latino multiculturalism, the Young Lords facilitated connections between activists of differing racial and cultural backgrounds.

The Federal Bureau of Investigation's COINTELPRO (Counterintelligence Program), which targeted Puerto Rican independence activists, many of whom were also active in the Young Lords, took a toll on the organization. In January, 1971, the group split over whether to open chapters in Puerto Rico or continue working only in U.S. communities. Two island chapters were started but did not survive long. In July, 1972, the Young Lords Party changed its name to the Puerto Rican Revolutionary Workers Organization and shifted to labor organizing. By 1976, it had dissolved.

Vanessa Tait

See also: Black Panther Party; Chicano movement; Latinos in the United States.

Z

Zionism

In 1882, after a series of pogroms (organized persecutions of Jews) in Russia, Jewish youths formed a group called the Woveveiiyyon ("Lovers of Zion") to promote immigration to Palestine. "Zion" is the ancient Hebrew poetic term for the abode of the faithful, specifically, Jerusalem and the Holy Land. The Woveveiiyyon began what was called "practical Zionism."

In 1896, after witnessing anti-Semitic demonstrations in Paris resulting from the Dreyfus affair, Theodor Herzl wrote *The Jewish State*, in which he reasoned that if an army officer (Alfred Dreyfus) could be falsely convicted of treason in as supposedly enlightened and ethical a country as France, simply because he was Jewish, there was no hope for Jews to live in peace anywhere except in an independent Jewish national state. Subsequently, Herzl organized "political Zionism" on a worldwide scale at the First Zionist Congress in Basel, Switzerland, in 1897.

After Herzl's death in 1904, Zionist leaders worked tirelessly in the face of Arab hostility and the horrors of the Holocaust to bring about the founding of the State of Israel on May 14, 1948. By the 1980's, practically all Jews of the Diaspora had become committed to Zionism, or at least to its mission of supporting Israel and human rights for Jews.   *Andrew C. Skinner*

See also: Anti-Semitism; Diaspora; Holocaust; Israeli Americans; Jewish Americans; Judaism; Pogrom.

Zoning

Zoning affords local governments the power to address a range of justice issues, including the affordability of housing, the integration of neighborhoods, and the preservation of quality of life; however, zoning also raises legal questions about just compensation for the "taking" of a property's use.

Almost all land in the incorporated cities and towns of the United States, and much land in the surrounding counties, is subject to land-use controls established by local ordinances. Zoning is the designating of the various parcels of land for specific purposes, such as residential, commercial, industrial, and open space. In addition to specifying permissible use, zoning ordinances typically regulate the acceptable types of construction and other improvements on the property. The benefits of zoning are obvious in terms of community planning, as they facilitate the logical and orderly development of neighborhoods, commercial districts, park lands, and sanitation districts. Zoning permits long-range planning and allows purchasers of property to know the nature of the surrounding areas once it is built out—possibly some decades in the future.

Beyond its practical benefits, zoning involves several justice issues. Particularly in terms of residential zoning, housing affordability and discrimination are relevant. By specifying maximum density (units per acre) of residential construction, zoning affects the affordability of housing through land costs. Low-density housing requirements can make housing prohibitively expensive for lower-income households. Off-street parking requirements, floor area ratios, and other zoning standards may add to housing costs. Highly restrictive zoning may effectively turn neighborhoods and even entire towns into elite enclaves. Some have gone so far as to charge that such situations amount to *de facto* racial discrimination. Conversely, a broad range of residential zoning standards in a single area (for example, including apartments, condominiums, mobile homes, and single-family homes) can encourage the creation of financially and racially integrated neighborhoods. Federal and various state fair housing laws prohibit intentional discrimination through zoning, but it is difficult to distinguish between regulations which stem from legitimate purposes, such as public health and safety, and those which unfairly place excessive "quality of life" standards above the need for affordable housing within a region.

Zoning also raises justice issues for the owners of land. By definition, land use controls such as zoning place some limits on the rights of ownership. This fact raises questions about just compensation: Do governmental restrictions upon one's land constitute a "taking" of all or part of the land's value, thus requiring compensation? Moreover, how should compensation, if necessary, be calculated? Over time, the courts have broadened the tolerable level of abridgment of property rights in the public interest. Nevertheless, standards vary from court to court and from place to place, leaving much room for controversy. *Steve D. Boilard*

See also: Housing; Redlining; Restrictive or racial covenants.

Zoot-suit riots

The zoot-suit riots occurred June 4-10, 1943, when approximately two hundred U.S. Army and Navy personnel attacked Mexican American youths in the streets of East Los Angeles. The zoot suit, an oversized, brightly colored suit accompanied by a large, feathered hat, was a fad among the youth of the Mexican American community who called themselves Pachucos. The attacks on youth wearing zoot suits were spurred by anti-immigrant sentiment in the Los Angeles area, as well as by the intensely negative portrayal of the Mexican American community by the media during the Sleepy Lagoon murder case, in which several Mexican American gang members were accused of the murder of a teenage boy. At the height of the riots, mobs of approximately one thousand servicemen and civilians dragged Mexican American youth from movie theaters, stripped them of their clothing, beat them, and left them naked in the streets. The Los Angeles police, in most cases, watched the attacks and did not attempt to intervene or protect the Pachucos. Once the disturbance subsided, the Los Angeles City Council's sole response was the passage of an ordinance that banned the wearing of zoot suits. The zoot-suit riots became a rallying point for Mexican Americans' struggle for civil rights during the Chicano movement of the 1950's and 1960's. *Jason Pasch*

See also Chicano movement; Latinos in the United States.

Pioneers of Intergroup Relations

African Americans

Abernathy, Ralph David (1926-1990): Christian minister and civil rights activist; became close friends with Martin Luther King, Jr., when both took Baptist pastorates in Montgomery, Alabama, around 1951; helped coordinate the Montgomery bus boycott in 1955 and organize the Southern Christian Leadership Conference (SCLC) in 1957; succeeded King as president of the SCLC, 1968-1977; stood unsuccessfully for Congress in 1977; published a controversial autobiography, *And the Walls Came Tumbling Down* (1989), which included details of King's extramarital affairs.

Ali, Muhammad (1942-): Boxer; born Cassius Marcellus Clay, Jr., started boxing at an early age in Louisville, Kentucky; won Olympic gold medal as a light-heavyweight in 1960; converted to the Black Muslim religion and changed his name in 1964; won heavyweight championship four times (1964, 1967, 1974, 1978); stripped of title when he refused induction into the U.S. Army in 1967, though the U.S. Supreme Court reversed the draft evasion conviction in 1971; became a symbol of black pride during the 1960's.

Angelou, Maya (1928-): Novelist, poet; born Marguerite Johnson, she worked as a nightclub singer in New York and San Francisco, as an editor for the English-language *Arab Observer* (Cairo), and as a teacher of music and drama in Ghana; became a national figure with publication of the first volume of her autobiography, *I Know Why the Caged Bird Sings* (1970), detailing her experience of southern racism and sexual abuse; nominated for an Emmy Award for her performance as Nyo Boto in the television series *Roots* (1977); invited to read her poem "On the Pulse of Morning" at the inauguration of President Bill Clinton in 1993.

Asante, Molefi Kete (1942-): Scholar; born Arthur Lee Smith, Jr., but legally changed his name in 1975; after receiving a doctoral degree in communications from the University of California, Los Angeles (UCLA) in 1968, taught at Purdue, UCLA, State University of New York, Howard University, and Temple University; named director of the Center for Afro-American Studies at UCLA; wrote more than two dozen books, including *Afrocentricity: The Theory of Social Change* (1980), *African Culture: The Rhythms of Unity* (1985), and *The Historical and Cultural Atlas of African-Americans* (1991); was founding editor of the *Journal of Black Studies*.

Baker, Josephine (1903-1986): Civil rights activist; after graduating as valedictorian with a bachelor's degree from Shaw Boarding School in 1927, moved to New York City where she became deeply involved with progressive politics; became director of the Young Negroes Cooperative League in 1931, helping to provide reasonably priced food to members during the Depression (1930's); worked with the literacy program of the Works Progress Administration; set up and directed branch offices of the National Association for the Advancement of Colored People during the 1940's; moved to Atlanta to work with the Southern Christian Leadership Conference in 1958; was unofficial adviser to the Student Nonviolent Coordinating Committee in the 1960's; helped organize the Mississippi Freedom Democratic Party; raised money for freedom fighters in Rhodesia and South Africa.

Baldwin, James Arthur (1924-1987): Author and playwright; often praised for his ability to make readers feel the destructive power of racial prejudice on both blacks and whites; his books include two autobiographical works, *Notes of a Native Son* (1955) and *Nobody Knows My Name* (1961); several powerful novels, including *Go Tell It on the Mountain* (1953), *Another Country* (1962), and *Just Above My Head* (1979); and a number of plays, including *Blues for Mister Charlie* (1964) and *The Amen Corner* (1964); spent the final years of his life in France, where he was made commander of the Legion of Honor, France's highest civilian award.

Baraka, Imamu Amiri (1934-): Poet, playwright; born LeRoi Jones, founded *Yugen* magazine and Totem Press in 1958 and the Black Arts Repertory Theater in 1964; achieved fame with honest treatment of racism in plays such as *Dutchman* (1964), *The Slave* (1966), and *Four Revolutionary Plays* (1968); was leading spokesperson for the Black Power movement in Newark, New Jersey, heading the activist Temple of Kawaida; chair of the National Black Political Convention in 1972.

Bethune, Mary McLeod (1875-1955): Educator; after teaching at various schools in Georgia and Florida, founded the Daytona Educational and Industrial School for Negro Girls in 1904 and McLeod Hospital in 1911; the Daytona school merged with the Cookman Institute to become Bethune-Cookman College in 1922, with Bethune serving as president until 1942; served on conferences under Herbert Hoover in the 1920's; served as director of the Division of Negro Affairs of the National Youth Administration, 1936-1944; was special assistant to the Secretary of War during World War II; served as special adviser on minority affairs to Franklin Roosevelt, 1935-1944;

played important roles in the National Urban League, National Association for the Advancement of Colored People, and National Council of Negro Women.

Bond, Julian (1940-): Politician, civil rights activist; student founder of the Committee on Appeal for Human Rights; attracted attention of Martin Luther King, Jr., and helped found the Student Nonviolent Coordinating Committee, serving as its first director of communications, 1961-1966; was Democratic member of the Georgia house of representatives, 1965-1975, and the Georgia senate, 1975-1987; helped found the Southern Poverty Law Center in 1971; served as president of the Atlanta branch of the National Association for the Advancement of Colored People (NAACP), 1974-1989; appointed chair of the NAACP in 1998; hosted the television program *America's Black Forum* and narrated the Public Broadcasting Service civil rights series *Eyes on the Prize*.

Bradley, Thomas (1917-1998): Politician; held various positions with the Los Angeles Police Department, 1940-1961; after earning a law degree in the 1950's, became the first African American elected to the Los Angeles City Council, 1963-1973; served as mayor of Los Angeles, 1973-1989; was a founding member of the Black Achievers Committee of the National Association for the Advancement of Colored People.

Braun, Carol Moseley (1947-): Politician; assistant U.S. attorney for the northern district of Illinois, 1973-1977; served as Illinois state representative, 1979-1987, establishing a reputation as an ardent supporter of civil rights legislation; was Cook County recorder of deeds, 1987-1993; became first African American woman to be elected to the U.S. Senate (Democrat, Illinois) in 1992. She served from 1993-1999.

Brown, H. Rap (1943-): Civil rights activist; became leader of the Student Nonviolent Coordinating Committee in 1967; charged with inciting riot in Cambridge, Maryland, in 1968 and convicted of carrying a gun across state lines; published *Die Nigger Die* (1969); while in prison for a robbery conviction, converted to Islam, taking the name Jamil Abdullah Al-Amin; leader of Community Mosque in Atlanta, Georgia.

Bruce, Blanche Kelso (1841-1898): Politician; born a slave, after the Civil War built a fortune as a plantation owner; served in various local and state positions in Mississippi; was a U.S. senator from Mississippi (Republican), 1875-1881, and became the first African American to serve a full term; was a staunch defender of black, Chinese, and American Indian rights; worked with U.S. register of treasury, 1881-1889, 1895-1898; worked as recorder of deeds, District of Columbia, 1889-1895.

Bunche, Ralph (1904-1971): Diplomat; head of the department of political science, Howard University, 1928-

1932; during World War II served as senior social analyst for the Office of the Coordinator of Information in African and Far Eastern Affairs and with the African section of the Office of Strategic Services; recognized as a colonial expert when he joined the State Department in 1944; served as delegate or adviser to nine international conferences in four years; was chief assistant on the United Nations Palestine Commission; became first African American to receive the Nobel Peace Prize in 1950, for his role in the Arab-Israeli cease-fire of 1948-1949; served as U.N. undersecretary of Special Political Affairs, 1957-1967, and undersecretary general of the United Nations, 1968-1971.

Carmichael, Stokely (1941-1998): Political activist; born in Trinidad; after attending Howard University, he became an accomplished organizer for the Student Nonviolent Coordinating Committee (SNCC) of which he was elected chair in 1966; popularized the controversial phrase "black power" as well as radical policies, which led to his expulsion from SNCC in 1968; joined the Black Panther Party in 1968, but resigned the following year and moved to Guinea, Africa; since the 1970's consistently supported Pan-Africanism; changed his name in 1978 to Kwame Toure, in honor of African leaders Sékou Touré and Kwame Nkrumah.

Chavis, Benjamin (1948-): Civil rights activist; after training as a theologian, became a civil rights organizer for the Southern Christian Leadership Conference and the United Church of Christ; indicted in 1971 as one of the Wilmington Ten for the firebombing of a store in Wilmington, Delaware; convicted but granted parole, his conviction was reversed in 1980; appointed executive director of the Commission for Racial Justice in 1985; served as executive director of the National Association for the Advancement of Colored People, 1993-1994, a position from which he was forced to resign because of a financial scandal; served as national director of the 1995 Million Man March.

Chisholm, Shirley (1924-): Politician; after an early career in child care and education, elected New York State assemblywoman in 1964; served as U.S. representative (Democrat), 1969-1983, becoming the first African American woman in Congress; published her autobiography, *Unbossed and Unbought* (1970); cofounded the National Political Congress of Black Women.

Cleaver, Eldridge (1935-1998): Civil rights activist; after serving a prison sentence from 1958 to 1966, joined the Black Panther Party and became one of the most vocal proponents of the doctrine of black power; his *Soul on Ice* (1968) became one of the most powerful statements of the movement; after involvement in a

1968 shooting, fled to Algeria; returned to the United States in 1975.

Cone, James (1938-): Theologian; faculty member at Union Theological Seminary from 1969; provided systematic case for divine support of the black liberation struggle in the United States and elsewhere; wrote many books, including *Black Theology and Black Power* (1969), *For My People: Black Theology and the Black Church* (1984), and *Martin and Malcolm and America: A Dream or a Nightmare?* (1991).

Cosby, Bill (1937-): Actor, comedian; by the mid-1960's, was playing top nightclubs with his comedy routine and regularly appearing on television; became first African American star of prime time television with three-time Emmy-winning role in *I Spy* (1965-1968); throughout the 1970's appeared in films and television series and in Las Vegas, Reno, and Tahoe nightclubs; *The Cosby Show* (1985-1992) presented upper-middle-class black family life to mainstream American audiences; earned five Grammy Awards; wrote *Fatherhood* (1986) and *Time Flies* (1987).

Crummell, Alexander (1819-1898): Christian minister, author; born in New York City; after earning a degree at Queens College, Cambridge, in England, served as professor of mental and moral science at the College of Liberia, 1853-1873; was minister of St. Luke's Protestant Episcopal Church in Washington, D.C., 1876-1898; helped found the American Negro Academy in 1897; published many books, including *Future of Africa* (1862) and *Africa and America* (1892).

Davis, Angela (1944-): Political activist, scholar; after an extensive education at Brandeis University, the Sorbonne, and the University of Frankfurt, took a teaching job at the University of California, Los Angeles; joined the Communist Party in 1969; became involved with the Black Panther Party and was implicated in a courtroom shooting in 1970; went underground but eventually was arrested; acquitted of all charges in 1972; cochair of the National Alliance against Racism and Political Repression; wrote *If They Come in the Morning* (1971), *Women, Race, and Class* (1983), and *Women, Culture, and Politics* (1989).

Delany, Martin Robison (1812-1885): Doctor, author, abolitionist; born in West Virginia but fled north when it was learned that he could read; edited *The Mystery* and *The North Star* in support of the antislavery movement; disappointed with treatment of blacks in the United States, he recommended founding an African American colony in Africa or South America; commissioned first black major in the U.S. Army in 1863; published *Principal of Ethnology: The Origin of Races and Color* (1879).

Douglass, Frederick (c. 1817-1895): Abolitionist; fled slavery in 1838; brilliant orator who became famous as an agent of the Massachusetts Anti-Slavery Society in the 1840's; published *Narrative of the Life of Frederick Douglass* (1845); lectured in England and Ireland, 1845-1847, earning enough money to purchase his freedom; founded and served as coeditor of *The North Star*, 1847-1860 (*Frederick Douglass's Paper* from 1851); opposed radical abolitionism of W. L. Garrison and John Brown; was U.S. marshal for District of Columbia, 1877-1881; was recorder of deeds, District of Columbia, 1881-1886; served as U.S. minister to Haiti, 1889-1891.

Du Bois, W. E. B. (1868-1963): Civil rights activist, scholar, author; leader of the Niagara Movement, 1905-1909; helped found the National Association for the Advancement of Colored People (NAACP), 1909; acted as director of publications for the NAACP and editor of *The Crisis*, 1909-1934; was a professor of sociology at Atlanta University, 1932-1944; served as head of special research department of the NAACP, 1944-1948; dissatisfied with the pace of racial change, joined the Communist Party and emigrated to Africa in 1961 to become editor in chief of the Pan-Africanist *Encyclopedia Africana*, sponsored by Ghanaian president Kwame Nkrumah; wrote numerous books, including *The Souls of Black Folk* (1903), *The Negro* (1915), *The Gift of Black Folk* (1924), *Color and Democracy* (1945), *The World and Africa* (1947), and the *Black Flame* trilogy (1957-1961).

Evers, Medgar (1925-1963): Civil rights activist; appointed Mississippi field secretary of the National Association for the Advancement of Colored People, 1954; actively fought for enforcement of school integration and advocated the right of blacks to vote and the boycotting of merchants who discriminated against African Americans; when murdered in 1963 became one of the first martyrs of the Civil Rights movement.

Farmer, James (1920-): Civil rights leader; organizer of the Congress of Racial Equality (CORE), 1942, the first major nonviolent protest organization; staged the first successful sit-in, at a Chicago restaurant in 1943; program director of the National Association for the Advancement of Colored People, 1959-1961; introduced the tactic of the Freedom Ride in 1961 to test principles of desegregation; left CORE in 1966; appointed assistant secretary of Health, Education, and Welfare in 1969; became associate director of the Coalition of American Public Employees in 1976.

Farrakhan, Louis (1933-): Minister; born Louis Eugene Walcott; joined the Nation of Islam in the 1950's; denounced Malcolm X (following his split with Elijah Muhammad) and succeeded him as leader of the Harlem mosque; left Nation of Islam when it began to accept whites in the mid-1970's, founding a rival organization, later known by the same name;

supported Jesse Jackson in the 1984 presidential campaign, marking a turning point in Black Muslim political involvement; organized 1995 Million Man March.

Father Divine (1879-1965): Religious leader; probably born George Baker; early life mysterious; joined various Christian sects before returning to native Georgia around 1910 to proclaim himself a "divine messenger"; driven from Georgia, settled in New York City in 1915, where he fed the poor and homeless and established a communitarian religious group based on racial equality; his Peace Mission movement spread in the 1930's and 1940's, becoming a cult in which Father Divine was worshiped as God incarnate on earth.

Forten, James (1766-1842): Abolitionist, entrepreneur; born of free parents in Philadelphia, served aboard a privateer during the American Revolution; captured and held prisoner for seven months; while in England became acquainted with abolitionist philosophy; by 1798 owned a prosperous maritime company; became active in the abolitionist movement in the 1830's, including membership in the American Anti-Slavery Society; helped raise funds for William Lloyd Garrison's newspaper *The Liberator*; founded the American Moral Reform Society.

Fortune, T. Thomas (1856-1928): Journalist, editor; worked in various positions for the *New York Sun* from 1878; founded the *New York Age* (1883), the leading black journal of opinion in the United States; crusaded against school segregation; joined Booker T. Washington in organizing the National Negro Business League in 1900; coined the term "Afro-American" as a substitute for "Negro" in the New York press.

Garvey, Marcus (1887-1940): Black nationalist leader; Jamaican-born founder of the Universal Negro Improvement Association (UNIA) in 1914; came to United States in 1916, founding branches of the UNIA in northern ghettos; at the UNIA's first convention in New York City in 1920, outlined plan for the establishment of an African nation-state for American blacks; preached racial pride through civil rights and economic self-sufficiency; convicted of fraud in 1925; sentence commuted by President Calvin Coolidge and deported to Jamaica in 1927, where he continued to be active in progressive politics.

Gordy, Berry, Jr. (1929-   ): Songwriter, producer; served with U.S. Army in Korea; after a number of failed or unsatisfying jobs in Detroit, Michigan, began writing hit songs with his sister Gwen and Billy Davis; formed Motown Record Corporation and a number of related businesses in 1959; by the mid-1960's had brought black soul music to mainstream American audiences with highly polished performances by artists such as the Supremes, Smokey Robinson, the Four Tops, the Marvelettes, Marvin Gaye, the Jackson Five,

Lionel Richie, and Stevie Wonder; inducted into the Rock and Roll Hall of Fame in 1988.

Grace, Charles Emmanuel "Sweet Daddy" (1881-1960): Religious leader; born Marcelino Manoel de Graca in the Cape Verde Islands; established the United House of Prayer for All People (c. 1921), with ministry style rooted in faith healing and speaking in tongues; products such as "Daddy Grace" coffee, tea, and creams were believed to heal; by 1960, his church had some 25,000 adherents in 375 congregations.

Graves, Earl (1935-   ): Publisher, editor; officer, U.S. Army Green Berets, 1957-1960; administrative assistant to Robert F. Kennedy, 1964-1968; launched *Black Enterprise* (1970) to provide African Americans with practical help for succeeding in business; by the late 1990's, *Black Enterprise* had a subscription base of more than 300,000; wrote *How to Succeed in Business Without Being White* (1997).

Haley, Alex (1921-1992): Journalist, author; chief journalist for the U.S. Coast Guard, 1952-1959; interviewed Malcolm X for *Playboy*, which led to his first book, *The Autobiography of Malcolm X* (1965); spent a dozen years researching family history, leading to publication of the novel *Roots* (1976), based on the life of a Mandingo youth named Kunta Kinte; the novel led to a twelve-hour television series, hundreds of interviews and articles, instructional packets and tapes, and sparked intense interest in African American genealogy and history.

Hamer, Fannie Lou (1917-1977): Civil rights activist; after forty years of work on the same plantation, lost her job when she tried to vote; began working with the Student Nonviolent Coordinating Committee to register black voters in 1962; helped form the Mississippi Freedom Democratic Party and spoke eloquently in favor of seating black delegates to the Democratic National Convention in 1964; became one of the first delegates to the Democratic convention in 1968; founded Freedom Farms Corporation, 1969; toured and spoke widely on behalf of civil rights legislation.

Hill, Anita (1956-   ): Professor of law; a relatively unknown law professor at the University of Oklahoma when she gained national attention during Senate confirmation hearings for U.S. Supreme Court justice nominee Clarence Thomas in 1991; charged that she had been sexually harassed when working for Thomas at the Equal Employment Opportunities Commission in the early 1980's; withstood attempts by some lawmakers to have the University of Oklahoma Law School fire her; spoke widely around the country throughout the 1990's in favor of civil rights and women's rights.

Hooks, Benjamin (1925-   ): Lawyer, preacher, civil rights leader; first African American to serve as judge in criminal court in Shelby County, Tennessee; served as executive director of the National Association for the Advancement of Colored People, 1977-1992, where he vigorously promoted integration, pro-African foreign policy, and employment legislation.

Hughes, Langston (1902-1967): Writer; after dropping out of Columbia University, wrote poetry and worked as a cabin boy on a freighter; major figure in the 1920's Harlem Renaissance; "The Negro Writer and the Racial Mountain" (1926) established an early ethic of black pride; wrote in many fields, including poetry (*The Weary Blues*, 1926; *Fine Clothes to the Jew*, 1927; *Shakespeare in Harlem*, 1942; *Montage of a Dream Deferred*, 1951); librettos (*Street Scene*, 1947); plays (*Mulatto*, 1935); and autobiography (*The Big Sea*, 1940; *I Wonder as I Wander*, 1956).

Innis, Roy (1934-   ): Civil rights leader; joined Congress of Racial Equality (CORE) in 1963, becoming national director in 1968; founded Harlem Commonwealth Council designed to promote black businesses; controversy over recruitment of black Vietnam veterans for the civil war in Angola and misappropriation of funds led to important defections from CORE, which became largely inactive in the 1980's.

Jackson, Jesse (1941-   ): Civil rights activist, Baptist minister; joined the Southern Christian Leadership Conference (SCLC) in 1965; served as executive director of SCLC's Operation Breadbasket, 1967-1971; founded Operation PUSH (People United to Save Humanity) in 1971; his PUSH-EXCEL program for encouraging young students to improve academically received funding from the administration of U.S. president Jimmy Carter, 1977-1981; ran for the Democratic nomination for president in 1984 and 1988; finished a strong second to Michael Dukakis in 1988, demonstrating the viability of an African American candidate; continued to press for child care, health care reform, housing reform, and statehood for the District of Columbia.

Johnson, Jack (1878-1946): Boxer; first black heavyweight champion, 1908-1915; became the center of racial controversy as the public called for Jim Jeffries, the white former champion, to come out of retirement; Johnson defeated Jeffries in 1910.

Johnson, James Weldon (1871-1938): Poet, diplomat, civil rights leader; as a young man known principally as a lyricist for popular songs, including "Lift Every Voice and Sing" (1899); served as U.S. consul in Puerto Cabello, Venezuela, 1906-1909, and Corinto, Nicaragua, 1909-1912; was executive secretary of the National Association for the Advancement of Colored People, 1920-1930; wrote many books, including *The Autobiography of an Ex-Colored Man* (1912), *The Book of American Negro Poetry* (1922), *God's Trombones* (1927), and *Negro Americans, What Now* (1934).

Johnson, John H. (1918-   ): Publisher; addressed the need for mainstream black publications with the establishment of the *Negro Digest* (1942) and *Ebony* (1945); member of advisory council of Harvard Graduate School of Business; director for the Chamber of Commerce of the United States.

Jordan, Vernon (1935-   ): Lawyer, civil rights leader; field secretary for the Georgia Branch of the National Association for the Advancement of Colored People, 1962-1964; director of the Voter Education Project of the Southern Regional Council, 1964-1968; appointed executive director of the United Negro College Fund, 1970-1972; served as executive director of the National Urban League, 1972-1981; became political confidante of President Bill Clinton in 1992.

King, Martin Luther, Jr. (1929-1968): Civil rights activist, Baptist minister; received doctorate from Crozer Theological Seminary, 1955; accepted pastorate of the Dexter Avenue Baptist Church in Montgomery, Alabama, in 1956; organized the Montgomery bus boycott in 1956; founded the Southern Christian Leadership Conference, serving as first president in 1957; was copastor of Ebenezer Baptist Church, Atlanta, 1960-1968; arrested for protesting segregation and unfair hiring practices in Birmingham, Alabama, in 1963, leading to his classic "Letter from a Birmingham Jail"; delivered his "I Have a Dream" speech at the historic March on Washington in 1963; *Time* Man of the Year in 1963; awarded Nobel Peace Prize in 1964; began to speak out forcefully against the Vietnam War and urban poverty, leading many black leaders to question his tactics in achieving full civil rights; assassinated in Memphis, Tennessee, in 1968; consistently promoted a policy of nonviolent protest.

Lee, Spike (1957-   ): Filmmaker; while attending New York University's Institute of Film and Television, won the Student Award presented by the Academy of Motion Picture Arts and Sciences for *Joe's Bed-Sty Barbershop: We Cut Heads* (1982); his controversial films, highlighting past and present struggles of African Americans in a land of alien values, include *She's Gotta Have It* (1986), *Do the Right Thing* (1989), *Mo' Better Blues* (1990), *Malcolm X* (1992), and *He Got Game* (1998).

Locke, Alain (1886-1954): Philosopher, writer; after study at Harvard University, Oxford University, and the University of Berlin, served on faculty at Howard University, 1912-1953; celebrated black cultural contributions in works such as *The New Negro: An Interpretation* (1925) and a special issue of the journal *Survey Graphic*, which announced the arrival of a "Harlem Renaissance" and published work by Langston Hughes, Zora Neale Hurston, and W. E. B. Du Bois; also wrote or edited *Race Contacts and Inter-Racial Relations* (1916), *Opportunity* (an annual review of the state of black writing), *Negro Art: Past and Present* (1936), and *The Negro and His Music* (1940).

Lowery, Joseph E. (1924-   ): Pastor, civil rights leader; pastor of the Warren Street Church in Birmingham, Alabama, 1952-1961; cofounder of the Southern Negro Leaders Conference (later the Southern Christian Leadership Conference, SCLC) in 1957, serving as its first vice president under Martin Luther King, Jr.; became president of the SCLC in 1977; pastor of Cascade United Methodist Church in Atlanta from 1986.

McKissick, Floyd (1922-1991): Lawyer, civil rights leader; sued the University of North Carolina at Chapel Hill for admission to their law school and became the first African American to earn a degree there; head of Congress on Racial Equality, 1966-1968; between 1968 and 1980 worked unsuccessfully to establish a new and self-sufficient community in Warren County, North Carolina, known as Soul City.

Malcolm X (1925-1965): Black nationalist; born Malcolm Little, to a family committed to Marcus Garvey's United Negro Improvement Association; after his father's murder, left school for New York, where he was convicted of burglary; converted to Nation of Islam while in prison; a brilliant speaker, he began making provocative, anti-white statements, for which he was expelled from the Nation of Islam by Elijah Muhammad; formed Organization of Afro-American Unity and Muslim Mosque Inc. in 1964; after pilgrimage to Mecca, converted to orthodox Islam, took the name El-Hajj Malik El-Shabazz, and moderated his views; shot to death by Black Muslims; author (with Alex Haley) of *The Autobiography of Malcolm X* (1965).

Marshall, Thurgood (1908-1993): Lawyer, judge, civil rights activist; served as chief legal counsel for the National Association for the Advancement of Colored People, 1938-1961; played key role in *Brown v. Board of Education* case (1954), in which the U.S. Supreme Court overturned the "separate but equal" doctrine in public education; won twenty-nine of the thirty-two cases he argued before the Supreme Court; became federal circuit judge, 1961-1967; appointed first African American associate justice of the U.S. Supreme Court, 1967-1991.

Meredith, James (1933-   ): Civil rights activist; became first African American to attend the University of Mississippi in 1962, generating riots and the stationing of federal troops on the campus; led march to encourage black voter registration in 1966, shot by sniper, but recovered; wrote *Three Years in Mississippi* (1966).

Morrison, Toni (1931-   ): Writer; born Chloe Anthony Wofford; incorporated African and African American folklore, legend, and mythology into her novels; works contain many autobiographical references; *Beloved* (1987), which examines the brutality of American slavery, won the Pulitzer Prize in fiction in 1988 and became a motion picture in 1998; won Nobel Prize in Literature in 1993; also wrote *The Bluest Eye* (1970), *Sula* (1974), *Song of Solomon* (1977), *Tar Baby* (1981), *Jazz* (1992), and *Paradise* (1998).

Muhammad, Elijah (1897-1975): Religious leader and black nationalist; born Elijah Poole to a former slave; became chief assistant to W. D. Fard, founder of the Lost-Found Nation of Islam, in 1930; upon Fard's disappearance in 1934, succeeded to leadership of the Nation of Islam; preached racial segregation, black integrity, and the need for economic independence from whites; support for Japan in World War II and the conviction of three members of the Nation of Islam for the assassination of Malcolm X led to unfavorable press coverage, but the movement continued to grow, especially among the underemployed of the major cities.he major cities.

Newton, Huey P. (1942-1989): Black activist; cofounder, with Bobby Seale, of the Black Panther Party for Self-Defense in 1966, which became a major force in California politics; convicted of manslaughter in the 1967 killing of an Oakland police officer, but the conviction was later overturned; helped elect Lionel Wilson as first black mayor of Oakland in 1977; frequently in legal trouble throughout the 1970's and 1980's; killed by a drug dealer.

Owens, Jesse (1913-1980): Track and field athlete; one of the first great all-around track and field athletes, earned four gold medals in the 1936 Berlin Olympics (100- and 200-meter races, 400-meter relay, broad jump); became internationally famous when German leader Adolf Hitler refused for racial reasons to present the medals; traveled and spoke widely on the value of sport in breaking down racial barriers.

Parks, Rosa Louise McCauley (1913-   ): Civil rights activist; secretary of the Montgomery, Alabama, chapter of the National Association for the Advancement of Colored People in the 1950's; arrested and fined for refusing to give up her seat to a white person, sparking a 382-day citywide bus boycott aimed at desegregating public transportation; harassment led Parks and her family to move to Detroit, Michigan, where she worked in the office of Congressman John Conyers and continued to campaign for civil rights.

Patterson, Frederick D. (1901-1988): Educator; faculty member, and later president of, Tuskegee Institute from 1928; chair of the R. R. Moton Memorial Institute; organized United Negro College Fund in 1944 to aid historically black colleges and universities.

Payne, Daniel Alexander (1811-1893): Educator, bishop; born to free parents, opened a school for blacks in Charleston, South Carolina, in 1829; after his school was closed by an act of the South Carolina legislature, traveled north to study, delivering powerful abolitionist speeches throughout the 1840's and 1850's; elected bishop of the African Methodist Episcopal Church in 1852; bought Wilberforce University from the Methodist Episcopal Church in 1863 and devoted the rest of his life to developing the university and overseeing missionary endeavors; wrote *Recollections of Seventy Years* (1888) and *History of the African Methodist Episcopal Church* (1891).

Powell, Adam Clayton, Jr. (1908-1972): Politician; instrumental in securing better treatment for African Americans in Harlem during the Depression (1930's); succeeded his father as pastor of the Abyssinian Baptist Church in 1936; served in various New York posts until 1944 when he was elected to the U.S. House of Representatives, 1945-1967, 1969-1971; sponsored more than fifty pieces of social legislation, many aimed at ending discrimination against minorities; became chairman of House Committee on Education and Labor in 1960; censured in the House and unseated in 1967 for misuse of public funds but readmitted the following year.

Powell, Colin (1937-   ): Military leader; served two tours of duty in Vietnam during the 1960's; military assistant to the secretary of defense in 1983; national security adviser to President Ronald Reagan, 1987-1989; served as chairman of the joint chiefs of staff, 1989-1993, from which position he gained international recognition for his role in conducting the Persian Gulf War (1991); popularity and vocal support for personal responsibility made him an attractive political candidate; addressed the 1996 Republican National Convention in San Diego, heightening rumors that he might one day run for high office.

Robeson, Paul (1898-1976): Singer, actor; son of a runaway slave; after earning a law degree from Columbia University, was discovered by playwright Eugene O'Neill and became a successful stage actor in the 1920's; performance in *Emperor Jones* (1923) led to a successful singing career, including 1925 concert debut of all-African-American music; active in national and international civil and human rights campaigns, he spoke out vigorously for independence for African colonies; trips to the Soviet Union and other association with Communists led to the revocation of his passport in 1950 and a decline in his career; regained passport after an eight-year legal battle in 1958 and moved to London, where he lived until 1963; wrote *Here I Stand* (1958).

Robinson, Jackie (1919-1972): Baseball player; after a stellar career at the University of California, Los Angeles, left in his junior year to play professional football for the Los Angeles Bulldogs, and then to serve as a lieutenant in the U.S. Army during World War II; played baseball with the Kansas City Monarchs of the Negro American League in 1945; became the first black player in modern major league baseball in 1947, beginning a ten-year career with the Brooklyn Dodgers; responded to much public hostility with grace and outstanding play, paving the way for expansion of opportunities for black athletes; inducted into Baseball Hall of Fame in 1962.

Rustin, Bayard (1910-1987): Civil rights leader; organizer of the Young Communist League, 1936-1941; worked with James Farmer in the Chicago Committee of Racial Equality, which developed into the Congress of Racial Equality; was a founding member of the Southern Christian Leadership Conference, 1963; served as organizational coordinator of the 1963 March on Washington; was executive director of the A. Philip Randolph Institute, 1964-1979; founded Organization for Black Americans to Support Israel in 1975; consistent supporter of nonviolent change.

Scott, Dred (1795-1858): Slave, abolitionist; attempted to escape and buy freedom; with help from attorneys, sued for his freedom on the grounds that he had accompanied his master into the free state of Illinois; U.S. Supreme Court ruled in 1857 that Scott, as a slave, was not a legal citizen and therefore had no standing before the courts; freed by owner shortly before his death.

Seale, Bobby (1936-   ): Black activist; cofounder, with Huey P. Newton, of the Black Panther Party for Self-Defense in 1966; mistrial declared in his 1971 trial for the kidnapping and killing of a suspected police informant; disenchanted with revolutionary politics, left the Panthers in 1974; wrote *Seize the Time: The Story of the Black Panther Party* (1970) and *A Lonely Rage: The Autobiography of Bobby Seale* (1978).

Sharpton, Al (1954-   ): Pentecostal minister, social activist; after gaining prominence for his preaching in Brooklyn, became active in the Civil Rights movement; appointed youth director of Jesse Jackson's Operation Breadbasket; briefly served as a bodyguard for singer James Brown and became involved with fight promoter Don King; founded the National Youth Movement (later the United African Movement) in 1971; involved with many high-profile racial incidents in New York City, including the Bernhard Goetz murder trial in 1984, the Howard Beach killing in 1986, the Tawana Brawley affair in 1987, and the Bensonhurst killing in 1989; controversial figure whose motives have been questioned.

Truth, Sojourner (c. 1797-1883): Abolitionist; born Isabella Baumfree, she was freed by the New York State Emancipation Act in 1827; preached and lectured widely to abolitionist audiences, taking the name Sojourner Truth in 1843; raised money to aid runaway slaves and soldiers during the Civil War; served as councilor with the National Freedmen's Relief Association, 1864; dictated *The Narrative of Sojourner Truth* (1850).

Tubman, Harriet (c. 1820-1913): Civil rights activist; born Araminta Ross, escaped slavery in 1848; rescued more than three hundred slaves before the Civil War in nineteen forays along the Underground Railroad; aided John Brown in recruiting soldiers for his raid on Harper's Ferry, 1858; spoke widely on emancipation and women's rights after 1860; served as nurse and spy for the Union army during the Civil War; buried with military honors.

Turner, Henry McNeal (1834-1915): Religious leader; born to free parents; tutored by lawyers for whom he worked as a janitor; became a preacher in the Methodist Episcopal Church South, 1853; switched affiliation and preached for African Methodist Episcopal (AME) churches in Baltimore, Maryland, and Washington, D.C., 1858-1863; was chaplain of First U.S. Colored Troops, 1863; served as Georgia state representative, 1868-1869, 1870; elected AME bishop in 1880; supported voting rights for blacks and advocated a return to Africa when the Civil Rights Act was overturned by the Supreme Court in 1883; proclaimed that "God is a Negro"; forerunner of modern black theology.

Walker, Alice (1944-   ): Writer; poet; her works deal principally with the experience of black women living in a racist and sexist society; early books were critically acclaimed, though she did not become widely popular until she published her third novel, *The Color Purple* (1982), which won a Pulitzer Prize in fiction and was adapted to film in 1985; champion of the works of Zora Neale Hurston; published in several genres, including poetry: *Once* (1968) and *Revolutionary Petunias and Other Poems* (1973); novels: *The Third Life of Grange Copeland* (1970), *Meridian* (1976), and *Possessing the Secret of Joy* (1992); short stories: "In Love and Trouble" (1973) and "You Can't Keep a Good Woman Down" (1976); and criticism: *A Zora Neale Hurston Reader* (1980).

Washington, Booker T. (1856-1915): Educator, political activist; born a slave, became committed to the idea that education would raise African Americans to equality; taught American Indians at Hampton Institute, 1879-1881; founded Tuskegee Normal and Industrial Institute, 1881, and served as its president; founded National Negro Business League, 1900; advised Presidents William Howard Taft and Theodore Roosevelt on racial issues; promoted what is sometimes called the "Atlanta Compromise," accepting segregation of African Americans in return for economic opportunities; his conservative racial views appealed to many white Americans who feared more radical change; wrote *Up from Slavery* (1901); opposed by W. E. B. Du Bois.

Wells-Barnett, Ida B. (1862-1931): Editor; editor and part owner of the black newspaper *Memphis Free Speech* from 1889; campaigned vigorously against lynching, leading to a mob attack on the newspaper's offices; with Frederick Douglass and Ferdinand L. Barnett, wrote "The Reason Why the Colored American Is Not in the World's Columbian Exposition" (1893); published the antilynching pamphlet, "Red Record" (1895); defended W. E. B. Du Bois's criticism of Booker T. Washington in *The Souls of Black Folk*; helped found the National Association for the Advancement of Colored People, 1909.

Wilkins, Roy (1901-1981): Journalist, civil rights leader; on the staff of the Kansas City *Call*, 1923-1931; served as assistant executive secretary of the National Association for the Advancement of Colored People (NAACP), 1931-1955; succeeded W. E. B. Du Bois as editor of *The Crisis*, 1934-1949; was executive secretary of the NAACP, 1955-1964; served as executive director of the NAACP, 1965-1977; chairman of the Leadership Conference on Civil Rights.

Woodson, Carter (1875-1950): Scholar; known as the "Father of Modern Black History"; formed the Association for the Study of Negro Life and History (later the Association for the Study of Afro-American Life and History), 1915, which established the *Journal of Negro History* (1916); founded Associated Publishers, 1920, and Negro History Bulletin, 1921; created Negro History Week (later Black History Month); wrote many books, including *The Education of the Negro Prior to 1861* (1915); *The Negro in Our History* (1922), *The Miseducation of the Negro* (1933), and *African Heroes and Heroines* (1939).

Wright, Richard (1908-1960): Novelist; member of the Communist Party, 1933-1944; used personal experience from his Mississippi youth to dramatize the brutal effects of racism in books such as *Uncle Tom's Children* (Best Work of Fiction by a Works Progress Administration writer, 1938), *Native Son* (1940), and the largely autobiographical *Black Boy* (1945); moved to Paris in 1946; there continued writing, including *The Outsider* (1953), *Black Power* (1954), *White Man Listen* (1957), and *Eight Men* (1961); *American Hunger* (1977) was a continuation of his autobiography.

Young, Andrew (1932-   ): Civil rights activist, politician, diplomat; aide and confidant of Martin Luther King, Jr., in the early 1960's; was executive vice president of the Southern Christian Leadership Conference, 1967; served as Georgia state representative, 1973-1977; was U.S. ambassador to the United Nations, 1977-1979; served as mayor of Atlanta, 1981-1989; chair of the Atlanta Committee for the Olympic Games.

Young, Whitney (1921-1971): Educator, civil rights leader; executive director of the St. Paul chapter of the Minnesota Urban League, 1950-1954; was dean of Atlanta University School of Social Work, 1954-1961; served as executive director of National Urban League, 1961-1971; called for a "domestic Marshall Plan" to end black poverty, and helped President Lyndon B. Johnson craft his War on Poverty; received Medal of Freedom in 1969; wrote *To Be Equal* (1964) and *Beyond Racism* (1969).

Hispanic Americans

Anaya, Rudolfo (1937-): Writer; earned degrees at the University of New Mexico (1963, 1968, 1972); taught in public schools, 1963-1970; on faculty, University of New Mexico, since 1974; wrote of the spirituality of the Chicano tradition in novels such as *Bless Me, Ultima* (1972), *Heart of Aztlan* (1976), and *Tortuga* (1979).

Avila, Joaquín (1948-): Lawyer; Alaska supreme court clerk, 1973-1974; staff attorney, Mexican American Legal Defense and Education Fund (MALDEF), San Francisco, 1974-1976; associate counsel, MALDEF, Texas, 1976-1982; largely responsible for extension of the Voting Rights Act of 1982; served as president, MALDEF, 1982-1985.

Baca Zinn, Maxine (1942-): Sociologist; professor of sociology, University of Michigan at Flint, 1975-1987; research professor in residence, Memphis State University in Memphis, 1987; senior research associate, Julian Samora Research Institute, 1990; professor of sociology, University of Michigan at East Lansing, since 1990; through sociological research on Latino families and Mexican American women, became a pioneer of Chicana feminism in the mid-1970's.

Badillo, Herman (1929-): Born in Puerto Rico; sent to United States as a boy in 1940; gained national recognition during unsuccessful race for mayor of New York City; served as U.S. representative (Democrat) from New York, 1971-1978; first Puerto Rican elected as a voting member of Congress; appointed deputy mayor of New York City in 1978.

Cavazos, Lauro (1927-): Educator, government official; dean of Tufts University School of Medicine; president of Texas Tech University; appointed secretary of education by President Bush, 1988-1990, the first Hispanic named to the cabinet; instrumental in the creation of the President's Council on Educational Excellence for Hispanic Americans.

Chacón, Eusebio (1869-1948): Writer; earned law degree from Notre Dame; wrote passionately of Hispanic culture in works such as *El hijo de la tempestad* (son of the storm, 1892) and *Tras la tormenta la calma* (the calm after the storm, 1892).

Chávez, César (1927-1993): Labor organizer; after his parents lost their farm during the Depression (1930's), raised as a migrant worker; general director, Community Service Organization, 1958-1962; established the National Farm Workers Association, 1962, which merged with another organization to become the United Farm Workers Organizing Committee, 1966, later the United Farm Workers of America; led strikes and boycotts from 1965 to improve wages and working conditions for migrant workers; committed to nonviolent tactics.

Chávez, Dennis (1888-1962): Politician; born in New Mexico; largely self-educated; earned law degree at Georgetown University in 1920; served as U.S. representative (Democrat), 1933-1935; appointed to the U.S. Senate in 1936, then elected, 1937-1962; first Hispanic U.S. senator; opposed U.S. entry into World War II; drafted a bill creating the Fair Employment Practices Commission.

Cisneros, Henry (1947-): Politician; after earning graduate degrees from Harvard University and George Washington University, joined faculty of University of Texas at San Antonio, 1974; was a member of San Antonio City Council, 1975-1981, emphasizing cooperation between white and Latino residents; served as mayor of San Antonio, 1981-1989, becoming the first Hispanic mayor of a major U.S. city; was secretary of Housing and Urban Development, 1993-1996; indicted for conspiracy and obstruction of justice in 1997.

Fernández, Ricardo (1940-): Educator; born in Puerto Rico; earned advanced degrees at Princeton University; on faculty at University of Wisconsin, 1973-1990; president, Lehman College of the City University of New York since 1990; president of the board of directors, Multicultural Training and Advocacy since 1986; was president, National Association for Bilingual Education, 1980-1981; produced pioneering reports on Hispanic education.

García, Héctor Pérez (1914-1996): Doctor, civil rights activist; earned medical degree at University of Texas in 1940; founder of the American GI Forum, 1948; founder of Political Association of Spanish Speaking Organizations; alternative ambassador to the United Nations in 1964; commissioner, U.S. Commission on Civil Rights in 1968; active in many human and civil rights organizations, including League of United Latin American Citizens, Texas Advisory Committee to the U.S. Commission on Civil Rights, and Advisory Council to Veterans Administration.

Gómez-Quiñones, Juan (1942-): Poet, historian, civil rights activist; born in Mexico; professor of history, University of California, Los Angeles (UCLA), 1969; director of Chicano Studies Research Center, UCLA; cofounder, United Mexican American Students; cofounder/director, Chicano Legal Defense.

González, Henry Barbosa (1916-): Politician; born in San Antonio, Texas, to Mexican parents; earned law degree at St. Mary's University in 1943; was a member, San Antonio City Council, 1953-1956; elected to the Texas state senate in 1956, becoming the first Mexican American state senator in 110 years; served as U.S. representative from Texas beginning 1961; vigorous supporter of civil rights campaigns of Presidents John F. Kennedy and Lyndon B. Johnson in the 1960's.

Gonzáles, Rodolfo "Corky" (1928-): Social activist; founded the Crusade for Justice in 1965 in Denver, providing medical and legal aid to Mexican Americans; proposed an independent Mexican American nation, or independent communities where Mexican Americans could control their own affairs; his poem "I Am Joaquin" (1967) became a symbol of the emerging Chicano movement.

Gutiérrez, José Ángel (1944-): Educator, civil rights activist; founder of La Raza Unida Party, 1970; cofounder of Mexican American Unity Council, 1968; cofounder of Mexican American Youth Organization, 1967; served as associate professor, Western Oregon State College, 1982-1986; was executive director, Greater Dallas Legal and Community Development Foundation, 1986; administrative law judge, city of Dallas, Texas, 1990.

Hernández, Antonia (1948-): Lawyer; born in Coahuila, Mexico; earned law degree at University of California, Los Angeles, in 1974; staff counsel to U.S. Senate Judiciary Committee, 1978-1981; served as staff attorney, Mexican American Legal Defense and Education Fund (MALDEF), Washington, D.C., 1981-1983; employment litigation director, MALDEF, Los Angeles, 1983-1985; president and general counsel, MALDEF, since 1985.

Hidalgo, Hilda (1928-): Educator, social activist; director, Group Work and Tutorial Division of the Child Service Association, Newark, New Jersey, 1964; founding member, Puerto Rican Congress of New Jersey, 1975; professor of public administration and social work, Rutgers University, 1977-1992; wrote *Rehabilitation in the 80's: Understanding the Hispanic Disabled* (1982); served on editorial boards for *Journal of Gay and Lesbian Psychotherapy, Affilia: The Journal of Women and Social Work*, and *Society and Culture*.

Huerta, Dolores (1930-): Labor leader; lobbyist for the Community Service Organization (CSO) in the late 1950's and early 1960's; cofounder of the National Farmworkers of America (NFWA), 1962, which later became the United Farm Workers of America (UFA); held many offices in the NFWA and UFA; helped lead the strike against California grape growers, 1965-1970, negotiating the contracts that led to a settlement; UFA activism helped lead to the passage of the Agricultural Labor Relations Act in 1975, guaranteeing the right of California farmworkers to deal with matters of union representation.

Magón, Ricardo Flores (1873-1922): Politician, journalist; founded the Partido Liberal Mexicano (PLM); attempted to invade Mexico from Texas, 1891-1892; fled to Laredo, Texas, 1904; his newspaper *Regeneracion* advocated the overthrow of Porfirio Díaz in Mexico and labor reform in the United States; jailed for violating neutrality laws, 1907-1910; moved to Los Angeles and launched armed invasion of Baja California upon the outbreak of revolution in Mexico, 1910; imprisoned for espionage, 1918-1922.

Martínez, Vilma (1943-): Lawyer, civil rights leader; counsel with the Legal Defense and Educational Fund of the National Association for the Advancement of Colored People, 1967-1970; equal employment opportunity counselor, New York State Division of Human Rights, 1970-1971; general counsel and president of Mexican American Legal Defense and Education Fund, 1973-1982, where she was instrumental in securing extension of the 1965 Voting Rights Act to Mexican Americans; consultant to the U.S. Census Bureau, 1975-1981; member of the California Board of Regents, 1976-1990.

Montoya, Joseph (1915-1978): Politician; born in New Mexico; earned law degree from Georgetown University in 1938; New Mexico representative (Democrat), 1937-1941, senator, 1941-1947; lieutenant-governor, 1946-1950, 1954-1957; U.S. representative, 1957-1964; U.S. senator, 1964-1977; best known for his work on the Senate Agricultural Committee.

Moreno, Luisa (1907-c. 1990): Labor organizer; born in Guatemala; began organizing Hispanic garment workers in New York City in the 1930's; led a successful pecan shellers' strike of the United Cannery, Agricultural, Packing and Allied Workers of America, gaining favorable notice of the leadership and eventually rising to be international vice president; helped launch the National Congress of the Spanish Speaking People (also known as El Congresso) in 1938, the first Mexican American civil rights organization; suspected of being a communist and deported in the 1950's under terms of the McCarran-Walter Immigration Act; died in Mexico.

Palés Matos, Luis (1898-1959): Puerto Rican poet; worked as a secretary, bookkeeper, and journalist as he developed his poetic craft; founded the short-lived San Juan avant-garde literary movement, Diepalismo, in 1921; from the mid-1920's, developed (with Nicolas Guillen) the literary movement known as Negrismo, exalting black contributions to Latin American history and culture, which was controversial because he was white; abandoned Negrista poetry in the 1940's; wrote *Drumbeats of Kink and Blackness* (1937), *Poesia 1915-1956* (1957).

Perales, César (1940-   ): Government official, lawyer; director, Criminal Justice Coordinating Council, New York City Office of the Mayor, 1976-1977; regional director, Department of Health, Education and Welfare (HEW), 1977-1979; assistant secretary, HEW, 1979-1980; president, Puerto Rican Legal Defense and Education Fund, 1981-1983; commissioner, New York State Department of Social Services since 1983.

Rivera, Geraldo (1943-   ): Journalist; earned law degree at the University of Pennsylvania and a degree in journalism at Columbia University; began career as reporter for WABC-TV in New York City in 1970; host of the television talk show *Geraldo* (1987-1996) and *The Geraldo Rivera Show* (1996-1998); has won ten Emmys for broadcast journalism.

Rodríguez, Armando Osorio (1929-   ): Judge, social activist; directing attorney, California Rural Legal Assistance, 1965-1967; chairman and board member, California Rural Legal Assistance, 1969-1987; judge, Fresno Municipal Court, 1975-1978, since 1980; judge, Fresno Superior Court, 1978-1980; board chair and member, Migrant Legal Service Project, since 1988.

Roybal, Edward (1916-   ): Politician; raised in Los Angeles, served in the Civilian Conservation Corps during the Depression (1930's) and in the Army during World War II (1944-1945); cofounder, Community Service Organization, 1947; member, Los Angeles City Council, 1949-1962, the first Mexican American to serve there since 1881; opposed city development that adversely affected Mexican American families; U.S. representative (Democrat), 1963-1993; introduced legislation leading to the Bilingual Education Act of 1967; founding member of Congressional Hispanic Caucus, 1976.

Vásquez, Tiburcio (1835-1875): Bandit; allegedly driven to crime by white injustice, became a Mexican American folk hero as he stole cattle and robbed California Anglos; captured in 1874 and executed the following year.

Asian Americans

Arai, Clarence Takeya (1901-1964): Lawyer, activist; earned law degree from University of Washington in 1924; president, Seattle Progressive Citizens League, 1928, leading to foundation of the National Council of Japanese American Citizens League in 1930; interned during World War II at a camp in Idaho.

Ariyoshi, George (1926-   ): Politician, attorney; born in Honolulu, Hawaii, to Japanese immigrants; entered U.S. Army in 1944, working with U.S. military intelligence in Japan after World War II; after earning law degree from University of Michigan Law School in 1952, returned to Hawaii, where he served as a territorial representative, 1954-1958, and a territorial senator, 1958-1959; upon admittance of Hawaii as a state in the union, served as U.S. senator, 1959-1973; senate majority leader, 1965; governor of Hawaii, 1974-1986; first Japanese American to be elected governor of a state.

Bulosan, Carlos (1911-1956): Writer, labor activist; migrated from the Philippines; worked in an Alaskan cannery and as a migrant field hand before becoming a respected author; published the radical literary magazine *The New Tide* (1934); at first applauded American opportunities, even for migrant workers, but later became disillusioned; editor of highly political yearbook of United Cannery and Packing House Workers of America (1950); best known for three novels, *The Voice of Bataan* (1943), *The Laughter of My Father* (1944), and *America Is in the Heart* (1946).

Chin, Frank (1940-   ): Writer, playwright; produced *The Chickencoop Chinaman* (1972), becoming the first Asian American playwright to reach the New York stage; founded the Asian American Theatre Workshop in San Francisco in 1973; opposed to the Asian American literature of popular authors such as Maxine Hong Kingston and Amy Tan, which he considers to be founded in Western philosophy and tradition; *The Year of the Dragon* (1974) dealt with the disintegration of a Chinese American family; organized Day of Remembrance in 1978, bringing Japanese American leaders and activists together to publicize grievances suffered during World War II; with others edited *Aiiieeeee! An Anthology of Asian American Writers* (1974).

D'Souza, Dinesh (1961-   ): Author; born in Bombay; came to the United States in 1978 to complete his high school education; while in college edited the *Dartmouth Review* (1981), often perceived as being insensitive to minorities; contributed articles to prominent conservative political journals; assistant to domestic policy chief Gary Bauer during the administration of President Ronald Reagan, 1987-1989; best known for his *Illiberal Education: The Politics of Race and Sex on Campus* (1991), a bestseller that fueled a national debate on political correctness and the best means of creating fair rules for a diverse society.

Fang, John T. C. (1925-1992): Journalist, publisher; born in China, fled to Taiwan when communists assumed power in 1949; served as reporter and associate editor of *New Life Daily News* (Taiwan); managing editor of *Chinese Daily Post* (San Francisco) in the 1950's and 1960's; in the 1970's published *Young China Daily News*, founded by Sun Yat-sen early in the twentieth century; established *Asian Weekly* (1979), which became the paper of record among Asian Americans;

beginning in 1984, prepared special editions during presidential elections, highlighting ethnic concerns.

Fong, Hiram L. (1906-   ): Politician; born to Chinese immigrants in Honolulu, Hawaii; earned law degree from Harvard in 1935; rose to rank of major, U.S. Army Air Corps, 1942-1944; Hawaiian territorial representative, 1938-1954; first Asian American elected to the U.S. senate (Republican), 1959-1977; helped establish the University of Hawaii's East West Center; instrumental in framing immigration reforms, 1965.

Harano, Ross Masao (1942-   ): Activist, businessman; born in California, his family was forcibly relocated to Arkansas; after growing up in Chicago, went into banking and international trade; served as equal opportunity officer, director of advisory councils, and chief of the crime victims division of the Illinois Office of the Attorney General, 1988-1993; president, Illinois Ethnic Coalition; chairperson, Chicago Chapter of the Japanese American Citizens League; president, Chicago World Trade Center.

Hayakawa, S. I. (1906-1992): Politician, educator; born in British Columbia to Japanese immigrants; received degrees from University of Manitoba in 1927 and McGill University in 1928 before moving to United States to earn a doctorate at the University of Wisconsin in 1935; as Canadian citizen was spared internment during World War II; president of San Francisco State University, 1968; U.S. senator (Republican) for California, 1977-1983; special adviser to the secretary of state for East Asian and Pacific affairs, 1983-1990; wrote *Language in Action* (1941), a seminal text in semantics.

Hayashi, Dennis (1952-   ): Born in Los Angeles to Japanese American parents who were interned during World War II; earned law degree at Hastings College in 1978; worked for the Asian Law Caucus, 1979-1991; has defended the civil rights of Pacific Islanders, Vietnamese, Japanese, and other Asian Americans; cofounder of National Network Against Asian American Violence; appointed director of the Office of Civil Rights, 1993.

Hayslip, Le Ly (1949-   ): Author, humanitarian; born to a devout Buddhist family in central Vietnam; arrested and brutalized by the French, the South Vietnamese, and the Viet Cong; came to the United States in 1970; founded East Meets West, an organization for improving relations between Vietnam and the United States and for bettering the lives of Vietnamese; founded hospitals, clinics, and schools in Vietnam; wrote memoirs of life in Vietnam and the United States: *When Heaven and Earth Changed Places* (1989) and *Child of War, Woman of Peace* (1993).

Hirano, Irene Yasutake (1948-   ): Administrator, social activist; born in Los Angeles, her father's family was interned during World War II; associate director of Asian Women's Center, 1972-1975; executive director of T.H.E. Clinic for Women, Los Angeles, providing medical help and counseling to poor women; president, Asian Women's Network, Los Angeles, 1980; director and president of the Japanese American National Museum since 1988.

Hongo, Florence M. (1928-   ): Educator, social activist; born in California; interned in a Colorado camp during World War II; organized the Japanese American Curriculum Project in 1969 (from 1994, the Asian American Curriculum Project), which produced the controversial *Japanese Americans, the Untold Story* (1970); after the state refused to accept the work as a supplemental textbook, began distributing books, filmstrips, and other literature designed to produce full information about the internment of Japanese Americans.

Igasaki, Paul M. (1955-   ): Lawyer, social activist; born in Chicago; moved to California to attend Martin Luther King, Jr., School of Law at the University of California, Davis; lawyer, Legal Services of Northern California, 1980-1985; Washington, D.C., representative for the Japanese American Citizens League; executive director of the Asian Law Caucus, 1991-1994; chairman of the Equal Employment Opportunity Commission, 1994.

Inouye, Daniel (1924-   ): Politician; born in Honolulu, Hawaii; joined U.S. Army, where he distinguished himself in combat in Europe, 1943-1945; earned a law degree at George Washington University Law School in 1952; majority leader in Hawaii territorial house, 1954-1958; U.S. representative (Democrat), 1959-1963; U.S. senator since 1963; strong supporter of President Lyndon B. Johnson's social welfare program; gained national attention as member of the senate Watergate committee in 1973; chair of senate Iran-Contra committee; chaired the Committee on Indian Affairs.

Kingston, Maxine Hong (1940-   ): Writer; raised in a Chinese immigrant family, utilized Cantonese stories and myths and personal experience to create works in which the boundaries between fiction and autobiography are obscured; *The Woman Warrior: Memoirs of a Girlhood Among Ghosts* (1976) and *China Men* (1980) explore the feminine and masculine sides of the Chinese American experience.

Kitano, Harry H. L. (1926-   ): Scholar; raised in San Francisco; interned in Topaz, Utah, during World War II; earned Ph.D. at University of California, Berkeley, in 1958; on faculty at University of California, Los Angeles, where he has twice been director of the Asian American Studies Center; wrote many important sociological studies of Japanese Americans, including *Japanese Americans: Evolution of a Sub-Culture* (1969).

Kochiyama, Yuri (1921-   ): Political activist; born in California; interned in Arkansas during World War II; joined National Association for the Advancement of Colored People during the 1950's; moved to Harlem in 1960 during the Civil Rights movement, working for better community education and working conditions; met Malcolm X and joined his Organization for Afro-American Unity in 1964; supported solidarity between Asians, African Americans, and Hispanics.

Kumar, K. V. (1945-   ): Businessperson, political activist; born in Bangalore, India; came to United States as a student in 1968, working as messenger for international organizations; priest at Vittala Hindu temple, Washington, D.C.; founded the National Indian American Chamber of Commerce in 1991 to assist more than 100,000 Indian-owned or -operated businesses; active in Republican politics.

Le Xuan Khoa (1931-   ): Educator, community leader; born in Vietnam; deputy minister for culture and education in South Vietnam; vice-president, University of Saigon; came to United States as a refugee in 1975; chief executive of Southeast Asia Refugee Action Center since 1980; editor in chief of *The Bridge*, reporting on refugee issues; frequently has testified to U.S. Congress on immigration issues.

Makino, Fred Kinzaburo (1877-1953): Publisher, community leader; born in Japan to an English merchant and a Japanese woman; sent to Hawaii in 1899, where he opened a drugstore; played a key role in the Higher Wage Association and the plantation strike of 1909; started the newspaper *Hawaii Hochi* in 1912 in support of Japanese laborers; fought against restrictions on Japanese-language schools in Hawaii.

Manlapit, Pablo (1891-1969): Migrated from the Philippines to Hawaii as a plantation laborer in 1910; founded Filipino Federation of Labor in 1911 and Filipino Unemployed Association in 1913; helped organize strike of plantation workers in Hawaii in 1920, the first major strike involving workers of multiple ethnic groups; convicted in 1924 following strike violence but paroled in 1927 with the requirement of leaving Hawaii; organized Filipino workers in California, 1927-1932; forced to return to the Philippines in 1934.

Masaoka, Mike Masaru (1915-1991): Social activist, community leader; raised in Utah, where he became a Mormon; executive secretary of the Japanese American Citizens League, 1941; advised U.S. government on administration of World War II internment camps for Japanese Americans; fought for admission of Nisei (second-generation, U.S.-born Japanese Americans) into American armed forces; as a lobbyist, played a key role in Japanese American Evacuation Claims Act, 1948, and McCarran-Walter Immigration and Naturalization Act, 1952; wrote *They Call Me Moses Masaoka* (1987).

Matsunaga, Masayuki "Spark" (1916-1990): Politician; born in Hawaii; served in U.S. Army during World War II, earning bronze star and purple heart; earned law degree from Harvard University in 1952; representative to the Hawaiian territorial legislature, 1954-1959; U.S. representative (Democrat), 1963-1977; U.S. senator, 1977-1990.

Mink, Patsy (1927-   ): Politician; born Patsy Takemoto in Hawaii; earned law degree at the University of Chicago in 1951, returning to Hawaii to open private practice; territorial representative, 1956; U.S. representative, 1965-1977, since 1990; member of Honolulu city council, 1983-1987.

Mukherjee, Bharati (1940-   ): Writer; born into the Brahman caste in India, settled first in Canada, then in the United States; most of her works deal with the location of identity when faced with a multiethnic experience; wrote novels: *The Tiger's Daughter* (1972), *Wife* (1975); nonfiction: *Days and Nights in Calcutta* (1977) and *The Sorrow and the Terror* (1987), both cowritten with her husband, Clark Blaise; and short stories: *Darkness* (1985).

Omura, James Matsumoto (1912-1994): Journalist; born in Washington State; founded magazine, *Current Life* (1940), which published poetry, fiction, and news articles by Japanese American writers; at the Tolan Committee hearings, spoke out against forcible removal of Japanese Americans from the West Coast.

Pran, Dith (1942-   ): Journalist; born in Cambodia; worked as an interpreter for U.S. military in 1960's; hired by *The New York Times* as photographer and assistant to Sydney Schanberg in covering the Vietnam War in the early 1970's; could not escape when United States evacuated Cambodia in 1975; miraculously survived during Pol Pot's regime, 1975-1979, emigrating to United States; actively involved in heightening awareness of Cambodian problems.

Rhee, Syngman (1875-1965): Politician, Korean nationalist; first Korean to receive a Ph.D. from an American university (Princeton); principal, Korean Community School, Hawaii, 1913, where he established a newspaper and a Korean community society; president of the provisional Korean government in exile, 1919-1941; chairman, Korean Commission in Washington, D.C., 1941-1945; president of Republic of Korea, 1948-1960.

Santos, Bienvenido (1911-   ): Filipino American writer; following a secondary teaching career in the Philippines, came to the United States as cultural attache to the Philippine Embassy in Washington, D.C., 1942-1945; returned to the Philippines, and over the next twenty-five years taught at universities in both the Philippines and the United States; while lecturing in the United States in 1972, martial law was declared in the Philippines and universities were closed, forcing him into exile; his books, short stories, and novels deal with the cultural difficulties of Filipinos who are unable to fully recover their culture because of contact with the United States; books include *You Lovely People* (1955), *Brother My Brother* (1960), *Villa Magdalena* (1965), and *Scent of Apples: A Collection of Stories* (1979).

Saund, Dalip Singh (1899-1973): Politician; came to United States in 1920; after earning a Ph.D. in mathematics, raised produce in California; naturalized in 1946; first mainland Asian immigrant to win a seat in the U.S. House of Representatives (Democrat, California), 1957-1963.

Takaki, Ronald (1939-   ): Born in Honolulu, Hawaii; involved in the Free Speech movement in 1964; joined faculty of University of California, Los Angeles (UCLA), 1967; helped establish a multicultural atmosphere at UCLA, developing a course on the history of racial inequality and establishing centers for Chicano, Asian American, Native American, and African American studies; joined faculty at University of California, Berkeley, in 1972; an award-winning author, he has produced many works on ethnic studies, including *A Pro-Slavery Crusade* (1970); *Iron Cages: Race and Culture in Nineteenth Century America* (1979), *Strangers from a Different Shore: A History of Asian Americans* (1989), and *A Different Mirror: A History of Multicultural America* (1993).

Tan, Amy (1952-   ): Chinese American writer; born in the United States to wealthy Chinese immigrants, her highly acclaimed first novel, *The Joy Luck Club* (1989), portrays the struggle of Chinese American women to recover their traditional culture; also wrote *The Kitchen God's Wife* (1991), and *The Hundred Secret Senses* (1995).

Uno, Edison (1929-1976): Educator, social activist; born in California; interned in Colorado and Texas during World War II; at age eighteen became president of the East Los Angeles chapter of the Japanese American Citizens League; worked to repeal Title II of the Internal Security Act of 1950 in the early 1970's; played a major role in the redress movement.

Yatabe, Thomas T. (1897-   ): One of the first Japanese Americans born on the mainland; ordered to attend racially segregated schools in San Francisco in 1906; cofounder of the American Loyalty League in 1918, forerunner of the Japanese American Citizens League (JACL); first president of the JACL, 1934; interned during World War II but continued to preach loyalty to the U.S. government; founded Chicago chapter of JACL following resettlement there, 1943.

Native Americans

American Horse (c. 1801-1876): Oglala Lakota Sioux leader; assisted Oglala chiefs in leading warriors and governing the community; actively resisted white encroachment following the Homestead Act of 1862; killed at the Battle of Slim Buttes in retaliation for the death of Custer at Little Big Horn.

Banks, Dennis (1937-   ): Anishinabe Ojibwa activist; entered the U.S. Air Force, serving in Japan, 1953; after the questionable administration of justice in a robbery conviction, founded with George Mitchell and Clyde Bellecourt the American Indian Movement (AIM), 1968, to assist Native Americans in securing legal and economic rights; planned controversial and confrontational tactics, including occupation of Alcatraz Island in 1969, day of mourning at Plymouth, Massachusetts, 1970, and the armed occupation of Wounded Knee, site of an 1890 Indian massacre; served fourteen months in a South Dakota penitentiary, 1984-1985, for involvement in a 1973 riot; throughout the 1980's and 1990's raised awareness of the concerns of Native Americans with organized walks and runs; wrote his autobiography, *Sacred Soul* (1988).

Black Hawk (c. 1767-1838): Northern Sauk and Fox leader; refused to accept treaties signed by southern Sauk and Fox; in an attempt to preserve Illinois and Wisconsin homeland, joined Tecumseh's tribal confederacy and sided with the British during the War of 1812; after U.S. government takeover of tribal lands, led a brief struggle to regain them in 1832; captured and taken to Washington, D.C., to meet with President Andrew Jackson; dictated his autobiography to trader Antoine LeClaire (*Life of Ma-ka-tai-me-she-kia-kiak: The Autobiography of Black Hawk*, 1833).

Bonnin, Gertrude Simmons (Zitkala-Sa, 1875-1938): Yankton Sioux educator, writer, activist; born on the South Dakota Yankton reservation to a Yankton Sioux mother and a white father; educated in Quaker institutions in Indiana; around 1900 began preserving her culture through the publication of stories and essays in books and periodicals such as *Atlantic* and *Harper's Magazine*; elected secretary of the Society of American Indians (SAI), 1916; opposition to the use of peyote in religious ceremonies led to her split with the SAI in 1920; founded the National Council of American Indians in 1926; collected writings include *Old Indian Legends* (1902) and *American Indian Stories* (1921).

Bruce, Louis R. (1906-1989): Oglala Sioux/Mohawk government official; born on Oglala Sioux reservation at Pine Ridge, South Dakota, to a Mohawk father and Oglala Sioux mother; raised on the Onondaga Reservation near Syracuse, New York, where his father held a pastorate; after graduating from Syracuse University in 1930, became a manager in a clothing store; director, Indians for the National Youth Administration, New York State, 1935-1941; created the National American Indian Youth Conference in 1957;

appointed commissioner of the Bureau of Indian Affairs, 1969-1972.

Cloud, Henry Roe (Wonah'ilayhunka, 1884-1950): Winnebago educator, administrator; born in Nebraska; parents died shortly after his conversion to Christianity; while at Yale University, adopted by missionary Dr. Walter C. Roe; became first Native American to graduate from Yale University in 1910; received divinity degree from Auburn Theological Seminary in 1913; chaired delegation of Winnebagos to President William H. Taft, 1912-1913; established the Roe Indian Institute (later American Indian Institute) in Wichita, Kansas, in 1915; coauthored the Meriam Report (1928); supervisor of Indian education at the Bureau of Indian Affairs, 1936-1947; superintendent of the Umatilla Indian Agency, Pendleton, Oregon.

Cochise (c. 1812-1874): Chiracahua Apache tribal leader; born in Arizona territory; came to the attention of U.S. Army when accused of a kidnapping in 1861, sparking a series of Apache wars; with father-in-law Mangas Coloradas led Apache resistance; surrendered in 1871.

Cornplanter (Kayenhtwanken, c. 1732-1836): Seneca tribal leader; son of a white trader and a Seneca woman; unanimous selection as chief of Seneca, one of the Iroquois tribes; led Iroquois to ally with the French in the French and Indian War (1755-1759) and the British in the American Revolution (1775-1783); became more peaceful toward settlers, working as an emissary for George Washington in 1791 and negotiating a peace treaty between the Northwest tribes and the U.S. government; lost influence with tribe because of conciliatory stance; dictated many Iroquois legends late in life.

Crazy Horse (Tashunca-uitko, c. 1842-1877): Oglala Sioux leader; war leader during Red Cloud's War (1866-1868); refused to enter reservation in 1875 and led the Sioux and Cheyenne into war in 1876; best known for defeating Custer at the Battle of Little Big Horn in 1876; surrendered and murdered in 1877.

Deer, Ada E. (1935-): Menominee social worker, educator, social activist; born on the Menominee Indian Reservation, Wisconsin, of mixed Anglo-Indian parentage; first Native American to receive a Masters of Social Work from Columbia University; after serving as a social worker in New York City and Minneapolis, became Community Service Coordinator for the Bureau of Indian Affairs (BIA), Minnesota, 1964-1967; founding member of Determination of Rights and Unity for Menominee Shareholders, 1970; chair of Menominee tribe and head of Menominee Restoration Committee, 1974-1976; narrowly lost an attempt to become the first Native American woman in the U.S. Congress, 1992; first woman head of the BIA, 1993.

Deloria, Vine, Jr. (1933-): Yankton Sioux writer; born in South Dakota, served in U.S. Marine Corps, 1954-1956; executive director, National Congress of American Indians, 1964-1967; earned law degree at University of Colorado in 1970; on faculties at Western Washington State College, 1970-1972, University of California, Los Angeles, 1972-1974, University of Arizona, 1978-1990, and University of Colorado since 1990; chairperson, Institute for the Development of Indian Law, 1970-1978; in his extensive writings presents the case for Indian self-determination; wrote *Custer Died for Your Sins: An Indian Manifesto* (1969), *We Talk, You Listen: New Tribes, New Turf* (1970), *God Is Red: A Native View of Religion* (1973), and *American Indian Policy in the Twentieth Century* (1985).

Eastman, Charles Alexander (Hakadah, 1858-1939): Santee Sioux writer, doctor; born in Minnesota of mixed Sioux and white parentage; fled with his family to British Columbia following Sioux Indian Uprising in 1862; returned to the United States in 1873; earned doctorate at Boston University and became physician at Pine Ridge Agency, South Dakota, 1890-1893; Washington, D.C., lobbyist for Santee Sioux, 1897-1900; physician at Crow Creek Reservation, 1900-1903; Indian inspector, Bureau of Indian Affairs, 1923-1925; the most eloquent Native American writer of his age, published ten books, including *Indian Boyhood* (1902), *From the Deep Woods to Civilization* (1916), and *Indian Heroes and Great Chieftains* (1918).

Harjo, Joy (1951-): Muscogee Creek writer, artist; attended boarding school at the Institute of American Indian Arts, Santa Fe, 1967; after graduating from the University of New Mexico in 1976, was faculty member at University of Colorado, 1985-1988, University of Arizona, 1988-1990, and University of New Mexico beginning 1990; widely acclaimed poetry draws upon the symbols and mystical elements of traditional Native American culture; throughout the 1980's worked extensively with the Native American Public Broadcasting Consortium; wrote *What Moon Drove Me to This* (1980), *Secrets from the Center of the World* (1989), *In Mad Love and War* (1990), and *The Woman Who Fell from the Sky* (1994).

Harris, LaDonna (1931-): Comanche political activist; born in Temple, Oklahoma, to an Irish-American father and a Cherokee mother but raised by her Cherokee grandparents; created Oklahomans for Indian Opportunity, which organized members of sixty tribes in 1965; chair, National Women's Advisory Council of the War on Poverty in 1967 and National Council on Indian Opportunity in 1968; founded Americans for Indian Opportunity in 1970; served as special adviser to the Office for Economic Opportunity during the administration of President Jimmy

Carter, 1977-1981, establishing the controversial Council for Energy Resources Tribes.

Joseph, Chief (Hinmaton Yalatkit, c. 1840-1904): Chief of the Nez Perce; educated at a Christian school; became chief at age thirty; refused treaty offer of 1868 removing Nez Perce from their lands; eventually led a band of Nez Perce in an unsuccessful escape to Canada, 1877; made two trips to Washington, D.C., to plead with President Theodore Roosevelt for better lands.

McGillivray, Alexander (c. 1759-1793): Creek leader and diplomat; born in Alabama to a Scottish trader and a Creek mother, learned English at an early age; organized southern Creek cooperation with the British during the American Revolution; throughout the mid-1780's negotiated with northern tribes, and the governments of the United States, Georgia, and Spain to limit further expansion into Creek territories; opposed sale of Creek lands; negotiated the Treaty of New York in 1790, establishing direct relations between the U.S. government and the Creek nation.

Mankiller, Wilma Pearl (1945-): Cherokee tribal leader; born at Tahlequah, Oklahoma, to a Cherokee father and a Dutch-Irish mother; family's relocation to California led her to reflect on her great-grandfather's removal on the Trail of Tears, 1838-1839; energized by the Indian occupation of Alcatraz Island by fellow San Francisco State College student Richard Oakes; returned to Oklahoma in 1976; became principal chief of the Cherokee in 1985, the first woman to hold that position.

Means, Russell (1939-): Lakota Sioux activist; born on the Pine Ridge Reservation in South Dakota, experienced racial taunting while attending San Leandro High School in California; director, American Indian Center, 1969; met Dennis Banks, cofounder of the radical American Indian Movement (AIM), and established its second chapter in Cleveland, Ohio; engaged in confrontational tactics to attract attention to Native American concerns; widespread conflict over reservation abuses led to the armed occupation of the community of Wounded Knee in 1973; acquitted of murder charges in 1976; left AIM in 1988 to form the American Indian Anti-Defamation League.

Opechancanough (c. 1544-1644): Powhatan-Renape leader; befriended John Smith in 1607; negotiated between English settlers and various Indian tribes, 1607-1618; disillusioned, led rebellions against the English in 1622 and 1644; murdered while a prisoner.

Parker, Ely Samuel (Hasanoanda, c. 1828-1895): Seneca tribal leader, government official; born on the Tonawanda Indian Reservation, the son of a Seneca chief; because of recognized abilities, was chosen as a young man to assist Seneca delegations to New York State and the U.S. federal government; met and assisted Lewis Henry Morgan in the collection of data on the Seneca in 1844, leading to Morgan's anthropological study, *League of the Ho-de-no-sau-nee, or Iroquois* (1851); denied admittance to the New York bar; became an engineer, finally accepting a position in Galena, Illinois in 1857, where he met Ulysses S. Grant; commissioned a captain in the Union army in 1863, eventually becoming Grant's military secretary; commissioner of Indian Affairs, 1869-1871.

Parker, Quanah (c. 1845-1911): Comanche leader; born to a Comanche warrior and a white captive; great hunter and warrior, who encouraged Comanche to accommodate themselves to new circumstances following their surrender to the U.S. government in 1875; recommended the leasing of reservation grazing lands to Texas cattlemen; shrewd businessman and negotiator.

Pitchlynn, Peter Perkins (Hatchootucknee, 1806-1881): Choctaw leader and diplomat; one-quarter Choctaw, was born into a bicultural elite in Mississippi; helped create Choctaw constitution in 1826; moved to Oklahoma with Choctaws in 1831; helped draft first western constitution in 1834; established Choctaw national school system in 1840's; elected chief in 1864.

Porter, Pleasant (1840-1907): Creek leader; born of mixed Creek and white parentage; served in the Confederate army during the Civil War, rising from private to second lieutenant; became wealthy in business; appointed superintendent of schools in Creek nation in 1867; defended Creek constitutionalism by commanding national militia in times of crisis, 1871, 1876, 1882-1883; Creek lobbyist in Washington, D.C., 1872-1890's; elected principal Creek chief, 1899, 1903; president of constitutional convention that designed proposal for state of Sequoyah in 1905.

Powhatan (Wahunsunacock, c. 1550-1618): Virginia Indian leader; paramount chief of eastern Virginia (Confederacy of Powhatan) when English settlers arrived in 1607; father of Pocahontas and brother of Opechancanough; English encroachment led to the first Anglo-Powhatan War (1610-1614).

Pushmataha (1764-1824): Choctaw chief; signed Treaty of Mount Dexter in 1805, ceding tribal lands in Alabama and Mississippi; opposed Tecumseh's confederation in 1811; allied with U.S. government during Creek War (1813-1814).

Red Cloud (Makhpia-sha, 1822-1909): Oglala Sioux chief; born along Platte River, his early life obscure; forced United States to abandon Bozeman Trail in 1866; made peace at Fort Laramie when government abandoned Bozeman forts in 1868; made four trips to Washington, D.C., before finally agreeing to resettle on the Pine Ridge Reservation in South Dakota in 1878.

Red Jacket (Sagoyewátha, c. 1756-1830): Seneca leader; born in New York; spokesperson for the British during the American Revolution; in 1780's assumed ceremonial title of council orator; after the revolution maintained a moderate stance, suggesting neutrality for the Iroquois in U.S.-Canadian disputes.

Ross, John (Coowescoowe, 1790-1866): Cherokee chief; son of Scotch father and part Cherokee mother; president, National Council of Cherokees, 1819-1826; chief of Cherokee nation, 1828-1866; forced to lead Cherokee nation on Trail of Tears to Oklahoma, 1838-1839; reluctantly brought Cherokee into the Confederacy during the Civil War in 1861; captured and taken to Washington, D.C., where he became friends with Abraham Lincoln.

Seattle (Seathl, c. 1788-1866): Duwamish, Suquamish, Lushootseed warrior and diplomat; born into the intertribal nobility of the Puget Sound area of Washington State; resisted encroachment by the Hudson's Bay Company; converted to Catholicism in 1838; appointed by U.S. leaders as head chief of the region following settlement of U.S.-Canadian land dispute.

Sequoyah (c. 1770-1843): Cherokee leader; born to a white man and a Cherokee woman who was sister to several chiefs; moved from North Carolina to Alabama to escape encroachment of whites; worked on a written Cherokee language, 1809-1821, which would better allow the tribe to deal with modern conditions; moved to Arkansas in 1818 to resist white encroachment; led delegation to Washington, D.C., to negotiate the exchange of Arkansas lands for Oklahoma territory; negotiated peace between western and eastern Cherokees in 1839.

Sitting Bull (Tatanka Iyotake, 1831-1890): Sioux leader; recognized early in life as a powerful warrior; became chief of the Hunkpapa Sioux; fought against white encroachment throughout the 1860's; appointed chief of the entire Sioux nation in 1867; refused U.S. government order to evacuate Sioux lands for the reservation in 1876, leading to the annihilation of Custer's force at Little Big Horn in 1876; surrendered to government forces in 1881, imprisoned, then sent to the Standing Rock Reservation in 1883; during the Ghost Dance movement, killed during an attempted arrest in 1890.

Tecumseh (1768-1813): Shawnee warrior, military leader; after his father's murder by white settlers in 1774, adopted by Blackfish, who raised him with several white boy captives, including Daniel Boone; fought settlers in Kentucky and Ohio who encroached on Shawnee lands in the 1780's; refused to recognize the Treaty of Greenville of 1795, which ceded huge tracts of Indian land in the upper Midwest; with his brother Elskatawa, formed a confederation of tribes for mu-

tual defense; joined the British during the War of 1812; killed at the Battle of the Thames River.

Ward, Nancy (Nanye-hi, c. 1738-c. 1824): Cherokee leader; as a young woman, led Cherokees in battle against the Creeks in 1755; accorded the title Ghigau (Beloved Woman); negotiator of the Treaty of Hopewell in 1785, first Cherokee treaty with the newly formed country; urged Cherokee to sell no more land to U.S. government in 1808; married Bryant Ward, an Irish trader.

Other Significant Figures

Allport, Gordon (1897-1967): Psychologist; on faculty at Harvard University, 1930-1967; helped establish department of social relations at Harvard; wrote pathbreaking studies on the development of personality; wrote many books, including *Personality: A Psychological Interpretation* (1937), *Nature of Personality* (1950), *Nature of Prejudice* (1954).

Baron, Salo Wittmayer (1895-1989): Historian; born in Galicia; earned doctorates in philosophy, law, and political science at the University of Vienna; emigrated to the United States in 1926; joined the faculty of Columbia University in 1926; held the first chair in Jewish history at a U.S. university; placed Jewish history in a broad world context, emphasizing Jewish resourcefulness and creativity; at various times president of American Academy of Jewish Research, the Conference on Jewish Social Studies, and the American Jewish Historical Society; wrote *A Social and Religious History of the Jews* (1937) and *The Russian Jew Under the Tsars and Soviets* (1964).

Bellow, Saul (1915-   ): Writer; born in Quebec to Russian immigrants; moved to Chicago in 1924; frequently wrote on the nature of the Jewish cultural experience; on faculty at Minnesota University and Chicago University in 1962; awarded Nobel Prize in Literature in 1976; won National Book Awards for fiction with *The Adventures of Augie March* (1954), *Herzog* (1964), and *Mr. Sammler's Planet* (1971); also wrote *Henderson the Rain King* (1959), *Humboldt's Gift* (1975), and *To Jerusalem and Back* (1976).

Brown, John (1800-1859): Abolitionist; joined antislavery forces in Kansas in 1855; murdered five proslavery advocates in 1856 in retaliation for a previous massacre; established plan for a slave refuge state; seized U.S. government arsenal at Harper's Ferry, Virginia, in 1859, hoping to incite a slave insurrection; convicted of treason and hanged.

Cahan, Abraham (1860-1951): Journalist; born in the Russian empire, fled to the United States escaping Tsarist persecution; worked for Joseph Pulitzer's *World*; founded Yiddish newspaper *Vorwarts!* (*Jewish Daily Forward*), in 1897, which he edited for fifty years; a staunch socialist, who nevertheless spoke out against the brutality of Stalin's regime in Russia; explored the Jewish immigrant experience in the novels *Imported Bridegroom* (1898), *The White Terror and the Red* (1905), *The Rise of David Levinsky* (1907).

Collier, John (1884-1968): Sociologist, educator; executive secretary, American Indian Defense Association, 1923-1933; editor, *American Indian Life*, 1926-1933; U.S. Commissioner of Indian Affairs, 1933-1945, responsible for passage of Indian Reorganization Act in 1934; director, National Indian Institute, 1945-1950; president, Institute of Ethnic Affairs, 1947-1968; wrote *Indians of the Americas* (1947), *Patterns and Ceremonials of the Indians of the Southwest* (1949).

Duke, David (1950-   ): Ku Klux Klan leader, politician; graduated from Louisiana State University; grand wizard of the Ku Klux Klan, 1975-1980; ties to the American Nazi Party; Louisiana state representative (Republican), 1989-1991; made strong bid for the U.S. senate in 1990 with a message of racial resentment, garnering 44 percent of the vote; ran for U.S. president in 1992 with little support.

Garrison, William Lloyd (1805-1879): Journalist, abolitionist; published *The Liberator* (1831-1865); founder American Anti-Slavery Society in 1833, president of that organization 1843-1865; opposed Compromise of 1850 and encouraged separation of North and South; after Civil War, campaigned against mistreatment of Indians and in favor of women's suffrage.

Glazer, Nathan (1923-   ): Sociologist; on faculty at Harvard's Graduate School of Education, 1968; early books were oriented toward Zionism and socialism, though he became a neoconservative in the 1970's; best known for *Beyond the Melting Pot* (1963), written with Daniel Patrick Moynihan, and *Affirmative Discrimination* (1976).

Howard, Oliver Otis (1830-1909): U.S. Army officer; entered Army in 1854; fought in the Civil War, being promoted to brigadier general in 1861; commissioner, Bureau of Refugees, Freedmen, and Abandoned Lands, 1865-1874; founder and president of Howard University, 1869-1874; commander in campaign against Chief Joseph, 1877; superintendent at West Point, 1881-1882; considered one of the few "humanitarian" generals who campaigned on behalf of Indian rights.

Jackson, Helen Hunt (1830-1885): Writer; documented U.S. government mismanagement of Indian affairs in *A Century of Dishonor* (1881), presenting copies to all members of Congress; special commissioner to investigate Indian affairs; in *Ramona* (1884) personalized mistreatment of the Indians.

Johnson, Lyndon Baines (1908-1973): Politician; Texas state administrator, National Youth Administration, 1935-1937; U.S. representative (Democrat) from Texas, 1937-1949, then senator, 1949-1961; majority leader, 1955-1961; U.S. vice-president, 1961-1963; U.S. president, 1963-1969; crafted Great Society reform proposals, including the Civil Rights Act of 1964 and the Voting Rights Act of 1965, designed to ensure that African Americans received their full civil rights; established Department of Housing and Urban Development; appointed Thurgood Marshall as first black Supreme Court justice in 1967.

Kahane, Meir (1932-1990): Rabbi, Jewish activist; earned law degree from New York University; in 1960's founded Jewish Defense League, advocating use of violence in securing Jewish rights; emigrated to Israel in 1971 and was elected to the Israeli parliament in 1981; assassinated in New York City; wrote *The Jewish Stake in Vietnam* (1967).

Kaplan, Mordecai (1881-1983): Conservative Jewish leader; born in Lithuania; immigrated to United States in 1889; graduated from City College of New York in 1900 and Columbia graduate school in 1902; ordained at the Jewish Theological Seminary in 1902, where he joined the faculty in 1909 and became dean of the teachers institute there in 1931; organized the first Jewish center in the United States, in New York, 1916; established the Society for the Advancement of Judaism in 1922; led the Reconstructionist movement, publishing *Judaism as a Civilization* (1934) and the biweekly *The Reconstructionist* (1935); also wrote *Judaism in Transition* (1936) and *Future of the American Jew* (1948).

Kennedy, John F. (1917-1963): Politician; after graduating from Harvard in 1940, became a naval officer during World War II; U.S. representative (Democrat) from Massachusetts, 1947-1953, then senator, 1953-1960; first Roman Catholic elected president of United States, 1961-1963; in 1961 established Peace Corps and the Alliance for Progress in Latin America; federalized Alabama national guard to ensure integration of schools in 1963; initiated legislation integrating hotels and restaurants to afford equal access to all races; assassinated in 1963.

Kennedy, Robert F. (1925-1968): Politician, lawyer; managed the 1960 presidential campaign of his brother, John F. Kennedy; U.S. attorney general, 1961-1964; ardent supporter of civil rights; U.S. senator from New York (Democrat), 1965-1968; assassinated; wrote *The Enemy Within* (1960), *Just Friends and Brave Enemies* (1962), *To Seek a Newer World* (1967).

Lincoln, Abraham (1809-1865): Politician; after a boyhood on pioneer farms in the Midwest, was in 1834 elected to the Illinois state legislature; served as U.S. representative from Illinois, 1847-1849, where he spoke out against the Mexican War; defeated for the

Senate in 1858 but established his position against slavery in the campaign; president of the United States, 1861-1865; issued Emancipation Proclamation in 1862, freeing slaves in rebellious territories as of January 1, 1863; assassinated by John Wilkes Booth.

Malamud, Bernard (1914-1986): Writer; frequently examined the moral strength of Judaism in urban environments; won Pulitzer Prize in fiction for *The Fixer* (1966); on faculty of Oregon State University, 1949-1961, and Bennington College, 1961-1986; also wrote *The Natural* (1952), *The Magic Barrel* (1958), *The Tenants* (1971), *Dubin's Lives* (1979).

Park, Robert Ezra (1864-1944): Sociologist, journalist; reporter and editor in Minneapolis, Chicago, and Detroit, 1887-1898; on faculty at Harvard, 1904-1905, University of Chicago, 1914-1933, and Fisk University, 1936-1943; secretary to Booker T. Washington; became an expert in the study of African American sociology; wrote *The Immigrant Press and Its Control* (1922), *Race and Culture* (1950), *Human Communities* (1952).

Roth, Philip (1933-   ): Writer; first major Jewish American writer to look frankly into middle-class Jewish life; most famous works include *Goodbye, Columbus and Five Short Stories* (1959), *Portnoy's Complaint* (1969), and *Operation Shylock* (1993).

Ruppin, Arthur (1876-1943): Scholar; helped establish the concept of Jewish studies in the United States; served as official in and adviser to many Zionist agencies; began teaching a course in sociology of the Jews in 1926 at Hebrew University; wrote *Die Juden der Gegenwart* (1904); *Die Soziologie der Juden* (1930-1931).

Schechter, Soloman (1847-1915): Leader of Conservative Judaism; born in Romania and educated in Vienna, Berlin, and London; appointed lecturer in Talmudics at Cambridge University, England, in 1890; moved to the United States to become president of the Jewish Theological Seminary of America in Philadelphia in 1902; supported the Zionist movement as a check on assimilation; founded the United Synagogue of America in 1913; wrote *The Wisdom of Ben Sira* (1899).

Singer, Isaac Bashevis (1904-1991): American Jewish journalist, writer; born in Poland, withdrew from rabinical seminary to work as a translator and proofreader for a Warsaw newspaper; moved to United States in 1935 and began working for the *Jewish Daily Forward*, a Yiddish-language newspaper; naturalized as a U.S. citizen in 1943 but continued to write in Yiddish; attempted to blend his old-world Jewish heritage with modern sensibilities; earned Nobel Prize in Literature in 1978; wrote many books, including *Satan in Goray* (1935), *The Family Moskat* (1950), *The Slave* (1962), and *Enemies, a Love Story* (1972).

Stevens, Thaddeus (1792-1868): Politician, lawyer; U.S. representative from Pennsylvania (Republican), 1849-1853, 1859-1868; abolitionist; opposed fugitive slave laws; led Radical Republican plan of reconstruction after the Civil War; instrumental in framing the Fourteenth Amendment to the Constitution in 1868 and the military reconstruction acts in 1867; proposed impeachment of President Andrew Johnson.

Wallace, George (1919-1998): Politician; after graduating from University of Alabama Law School in 1942, joined U.S. Army Air Force, 1942-1945; served in Alabama legislature, 1947-1953; served as state judge, 1953-1958, as governor, 1963-1967, 1971-1979, 1983-1987, pledged "segregation forever" but changed his views and received many black votes in the 1980's; ran for president of United States on an anti-civil rights ticket (American Independent Party, 1968), receiving almost 10 million popular votes and 46 electoral votes; shot during 1972 presidential primaries.

Whipple, Henry B. (1822-1901): Christian bishop; Episcopal bishop of Minnesota, 1859; convinced of government cruelty and corruption in dealing with Indians, appealed to Presidents James Buchanan, Abraham Lincoln, and Ulysses S. Grant, leading eventually to Indian Appropriations Act of 1869 and an ostensible peace policy.

Wiesel, Elie (1928-   ): Educator, writer; born in Romania; deported to Auschwitz with his parents and three sisters in 1944; watched his father die of starvation and disease and mother and sister die in gas chambers; worked as journalist in France before moving to the United States in 1956 and becoming a naturalized citizen in 1963; on faculty at City College, City University of New York, 1972-1976, Yale University, 1982-1983, and Boston University since 1976; chair, U.S. President's Commission on the Holocaust, 1979-1980; received Nobel Peace Prize, 1986; author of many books, including his Holocaust memoir, *Night* (1960), *Dawn* (1961), *The Accident* (1962), *The Town Beyond the Wall* (1964), *A Beggar in Jerusalem* (1970), *Souls on Fire* (1976), *The Fifth Son* (1985), and *Twilight* (1988).

Wirth, Louis (1897-1952): Sociologist; first Jewish president of the American Sociological Association; first president of the International Sociological Association; his first major work, *The Ghetto* (1928), viewed the Jewish community as retrograde and urged assimilation of Jews.

Wise, Isaac Mayer (1819-1900): Educator, leader of reform Judaism; raised and educated in Prague and Vienna; arrived in the United States in 1847; appointed president of Hebrew Union College in 1875; devoted the remainder of his life to building the college; named president of the Central Conference of American Rabbis in 1889.

Canadians

Big Bear (Mistahimaskwa, c. 1825-1888): Cree chief; born in Saskatchewan; concerned about the loss of traditional Indian lifestyle, refused to sign Treaty Number Six in 1876 and remained off the reservation until 1882 when destruction of the buffalo led to imminent starvation; Cree violence that he had tried to prevent led to his conviction for treason and a three-year sentence in Stoney Mountain Penitentiary, 1885.

Brant, Joseph (Thayendanegea, 1742-1807): Mohawk chief; served British in French and Indian War, Pontiac's War; interpreter for Sir William Johnson and the British Indian Department; rallied to the British cause in the American Revolution and made captain in 1780; convinced British to pay Iroquois for wartime losses in 1785; started first Episcopal church in upper Canada in 1786; unsuccessfully tried to organize confederacy of Iroquois and western tribes in order to block American expansion, 1783-1795.

Harper, Elijah (1949-   ): Cree activist; born in northern Manitoba; helped establish the native Canadian students' association at the University of Manitoba, 1970-1972; elected chief of the Red Sucker Lake Band, 1977-1981; member of the Manitoba legislature, 1981-1997; key figure in defeating the Meech Lake Accord in 1990; helped organize the movement for the establishment of National Aboriginal Day in 1996; came to symbolize the active defense of aboriginal interests.

Jones, Peter (Kahkewaquonaby, 1802-1856): Mississauga missionary; son of a white father and a Mississauga (Ojibwa) mother; converted to Christianity in 1823; made earliest translation of Bible from English into Ojibwa; chief of two Ojibwa bands; fought for Indian land rights; *Life and Journals* (1860) and *History of the Ojebway Indians* (1861) published posthumously.

Klein, Abraham Moses (1909-1972): Lawyer, poet, writer; born in Ukraine, raised in the Jewish immigrant district of Montreal; earned a degree from University of Montreal law school in 1933; editor and columnist of the *Canadian Jewish Chronicle* (1938-1955); visiting lecturer in poetry at McGill University, 1945-1948; suffered mental breakdown in early 1950's and gradually withdrew from society; wrote *The Hitleriad* (1944), *The Rocking Chair* (1948), and *The Second Scroll* (1951).

Kogawa, Joy (1935-   ): Writer, poet; born in Vancouver, British Columbia; interned in interior British Columbia during World War II; best known for her novel *Obasan* (1981), which realistically portrays the pain and alienation that Japanese Canadians suffered during World War II; also wrote *The Splintered Moon* (1967) and *Jericho Road* (1977).

Lévesque, René (1922-   ): Politician; born in Quebec, hosted *Point de Mire* (point of view), a public affairs television program, 1956-1959; during the 1960's, served in the Quebec legislature; formed the separatist organization that would become the Parti Québécois in 1967, arguing that independence alone could protect French speakers in Canada; prime minister of Quebec, 1976-1985.

Manuel, George (1921-1989): Shuswap tribal leader, civil rights activist; born in a Shuswap village in southern British Columbia; organized tribes in British Columbia in protest of the Canadian government's decision to stop payment for medical services to native Canadians; formed Aboriginal Native Rights Committee of the Interior Tribes in 1958; president, National Indian Brotherhood, 1970-1976; president of Union of British Columbian Indian Chiefs, 1977-1981, president of World Council of Indigenous Peoples in 1975 and 1981; wrote *The Fourth World* (1974).

Poundmaker (1842-1886): Cree tribal leader; adopted by Blackfoot chief Crowfoot (c. 1873); named subchief of the Sipiwininiwug; signed Treaty Number 6 with the Canadian government, allocating land to the Indians and providing for education in farming; joined in the second Riel Rebellion in 1885; tried for treason and imprisoned for seven months in 1885.

Riel, Louis, Jr. (1844-1885): Metis leader; born in Manitoba to a Metis father and a French mother; deeply religious, studied for the priesthood in Montreal, before withdrawing; returned to Manitoba when he was not allowed to marry the girl he loved, probably for racial reasons; fearing the destruction of Metis property rights following the sale of Hudson's Bay Company lands to the Canadian government, led the Metis in a rebellion in 1869; after failed negotiations, declared the Red River area independent under the name Assiniboia and was elected president; pardoned for his role in the rebellion in 1875; forced to remain in the United States, married a Metis woman and settled in Montana; executed for his part in a second Metis rebellion, 1884-1885.

Shtern, Sholem (1906-   ): Writer; developed a distinctively Jewish Canadian literature, with heavy Marxist overtones; wrote *In Kanade* (1960, 1963), detailing the Jewish immigrant experience.

Wiebe, Rudy (1934-   ): Writer; born in Saskatchewan to Russian immigrants; briefly edited the *Mennonite Brethren Herald* in the early 1960's; wrote widely on encounters between Anglo-Canadians and Mennonites, the Metis, and native Canadians; began teaching at the University of Alberta in 1967; wrote *Peace Shall Destroy Many* (1962), *The Blue Mountains of China* (1970), *The Temptations of Big Bear* (1973), *My Lovely Enemy* (1983), and *A Discovery of Strangers* (1994).

John Powell

Time Line

1619	The first blacks are brought to the Colony of Virginia as indentured servants
1641	The Massachusetts Colony recognizes the legality of slavery
1654	The first Jews arrive in New Amsterdam
1658	The first Jewish synagogue is established at Newport, in the religiously tolerant colony of Rhode Island
1662	The British government grants a monopoly to the Royal African Slave Company, marking the shift away from indentured servitude toward slavery
1662	The Virginia legislature rules that children of unions of slave and free parents are slave or free according to their mothers' status
1664	Maryland enacts the first law outlawing marriage between white women and black men
1688	Pennsylvania Mennonites protest slavery
1691	A Virginia law restricts manumissions to prevent the growth of a free black class
1705	Virginia bars African Americans and Indians from holding ecclesiastic, civil, or military offices
1712	A slave revolt in New York results in the execution of twenty-one slaves and the suicides of six others
1723	Virginia denies African Americans the right to vote
1758	The Colony of New Jersey establishes the first Indian reservation in North America
1763	The Treaty of Paris gives Britain control of the French colony of Quebec
1774	The Quebec Act expands Quebec's borders and protects French Canadian rights
1775	The first abolitionist organization in the United States, the Pennsylvania Society for the Abolition of Slavery, is formed
1793	Virginia outlaws entry of free African Americans into the state
1793	The Fugitive Slave Act requires the return of escaped slaves to their owners
1793	Invention of the cotton gin encourages the spread of slavery in the South
1808	The federal government bans importation of slaves into the United States, but illegal importation continues
1819	The U.S. government requires the tracking of the numbers of immigrants to the country
1820	Congress enacts the Missouri Compromise, under which Missouri is admitted to the Union as a slave state, Maine is admitted as a free state, and slavery is prohibited in the remaining territories north of Missouri's southern boundary
1822	Denmark Vesey is executed for conspiring to lead a slave insurrection in South Carolina
1824	The Bureau of Indian Affairs is established by the U.S. government as part of the War Department
1827	The first African American newspaper, *Freedman's Journal*, is published
1831	The Supreme Court's *Cherokee Nation v. Georgia* decision results in the forcible removal of Cherokees from Georgia to present-day Oklahoma
1831	Nat Turner leads a slave insurrection in Virginia
1832	The New England Anti-Slavery Society is organized
1837	The colonial Canadian government crushes a French-Canadian revolt in Quebec
1843	B'nai B'rith, an international Jewish service organization, is founded
1843	Sojourner Truth begins giving abolitionist lectures
1848	U.S. victory in the Mexican-American War leads to the annexation of the American southwest, with substantial Mexican and Indian populations

1849	The Bureau of Indian Affairs is transferred from the U.S. War Department to the Department of the Interior
1850	California establishes a $20 monthly licensing fee for foreign miners, seeking to limit Mexican and Chinese intrusions
1850	The Compromise of 1850 results in California's admission to the Union as a nonslave state and the entrance of Utah and New Mexico as undecided on the issue
1852	Harriet Beecher Stowe publishes *Uncle Tom's Cabin*, which attacks slavery
1854	The Young Men's Hebrew Association is founded
1854	The Republican Party is founded by antislavery members of the Whig, Democratic, and Free Soil parties
1857	The Supreme Court's *Dred Scott* decision declares that African Americans are not citizens of the United States and that the Missouri Compromise is unconstitutional
1859	Abolitionist John Brown is hanged after his raid on the federal arsenal at Harpers Ferry, Virginia
1861	The Civil War begins (April)
1863	President Abraham Lincoln issues the Emancipation Proclamation, declaring slaves in states still in rebellion against the Union to be free (January 1)
1865	The Civil War ends (April 9)
1865	Ratification of the Thirteenth Amendment to the U.S. Constitution prohibits slavery or other involuntary servitude (December)
1865	Southern states begin to enforce black laws, which severely limit liberties of newly freed African Americans
1865	The Ku Klux Klan is founded in Tennessee
1866	Congress enacts the Civil Rights Act of 1866, declaring that persons born in the United States are, without regard to race, citizens of the United States entitled to equal protection of the law
1866	The Five Civilized Tribes are forced to give up their western lands to other Indians, partly as punishment for aiding the Confederacy in the Civil War
1868	Ratification of the Fourteenth Amendment grants citizenship to all persons born in the United States, without regard to race, and requires states to accord individuals equal protection of the law and due process of the law (July)
1870	Ratification of the Fifteenth Amendment guarantees the right to vote without regard to race, color, or previous condition of servitude (February)
1871	Congress enacts the Ku Klux Klan Act in an attempt to restrain the violence perpetrated by the organization
1875	Congress enacts the Civil Rights Act of 1875, prohibiting racial discrimination in transportation, hotels, inns, theaters, and places of public amusement
1877	Reconstruction ends after President Rutherford B. Hayes withdraws the last Union troops from the South
1879	The Supreme Court's *Strauder v. West Virginia* decision holds that exclusion of African Americans from jury service violates the equal protection clause
1881	Booker T. Washington founds the Tuskegee Institute
1882	The Chinese Exclusion Act prohibits Chinese laborers from immigrating to the United States
1882	President Chester Arthur creates a Hopi reservation out of land in the middle of the Navajo reservation, leading to prolonged conflict
1883	The Supreme Court's *Civil Rights Cases* decision declares the Civil Rights Act of 1875 unconstitutional
1885	Tensions mount between Canadians of British and French descent following the execution of Louis Riel, a métis leader considered a hero by French Canadians
1886	The Supreme Court's *Yick Wo v. Hopkins* decision finds unconstitutional a municipality's discriminatory application of zoning laws against persons of Chinese ancestry
1889	Unassigned lands in the Indian Territory are opened to white settlement

1890	Federal troops massacre two hundred Sioux at Wounded Knee, South Dakota
1896	The Supreme Court's *Plessy v. Ferguson* decision establishes the separate-but-equal principle by holding that a legally mandated provision for separate railway cars for whites and blacks does not violate the equal protection clause
1898	Supreme Court's *United States v. Wong Kim Ark* decision finds that the Fourteenth Amendment provides that children of permanent Chinese residents of the United States are U.S. citizens
1898	The United States defeats Spain in the Spanish-American War and acquires the Philippines, Guam, and Puerto Rico
1899	The Supreme Court's *Cumming v. Richmond County Board of Education* decision holds that a school district can provide high school education for white students but not for blacks
1900	The Foraker Act makes Puerto Rico an unincorporated U.S. territory
1901	Inhabitants of the Indian Territory are made U.S. citizens
1905	The Niagara Movement, predecessor of the National Association for the Advancement of Colored People, is organized with the help of W. E. B. Du Bois
1906	Plantation owners begin to bring Filipino workers to Hawaii to replace recently banned Koreans
1907	Asian Indian sawmill workers are attacked and driven out of Bellingham, Washington
1907	Charles Curtis becomes the first Native American senator
1908	The Gentleman's Agreement restricts Japanese immigration to the United States
1909	The National Association for the Advancement of Colored People (NAACP) is founded
1911	The National Urban League is organized to protect the rights of African Americans who migrate to northern cities from the South
1915	The Supreme Court's *Guinn v. United States* decision invalidates state voter literacy requirements intended to prevent African Americans from voting
1915	*The Birth of a Nation*, pathbreaking feature film about the Civil War and Reconstruction, demonstrates the pervasiveness of anti-black racism in the United States
1916	Marcus Garvey arrives in the United States from Jamaica and becomes a leading advocate of black nationalism
1916	Madison Grant's book *The Passing of the Great Race* is published, representing a popular strain of racist literature aimed at peoples of the Balkans, Mediterranean basin, eastern Europe, and Asia
1917	Puerto Ricans become U.S. citizens but are denied the right to vote in presidential elections
1917	Immigration to the United States from the Asiatic Barred Zone, which includes most of Asia and the Pacific islands, is forbidden
1920	The American Civil Liberties Union (ACLU) is founded
1921	The Snyder Act defines the major duties of the Bureau of Indian Affairs, including provision of education, employment opportunities, medical care, and improvement of reservation lands
1922	The Supreme Court's *Ozawa v. United States* decision upholds a federal law that denies resident aliens the opportunity to obtain U.S. citizenship because of their race
1923	The Supreme Court's *Frick v. Webb* decision upholds a state law that prohibits persons of Japanese descent from owning real estate
1923	Supreme Court's *United States v. Bhagat Singh Thind* decision finds that a high caste Hindu is not a "white person" as defined in federal citizenship laws and thus is not entitled to U.S. citizenship
1924	The U.S. Bureau of Immigration establishes the Border Patrol to restrict illegal immigration from Mexico
1924	The Indian Citizenship Act grants citizenship to all Indians born in the territorial United States
1924	The Johnson-Reed Act sets an annual nationality immigration quota at 2 percent of the number of foreign-born Americans of each nationality residing in the United States according to the 1890 census

1924	The Oriental Exclusion Act bans Asians from immigrating to the United States
1927	The Supreme Court's *Gong Lum v. Rice* decision allows a state to segregate Chinese American students in schools with other "colored" students rather than in schools for whites
1927	The Supreme Court's *Nixon v. Herndon* decision finds unconstitutional the exclusion of blacks from voting in state Democratic primaries
1929	Several Mexican labor and social organizations merge to form the League of United Latin American Citizens (LULAC)
1930	Wallace Fard founds the Nation of Islam
1931	Trial of the Scottsboro Nine begins in Alabama
1934	The Tydings-McDuffie Act promises the Philippines independence in 1946 and limits Filipino immigration to the United States to an annual quota of fifty
1934	The Johnson-O'Malley Act enables federal and state governments to cooperate in providing services to Native Americans
1934	The Wheeler-Howard Indian Reorganization Act stops further loss of reservation lands and provides for limited self-government through elected tribal councils
1935	The Supreme Court's *Grovey v. Townsend* decision upholds a state Democratic Party's limitation of membership to whites
1935	Mary McLeod Bethune founds the National Council of Negro Women
1938	The Supreme Court's *Missouri ex rel. Gaines v. Canada* decision holds that refusal of a state to allow African Americans to attend a state's only public law school violates the equal protection clause
1939	The NAACP creates the Legal Defense and Educational Fund to oppose racially discriminatory laws, and Thurgood Marshall takes charge of these efforts
1940	Congress passes the Alien Registration Act
1941	In response to A. Philip Randolph's call for African Americans to march on Washington to protest racial discrimination in the armed forces, defense industries, and federal employment generally, President Franklin D. Roosevelt issues an executive order that temporarily establishes the Fair Employment Practices Committee
1942	Executive Order 9066 authorizes military commanders to remove "any and all persons" from designated military areas, leading to the forcible detention of some 110,000 Americans of Japanese ancestry in camps throughout the west
1942	The United States and Mexico conclude the Bracero Agreement, a program permitting temporary foreign laborers to work in the United States
1942	James Farmer and students at the University of Chicago establish the Congress of Racial Equality (CORE)
1943	Congress repeals the ban on Chinese immigrants
1943	In the so-called Zoot Suit Riots, following an alleged attack on U.S. sailors in Los Angeles, soldiers, sailors, and marines indiscriminately attack Mexican Americans for several days
1943	The Supreme Court's *Hirabayashi v. United States* decision upholds a curfew for Japanese Americans during World War II
1944	The Supreme Court's *Korematsu v. United States* decision holds that Japanese American internment during World War II does not violate the equal protection clause
1944	The Supreme Court's *Smith v. Allwright* decision finds that exclusion of African Americans from participation in party primaries violates the Constitution
1944	The National Congress of American Indians, the first national native political organization, is formed
1946	The Indian Claims Commission, an independent commission of the federal government, is formed to examine native land claims
1946	President Harry S Truman issues an executive order establishing the President's Committee on Civil Rights
1947	Jackie Robinson becomes the first African American to play major league baseball

1947	The President's Committee on Civil Rights produces a report entitled *To Secure These Rights*, which condemns racial discrimination in the United States
1947	The Crawford-Butler Act permits Puerto Ricans to elect their own governor
1948	When the Democratic Party National Convention adopts a strong civil rights plank, Southern Democrats withdraw to form the Dixiecrat Party, with Strom Thurmond as their presidential candidate
1948	The Supreme Court's *Shelley v. Kraemer* decision holds that the Constitution prevents state courts from enforcing racially restrictive real estate covenants
1948	President Harry S Truman signs Executive Order 9981 prohibiting racial discrimination in the armed forces and other federal employment
1948	The Japanese American Evacuation Claims Act authorizes a maximum payment of $2,500 to Japanese Americans who had been interned during World War II to compensate for lost property
1949	Luís Muñoz Marin is inaugurated as the first elected governor of Puerto Rico
1950	The Supreme Court's *Sweatt v. Painter* decision holds that Texas' attempt to establish a separate law school for blacks rather than admit black applicants to the University of Texas Law School violates the equal protection clause
1950-1953	U.S. troops in Korea establish ties with Koreans through marriage and collaboration
1952	Puerto Rico becomes a self-governing U.S. commonwealth
1952	The McCarran-Walter Act eliminates race as a bar to immigration but continues the national origins quota system
1952	The Relocation Services Program is established to aid Native Americans in finding urban employment and housing
1953	Congress passes the Termination Resolution, initiating an abortive attempt to end government support for certain Indian reservations
1954	The Supreme Court's *Brown v. Board of Education of Topeka, Kansas* decision finds that racial segregation in public schools violates the equal protection clause (May 17)
1955	The Interstate Commerce Commission bans racial segregation on interstate buses and trains
1955	Fifteen-year-old African American Emmett Till is murdered in Mississippi after allegedly flirting with a white woman; a jury ultimately acquits two white men charged with his murder
1955	The Supreme Court issues a second opinion in the *Brown v. Board of Education* case (*Brown II*), requiring desegregation of public schools "with all deliberate speed"
1955	Rosa Parks's defiance of segregated seating rules on a Montgomery, Alabama, bus touches off a year-long bus boycott
1956	Most southern members of Congress sign the "Southern Manifesto" denouncing the Supreme Court's *Brown v. Board of Education* decision
1957	Martin Luther King, Jr., and other African American leaders found the Southern Christian Leadership Conference (SCLC)
1957	Congress passes the first civil rights act since Reconstruction, banning discrimination in public places based on race, color, religion, or national origin
1957	After Arkansas' governor uses National Guard troops to block African American children from entering Little Rock's Central High School, President Dwight D. Eisenhower federalizes the guard and mobilizes additional federal armed forces to ensure that the school is peacefully integrated
1958	The Supreme Court's *Cooper v. Aaron* decision rejects state attempt to delay desegregation of public schools on the grounds of potential racial turmoil
1959	Hawaii is granted statehood
1959-1962	Following Fidel Castro's implementation of a Marxist government in Cuba, some 200,000 Cubans emigrate to the United States
1960	Student sit-ins begin at lunch counters in Greensboro, North Carolina

1960	Passage of the Civil Rights Act of 1960 expands protections of voting rights
1960	The Student Non-Violent Coordinating Committee (SNCC) is founded
1961	President John F. Kennedy issues an executive order that establishes the Equal Employment Opportunity Commission and requires businesses with government contracts to take "affirmative action" in the equal treatment of employees
1961	Freedom rides sponsored by CORE test the ban on segregation in interstate buses; riders are beaten, and a bus is burned in Birmingham, Alabama
1961-1975	Political, diplomatic, and personal ties resulting from American involvement in Vietnam lead to widespread Vietnamese immigration
1962	President John F. Kennedy signs an executive order banning racial discrimination in federally financed housing
1962	Voter registration drives begin in southern states under the direction of the Council of Federated Organizations (COFO)
1962	James Meredith enrolls in the University of Mississippi over the defiant protest of Governor Ross R. Barnett and in the face of mob violence
1962	César Chávez establishes the United Farm Workers labor organization to protect rights of Mexican American laborers
1963	During demonstrations in Birmingham, Alabama, Police Commissioner Eugene (Bull) Connor orders the use of dogs and fire hoses against demonstrators
1963	Medgar W. Evers, field secretary for the Mississippi NAACP, is assassinated (June 12)
1963	The March on Washington is sponsored by civil rights, labor, and religious organizations; featured speaker Martin Luther King, Jr., delivers his "I Have a Dream" speech (August 28)
1963	In his inaugural address, newly elected Alabama governor George C. Wallace declares "Segregation now, segregation tomorrow, segregation forever"
1963	Four African American girls are killed when a bomb explodes at the Sixteenth Street Baptist Church in Birmingham, Alabama (September 15)
1963	Reies López Tijerina forms the *Alianza Federal de Mercedes* (Federal Alliance of Land Grants) in California to regain lands taken from Mexican Americans
1964	The United States and Mexico end the Bracero Program
1964	The Council of Federated Organizations, a group of associated civil rights groups, organizes the Freedom Summer project to register African Americans to vote in Mississippi
1964	Ratification of the Twenty-fourth Amendment prohibits poll taxes in federal elections
1964	Civil rights workers James Chaney, Michael Schwerner, and Andrew Goodman are killed near Philadelphia, Mississippi (June)
1964	Supreme Court's *Griffin v. Prince Edward County School Board* decision finds that school districts cannot simply close public schools in an attempt to avoid desegregating them
1964	Congress passes the Civil Rights Act of 1964, which prohibits racial, religious, sexual, and other forms of discrimination in a variety of contexts
1964	Martin Luther King, Jr., is awarded the Nobel Peace Prize
1964	Supreme Court's *Heart of Atlanta Motel v. United States* decision upholds the power of Congress to prohibit racial discrimination in privately owned hotels and inns
1965	Malcolm X is assassinated (February 21)
1965	Martin Luther King, Jr., leads a march from Selma to Montgomery, Alabama, to protest voting discrimination (March)
1965	Congress passes the Voting Rights Act
1965	President Lyndon B. Johnson issues an executive order requiring businesses with federal contracts to undertake affirmative action measures

1965	The Immigration Act repeals discriminatory immigration laws against nonwhites, leading to large-scale immigration from Korea and India
1965	César Chávez leads grape pickers of California's San Joaquin Valley into a five-year strike, becoming the first Chicano activist to gain national prominence
1965	The Watts riot flares in Los Angeles
1965	Thurgood Marshall becomes solicitor general of the United States
1965	Congress amends the McCarran-Walter Act to abolish the national origins quota system
1966	The Supreme Court overrules the attempt by Georgia's legislature to deny Julian Bond a seat in the legislature because of his association with SNCC
1966	Massachussetts makes Edward W. Brooke the first black U.S. senator elected since Reconstruction
1966	The Black Panther Party is organized in Oakland, California, by Bobby Seale and Huey P. Newton
1966	Constance Bake Motley becomes the first African American woman appointed to serve as a federal judge
1966	Stokely Carmichael takes over leadership of SNCC and coins the phrase "Black Power" to advocate more militant responses to continued racial discrimination
1967	Sixty percent of Puerto Ricans vote to remain a U.S. commonwealth
1967	*Guess Who's Coming to Dinner*, a controversial film dealing explicitly with the question of racial prejudice in the United States, is released
1967	Thurgood Marshall is appointed by President Lyndon Johnson as the U.S. Supreme Court's first black justice
1967	Summer race riots disrupt many northern cities
1967	The Supreme Court's *Loving v. Virginia* decision holds that a state law barring interracial marriages is unconstitutional
1968	The Supreme Court's *Green v. County School Board* decision finds that a "freedom of choice" plan adopted by a school district does not satisfy the district's constitutional obligation to desegregate public schools
1968	The National Advisory Committee on Civil Disorders (the Kerner Commission) releases its report concerning urban riots, claiming as key reasons white racism and increasing racial and economic stratification
1968	The Supreme Court's *Jones v. Alfred H. Mayer Co.* decision finds that Congress has the power to prohibit racial discrimination in housing sales
1968	Martin Luther King, Jr., is assassinated in Memphis, Tennessee, a few days after leading a protest march for striking sanitation workers (April 4)
1968	Congress passes the American Indian Civil Rights Act, which guarantees to residents of reservations a variety of rights with respect to tribal authorities
1968	Congress passes the Civil Rights Act of 1968, which prohibits discrimination in the sale and rental of housing and in home financing
1968	René Lévesque forms a new party to promote Quebec sovereignty
1968	The first Mexican American studies program is established at California State College, Los Angeles
1968	The American Indian Movement, a radical Indian rights organization, is formed
1968	Shirley Chisholm of New York becomes the first African American woman elected to Congress
1969	Native Americans seize Alcatraz Island and hold it for eighteen months, demanding that it be made into a center of Native American culture
1969-1971	The Richard M. Nixon administration requires federal contractors to set specific goals and timetables for minority hiring
1970	José Angel Gutierrez helps establish *La Raza Unida*, a Texas-based political party aimed at securing Hispanic control of counties with majority Hispanic populations

1970	Chicano activists found La Raza Unida Party
1971	The Supreme Court's *Griffin v. Breckenridge* decision upholds a federal law punishing racially motivated assaults on public highways
1971	The Native American Rights Fund is created
1971	Jesse Jackson organizes Operation PUSH
1971	In *Griggs v. Duke Power Company*, the Supreme Court bans non-job-related tests that might unfairly screen minorities
1971	The Attica Prison riot leaves more than forty people dead
1971	Ratification of the Twenty-sixth Amendment to the U.S. Constitution lowers the minimum voting age to eighteen
1971	The Supreme Court's *Swann v. Charlotte-Mecklenburg Board of Education* decision authorizes busing to desegregate school district
1971	The Supreme Court's *Graham v. Richardson* decision invalidates state discrimination against aliens in the distribution of welfare benefits
1972	Indian rights activists seize the headquarters of the Bureau of Indian Affairs, accusing the agency of failing to protect native interests
1972	African American Angela Davis, a former UCLA professor, is acquitted of charges that she aided and abetted a courtroom shootout in California two years before
1972	Five hundred Native Americans travel to Washington in the "Trail of Broken Treaties" to protest federal policy toward Native Americans
1973	Congress passes the Ethnic Heritage Act to fund programs enhancing the image of various ethnic groups
1973	Cree Indians of Quebec gain a temporary injunction halting construction of a hydroelectric plant on James Bay that they claim violates guarantees of hunting and fishing rights
1973	Members of the American Indian Movement seize the South Dakota village of Wounded Knee in order to call attention to government violations of treaties made with Indian tribes
1973	The Supreme Court's *In re Griffiths* decision holds that a state cannot deny resident aliens the right to become lawyers
1974	The province of Quebec declares French its official language
1974	In *Lau v. Nichols*, the Supreme Court requires schools to teach children in a language they can understand
1974	Congress clarifies boundaries between Hopi and Navajo reservations in northeastern Arizona, leaving some twelve thousand Navajos on Hopi land
1976	The Supreme Court's *Hampton v. Wong Mow Sun* decision finds unconstitutional federal regulations limiting most federal civil-service positions to U.S. citizens and natives of Samoa
1976	The Supreme Court's *Washington v. Davis* decision holds that laws having a disproportionately burdensome effect on racial minorities are not subject to the same rigorous review as laws purposefully discriminating on grounds of race
1978	Three hundred Native Americans begin the "longest walk" to safeguard treaty rights
1978	In *Regents of the University of California v. Bakke*, the Supreme Court rules against the use of quotas to achieve racial balance in colleges and universities but allows an applicant's race to be considered in the admissions process
1978	The tightening of communist controls by the Vietnamese through Southeast Asia displaces many ethnic Chinese, Laotians, and Cambodians
1978	Congress establishes a single worldwide ceiling of 290,000 immigrants and a uniform system for determining preference
1978	Congress passes the American Indian Religious Freedom Act
1979	The Supreme Court's *United Steel Workers of America v. Weber* decision upholds the ability of private employers to adopt affirmative action plans

1979	The Islamic revolution in Iran causes thousands of Iranians to emigrate in the early 1980's
1979	Tensions between native whites and Vietnamese Americans peak when Vietnamese immigrants are acquitted of murder in the death of an American fisherman
1980	In *Fullilove v. Klutznick*, the Supreme Court upholds minority set-aside contracts established by Congress for federal programs
1980	The Refugee Act increases the refugee immigration allotment, paving the way for massive immigration from southeast Asia throughout the early 1980's
1980	The U.S. government agrees to pay more than $200 million to settle land claims by the Passamaquoddy and Penobscot tribes in Maine and eight Sioux tribes in South Dakota
1980	Castro allows 125,000 Marielitos to leave Cuba, including many unskilled workers, convicted criminals, and mentally ill people
1980	Race riots leave eighteen people dead in Miami after four Miami police officers are acquitted of charges of beating a black insurance executive to death
1982	The Supreme Court rules that Indian tribes have the right to tax mineral production on reservation lands
1982	Congress extends the effect of the Voting Rights Act of 1965
1982	The Supreme Court's *Plyler v. Doe* decision holds that a state's denial of public education to illegal aliens violates the equal protection clause
1984	Indian Land Consolidation Act bars American Indians from passing private property on reservations to heirs, in order to stop the division of reservation lands
1984	The Civil Rights Commission ends the use of quotas in employment promotions for African Americans
1985	Wilma Mankiller becomes the first female chief of a major Native American tribe
1985	The United States halts trade with South Africa after sustained public protests concerning the South African regime's racist policies
1986	The Supreme Court's *Batson v. Kentucky* decision holds that a prosecutor's attempt to disqualify possible jurors because of their race violates the equal protection clause of the Fourteenth Amendment
1986	In *Wygant v. Jackson Board of Education*, the Supreme Court rules that the jobs of newly hired black teachers cannot be protected by laying off senior white teachers
1986	Immigration Reform and Control Act prohibits employers from employing undocumented aliens and provides opportunities for illegal aliens who have resided continuously in the United States since before 1982 to become citizens
1986	A holiday honoring Martin Luther King, Jr., is celebrated officially for the first time
1987	Twenty thousand people participate in a racial brotherhood march in Cummings, Georgia, following disruption of an earlier march by the Ku Klux Klan
1987	The shooting of an unarmed black teenager by a white police officer leads to widespread protest from Montreal's black community
1987	The Meech Lake Accord, a proposed amendment to Canada's constitution recognizing Quebec as a "distinct society," is negotiated by provincial premiers; it will fail to be ratified by the 1990 deadline
1987	Three white teenagers are convicted of manslaughter following a racially motivated attack on three black men in the Howard Beach section of New York City a year earlier
1987	The Supreme Court's *McCleskey v. Kemp* decision holds that mere proof of a racially disproportionate impact of death penalty sentences on African Americans does not violate the Constitution
1988	A federal jury orders the Ku Klux Klan, the Southern White Knights, and eleven individuals to pay $1 million in damages to protesters attacked during a 1987 civil rights march
1988	In the wake of much controversy over bilingual education, state legislatures in Arizona, Colorado, and Florida pass laws making English the state language

1988	The Fair Housing Amendments Act establishes a procedure for imposing fines for those found guilty of housing discrimination based on race, color, sex, religion, or national origin
1988	The Canadian government resolves long-standing disputes with the tribal groups in Alberta, the Yukon, and the Northwest Territories, ceding various rights to some 20,000 square miles of territory
1988	Puyallup Indians in Washington state drop claims to three hundred acres of Tacoma territory in return for cash, land, and job training worth more than $160 million
1988	*La Presse*, the largest French-language newspaper in Canada, gives active support to a movement designed to prevent Hasidic Jews from building a synagogue in the affluent suburb of Outremont
1988	Lauro Cavazos is appointed secretary of education, becoming the first Hispanic member of a U.S. Cabinet
1988	The Civil Rights Restoration Act restricts federal funding to institutions that discriminate on the basis of race, gender, disability and age, reversing a 1984 Supreme Court decision that narrowed the scope of federal antidiscrimination laws
1988	Legislation provides $20,000 apiece for surviving Japanese Americans who were forcibly interned during World War II and $12,000 apiece for surviving Aleut Indians who were removed from the Aleutian and Pribilof Islands during the war
1988	The Canadian government agrees to award about $21,000 (Canadian) apiece to surviving Japanese Canadians who were forcibly relocated during World War II
1988	The House of Representatives extends antidiscrimination job protection to its own employees, overriding its previous exemption
1988	The city of Yonkers, New York, accepts a court-ordered plan to integrate both housing and schools, ending a legal battle begun in 1980
1989	The Supreme Court's *Richmond v. J. A. Croson, Co.* decision holds that state and local affirmative action programs must be subject to "strict scrutiny," a constitutional standard requiring the most compelling government justifications
1989	Douglas Wilder becomes the first elected black state governor in the United States
1989	In *Martin v. Wilks*, the Supreme Court allows white firefighters in Birmingham, Alabama, to challenge a 1981 court-approved affirmative action program designed to increase minority representation and promotion
1989	Stanford University and the Smithsonian Institution agree to return ancient Indian bones for reburial when they can be associated with specific tribes
1989	New York State Police troopers and FBI agents raid illegal Mohawk casinos on the Akwesasne reservation, which straddles the U.S.-Canadian border
1989	Racial unrest on the campus of the University of Massachusetts in Amherst leads to the introduction of mounted police patrols on campus
1989	In protest of the Supreme Court's decision in *Patterson v. McLean Credit* to limit the application of an 1866 civil rights law to job-discrimination cases, more than 35,000 protesters silently file past the Supreme Court Building and the Capitol
1989	William Barclay Allen resigns as chairman of the U.S. Commission on Civil Rights following a number of controversial actions, culminating in a California speech entitled "Blacks, Animals, and Homosexuals: Who Is a Minority?"
1989	Following a 1988 federal court ruling that Mississippi judicial districts must be redrawn, voters elect five black trial court judges
1989	Black honor student Yusuf Hawkins is killed in the predominantly Italian Brooklyn neighborhood of Bensonhurst when he and three friends are assaulted by about thirty white men
1989	A memorial inscribed with the names of forty people who died in the 1960's Civil Rights movement is dedicated in Montgomery, Alabama
1990	150 people march from Selma to Montgomery to mark the twenty-fifth anniversary of the historic march to gain equal voting rights for African Americans
1990	The Milwaukee, Wisconsin, school board votes to open two schools for blacks utilizing a special curriculum focusing on black culture and featuring programs designed to develop self-esteem and personal responsibility

1990	Armed Mohawk Indians protesting the extension of a city-owned golf course near Montreal erect barricades and disrupt traffic throughout the summer, highlighting grievances against the federal government
1990	President George Bush vetoes the Civil Rights Act, which would have overturned five recent Supreme Court rulings making it more difficult to win discrimination lawsuits against employers
1990	In a series of steps taken to improve relations between Indians and non-Indians, South Dakota celebrates its first Native Americans Day on October 8 and declares 1990 a year of reconciliation
1990	The Supreme Court upholds an Oregon ban on the use of the hallucinogenic drug Peyote in religious rituals, angering Native Americans who argue that the drug has been part of their worship for more than five hundred years
1990	Texas Hispanics lose a federal court appeal protesting county-wide election of judges
1990	Under a new law, the Justice Department begins collecting statistics on hate crimes in order to determine if changes in federal law are needed
1990	In *The Content of Our Character*, Shelby Steele presents an African American case against affirmative action, arguing that it contributes to a "victim-focused identity"
1990	Black activists boycott Korean American supermarkets in Brooklyn following charges that a black customer had been assaulted in one of the stores
1990	Using themes of racial resentment, former Ku Klux Klansman David Duke makes a strong showing in the U.S. Senate primary in Louisiana
1991	The Supreme Court's *Board of Education of Oklahoma City Public Schools v. Dowell* decision holds that a school district is entitled to have a desegregation order lifted when it has complied in good faith with a desegregation decree since it was entered and when vestiges of past discrimination have been eliminated to the extent practicable
1991	A U.S. district court strikes down a University of Wisconsin, Madison, policy banning speech demeaning to a person's race, sex, religion, color, creed, disability, sexual orientation or ancestry
1991	Dinesh D'Souza argues against political correctness and ideological education in *Illiberal Education: The Politics of Race and Sex on Campus*
1991	An advisory panel to the New York state commissioner of education publishes "One Nation, Many Peoples: A Declaration of Cultural Interdependence," calling for the inclusion of more nonwhite and non-European views in the public school curriculum
1991	An agreement is signed by the province of Ontario and leaders of the twelve "First Nations," recognizing the Indians' right to govern themselves
1991	Wisconsin state officials and Indian leaders end a seventeen-year legal battle by agreeing that the Chippewa are entitled to 50 percent of the harvestable natural resources in northern Wisconsin
1991	Rioting breaks out in a largely Hispanic neighborhood of Washington, D.C., following the wounding of a Hispanic man by a black female police officer
1991	President George Bush signs the Civil Rights Bill, making it easier for employees to sue employers for discrimination, but only after changes are made to a vetoed 1990 bill that might have created racial quotas
1991	Clarence Thomas succeeds Thurgood Marshall as the second black Supreme Court justice, despite protests from civil rights groups decrying his opposition to affirmative action programs and busing for school desegregation
1991	The National Civil Rights Museum, dedicated to the 1950's and 1960's struggle for racial equality in the United States, is opened in Memphis, Tennessee
1991	Frank Iacobucci is sworn in as the first Italian Canadian justice of the Canadian Supreme Court
1991	Eight FBI agents are disciplined and an internal review is initiated following a $1 million racial settlement with Donald Rochon, a black former agent
1991	The U.S. Education Department proposes regulations banning most race-based college scholarships
1991	Studies by the Urban Institute find that hiring and housing discrimination against blacks is "widespread and entrenched"

1991	The wounding of a Salvadoran immigrant by police leads to two days of rioting in Washington, D.C.
1991	The killing of a young Guyanese immigrant by an Orthodox Jewish driver leads to the retaliatory murder of an Australian Hasidic scholar by black youths and prompts four days of rioting
1991	The Persian Gulf War leads to immigration in the early 1990's of Iraqis who had assisted U.S. and NATO forces in expelling Iraq from Kuwait
1992	Four Los Angeles police officers are acquitted of charges stemming from the 1991 beating of black motorist Rodney King, touching off five days of rioting in Los Angeles that result in more than fifty deaths and $1 billion in property damage
1992	The Supreme Court prohibits criminal defendants from excluding potential jurors on the basis of race
1992	Ben Nighthorse Campbell of Colorado becomes the first Native American to win a U.S. Senate seat since 1929
1992	The FBI agrees to promote, reassign, or grant back pay to more than fifty black agents
1992	The U.S. Department of Education determines that the admissions policy of the University of California at Berkeley's law school violates the Civil Rights Act of 1964 by comparing prospective candidates only against others in their own racial group
1992	Following the killing of a black man, Raymond Lawrence, by a white police officer, rioters in Toronto go on a two-hour rampage in the city's first ever race riot
1992	In *Oh Canada! Oh Quebec! Requiem for a Divided Country*, Mordecai Richler criticizes French-speaking nationalists for suppressing the rights of English speakers in Quebec
1992	In settlement of the first case of mortgage discrimination, the Justice Department forces Decatur Federal Savings and Loan of Atlanta to pay $1 million to forty-eight black families who had been unfairly denied mortgages between 1988 and 1992
1992	In *United States v. Fordice*, the Supreme Court rules that remnants of segregation remain in the Mississippi system of higher education and that positive steps must be taken to remedy such segregation
1992	In *R.A.V. v. City of St. Paul*, the Supreme Court unanimously rules that a St. Paul, Minnesota, law making the use of racist language a criminal offense is a violation of First Amendment guarantees of free speech
1992	Celebration of the five hundredth anniversary of Christopher Columbus's first voyage to the Americas sparks widespread opposition from Native American and black leaders who argue that the Spanish explorer directly or indirectly introduced disease, imperial control, and slavery into the New World
1993	President Bill Clinton angers civil rights groups when he withdraws Lani Guinier's nomination for head of the Civil Rights Division of the Justice Department following opposition by critics who cite her radical proposals for helping minorities gain political power
1993	The Holocaust Memorial Museum opens in Washington, D.C.
1993	Shoney's restaurant company agrees to a $105 million settlement with 40,000 current or former employees who claim racial bias in hiring, firing, and promoting practices
1993	Los Angeles police officers Stacey Koon and Laurence Powell are sentenced to prison for violating the civil rights of Rodney King in a 1991 beating incident
1993	Canadian prime minister Brian Mulroney signs the final agreement leading to the creation of the large Inuit (Eskimo) territory of Nunavut, to be carved from the Northwest Provinces
1993	In *Wisconsin v. Mitchell*, the Supreme Court rules that states can punish racially motivated crimes more harshly than similar crimes not motivated by bias
1993	Some 75,000 civil rights activists march on Washington, D.C., to celebrate the thirtieth anniversary of the first march on Washington and call for a renewed commitment to civil rights
1993	The Supreme Court votes to return to a lower court a challenge to the creation of two strangely shaped congressional districts that favor minority candidates, arguing that such gerrymandering might violate the rights of white voters

1994	Seventy-three-year-old white supremacist Byron De La Beckwith is convicted of the 1963 murder of civil rights leader Medgar Evers and is sentenced to life in prison
1994	The parent Flagstar Company agrees to pay $45.7 million in a class-action settlement stemming from 4,300 racial bias complaints against Denny's restaurant chain
1994	President Bill Clinton, Vice President Al Gore, and most members of the Cabinet meet with elected leaders of 547 Native American tribes to discuss relations between tribal governments and the federal government
1994	A Washington judge agrees to allow tribal judgment of two Tlingit boys convicted of robbery and assault; the Kuye'di Kuiu Kwaan Tribal Court in Klawock, Alaska, imposes year-long banishment for each boy on separate uninhabited islands
1994	Canada's Royal Commission on Aboriginal Peoples concludes that the federal government was negligent in relocating seventeen Inuit families to a barren coast of Ellesmere Island, north of the Arctic Circle, during the 1950's
1994	A federal jury orders the city of Los Angeles to pay Rodney King $3.8 million in damages stemming from a 1991 beating by white police officers
1995	The Supreme Court's *Miller v. Johnson* decision finds that state congressional districts deliberately drawn to include a majority of African American residents violates equal protection
1995	Treaties with four of the Yukon's fourteen native bands provide certain land titles, recognition of aboriginal rights, and financial compensation, ending twenty-two years of negotiations between the Canadian government and native groups
1995	The Supreme Court upholds a lower-court ruling abolishing a University of Maryland scholarship program specifically designed for African American students
1995	Delegates to the annual convention of Southern Baptists, the nation's largest Protestant denomination, pass a resolution denouncing racism and apologizing for "historic acts of evil such as slavery"
1995	In *Adarand Constructors v. Peña*, the Supreme Court requires that federal contracts based on affirmative action set-asides are valid only in cases where those benefiting have suffered actual discrimination in the past
1995	Governor Pete Wilson abolishes some 150 boards that advised California state agencies on minority hiring
1995	The governing board of the University of California votes to end preferential treatment for minorities in their hiring process
1995	O. J. Simpson's acquittal of the 1994 murder of his wife and a companion divides the country along racial lines
1995	Approximately 700,000 people, mostly African American men, attend Louis Farrakhan's Million Man March, a Washington, D.C., rally highlighting male family responsibilities and addressing problems plaguing the black community in America
1995	Maryland Democratic Representative Kweisi Mfume becomes chief executive of the NAACP following longstanding controversies over improper financial practices of former directors William F. Gibson, Benjamin Chavis, and Benjamin L. Hooks
1996	The U.S. government returns four acres of land considered sacred by the Karuk Indians of Northwestern California; the land had been seized following a 1993 conviction for growing marijuana on the property
1996	At a Theater Communications Group conference, African American playwright August Wilson decries the lack of funding for minority theaters and suggests that many critics are incapable of appreciating works with minority themes
1996	The National Capital Commission agrees to remove a statue of a kneeling Canadian Indian from an Ottawa monument to explorer Samuel de Champlain after complaints from the Assembly of First Nations that it was demeaning
1996	The U.S. Department of the Interior releases the Delaware tribe from trusteeship of the Cherokee nation, a status which had been forced on the Delaware in 1979 in violation of an 1866 treaty
1996	Federal judges close one casino and rule that ten others in New Mexico are operating illegally because they have not received approval from the state legislature
1996	California voters approve Proposition 209, designed to end all forms of affirmative action in "the operation of public employment, public education, or public contracting"

1996	Mohawk Indians seize a public grade school in Hogansburg, New York, and form their own unified school district, leading to negotiations and a new eight-member council to address Native American grievances
1996	A U.S. Fifth Circuit Court of Appeals decision in *Hopwood v. Texas* bars the University of Texas Law School from considering race as a factor in the admissions process
1996	President Bill Clinton signs the Church Arson Prevention Act, making destruction of religious property "on the basis of race, color, or ethnicity" a federal crime
1996	Texaco Incorporated agrees to pay $176.1 million to settle a discrimation suit filed on behalf of 1,500 current and former black employees
1996	In winning a second term as president, Bill Clinton receives 84 percent of the African American vote and 72 percent of the Hispanic vote
1996	The Oakland, California, school board determines that the English dialect spoken by many African Americans is a separate language (Ebonics) based upon West African roots, thus qualifying for federal funds approved for bilingual education
1997	Louis Farrakhan holds an antiracism rally in Philadelphia at the invitation of Jewish mayor Edward Rendell, easing racial tensions stemming from accusations of a racially motivated attack on young blacks in the city's Grays Ferry neighborhood
1997	The Indian Land Consolidation Act (1984), which prohibited the passing to heirs of private property on reservation lands, is declared unconstitutional by the Supreme Court, which rules that it violates Fifth Amendment property rights
1997	Navajos living on the Hopi reservation are required to sign seventy-five-year leases on their property, to move, or to be relocated by the federal government
1997	The National Church Arson Task Force, appointed by President Clinton in 1996, reports that racism was only one of many factors contributing to more than four hundred church fires that had been set during the 1990's
1997	Winnie Madikizela-Mandela speaks at the Million Woman March, a Philadelphia rally organized to unify African American women against common community and family problems
1997	President Bill Clinton launches a year-long debate on race relations in America by appointing black historian John Hope Franklin to lead a panel consisting of three whites, two blacks, one Hispanic, and one Korean American
1998	Sam Bowers, a former Imperial Wizard of the Ku Klux Klan in Mississippi, is sentenced to life in prison for ordering the 1966 murder of civil rights activist Vernon Dahmer

John Powell

Bibliography

Plentiful resources cover the many aspects—theoretical, historical, political, social, and psychological—of interracial and interethnic relations in North America. Categorized below are more than two thousand books available in or through libraries, many suited to the general and high school audiences, many aimed at the undergraduate college student. Although all the "classic" theorists—from Allport to Gordon to Myrdal to Zangwill—are represented here, the listings give priority to resources published within the last two decades of the twentieth century, when research into North American intergroup dynamics and cultural studies reached a high point. Sources have been listed multiply only in approximately two dozen cases, when their titles clearly refer to more than one category identified below. The editors preferred, instead, to cross-reference those categories for which resources are likely to be found in a different section of the bibliography (for example, African American History. *See also* Civil Rights).

GENERAL AND THEORETICAL WORKS

See also Psychology, Attitudes, Personal Relations; Race Definitions; Racism, Prejudice, Discrimination

Abrahamson, Mark. *Urban Enclaves: Identity and Place in America.* New York: St. Martin's Press, 1996.

Abrahamson, Mark, Ephraim H. Mizruchi, and Carlton A. Hornung. *Stratification and Mobility.* New York: Macmillan, 1976.

Ackermann, Robert John. *Heterogeneities: Race, Gender, Class, Nation, and State.* Amherst: University of Massachusetts Press, 1996.

Alba, Richard D., ed. *Ethnicity and Race in the U.S.A.* Boston: Routledge & Kegan Paul, 1985.

Andersen, Margaret, and Patricia H. Collins, comps. *Race, Class, and Gender: An Anthology.* Belmont, Calif.: Wadsworth, 1992.

Appiah, Anthony, and Amy Gutmann. *Color Conscious: The Political Morality of Race.* Princeton, N.J.: Princeton University Press, 1996.

Auerbach, Susan, ed. *Encyclopedia of Multiculturalism.* White Plains, N.Y.: Marshall Cavendish, 1993.

Balibar, Étienne, and Immanuel Wallerstein. *Race, Nation, Class: Ambiguous Identities.* New York: Verso, 1991.

Banton, Michael. *Race Relations.* New York: Basic Books, 1967.

_____. *Racial and Ethnic Competition.* New York: Cambridge University Press, 1983.

_____. *Racial Theories.* 2d ed. New York: Cambridge University Press, 1998.

Barber, Bernard. *Social Stratification: A Comparative Analysis of Structure and Process.* New York: Harcourt, Brace and World, 1957.

Barrera, Mario. *Race and Class in the Southwest: A Theory of Racial Inequality.* Notre Dame: University of Notre Dame Press, 1976.

Barzun, Jacques. *Race: A Study in Superstition.* Rev. ed. New York: Harper & Row, 1965.

Bendix, Reinhard, and Seymour Martin Lipset, eds. *Class, Status, and Power.* 2d ed. New York: Free Press, 1966.

Berreman, Gerald D. *Caste and Other Inequities.* Meerut, India: Folklore Institute, 1979.

Blalock, Hubert M. *Race and Ethnic Relations.* Englewood Cliffs, N.J.: Prentice-Hall, 1982.

Blauner, Robert. *Racial Oppression in America.* New York: Harper & Row, 1972.

Bottomore, T. B. *Classes in Modern Society.* New York: Pantheon Books, 1966.

Bryjak, George J., and Michael P. Soroka. *Sociology: Cultural Diversity in a Changing World.* 2d ed. Boston: Allyn & Bacon, 1992.

Buenker, John D., and Lorman A. Ratner. *Multiculturalism in the United States: A Comparative Guide to Acculturation and Ethnicity.* Westport, Conn.: Greenwood Press, 1992.

Bullard, Robert D., and Glenn S. Johnson, eds. *Just Transportation: Dismantling Race and Class Barriers to Mobility.* Stoney Creek, Conn.: New Society Publishers, 1997.

Bullard, Robert D., et al. *We Speak for Ourselves: Social Justice, Race and Environment,* edited by Dan A. Alston. Washington, D.C.: Panos Institute, 1990.

Burke, Ronald K., ed. *American Public Discourse: A Multicultural Perspective.* Lanham, Md.: University Press of America, 1992.

Cashmore, Ellis, and Barry Troyna. *Introduction to Race Relations.* 2d ed. New York: Falmer Press, 1990.

Cashmore, Ernest. *Dictionary of Race and Ethnic Relations.* 4th ed. New York: Routledge, 1996.

Cecil, Andrew R. *Equality, Tolerance, and Loyalty: Virtues Serving the Common Purpose of Democracy.* Dallas: University of Texas at Dallas Press, 1990.

Clayton, Obie, Jr., ed. *An American Dilemma Revisited: Race Relations in a Changing World.* New York: Russell Sage Foundation, 1996.

Cohen, Jean. *Class and Civil Society.* Amherst: University of Massachusetts Press, 1982.

Coles, Robert. *Children in Crisis: A Study in Courage and Fear.* Boston: Little, Brown, 1967.

Collins, Randall. *Conflict Sociology.* New York: Academic Press, 1975.

Collins, Sheila D. *The Rainbow Challenge.* New York: Monthly Review Press, 1986.

Cose, Ellis. *Color-Blind: Seeing Beyond Race in a Race-Obsessed World.* New York: HarperCollins, 1997.

_____. *A Nation of Strangers.* New York: William Morrow, 1992.

Coser, Lewis A. *Continuities in the Study of Social Conflict.* New York: Free Press, 1967.

_____. *The Functions of Social Conflict.* Glencoe, Ill.: Free Press, 1956.

Cott, Nancy F., ed. *Intercultural and Interracial Relations.* New Providence: K. G. Saur, 1993.

Cox, Oliver Cromwell. *Caste, Class, and Race: A Study in Social Dynamics.* New York: Monthly Review Press, 1959.

_____. *Race Relations: Elements and Social Dynamics.* Detroit: Wayne State University Press, 1976.

Crenshaw, Kimberlé, ed. *Critical Race Theory: The Key Writings That Formed the Movement.* New York: W. W. Norton, 1995.

Crouch, Stanley. *The All-American Skin Game: Or, The Decoy of Race.* New York: Pantheon, 1995.

Cummings, Scott. *Left Behind in Rosedale: Race Relations and the*

Collapse of Neighborhood Institutions. Boulder, Colo.: Westview Press, 1998.

Delgado, Richard, ed. *Critical Race Theory: The Cutting Edge.* Philadelphia: Temple University Press, 1995.

Delgado, Richard, and Jean Stefancic, eds. *Critical White Studies: Looking Behind the Mirror.* Philadelphia: Temple University Press, 1997.

Dennis, Rutledge M., ed. *Research in Race and Ethnic Relations: A Research Annual.* Greenwich, Conn.: JAI Press, 1991.

Dewitt, Howard A. *The Fragmented Dream: Multicultural California.* Dubuque, Iowa: Kendall/Hunt, 1996.

Di Leonardo, Micaela. *The Varieties of Ethnic Experience.* Ithaca, N.Y.: Cornell University Press, 1984.

Dorn, Edwin. *Rules and Racial Equality.* New Haven, Conn.: Yale University Press, 1979.

Downs, James F., and Hermann K. Bleibtreu. *Human Variation.* Rev. ed. Beverly Hills, Calif.: Glencoe Press, 1972.

Dumont, Louis. *Homo Hierarchicus: The Caste System and Its Implications.* Translated by Mark Sainsbury, Louis Dumont, and Basia Gulati. Rev. English ed. Chicago: University of Chicago Press, 1980.

Dworkin, Anthony Gary, and Rosalind J. Gary, eds. *The Minority Report: An Introduction to Racial, Ethnic, and Gender Relations.* Rev. ed. Fort Worth: Harcourt Brace College Publications, 1998.

Dyson, Michael Eric. *Race Rules.* Reading, Mass.: Addison-Wesley, 1996.

Early, Gerald, ed. *Lure and Loathing: Essays in Race, Identity, and the Ambivalence of Assimilation.* New York: Penguin, 1993.

Farley, John E. *Majority-Minority Relations.* 3d ed. Englewood Cliffs, N.J.: Prentice Hall, 1995.

Farley, Reynolds, and Walter R. Allen. *The Color Line and the Quality of Life in America.* New York: Russell Sage Foundation, 1987.

Feagin, Joe R., and Clairece Booher Feagin. *Racial and Ethnic Relations.* 5th ed. Englewood Cliffs, N.J.: Prentice-Hall, 1996.

Fetzer, Philip L., ed. *The Ethnic Moment: The Search for Equality in the American Experience.* Armonk, N.Y.: M. E. Sharpe, 1997.

Fine, Michelle, et al. *Off White: Readings on Race, Power, and Society.* New York: Routledge, 1997.

Fischer, William C., ed. *Identity, Community, and Pluralism in American Life.* New York: Oxford University Press, 1997.

Franklin, John Hope. *Color and Race.* Boston: Houghton Mifflin, 1968.

_____. *The Color Line: Legacy for the Twenty-first Century.* Columbia: University of Missouri Press, 1993.

Freeman, Howard E., and Norman R. Kurtz, eds. *America's Troubles: A Casebook on Social Conflict.* Englewood Cliffs, N.J.: Prentice-Hall, 1969.

Friedman, Murray, and Nancy Isserman, eds. *The Tribal Basis of American Life: Racial, Religious, and Ethnic Groups in Conflict.* Westport, Conn.: Praeger, 1998.

Fuchs, Lawrence H. *The American Kaleidoscope: Race, Ethnicity, and the Civic Culture.* Hannover, N.H.: University Press of New England, 1990.

Gates, Henry Louis, Jr. *Loose Canons: Notes on the Culture Wars.* New York: Oxford University Press, 1992.

Geschwender, James. *Racial Stratification in America.* Dubuque, Iowa: Wm. C. Brown, 1978.

Giddens, Anthony. *The Class Structure of the Advanced Societies.* New York: Harper & Row, 1975.

_____. *The Constitution of Society: Outline of the Theory of Structuration.* Berkeley: Calif.: University of California Press, 1984.

Giddens, Anthony, and David Held. *Classes, Power, and Conflict: Classical and Contemporary Debates.* Berkeley: University of California Press, 1982.

Gilder, George F. *Visible Man: A True Story of Post-Racist America.* San Francisco: ICS Press, 1995.

Glazer, Nathan. *Ethnic Dilemmas, 1964-1982.* Cambridge, Mass.: Harvard University Press, 1983.

Glazer, Nathan, and Daniel Patrick Moynihan. *Beyond the Melting Pot: The Negroes, Puerto Ricans, Jews, Italians, and Irish of New York City.* Cambridge, Mass.: MIT Press, 1963.

_____, eds. *Ethnicity.* Cambridge, Mass.: Harvard University Press, 1975.

Goertz, Clifford. *The Interpretation of Cultures.* New York: Basic Books, 1973.

Goffman, Erving. *Stigma: Notes on the Management of Spoiled Identity.* Englewood Cliffs, N.J.: Prentice-Hall, 1963.

Goldberg, David Theo. *Racial Subjects: Writing on Race in America.* New York: Routledge, 1997.

Goldsby, Richard. *Race and Races.* New York: Macmillan, 1971.

Gomez, Rudolph, et al., eds. *The Social Reality of Ethnic America.* Lexington, Mass.: D. C. Heath, 1974.

Gordon, Milton M. *Assimilation in American Life: The Role of Race, Religion, and National Origins.* New York: Oxford University Press, 1964.

_____. *Human Nature, Class, and Ethnicity.* New York: Oxford University Press, 1978.

Gossett, Thomas F. *Race: The History of an Idea in America.* New York: Schocken Books, 1971.

Greeley, Andrew M. *Ethnicity, Denomination, and Inequality.* Beverly Hills, Calif.: Sage Publications, 1976.

_____. *Ethnicity in the United States: A Preliminary Reconnaissance.* New York: Wiley, 1974.

Grove, D. John. *The Race vs. Ethnic Debate: A Cross-National Analysis of Two Theoretical Approaches.* Denver: Center on International Race Relations, University of Denver, 1974.

Harris, Dean A., ed. *Multiculturalism from the Margins: Non-Dominant Voices on Difference and Diversity.* Westport, Conn.: Bergin & Garvey, 1995.

Hawley, Willis D., and Anthony Jackson, eds. *Toward a Common Destiny: Improving Race and Ethnic Relations in America.* San Francisco: Jossey-Bass, 1995.

Hewstone, Miles, and Rupert Brown, eds. *Contact and Conflict in Intergroup Encounters.* Oxford, England: Basil Blackwell, 1986.

Hill, Mike, ed. *Whiteness: A Critical Reader.* New York: New York University Press, 1997.

Hind, Robert J. "The Internal Colonial Concept." *Comparative Studies in Society and History* 26 (July, 1984): 543-568.

Hochschild, Jennifer L. *Facing Up to the American Dream: Race, Class, and the Soul of the Nation.* Princeton, N.J.: Princeton University Press, 1995.

Hollinger, David A. *Postethnic America: Beyond Multiculturalism.* New York: BasicBooks, 1995.

Holmes, Robert L., ed. *Nonviolence in Theory and Practice.* Belmont, Calif.: Wadsworth, 1990.

Horowitz, Donald. *Ethnic Groups in Conflict.* Berkeley: University of California Press, 1985.

Hughey, Michael W., ed. *New Tribalisms: The Resurgence of Race and Ethnicity*. New York: New York University Press, 1998.

Hunter, James Davison. *Culture Wars: The Struggle to Define America*. New York: Basic Books, 1991.

Jackson, John A., ed. *Social Stratification*. London: Cambridge University Press, 1968.

Jaret, Charles. *Contemporary Racial and Ethnic Relations*. New York: HarperCollins, 1995.

Jiobu, Robert. *Ethnicity and Assimilation*. Albany: State University of New York Press, 1988.

Jones, James E., Jr. *Race in America: The Struggle for Equality*. Madison: University of Wisconsin Press, 1993.

Katz, Irwin, and Patricia Gurin, eds. *Race and the Social Sciences*. New York: Basic Books, 1969.

Kaus, Mickey. *The End of Equality*. New York: Basic Books, 1992.

Kincheloe, Joe L., ed. *White Reign: Deploying Whiteness in America*. New York: St. Martin's Press, 1998.

Kinloch, Graham C. *The Dynamics of Race Relations*. New York: McGraw-Hill, 1974.

Kisubi, Alfred T., and Michael A. Burayidi. *Race and Ethnic Relations in the First Person*. Westport, Conn.: Praeger, 1998.

Kivisto, Peter. *Americans All: Race and Ethnic Relations in Historical, Structural, and Comparative Perspectives*. Belmont, Calif.: Wadsworth, 1995.

Knopke, Harry J., et al. *Opening Doors: Perspectives on Race Relations in Contemporary America*. Tuscaloosa: University of Alabama Press, 1991.

Kottak, Conrad Phillip, and Kathryn A. Kozaitis. *On Being Different: Diversity and Multiculturalism in the North American Mainstream*. Boston: McGraw-Hill, 1999.

Kozol, Jonathan. *Amazing Grace: The Lives of Children and the Conscience of a Nation*. New York: Crown, 1995.

Krauss, Irving. *Stratification, Class, and Conflict*. New York: Free Press, 1976.

Kromkowski, John A., ed. *Race and Ethnic Relations*. 6th ed. Guilford, Conn.: Dushkin, 1996.

Lambert, Wallace E., and Donald M. Taylor. *Coping with Cultural and Racial Diversity in Urban America*. New York: Praeger, 1990.

Lenski, Gerhard E. *Power and Privilege: A Theory of Social Stratification*. New York: McGraw-Hill, 1966.

Levy, Mark R., and Michael S. Kramer. *The Ethnic Factor*. New York: Simon & Schuster, 1972.

Lieberson, Stanley. *Ethnic Patterns in American Cities*. New York: Free Press, 1963.

Lieberson, Stanley, and Mary Waters. *From Many Strands: Ethnic and Racial Groups in Contemporary America*. New York: Russell Sage Foundation, 1990.

Lincoln, C. Eric, and Henry Louis Gates, Jr. *Coming Through the Fire: Surviving Race and Place in America*. Durham, N.C.: Duke University Press, 1996.

Locke, Alain Leroy. *Race Contacts and Interracial Relations: Lectures on the Theory and Practice of Race*. Washington, D.C.: Howard University Press, 1992.

Loury, Glenn C. *One by One from the Inside Out: Essays and Reviews on Race and Responsibility in America*. New York: Free Press, 1995.

Lyman, Stanford M. *Color, Culture, Civilization: Race and Minority Issues in American Society*. Urbana: University of Illinois Press, 1994.

Mack, Raymond W. *Race, Class, and Power*. 2d ed. New York: American Book Company, 1968.

McKee, James B. *Sociology and the Race Problem: The Failure of a Perspective*. Urbana: University of Illinois Press, 1993.

McLemore, S. Dale. *Racial and Ethnic Relations in America*. 5th ed. Boston: Allyn and Bacon, 1998.

McWilliams, Carey. *A Mask for Privilege*. Boston: Little, Brown, 1948.

Maharidge, Dale. *The Coming White Minority: California's Eruptions and America's Future*. New York: Times Books, 1996.

Marden, Charles F., Gladys Meyer, and Madeline H. Engel. *Minorities in American Society*. 6th ed. New York: HarperCollins, 1992.

Marger, Martin N. *Race and Ethnic Relations: American and Global Perspectives*. 2d ed. Belmont, Calif.: Wadsworth, 1991.

Mason, Philip. *Patterns of Dominance*. London: Oxford University Press, 1970.

_____. *Race Relations*. New York: Oxford University Press, 1970.

Masuoka, Jitsuichi, and Presten Valien, eds. *Race Relations: Problems and Theory, Essays in Honor of Robert E. Park*. Chapel Hill: University of North Carolina Press, 1971.

Mendus, Susan, ed. *Justifying Toleration: Conceptual and Historical Perspectives*. Cambridge, England: Cambridge University Press, 1988.

Meyers, Gustavus. *History of Bigotry in the United States*. Rev. ed. New York: Capricorn Books, 1960.

Miller, John J. *The Unmaking of Americans: How Multiculturalism Has Undermined the Assimilation Ethic*. New York: Free Press, 1998.

Mindel, Charles H., Robert W. Habenstein, and Roosevelt Wright, Jr., eds. *Ethnic Families in America*. 4th ed. Englewood Cliffs, N.J.: Prentice-Hall, 1998.

Monk, Richard C., ed. *Taking Sides: Clashing Views on Controversial Issues in Race and Ethnicity*. 2d ed. Guilford, Conn.: Dushkin, 1996.

Montagu, Ashley. *Race, Science, and Humanity*. Princeton, N.J.: Van Nostrand, 1963.

Morgan, Gordon D. *America Without Ethnicity*. Port Washington, N.Y.: Kennikat Press, 1981.

Myrdal, Gunnar. *An American Dilemma: The Negro Problem and American Democracy*. New York: Harper & Row, 1944; McGraw-Hill, 1964.

Nash, Gary B., and Richard Weiss, eds. *The Great Fear: Race in the Mind of America*. New York: Holt, Rinehart and Winston, 1970.

National Conference on Christians and Jews. *Taking America's Pulse: The National Conference Survey on Inter-Group Relations*. New York: Author, 1994.

Naylor, Larry L., ed. *Cultural Diversity in the United States*. Westport, Conn.: Bergin & Garvey, 1997.

Newman, William M. *American Pluralism*. New York: Harper & Row, 1973.

Oleksy, Elzbieta, ed. *American Cultures: Assimilation and Multiculturalism*. San Francisco: International Scholars, 1995.

Olzak, Susan. *The Dynamics of Ethnic Competition and Conflict*. Stanford, Calif.: Stanford University Press, 1992.

Olzak, Susan, and Joane Nagel. *Competitive Ethnic Relations*. Orlando, Fla.: Academic Press, 1986.

Omi, Michael, and Howard Winant. *Racial Formation in the United States*. 2d ed. New York: Routledge, 1994.

Outlaw, Lucius T., Jr. *On Race and Philosophy.* New York: Routledge, 1996.

Park, Robert Ezra. *Race and Culture.* Glencoe, Ill.: Free Press, 1950.

Parrillo, Vincent N. *Diversity in America.* Thousand Oaks, Calif.: Sage Publications, 1995.

_____. *Strangers to These Shores: Race and Ethnic Relations in the United States.* 5th ed. Boston: Allyn and Bacon, 1997.

Payne, Richard J. *Getting Beyond Race: The Changing American Culture.* Boulder, Colo.: Westview Press, 1998.

Perlmutter, Philip. *The Dynamics of American Ethnic, Religious, and Racial Group Life: An Interdisciplinary Overview.* Westport, Conn.: Praeger, 1996.

Pettigrew, Thomas F. *Racially Separate or Together?* New York: McGraw-Hill, 1971.

_____, ed. *The Sociology of Race Relations: Reflections and Reform.* New York: Free Press, 1980.

Pincus, Fred L., and Howard J. Ehrlich, eds. *Race and Ethnic Conflict.* Boulder, Colo.: Westview Press, 1994.

Rabinowitz, Howard N. *Race, Ethnicity, and Urbanization: Selected Essays.* Columbia: University of Missouri Press, 1994.

Ransford, H. Edward. *Race and Class in American Society: Black, Latino, Anglo.* 2d rev. ed. Cambridge, Mass.: Schenkman, 1994.

Rex, John. *Race Relations in Sociological Theory.* New York: Schocken Books, 1970.

Rex, John, and David Mason, eds. *Theories of Race and Ethnic Relations.* Cambridge: Cambridge University Press, 1986.

Rhea, Joseph Tilden. *Race Pride and the American Identity.* Harvard University Press, 1998.

Ringer, Benjamin B., and Elinor R. Lawless. *Race: Ethnicity and Society.* New York: Routledge, 1989.

Rose, Peter Isaac. *They and We: Racial and Ethnic Relations in the United States.* 5th ed. New York: McGraw-Hill, 1997.

Rossides, Daniel W. *Social Stratification: The American Class System in Comparative Perspective.* Englewood Cliffs, N.J.: Prentice-Hall, 1990.

Roth, Byron M. *Prescriptions for Failure: Race Relations in the Age of Social Science.* New Brunswick, N.J.: Transaction, 1994.

Rothenberg, Paula S. *Race, Class, and Gender in the United States: An Integrated Study.* 2d ed. New York: St. Martin's Press, 1992.

Rothman, Robert A. *Inequality and Stratification: Class, Color, and Gender.* 2d ed. Englewood Cliffs, N.J.: Prentice-Hall, 1993.

Rousseau, Jean-Jacques. *Discourse on the Origin of Inequality.* Translated by Donald A. Cress. Indianapolis: Hackett, 1992.

Rowan, Carl. *The Coming Race War in America: A Wake-up Call.* Boston: Little, Brown, 1996.

Russell, Cheryl. *The Official Guide to Racial and Ethnic Diversity.* Ithaca, N.Y.: New Strategist, 1997.

Ryan, William. *Blaming the Victim.* Rev. ed. New York: Vintage Books, 1976.

_____. *Equality.* New York: Pantheon Books, 1981.

Scarr. Sandra. *Race, Social Class, and Individual Differences.* Hillsdale, N.J.: Lawrence Erlbaum, 1981.

Schaffer, Richard T. *Race and Ethnicity in the United States.* New York: HarperCollins, 1995.

_____. *Racial and Ethnic Groups.* 5th ed. New York: HarperCollins, 1993.

Schmidt, Alvin J., and Dinesh D'Souza. *Menace of Multiculturalism: Trojan Horse in America.* Westport, Conn.: Praeger, 1997.

Scott, James C. *Domination and the Arts of Resistance.* New Haven, Conn.: Yale University Press, 1990.

Shibutani, Tamotsu, and Kian M. Kwan. *Ethnic Stratification.* New York: Macmillan, 1965.

Simpson, George, and J. Milton Yinger. *Racial and Cultural Minorities.* 5th ed. New York: Plenum Press, 1985.

Smith, Michael P., and Joe R. Feagin, eds. *The Bubbling Cauldron: Race, Ethnicity, and the Urban Crisis.* Minneapolis: University of Michigan Press, 1995.

Sniderman, Paul M., and Thomas Piazza. *The Scar of Race.* Cambridge, Mass.: Harvard University Press, 1993.

Sowell, Thomas. *Race and Culture: A World View.* New York: Basic Books, 1994.

Stanfield, John H., II, ed. *A History of Race Relations Research: First-Generation Recollections.* Newbury Park, Calif.: Sage Publications, 1993.

Steele, Shelby. *The Content of Our Character: A New Vision of Race in America.* New York: St. Martin's Press, 1990.

Steinberg, Stephen. *The Ethnic Myth: Race, Ethnicity, and Class in America.* New York: Atheneum, 1981.

Stone, John. *Racial Conflict in Contemporary Society.* Cambridge, Mass.: Harvard University Press, 1995.

Stuck, Mary, ed. *Issues in Diversity: Voices of the Silenced.* Acton, Mass.: Copley, 1990.

Sugrue, Thomas J. *The Origins of the Urban Crisis: Race and Inequality in Postwar Detroit.* Princeton, N.J.: Princeton University Press, 1996.

Tajfel, Henri. *Human Groups and Social Categories.* Cambridge, England: Cambridge University Press, 1981.

Takaki, Ronald T., ed. *From Different Shores: Perspectives on Race and Ethnicity in America.* 2d ed. New York: Oxford University Press, 1994.

Taylor, Jared. *Paved with Good Intentions: The Failure of Race Relations in Contemporary America.* New York: Carroll & Graf, 1992.

Thernstrom, Stephan, ed. *Harvard Encyclopedia of American Ethnic Groups.* Cambridge, Mass.: Harvard University Press, 1980.

Thomas, Gail E., ed. *Race and Ethnicity in America: Meeting the Challenge in the 21st Century.* Washington, D.C.: Taylor & Francis, 1995.

_____, ed. *U.S. Race Relations in the 1980's and 1990's.* New York: Hemisphere, 1990.

Vander Zanden, James W. *American Minority Relations.* 4th ed. New York: Alfred A. Knopf, 1983.

Wacker, R. Fred. *Ethnicity, Pluralism, and Race: Race Relations Theory in America Before Myrdal.* Westport, Conn.: Greenwood Press, 1983.

Warner, W. Lloyd, and Leo Srole. *The Social Systems of American Ethnic Groups.* New Haven, Conn.: Yale University Press, 1945.

Weber, Max. *Basic Concepts in Sociology.* Translated and introduced by H. P. Secher. 5th ed. New York: Citadel Press, 1968.

Welsing, Frances Cress. *Isis (Yssis) Papers: The Keys to the Colors.* Chicago: Third World Press, 1991.

Wilkinson, J. Harvie, III. *One Nation Indivisible: How Ethnic Separatism Threatens America.* Reading, Mass.: Addison-Wesley, 1997.

Williams, Mary E., ed. *Minorities.* San Diego, Calif.: Greenhaven Press, 1998.

Willie, Charles Vert. *The Caste and Class Controversy.* Dix Hills, N.Y.: General Hall, 1979.

_____. *Oreo: On Race and Marginal Men and Women*. Wakefield, Mass.: Parameter Press, 1975.

Wilson, William J. *The Declining Significance of Race*. Chicago: University of Chicago Press, 1978.

_____. *The Truly Disadvantaged: The Inner City, the Underclass, and Public Policy*. Chicago: University of Chicago Press, 1987.

_____. *When Work Disappears: The World of the New Urban Poor*. New York: Alfred A. Knopf, 1996.

Winant, Howard. *Racial Conditions: Politics, Theory, Comparisons*. Minneapolis: University of Minnesota Press, 1994.

Winborne, Wayne, and Renae Cohen. *Intergroup Relations in the United States: Research Perspectives*. Bloomsburg, Pa.: Haddon Craftsman, 1998.

Winkelman, Michael. *Ethnic Relations in the U.S.: A Sociohistorical Cultural Systems Approach*. Minneapolis: West, 1993.

Wrench, John. *Race Relations in the 1990s: Mapping Out an Agenda*. Coventry, England: Centre for Research in Ethnic Relations, University of Warwick, 1990.

Yetman, Norman, ed. *Majority and Minority: The Dynamics of Race and Ethnicity in American Life*. 5th ed. Boston: Allyn & Bacon, 1991.

Yinger, J. Milton. *Ethnicity: Source of Strength? Source of Conflict?* Albany: State University of New York Press, 1994.

Zangwill, Israel. *The Melting Pot*. New York: Macmillan, 1925.

AFFIRMATIVE ACTION

See also Economics; Education

Annals of the American Academy of Political and Social Science 523 (September, 1992). Special issue, Affirmative Action Revisited.

Badgett, M. V. Lee, Andrew F. Brimmer, Cecilia A. Conrad, and Heidi Hartmann. *Economic Perspectives on Affirmative Action*. Washington, D.C.: Joint Center for Political and Economic Studies, 1995.

Beckwith, Francis J., and Todd E. Jones, eds. *Affirmative Action: Social Justice or Reverse Discrimination?* Amherst, N.Y.: Prometheus, 1997.

Benokraitis, Nijole, and Joe R. Feagin. *Affirmative Action and Equal Opportunity: Action, Inaction, Reaction*. Boulder, Colo.: Westview Press, 1978.

Bolick, Clint. *The Affirmative Action Fraud: Can We Restore the American Civil Rights Vision?* Washington, D.C.: Cato Institute, 1996.

Bowen, William G., and Derek Bok. *The Shape of the River: Long-Term Consequences of Considering Race in College and University Admissions*. Princeton, N.J.: Princeton University Press, 1998.

Bowie, Norman E., ed. *Equal Opportunity*. Boulder, Colo.: Westview Press, 1988.

Burstein, Paul. "Affirmative Action, Jobs, and American Democracy: What Has Happened to the Quest for Equal Opportunity?" *Law and Society Review* 26, no. 4 (1992): 901-922.

Carter, Stephen L. *Reflections of an Affirmative Action Baby*. New York: Basic Books, 1992.

Clayton, Susan D., and Faye J. Crosby. *Justice, Gender and Affirmative Action*. Ann Arbor: University of Michigan Press, 1992.

Cohen, Carl. *Naked Racial Preferences: The Case Against Affirmative Action*. Lanham, Md.: Madison Books, 1995.

Delgado, Richard. *The Coming Race War? And Other Apocalyptic Tales of America After Affirmative Action and Welfare*. New York: New York University Press, 1996.

Dworkin, Ronald. "What Did *Bakke* Really Decide?" In *A Matter of Principle*. Cambridge, Mass.: Harvard University Press, 1985.

Eastland, Terry. *Ending Affirmative Action: The Case for Colorblind Justice*. New York: Basic Books, 1996.

Edley, Christopher F., Jr. *Not All Black and White: Affirmative Action, Race, and American Values*. New York: Hill & Wang, 1996.

Ezorsky, Gertrude. *Racism and Justice: The Case for Affirmative Action*. Ithaca, N.Y.: Cornell University Press, 1991.

Fiscus, Ronald J. *The Constitutional Logic of Affirmative Action*. Durham, N.C.: Duke University Press, 1992.

Fullinwider, Robert. *The Reverse Discrimination Controversy*. Totowa, N.J.: Rowman and Littlefield, 1980.

Glazer, Nathan. *Affirmative Discrimination: Ethnic Inequality and Public Policy*. New York: Basic Books, 1975.

Greene, Kathanne W. *Affirmative Action and Principles of Justice*. New York: Greenwood Press, 1989.

Greenwalt, Kent. *Discrimination and Reverse Discrimination*. New York: Alfred A. Knopf, 1983.

Horne, Gerald. *Reversing Discrimination: The Case for Affirmative Action*. New York: International, 1992.

Jackson, Charles C. "Affirmative Action: Controversy and Retrenchment." *The Western Journal of Black Studies* 16, no. 4 (Winter, 1992).

Jones, Augustus J. *Affirmative Talk, Affirmative Action: A Comparative Study of the Politics of Affirmative Action*. New York: Praeger, 1991.

Kahlenberg, Richard D. *The Remedy: Class, Race, and Affirmative Action*. New York: BasicBooks, 1996.

Leonard, Jonathan. "The Federal Anti-Bias Effort." In *Essays on the Economics of Discrimination*, edited by Emily P. Hoffman. Kalamazoo, Mich.: W. E. Upjohn Institute, 1991.

Lerner, Robert, and Althea K. Nigai. *Racial Preferences in Undergraduate Enrollment at the University of California, Berkeley, 1993-1995: A Preliminary Report*. Washington, D.C.: Center for Equal Opportunity, 1996.

Lynch, Frederick R. *The Diversity Machine: The Drive to Change the "White Male Workplace."* New York: Free Press, 1996.

McCormack, Wayne. *The Bakke Decision: Implications for Higher Education Admissions*. Washington, D.C.: American Council on Education and the Association of American Law Schools, 1978.

McWhirter, Darien A. *The End of Affirmative Action: Where Do We Go from Here?* New York: Carol Publishing Group, 1996.

Maguire, Daniel. *A Case for Affirmative Action*. Dubuque, Iowa: Shepherd, 1992.

Post, Robert, and Michael Paul Rogin, eds. *Race and Representation: Affirmative Action*. New York: Zone Books, 1998.

Roberts, Paul Craig, and Lawrence M. Stratton, Jr. *The New Color Line: How Quotas and Privilege Destroy Democracy*. Washington, D.C.: Regnery, 1995.

Rosenfeld, Michel. *Affirmative Action and Justice: A Philosophical and Constitutional Inquiry*. New Haven, Conn.: Yale University Press, 1991.

Sindler, Allan P. *Bakke, Defunis, and Minority Admissions: The Quest for Equal Opportunity*. New York: Longman, 1978.

Sowell, Thomas. *Preferential Policies: An International Perspective*. New York: William Morrow, 1990.

Steinberg, Stephen. *Turning Back: The Retreat from Racial Justice in American Thought and Policy.* Boston: Beacon Press, 1995.

Swain, Carol M., ed. *Race Versus Class: The New Affirmative Action Debate.* Lanham, Md.: University Press of America, 1996.

Thernstrom, Abigail. *Whose Votes Count? Affirmative Action and Minority Voting Rights.* Cambridge, Mass.: Harvard University Press, 1987.

U.S. Commission on Civil Rights. *Affirmative Action in 1980's: Dismantling the Process of Discrimination: A Statement of the United States Commission on Civil Rights.* Washington, D.C.: Author, 1981.

Urofsky, Melvin I. *A Conflict of Rights: The Supreme Court and Affirmative Action.* New York: Charles Scribner's Sons, 1991.

Zelnick, Bob. *Backfire: A Reporter's Look at Affirmative Action.* Chicago: Henry Regnery, 1996.

AFRICAN AMERICANS

See also General and Theoretical Works; Affirmative Action; Canada/Black Canadians; Caribbean Americans; Civil Rights; Hate and White Supremacy; History of Race Relations; Multiracialism and Biracialism; Psychology, Attitudes, Personal Relations; Race Definitions; Racism, Prejudice, Discrimination

General Studies

Allen, Bonnie. *We Are Overcome: Thoughts on Being Black in America.* New York: Crown, 1995.

Allen, Robert L. *Black Awakening in Capitalist America.* Garden City, N.Y.: Doubleday/Anchor, 1970.

America, Richard F. *Paying the Social Debt: What White America Owes Black America.* Westport, Conn.: Praeger, 1993.

Appiah, Kwame Anthony. *In My Father's House: Africa in the Philosophy of Culture.* New York: Oxford University Press, 1992.

Armour, Jody David. *Negrophobia and Reasonable Racism: The Hidden Costs of Being Black in America.* New York: New York University Press, 1997.

Asante, Molefi Kete. *The Afrocentric Idea.* Philadelphia: Temple University Press, 1987.

_____. *Afrocentricity.* Trenton, N.J.: Africa World Press, 1988.

Baldwin, James. *The Fire Next Time.* New York: Dell, 1963.

Berry, Mary Frances, and John Blassingame. *Long Memory: The Black Experience in America.* New York: Oxford University Press, 1982.

Blauner, Bob. *Black Lives, White Lives: Three Decades of Race Relations in America.* Berkeley: University of California Press, 1989.

Boxill, Bernard R. *Blacks and Social Justice.* Totowa, N.J.: Rowman & Allanheld, 1984.

Brock, Lisa, and Digna Castañeda Fuertes, eds. *Between Race and Empire: African-Americans and Cubans Before the Cuban Revolution.* Philadelphia: Temple University Press, 1998.

Brooks, Roy L. *Rethinking the American Race Problem.* Berkeley: University of California Press, 1990.

Broussard, Albert S. *Black San Francisco: The Struggle for Racial Equality in the West, 1900-1954.* Lawrence: University Press of Kansas, 1993.

Brown, Tony. *Black Lies, White Lies: The Truth According to Tony Brown.* New York: Wm. C. Morrow, 1995.

Carlson, Lewis H., and George A. Colburn, eds. *In Their Place: White America Defines Her Minorities, 1850-1950.* New York: Wiley, 1972.

Clark, Kenneth B. *Dark Ghetto: Dilemmas of Social Power.* New York: Harper & Row, 1965.

Cleaver, Eldridge. *Soul on Ice.* New York: McGraw-Hill, 1968.

Coleman, Jonathan. *Long Way to Go: Black and White in America.* New York: Atlantic Monthly Press, 1997.

Collier, Peter, and David Horowitz. *The Race Card: White Guilt, Black Resentment, and the Assault on Truth and Justice.* Rocklin, Calif.: Prima Publishing, 1997.

Croucher, Sheila. *Imagining Miami.* Charlottesville: University Press of Virginia, 1997.

Cruse, Harold. *Plural but Equal: A Critical Study of Blacks and Minorities in America's Plural Society.* New York: William Morrow, 1987.

Davis-Adeshoté, Jeanette, et al. *Black Survival in White America: From Past History to the Next Century.* Orange, N.J.: Bryant and Dillon, 1995.

Dorman, James H., and Robert R. Jones. *The Afro-American Experience.* New York: Wiley, 1974.

Du Bois, W. E. B. *The Souls of Black Folk.* 1903. Reprint. New York: Vintage Books, 1990.

Dunn, Marvin. *Black Miami in the Twentieth Century.* Tallahassee: University of Florida Press, 1997.

Dvorak, Katharine L. *An African American Exodus.* Brooklyn, N.Y.: Carlson, 1991.

Gaillard, Frye. *The Dream Long Deferred.* Chapel Hill: University of North Carolina Press, 1988.

Goldschmid, Marcel L., ed. *Black Americans and White Racism: Theory and Research.* New York: Holt, Rinehart and Winston, 1970.

Gubar, Susan. *Racechanges: White Skin, Black Face in American Culture.* New York: Oxford University Press, 1997.

Guerrero, Ed. *Framing Blackness.* Philadelphia: Temple University Press, 1993.

Hacker, Andrew. *Two Nations: Black and White, Separate, Hostile, Unequal.* New York: Charles Scribner's Sons, 1992.

Holden, Matthew. *The White Man's Burden.* New York: Chandler, 1973.

Johnson, Charles S. *The Negro in American Civilization: A Study of Negro Life and Race Relations in the Light of Social Research.* New York: Henry Holt, 1930.

Jordan, Winthrop D. *White over Black: American Attitudes Toward the Negro, 1550-1812.* New York: W. W. Norton, 1968, 1995.

Keyes, Alan L. *Masters of the Dream: The Strength and Betrayal of Black America.* New York: William Morrow, 1995.

Kochman, Thomas. *Black and White Styles in Conflict.* Chicago: University of Chicago Press, 1981.

Long, Richard A. *African Americans: A Portrait.* New York: Crescent Books, 1993.

Lyman, Stanford M. *The Black American in Sociological Thought.* New York: Putnam, 1972.

McWilliams, Carey. *Brothers Under the Skin.* Rev. ed. Boston: Little, Brown, 1964.

Mills, Charles W. *Blackness Visible: Essays on Philosophy and Race.* Ithaca, N.Y.: Cornell University Press, 1998.

Munford, Clarence J. *Race and Reparations: A Black Perspective for the Twenty-first Century.* Trenton, N.J.: Africa World Press, 1996.

Myrdal, Gunnar. *An American Dilemma: The Negro Problem and American Democracy.* New York: Harper & Row, 1944; McGraw-Hill, 1964.

Parsons, Talcott, and Kenneth B. Clark, eds. *The Negro American.* Boston: Houghton Mifflin, 1966.

Pettigrew, Thomas F. *A Profile of the Negro American.* Princeton, N.J.: D. Van Nostrand, 1964.

Pieterse, Jan Nederveen. *White on Black.* New Haven, Conn.: Yale University Press, 1992.

Ploski, Harry A., and James Williams, eds. *The Negro Almanac: A Reference Work on the African American.* Detroit, Mich.: Gale Research, 1989.

Schoem, David, ed. *Inside Separate Worlds: Life Stories of Young Blacks, Jews, and Latinos.* Ann Arbor: University of Michigan Press, 1991.

Shipler, David K. *A Country of Strangers: Blacks and Whites in America.* New York: Knopf, 1997.

Sigelman, Lee, and Susan Welch. *Black Americans' Views of Racial Inequality.* Cambridge, England: Cambridge University Press, 1991.

Silberman, Charles E. *Crisis in Black and White.* New York: Vintage Books, 1964.

Smith, Lillian. *Killers of the Dream.* New York: W. W. Norton, 1949.

Steele, Shelby. *A Dream Deferred: The Second Betrayal of Black Freedom in America.* New York: HarperCollins, 1998.

Thernstrom, Stephan, and Abigail Thernstrom. *America in Black and White: One Nation Indivisible.* New York: Random House, 1997.

West, Cornell. *Race Matters.* New York: Random House, 1993.

_____. *Restoring Hope: Conversations on the Future of Black America.* Boston: Beacon Press, 1997.

Wonkeryor, Edward Lama. *On Afrocentricity, Intercultural Communication, and Racism.* Lewiston, N.Y.: Edwin Mellin Press, 1998.

African American History
See also Civil Rights

Anderson, Eric, and Alfred A. Moss, Jr., eds. *The Facts of Reconstruction: Essays in Honor of John Hope Franklin.* Baton Rouge: Louisiana State University Press, 1991.

Aptheker, Herbert. *Anti-Racism in U.S. History: The First Two Hundred Years.* New York: Greenwood Press, 1992.

Bell, Howard Holman. *A Survey of the Negro Convention Movement, 1830-1861.* New York: Arno Press, 1969.

Benedict, Michael Les. *A Compromise of Principle: Congressional Republicans and Reconstruction, 1863-1869.* New York: W. W. Norton, 1974.

Bonnett, Aubrey W., and G. Llewellyn Watson, eds. *Emerging Perspectives on the Black Diaspora.* Lanham, Md.: University Press of America, 1990.

Brown, Richard H. *The Missouri Compromise: Political Statesmanship or Unwise Evasion?* Boston: D. C. Heath, 1964.

Carter, Dan T. *Scottsboro: A Tragedy of the American South.* Rev. ed. Baton Rouge: Louisiana State University Press, 1979.

_____. *When the War Was Over: The Failure of Self-Reconstruction in the South, 1865-1867.* Baton Rouge: Louisiana State University Press, 1985.

Chalmers, Allan Knight. *They Shall Be Free.* Garden City, N.Y.: Doubleday, 1951.

Collins, Bruce. *The Origins of America's Civil War.* New York: Holmes & Meier, 1981.

Conniff, Michael L., and Thomas J. Davis. *Africans in the Americas: A History of the Black Diaspora.* New York: St. Martin's Press, 1994.

Cox, LaWanda. *Lincoln and Black Freedom: A Study in Presidential Leadership.* Columbia: University of South Carolina Press, 1981.

Cox, LaWanda, and John H. Cox. *Politics, Principle, and Prejudice: Dilemma of Reconstruction America, 1865-1866.* New York: Free Press, 1963.

Cronon, E. David. *Black Moses: The Story of Marcus Garvey and the Universal Negro Improvement Association.* Madison: University of Wisconsin Press, 1955.

Crouch, Barry A. *The Freedmen's Bureau and Black Texans.* Austin: University of Texas Press, 1992.

Dykstra, Robert R. *Bright Radical Star: Black Freedom and White Supremacy on the Hawkeye Frontier.* Cambridge, Mass.: Harvard University Press, 1993.

Finkelman, Paul, ed. *Race, Law, and American History, 1700-1900.* 11 vols. New York: Garland, 1992.

Foner, Eric. *Nothing But Freedom: Emancipation and Its Legacy.* Baton Rouge: Louisiana State University Press, 1983.

_____. *Reconstruction: America's Unfinished Revolution.* New York: Harper & Row, 1988.

Franklin, John Hope. *The Emancipation Proclamation.* Garden City, N.Y.: Doubleday, 1963.

_____. *Reconstruction: After the Civil War.* Chicago: University of Chicago Press, 1961.

Franklin, John Hope, and Alfred A. Moss, Jr. *From Slavery to Freedom: A History of African Americans.* 7th ed. New York: McGraw-Hill, 1994.

Frazier, Thomas R., ed. *Afro-American History: Primary Sources.* New York: Harcourt, Brace & World, 1970.

Frederickson, George M. *The Arrogance of Race: Historical Perspectives.* Middletown, Conn.: Wesleyan University Press, 1988.

Garvey, Amy Jacques. *Garvey and Garveyism.* 1963. Reprint. New York: Collier, 1976.

Garvey, Marcus. *Philosophy and Opinions of Marcus Garvey.* Edited by Amy Jacques-Garvey, with new introduction by Robert A. Hill. New York: Atheneum, 1992.

Goodfriend, Joyce D. *Before the Melting Pot: Society and Culture in Colonial New York City, 1664-1730.* Princeton, N.J.: Princeton University Press, 1992.

Hamilton, Holman. *Prologue to Conflict: The Crisis and Compromise of 1850.* New York: W. W. Norton, 1964.

Harlan, Louis R. *Booker T. Washington in Perspective: Essays of Louis R. Harlan.* Edited by Raymond W. Smock. Jackson: University Press of Mississippi, 1988.

_____. *Booker T. Washington: The Making of a Black Leader, 1856-1901.* New York: Oxford University Press, 1972.

_____. *Booker T. Washington: The Wizard of Tuskegee, 1901-1915.* New York: Oxford University Press, 1983.

Hill, Robert A., and Barbara Bair, eds. *Marcus Garvey: Life and Lessons.* Berkeley: University of California Press, 1987.

Holman, Hamilton. *Prologue to Conflict: The Crisis and Compromise of 1850.* New York: W. W. Norton, 1966.

Holt, Michael. *The Political Crisis of the 1850's.* New York: W. W. Norton, 1978.

Hornsby, Alton, Jr. *Chronology of African-American History.* Detroit, Mich.: Gale Research, 1991.

Keegan, Frank L. *Blacktown, U.S.A.* Boston: Little, Brown, 1971.

Kellogg, Charles Flint. *NAACP: A History of the National Association for the Advancement of Colored People.* Baltimore: The Johns Hopkins University Press, 1964.

Kusmer, Kenneth L., ed. *Black Communities and Urban Development in America, 1720-1990.* New York: Garland, 1991.

Lasch-Quinn, Elisabeth. *Black Neighbors: Race and the Limits of Reform in the American Settlement House Movement, 1890-1945.* Chapel Hill: University of North Carolina Press, 1993.

Leckie, William H. *The Buffalo Soldiers: A Narrative of the Negro Cavalry in the West.* Norman: University of Oklahoma Press, 1967.

Lemann, Nicholas. *The Promised Land: The Great Black Migration and How It Changed America.* New York: Alfred A. Knopf, 1991.

Lewis, David Levering. *W. E. B. Du Bois: Biography of a Race, 1868-1919.* New York: Henry Holt, 1993.

Lewis, Rupert, and Maureen Warner-Lewis, eds. *Garvey: Africa, Europe, the Americas.* Kingston, Jamaica: Institute of Social and Economic Research, University of the West Indies, 1986.

Lofgren, Charles A. *The Plessy Case: A Legal-Historical Interpretation.* New York: Oxford University Press, 1987.

Lubiano, Wahneema, ed. *The House That Race Built: Black Americans, U.S. Terrain.* New York: Pantheon, 1997.

McPherson, James M. *The Battle Cry of Freedom: The Civil War Era.* Oxford, England: Oxford University Press, 1988.

_____. *The Negro in the Civil War.* New York: Vintage Books, 1965.

_____. *Ordeal by Fire: The Civil War and Reconstruction.* 2d ed. New York: McGraw-Hill, 1992.

_____. *The Struggle for Equality: Abolitionists and the Negro in the Civil War and Reconstruction.* Princeton, N.J.: Princeton University Press, 1964.

Magdol, Edward. *A Right to the Land: Essays on the Freedmen's Community.* Westport, Conn.: Greenwood Press, 1977.

Mathurin, Owen Charles. *Henry Sylvester Williams and the Origins of the Pan-African Movement, 1869-1911.* Westport, Conn.: Greenwood Press, 1976.

Meier, August. *Negro Thought in America, 1880-1915: Racial Ideologies in the Age of Booker T. Washington.* Ann Arbor: University of Michigan Press, 1988.

Miller, Loren. *The Petitioners: The Story of the Supreme Court of the United States and the Negro.* New York: Pantheon Books, 1966.

Modern Black Nationalism: From Marcus Garvey to Louis Farrakhan. New York: New York University Press, 1997.

Moses, Wilson Jeremiah. *The Golden Age of Black Nationalism, 1850-1925.* New York: Oxford University Press, 1978.

Nevins, Allen. *A House Dividing, 1852-1857.* Vol. 2 in *Ordeal of the Union.* New York: Charles Scribner's Sons, 1947.

Nieman, Donald G. *Promises to Keep: African-Americans and the Constitutional Order, 1776 to the Present.* New York: Oxford University Press, 1991.

Norris, Clarence, and Sybil D. Washington. *The Last of the Scottsboro Boys.* New York: Putnam, 1979.

Oates, Stephen B. *Our Fiery Trial: Abraham Lincoln, John Brown, and the Civil War Era.* Amherst: University of Massachusetts Press, 1979.

Ovington, Mary White, et al. *Black and White Sat Down Together: The Reminiscences of an NAACP Founder.* New York: Feminist Press of City University of New York, 1996.

Patterson, Haywood, and Earl Conrad. *Scottsboro Boy.* Garden City, N.Y.: Doubleday, 1950.

Potter, David M. *The Impending Crisis, 1848-1861.* Completed and edited by Don. E. Fehrenbacher. New York: Harper & Row, 1976.

Quarles, Benjamin. *Lincoln and the Negro.* New York: Oxford University Press, 1962.

_____. *The Negro in the Civil War.* Boston: Little, Brown, 1953.

Rabinowitz, Howard N., and George W. Frederickson. *Race Relations in the Urban South, 1865-1890.* New York: Oxford University Press, 1996.

Rymer, Russ. *American Beach: A Saga of Race, Wealth, and Memory.* New York: HarperCollins, 1998.

Shropshire, Kenneth L., and Kellen Winslow. *In Black and White: Race and Sports in America.* New York: New York University Press, 1996.

Stampp, Kenneth, ed. *The Causes of the Civil War.* Rev. ed. Englewood Cliffs, N.J.: Prentice-Hall, 1974.

_____. *The Era of Reconstruction, 1865-1877.* New York: Alfred A. Knopf, 1965.

Tygiel, Jules. *Baseball's Great Experiment: Jackie Robinson and His Legacy.* New York: Vintage, 1984.

Van Sertima, Ivan, ed. *African Presence in Early America.* New Brunswick, N.J.: Transaction, 1992.

Walvin, James. *Black and White: The Negro and English Society, 1555-1945.* London: Penguin Press, 1973.

Williams, Vernon J. *From a Caste to a Minority: Changing Attitudes of American Sociologists Toward Afro-Americans, 1896-1945.* New York: Greenwood Press, 1989.

Wood, Peter H. *Black Majority: Negroes in Colonial South Carolina from 1670 Through the Stono Rebellion.* New York: W. W. Norton, 1974.

African Americans and Other Minorities

Berman, Paul, ed. *Blacks and Jews: Alliance and Arguments.* New York: Delacorte Press, 1994.

Collum, Danny Duncan. *Black and White Together: The Search for Common Ground.* Maryknoll, N.Y.: Orbis Books, 1996.

Daughtry, Herbert D., Sr. *No Monopoly on Suffering: Blacks and Jews in Crown Heights.* Trenton, N.J.: Africa World Press, 1997.

Diner, Hasia R. *In the Almost Promised Land: American Jews and Blacks, 1919-1935.* Westport, Conn.: Westview, 1977.

Forbes, Jack D. *Black Africans and Native Americans: Color, Race, and Caste in the Evolution of Red-Black Peoples.* Urbana: University of Illinois Press, 1993.

Halliburton, R., Jr. *Red over Black: Black Slavery Among the Cherokee Indians.* Westport, Conn.: Greenwood Press, 1977.

Hentoff, Nat, ed. *Black Anti-Semitism and Jewish Racism.* New York: Richard W. Baron, 1969.

Hoover, Dwight W. *The Red and the Black.* Chicago: Rand McNally, 1976.

Katz, William Loren. *Black Indians: A Hidden Heritage.* New York: Atheneum, 1986.

Kaufman, Jonathan. *Broken Alliance: The Turbulent Times Between Blacks and Jews in America.* New York: Scribner's, 1988.

Lerner, Michael, and Cornel West. *Jews and Blacks: Let the Healing Begin.* New York: G. P. Putnam's Sons, 1995.

Lieberson, Stanley. *A Piece of the Pie: Blacks and White Immigrants Since 1880.* Berkeley: University of California Press, 1980.

Littlefield, Daniel F., Jr. *Africans and Creeks: From the Colonial Period to the Civil War.* Westport, Conn.: Greenwood Press, 1979.

_____. *Africans and Seminoles: From Removal to Emancipation.* Westport, Conn.: Greenwood Press, 1978.

Ownby, Ted, ed. *Black and White Cultural Interaction in the Antebellum South.* Jackson: University Press of Mississippi, 1993.

Phillips, William M., Jr. *An Unillustrious Alliance: The African American and Jewish American Communities.* Westport, Conn.: Greenwood Press, 1991.

Piatt, Bill, et al. *Black and Brown in America: The Case for Cooperation.* New York: New York University Press, 1997.

Saito, Leland T. *Race and Politics: Asian Americans, Latinos, and Whites in a Los Angeles Suburb.* Urbana: University of Illinois Press, 1998.

Salzman, Jack, and Cornel West, eds. *Struggles in the Promised Land: Towards a History of Black-Jewish Relations in the United States.* New York: Oxford University Press, 1997.

Waldinger, Roger. *Still the Promised City? African-Americans and the New Immigrants in Post-Industrial New York.* Cambridge, Mass.: Harvard University Press, 1996.

Williams, Richard E. *Hierarchical Structures and Social Value: The Creation of Black and Irish Identities in the United States.* Cambridge, England: Cambridge University Press, 1990.

Family and Community

Billingsley, Andrew. *Black Families in White America.* Englewood Cliffs, N.J.: Prentice-Hall, 1968.

Blackwell, James. *The Black Community: Diversity and Unity.* New York: Harper & Row, 1975.

David, Jay, ed. *Growing Up Black: From Slave Days to the Present, Twenty-five African-Americans Reveal the Trials and Triumphs of Their Childhoods.* New York: Avon Books, 1992.

Ellison, Ralph. *Invisible Man.* New York: Random House, 1952.

Frazier, Edward Franklin. *The Negro Family in the United States.* Chicago: University of Chicago Press, 1939.

Griffin, John Howard. *Black Like Me.* Boston: Houghton Mifflin, 1961.

Haizlip, Shirlee Taylor. *The Sweeter the Juice.* New York: Simon & Schuster, 1994.

Hamblin, Ken. *Pick a Better Country; An Unassuming Colored Guy Speaks His Mind About America.* New York: Simon & Schuster, 1996.

Hill, Robert, ed. *Research on the African-American Family: A Holistic Perspective.* Westport, Conn.: Auburn House, 1993.

Horton, James Oliver. *Free People of Color: Inside the African American Community.* Washington, D.C.: Smithsonian Institution Press, 1993

McAdoo, Harriette Pipes, ed. *Black Families.* 3d ed. Thousand Oaks, Calif.: Sage, 1997.

McCall, Nathan. *Makes Me Wanna Holler: A Young Black Man in America.* New York: Random House, 1994.

Page, Clarence. *Showing My Color: Impolite Essays on Race and Identity.* New York: HarperCollins, 1996.

Parks, Gordon. *Born Black.* Philadelphia: Lippincott, 1971.

Perkins, John, and Thomas A. Tarnants III. *He's My Brother: A Black Activist and a Former Klansman Tell Their Stories.* Grand Rapids, Mich.: Chosen Books, 1994.

Powell, Colin L. *My American Journey.* New York: Random House, 1995.

Staples, Robert. *Black Families at the Crossroads.* San Francisco: Jossey-Bass, 1993.

Warner, Lee H. *Free Men in an Age of Servitude: Three Generations of a Black Family.* Lexington: University Press of Kentucky, 1992.

Politics

Conti, Joseph G., and Brad Stetson. *Challenging the Civil Rights Establishment: Profiles of a New Black Vanguard.* Westport, Conn.: Praeger, 1993.

Cross, Theodore. *The Black Power Imperative: Racial Inequality and the Politics of Nonviolence.* New York: Faulkner, 1984.

Dawson, Michael C. *Behind the Mule: Race and Class in African-American Politics.* Princeton, N.J.: Princeton University Press, 1994.

Faryna, Stan, Brad Stetson, and Joseph G. Conti, eds. *Black and Right: The New Bold Voice of Black Conservatives in America.* Westport, Conn.: Greenwood, 1997.

Gilroy, Paul, and Houston A. Baker. *There Ain't No Black in the Union Jack: The Cultural Politics of Race and Nation.* Chicago: Chicago University Press, 1991.

Ginzberg, Eli, and Alfred S. Eichner. *Troublesome Presence: Democracy and Black Americans.* New Brunswick, N.J.: Transaction, 1993.

Hine, Darlene Clark. *Black Victory: The Rise and Fall of the White Primary in Texas.* Millwood, N.Y.: KTO Press, 1979.

Jewell, K. Sue. *From Mammy to Miss America and Beyond: Cultural Images and the Shaping of U.S. Social Policy.* New York: Routledge, 1993.

Lawson, Steven F. *Black Ballots: Voting Rights in the South, 1944-1969.* New York: Columbia University Press, 1976.

_____. *In Pursuit of Power: Southern Blacks and Electoral Politics, 1965-1982.* New York: Columbia University Press, 1985.

McKissick, Floyd B. *Three-fifths of a Man.* New York: Macmillan, 1969.

Marable, Manning. *Beyond Black and White: Transforming African-American Politics.* London and New York: Verso, 1995.

_____. *Race, Reform, and Rebellion: The Second Reconstruction in Black America, 1945-1991.* Jackson: University Press of Mississippi, 1991.

Merelman, Richard M. *Representing Black Culture: Racial Conflict and Cultural Politics in the United States.* New York: Routledge, 1995.

Norton, Philip. *Black Nationalism in America.* Hull, Humberside, England: Department of Politics, University of Hull, 1983.

Orfield, Gary, and Carol Ashkinaze. *The Closing Door: Conservative Policy and Black Opportunity.* Chicago: University of Chicago Press, 1991.

Perkins, Joseph, ed. *A Conservative Agenda for Black Americans.* Washington, D.C.: Heritage Foundation, 1990.

Persons, Georgia A., ed. *Dilemmas of Black Politics: Issues of Leadership and Strategy.* New York: HarperCollins, 1993.

Reed, Adolph L. *The Jesse Jackson Phenomenon: The Crisis of Purpose in Afro-American Politics.* New Haven, Conn.: Yale University Press, 1986.

Singh, Robert. *The Farrakhan Pheonomenon: Race, Reaction, and the Paranoid Style in American Politics.* Washington, D.C.: Georgetown University, 1997.

Smith, T. Alexander, and Lenahan O'Connell. *Black Anxiety,*

White Guilt, and the Politics of Status Frustration. Westport, Conn.: Praeger, 1997.

Sonenshein, Raphael J. *Politics in Black and White: Race and Power in Los Angeles.* Princeton, N.J.: Princeton University Press, 1993.

Swain, Carol M. *Black Faces, Black Interests: The Representation of African Americans in Congress.* Cambridge, Mass.: Harvard University Press, 1993.

Tate, Katherine. *From Protest to Politics: The New Black Voters in American Elections.* Cambridge, Mass.: Harvard University Press, 1994.

Walton, Hanes, Jr. *Black Politics.* Philadelphia: J. B. Lippincott, 1972.

Religion and the Black Church

Allen, Richard. *The Life, Experience, and Gospel Labors of the Right Reverent Richard Allen.* 1833. Reprint. Nashville, Tenn.: Abingdon Press, 1983.

Cone, James H. *Black Theology and Black Power.* New York: Seabury Press, 1969.

_____. *A Black Theology of Liberation.* 20th anniversary ed. Maryknoll, N.Y.: Orbis Books, 1990.

Evans, James H., Jr. *Spiritual Empowerment in Afro-American Literature.* Lewiston, N.Y.: Edwin Mellen, 1987.

Fitts, LeRoy. *A History of Black Baptists.* Nashville, Tenn.: Broadman Press, 1985.

Frazier, E. Franklin, and C. Eric Lincoln. *The Negro Church in America: The Black Church Since Frazier.* New York: Schocken Books, 1974.

George, Carol V. R. *Segregated Sabbaths: Richard Allen and the Rise of Independent Black Churches, 1760-1840.* New York: Oxford University Press, 1973.

Lee, Martha F. *The Nation of Islam: An American Millenarian Movement.* Lewiston, N.Y.: Edwin Mellen Press, 1988.

Lincoln, C. Eric. *The Black Muslims in America.* Rev. ed. Boston: Beacon Press, 1973.

Lincoln, C. Eric, and Lawrence H. Mamiya. *The Black Church in the African-American Experience.* Durham, N.C.: Duke University Press, 1990.

Luker, Ralph E. *The Social Gospel in Black and White: American Racial Reform, 1885-1912.* Chapel Hill: University of North Carolina Press, 1991.

Marsh, Clifton E. *From Black Muslims to Muslims: The Transition From Separatism to Islam, 1930-1980.* Metuchen, N.J.: Scarecrow Press, 1984.

Muhammad, Elijah. *The Supreme Wisdom.* 2 vols. Brooklyn: Temple of Islam, 1957.

Mukenge, Ida Rousseau. *The Black Church in Urban America.* Lanham, Md.: University Press of America, 1983.

Paris, Peter J. *The Social Teaching of the Black Churches.* Philadelphia: Fortress Press, 1985.

Phillips, C. H. *The History of the Colored Methodist Episcopal Church in America.* 1898. Reprint. New York: Arno Press, 1972.

Sernett, Milton C. *Afro-American Religious History: A Documentary Witness.* Durham, N.C.: Duke University Press, 1985.

Seymour, Robert E., Jr. *"Whites Only": A Pastor's Retrospective on Signs of the New South.* Valley Forge, Pa.: Judson Press, 1991.

Smith, Theophus H. *Conjuring Culture: Biblical Formations of Black America.* New York: Oxford University Press, 1994.

Wesley, Charles. *Richard Allen: Apostle of Freedom.* Washington, D.C.: Associated Publishers, 1935.

Wilmore, Gayraud S., ed. *African American Religious Studies: An Interdisciplinary Anthology.* Durham, N.C.: Duke University Press, 1989.

_____, ed. *Black Religion and Black Radicalism.* 2d ed. Maryknoll, N.Y.: Orbis Books, 1983.

Slavery

Abbott, Richard H. *Cotton and Capital: Boston Businessmen and Antislavery Reform, 1854-1868.* Amherst: University of Massachusetts Press, 1991.

Angle, Paul M., ed. *Created Equal? The Complete Lincoln-Douglas Debates of 1858.* Chicago: University of Chicago Press, 1958.

Aptheker, Herbert. *American Negro Slave Revolts.* 1943. Rev. ed. New York: Columbia University Press, 1969.

Ball, Edward. *Slaves in the Family.* New York: Farrar, Straus & Giroux, 1998.

Barber, John Warner. *A History of the Amistad Captives.* New York: Arno Press, 1969.

Barnes, Gilbert Hobbs. *The Antislavery Impulse: 1830-1844.* New York: Harcourt, Brace & World, 1964.

Bender, Thomas, ed. *The Antislavery Debate: Capitalism and Abolitionism as a Problem in Historical Interpretation.* Berkeley: University of California Press, 1992.

Berlin, Ira. *Many Thousands Gone: The First Two Centuries of Slavery in North America.* Cambridge, Mass.: Belknap Press, 1998.

Berlin, Ira, et al. *Slaves No More: Three Essays on Emancipation and the Civil War.* Cambridge, England: Cambridge University Press, 1992.

Blackburn, Robin. *The Overthrow of Colonial Slavery, 1776-1848.* New York: Verso, 1988.

Blassingame, John W. *The Slave Community: Plantation Life in the Antebellum South.* New York: Oxford University Press, 1972.

Blassingame, John W., and John R. McKivigan, eds. *The Frederick Douglass Papers.* Series 1, *Speeches, Debates, and Interviews.* Vol. 3, *1855-1863.* New Haven, Conn.: Yale University Press, 1991.

Bontemps, Arna, ed. *Great Slave Narratives.* Boston: Beacon Press, n.d.

Boskin, Joseph. *Into Slavery: Racial Decisions in the Virginia Colony.* Philadelphia: J. B. Lippincott, 1976.

Boyer, Richard O. *The Legend of John Brown: A Biography and a History.* New York: Alfred A. Knopf, 1972.

Buckmaster, Henrietta. *Let My People Go: The Story of the Underground Railroad and the Growth of the Abolition Movement.* Boston: Beacon Press, 1941.

Campbell, Stanley. *The Slave Catchers: Enforcement of the Fugitive Slave Law, 1850-1860.* Chapel Hill: University of North Carolina Press, 1970.

Catterall, Helen T., ed. *Judicial Cases Concerning American Slavery and the Negro.* 5 vols. New York: Octagon Books, 1968.

Curtin, Philip D. *The Atlantic Slave Trade.* Madison: University of Wisconsin Press, 1969.

Daniel, Pete. *The Shadow of Slavery: Peonage in the South, 1901-1969.* Urbana: University of Illinois Press, 1972.

Davis, David Brion. *The Problem of Slavery in the Age of Revolution, 1770-1823.* Ithaca, N.Y.: Cornell University Press, 1975.

_____. *The Problem of Slavery in Western Culture.* Ithaca, N.Y.: Cornell University Press, 1966.

_____. *Slavery and Human Progress.* New York: Oxford University Press, 1984.

Degler, Carl N. *Neither Black Nor White: Slavery and Race Relations in Brazil and the United States.* 1971. Madison: University of Wisconsin Press, 1986.

Duberman, Martin, ed. *The Antislavery Vanguard: New Essays on the Abolitionists.* Princeton, N.J.: Princeton University Press, 1965.

Elkins, Stanley M. *Slavery: A Problem in American Institutional and Intellectual Life.* Chicago: University of Chicago Press, 1959.

Eltis, David, and James Walvin, eds. *The Abolition of the Atlantic Slave Trade: Origins and Effects in Europe, Africa, and the Americas.* Madison: University of Wisconsin Press, 1981.

Faust, Drew Gilpin. *The Ideology of Slavery: Proslavery Thought in the Antebellum South, 1830-1860.* Baton Rouge: Louisiana State University Press, 1981.

Filler, Louis. *The Crusade Against Slavery, 1830-1860.* New York: Harper & Row, 1960.

Finkelman, Paul, ed. *Slavery and the Founders: Race and Liberty in the Age of Jefferson.* Armonk, N.Y.: M. E. Sharpe, 1996.

Finley, Moses I. *Ancient Slavery and Modern Ideology.* New York: Viking Press, 1980.

Fogel, Robert. *Without Consent or Contract: The Rise and Fall of American Slavery.* New York: W. W. Norton, 1989.

Franklin, Raymond S. *Shadows of Race and Class.* Minneapolis: University of Minnesota Press, 1991.

Friedman, Lawrence J. *Gregarious Saints: Self and Community in American Abolitionism, 1830-1870.* New York: Cambridge University Press, 1982.

Frost, J. William, ed. *The Quaker Origins of Antislavery.* Norwood, Pa.: Norwood Editions, 1980.

Gara, Larry. *The Liberty Line: The Legend of the Underground Railroad.* Lexington: University of Kentucky Press, 1961.

Genovese, Eugene D. *Roll, Jordan, Roll: The World the Slaves Made.* New York: Pantheon Books, 1974.

_____. *The Slaverholders' Dilemma: Freedom and Progress in Southern Conservative Thought, 1820-1860.* Columbia: University of South Carolina Press, 1992.

Giddings, Joshua R. *The Exiles of Florida: Or, The Crimes Committed by Our Government Against the Maroons Who Fled from South Carolina and Other Slave States, Seeking Protection Under Spanish Laws.* 1858. Reprint. Gainesville: University of Florida Press, 1964.

Goldwin, Robert A., and Art Kaufman. *Slavery and Its Consequences: The Constitution, Equality, and Race.* Washington, D.C.: American Enterprise Institute Press, 1988.

Goodheart, Lawrence, Richard D. Brown, and Stephen Rabe, eds. *Slavery in American Society.* 3d ed. Lexington, Mass.: Heath, 1993.

Goodman, Paul. *Of One Blood: Abolitionism and the Origins of Racial Equality.* Berkeley: University of California Press, 1998.

Gutman, Herbert. *The Black Family in Slavery and Freedom, 1750-1925.* New York: Pantheon, 1976.

Harris, Marvin. *Patterns of Race Relations in America.* New York: Walker, 1964.

Hoetink, H. *Slavery and Race Relations in the Americas: Notes on Their Nature and Nexus.* New York: Harper & Row, 1973.

Holzer, Harold, ed. *The Lincoln-Douglas Debates: The First Complete, Unexpurgated Text.* New York: HarperCollins, 1993.

Howard, Warren S. *American Slavers and the Federal Law: 1837-1862.* Berkeley: University of California Press, 1963.

Huggins, Nathan Irvin. *Slave and Citizen: The Life of Frederick Douglass.* Boston: Little, Brown, 1980.

James, Sydney V. *A People Among Peoples: Quaker Benevolence in Eighteenth Century America.* Cambridge, Mass.: Harvard University Press, 1963.

Jenkins, William S. *Pro-Slavery Thought in the Old South.* Chapel Hill: University of North Carolina Press, 1935.

Kolchin, Peter. *American Slavery: 1619-1877.* New York: Hill & Wang, 1993.

Kraditor, Aileen S. *Means and Ends in American Abolitionism: Garrison and His Critics on Strategy and Tactics, 1834-1850.* New York: Vintage Books, 1970.

Kraut, Alan M., ed. *Crusaders and Compromisers: Essays on the Relationship of the Antislavery Struggle to the Antebellum Party System.* Westport, Conn.: Greenwood Press, 1983.

Levine, Alan J. *Race Relations Within Western Expansion.* Westport, Conn.: Praeger, 1996.

Litwack, Leon F. *Been in the Storm So Long: The Aftermath of Slavery.* New York: Alfred A. Knopf, 1979.

_____. *North of Slavery: The Negro in the Free States: 1790-1860.* Chicago: University of Chicago Press, 1961.

McGary, Howard, and Bill E. Lawson. *Between Slavery and Freedom: Philosophy and American Slavery.* Bloomington: Indiana University Press, 1992.

McKivigan, John R. *The War Against Proslavery Religion: Abolitionism and the Northern Churches, 1830-1865.* Ithaca, N.Y.: Cornell University Press, 1984.

MacLeod, Duncan J. *Slavery, Race, and the American Revolution.* London: Cambridge University Press, 1974.

McManus, Edgar J. *A History of Negro Slavery in New York.* Syracuse, N.Y.: Syracuse University Press, 1966.

Martin, Christopher. *The "Amistad" Affair.* New York: Abelard-Schuman, 1970.

Martin, Waldo E. *The Mind of Frederick Douglass.* Chapel Hill: University of North Carolina Press, 1984.

Melish, Joanne Pope. *Disowning Slavery: Gradual Emancipation and "Race" in New England, 1780-1860.* Ithaca: Cornell University Press, 1998.

Meltzer, Milton, ed. *Frederick Douglass, in His Own Words.* San Diego, Calif.: Harcourt, Brace, 1995.

Merrill, Walter M. *Against Wind and Tide: A Biography of William Lloyd Garrison.* Cambridge, Mass.: Harvard University Press, 1963.

Morgan, Edmund S. *American Slavery, American Freedom: The Ordeal of Colonial Virginia.* New York: W. W. Norton, 1975.

Morris, Thomas D. *Free Men All: The Personal Liberty Laws of the North, 1780-1861.* Baltimore: The Johns Hopkins University Press, 1974.

Mullin, Michael. *Africa in America: Slave Acculturation and Resistance in the American South and the British Caribbean, 1736-1831.* Urbana: University of Illinois Press, 1992.

Nye, Russel B. *William Lloyd Garrison and the Humanitarian Reformers.* Boston: Little, Brown, 1955.

Oakes, James. *The Ruling Race: A History of American Slaveholders.* New York: Alfred A. Knopf, 1982.

_____. *Slavery and Freedom: An Interpretation of the Old South.* New York: Alfred A. Knopf, 1990.

Owen, Robert Dale. *The Wrong of Slavery, the Right of Emancipation, and the Future of the African Race in the United States.* Philadelphia: J. B. Lippincott, 1864.

Owens, William A. *Black Mutiny: The Revolt on the Schooner "Amistad."* Philadelphia: Pilgrim Press, 1968.

Patterson, Orlando. *Slavery and Social Death: A Comparative Study.* Cambridge, Mass.: Harvard University Press, 1982.

_____. *The Sociology of Slavery.* Rutherford, N.J.: Fairleigh Dickinson University Press, 1975.

Perry, Lewis, and Michael Fellman, eds. *Antislavery Reconsidered: New Perspectives on the Abolitionists.* Baton Rouge: Louisiana State University Press, 1979.

Phillips, Ulrich B. *American Negro Slavery.* Baton Rouge: Louisiana State University Press, 1966.

Phillips, William D. *Slavery from Roman Times to the Early Transatlantic Trade.* Minneapolis: University of Minnesota Press, 1985.

Quarles, Benjamin. *Black Abolitionists.* New York: Oxford University Press, 1969.

Rawley, James A. *The Transatlantic Slave Trade: A History.* New York: W. W. Norton, 1981.

Rogers, William B. *"We Are All Together Now": Frederick Douglass, William Lloyd Garrison, and the Prophetic Tradition.* New York: Garland, 1995.

Schwartz, Philip J. *Twice Condemned: Slaves and the Criminal Laws of Virginia, 1705-1865.* Baton Rouge: Louisiana State University Press, 1988.

Shaw, Robert B. *A Legal History of Slavery in the United States.* Potsdam, N.Y.: Northern Press, 1991.

Siebert, Wilbur H. *The Underground Railroad from Slavery to Freedom.* 1898. Reprint. New York: Arno Press, 1968.

Smith, John D. *Black Slavery in the Americas: An Interdisciplinary Bibliography, 1865-1980.* 2 vols. Westport, Conn.: Greenwood Press, 1982.

Sorin, Gerald. *Abolitionism: A New Perspective.* New York: Praeger, 1972.

Stampp, Kenneth M. *The Peculiar Institution: Slavery in the Ante-Bellum South.* New York: Alfred A. Knopf, 1956.

Stewart, James Brewer. *Holy Warriors: The Abolitionists and American Slavery.* New York: Hill & Wang, 1976.

_____. *William Lloyd Garrison and the Challenge of Emancipation.* Arlington Heights, Ill.: Harlan Davidson, 1992.

Still, William. *The Underground Railroad.* 1872. Reprint. Chicago: Johnson, 1972.

Stuckey, Sterling. *Slave Culture.* New York: Oxford University Press, 1987.

Styron, William. *Confessions of Nat Turner.* New York: Random House, 1967.

Thomas, John L. *The Liberator: William Lloyd Garrison, A Biography.* Boston: Little, Brown, 1963.

Tise, Larry E. *Proslavery: A History of the Defense of Slavery in America, 1701-1840.* Athens: University of Georgia Press, 1987.

Tushnet, Mark V. *The American Law of Slavery, 1810-1860: Considerations of Humanity and Interest.* Princeton, N.J.: Princeton University Press, 1981.

Washington, Booker T. *Up from Slavery.* 1901. Reprint. New York: Gramercy Books, 1993.

Watson, Alan. *Slave Law in the Americas.* Athens: University of Georgia Press, 1989.

White, Shane. *Somewhat More Independent: The End of Slavery in New York City, 1770-1810.* Athens: University of Georgia Press, 1991.

Wilson, Carol. *Freedom at Risk: The Kidnapping of Free Blacks in America, 1780-1865.* Lexington: University Press of Kentucky, 1994.

Woodward, C. Vann. *American Counterpoint: Slavery and Racism in the North-South Dialogue.* Boston: Little, Brown, 1971.

Zilversmit, Arthur. *The First Emancipation: The Abolition of Slavery in the North.* Chicago: University of Chicago Press, 1967.

The South and Segregation

Baer, Hans A., and Yvonne Jones, eds. *African Americans in the South: Issues of Race, Class, and Gender.* Athens: University of Georgia Press, 1992.

Bartley, Numan V. *The New South: 1945-1980.* Baton Rouge: Louisiana State University Press, 1995.

Bayor, Ronald H. *Race and the Shaping of Twentieth-Century Atlanta.* Chapel Hill: University of North Carolina Press, 1996.

Davis, Allison, Burleigh B. Gardner, and Mary R. Gardner. *Deep South: A Social Anthropological Study of Caste and Class.* Chicago: University of Chicago Press, 1941.

Dollard, John. *Caste and Class in a Southern Town.* New Haven, Conn: Yale University Press, 1947.

Fossett, Mark A., and Therese Siebert. *Long Time Coming: Racial Inequality in the Nonmetropolitan South, 1940-1990.* Boulder, Colo.: Westview Press, 1997.

Goldfield, David R. *Black, White, and Southern: Race Relations in Southern Culture, 1940 to the Present.* Baton Rouge: Louisiana State University Press, 1990.

_____. *Region, Race and Cities: Interpreting the Urban South.* Baton Rouge: Louisiana State University Press, 1997.

Hale, Grace Elizabeth. *Making Whiteness: The Culture of Segregation in the South, 1890-1940.* New York: Pantheon, 1998.

Larson, Edward J. *Sex, Race, and Science: Eugenics in the Deep South.* Baltimore: The Johns Hopkins University Press, 1995.

McLaurin, Melton A. *Separate Pasts: Growing Up White in the Segregated South.* Athens: University of Georgia Press, 1987.

McMillen, Neil R. *Dark Journey: Black Mississippians in the Age of Jim Crow.* Urbana: University of Illinois Press, 1990.

Newby, I. A. *Jim Crow's Defense.* Baton Rouge: Louisiana State University Press, 1965.

Odum, Howard W. *Race and Rumors of Race: The American South in the Early Forties.* Baltimore: Johns Hopkins University Press, 1997.

Rasmussen, R. Kent. *Farewell to Jim Crow: The Rise and Fall of Segregation in America.* New York: Facts on File, 1997.

Stokes, Melvyn, and Rick Halpern, eds. *Race and Class in the American South Since 1890.* Providence, R.I.: Berg, 1994.

Williamson, Joel. *A Rage for Order: Black-White Relations in the American South Since Emancipation.* New York: Oxford University Press, 1986.

Wilson, Theodore B. *The Black Codes of the South.* Tuscaloosa: University of Alabama Press, 1965.

Woodward, C. Vann. *The Strange Career of Jim Crow.* 3d rev. ed. New York: Oxford University Press, 1974.

AMERICAN INDIANS

See also Canada/Aboriginals

General Studies and Modern Issues

Allen, Paula Gunn, ed. *Studies in American Indian Literature: Critical Essays and Course Designs.* New York: Modern Language Association of America, 1983.

Ambler, Marjane. *Breaking the Iron Bonds: Indian Control of Energy Development.* Lawrence: University Press of Kansas, 1990.

Arnold, Robert D., et al. *Alaska Native Land Claims.* Anchorage: Alaska Native Foundation, 1978.

Barsh, Russel Lawrence, and James Youngblood Henderson. *The Road: Indian Tribes and Political Liberty.* Berkeley: University of California Press, 1980.

Bataille, Gretchen M., and Charles L. P. Silet. *The Pretend Indians: Images of Native Americans in the Movies.* Ames: Iowa State University Press, 1980.

Berkhofer, Robert F., Jr. *Salvation and the Savage.* Lexington: University Press of Kentucky, 1965.

_____. *The White Man's Indian: Images of the American Indian from Columbus to the Present.* New York: Vintage Books, 1979.

Berry, Mary Clay. *The Alaska Pipeline: The Politics of Oil and Native Land Claims.* Bloomington: Indiana University Press, 1975.

Bolt, Christine. *American Indian Policy and American Reform.* London: Allen & Unwin, 1987

Brandon, William. *The Indian in American Culture.* New York: Harper & Row, 1974.

Brophy, W. A., and S. D. Aberle. *The Indian.* Norman: University of Oklahoma Press, 1966.

Cahn, Edgar S., and David W. Hearne. *Our Brother's Keeper: The Indian in White America.* New York: New American Library, 1975.

Canby, William C. *American Indian Law in a Nutshell.* Minneapolis: West, 1981.

Case, David S. *Alaska Natives and American Laws.* Fairbanks: University of Alaska Press, 1984.

Churchill, Ward, and Jim Vander Wall. *Agents of Repression: The FBI's Secret Wars Against the Black Panther Party and the American Indian Movement.* Boston: South End Press, 1988.

Cohen, Fay G. *Treaties on Trial: The Continuing Controversy Over Northwest Indian Fishing Rights.* Seattle: University of Washington Press, 1986.

Cohen, Felix S. *Handbook of Federal Indian Law.* Washington, D.C.: Government Printing Office, 1942.

Collier, John. *Indians of the Americas.* New York: W. W. Norton, 1947.

Cornelius, Judy, and William Eadington, eds. *Indian Gaming and the Law.* 2d ed. Reno: University of Nevada, 1998.

Cornell, Stephen. *The Return of the Native: American Indian Political Resurgence.* New York: Oxford University Press, 1988.

Costo, Rupert, and Jeannette Henry Costo, eds. *The Missions of California: A Legacy of Genocide.* San Francisco: Indian Historian Press, 1987.

Deloria, Vine, Jr. *American Indian Policy in the Twentieth Century.* Norman: University of Oklahoma Press, 1985.

_____. *Behind the Trail of Broken Treaties: An Indian Declaration of Independence.* 2d ed. Norman: University of Oklahoma Press, 1987.

_____. *Custer Died for Your Sins: An Indian Manifesto.* New York: Macmillan, 1969.

Deloria, Vine, Jr., and Clifford Lytle. *The Nations Within: The Past and Future of American Indian Sovereignty.* New York: Pantheon Books, 1984.

_____. *American Indians, American Justice.* Austin: University of Texas Press, 1983.

Dutton, Bertha P. *American Indians of the Southwest.* Rev. ed. Albuquerque: University of New Mexico Press, 1983.

Ellis, Richard N. *The Western American Indian.* Lincoln: University of Nebraska Press, 1972.

Embree, Edwin R. *Indians of the Americas.* 1934. Reprint. New York: Collier Books, 1970.

Fey, Harold, and D'Arcy McNickle. *Indians and Other Americans: Two Ways of Life Meet.* Rev. ed. New York: Harper & Row, 1970.

Fischbacher, Theodore. *A Study of the Role of the Federal Government in the Education of the American Indian.* San Francisco: R&E Research Associates, 1974.

Fortunate Eagle, Adam (Adam Nordwall). *Alcatraz! Alcatraz! The Indian Occupation of 1969-1971.* Berkeley, Calif.: Heyday Books, 1992.

Hertzberg, Hazel W. *The Search for an American Indian Identity: Modern Pan-Indian Movements.* Syracuse, N.Y.: Syracuse University Press, 1971.

Heth, Charlotte, and Susan Guyette. *Issues for the Future of American Indian Studies.* Los Angeles: American Indian Studies Center, University of California, Los Angeles, 1985.

Hilger, Michael. *The American Indian in Film.* Metuchen, N.J.: Scarecrow Press, 1986.

Hodgkinson, Harold L. *The Demographics of American Indians: One Percent of the People, Fifty Percent of the Diversity.* Washington, D.C.: Center for Demographic Policy, Institute for Educational Leadership, 1990.

Hoffman, Fred. *The American Indian Family: Strengths and Stresses.* Isleta, N.Mex.: American Indian Social Research and Development Associates, 1981.

Hoover, Dwight W. *The Red and the Black.* Chicago: Rand McNally, 1976.

Hornung, Rick. *One Nation Under the Gun: Inside the Mohawk Civil War.* New York: Pantheon Books, 1991.

Hudson, Charles. *The Southeastern Indians.* Knoxville: University of Tennessee Press, 1976.

Iverson, Peter. *The Navajos.* New York: Chelsea House, 1990.

Josephy, Alvin M., Jr. *500 Nations: An Illustrated History of the North American Indians.* New York: Alfred A. Knopf, 1994.

_____. *The Indian Heritage of America.* New York: Alfred A. Knopf, 1968.

_____. *Now That the Buffalo's Gone: A Study of Today's American Indians.* Norman: University of Oklahoma Press, 1984.

_____. *Red Power: The American Indians' Fight for Freedom.* New York: American Heritage Press, 1971.

Kroeber, Alfred Louis. *Handbook of the Indians of California.* New York: Dover, 1976.

LaBarre, Weston. *The Peyote Cult.* 1938. Reprint. Hamden, Conn.: Shoestring Press, 1964.

Legters, Lyman, and Fremont J. Lyden, eds. *American Indian Policy: Self-Governance and Economic Development.* Westport, Conn.: Greenwood Press, 1994.

McNickle, D'Arcy. *The Indian Tribes of the United States.* London: Oxford University Press, 1962.

Magill, Frank N., and Harvey Markowitz, eds. *Ready Reference: American Indians.* Pasadena, Calif.: Salem Press, 1995.

Mankiller, Wilma, and Michael Wallis. *Mankiller: A Chief and Her People.* New York: St. Martin's Press, 1993.

Matthiessen, Peter. *In the Spirit of Crazy Horse.* 2d ed. New York: Viking Press, 1991.

Meredith, Howard. *Modern American Indian Tribal Government and Politics.* Tsaile, Ariz.: Navajo Community College Press, 1993.

Meriam, Lewis, et al. *The Problem of Indian Administration* [Meriam Report]. Baltimore: The Johns Hopkins University Press, 1928.

Meyer, William. *Native Americans.* New York: International, 1971.

Mintz, Steven, ed. *Native American Voices.* St. James, N.Y.: Brandywine Press, 1995.

Mulroy, Kevin. *Freedom on the Border: The Seminole Maroons in Florida, the Indian Territory, Coahuila, and Texas.* Lubbock: Texas Tech University Press, 1993.

Nichols, Roger L. *The American Indian Past and Present.* 4th ed. New York: McGraw-Hill, 1992.

O'Brien, Sharon. *American Indian Tribal Governments.* Norman: University of Oklahoma Press, 1989.

Olson, James S. *Encyclopedia of American Indian Civil Rights.* Greenwood, 1997.

Olson, James S., and Raymond Wilson. *Native Americans in the Twentieth Century.* Provo, Utah: Brigham Young University, 1984.

Paredes, J. Anthony, ed. *Indians of the Southeastern United States in the Late Twentieth Century.* Tuscaloosa: University of Alabama Press, 1992.

Reddy, Marlita A., ed. *Statistical Record of Native North Americans.* Detroit: Gale Research, 1993.

Shattuck, Petra T., and Jill Norgren. *Partial Justice: Federal Indian Law in a Liberal Constitutional System.* New York: Berg, 1991.

Slotkin, James. *The Peyote Religion.* Glencoe, Ill.: Free Press, 1956

Smith, Jane F., and Robert Kvasnicka, eds. *Indian-White Relations: A Persistent Paradox.* Proceedings of the National Archives Conference. Washington, D.C.: Howard University Press, 1976.

Snipp, C. Matthew. *American Indians: The First of This Land.* New York: Russell Sage Foundation, 1989.

Sorkin, Alan L. *American Indians and Federal Aid.* Washington, D.C.: Brookings Institution, 1971.

_____. *The Urban American Indian.* Lexington, Mass.: D.C. Heath, 1978.

Spicer, Edward H. *The American Indians.* Cambridge, Mass.: Belknap Press of Harvard University Press, 1980.

Stedman, Raymond William. *Shadows of the Indian Stereotypes in American Culture.* Norman: University of Oklahoma Press, 1982.

Sturtevant, William C., ed. *Handbook of North American Indians.* Washington, D.C.: Smithsonian Institution, 1978.

Taylor, Theodore W. *American Indian Policy.* Mt. Airy, Md.: Lomond, 1983.

Underhill, Ruth. *The Navajos.* Rev. ed. Norman: University of Oklahoma Press, 1967.

_____. *Red Man's America.* Chicago: University of Chicago Press, 1953.

U.S. Congress. Senate. Committee on Labor and Public Welfare. Special Subcommittee on Indian Education. *Indian Education: A National Tragedy, a National Challenge.* Washington, D.C.: Government Printing Office, 1969.

U.S. Department of Education Task Force. *Indian Nations at Risk: An Educational Strategy for Change.* Washington, D.C.: U.S. Government Printing Office, 1991.

Voices from Wounded Knee, 1973: In the Words of the Participants. Rooseveltown, N.Y.: Akwesasne Notes, 1974.

Waldman, Carl. *Atlas of the North American Indian.* New York: Facts On File, 1985.

_____. *Encyclopedia of Native American Tribes.* New York: Facts On File, 1988.

Walke, Roger. *Gambling on Indian Reservations.* Washington, D.C.: Congressional Research Service, Library of Congress, 1989.

Washburn, Wilcomb E., ed. *The Indian in America.* New York: Harper & Row, 1975.

Weyler, Rex. *Blood of the Land: The U.S. Government and Corporate War Against the First Nations.* 2d ed. Philadelphia: New Society Publishers, 1992.

Wilkinson, Charles F. *American Indians, Time, and the Law: Native Societies in a Modern Constitutional Democracy.* New Haven, Conn.: Yale University Press, 1987.

Williams, Robert A., Jr. *The American Indian in Western Legal Thought: The Discourses of Conquest.* New York: Oxford University Press, 1990.

History of American Indians

Adams, Alexander B. *Geronimo: A Biography.* New York: G. P. Putnam's Sons, 1971.

Adkison, Norman B. *Indian Braves and Battles with More Nez Perce Lore.* Grangeville: Idaho County Free Press, 1967.

_____. *Nez Perce Indian War and Original Stories.* Grangeville, Idaho: Idaho County Free Press, 1966.

Allen, Robert S. *His Majesty's Indian Allies.* Toronto: Dundurn Press, 1992.

Anderson, William L., ed. *Cherokee Removal: Before and After.* Athens: University of Georgia Press, 1991.

Andrist, Ralph K. *The Long Death: The Last Days of the Plains Indians.* New York: Macmillan, 1964.

Armstrong, Virginia Irving, comp. *I Have Spoken: American History Through the Voices of the Indians.* Chicago: Swallow Press, 1971.

Auth, Stephen F. *The Ten Years War: Indian-White Relations in Pennsylvania, 1755-1765.* New York: Garland, 1989.

Axelrod, Alan. *Chronicle of the Indian Wars: From Colonial Times to Wounded Knee.* New York: Prentice-Hall, 1993.

Axtell, James. *The European and the Indian: Essays in the Ethnohistory of Colonial North America.* Oxford, England: Oxford University Press, 1981.

Bailey, L. R. *Indian Slave Trade in the Southwest.* Los Angeles: Westernlore Press, 1966.

Bailey, Paul. *Wovoka: The Indian Messiah.* Los Angeles: Westernlore Press, 1957.

Beal, Merrill D. *I Will Fight No More Forever: Chief Joseph and the Nez Perce War.* Seattle: University of Washington Press, 1963.

Billington, Ray Allen. *Westward Expansion.* New York: Macmillan, 1949.

Biolsi, Thomas. *Organizing the Lakota: The Political Economy of the New Deal on the Pine Ridge and Rosebud Reservations.* Tucson: University of Arizona Press, 1992.

Brady, Cyrus. *Indian Fights and Fighters.* Lincoln: University of Nebraska Press, 1971.

Brill, Charles. *Conquest of the Southern Plains.* Millwood, N.Y.: Kraus Reprint, 1975.

Browman, David L., ed. *Early Native Americans: Prehistoric Demography, Economy, and Technology.* New York: Mouton, 1980.

Brown, Dee. *Bury My Heart at Wounded Knee: An Indian History of the American West.* New York: Holt, Rinehart & Winston, 1970.

Casas, Bartolome de las. *The Tears of the Indians.* Translated by John Phillips. Stanford, Calif.: Academic Reprints, 1953.

Chalmers, Harvey, II. *The Last Stand of the Nez Perce.* New York: Twayne, 1962.

Clark, Blue. *"Lone Wolf v. Hitchcock": Treaty Rights and Indian Law at the End of the Nineteenth Century.* Lincoln: University of Nebraska Press, 1994.

Cook, Sherburne Friend. *The Conflict Between the California Indian and White Civilization.* 4 vols. Berkeley: University of California Press, 1943.

Crane, Verner. *The Southern Frontier, 1670-1732.* Ann Arbor: University of Michigan Press, 1929.

Cument, James, ed. *Scholastic Encyclopedia of the North American Indian.* New York: Scholastic, 1996.

Debo, Angie. *A History of the Indians in the United States.* Norman: University of Oklahoma Press, 1989.

Dillon, Richard H. *North American Indian Wars.* New York: Facts On File, 1983.

Dippie, Brian. *The Vanishing American.* Middletown, Conn.: Wesleyan University Press, 1982.

Dowd, Gregory Evans. *A Spirited Resistance.* Baltimore: The Johns Hopkins University Press, 1992.

Edmunds, R. David. *Tecumseh and the Quest for Indian Leadership.* Boston: Little, Brown, 1984.

Ehle, John. *Trail of Tears: The Rise and Fall of the Cherokee Nation.* New York: Doubleday, 1988.

Faulk, Odie B. *Crimson Desert: Indian Wars of the American Southwest.* New York: Oxford University Press, 1974.

Fixico, Donald L. *Termination and Relocation: Federal Policy, 1945-1966.* Albuquerque: University of New Mexico Press, 1986.

Forbes, Jack D. *Black Africans and Native Americans: Color, Race, and Caste in the Evolution of Red-Black Peoples.* New York: Basil Blackwell, 1988.

Foreman, Grant. *Indian Removal: The Emigration of the Five Civilized Tribes of Indians.* 1932. 2d ed. Norman: University of Oklahoma Press, 1953.

Fritz, Henry E. *The Movement for Indian Assimilation, 1860-1890.* Philadelphia: University of Pennsylvania Press, 1963.

Grinde, Donald A., Jr. *The Iroquois and the Founding of the American Nation.* San Francisco: Indian Historian Press, 1977.

Harvey, Karen D., and Lisa D. Harjo. *Indian Country: A History of Native People in America.* Golden, Colo.: North American Press, 1994.

Hoxie, Frederick E. *A Final Promise: The Campaign to Assimilate the Indians, 1880-1920.* Lincoln: University of Nebraska Press, 1984.

_____. *Indians in American History.* Wheeling, Ill.: Harlan Davidson, 1988.

Jackson, Helen. *A Century of Dishonor: A Sketch of the United States Government's Dealings with Some of the Indian Tribes.* 1880. Reprint. New York: Barnes & Noble, 1993.

Josephy, Alvin M., Jr. *The Indian Heritage of America.* New York: Bantam, 1968.

_____. *The Patriot Chiefs: A Chronicle of American Indian Resistance.* Rev. ed. New York: Penguin Books, 1993.

Katz, William Loren. *Black Indians: A Hidden Heritage.* New York: Atheneum, 1986.

Kelley, Robert. *American Protestantism and United States Indian Policy.* Lincoln: University of Nebraska Press, 1983.

Lazarus, Edward. *Black Hills, White Justice: The Sioux Nation Versus the United States, 1775 to the Present.* New York: HarperCollins, 1991.

Leach, Douglas Edward. *Flintlock and Tomahawk: New England in King Philip's War.* New York: Norton Library Edition, 1966.

Littlefield, Daniel F., Jr. *Africans and Creeks: From the Colonial Period to the Civil War.* Westport, Conn.: Greenwood Press, 1979.

_____. *Africans and Seminoles: From Removal to Emancipation.* Westport, Conn.: Greenwood Press, 1978.

McDonnell, Janet A. *The Dispossession of the American Indian, 1887-1934.* Bloomington: Indiana University Press, 1991.

McPherson, Robert S. *The Northern Navajo Frontier, 1860-1900: Expansion Through Adversity.* Albuquerque: University of New Mexico Press, 1988.

Mooney, James. *The Ghost-Dance Religion and the Sioux Outbreak of 1890.* 1896. Reprint. Chicago: University of Chicago Press, 1965.

Nabokov, Peter, ed. *Native American Testimony: A Chronicle of Indian-White Relations from Prophecy to the Present, 1492-1992.* New York: Viking Penguin, 1991.

Nash, Gary B. *Red, White, and Black: The Peoples of Early America.* Englewood Cliffs, N.J.: Prentice-Hall, 1974.

Neihardt, John G. *Black Elk Speaks: Being the Life Story of a Holy Man of the Oglala Sioux.* 1932. Reprint. Lincoln: University of Nebraska Press, 1979.

Otis, Delos S. *The Dawes Act and the Allotment of Indian Lands.* Edited by Francis Paul Prucha. Norman: University of Oklahoma Press, 1973.

Perdue, Theda. *Slavery and the Evolution of Cherokee Society, 1540-1886.* Knoxville: University of Tennessee Press, 1979.

Philp, Kenneth R. *John Collier's Crusade for Indian Reform, 1920-1954.* Tucson: University of Arizona Press, 1977.

Porter, C. Fayne. *Our Indian Heritage: Profiles of Twelve Great Leaders.* Philadelphia: Chilton Books, 1964.

Pratt, Richard H. *Battlefield and Classroom: Four Decades with the American Indian, 1867-1904,* edited by Robert M. Utley. New Haven, Conn.: Yale University Press, 1964.

Prucha, Francis Paul. *American Indian Treaties: The History of a Political Anomaly.* Berkeley: University of California Press, 1994.

_____, ed. *Americanizing the American Indians: Writings of the "Friends of the Indian" 1880-1900.* Lincoln: University of Nebraska Press, 1973.

_____. *The Great Father: The United States Government and the American Indians.* 2 vols. Lincoln: University of Nebraska Press, 1984.

_____. *Indian Policy in the United States: Historical Essays.* Lincoln: University of Nebraska Press, 1981.

_____. *The Sword of the Republic.* New York: Macmillan, 1969.

Ray, Dorothy Jean. *The Eskimos of Bering Strait, 1650-1898.* Seattle: University of Washington Press, 1975.

Stagg, Jack. *Anglo-Indian Relations in North America to 1763 and an Analysis of the Royal Proclamation of 7 October 1763.* Ottawa: Research Branch, Indian and Northern Affairs Canada, 1981.

Stannard, David E. *American Holocaust.* New York: Oxford University Press, 1992.

Stuart, Paul. *Nations Within a Nation: Historical Statistics of American Indians.* New York: Greenwood Press, 1987.

Svaldi, David. *Sand Creek and the Rhetoric of Extermination: A Case Study in Indian-White Relations.* Lanham, Md.: University Press of America, 1989.

Taylor, Graham D. *The New Deal and American Indian Tribalism: The Administration of the Indian Reorganization Act, 1934-1945.* Lincoln: University of Nebraska Press, 1980.

Thomas, David Hurst, et al. *The Native Americans: An Illustrated History.* Atlanta, Ga.: Turner Publishing, 1993.

Thornton, Russell. *American Indian Holocaust and Survival: A Population History Since 1492.* Norman: University of Oklahoma Press, 1987.

Tyler, Lyman S. *A History of Indian Policy.* Washington, D.C.: U.S. Government Printing Office, 1973.

Utley, Robert M. *The Indian Frontier of the American West, 1846-1890.* Albuquerque: University of New Mexico Press, 1984.

Utley, Robert M., and Wilcomb E. Washburn. *The Indian Wars.* Boston: Houghton Mifflin, 1985.

Washburn, Wilcomb E. *The Assault on Indian Tribalism: The General Allotment Law (Dawes Act) of 1887.* Philadelphia: J. B. Lippincott, 1975.

_____, ed. *History of Indian-White Relations.* Vol. 4 in *Handbook of North American Indians,* edited by William C. Sturtevant. Washington, D.C.: Smithsonian Institution Press, 1988.

Weatherford, Jack. *Native Roots: How the Indians Enriched America.* New York: Fawcett Columbine, 1991.

Wunder, John R. *"Retained by the People": A History of the American Indians and the Bill of Rights.* New York: Oxford University Press, 1994.

ARAB AMERICANS

See also Canada/Arab Canadians

Abraham, Sameer Y., and Nabeel Abraham, eds. *The Arab World and Arab-Americans: Understanding a Neglected Minority.* Detroit, Mich.: Center for Urban Studies, Wayne State University, 1981.

_____, eds. *Arabs in the New World: Studies on Arab-American Communities.* Detroit, Mich.: Center for Urban Studies, Wayne State University, 1983.

Abu-Lagan, Baha, and Michael W. Suleiman, eds. *Arab Americans: Continuity and Change.* Belmont, Mass.: Association of Arab-American University Graduates, 1989.

The Arab American Directory. 2d ed. Alexandria, Va.: Arab Media House, 1997.

Ashabranner, Brent. *An Ancient Heritage: The Arab-American Minority.* New York: HarperCollins, 1991.

Aswad, Barbara, ed. *Arab-Speaking Communities in American Cities.* New York: Center for Migration Studies of New York, 1974.

Barboza, Steven, ed. *American Jihad.* New York: Doubleday, 1994.

Burghuthi, Iyad. *Palestinian Americans: Soci-political Attitudes of Palestinian Americans Towards the Arab-Israeli Conflict.* Durham: Center for Middle Eastern & Islamic Studies, University of Durham, 1989.

Chan, Carole. *Salaam Means Peace: An Introduction to Arab Americans.* Los Angeles, Calif.: Los Angeles County Commission on Human Relations, 1991.

Hagopian, Elaine Catherine, and Ann Paden, eds. *The Arab Americans: Studies in Assimilation.* Wilmette, Ill.: Medina University Press International, 1969.

Hanania, Ray. *I'm Glad I Look Like a Terrorist: Growing Up Arab in America.* Tinley Park, Ill.: Urban Strategies Group, 1996.

Hooglund, Eric J., ed. *Crossing the Waters: Arabic-Speaking Immigrants to the United States Before 1940.* Washington, D.C.: Smithsonian Institution Press, 1987.

Los Angeles County Commission on Human Relations. *Violence and Intimidation—Rising Bigotry Toward Arabs and Muslims: A Report of a Public Hearing.* Los Angeles: Author, 1991.

McCarus, Ernest, ed. *The Development of Arab-American Identity.* Ann Arbor: University of Michigan Press, 1994.

Macron, Mary. *A Celebration of Life: Memories of an Arab-American in Cleveland.* ADC Issues 7. Washington, D.C.: American-Arab Anti-Discrimination Committee, [1986?].

Mehdi, Beverlee Turner, ed. *The Arabs in America, 1492-1977: A Chronology and Fact Book.* Dobbs Ferry, N.Y.: Oceana, 1978.

Michalak, Laurence O. *Cruel and Unusual: Negative Images of Arabs in American Popular Culture.* 2d ed. ADC Issues 15. Washington, D.C.: ADC Research Institute, [1983?].

Naff, Alixa. *The Arab Americans.* New York: Chelsea House, 1988.

Orfalea, Gregory. *Before the Flames: A Quest for the History of Arab Americans.* Austin: University of Texas Press, 1988.

Sawaie, Mohammed, ed. *Arabic-Speaking Immigrants in the United States and Canada: A Bibliographic Guide with Annotation.* Lexington, Ky.: Mazda Publishers, 1985.

Shain, Yossi. *Arab-Americans in the 1990's: What Next for the Diaspora?* Tel Aviv: Tel Aviv University, Tami Steinmetz Center for Peace Research, 1996.

Suleiman, Michael W. "Arab Americans: A Community Profile." In *Islam in North America: A Sourcebook,* edited by Michael A. Koszegi and J. Gordon Melton. New York: Garland, 1992.

Zogby, James, ed. *Taking Root, Bearing Fruit: The Arab-American Experience.* Washington, D.C.: American-Arab Anti-Discrimination Committee, 1984.

ASIAN AMERICANS

See also Canada/Asian Canadians

General Studies

Aguilar-San Juan, Karin, ed. *The State of Asian America: Activism and Resistance in the 1990s.* Boston, Mass.: South End Press, 1994.

Ancheta, Angelo N. *Race, Rights, and the Asian American Experience.* New Brunswick, N.J.: Rutgers University Press, 1998.

Anwar, Muhammad. *Between Cultures: Continuity and Change in the Lives of Young Asians.* New York: Routledge, 1998.

Barringer, Herbert R., Robert W. Gardner, and Michael J. Levin. *Asian and Pacific Islanders in the United States.* New York: Russell Sage, 1993.

Cao, Lan, and Himilce Novas. *Everything You Need to Know About Asian American History.* New York: Penguin, 1996.

Chan, Sucheng. *Asian Americans: An Interpretive History.* Boston: Twayne, 1991.

Curry, Charles F. *Alien Land Laws and Alien Rights.* Washington, D.C.: U.S. Government Printing Office, 1921.

Endo, R., S. Sue, and N. Wagner, eds. *Asian Americans: Social and Psychological Perspectives.* Palo Alto, Calif.: Science & Behavior Books, 1980.

Eoyang, Eugene C. *Coat of Many Colors: Reflections on Diversity by a Minority of One.* Boston: Beacon Press, 1995.

Espiritu, Yen Le. *Asian American Panethnicity: Bridging Institutions and Identities.* Philadelphia: Temple University Press, 1992.

Ferguson, Ted. *A White Man's Country.* Toronto: Doubleday, 1975.

Flynn, James R. *Asian Americans: Achievement Beyond IQ.* Mahwah, N.J.: Lawrence Erlbaum Associates, 1991.

Foner, Philip, and Daniel Rosenberg. *Racism, Dissent, and Asian Americans from 1850 to the Present.* Westport, Conn.: Greenwood Press, 1993.

Fong, Timothy P. *The Contemporary Asian American Experience: Beyond the Model Minority.* Upper Saddle River, N.J.: Prentice-Hall, 1998.

Friday, Chris. *Organizing Asian American Labor.* Philadelphia: Temple University Press, 1994.

Fu, Danling. *My Trouble Is English: Asian Students and the American Dream.* Portsmouth, N.H.: Boynton/Cook, 1995.

Haas, Michael. *Institutional Racism: The Case of Hawai'i.* Westport, Conn.: Praeger, 1992.

_____, ed. *Multicultural Hawai'i: The Fabric of a Multiethnic Society.* New York: Garland, 1998.

Kitano, Harry H. L., and Roger Daniels. *Asian Americans.* Englewood Cliffs, N.J.: Prentice-Hall, 1988.

Knoll, Tricia. *Becoming Americans: Asian Sojourners, Immigrants, and Refugees in the Western United States.* Portland: Coast to Coast Books, 1982.

Lee, Stacey J. *Unraveling the "Model Minority" Stereotype: Listening to Asian American Youth.* New York: Teachers College Press, 1996.

Lott, Juanita Tamayo. *Asian Americans: From Racial Category to Multiple Identities.* Walnut Creek, Calif.: Altamira Press, 1998.

Marchetti, Gina. *Romance and the "Yellow Peril": Race, Sex, and Discursive Strategies in Hollywood Fiction.* Berkeley: Unversity of California Press, 1993.

Matsuoka, Fumitaka. *Out of Silence: Emerging Themes in Asian American Churches.* Cleveland: United Church Press, 1995.

Ng, Franklin, ed. *Asian American Interethnic Relations and Politics.* New York: Garland, 1998.

Ng, Wendy L., ed. *Reviewing Asian America: Locating Diversity.* Pullman: Washington State University Press, 1995.

Paisano, Edna L. *We the American-Asians.* Washington, D.C.: U.S. Department of Commerce Economics and Statistics Administration, Bureau of the Census, 1993.

Said, Edward. *Orientalism.* New York: Random House, 1978.

Saito, Leland T. *Race and Politics: Asian Americans, Latinos, and Whites in a Los Angeles Suburb.* Urbana: University of Illinois Press, 1998.

Sue, Stanley, and James K. Morishima. *The Mental Health of Asian Americans.* San Francisco: Jossey-Bass, 1982.

Takaki, Ronald T. *Strangers from a Different Shore: A History of Asian Americans.* Boston: Little, Brown, 1989.

Walker-Moffat, Wendy. *The Other Side of the Asian American Success Story.* San Francisco: Jossey-Bass, 1995.

Wei, William. *The Asian American Movement.* Philadelphia: Temple University Press, 1993.

Woo, Deborah. *The Glass Ceiling and Asian Americans: A Research Monograph.* Washington, D.C.: Glass Ceiling Commission, U.S. Department of Labor, 1995.

Chinese Americans

Barth, Gunther. *Bitter Strength: A History of the Chinese in the United States, 1850-1870.* Cambridge, Mass.: Harvard University Press, 1964.

Chan, Anthony. *Gold Mountain: The Chinese in the New World.* Vancouver: New Star Books, 1983.

Chan, Sucheng, ed. *Entry Denied: Exclusion and the Chinese Community in America, 1882-1943.* Philadelphia: Temple University Press, 1991.

Chinn, Thomas W. *Bridging the Pacific: San Francisco Chinatown and Its People.* San Francisco: Chinese Historical Society of America, 1989.

Coolidge, Mary Roberts. *Chinese Immigration.* New York: Henry Holt, 1909.

Daniels, Roger. *Asian America: Chinese and Japanese in the United States Since 1850.* Seattle: University of Washington Press, 1988.

Dillon, Richard H. *The Hatchet Men: The Story of the Tong Wars in San Francisco Chinatown.* New York: Coward-McCann, 1962.

Hoexter, Corinne K. *From Canton to California: The Epic of Chinese Immigration.* New York: Four Winds Press, 1976.

Kinkead, Gwen. *Chinatown: A Portrait of a Closed Society.* New York: HarperCollins, 1992.

Mangiafico, Luciano. *Contemporary American Immigrants: Patterns of Filipino, Korean, and Chinese Settlement in the United States.* New York: Praeger, 1988.

McKenzie, Roderick Duncan. *Oriental Exclusion: The Effect of American Immigration Laws, Regulations, and Judicial Decisions upon the Chinese and Japanese on the American Pacific Coast, 1885-1940.* New York: J. S. Ozer, 1971.

Miller, Stuart Creighton. *The Unwelcome Immigrant: The American Image of the Chinese, 1785-1882.* Berkeley: University of California Press, 1969.

Sung, Betty Lee. *The Adjustment Experience of Chinese Immigrant Children in New York City.* Staten Island, N.Y.: Center for Migration Studies, 1987.

_____. *Mountain of Gold: The Story of the Chinese in America.* New York: I Company, 1967.

Toff, Nancy, ed. *The Japanese Americans, the Korean Americans, the Chinese Americans.* New York: Chelsea House, 1989.

Tsai, Shih-Shan Henry. *The Chinese Experience in America.* Bloomington: Indiana University Press, 1986.

Tung, William L. *The Chinese in America, 1820-1973.* Dobbs Ferry, N.Y.: Oceana Press, 1974.

Zhou, Min. *Chinatown: The Socio-Economic Potential of an Urban Enclave.* Philadelphia: Temple University Press, 1992.

Filipino Americans

Brands, H. W. *Bound to Empire: The United States and the Philippines.* New York: Oxford University Press, 1992.

DeWitt, Howard A. *Anti-Filipino Movements in California: A History, Bibliography, and Study Guide.* San Francisco: R&E Research Associates, 1976.

Espiritu, Yen Le. *Filipino American Lives.* Philadelphia: Temple University Press, 1995.

Ignacio, Lemuel F. *Asian Americans and Pacific Islanders.* San Jose, Calif.: Pilipino Development Associates, 1976.

Karnov, Stanley. *In Our Image: America's Empire in the Philippines.* New York: Random House, 1989.

Mangiafico, Luciano. *Contemporary American Immigrants: Patterns of Filipino, Korean, and Chinese Settlement in the United States.* New York: Praeger, 1988.

Miller, Stuart Creighton. *"Benevolent Assimilation": The American*

Conquest of the Philippines, 1899-1903. New Haven, Conn.: Yale University Press, 1982.

Root, Maria P. P., ed. *Filipino Americans: Transformation and Identity.* Newbury Park, Calif.: Sage Publications, 1997.

Salamanca, Bonifacio S. *The Filipino Reaction to American Rule, 1901-1913.* Quezon City, Philippines: New Day Publishers, 1984.

San Juan, Epifanio, et al. *From Exile to Diaspora: Versions of the Filipino Experience in the United States.* Boulder, Colo.: Westview Press, 1998.

Toff, Nancy, ed. *The Filipino Americans.* New York: Chelsea House, 1989.

Japanese Americans

Christgau, John. *"Enemies": World War II Alien Internment.* Ames: Iowa State University Press, 1985.

Chuman, Frank F. *The Bamboo People: The Law and Japanese-Americans.* Del Mar, Calif.: Publisher's Inc., 1976.

Collins, Donald E. *Native American Aliens, Disloyalty and the Renunciation of Citizenship by Japanese Americans During World War II.* Westport, Conn.: Greenwood Press, 1985.

Connor, John W. *Tradition and Change in Three Generations of Japanese Americans.* Chicago: Nelson-Hall, 1977.

Conroy, Hilary. *The Japanese Frontier in Hawaii, 1868-1898.* Berkeley: University of California Press, 1953.

Daniels, Roger. *Asian America: Chinese and Japanese in the United States Since 1850.* Seattle: University of Washington Press, 1988.

_____. *Concentration Camps, North America: Japanese in the United States and Canada During World War II.* 1981. Reprint. Malabar, Fla.: Robert E. Krieger, 1989.

_____. *The Politics of Prejudice: The Anti-Japanese Movement in California, and the Struggle for Japanese Exclusion.* Berkeley: University of California Press, 1962.

Drinnon, Richard. *Keeper of Concentration Camps: Dillon S. Myer and American Racism.* Berkeley: University of California Press, 1987.

Fugita, Stephen S., and David J. O'Brien. *Japanese American Ethnicity: The Persistence of Community.* Seattle: University of Washington Press, 1991.

Gulick, Sidney L. *The American Japanese Problem.* New York: Scribner's, 1914.

Hatamiya, Leslie T. *Righting a Wrong: Japanese Americans and the Passage of the Civil Liberties Act of 1988.* Stanford, Calif.: Stanford University Press, 1993.

Hoobler, Dorothy, Thomas Hoobler, and George Takei. *The Japanese American Family Album.* New York: Oxford University Press, 1996.

Hosokawa, Bill. *JACL in Quest of Justice.* New York: William Morrow, 1982.

_____. *Nisei: The Quiet Americans.* New York: William Morrow, 1969.

Ichihashi, Yamato. *The American Immigration Collection: Japanese in the United States.* 1932. Reprint. New York: Arno Press, 1969.

Johnson, Herbert B. *Discrimination Against the Japanese in California.* Berkeley, Calif.: Courier, 1907.

Kitano, Harry. *The Japanese Americans.* New York: Chelsea House, 1987.

Levine, Gene N., and Colbert Rhodes. *The Japanese American Community.* New York: Praeger, 1981.

Lind, Andrew W. *Hawaii's Japanese.* Princeton, N.J.: Princeton University Press, 1946.

McClatchy, V. S. *Japanese Immigration and Colonization.* Reprint. San Francisco: R&E Research Associates, 1970.

McKenzie, Roderick Duncan. *Oriental Exclusion: The Effect of American Immigration Laws, Regulations, and Judicial Decisions upon the Chinese and Japanese on the American Pacific Coast, 1885-1940.* New York: J. S. Ozer, 1971.

McWilliams, Carey. *Prejudice: Japanese-Americans, Symbol of Racial Intolerance.* Boston: Little, Brown, 1944.

Makabe, Tomoko. *Picture Brides: Japanese Women in Canada.* Toronto: Multicultural History Society of Ontario, 1995.

Manchester-Boddy, E. *Japanese in America.* San Francisco: R&E Research Associates, 1970.

Masaoka, Mike, with Bill Hosokawa. *They Call Me Moses Masaoka: An American Saga.* New York: William Morrow, 1987.

Montero, Darrel. *Japanese Americans: Changing Patterns of Ethnic Affiliation over Three Generations.* Boulder, Colo.: Westview Press, 1980.

Mura, David. *Turning Japanese: Memoirs of a Sansei.* New York: Atlantic Monthly Press, 1991.

Myer, Dillon S. *Uprooted Americans: The Japanese Americans and the War Relocation Authority During World War II.* Tucson: University of Arizona Press, 1971.

Nakayama, Gordon. *Issei.* Toronto: NC Press, 1984.

Niiya, Brian, ed. *Japanese American History: An A-to-Z Reference from 1868 to the Present.* New York: Japanese American National Museum and Facts On File, 1993.

O'Brien, David J., and Stephen Fugita. *The Japanese American Experience.* Bloomington: Indiana University Press, 1991.

Okazaki, Robert. *The Nisei Mass Evacuation Group and the P.O.W. Camp 101: The Japanese Canadian Community's Struggle for Justice and Human Rights During World War II.* Scarborough, Ont.: Markham, 1996.

Pajus, Jean. *The Real Japanese California.* San Francisco: R&E Research Associates, 1971.

Petersen, Willima. *Japanese Americans: Oppression and Success.* New York: Random House, 1971.

Smith, Bradford. *Americans from Japan.* New York: J. B. Lippincott, 1948.

Strong, Edward K., Jr. *The Second-Generation Japanese Problem.* Stanford, Calif.: Stanford University Press, 1934.

Takahasi, Jere. "Japanese American Responses to Race Relations: The Formation of Nisei Perspectives." *Amerasia Journal* 9, no. 1 (Spring/Summer, 1982): 29-57.

Toff, Nancy, ed. *The Japanese Americans, the Korean Americans, the Chinese Americans.* New York: Chelsea House, 1989.

U.S. Department of the Interior, War Relocation. *Authority, Myths, and Facts About the Japanese American.* Washington, D.C.: U.S. Government Printing Office, 1945.

Wilson, Robert A., and Bill Hosokawa. *East to America: A History of the Japanese in the United States.* New York: William Morrow, 1980.

Korean Americans

Abelmann, Nancy, and John Lie. *Blue Dreams: Korean Americans and the Los Angeles Riots.* Cambridge, Mass.: Harvard University Press, 1995.

Choy, Bong-youn. *Koreans in America.* Chicago: Nelson-Hall, 1979.

Kim, Illsoo. "The Koreans: Small Business in an Urban Frontier." In *New Immigrants in New York*, edited by Nancy Foner. New York: Columbia University Press, 1987.

Kim, Warren Y. *Koreans in America*. Seoul: Po Chin Chai Printing Co., 1971.

Lee, Lauren. *Korean Americans*. New York: Marshall Cavendish, 1995.

Light, Ivan, and Edna Bonacich. *Immigrant Entrepreneurs: Koreans in Los Angeles, 1965-1982*. Berkeley: University of California Press, 1988.

Mangiafico, Luciano. *Contemporary American Immigrants: Patterns of Filipino, Korean, and Chinese Settlement in the United States*. New York: Praeger, 1988.

Min, Pyong Gap. *Caught in the Middle: Korean Merchants in America's Multiethnic Cities*. Berkeley: University of California Press, 1996.

Patterson, Wayne. *The Korean Frontier in America: Immigration to Hawaii, 1896-1910*. Honolulu: University of Hawaii Press, 1988.

Takaki, Ronald T. *From the Land of Morning Calm: The Koreans in America*. New York: Chelsea House, 1994.

Toff, Nancy, ed. *The Japanese Americans, the Korean Americans, the Chinese Americans*. New York: Chelsea House, 1989.

Yoon, In-Jin. *On My Own: Korean Businesses and Race Relations in America*. Chicago: University of Chicago Press, 1997.

South Asian Americans

Gibson, Margaret A. *Accommodation Without Assimilation: Sikh Immigrants in an American High School*. Ithaca, N.Y.: Cornell University Press, 1988.

Helweg, Arthur W., and Usha M. Helweg. *An Immigrant Success Story: East Indians in the United States*. Philadelphia: University of Pennsylvania Press, 1990.

La Brack, Bruce. *The Sikhs of Northern California 1904-1974*. New York: AMS Press, 1988.

Southeast Asian Americans

Bass, Thomas. *Vietnamerica: The War Comes Home*. New York: Soho Press, 1996.

Caplan, Nathan S., et al. *Children of the Boat People*. Ann Arbor: University of Michigan Press, 1991.

_____. *The Boat People and Achievement in America: A Study of Family Life, Hard Work, and Cultural Values*. Ann Arbor: University of Michigan Press, 1989.

Esterik, Penny Van. *Taking Refuge: Lao Buddhists in North America*. Tempe: Arizona State University Press, 1992.

Faderman, Lillian, with Ghia Xiong. *I Begin My Life All Over: The Hmong and the American Immigrant Experience*. Boston: Beacon, 1998.

Fadiman, Anne. *The Spirit Catches You and You Fall Down: A Hmong Child, Her American Doctors, and the Collision of Two Cultures*. New York: Farrar, Straus & Giroux, 1997.

Haines, David W., ed. *Refugees as Immigrants: Cambodians, Laotians, and Vietnamese in America*. Totowa, N.J.: Rowman and Littlefield, 1989.

Kibria, Nazli. *Family Tightrope: The Changing Lives of Vietnamese Americans*. Princeton, N.J.: Princeton University Press, 1993.

Long, Patrick Du Phuoc, with Laura Richard. *The Dream Shattered: Vietnamese Gangs in America*. Boston: Northeastern University Press, 1996.

Montero, Darrel. *Vietnamese Americans: Patterns of Resettlement and Socioeconomic Adaptation in the United States*. Boulder, Colo.: Westview Press, 1979.

Rutledge, Paul James. *The Vietnamese Experience in America*. Bloomington: Indiana University Press, 1992.

Sherman, Spenceer. "The Hmong in America: Laotian Refugees in the Land of the Giants." In *National Geographic* (October, 1988).

Toff, Nancy, ed. *The Indo-Chinese Americans*. New York: Chelsea House Publishers, 1989.

Zhou, Min, and Carl L. Bankston III. *Growing Up American: How Vietnamese Children Adapt to Life in the United States*. New York: Russell Sage, 1998.

CANADA

General Studies

Berry, J. W., and J. A. Laponce, eds. *Ethnicity and Culture in Canada: The Research Landscape*. Toronto: University of Toronto Press, 1994.

Billingsley, Brenda, and Leon Muszynski. *No Discrimination Here? Toronto Employers and the Multi-Racial Workforce*. Toronto: Social Planning Council of Metropolitan Toronto/Uran Alliance on Race Relations, 1985.

Bissoondath, Neil. *Selling Illusions: The Cult of Multiculturalism in Canada*. Toronto: Penguin Books, 1994.

Bothwell, Robert, Ian Drummond, and John English. *Canada: 1900-1945*. Toronto: University of Toronto Press, 1987.

_____. *Canada Since 1945: Power, Politics, and Provincialism*. Rev. ed. Toronto: University of Toronto Press, 1989.

Boyko, John. *Last Steps to Freedom: The Evolution of Canadian Racism*. 2d rev. ed. Winnipeg: J. Gordon Shillingford, 1998.

Brebner, J. Bartlet. *Canada: A Modern History*, revised by Donald C. Masters. Ann Arbor: University of Michigan Press, 1970.

Canadian Human Rights Foundation. *Multiculturalism and the Charter: A Legal Perspective*. Toronto: Carswell, 1987.

Canadian Multiculturalism: Issues and Trends. Ottawa: Library of Parliament, Research Branch, 1997.

Chiswick, Barry R., ed. *Immigration, Language, and Ethnicity: Canada and the United States*. Washington, D.C.: AEI Press, 1992.

Cook, Ramsay, and Robert Craig Brown. *Canada, 1896-1921: A Nation Transformed*. Toronto: McClelland and Stewart, 1991.

Driedger, Leo, ed. *Ethnic Canada: Identities and Inequalities*. Toronto: Copp, Clark and Pittman, 1987.

_____. *The Ethnic Factor: Identity in Diversity*. Toronto: McGraw-Hill Ryerson, 1989.

_____. *Multi-Ethnic Canada: Identities and Inequalities*. Toronto: Oxford University Press, 1996.

Elliott, Jean Leonard. *Unequal Relations: An Introduction to Race and Ethnic Dynamics in Canada*. Scarborough, Ont.: Prentice-Hall Canada, 1992.

Fleras, Augie, and Jean Leonard Elliott. *Multiculturalism in Canada: The Challenge to Diversity*. Scarborough, Ont.: Nelson Canada, 1992.

Francis, R. Douglas, and Donald B. Smith, eds. *Readings in Canadian History: Pre-Confederation*. 2d ed. Toronto: Holt, Rinehart and Winston of Canada, 1986.

Halli, Shiva S., Frank Trovato, and Leo Driedger, eds. *Ethnic Demography: Canadian Immigrant, Racial, and Cultural Variations.* Ottawa: Carleton University Press.

Hawkins, Freda. *Canada and Immigration: Public Policy and Public Concern.* 2d ed. Kingston, Ont.: McGill-Queen's University Press, 1988.

Hill, Daniel G., and Marvin Schiff. *Human Rights in Canada: A Focus on Racism.* 3d ed. Ottawa: Canadian Labour Congress and the Human Rights Research and Education Center, University of Ottawa, 1988.

Keohane, Kieran. *Symptoms of Canada: An Essay on the Canadian Identity.* Toronto: University of Toronto Press, 1998.

Li, Peter S., ed. *Race and Ethnic Relations in Canada.* Don Mills, Ont.: Oxford University Press Canada, 1990.

Li, Peter S., and B. Singh Bolaria, and John Boyko, eds. *Racial Minorities in Multicultural Canada.* Toronto: Garamond Press, 1983.

McInnes, Edgar. *Canada: A Political and Social History.* 4th ed. Toronto: Holt, Rinehart and Winston of Canada, 1982.

Milne, David. *The Canadian Constitution.* Toronto: Lorimer, 1990.

Noivo, Edite. *Inside Ethnic Families: Three Generations of Portuguese-Canadians.* Montreal: McGill-Queen's University Press, 1998.

Palmer, Howard. *Patterns of Prejudice: A History of Nativism in Alberta.* Toronto: McClelland and Stewart, 1982.

Reitz, Jeffrey, and Raymond Breton. *The Illusion of Difference: Realities of Ethnicity in Canada and the United States.* Toronto: C. D. Howe Institute, 1994.

Report of the Commission on Systemic Racism in the Ontario Criminal Justice System: A Community Summary. Toronto: The Commission, 1995.

Weiner, Nan. *Employment Equity: Making It Work.* Toronto: Butterworths, 1993.

Whitaker. Reginald. *Double Standard: The Secret History of Canadian Immigration.* Toronto: Lester & Orpen Dennys, 1987.

Woodcock, George. *The Canadians.* Cambridge, Mass.: Harvard University Press, 1979.

Aboriginals

See also American Indians

Bartlett, Richard H. *Indian Reserves and Aboriginal Lands in Canada.* Saskatoon, Canada: University of Saskatchewan, Native Law Center, 1990.

Beal, Bob, and Rod Macleod. *Prairie Fire: The 1885 North-West Rebellion.* Edmonton: Hurtig, 1984.

Bowsfield, Hartfield. *Louis Riel: The Rebel and the Hero.* Toronto: Oxford University Press, 1971.

Carter, Sarah. *Lost Harvest: Prairies, Indian Reserve Farmers, and Government Policy.* Montreal: McGill-Queen's University Press, 1990.

Dickason, Olive Patricia. *Canada's First Nations: A History of Founding Peoples from Earliest Times.* Norman: University of Oklahoma Press, 1992.

Dickerson, Mark O. *Whose North? Political Change, Political Development, and Self-Government in the Northwest Territories.* Vancouver: University of British Columbia Press, 1992.

First Nations in Canada/Les Premières nations du Canada. Ottawa, Ont.: Minister of Public Works and Government Services, 1997.

Flanagan, Thomas. *Louis "David" Riel: Prophet of the New World.* Toronto: University of Toronto Press, 1979.

_____. *Riel and the Rebellion: 1885 Reconsidered.* Saskatoon: Western Producer Prairie Books, 1983.

Fleras, Augie. *Unequal Relations: An Introduction to Race, Ethnic, and Aboriginal Dynamics in Canada.* 2d ed. Scarborough, Ont.: Prentice Hall Canada, 1996.

Frideres, James. *Canada's Indians: Contemporary Conflicts.* Scarborough, Ontario: Prentice Hall of Canada, 1974.

Getty, Ian, and Antoine Lussier, eds. *As Long as the Sun Shines and Water Flows: A Reader in Canadian Native Studies.* Vancouver: University of British Columbia Press, 1983.

Giraud, Marcel. *The Metis in the Canadian West.* Translated by George Woodcock. 2 vols. Lincoln: University of Nebraska Press, 1986.

Grant, John Webster. *Moon of Wintertime: Missionaries and the Indians of Canada in Encounter Since 1543.* Toronto: University of Toronto Press, 1984.

Howard, Joseph Kinsey. *Strange Empire: Louis Riel and the Métis People.* Toronto: J. Lewis and Samuel, 1974.

Howard, Richard. *Riel.* Toronto: Clarke, Irwin, 1967.

Indians and Inuit of Canada/Les Indiens et les Inuit du Canada. Ottawa, Ont.: Indian and Northern Affairs, 1990.

Inuit Tapirisat of Canada. *The Inuit of Canada.* Hull, Quebec: Author, 1995.

Josee, Normand. *A Profile of the Metis.* Ottawa: Statistics Canada, 1996.

Long, J. Anthony, and Menno Boldt, in association with Leroy Little Bear. *Governments in Conflict? Provinces and Indian Nations in Canada.* Toronto: University of Toronto Press, 1988.

McDougall, John. *In the Days of the Red River Rebellion.* Edmonton: University of Alberta Press, 1983.

McMillan, Alan D. *Native Peoples and Cultures of Canada: An Anthropological Overview.* Vancouver: Douglas & McIntyre, 1988.

Miller, J. R. *Skyscrapers Hide the Heavens: A History of Indian-White Relations in Canada.* Rev. ed. Toronto: University of Toronto Press, 1991.

_____. *Sweet Promises: A Reader on Indian-White Relations in Canada.* Toronto: University of Toronto Press, 1991.

Morris, Alexander. *The Treaties of Canada with the Indians of Manitoba and the North-West Territories.* Toronto: Belfords, Clark & Co., 1880. Reprint. Toronto: Coles, 1971.

Morrison, Andrea P., with Irwin Cotler. *Justice for Natives Searching for Common Ground.* Montreal: McGill-Queen's University Press, 1997.

Morse, Bradforse W. *Aboriginal Peoples and the Law: Indian, Metis and Inuit Rights in Canada.* Rev. ed. Ottawa: Carleton University Press, 1989.

Purich, Donald J. *The Inuit and Their Land: The Story of Nunavut.* Toronto: James Lorimer, 1992.

_____. *The Metis.* Toronto: James Lorimer, 1988.

Read, Colin, and Ronald J. Stagg, eds. *The Rebellion of 1837 in Upper Canada: A Collection of Documents.* Toronto: Champlain Society in Cooperation with the Ontario Heritage Foundation, 1985.

Riel, Louis. *The Collected Writings of Louis Riel.* Edited by George F. G. Stanley. Edmonton: University of Alberta Press, 1985.

Royal Commission on Aboriginal Peoples [Canada]. *Looking*

Forward, Looking Back; Restructuring the Relationship; Gathering Strength; Perspectives and Realities; and *Renewal: A Twenty Year Commitment.* Ottawa, Ont.: Canada Communication Group, 1996.

Satzewich, Vic, and Terry Wotherspoon. *First Nations: Race, Class, and Gender Relations.* Scarborough, Ont.: Nelson Canada, 1993.

Sealely, D. Bruce, and Antoine Lussier. *The Metis: Canada's Forgotten People.* Winnipeg: Pemmican Publishers, 1981.

Siggins, Maggie. *Riel: A Life of Revolution.* Toronto: HarperCollins, 1994.

Stanley, George F. G. *The Birth of Western Canada: A History of the Riel Rebellions.* 2d ed. Toronto: University of Toronto Press, 1960.

Tennant, Paul. *Aboriginal Peoples and Politics: The Indian Land Question in British Columbia, 1849-1989.* Vancouver: University of British Columbia Press, 1990.

Titley, E. Brian. *A Narrow Vision: Duncan Campbell Scott and the Administration of Indian Affairs in Canada.* Vancouver: University of British Columbia Press, 1986.

Arab Canadians

See also Arab Americans

Abu-Laban, Baha. *An Olive Branch on the Family Tree: The Arabs in Canada.* Toronto: McClelland and Stewart, 1980.

Asian Canadians

See also Asian Americans

Adachi, Ken. *The Enemy That Never Was: A History of the Japanese Canadians.* Toronto: McClelland & Stewart, 1991.

Anderson, Kay J. *Vancouver's Chinatown: Racial Discourse in Canada, 1875-1980.* Buffalo, N.Y.: McGill-Queen's University Press, 1991.

Buchignani, Norman, and Doreen M. Indra, with Ram Srivastiva. *Continuous Journey: A Social History of South Asians in Canada.* Toronto: McClelland and Stewart, 1985.

Chandrasekhar, S. *From India to Canada: A Brief History of Immigration, Problems of Discrimination, Admission, and Assimilation.* La Jolla, Calif.: A Population Review Book, 1986.

Chu, Garrick, ed. *Inalienable Rice: A Chinese and Japanese Canadian Anthology.* Vancouver: Intermedia Press, 1980.

Dorais, Louis-Jacques, Lise Pilon Le, and Nguyen Huy. *Exile in a Cold Land: A Vietnamese Community in Canada.* New Haven, Conn.: Yale Center for International and Area Studies, 1987.

Johnston, Hugh. *The Voyage of the Komagata Maru: The Sikh Challenge to Canada's Colour Bar.* Delhi, India: Oxford University Press, 1979.

Kobayashi, Cassandra, and Roy Miki, eds. *Spirit of Redress: Japanese Canadians in Conference.* Vancouver, B.C.: JC Publications, 1989.

Lai, David Chuenyan. *Chinatowns: Towns Within Cities in Canada.* Vancouver: University of British Columbia Press, 1988.

Makabe, Tomoko. *The Canadian Sansei.* Toronto: University of Toronto Press, 1998.

Ward, W. Peter. *White Canada Forever: Popular Attitudes and Public Policy Toward Orientals in British Columbia.* Montreal: McGill-Queen's University Press, 1990.

Wickberg, Edgar, ed. *From China to Canada: A History of the Chinese Communities in Canada.* Toronto: McClelland & Stewart, 1982.

Black Canadians

See also African Americans

Alexander, Ken, and Avis Glaze. *The African-Canadian Experience.* Toronto: Umbrella Press, 1996.

Henry, Frances. *The Caribbean Diaspora in Toronto: Learning to Live with Racism.* Buffalo, N.Y.: University of Toronto Press, 1995.

Winks, Robin W. *The Blacks in Canada: A History.* Montreal: McGill-Queen's University Press, 1971.

French Canadians and the Quebec Question

See also Language and Bilingualism

Bastarache, Michael, et al. *Language Rights in Canada.* Montreal, Quebec: Editions Yvon Blais, 1987.

Behiels, Michael. *Prelude to Quebec's Quiet Revolution: Liberalism Versus Neo-Nationalism, 1945-1960.* Montreal: McGill-Queen's University Press, 1985.

Bouchard, Lucien. *On the Record.* Translated by Dominique Clift. Toronto: Stoddart, 1994.

Bourhis, Richard Y., ed. *Conflict and Language Planning in Quebec.* Clevedon, Avon, England: Multilingual Matters, 1984.

Cohen, Andrew. *A Deal Undone.* Vancouver, B.C.: Douglas and McIntyre, 1990.

Coyne, Deborah. *Roll of the Dice.* Toronto: Lorimer, 1992.

Daniels, Dan, ed. *Quebec, Canada and the October Crisis.* Montreal: Black Rose Books, 1973.

Fraser, Graham. *René Lévesque and the Parti Québécois in Power.* Toronto: Macmillan, 1984.

Gagnon, Alain-G., and Mary Beth Montcalm. *Quebec Beyond the Quiet Revolution.* Scarborough, Ont.: Nelson Canada, 1990.

Gougeon, Gilles. *A History of Quebec Nationalism.* Translated by Louisa Blair, Robert Chodos, and Jane Obertino. Toronto: James Lorimer, 1994.

Johnson, William. *A Canadian Myth: Québec, Between Canada and the Illusion of Utopia.* Montreal: Robert Davies, 1994.

Laczko, Leslie S. *Pluralism and Inequality in Quebec.* Toronto: University of Toronto Press, 1995.

Mathews, Georges. *Quiet Resolution: Quebec's Challenge to Canada.* Toronto: Summerhill, 1990.

Monahan, Patrick. *Meech Lake: The Inside Story.* Toronto: University of Toronto Press, 1991.

Pelletier, Gérard. *The October Crisis.* Translated by Joyce Marshall. Montreal: McClelland and Stewart, 1971.

Purves, Grant. *Official Bilingualism in Canada.* Ottawa, Ont.: Library of Parliament, Research Branch, 1992.

Rotstein, Abraham, ed. *Power Corrupted: The October Crisis and the Repression of Quebec.* Toronto: New Press, 1971.

Saywell, John. *The Rise of the Parti Québécois, 1967-1976.* Toronto: University of Toronto Press, 1977.

Schneiderman, David, ed. *Language and the State: The Law and Politics of Identity.* Cowansville, Quebec: Editions Yvon Blais, 1991.

Thomson, Dale C. *Jean Lesage and the Quiet Revolution.* Toronto: Macmillan, 1984.

Valaskakis, Kimon, and Angéline Fournier. *The Delusion of Sovereignty.* Translated by George Tombs. Montreal: Robert Davies, 1995.

Ward, Mason, and Jean Falardeau, eds. *Canadian Dualism: Studies of English-French Relations.* Toronto: University of Toronto Press, 1960.

Wardhaugh, Ronald. *Language and Nationhood: The Canadian Experience.* Vancouver, B.C.: New Star Books, 1983.

Young, Robert. *The Secession of Quebec and the Future of Canada.* Montreal: McGill-Queen's University Press, 1995.

Jewish Canadians

See also Jewish Americans

Arbella, Irving, and Harold Troper. *None Is Too Many: Canada and the Jews of Europe, 1933-1948.* Toronto: Lester and Orpen Dennys, 1982.

Elazar, Daniel J., and Harold M. Waller's *Maintaining Consensus: The Canadian Jewish Polity in the Postwar World.* Lanham, Md.: University Press of America, 1990.

Rosenberg, Stuart E. *The Jewish Community in Canada.* Vol. 1, *A History.* Toronto: McClelland and Stewart, 1970.

Weinfeld, J., W. Shaffir, and I. Cotler, eds. *The Canadian Jewish Mosaic.* Toronto and New York: John Wiley & Sons, 1981.

Women in Canada

See also Women and Gender Issues

Stephenson, Marylee, ed. *Women in Canada.* Don Mills, Ontario: General, 1977.

Swyripa, Frances. *Wedded to the Cause: Ukrainian-Canadian Women and Ethnic Identity, 1891-1991.* Toronto: University of Toronto Press, 1993.

CARIBBEAN AMERICANS

See also Latinos

General Studies

Afro-Latin Americans Today: No Longer Invisible. London: Minority Rights Group, 1995.

Bonnett, Aubrey W. *Institutional Adaptation of West Indian Immigrants to America.* Washington, D.C.: University Press of America, 1982.

Glissant, Édouard, et al. *Caribbean Discourse: Selected Essays.* Translated by J. Michael Dash. Charlottesville: University Press of Virginia, 1989.

Helg, Aline. *Our Rightful Share: The Afro-Cuban Struggle for Equality, 1886-1912.* Chapel Hill: University of North Carolina Press, 1995.

Henry, Frances. *The Caribbean Diaspora in Toronto: Learning to Live with Racism.* Buffalo, N.Y.: University of Toronto Press, 1995.

Hulme, Peter. *Colonial Encounters: Europe and the Native Caribbean, 1492-1797.* New York: Methuen, 1986.

Kasinitz, Philip. *Caribbean New York: Black Immigrants and the Politics of Race.* Ithaca, N.Y.: Cornell University Press, 1992.

Keegan, William F., ed. *Earliest Hispanic/Native American Interactions in the Caribbean.* New York: Garland, 1991.

Las Casas, Bartolomé de. *History of the Indies.* Edited and translated by Andrée Collard. New York: Harper & Row, 1971.

Levine, Robert M. *Race and Ethnic Relations in Latin American and the Caribbean: An Historical Dictionary and Bibliography.* Metuchen, N.J.: Scarecrow, 1980.

Lewis, Gordon K. *The Growth of the Modern West Indies.* New York: Monthly Review Press, 1968.

Nicholls, David. *Haiti in the Caribbean Context: Ethnicity, Economy, and Revolt.* New York: St. Martin's Press, 1985.

Palmer, Ransford W. *Pilgrims from the Sun: West Indian Migration to America.* New York: Twayne Publishers, 1995.

Thompson, Alvin O. *The Haunting Past: Politics, Economics and Race in Caribbean Life.* Armonk, N.Y.: M. E. Sharpe, 1997.

Tyler, S. Lyman. *Two Worlds: The Indian Encounter with the European, 1492-1509.* Salt Lake City: University of Utah Press, 1988.

Vickerman, Milton. *Crosscurrents: West Indian Immigrants and Race.* New York: Oxford University Press, 1998.

Watkins-Owens, Irma. *Blood Relations: Caribbean Immigrants and the Harlem Community, 1900-1930.* Bloomington: Indiana University Press, 1996.

Dominicans

Atkins, G. Pope, and Larman C. Wilson. *The Dominican Republic and the United States: From Imperialism to Transnationalism.* University of Georgia Press, 1998.

Guarnizo, Luis E. "Dominicanyorks." In *Challenging Fronteras,* edited by Mary Romero, Pierrette Hondagneu-Sotelo, and Vilma Ortiz. New York: Routledge, 1997.

James, Cyril L. R. *The Black Jacobins: Toussaint L'Ouverture and the San Domingo Revolution.* New York: Vintage Books, 1989.

Pessar, Patricia. *A Visa for a Dream.* Boston: Allyn & Bacon, 1995.

Pons, Frank Moya. *The Dominican Republic: A National History.* New Rochelle, N.Y.: Hispaniola Books, 1995.

Haitians

Bellegarde-Smith, Patrick. *Haiti: The Breached Citadel.* Boulder, Colo.: Westview Press, 1990.

Farmer, Paul. *The Uses of Haiti.* Monroe, Maine: Common Courage Press, 1994.

Fick, Carolyn E. *The Making of Haiti: The Saint Domingue Revolution from Below.* Knoxville: University of Tennessee Press, 1990.

Miller, Jake. *The Plight of Haitian Refugees.* New York: Praeger, 1984.

Nicholls, David. *From Dessalines to Duvalier: Race, Colour, and National Independence in Haiti.* 3d ed. London: Macmillan Caribbean, 1996.

Ott, Thomas O. *The Haitian Revolution, 1789-1804.* Knox-ville: University of Tennessee Press, 1973.

Stepick, Alex. *Haitian Refugees in the U.S.* London: Minority Rights Group, 1982.

Wilentz, Amy. *The Rainy Season: Haiti Since Duvalier.* New York: Simon & Schuster, 1989.

CENSUS ISSUES

Abramowitz, Molly. *Census '90 Basics.* Washington, D.C.: U.S. Dept. of Commerce, Bureau of the Census, 1990.

Anderson, Margo J. *The American Census: A Social History.* New Haven, Conn.: Yale University Press, 1988.

Bryant, Barbara Everett, and William Dunn. *Moving Power and Money: The Politics of Census Taking.* Ithaca, N.Y.: New Strategic Publications, 1995.

Choldin, Harvey M. *Looking for the Last Percent: The Controversy over Census Undercounts.* New Brunswick, N.J.: Rutgers University Press, 1994.

Citro, Constance F., and Michael L. Cohen, eds. *The Bicentennial Census: New Directions for Methodology in 1990.* Washington, D.C.: National Academy Press, 1985.

Robey, Bryant. *Two Hundred Years and Counting: The 1990 Census.* Washington, D.C.: Population Reference Bureau, 1989.

U.S. General Accounting Office. *Federal Formula Programs: Outdated Population Data Used to Allocate Most Funds.* Washington, D.C.: U.S. General Accounting Office, 1990.

Webster, Yehudi O. *The Racialization of America.* New York: St. Martin's Press, 1992.

CIVIL RIGHTS

See also Affirmative Action; Economics; Education; specific ethnicities

General Studies

Abernathy, Ralph. *And the Walls Came Tumbling Down.* New York: Harper & Row, 1989.

Ashmore, Harry S. *"Civil Rights and Wrongs": A Memoir of Race and Politics, 1944-1996.* Rev. and expanded ed. Columbia: University of South Carolina Press, 1997.

Bartley, Numan V. *The Rise of Massive Resistance: Race and Politics in the South During the 1950's.* Baton Rouge: Louisiana State University Press, 1969.

Bates, Daisy. *The Long Shadow of Little Rock: A Memoir.* New York: David McKay, 1962.

Blaustein, Albert P., and Robert L. Zangrando, eds. *Civil Rights and the American Negro: A Documentary History.* New York: Trident Press, 1968.

Bloom, Jack D. *Class, Race, and the Civil Rights Movement.* Bloomington: Indiana University Press, 1987.

Blossom, Virgil T. *It Has Happened Here.* New York: Harper and Brothers, 1959.

Blumberg, Rhoda L. *Civil Rights: The 1960s Freedom Struggle.* Boston: Twayne, 1984.

Burk, Robert Frederick. *The Eisenhower Administration and Black Civil Rights.* Knoxville: University of Tennessee Press, 1984.

Burns, W. Haywood. *The Voices of Negro Protest in America.* New York: Oxford University Press, 1963.

Carmichael, Stokely, and Charles V. Hamilton. *Black Power: The Politics of Liberation in America.* New York: Random House, 1967.

Carson, Clayborne. *In Struggle: SNCC and the Black Awakening of the 1960's.* Cambridge: Mass.: Harvard University Press, 1981.

Carson, Clayborne, et al., eds. *Eyes on the Prize Civil Rights Reader: Documents, Speeches, and Firsthand Accounts from the Black Freedom Struggle, 1954-1990.* New York: Penguin, 1991.

Chappell, David L. *Inside Agitators: White Southerners in the Civil Rights Movement.* Baltimore: The Johns Hopkins University Press, 1994.

Chong, Dennis. *Collective Action and the Civil Rights Movement.* Chicago: University of Chicago Press, 1991.

Churchill, Ward, and Jim Vander Wall. *Agents of Repression: The FBI's Secret Wars Against the Black Panther Party and the American Indian Movement.* Boston: South End Press, 1988.

Couto, Richard A. *Ain't Gonna Let Nobody Turn Me Round: The Pursuit of Racial Justice in the Rural South.* Philadelphia: Temple University Press, 1991.

D'Emilio, John. *The Civil Rights Struggle: Leaders in Profile.* New York: Facts On File, 1979.

Dees, Morris. *The Gathering Storm.* New York: HarperCollins, 1996.

Dees, Morris, with Steve Fiffer. *A Season for Justice: The Life and Times of Civil Rights Lawyer Morris Dees.* New York: Maxwell Macmillan International, 1991.

Dittmer, John. *Local People: The Struggle for Civil Rights in Mississippi.* Urbana: University of Illinois Press, 1994.

Draper, Alan. *Conflict of Interests: Organized Labor and the Civil Rights Movement in the South, 1954-1968.* Ithaca, N.Y.: ILR Press, 1994.

Dunbar, Leslie W. *Minority Report: What Has Happened to Blacks, American Indians, and Other Minorities in the Eighties.* New York: Pantheon, 1984.

Farmer, James. *Freedom—When?* New York: Random House, 1965.

_____. *Lay Bare the Heart: The Autobiography of the Civil Rights Movement.* New York: New American Library, 1985.

Finch, Minnie. *The NAACP: Its Fight for Justice.* Metuchen, N.J.: Scarecrow Press, 1981.

Forman, James. *The Making of Black Revolutionaries.* 1972. 2d ed. Washington, D.C.: Open Hand, 1985.

Freyer, Tony. *The Little Rock Crisis: A Constitutional Interpretation.* Westport, Conn.: Greenwood Press, 1984.

Garrow, David J., ed. *We Shall Overcome: The Civil Rights Movement in the United States in the 1950's and 1960's.* 3 vols. Brooklyn, N.Y.: Carlson, 1989.

Graham, Hugh Davis. *The Civil Rights Era: Origins and Development of National Policy.* New York: Oxford University Press, 1990.

Hamilton, Charles, and Stokely Carmichael. *Black Power.* New York: Random House, 1967.

Harvey, James C. *Black Civil Rights During the Johnson Administration.* Jackson: University and College Press of Mississippi, 1973.

Higham, John, ed. *Civil Rights and Social Wrongs: Black-White Relations Since World War II.* University Park: Pennsylvania State University Press, 1997.

Hill, Herbert, and James E. Jones, Jr., eds. *Race in America: The Struggle for Equality.* Madison: University of Wisconsin Press, 1993.

Kosof, Anna. *The Civil Rights Movement and Its Legacy.* New York: Watts, 1989.

Levy, Peter B. *The Civil Rights Movement.* Westport, Conn.: Greenwood Press, 1998.

McKissack, Pat, and Fredrick McKissack. *The Civil Rights Movement in America from 1865 to the Present.* 2d ed. Chicago: Children's Press, 1991.

McMillen, Neil R. *The Citizens' Council: Organized Resistance to the Second Reconstruction, 1954-1964.* Urbana: University of Illinois Press, 1971.

Marsh, Charles. *God's Long Summer: Stories of Faith and Civil Rights.* Princeton, N.J.: Princeton University Press, 1997.

Meier, August, and Elliot Rudwick. *CORE: A Study in the Civil Rights Movement, 1942-1968.* Urbana: University of Illinois Press, 1975.

Meredith, James H. *Three Years in Mississippi.* Bloomington: Indiana University Press, 1966.

Meriwether, Louise. *Don't Ride the Bus on Mondays: The Rosa Parks Story.* Englewood Cliffs, N. J.: Prentice Hall, 1973.

Miller, Marilyn. *The Bridge at Selma.* Morristown, N.J.: Silver Burdett, 1985.

Morris, Aldon B. *The Origins of the Civil Rights Movement: Black Communities Organizing for Change.* New York: Free Press, 1984.

Newton, Huey P. *To Die for the People.* New York: Random House, 1972.

_____. *War Against the Panthers: A Study of Repression in America.* 1980. New York: Harlem River Press: 1996?

O'Neill, William L. *Coming Apart: An Informal History of America in the 1960's.* Chicago: Quadrangle Books, 1971.

O'Reilly, Kenneth. *Racial Matters: The FBI's Secret File on Black America, 1960-1972.* New York: Free Press, 1989.

Oppenheimer, Martin. *The Sit-In Movement of 1960.* Brooklyn, N.Y.: Carlson, 1989.

Powledge, Fred. *Free at Last? The Civil Rights Movement and the People Who Made It.* Boston: Little, Brown, 1991.

Price, Steven D., comp. *Civil Rights, 1967-68.* Vol. 2. New York: Facts On File, 1973.

Record, Wilson, and Jane Cassels Record, eds. *Little Rock, U.S.A.* San Francisco: Chandler, 1960.

Robinson, Jo Ann Gibson. *The Montgomery Bus Boycott and the Women Who Started It: The Memoir of Jo Ann Gibson Robinson.* Knoxville: University of Tennessee Press, 1987.

Rothschild, Mary Aickin. *A Case of Black and White: Northern Volunteers and the Southern Freedom Summers, 1964-1965.* Westport, Conn.: Greenwood Press, 1982.

Seale, Bobby. *Seize the Time: The Story of the Black Panther Party and Huey P. Newton.* New York: Random House, 1968.

Sitkoff, Harvard. *The New Deal for Blacks: The Emergence of Civil Rights as a National Issue.* New York: Oxford University Press, 1978.

_____. *The Struggle for Black Equality, 1954-1980.* New York: Hill and Wang, 1993.

U.S. Commission on Civil Rights. *The Tarnished Golden Door: Civil Rights Issues in Immigration.* Washington, D.C.: U.S. Government Printing Office, 1980.

Van Dyke, Vernon. *The Human Rights, Ethnicity, and Discrimination.* Westport, Conn.: Greenwood Press, 1985.

Weisbrot, Robert. *Freedom Bound: A History of America's Civil Rights Movement.* New York: W. W. Norton, 1990.

Wexler, Sanford. *The Civil Rights Movement: An Eyewitness History.* New York: Facts On File, 1993.

Williams, Juan. *Eyes on the Prize: America's Civil Rights Years, 1954-1965.* New York: Viking, 1987.

Wunder, John R. *"Retained by the People": A History of American Indians and the Bill of Rights.* New York: Oxford University Press, 1994.

Young, Andrew. *An Easy Burden: The Civil Rights Movement and the Transformation of America.* New York: HarperCollins, 1996.

Civil Rights Law

Abernathy, Charles F. *Civil Rights and Constitutional Litigation: Cases and Materials.* 2d ed. St. Paul, Minn.: West, 1992.

Abernathy, M. Glenn. *Civil Liberties Under the Constitution.* 5th ed. Columbia: University of South Carolina Press, 1989.

Bardolph, Richard, ed. *The Civil Rights Record: Black Americans and the Law, 1849-1870.* New York: Thomas Crowell, 1970.

Bell, Derrick A., Jr. *Race, Racism, and American Law.* 2d ed. Boston: Little, Brown, 1980.

Berman, Daniel M. *A Bill Becomes a Law: Congress Enacts Civil Rights Legislation.* New York: Macmillan, 1966.

Berry, Mary Frances. *Black Resistance/White Law: A History of Constitutional Racism in America.* Rev. ed. New York: Penguin, 1994.

Curtis, Michael Kent. *No State Shall Abridge.* Durham, N.C.: Duke University Press, 1986.

Davidson, Chandler, and Bernard Grofman, eds. *Quiet Revolution in the South: The Impact of the Voting Rights Act, 1965-1990.* Princeton, N.J.: Princeton University Press, 1994.

Flagg, Barbara J. *Was Blind, but Now I See: White Race Consciousness and the Law.* New York: New York University Press, 1998.

Grofman, Bernard, and Chandler Davidson, eds. *Controversies in Minority Voting: The Voting Rights Act in Perspective.* Washington, D.C.: Brookings Institution, 1992.

Halpern, Steven C. *On the Limits of the Law: The Ironic Legacy of Title VI of the 1964 Civil Rights Act.* Baltimore: The Johns Hopkins University Press, 1995.

Hoemann, George H. *What God Hath Wrought: The Embodiment of Freedom in the Thirteenth Amendment.* New York: Garland Press, 1987.

Hyman, Harold M., and William M. Wiecek. *Equal Justice Under Law: Constitutional Development, 1835-1875.* New York: Harper & Row, 1982.

Kull, Andrew. *The Color-Blind Constitution.* Cambridge, Mass.: Harvard University Press, 1992.

Lively, Donald E. *The Constitution and Race.* New York: Praeger, 1992.

McDonald, Laughlin. *Rights of Racial Minorities: The Basic ACLU Guide to Racial Minority Rights.* 2d ed. Carbondale: Southern Illinois University Press, 1993.

Nelson, William. *The Fourteenth Amendment.* Cambridge, Mass.: Harvard University Press, 1988.

Reams, Bernard D., Jr., and Paul E. Wilson, eds. *Segregation and the Fourteenth Amendment in the States: A Survey of State Segregation Laws, 1865-1953, Prepared for United States Supreme Court in re Brown vs. Board of Education of Topeka.* Buffalo, N.Y.: W. S. Hein, 1975.

Roberts, Ronald S. *Clarence Thomas and the Tough Love Crowd: Counterfeit Heroes and Unhappy Truths.* New York: New York University Press, 1995.

Tushnet, Mark V. *Making Civil Rights Law: Thurgood Marshall and the Supreme Court, 1936-1961.* New York: Oxford University Press, 1994.

U.S. Commission on Civil Rights. *The Voting Rights Act: Unfulfilled Goals.* Washington, D.C.: Government Printing Office, 1981.

Whalen, Charles, and Barbara Whalen. *The Longest Debate: A Legislative History of the 1964 Civil Rights Act.* Washington, D.C.: Seven Locks Press, 1985.

Desegregation

See also African Americans/The South and Segregation; Civil Rights/Civil Rights Law; Civil Rights/The Military

Armor, David J. *Forced Justice: School Desegregation and the Law.* New York: Oxford University Press, 1995.

Barnes, Catherine A. *Journey from Jim Crow: The Desegregation of Southern Transit.* New York: Columbia University Press, 1981.

Barrett, Russell H. *Integration at Ole Miss.* Chicago: Quadrangle Press, 1965.

Brooks, Roy L. *Integration or Separation? A Strategy for Racial Equality.* Cambridge, Mass.: Harvard University Press, 1996.

Clark, E. Culpepper. *The Schoolhouse Door: Segregation's Last Stand at the University of Alabama.* New York: Oxford University Press, 1993.

Cohodas, Nadine. *The Band Played Dixie: Race and the Liberal Conscience at Ole Miss.* New York: Free Press, 1997.

Hochschild, Jennifer L. *The New American Dilemma: Liberal Democracy and School Desegregation.* New Haven, Conn.: Yale University Press, 1984.

Hughes, Larry W., William M. Gordon, and Larry W. Hillman. *Desegregating American Schools.* New York: Longman, 1980.

Jacoby, Tamar. *Someone Else's House: America's Unfinished Struggle for Integration.* New York: Free Press, 1998.

Jones, Leon. *From Brown to Boston: Desegregation in Education, 1954-1974.* Metuchen, N.J.: Scarecrow Press, 1979.

Kluger, Richard. *Simple Justice: The History of Brown v. Board of Education and Black America's Struggle for Equality.* New York: Alfred A. Knopf, 1976.

Kohn, Howard. *We Had a Dream: A Tale of the Struggles for Integration in America.* New York: Simon & Schuster, 1998.

Loevy, Robert D. *To End All Segregation: The Politics of the Passage of the Civil Rights Act of 1964.* Lanham, Md.: University Press of America, 1990.

Metcalf, George R. *From Little Rock to Boston: The History of School Desegregation.* Westport, Conn.: Greenwood Press, 1983.

Molotch, Harvey. *Managed Integration: Dilemmas of Doing Good in the City.* Berkeley: University of California Press, 1972.

Patterson, Orlando. *The Ordeal of Integration: Progress and Resentment in America's Racial Crisis.* Counterpoint, dist. by Publishers Group West, 1997.

Rasmussen, R. Kent. *Farewell to Jim Crow: The Rise and Fall of Segregation in America.* New York: Facts on File, 1997.

Schwartz, Bernard. *Swann's Way: The School Busing Case and the Supreme Court.* New York: Oxford University Press, 1986.

Small, Stephen. *Racialized Barriers: The Black Experience in the United States and England in the 1980's.* London: Routledge, 1994.

Wicker, Tom. *Tragic Failure: Racial Integration in America.* New York: William Morrow, 1996.

Wilkinson, J. Harvie, III. *From "Brown" to "Bakke": The Supreme Court and School Integration: 1954-1978.* New York: Oxford University Press, 1979.

Wolters, Raymond. *The Burden of Brown: Thirty Years of School Desegregation.* Knoxville: University of Tennessee Press, 1984.

Ziegler, Benjamin, ed. *Desegregation and the Supreme Court.* Boston: D. C. Heath, 1958.

Malcolm X

Breitman, George, Herman Porter, and Baxter Smith. *The Assassination of Malcolm X.* New York: Pathfinder Press, 1976.

Carson, Clayborne. *Malcolm X: The FBI Files.* New York: Carroll & Graff, 1991.

Clark, John Henrick, ed. *Malcolm X: The Man and His Times.* Trenton, N.J.: African World Press, 1990.

Clark, Kenneth B., ed. *The Negro Protest: James Baldwin, Malcolm X, Martin Luther King Talk with Kenneth B. Clark.* Boston: Beacon Press, 1963.

Malcolm X. *By Any Means Necessary: Speeches, Interviews and a Letter by Malcolm X.* Edited by George Breitman. New York: Pathfinder, 1970.

Malcolm X with Alex Haley. *The Autobiography of Malcolm X.* New York: Ballantine Books, 1965.

Martin Luther King, Jr.

Ansbro, John J. *Martin Luther King, Jr.: The Making of a Mind.* Maryknoll, N.Y.: Orbis Books, 1982.

Branch, Taylor. *Parting the Waters: America in the King Years, 1954-1963.* New York: Simon & Schuster, 1988.

Clark, Kenneth B., ed. *The Negro Protest: James Baldwin, Malcolm X, Martin Luther King Talk with Kenneth B. Clark.* Boston: Beacon Press, 1963.

Colaiaco, James A. *Martin Luther King, Jr.: Apostle of Militant Nonviolence.* New York: St. Martin's Press, 1988.

Fairclough, Adam. *Martin Luther King, Jr.* Athens: University of Georgia Press, 1990.

_____. *To Redeem the Soul of America: The Southern Christian Leadership Conference and Martin Luther King, Jr.* Athens: University of Georgia Press, 1987.

Frank, Gerold. *An American Death: The True Story of the Assassination of Dr. Martin Luther King, Jr.* Garden City, N.Y.: Doubleday, 1972.

Garrow, David J. *Bearing the Cross: Martin Luther King, Jr., and the Southern Christian Leadership Conference.* New York: William Morrow, 1986.

_____. *Protest at Selma: Martin Luther King, Jr., and the Voting Rights Act of 1965.* New Haven: Yale University Press, 1978.

Hanigan, James P. *Martin Luther King, Jr., and the Foundations of Nonviolence.* Lanham, Md.: University Press of America, 1984.

King, Martin Luther, Jr. *Stride Toward Freedom: The Montgomery Story.* New York: Harper & Row, 1958.

Lewis, David L. *King: A Critical Biography.* New York: Praeger, 1970.

McPhee, Penelope, and Flip Schulke. *King Remembered.* New York: Pocket Books, 1986.

Oates, Stephen B. *Let the Trumpet Sound: The Life of Martin Luther King, Jr.* New York: Harper & Row, 1982.

Oppenheimer, Martin. *Martin Luther King, Jr., and the Civil Rights Movement.* University of Pennsylvania, 1963.

Peake, Thomas R. *Keeping the Dream Alive: A History of the Southern Christian Leadership Conference from King to the Nineteen-Eighties.* New York: Peter Lang, 1987.

Ward, Brian, and Tony Badger. *The Making of Martin Luther King and the Civil Rights Movement.* Washington Square, N.Y.: New York University Press, 1996.

The Military

Bogart, Leo. *Social Research and Desegregation of the United States Army.* Chicago: Markham, 1969.

Brandt, Nat. *Harlem at War: The Black Experience in WWII.* Syracuse, N.Y.: Syracuse University Press, 1996.

Dalifiume, Richard. *Desegregation of the U.S. Armed Forces: Fighting on Two Fronts, 1939-1953.* Columbia: University of Missouri Press, 1969.

Mershon, Sherie, and Steven L. Schlossman. *Foxholes and Color Lines: Desegregating the U.S. Armed Forces.* Baltimore: The Johns Hopkins University Press, 1998.

Moskos, Charles C. *All That We Can Be: Black Leadership and Racial Integration the Army Way.* New York: Basic Books, 1996.

Nalty, Bernard C. *Strength for the Fight: A History of Black Americans in the Military.* New York: Free Press, 1986.

Stillman, Richard. *Integration of the Negro in the U.S. Armed Forces.* New York: Frederick A. Praeger, 1968.

U.S. Department of Defense. Office of the Deputy Assistant Secretary of Defense for Civilian Personnel Policy/Equal Opportunity. *Black Americans in Defense of Our Nation.* Washington, D.C.: Government Printing Office, 1991.

CRIME

See also Hate and White Supremacy

Abraham, Henry J. *Freedom and the Court.* New York: Oxford University Press, 1967.

Baldus, David C., George Woodworth, and Charles A. Pulaska, Jr.. *Equal Justice and the Death Penalty.* Boston: Northeastern University Press, 1990.

Barker, Thomas, and David L. Carter. *Police Deviance.* 2d ed. Cincinnati, Ohio: Anderson, 1991.

Bell, Derrick A. *Faces at the Bottom of the Well: The Permanence of Racism.* New York: Basic Books, 1992.

_____. *Race, Racism and American Law.* 2d ed. Boston, Mass.: Little, Brown, 1977.

Brenner, Robert N., and Marjorie Kravitz, eds. *A Community Concern: Police Use of Deadly Force.* Washington, D.C.: United States Department of Justice, 1979.

Clarke, James W. *The Lineaments of Wrath: Race, Violent Crime, and American Culture.* New Brunswick, N.J.: Transaction, 1998.

Cose, Ellis, ed. *The Darden Dilemma: Twelve Black Writers on Justice, Race, and Conflicting Loyalties.* New York: HarperPerennial, 1997.

Denney, David. *Racism and Anti-Racism in Probation.* New York: Routledge, 1992.

Dudley, William, ed. *Police Brutality.* San Diego: D. L. Bender, 1991.

Dulaney, W. Marvin. *Black Police in America.* Bloomington: Indiana University Press, 1996.

Elliston, Frederick, and Michael Feldberg, eds. *Moral Issues in Police Work.* Totowa, N.J.: Rowman & Allen, 1985.

Finkelman, Paul, ed. *Race and Criminal Justice.* New York: Garland, 1992.

Free, Marvin, Jr. *African Americans and the Criminal Justice System.* New York: Garland, 1996.

Fukarai, Hirosaki, Edgar W. Butler, and Richard Krooth. *Race and the Jury: Racial Disenfranchisement and the Search for Justice.* New York: Plenum, 1993.

Gibbs, Jewelle Taylor. *Race and Justice: Rodney King and O.J. Simpson in a House Divided.* San Francisco: Jossey-Bass, 1996.

Hastie, Reid, Steven D. Penrod, and Nancy Pennington. *Inside the Jury.* Cambridge, Mass.: Harvard University Press, 1983.

Hawkins, Darnell F., ed. *Ethnicity, Race, and Crime: Perspectives Across Time and Place.* Albany, N.Y.: State University of New York Press, 1995.

Huff, C. Ronald, ed. *Gangs in America.* Newbury Park, Calif.: Sage Publications, 1990.

Hutchinson, Earl Ofari. *The Crisis in Black and Black.* Middle Passage, 1998.

Kennedy, Randall. *Race, Crime, and the Law.* New York: Pantheon, 1997.

Khalifah, H. Khalif, ed. *Rodney King and the L.A. Rebellion: Analysis and Commentary by Thirteen Best-Selling Black Writers.* Hampton, Va.: U.B. & U.S. Communications Systems, 1992.

Klein, Stephen P., Susan Turner, and Joan Petersilia. *Race Equity in Sentencing.* Santa Monica, Calif.: Rand Corporation, 1988.

Loftus, Elizabeth F. *Eyewitness Testimony.* Cambridge, Mass.: Harvard University Press, 1979.

Lusane, Clarence. *Pipe Dream Blues: Racism and the War on Drugs.* Boston: South End Press, 1991.

Lynch, Michael J., and E. Britt Patterson, eds. *Justice with Prejudice: Race and Criminal Justice in America.* Guilderland, N.Y.: Harrow and Heston, 1996.

_____, eds. *Race and Criminal Justice.* New York: Harrow and Heston, 1991.

McKanna, Clare V., Jr. *Homicide, Race, and Justice in the American West, 1880-1920.* Tucson: University of Arizona Press, 1997.

McNeely, R. L., and Carl E. Pope, eds. *Race, Crime, and Criminal Justice.* Beverly Hills, Calif.: Sage Publications, 1981.

Mann, Coramae Richey. *Unequal Justice: A Question of Color.* Bloomington: University of Indiana, 1988.

Miller, Jerome G. *Search and Destroy.* New York: Cambridge, 1996.

O'Kane, James M. *The Crooked Ladder: Gangsters, Ethnicity, and the American Dream.* New Brunswick N.J.: Transaction, 1992.

Owens, Tom, with Rod Browning. *Lying Eyes: The Truth Behind the Corruption and Brutality of the LAPD and the Beating of Rodney King.* New York: Thunder's Mouth Press, 1994.

Paul, Arnold, ed. *Black Americans and the Supreme Court Since Emancipation: Betrayal or Protection?* New York: Holt, Rinehart and Winston, 1972.

Petersilia, Joan. *Racial Disparities in the Criminal Justice System.* Santa Monica, Calif.: Rand Corporation, 1983.

Pinderhughes, Howard. *Race in the Hood: Conflict and Violence Among Urban Youth.* Minneapolis: University of Minnesota Press, 1997.

Razack, Sherene H. *Looking White People in the Eye: Gender, Race, and Culture in Courtrooms and Classrooms.* Toronto: University of Toronto Press, 1998.

Report of the Commission on Systemic Racism in the Ontario Criminal Justice System: A Community Summary. Toronto: The Commission, 1995.

Reynolds, Gerald A. *Race and the Criminal Justice System: How Race Affects Jury Trials.* Washington, D.C.: Center for Equal Opportunity, 1996.

Skolnick, Jerome H., and James J. Fyfe. *Above the Law: Police and the Excessive Use of Force.* New York: Free Press, 1993.

Toch, Hans, ed. *Psychology of Crime and Criminal Justice.* New York: Holt, Rinehart and Winston, 1979.

Tonry, Michael. *Ethnicity, Crime, and Immigration: Comparative and Cross-National Perspectives.* Chicago: University of Chicago Press, 1997.

_____. *Malign Neglect: Race, Crime, and Punishment in America.* New York: Oxford University Press, 1995.

Walker, Samuel, Cassia Spohn, and Miriam DeLeone. *The Color of Justice: Race, Ethnicity, and Crime in America.* Belmont, Calif.: Wadsworth, 1996.

Wilbanks, William. *The Myth of a Racist Criminal Justice System.* Monterey, Calif.: Brooks/Cole, 1987.

ECONOMICS

See also Affirmative Action; Civil Rights

General Studies

America, Richard F. *The Wealth of the Races: The Present Value of Benefits from Past Injustices.* New York: Greenwood Press, 1990.

Banner-Haley, Charles T. *The Fruits of Integration: Black Middle-Class Ideology and Culture, 1960-1990.* Jackson: University Press of Mississippi, 1994.

Becker, Gary S. *The Economics of Discrimination.* 2d ed. Chicago: University of Chicago Press, 1971.

Benjamin, Lois. *The Black Elite: Facing the Color Line in the Twilight of the Twentieth Century.* Chicago: Nelson-Hall, 1991.

Bonacich, Edna, and John Modell. *The Economic Basis of Ethnic Solidarity.* Berkeley: University of California Press, 1980.

Bonacich, Edna. "A Theory of Middleman Minorities." *American Sociological Review* 38 (October, 1973): 583-594.

Burman, Stephen. *The Black Progress Question: Explaining the African American Predicament.* Newbury Park, Calif.: Sage Publications, 1995.

Carnoy, Martin. *Faded Dreams: The Politics and Economics of Race in America.* New York: Cambridge University Press, 1994.

Caskey, John P. *Fringe Banking: Check Cashing Outlets, Pawnshops, and the Poor.* New York: Russell Sage Foundation, 1994.

Cherry, Robert. *Discrimination: Its Economic Impact on Blacks, Women, and Jews.* Lexington, Mass.: Lexington Books, 1989.

Domhoff, G. William. *The Powers That Be.* New York: Random House, 1978.

Farley, Reynolds. *Blacks and Whites: Narrowing the Gap?* Cambridge, Mass.: Harvard University Press, 1984.

Feagin, Joe R., and Melvin P. Sikes. *Living with Racism: The Black Middle Class Experience.* Boston: Beacon Press, 1994.

Forbes, H. D. *Ethnic Conflict: Commerce, Culture, and the Contact Hypothesis.* New Haven, Conn.: Yale University Press, 1997.

Franklin, Raymond S., and Solomon Resnik. *The Political Economy of Racism.* New York: Holt, Rinehart and Winston, 1973.

Frazier, E. Franklin. *Black Bourgeoisie.* Glencoe, Ill.: Free Press, 1957.

Gans, Herbert. *The Urban Villagers.* Rev. ed. New York: Free Press, 1982.

Jaynes, Gerald D., and Robin M. Williams, eds. *A Common Destiny: Blacks and American Society.* Washington, D.C.: National Academy Press, 1988.

Levitan, Sar A., William B. Johnston, and Robert Taggart. *Still a Dream: The Changing Status of Blacks Since 1960.* Cambridge, Mass.: Harvard University Press, 1975.

Lewis, W. Arthur. *Racial Conflict and Economic Development.* Cambridge, Mass.: Harvard University Press, 1985.

Light, Ivan. *Ethnic Enterprise in America.* Berkeley: University of California Press, 1972.

_____. *Immigrant Entrepreneurs: Koreans in Los Angeles.* Berkeley: University of California Press, 1988.

Mandle, Jay R. *Not Slave, Not Free: The African American Economic Experience Since the Civil War.* Durham, N.C.: Duke University Press, 1992.

Mills, C. Wright. *White Collar.* New York: Oxford University Press, 1951.

Murray, Charles. *Losing Ground: American Social Policy, 1950-1980.* New York: Basic Books, 1984.

Oliver, Melvin L., and Thomas M. Shapiro. *Black Wealth, White Wealth: A New Perspective on Racial Inequality.* New York: Routledge, 1995.

Ong, Paul, ed. *Economic Diversity: Issues and Policies.* Los Angeles: Leadership Education for Asian Pacifics, 1994.

Perlo, Victor. *Economics of Racism U.S.A.: Roots of Black Inequality.* 2d ed. New York: International Publishers, 1976.

Peterson, Paul, ed. *The New Urban Reality.* Washington, D.C.: Brookings Institution, 1985.

Pinkney, Alphonso. *The Myth of Black Progress.* New York: Cambridge University Press, 1984.

Reich, Michael. *Racial Inequality: A Political-Economic Analysis.* Princeton, N.J.: Princeton University Press, 1981.

Roediger, David. *Towards the Abolition of Whiteness.* London: Verso, 1994.

Smith, James P., and Finis R. Welch. *Closing the Gap: Forty Years of Economic Progress for Blacks.* Santa Monica, Calif.: Rand Corporation, 1986.

Sowell, Thomas. *The Economics and Politics of Race: An International Perspective.* New York: William Morrow, 1983.

_____. *Markets and Minorities.* New York: Basic Books, 1981.

_____. "Middleman Minorities." *The American Enterprise* 4 (May/June, 1993): 30-41.

_____. *Race and Economics.* New York: David McKay, 1975.

Squires, Gregory D. *Capital and Communities in Black and White: The Intersections of Race, Class, and Uneven Development.* Albany: State University of New York Press, 1994.

_____, ed. *From Redlining to Reinvestment: Community Responses to Urban Disinvestment.* Philadelphia: Temple University Press, 1992.

Weber, Max. *The Protestant Ethic and the Spirit of Capitalism.* Translated by Talcott Parsons, with a foreword by R. H. Tawney. New York: Charles Scribner's Sons, 1958.

_____. *The Theory of Social and Economic Organization.* Edited and introduced by Talcott Parsons. Translated by A. M. Henderson and Talcott Parsons. Glencoe, Ill.: Free Press, 1947.

Willie, Charles Vert. *Race, Ethnicity, and Socioeconomic Status: A Theoretical Analysis of Their Interrelationship.* Bayside, N.Y.: General Hall, 1983.

Wilson, William Julius. *The Declining Significance of Race: Blacks and Changing American Institutions.* Chicago: University of Chicago Press, 1978.

Employment and Labor

Asher, Robert, and Charles Stephenson. *Labor Divided: Race and Ethnicity in United States Labor Struggles, 1835-1960.* Albany: State University of New York Press, 1990.

Blumrosen, Alfred. *Modern Law: The Law Transmission System and Equal Employment Opportunity.* Madison: University of Wisconsin Press, 1993.

Brown, Cliff. *Racial Conflicts and Violence in the Labor Market: Roots in the 1919 Steel Strike.* New York: Garland, 1998.

Cheng, Lucie, and Edna Bonacich. *Labor Immigration Under Capitalism.* Berkeley: University of California Press, 1984.

Cross, H., G. Keeney, J. Mell, and W. Zimmerman. *Employer Hiring Practices: Differential Treatment of Hispanic and Anglo Job Seekers.* Washington, D.C.: Urban Institute, 1990.

Davis, George, and Glegg Watson. *Black Life in Corporate America: Swimming in the Mainstream.* New York: Doubleday, 1985.

DeFreitas, Gregory. *Inequality at Work: Hispanics in the U.S. Labor Force.* New York: Oxford University Press, 1991.

Edid, Maralyn. *Farm Labor Organizing: Trends and Prospects.* Ithaca, N.Y.: ILR Press, 1994.

Equal Employment Opportunity Act of 1972. Washington, D.C.: U.S. Government Printing Office, 1972.

Fernandez, John P., and Jules Davis. *Race, Gender, and Rhetoric:*

The True State of Race and Gender Relations in Corporate America. New York: McGraw-Hill, 1999.

Hartigan, John A., and Alexandra K. Wigdor, eds. *Fairness in Employment Testing: Validity Generalizations, Minority Issues, and the General Aptitude Test Battery.* Washington, D.C.: National Academy Press, 1989.

Kent, Ronald C., et al. *Culture, Gender, Race and U.S. Labor History.* Westport, Conn.: Greenwood Press, 1993.

Levitan, Sar A., Garth L. Mangum, and Ray Marshall. *Human Resources and Labor Markets.* 2d ed. New York: Harper & Row, 1976.

Libeau, Vera A. *Minority and Female Membership in Referral Unions, 1974.* Washington, D.C.: Equal Employment Opportunity Commission, 1977.

Meister, Dick, and Anne Loftis. *A Long Time Coming: The Struggle to Unionize America's Farm Workers.* New York: Macmillan, 1977.

Practising Law Institute. *The Civil Rights Act of 1991: Its Impact on Employment Discrimination Litigation.* New York: Author, 1992.

Sedmak, Nancy J. *Primer on Equal Employment Opportunity.* 6th ed. Washington, D.C.: Bureau of National Affairs, 1994.

Shulman, Steven, and William Darity, Jr., eds. *The Question of Discrimination: Racial Inequality in the U.S. Labor Market.* Middletown, Conn.: Wesleyan University Press, 1989.

Singer, M. *Diversity-Based Hiring: An Introduction from Legal, Ethical and Psychological Perspectives.* Brookfield, Vt.: Ashgate, 1993.

Stith, Anthony, and Tonya A. Martin, eds. *Breaking the Glass Ceiling: Racism and Sexism in Corporate America: The Myths, the Realities and the Solutions.* Orange, N.J.: Bryant & Dillon, 1996.

Turner, Margery Austin, Michael Fix, and Raymond J. Struyk. *Opportunities Denied: Discrimination in Hiring.* Washington, D.C.: Urban Institute, 1991.

Twomey, David. *Equal Employment Opportunity Law.* 2d ed. Cincinnati: South-Western Publishing Co., 1990.

U.S. Commission on Civil Rights. *Unemployment and Underemployment Among Blacks, Hispanics, and Women.* Washington, D.C.: U.S. Government Printing Office, 1982.

U.S. Equal Employment Opportunity Commission. *EEOC Compliance Manual.* Chicago: Commerce Clearing House, 1995.

Housing

Barak, Gregg. *Gimme Shelter: A Social History of Homelessness in Contemporary America.* New York: Praeger, 1991.

Bullard, Charles, J. Eugene Grigsby III, and Charles Lee, eds. *Residential Apartheid: The American Legacy.* Los Angeles: UCLA Center for Afro-American Studies, 1994.

Haar, Charles M. *Suburbs Under Siege: Race, Space, and Audacious Judges.* Princeton, N.J.: Princeton University Press, 1996.

Harrison, M. L. *Housing, "Race," Social Policy, and Empowerment.* Brookfield: Avebury, 1995.

Kirp, David L., John Dwyer, and Larry Rosenthal. *Our Town: Race, Housing, and the Soul of Suburbia.* New Brunswick, N.J.: Rutgers University Press, 1996.

Kushner, James A. *Fair Housing: Discrimination in Real Estate, Community Development, and Revitalization.* New York: McGraw-Hill, 1983.

Metcalf, Georg. *Fair Housing Comes of Age.* New York: Greenwood Press, 1988.

Schwemm, Robert G., ed. *The Fair Housing Act After Twenty Years.* New Haven, Conn.: Yale Law School, 1989.

Yinger, John. *Closed Doors, Opportunities Lost: The Continuing Costs of Housing Discrimination.* New York: Russell Sage Foundation, 1995.

Poverty

Boger, John Charles, and Judith Welch Wegner, eds. *Race, Poverty, and American Cities.* Chapel Hill: University of North Carolina Press, 1996.

Burton, C. Emory. *The Poverty Debate: Politics and the Poor in America.* Westport, Conn.: Praeger, 1992.

Caplovitz, David. *The Poor Pay More: Consumer Practices of Low-Income Families.* New York: Free Press, 1963.

Cottingham, Clement, ed. *Race, Poverty, and the Urban Underclass.* Lexington, Mass.: Lexington Books, 1982.

Devine, Joel A., and James D. Wright. *The Greatest of Evils: Urban Poverty and the American Underclass.* New York: Aldine de Gruyter, 1993.

Duncan, Cynthia M., ed. *Rural Poverty in America.* New York: Auburn House, 1992.

Ellwood, David T. *Poor Support: Poverty in the American Family.* New York: Basic Books, 1988.

Gans, Herbert J. *People, Plans, and Policies: Essays on Poverty, Racism, and Other National Urban Problems.* New York: Columbia University Press, 1991.

Harrington, Michael. *The New American Poverty.* New York: Penguin Books, 1985.

_____. *The Other America: Poverty in the United States.* New York: Macmillan, 1971.

Harris, Fred R., and Roger W. Wilkins, eds. *Quiet Riots: Race and Poverty in the United States: Twenty Years After the Kerner Report.* New York: Pantheon, 1988.

Hartman, Chester, ed. *Double Exposure: Poverty and Race in America.* Armonk, N.Y.: M. E. Sharpe, 1997.

Hudson, Michael, ed. *Merchants of Misery: How Corporate America Profits from Poverty.* Monroe, Maine: Common Courage Press, 1996.

Jencks, Christopher. *Rethinking Social Policy: Race, Poverty, and the Underclass.* Cambridge, Mass.: Harvard University Press, 1992.

Jencks, Christopher, and Paul E. Peterson, eds. *The Urban Underclass.* Washington, D.C.: Brookings Institution, 1991.

Jones, Jacqueline. *The Dispossessed: America's Underclass from the Civil War to the Present.* New York: Basic Books, 1992.

Kozol, Jonathan. *Rachel and Her Children: Homeless Families in America.* New York: Crown, 1988.

Marable, Manning. *How Capitalism Underdeveloped Black America.* Boston: South End Press, 1983.

Massey, Douglas S., and Nancy A. Denton. *American Apartheid: Segregation and the Making of the Underclass.* Cambridge, Mass.: Harvard University Press, 1993.

Mead, Lawrence M. *The New Politics of Poverty: The Nonworking Poor in America.* New York: Basic Books, 1992.

Nightingale, Carl Husemoller. *On the Edge: A History of Poor Black Children and Their American Dream.* New York: Basic Books, 1993.

Patterson, James T. *America's Struggle Against Poverty, 1900-1985.* Cambridge, Mass.: Harvard University Press, 1986.

Rodgers, Harrell R., Jr. *Poor Women, Poor Families: The Economic Plight of America's Female-Headed Households.* Rev. ed. Armonk, N.Y.: M. E. Sharpe, 1990.

Rossi, Peter H. *Down and Out in America: The Origins of Homelessness.* Chicago: University of Chicago Press, 1989.

Sandefur, Gary, and Marta Tienda. *Divided Opportunities: Minorities, Poverty, and Social Policy.* New York: Plenum Press, 1988.

Snow, David A., and Leon Anderson. *Down on Their Luck: A Study of Homeless Street People.* Berkeley: University of California Press, 1993.

Wilson, William J. *The Truly Disadvantaged: The Inner City, the Underclass, and Public Policy.* Chicago: University of Chicago Press, 1987.

_____. *When Work Disappears: The World of the New Urban Poor.* New York: Random House, 1996.

Welfare

Caputo, Richard K. *Welfare and Freedom American Style II: The Role of the Federal Government, 1941-1980.* Lanham, Md.: University Press of America, 1994.

Feagin, Joe R. *Subordinating the Poor: Welfare and American Beliefs.* Englewood Cliffs, N.J.: Prentice Hall, 1975.

Komisar, Lucy. *Down and Out in the USA: A History of Public Welfare.* Rev. ed. New York: Franklin Watts, 1977.

Noble, Charles. *Welfare as We Knew It: A Political History of the American Welfare State.* New York: Oxford University Press, 1997.

Quadagno, Jill. *The Color of Welfare: How Racism Undermined the War on Poverty.* New York: Oxford University Press, 1994.

Rein, Mildred. *Dilemmas of Welfare Policy: Why Work Strategies Haven't Worked.* New York: Praeger, 1982.

Tarantino, Thomas Howard, and Dismas Becker, eds. *Welfare Mothers Speak Out: We Ain't Gonna Shuffle Anymore.* New York: W. W. Norton, 1972.

Trattner, Walter I. *From Poor Law to Welfare State: A History of Social Welfare in America.* 5th ed. New York: Free Press, 1994.

EDUCATION

See also Language and Bilingualism

American Sociological Association. *Teaching Race and Ethnic Relations: Syllabi and Instructional Materials.* 2d ed. Washington, D.C.: Author, 1990.

Anderson, Talmadge. *Introduction to African American Studies.* Dubuque, Iowa: Kendall/Hunt, 1994.

Aronson, Elliot, et al. *The Jigsaw Classroom.* Beverly Hills, Calif.: Sage Publications, 1978.

Atkinson, Pansye S. *Brown vs. Topeka: An African American's View: Desegregation and Miseducation.* Chicago: African American Images, 1993.

Ballantine, Jeanne H., ed. *The Sociology of Education: A Systematic Analysis.* Englewood Cliffs, N.J.: Prentice-Hall, 1983.

Banks, James A. *Multiethnic Education: Theory and Practice.* 2d ed. Boston: Allyn & Bacon, 1988.

_____. *Teaching Strategies for Ethnic Studies.* Boston: Allyn & Bacon, 1979.

Banks, James A., and Cherry A. McGee Banks. *Multicultural Education: Issues and Perspectives.* Boston: Allyn & Bacon, 1989.

Barnett, Marqueritz R., ed. *Readings on Equal Education.* New York: AMS Press, 1984.

Bartley, Gayle, et al. *Drawing on Diversity: A Handbook for and by Boston Teachers in Multicultural, Multiracial Classrooms.* Boston: Boston Public Schools, 1990.

Bell, Derrick, ed. *Shades of Brown: New Perspectives on School Desegregation.* New York: Teachers College Press, 1980.

Bernstein, Richard. *Dictatorship of Virtue: Multiculturalism, and the Battle for America's Future.* New York: Alfred A. Knopf, 1994.

Berry, Gordon LaVern, and Joy Keiko Asamen, eds. *Black Students: Psychosocial Issues and Academic Achievement.* Newbury Park, Calif.: Sage Publications, 1989.

Biegel, Stuart. "The Parameters of the Bilingual Education Debate in California Twenty Years After *Lau v. Nichols.*" *Chicano-Latino Law Review* 14 (Winter, 1994): 48-60.

Blackwell, James Edward. *Dynamics of Minority Education: An Index to the Status of Race and Ethnic Relations in the United States.* Boston: William Monroe Trotter Institute, University of Massachusetts, 1988.

Bloom, Allan. *The Closing of the American Mind: How Higher Education Has Failed Democracy and Impoverished the Souls of Today's Students.* New York: Simon & Schuster, 1987.

Bond, Horace Mann. *Education for Freedom: A History of Lincoln University.* Princeton, N.J.: Princeton University Press, 1976.

Bull, Barry L., Royal T. Fruehling, and Virgie Chattergy. *The Ethics of Multicultural and Bilingual Education.* New York: Columbia University Press, 1992.

Bunzel, John H. *Race Relations on Campus: Stanford Students Speak Out.* Stanford, Calif.: Stanford Alumni Association, 1992.

Butler, Johnnela E., and John C. Walter. *Transforming the Curriculum: Ethnic Studies and Women's Studies.* Albany, N.Y.: State University of New York Press, 1991.

Campbell, Duane E. *Choosing Democracy: A Practical Guide to Multicultural Education.* Upper Saddle River, N.J.: Prentice Hall, 1996.

Caplan, Nathan, Marcella H. Choy, and John K. Whitmore. *Children of the Boat People: A Study of Educational Success.* Ann Arbor: University of Michigan Press, 1991.

Carnegie Foundation for the Advancement of Teaching. *Tribal Colleges: Shaping the Future of Native America.* Princeton, N.J.: Author, 1989.

Chiong, Jane Ayers. *Racial Categorization of Multiracial Children in Schools.* Westport, Conn.: Bergin & Garvey, 1998.

Coleman, James S., et al. *Equality of Educational Opportunity* [Coleman Report]. Washington, D.C.: U.S. Government Printing Office, 1966.

Cooper, Harris M., and Thomas L. Good. *Pygmalion Grows Up: Studies in the Expectation Communication Process.* New York: Longman, 1983.

Council on Terracial Books for Children. *Stereotypes, Distortions, and Omissions in U.S. History Textbooks.* New York: Racisim and Sexism Resource Center for Educators, 1977.

Crawford, James. *Bilingual Education: History, Politics, Theory, and Practice.* Trenton, N.J.: Crane, 1989.

Crouse, James, and Dale Trusheim. *The Case Against the SAT.* Chicago: University of Chicago Press, 1988.

Cummins, James. *Empowering Language Minority Students.* Sacramento: California Association for Bilingual Education, 1989.

Dalton, Jon C., ed. *Racism on Campus: Confronting Racial Bias Through Peer Interventions.* San Francisco: Jossey-Bass, 1991.

Daves, Charles W., ed. *The Uses and Misuses of Tests.* San Francisco: Jossey-Bass, 1984.

Davidson, Florence H., and Miriam M. Davidson. *Changing

Childhood Prejudice: The Caring Work of the Schools. Westport, Conn.: Greenwood Press, 1994.

Day, Frances Ann. *Multicultural Voices in Contemporary Literature.* Portsmouth, N.H.: Heinemann, 1994.

Derman-Sparks, Louise, et al. *Teaching/Learning Anti-Racism: A Developmental Approach.* New York: Teachers College Press, 1997.

Dreeben, Robert. *On What Is Learned in School.* Reading, Mass.: Addison-Wesley, 1968.

D'Souza, Dinesh. *Illiberal Education: The Politics of Race and Sex on Campus.* New York: Maxwell Macmillan International, 1991.

Feagin, Joe R., et al. *The Agony of Education: Black Students at White Colleges and Universities.* New York: Routledge, 1996.

Ford, Donna V. *Reversing Underachievement Among Gifted Black Students: Promising Practices and Programs.* New York: Teachers College Press, 1996.

Formisano, Ronald P. *Boston Against Busing: Race, Class, and Ethnicity in the 1960's and 1970's.* Chapel Hill: University of North Carolina Press, 1991.

Gaber, Ivor, and Jane Aldridge, eds. *In the Best Interests of the Child: Culture, Identity and Transracial Adoption.* London: Free Association Books, 1994.

Gill, Dawn, et al., eds. *Racism and Education: Structures and Strategies.* Newbury Park, Calif.: Sage Publications, 1992.

Gill, Walter. *Issues in African American Education.* Nashville, Tenn.: One Horn Press, 1991.

Graff, Gerald. *Beyond the Culture Wars: How Teaching the Conflicts Can Revitalize American Education.* New York: W. W. Norton, 1992.

Graglia, Lino A. *Disaster by Decree: The Supreme Court Decisions on Race and the Schools.* Ithaca, N.Y.: Cornell University Press, 1976.

Hill, David. *Teaching in Multiracial Schools: A Guidebook.* London: Methuen, 1976.

Hill, Leven, ed. *Black American Colleges and Universities.* Detroit, Mich.: Gale Research, 1994.

Hirsch, E. D., Jr. *Cultural Literacy: What Every American Needs to Know.* Boston: Houghton Mifflin, 1987.

Hirschfeld, Lawrence A. *Race in the Making: Cognition, Culture and the Child's Construction of Human Kind.* Cambridge, Mass.: MIT Press, 1996.

Hoffmann, Banesh. *The Tyranny of Testing.* New York: Crowell-Collier, 1962.

Holmes, Robyn M. *How Young Children Perceive Race.* Thousand Oaks, Calif.: Sage Publications, 1995.

Hurn, Christopher J. *The Limits and Possibilities of Schooling: An Introduction to the Sociology of Education.* 3d ed. Boston: Allyn & Bacon, 1993.

Jacoby, Russell, and Naomi Glauberman, eds. *The Bell Curve Debate: History, Documents, Opinions.* New York: Times Books (Random House), 1995.

Jensen, Arthur. *Bias in Mental Testing.* New York: Free Press, 1980.

Jones-Wilson, Faustine C. *The Encyclopedia of African American Education.* Westport, Conn.: Greenwood Press, 1996.

Kamin, Leon J. *The Science and Politics of IQ.* New York: Halsted Press, 1974.

Koretz, Daniel. *Trends in the Postsecondary Enrollment of Minorities.* Santa Monica, Calif.: Rand Corporation, 1990.

Kozol, Jonathan. *Death at an Early Age: The Destruction of the Hearts and Minds of Negro Children in the Boston Public Schools.* Boston: Houghton, Mifflin, 1967.

_____. *Savage Inequalities.* New York: Crown, 1991.

La Belle, Thomas J., and Christopher R. Ward. *Ethnic Studies and Multiculturalism.* Albany: State University of New York Press, 1996.

Lefkowitz, Mary. *Not Out of Africa: How Afrocentrism Became an Excuse to Teach Myth.* New York: Basic Books, 1996.

Levin, Michael. *Why Race Matters: Race Differences and What They Mean.* Westport, Conn.: Praeger, 1997.

Margo, Robert A. *Race and Schooling in the South, 1880-1950: An Economic History.* Chicago: University of Chicago Press, 1990.

Moran, Rachel F. "Of Democracy, Devaluation, and Bilingual Education." *Creighton Law Review* 26 (February, 1993): 255-319.

Mwadilitu, Mwalimi I. [Alexander E. Curtis]. *Richard Allen: The First Exemplar of African American Education.* New York: ECA Associates, 1985.

Nairn, Allan. *The Reign of ETS: The Corporation That Makes Up Minds.* Washington, D.C.: The Ralph Nader Report on the Educational Testing Service, 1980.

Nettles, Michael T., and Arie L. Nettles, eds. *Equity and Excellence in Educational Testing and Assessment.* Boston: Kluwer Academic, 1995.

Oakes, Jeannie. *Keeping Track: How Schools Structure Inequality.* New Haven: Yale University Press, 1985.

Oishi, Sabine, et al. *Effects of Student Teams and Individualized Instruction on Cross-Race and Cross-Sex Friendships.* Baltimore: Center for Social Organization of Schools, Johns Hopkins University, 1983.

Olsen, Laurie. *Crossing the Schoolhouse Border: Immigrant Students and the California Public Schools.* San Francisco: California Tomorrow, 1988.

Orlando, Carlos J., and Virginia P. Collier. *Bilingual and ESL Classrooms: Teaching in Multicultural Contexts.* New York: McGraw-Hill, 1985.

Pai, Young. *Cultural Foundations of Education.* Columbus, Ohio: Charles E. Merrill, 1990.

Porter, Rosalie P. *Forked Tongue: The Politics of Bilingual Education.* New York: Basic Books, 1990.

Pratt, Richard H. *Battlefield and Classroom: Four Decades with the American Indian, 1867-1904.* Edited by Robert M. Utley. New Haven, Conn.: Yale University Press, 1964.

Razack, Sherene H. *Looking White People in the Eye: Gender, Race, and Culture in Courtrooms and Classrooms.* Toronto: University of Toronto Press, 1998.

Reddy, Maureen T. *Everyday Acts Against Racism: Raising Children in a Multiracial World.* Seattle: Seal Press, 1996.

Rippa, S. Alexander. *Education in a Free Society: An American History.* 7th ed. New York: Longman, 1992.

Roebuck, Julian, and Komanduri Murty. *Historically Black Colleges and Universities: Their Place in American Higher Education.* Westport, Conn.: Praeger, 1993.

Rossell, Christine H., and Willis D. Hawley, eds. *The Consequences of School Desegregation.* Philadelphia: Temple University Press, 1983.

Sadker, Myra P., and David M. Sadker. *Teachers, Schools, and Society.* 2d ed. New York: McGraw-Hill, 1991.

Seller, Maxine, and Lois Weis, eds. *Beyond Black and White: New Faces and Voices in U.S. Schools.* Albany: State University of New York Press, 1997.

Spring, Joel. *American Education: An Introduction to Social and*

Political Aspects. 4th ed. New York: Longman, 1989.

Tesconi, Charles A., Jr., and Emanuel Hurwitz, Jr. *Education for Whom? The Question of Equal Educational Opportunity.* New York: Dodd, Mead, 1974.

Troyna, Barry. *Racism and Education: Research Perspectives.* Philadelphia: Open University Press, 1993.

Troyna, Barry, and Richard Hatcher. *Racism in Children's Lives: A Study of Mainly-White Primary Schools.* New York: Routledge in association with National Children's Bureau, 1992.

Tucker, William H. *The Science and Politics of Racial Research.* Urbana: University of Illinois Press, 1994.

U.S. Commission on Civil Rights. *A Better Chance to Learn: Bilingual-Bicultural Education.* Washington, D.C.: Author, 1975.

Walsh, Catherine. *Pedagogy and the Struggle for Voice.* New York: Bergin and Garvey, 1991.

Webster, Yehudi O. *Against the Multicultural Agenda: A Critical Thinking Alternative.* Westport, Conn.: Praeger, 1997.

Weis, Lois, ed. *Class, Race, and Gender in American Education.* Albany: State University of New York Press, 1988.

Willie, Charles Vert. *The Ivory and Ebony Towers: Race Relations and Higher Education.* Lexington, Mass., Lexington Books, 1981.

Wollenberg, Charles. *All Deliberate Speed: Segregation and Exclusion in California Schools, 1855-1975.* Berkeley: University of California Press, 1976.

Woolfolk, Anita E. *Educational Psychology.* Needham Heights, Mass.: Allyn & Bacon, 1993.

Wurzel, Jaime S., ed. *Toward Multiculturalism: A Reader in Multicultural Education.* Yarmouth, Maine: Intercultural Press, 1988.

Zweigenhaft, Richard L., and G. William Domhoff. *Blacks in the White Establishment? A Study of Race and Class in America.* New Haven, Conn.: Yale University Press, 1991.

EUROPEAN AMERICANS

German Americans

Franck, Irene M. *The German American Heritage.* New York: Facts On File, 1988.

Lich, Glen E., and Dona B. Reeves. *German Culture in Texas.* Boston: Twayne, 1980.

Ripley, LaVern. *The German-Americans.* Boston: Twayne, 1976.

Sachese, Julius F. *History of the German Role in the Discovery, Exploration, and Settlement of the New World.* Reprint. *Germany and America, 1450-1700.* Edited by Don H. Tolzman. New York: Heritage Books, 1991.

Wilk, Gerard. *Americans from Germany.* New York: German Information Center, 1976.

Irish Americans

Adams, William F. *Ireland and Irish Emigration to the New World.* New Haven, Conn.: Yale University Press, 1932.

Akenson, Donald H. *The United States and Ireland.* Cambridge, Mass.: Harvard University Press, 1973.

Bagenal, Philip. *The American Irish and Their Influence on Irish Politics.* London: Kegan Paul, Trench & Company, 1882. Reprint. New York: Jerome S. Ozer, 1971.

Bimba, Anthony. *The Molly Maguires.* New York: International Publishers, 1932.

Broehl, Wayne G., Jr. *The Molly Maguires.* Cambridge, Mass.: Harvard University Press, 1964.

Clark, Dennis. *Hibernia America: The Irish and Regional Cultures.* Contributions in Ethnic Studies 14. New York: Greenwood Press, 1986.

Dickson, Robert J. *Ulster Immigration to Colonial America, 1718-1773.* London: Routledge, 1966.

Diner, Hasia. *Erin's Daughters in America: Irish Immigrant Women in the Nineteenth Century.* Baltimore: The Johns Hopkins University Press, 1983.

Dinsmore, John W. *The Scotch-Irish in America.* Chicago: Winona Pulbishing, 1906.

Fallows, Marjorie. *Irish Americans: Identity and Assimilation.* Englewood Cliffs, N.J.: Prentice-Hall, 1979.

Ford, Henry J. *The Scotch-Irish in America.* Princeton, N.J.: Princeton University Press, 1915.

Greeley, Andrew M. *The Irish Americans: The Rise to Money and Power.* New York: Harper & Row, 1981.

————. "The Success and Assimilation of Irish Protestants and Irish Catholics in the United States." *Sociology and Social Research* 72, no. 4 (July, 1988): 231.

Griffin, William D. *A Portrait of the Irish in America.* New York: Charles Scribner's Sons, 1981.

Hechter, Michael. *Internal Colonialism: The Celtic Fringe in British National Development, 1536-1966.* Berkeley: University of California Press, 1975.

Hershkowitz, Leo. *Tweed's New York.* New York: Doubleday/Anchor, 1987.

Ignatiev, Noel. *How the Irish Became White.* New York: Routledge, 1995.

Knobel, Dale T. *Paddy and the Republic: Ethnicity and Nationality in Antebellum America.* Middletown, Conn.: Wesleyan University Press, 1986.

Leslie, Shane. *The Irish Issue in Its American Aspect.* New York: Scribner's, 1919.

Leyburn, James G. *The Scotch-Irish.* Chapel Hill: University of North Carolina Press, 1962.

McCaffrey, Lawrence J. *The Irish Diaspora in America.* Washington, D.C.: Catholic University of America Press, 1984.

McGee, Thomas D'Arcy. *A History of Irish Settlers in North America.* Boston: Office of American Celt, 1851.

Shannon, William V. *The American Irish.* New York: Macmillan, 1963.

Shrier, Arnold. *Ireland and the American Emigration, 1850-1900.* Minneapolis: University of Minnesota Press, 1958.

Thernstrom, Stephan. *The Other Bostonians.* Cambridge, Mass.: Harvard University Press, 1973.

Williams, Richard E. *Hierarchical Structures and Social Value: The Creation of Black and Irish Identities in the United States.* Cambridge, England: Cambridge University Press, 1990.

Wittke, Carl. *The Irish in America.* Baton Rouge: Louisiana State University Press, 1956.

Italian Americans

Alba, Richard. *Italian Americans.* Englewood Cliffs, N.J.: Prentice Hall, 1985.

Brown, Mary Elizabeth. *Churches, Communities, and Children: Italian Immigrants in the Archdiocese of New York, 1880-1945.* Staten Island, N.Y.: CMS, 1995.

Child, Irvin L. *Italian or American?* New Haven, Conn.: Yale University Press, 1943.

Cordasco, Francesco, and Eugene Bucchioni, eds. *The Italians.* Clifton, N.J.: Augustus M. Kelley, 1974.

Crispino, James A. *The Assimilation of Ethnic Groups: The Italian Case.* Staten Island, N.Y.: Center for Migration Studies, 1980.

Curtis, Lewis P., Jr. *Apes and Angels: The Irish in Victorian Caricature.* Washington, D.C.: Smithsonian Institution Press, 1971.

Di Franco, Philip. *The Italian American Experience.* New York: Tom Doherty Associates, 1988.

Gambino, Richard. *Blood of My Blood.* Garden City, N.Y.: Doubleday/Anchor, 1975.

Iacovetta, Franca. *Such Hardworking People: Italian Immigrants in Postwar Toronto.* Montreal: McGill-Queen's University Press, 1992.

Iorizzo, Luciano J., and Salvatore Mondello. *The Italian-Americans.* New York: Twayne, 1971.

Johnson, Colleen L. *Growing Up and Growing Old in Italian American Families.* New Brunswick, N.J.: Rutgers University Press, 1985.

LaRuffia, Anthony L. *Monte Carmelo: An Italian-American Community in the Bronx.* New York: Gordon & Breach, 1988.

Lopreato, Joseph. *Italian Americans.* New York: Random House, 1970.

Lord, Eliot, John J. D. Tranor, and Samuel J. Barrows. *The Italian in America.* Reprint ed. San Francisco: R&E Associates, 1970.

Macphee, Sylvai Pellini. *Changing Perspectives of Italian Americans.* Cambridge, Mass.: Center for Community Economic Development, 1974.

Mangione, Jerre, and Ben Morreale. *La Storia: Five Centuries of the Italian American Experience.* New York: HarperCollins, 1992.

Mormino, Gary Ross. *Immigrants on the Hill: Italian Americans in St. Louis, 1882-1982.* Urbana: University of Illinois Press, 1986.

Nelli, Humbert S. *The Italians In Chicago, 1880-1930.* New York: Oxford University Press, 1970.

Puzo, Mario. *The Godfather.* New York: G. P. Putman's Sons, 1969.

Rieder, Jonathan. *Canarsie: The Jews and Italians of Brooklyn Against Liberalism.* Cambridge, Mass.: Harvard University Press, 1985.

Rolle, Andrew F. *The American Italian.* Belmont, Calif.: Wadsworth, 1972.

Stella, Antonia. *Some Aspects of Italian Immigration to the United States.* Reprint ed. San Francisco: R&E Associates, 1970.

Tardi, Susanna. *Family and Society: The Case of the Italians in New Jersey.* Ann Arbor, Mich.: UMI Dissertation Service, 1991.

Tomasi, Silvano, and M. H. Engel, eds. *The Italian Experience in the United States.* New York: Center for Migration Studies, 1970.

Yans-McLaughlin, Virginia. *Family and Community—Italian Immigrants in Buffalo, 1880-1930.* Ithaca, N.Y.: Cornell University Press, 1971.

Polish Americans

Bukowiczyk, John J. *Polish Americans and Their History: Community, Culture, and Politics.* Pittsburgh, Pa.: University of Pittsburgh Press, 1996.

Erdmans, Mary Patrice. *Opposite Poles: Immigrants and Ethnics in Polish Chicago, 1976-1990.* University Park: Pennsylvania State University Press, 1998.

Lopata, Helena Z. *Polish Americans: Status Competition in an Ethnic Community.* Englewood Cliffs, N.J.: Prentice-Hall, 1976.

Thomas, William I., and Florian Znaniecki. *The Polish Peasant in Europe and America.* Boston: Richard G. Badger, 1918. Reprint. Urbana: University of Illinois Press, 1996.

Russian and Other Slavic Americans

Balch, Emily Greene. *Our Slavic Fellow Citizens.* New York: Charities Publication Committee, 1910. Reprint. New York: Arno Press, 1969.

Chevigny, Hector. *Russian America: The Great Alaskan Venture, 1741-1867.* New York: Viking Press, 1965.

Hardwick, Susan Wiley. *Russian Refuge: Religion, Migration, and Settlement on the North American Pacific Rim.* Chicago: University of Chicago Press, 1993.

Kuropas, Myron B. *Ukrainian Americans: Roots and Aspirations, 1884-1954.* Buffalo, N.Y.: University of Toronto Press, 1991.

Lucassen, Leo, et al. *Gypsies and Other Itinerant Groups: A Socio-Historical Approach.* New York: St. Martin's Press, 1998.

Magocsi, Paul R. *The Russian Americans.* New York: Chelsea House Publications, 1987.

Wertsman, Vladimir. *The Russians in America: A Chronology and Fact Book.* Dobbs Ferry, N.Y.: Oceana Publications, 1977.

Scandinavian Americans

Acrelius, Israel. *A History of New Sweden.* 1759. Reprint. Translated by William M. Reynolds. Philadelphia: The Historical Society of Pennsylvania, 1874.

Enterline, James Robert. *Viking America: The Norse Crossings and Their Legacy.* Epilogue by Thor Heyerdahl. Garden City, N.Y.: Doubleday, 1972.

Magnusson, Magnus, and Hermann Palsson, eds. and trans. *The Vinland Sagas: The Norse Discovery of America.* New York: Penguin Books, 1980.

Wahlgren, Erik. *The Vikings and America.* London: Thames & Hudson, 1986.

Wuorinen, John H. *The Finns on the Delaware, 1638-1655: An Essay in Colonial American History.* Philadelphia: University of Pennsylvania Press, 1938.

"White" Americans

Alba, Richard D. *Ethnic Identity: The Transformation of White America.* New Haven, Conn.: Yale University Press, 1990.

Baltzell, E. Digby. *The Protestant Establishment.* New York: Random House, 1966.

Berthoff, Rowland. *British Immigrants in Industrial America, 1790-1950.* Cambridge, Mass.: Harvard University Press, 1953.

Handlin, Oscar. *Boston's Immigrants 1790-1880: A Study in Acculturation.* Cambridge, Mass.: The Belknap Press of Harvard University Press, 1959.

Helms, Janet E. *A Race Is a Nice Thing to Have: A Guide to Being a White Person or Understanding the White Persons in Your Life.* Topeka, Kans.: Content Communications, 1992.

Horsman, Reginald. *Race and Manifest Destiny: Origins of American Racial Anglo-Saxionism.* Cambridge, Mass.: Harvard University Press, 1981.

Jacobson, Matthew Frye. *Whiteness of a Different Color: European Immigrants and the Alchemy of Race.* Cambridge, Mass.: Harvard University Press, 1998.

Kaplan, Jeffrey, and Tore Bjøro, eds. *Nation and Race: The Developing Euro-American Racist Subculture.* Boston: Northeastern University Press, 1998.

Marrus, Michael Robert. *The Unwanted: European Refugees in the Twentieth Century.* New York: Oxford University Press, 1985.

Tate, Thad W., and David L. Ammerman. *The Chesapeake in the*

Seventeenth Century: Essays on the Anglo-American Society. Chapel Hill: University of North Carolina Press, 1979.

HATE AND WHITE SUPREMACY

See also Crime; Racism, Prejudice, Discrimination

Allen, Irving Lewis. *Unkind Words: Ethnic Labeling from Redskin to WASP.* New York: Bergin & Garvey, 1990.

Almaguer, Tomás. *Racial Fault Lines: The Historical Origins of White Supremacy in California.* Berkeley: University of California Press, 1994.

Baird, Robert M., and Stuart E. Rosenbaum, eds. *Bigotry, Prejudice and Hatred: Definitions, Causes, and Solutions.* Buffalo, N.Y.: Prometheus Books, 1992.

Bennett, Lerone, Jr. *Confrontation: Black and White.* Baltimore: Penguin, 1966.

Boesel, David, and Peter H. Rossi, eds. *Cities Under Siege: An Anatomy of the Ghetto Riots, 1964-1968.* New York: Basic Books, 1971.

Bridges, Tyler. *The Rise of David Duke.* Jackson: University Press of Mississippi, 1994.

Brundage, W. Fitzhugh. *Lynching in the New South: Georgia and Virginia, 1880-1930.* Urbana: University of Illinois Press, 1993.

_____, ed. *Under Sentence of Death: Lynching in the South.* Chapel Hill: University of North Carolina Press, 1997.

Button, James W. *Black Violence: Political Impact of the 1960's Riots.* Princeton, N.J.: Princeton University Press, 1978.

Cannon, Lou. *Official Negligence: How Rodney King and the Riots Changes Los Angeles and the LAPD.* New York: Times Books, 1998.

Capeci, Dominic J., Jr. *The Harlem Riot of 1943.* Philadelphia: Temple University Press, 1977.

Cobbs, Elizabeth H., and Petric J. Smith. *Long Time Coming: An Insider's Story of the Birmingham Church Bombing That Rocked the World.* Birmingham, Ala.: Crane Hill, 1994.

Connery, Robert, ed. *Urban Riots.* New York: Vintage Books, 1969.

Daniels, Jessie. *White Lies: Race, Class, Gender and Sexuality in White Supremacist Discourse.* New York: Routledge, 1997.

Feagin, Joe R., and Harlan Hahn. *Ghetto Revolts.* New York: Macmillan, 1973.

Feldberg, Michael. *The Philadelphia Riots of 1844: A Study of Ethnic Conflict.* Westport, Conn.: Greenwood Press, 1975.

Ferber, Abby L. *White Man Falling: Race, Gender, and White Supremacy.* Lanham, Md.: Rowman & Littlefield, 1998.

Fine, Sidney. *Violence in the Model City: The Cavanaugh Administration, Race Relations and the Detroit Riot of 1967.* Ann Arbor: University of Michigan Press, 1989.

Finkelman, Paul, ed. *Lynching, Racial Violence, and Law.* New York: Garland, 1992.

Frederickson, George M. *White Supremacy: A Comparative Study in American and South African History.* New York: Oxford University Press, 1980.

Gale, Dennis E. *Understanding Urban Unrest: From Reverend King to Rodney King.* Newbury Park, Calif.: Sage Publications, 1996.

Gates, Henry Louis, Jr., ed. *Speaking of Race, Speaking of Sex: Hate Speech, Civil Rights, and Civil Liberties.* New York: New York University Press, 1994.

Ginzburg, Ralph. *100 Years of Lynchings.* Baltimore: Black Classic Press, 1997.

Giroux, Henry A. *Fugitive Cultures: Race, Violence, and Youth.* New York: Routledge, 1996.

Gooding-Williams, Robert, ed. *Reading Rodney King/Reading Urban Uprising.* New York: Routledge, 1993.

Grimshaw, Allen D. *Racial Violence in the United States.* Chicago: Aldine Publishing, 1969.

Hamm, Mark S. *American Skinheads: The Criminology and Control of Hate Crime.* Westport, Conn.: Praeger, 1993.

Higham, John. *Strangers in the Land: Patterns of American Nativism, 1860-1925.* New Brunswick, N.J.: Rutgers University Press, 1955.

Horne, Gerald. *Fire This Time: The Watts Uprising and the 1960s.* Charlottesville: University Press of Virginia, 1995.

Howard, Walter T. *Lynchings: Extralegal Violence in Florida During the 1930s.* London: Susquehanna University Press, 1995.

Kotlowitz, Alex. *The Other Side of the River: A Story of Two Towns, a Death, and America's Dilemma.* New York: Nan A. Talese, 1998.

Kronenwetter, Michael. *United They Hate: White Supremacist Groups in America.* New York: Walker, 1992.

Lee, Alfred McClung. *Race Riot, Detroit 1943.* 1943. Reprint. New York: Octagon Books, 1968.

Levin, Jack, and Jack McDevitt. *Hate Crimes: The Rising Tide of Bigotry and Bloodshed.* New York: Plenum Press, 1993.

Los Angeles Times editors. *Understanding the Riots: Los Angeles Before and After the Rodney King Case.* Los Angeles: Los Angeles Times, 1992.

MacKinnon, Catharine A. *Only Words.* Cambridge, Mass.: Harvard University Press, 1993.

Madhubuti, Haki R., ed. *Why L.A. Happened: Implications of the '92 Los Angeles Rebellion.* Chicago: Third World Press, 1993.

Matsuda, Mari J. *Words That Wound: Critical Race Theory, Assaultive Speech, and the First Amendment.* Boulder, Colo.: Westview Press, 1993.

McGovern, James R. *Anatomy of a Lynching: The Killing of Claude Neal.* Baton Rouge: Louisiana State University Press, 1982.

National Advisory Commission on Civil Disorders [Kerner Commission]. *Report.* New York: Bantam, 1968.

Novick, Michael. *White Lies, White Power: The Fight Against White Supremacy and Reactionary Violence.* Monroe, Maine: Common Courage Press, 1995.

Pinkney, Alphonso. *Lest We Forget: White Hate Crimes, Howard Beach, and Other Racial Atrocities.* Chicago: Third World Press, 1994.

Porter, Bruce, and Marvin Dunn. *The Miami Riot of 1980: Crossing the Bounds.* Lexington, Mass.: D. C. Heath, 1984.

Raper, Arthur. *The Tragedy of Lynching.* New York: Arno Press, 1969.

Schwartz, Alan M., ed. *Hate Groups in America: A Record of Bigotry and Violence.* New York: Anti-Defamation League of B'nai B'rith, 1988.

Sears, David O., and John B. McConahay. *The Politics of Violence: The New Urban Blacks and the Watts Riot.* Boston: Houghton Mifflin, 1973.

Tolnay, Stewart E., and E. M. Beck. *A Festival of Violence: An Analysis of Southern Lynchings, 1882-1930.* Urbana: University of Illinois Press, 1995.

U.S. Commission on Civil Rights. Michigan State Advisory Committee. *Hate Groups in Michigan: A Sham or a Shame? A Report.* Washington, D.C.: Author, 1982.

Williams-Myers, A. J. *Destructive Impulses: An Examination of an American Secret in Race Relations: White Violence.* Lanham, Md.: University Press of America, 1995.

Zangrando, Robert. *The NAACP Crusade Against Lynching, 1909-1950.* Philadelphia: Temple University Press, 1980.

The Ku Klux Klan

Alexander, Charles C. *The Ku Klux Klan in the Southwest.* Norman: University of Oklahoma Press, 1995.

Chalmers, David M. *Hooded Americanism: The First Century of the Ku Klux Klan.* 3d ed. Durham, N.C.: Duke University Press, 1987.

Davis, Daryl. *Klan-Destine Relationships: A Black Man's Odyssey in the Ku Klux Klan.* Far Hills, N.J.: New Horizon Press, 1998.

Ezekiel, Raphael S. *The Racist Mind: Portraits of American Neo-Nazis and Klansmen.* New York: Viking, 1995.

George, John, and Laird Wilcox. *Nazis, Communists, Klansmen, and Others on the Fringe: Political Extremism in America.* Buffalo, N.Y.: Prometheus Books, 1992.

Jenkins, William D. *Steel Valley Klan: The Ku Klux Klan in Ohio's Mahoning Valley.* Kent, Ohio: Kent State University Press, 1990.

Kennedy, Stetson. *I Rode with the Ku Klux Klan: The Klan Unmasked.* Gainesville: University Presses of Florida, 1990.

Lay, Shawn. *Hooded Knights on the Niagara: The Ku Klux Klan in Buffalo, New York.* New York: New York University Press, 1995.

_____, ed. *The Invisible Empire in the West: Toward a New Historical Appraisal of the Ku Klux Klan of the 1920s.* Urbana: University of Illinois Press, 1992.

Lutholtz, M. William. *Grand Dragon: D. C. Stephenson and the Ku Klux Klan in Indiana.* West Lafayette, Ind.: Purdue University Press, 1991.

MacLean, Nancy. *Behind the Mask of Chivalry: The Making of the Second Ku Klux Klan.* New York: Oxford University Press, 1994.

Mecklin, John Moffatt. *The Ku Klux Klan: A Study of the American Mind.* New York: Harcourt, Brace, 1924.

Nelson, Jack. *Terror in the Night: The Klan's Campaign Against the Jews.* New York: Simon & Schuster, 1993.

Newton, Michael, and Judy Newton. *The Ku Klux Klan: An Encyclopedia.* New York: Garland, 1991.

Randel, William. *The Ku Klux Klan: A Century of Infamy.* Philadelphia: Chilton Books, 1965.

Ridgeway, James. *Blood in the Face: The Ku Klux Klan, Aryan Nations, Nazi Skinheads, and the Rise of a New White Culture.* Rev. ed. New York: Thunder's Mouth Press, 1995.

Ruiz, Jim. *The Black Hood of the Ku Klux Klan.* San Francisco: Austin & Winfield, 1998.

Smith, John David, ed. *Disfranchisement Proposals and the Ku Klux Klan.* New York: Garland, 1993.

Southern Poverty Law Center, comp. *The Ku Klux Klan: A History of Racism and Violence.* 4th ed. Montgomery, Ala.: Klanwatch, 1991.

Stanton, Bill. *Klanwatch: Bringing the Ku Klux Klan to Justice.* New York: Weidenfeld, 1991.

Trelease, Allen W. *White Terror: The Ku Klux Klan Conspiracy and the Southern Reconstruction.* Baton Rouge: Louisiana State University Press, 1995.

Tucker, Richard K. *The Dragon and the Cross: The Rise and Fall of the Ku Klux Klan in Middle America.* Hamden, Conn.: Archon Books, 1991.

Turner, John. *The Ku Klux Klan: A History of Racism and Violence.* Montgomery, Ala.: Southern Poverty Law Center, 1982.

Wade, Wyn Craig. *The Fiery Cross: The Ku Klux Klan in America.* New York: Simon & Schuster, 1987.

HISTORY OF RACE RELATIONS

See also African Americans/Slavery; African Americans/The South and Segregation; American Indians/History of American Indians; specific ethnicities

Binder, Frederick M., and David M. Reimers. *All the Nations Under Heaven: An Ethnic and Racial History of New York City.* New York: Columbia University Press, 1995.

Blum, John Morton. *V Was for Victory: Politics and American Culture During World War II.* New York: Harcourt Brace Jovanovich, 1976.

Bourne, Russell. *The Red King's Rebellion: Racial Politics in New England, 1675-1678.* New York: Oxford University Press, 1990.

Brack, Gene M. *Mexico Views Manifest Destiny, 1821-1846: An Essay on the Origins of the Mexican War.* Albuquerque: University of New Mexico Press, 1975.

Church, Benjamin. *Diary of King Philip's War, 1675-76.* Tercentary ed. Chester, Conn.: Pequot Press, 1975.

Craven, Wesley Frank. *White, Red, and Black: The Seventeenth Century Virginian.* Charlottesville: University Press of Virginia, 1971.

Dinnerstein, Leonard, and Frederic Cole Jaher, eds. *Uncertain Americans: Readings in Ethnic History.* Rev. ed. New York: Oxford University Press, 1977.

Hanke, Lewis. *The Spanish Struggle for Justice in the Conquest of America.* Boston: Little, Brown, 1965.

Hill, Winifred Storrs. *Tarnished Gold: Prejudice During the California Gold Rush.* San Francisco: International Scholars Publications, 1996.

International Seminar of North American History. *From "Melting Pot" to Multiculturalism: The Evolution of Ethnic Relations in the United States and Canada.* Proceedings of the International Seminar of North American History. April 12-16, 1989. Rome: Bulzoni Editore, 1990.

James, C. L. R. *Fighting Racism in World War II.* New York: Monad Press, 1991.

Krenn, Michael L., ed. *Race and U.S. Foreign Policy.* 4 vols. New York: Routledge, 1998.

Lindqvist, Sven. *The Skull Measurer's Mistake: And Other Portraits of Men and Women Who Spoke Out Against Racism,* translated by Joan Tate. New York: New Press, 1997.

Marable, Manning. *Blackwater: Historical Studies in Race, Class Consciousness, and Revolution.* Niwot: University Press of Colorado, 1993.

Perlmutter, Philip. *Divided We Fall: A History of Ethnic, Religious, and Racial Prejudice in America.* Ames: Iowa State University Press, 1992.

Pinsker, Sanford. *Worrying About Race, 1985-1995: Reflections During a Troubled Time.* New York: Whitston, 1996.

Polenberg, Richard. *One Nation Divisible: Class, Race, and Ethnicity in the United States Since 1938.* New York: Penguin, 1980.

Saxton, Alexander. *The Rise and Fall of the White Republic: Class Politics and Mass Culture in Nineteenth-Century America.* New York: Verso, 1990.

Smith, John David. *The Eugenic Assault on America: Scenes in Red, White, and Black.* Fairfax, Va.: George Mason University Press, 1993.

Sowell, Thomas. *Ethnic America: A History.* New York: Basic Books, 1981.

Steinfield, Melvin, comp. *Cracks in the Melting Pot: Racism and*

Discrimination in American History. Beverly Hills, Calif.: Glencoe, 1970.

Stewart, Kenneth L. *Race and Ethnic Relations in America*. Bellvue, Wash.: MicroCase Corp., 1997.

Takaki, Ronald T. *A Different Mirror: A History of Multicultural America*. Boston: Little, Brown, 1993.

Vaughan, Alden T. *The Roots of American Racism: Essays on the Colonial Experience*. New York: Oxford University Press, 1995.

Williams, Lou Falkner. *The Great South Carolina Ku Klux Klan Trials, 1871-1872*. Athens: University of Georgia Press, 1996.

IMMIGRATION AND IMMIGRANTS

See also Refugees; specific ethnicities

Aleinikoff, Thomas A., and David A. Martin. *Immigration: Process and Policy*. 2d ed. Saint Paul, Minn.: West, 1991.

Apraku, Kofi Konadu. *African Emigrés in the United States: A Missing Link in Africa's Social and Economic Development*. New York: Praeger, 1991.

Bean, Frank D., Georges Vernez, and Charles B. Keely. *Opening and Closing the Doors: Evaluating Immigration Reform and Control*. Washington, D.C.: Rand Corporation and the Urban Institute, 1989.

Bernard, William S., ed. *American Immigration Policy*. Port Washington, N.Y.: Kennikat Press, 1969.

Bodnar, John. *The Transplanted: A History of Immigrants in Urban America*. Bloomington: Indiana University Press, 1985.

Bolino, August C. *The Ellis Island Source Book*. Washington, D.C.: Kensington Historical Press, 1985.

Borjas, George J. *Friends or Strangers: The Impact of Immigrants on the U.S. Economy*. New York: Basic Books, 1990.

Briggs, Vernon M. *Mass Immigration and the National Interest*. Armonk, N.Y.: M. E. Sharpe, 1992.

Briggs, Vernon M., Jr., and Stephen Moore. *Still an Open Door? U.S. Immigration Policy and the American Economy*. Washington, D.C.: American University Press, 1994.

Brimelow, Peter. *Alien Nation*. New York: Random House, 1995.

Brownstone, David M., Irene M. Franck, and Douglas L. Brownstone, eds. *Island of Hope, Island of Tears*. New York: Penguin Books, 1986.

Coppa, Frank J., and Thomas J. Curran, eds. *The Immigrant Experience in America*. Boston: Twayne, 1976.

Crewdson, John. *The Tarnished Door: The New Immigrants and the Transformation of America*. New York: Times Books, 1983.

Curran, Thomas J. *Xenophobia and Immigration, 1820-1930*. Boston: Twayne, 1975.

D'Innocenzo, Michael, and Josef P. Sirefman, eds. *Immigration and Ethnicity: American Society—"Melting Pot" or "Salad Bowl"?* Westport, Conn.: Greenwood Press, 1992.

Daniels, Roger. *Coming to America: A History of Immigration and Ethnicity in American Life*. New York: HarperCollins, 1990.

_____. *Not Like Us: Immigrants and Minorities in America, 1890-1924*. Chicago: Ivan R. Dee, 1997.

Dinnerstein, Leonard, Roger H. Nichols, and David H. Reimers. *Natives and Strangers: Blacks, Indians, and Immigrants in America*. 2d ed. New York: Oxford University Press, 1990.

Divine, Robert A. *American Immigration Policy, 1924-1952*. New Haven, Conn.: Yale University Press, 1957. Reprint. New York: Da Capo Press, 1972.

Edmonston, Barry, and Jeffrey S. Passel, eds. *Immigration and Ethnicity: The Integration of America's Newest Arrivals*. Washington, D.C.: Urban Institute Press, 1994.

Ehrlich, Paul R., Loy Bilderback, and Anne H. Ehrlich. *The Golden Door: International Migration, Mexico, and the United States*. New York: Ballantine Books, 1978.

Fix, Michael, and Jeffrey S. Passel. *Immigration and Immigrants: Setting the Record Straight*. Washington, D.C.: Urban Institute, 1994.

Frank D. Bean, Georges Vernez, and Charles B. Keely. *Opening and Closing the Doors: Evaluating Immigration Reform and Control*. Washington, D.C.: Rand Corporation and the Urban Institute, 1989.

Franklin, Frank George. *The Legislative History of Naturalization in the United States: From the Revolutionary War to 1861*. Chicago: University of Chicago Press, 1906.

Glazer, Nathan, ed. *Clamor at the Gates: The New American Immigration*. San Francisco: ICS Press, 1985.

Handlin, Oscar. *The Uprooted*. 1951. 2d enlarged ed. Boston: Little, Brown, 1973.

Hansen, Marcus Lee. *The Immigrant in American History*. Cambridge, Mass.: Harvard University Press, 1940.

Harper, Elizabeth J. *Immigration Laws of the United States*. 3d ed. Indianapolis: Bobbs-Merrill, 1975.

Henderson, George, and Thompson Olasiji. *Migrants, Immigrants, and Slaves: Racial and Ethnic Groups in America*. Lanham, Md.: University Press of America, 1995.

Hofstetter, Richard R., ed. *U.S. Immigration Policy*. Durham, N.C.: Duke University Press, 1984.

Horowitz, Donald L., and Gerard Noiriel, eds. *Immigrants in Two Democracies: French and American Experience*. New York: New York University Press, 1992.

Hull, Elizabeth. *Without Justice for All*. Westport, Conn.: Greenwood Press, 1985.

Jones, Maldwyn Allen. *American Immigration*. 2d ed. Chicago: University of Chicago Press, 1992.

LeMay, Michael C. *From Open Door to Dutch Door: An Analysis of U.S. Immigration Policy Since 1820*. New York: Praeger, 1987.

Long, Robert Emmett, ed. *The Reference Shelf: Immigration*. New York: H. W. Wilson, 1996.

Maldonado, Lionel, and Joan Moore. *Urban Ethnicity in the United States*. Beverly Hills, Calif.: Sage Publications, 1985.

Masud-Piloto, Felix R. *From Welcomed Exiles to Illegal Immigrants*. Lanham, Md.: Rowman & Littlefield, 1996.

Novotny, Ann. *Strangers at the Door: Ellis Island, Castle Garden, and the Great Migration to America*. Riverside, Conn.: Chatham Press, 1971.

Nugent, Walter. *Crossings: The Great Transatlantic Migrations, 1870-1914*. Bloomington: Indiana University Press, 1992.

Papademetriou, Demetrios G., and Mark J. Miller, eds. *The Unavoidable Issue: U.S. Immigration Policy in the 1980's*. Philadelphia: Institute for the Study of Human Issues, 1983.

Pedraza, Silvia, and Rubén G. Rumbaut, eds. *Origins and Destinies: Immigration, Race, and Ethnicity in America*. Belmont, Calif.: Wadsworth, 1996.

Perea, Juan F. ed. *Immigrants Out! The New Nativism and the Anti-Immigrant Impulse in the United States*. New York: New York University Press, 1996.

Portes, Alejandro, ed. *The New Second Generation*. New York: Russell Sage Foundation, 1996.

Portes, Alejandro, and Rubén G. Rumbaut. *Immigrant America: A Portrait.* Berkeley: University of California Press, 1990.

Reeves, Pamela. *Ellis Island: Gateway to the American Dream.* New York: Crescent Books, 1991.

Reimers, David M. *Still the Golden Door: The Third World Comes to America.* 2d ed. New York: Columbia University Press, 1992.

Rose, Peter Isaac. *Tempest-Tost: Race, Immigration, and the Dilemmas of Diversity.* New York: Oxford University Press, 1997.

Shenton, James Patrick, and Patrick Kenny. *Ethnicity and Immigration.* Rev. ed. Washington, D.C.: American Historical Association, 1997.

Simcox, David E., ed. *U.S. Immigration in the 1980's: Reappraisal and Reform.* Washington, D.C.: Center for Immigration Studies, 1988.

Simon, Rita J., and Susan H. Alexander. *The Ambivalent Welcome: Print Media, Public Opinion, and Immigration.* Westport, Conn.: Praeger, 1993.

U.S. Commission on Civil Rights. *The Tarnished Golden Door: Civil Rights Issues in Immigration.* Washington, D.C.: U.S. Government Printing Office, 1980.

Ueda, Reed. *Postwar Immigrant America: A Social History.* Boston: St. Martin's Press, 1994.

Waldinger, Roger. *Through the Eye of the Needle: Immigrants and Enterprise in New York's Garment Trades.* New York: New York University Press, 1986.

Wittke, Carl. *We Who Built America.* Rev. ed. Cleveland: Case Western Reserve University Press, 1964.

Yans-McLaughlin, Virginia, ed. *Immigration Reconsidered.* New York: Oxford University Press, 1990.

IRANIAN AMERICANS

Ansari, Maboud. *The Making of the Iranian Community in America.* New York: Pardis Press, 1992.

Benjamin, Mooshie Sargis. *The Persian Yankee.* New York: Vantage Press, 1956.

Dadgar, Ali Reza, et al. *Labyrinth of Exile: Recent Works.* Los Angeles: University of California, Fowler Museum of Cultural History, 1994.

Kelley, Ron, ed. *Irangeles: Iranians in Los Angeles.* Berkeley: University of California Press, 1993.

JEWISH AMERICANS

See also Canada/Jewish Canadians

Améry, Jean. *At the Mind's Limits: Contemplations by a Survivor on Auschwitz and Its Realities.* Translated by Sidney Rosenfeld and Stella P. Rosenfeld. Bloomington: Indiana University Press, 1980.

Arbella, Irving, and Harold Troper. *None Is Too Many: Canada and the Jews of Europe, 1933-1948.* Toronto: Lester and Orpen Dennys, 1982.

Baum, Charlotte, Paula Hyman, and Sonya Michel. *The Jewish Woman in America.* New York: Dial Press, 1976.

Bauman, Zygmunt. *Modernity and the Holocaust.* Ithaca, N.Y.: Cornell University Press, 1989.

Bell, Leland V. *In Hitler's Shadow: The Anatomy of American Nazism.* Port Washington, N.Y.: Kennikat Press, 1973.

Berenbaum, Michael. *The World Must Know: The History of the Holocaust as Told in the United States Holocaust Memorial Museum.* Boston: Little, Brown, 1993.

Berman, Paul, ed. *Blacks and Jews: Alliance and Arguments.* New York: Delacorte Press, 1994.

Bernheimer, Charles S., ed. *The Russian Jews in the United States.* Philadelphia: John Winston, 1905.

Birmingham, Stephen. *"Our Crowd": The Great Jewish Families of New York.* New York: Harper & Row, 1967.

Blau, J. L. *Judaism in America.* Chicago: University of Chicago Press, 1976.

Brenner, Lenni. *Jews in America Today.* Secaucus, N.J.: Lyle Stuart, 1986.

Brettschneider, Marla, ed. *The Narrow Bridge: Jewish Views on Multiculturalism.* New Brunswick, N.J.: Rutgers University Press, 1996.

Brodkin, Karen. *How Jews Became White Folks and What That Says About Race in America.* New Brunswick, N.J.: Rutgers University Press, 1998.

Cohen, Bernard. *Sociocultural Changes in American Jewish Life as Reflected in Selected Jewish Literature.* Rutherford, N.J.: Fairleigh Dickinson University Press, 1972.

Cohen, George. *The Jews in the Making of America.* Boston: Stratford, 1924.

Cohen, Werner. *Encounter with Emancipation: The German Jews in the United States, 1830-1914.* Philadelphia: Jewish Publication Society of America, 1984.

Cott, Nancy, and Elizabeth Pleck, eds. *A Heritage of Her Own.* New York: Simon & Schuster, 1979.

Daughtry, Herbert D. *No Monopoly on Suffering: Blacks and Jews in Crown Heights.* Trenton, N.J.: Africa World Press, 1997.

Davies, Alan, ed. *Anti-Semitism in Canada: History and Interpretation.* Waterloo, Ont.: Wilfrid Laurier University Press, 1992.

Dawidowicz, Lucy S. *The War Against the Jews: 1933-1945.* New York: Holt, Rinehart & Winston.

Diner, Hasia R. *In the Almost Promised Land: American Jews and Blacks, 1919-1935.* Westport, Conn.: Westview, 1977.

Dinnerstein, Leonard. *Uneasy at Home: Antisemitism and the American Jewish Experience.* New York: Columbia University Press, 1987.

Downs, Donald Alexander. *Nazis in Skokie: Freedom, Community, and the First Amendment.* Notre Dame, Ind.: University of Notre Dame Press, 1985.

Elazar, Daniel J., and Harold M. Waller's *Maintaining Consensus: The Canadian Jewish Polity in the Postwar World.* Lanham, Md.: University Press of America, 1990.

Feingold, Henry L. *Zion in America.* New York: Twayne, 1974.

Ferrarotti, Franco. *The Temptation to Forget: Racism, Anti-Semitism, Neo-Nazism.* Westport, Conn.: Greenwood Press, 1994.

Foster, Arnold, and Benjamin R. Epstein. *The New Anti-Semitism.* New York: McGraw-Hill, 1974.

Friedman, Murray. *What Went Wrong: The Creation and Collapse of the Black-Jewish Alliance.* New York: Free Press, 1995.

Friedman, Saul S. *Jews and the American Slave Trade.* New Brunswick, N.J.: Transaction, 1998.

Gerber, David A., *Anti-Semitism in American History.* Chicago: University of Illinois Press, 1986.

Glazer, Nathan. *New Perspectives in American Jewish Sociology.* New York: American Jewish Committee, 1987.

Glock, Charles Y., and Rodney Stark. *Christian Beliefs and Anti-Semitism.* New York: Harper & Row, 1966.

Goldberg, Nathan. *Occupational Patterns of American Jewry.* New York: Jewish Teachers Seminary Press, 1947.

Golden, Harry. *A Little Girl Is Dead.* Cleveland: World Publishing, 1965.

Goldscheider, Calvin, and Sidney Goldstein. *The Jewish Community of Rhode Island.* Providence: Jewish Foundation of Rhode Island, 1988.

Grayzel, Solomon. *A History of the Contemporary Jews from 1900 to the Present.* New York: Meridian Books, 1962.

Gutman, Israel, et al., eds. *Encyclopedia of the Holocaust.* 4 vols. New York: Macmillan, 1990.

Heitzmann, William R. *American Jewish Voting Behavior.* San Francisco: R&E Research Associates, 1975.

Hentoff, Nat, ed. *Black Anti-Semitism and Jewish Racism.* New York: Richard W. Baron, 1969.

Hershkowitz, Leo. "Judaism." In *The Encyclopedia of the North American Colonies,* edited by Jacob Ernest Cook. Vol. 3. New York: Charles Scribner's Sons, 1993.

Hertzberg, Arthur. *The Jews in America.* New York: Simon & Schuster, 1989.

Hilberg, Raul. *The Destruction of the European Jews.* Rev. ed. 3 vols. New York: Holmes & Meier, 1985.

Howe, Irving. *World of Our Fathers.* New York: Harcourt Brace Jovanovich, 1976.

Isaacs, Stephen D. *Jews and American Politics.* Garden City, N.Y.: Doubleday, 1974.

Karpf, Maurice J. *Jewish Community Organization in the United States.* New York: Arno, 1971.

Kaufman, Jonathan. *Broken Alliance: The Turbulent Times Between Blacks and Jews in America.* New York: Scribner's, 1988.

Korman, Abraham K. *The Outsiders: Jews and Corporate America.* Lexington, Mass.: Lexington Books, 1988.

Learski, Rufus. *The Jews in America.* New York: KTAV Publishing House, 1972.

Lerner, Michael, and Cornel West. *Jews and Blacks: A Dialogue on Race, Religion, and Culture in America.* New York: Plume, 1996.

Lipset, Martin, and Earl Raab. *Jews and the New American Scene.* Cambridge, Mass.: Harvard University Press, 1995.

Marcus, Jacob R. *The Colonial American Jew, 1492-1776.* 3 vols. Detroit, Mich.: Wayne State University Press, 1970.

Marrus, Michael Robert. *The Unwanted: European Refugees in the Twentieth Century.* New York: Oxford University Press, 1985.

Martire, Gregory, and Ruth Clark. *Anti-Semitism in the United States: A Study of Prejudice in the 1980's.* New York: Praeger, 1982.

Mayer, Egon. *Love and Tradition: Marriage Between Jews and Christians.* New York: Plenum Press, 1985.

Medoff, Rafael. *Zionism and the Arabs: An American Jewish Dilemma, 1898-1948.* Westport, Conn.: Praeger, 1997.

Meltzer, Milton. *Never to Forget: The Jews of the Holocaust.* New York: Harper & Row, 1976.

Mendes-Flohr, Paul R., and Jehuda Reinharz, eds. *The Jew in the Modern World: A Documentary History.* New York: Oxford University Press, 1980.

Nelson, Jack. *Terror in the Night: The Klan's Campaign Against the Jews.* New York: Simon & Schuster, 1993.

Oppenheim, Samuel. *The Early History of the Jews in New York, 1654-1664.* New York: American Jewish Historical Society, 1909.

Parkes, James. *End of an Exile: Israel, the Jews, and the Gentile World.* Marblehead, Mass.: Micah Publications, 1982.

Patai, Raphael. *The Vanished Worlds of Jewry.* New York: Macmillan, 1980.

Phillips, William M. *An Unillustrious Alliance: The African American and Jewish American Communities.* New York: Greenwood Press, 1991.

Plesur, Milton. *Jewish Life in Twentieth Century America.* Chicago: Nelson-Hall, 1982.

Pogrebin, Letty Cottin. *Deborah, Golda, and Me: Being Female and Jewish in America.* New York: Crown, 1991.

Quinley, Harold E., and Charles Y. Glock. *Anti-Semitism in America.* New York: Free Press, 1979.

Rader, Jacob Marcus. *The Colonial American Jew, 1492-1776.* 3 vols., Detroit: Wayne State University Press, 1950, 1953, 1970.

Rieder, Jonathan. *Canarsie: The Jews and Italians of Brooklyn Against Liberalism.* Cambridge, Mass.: Harvard University Press, 1985.

Rittner, Carol, and John K. Roth, eds. *Different Voices: Women and the Holocaust.* New York: Paragon House, 1993.

Rogin, Michael P. *Blackface, White Noise: Jewish Immigrants in the Hollywood Melting Pot.* Berkeley: California University Press, 1996.

Ross, Robert W. *So It Was True: American Protestant Press and the Nazi Persecution of the Jews.* Minneapolis: University of Minnesota Press, 1980.

Rubenstein, Richard L. *The Cunning of History: The Holocaust and the American Future.* New York: Harper & Row, 1987.

Rubenstein, Richard L., and John K. Roth. *Approaches to Auschwitz: The Holocaust and Its Legacy.* Atlanta: John Knox Press, 1987.

Sachar, Howard M. *A History of the Jews in America.* New York: Alfred A. Knopf, 1992.

Salzman, Jack, and Cornel West, eds. *Struggles in the Promised Land: Towards a History of Black-Jewish Relations in the United States.* New York: Oxford University Press, 1997.

Schoem, David, ed. *Inside Separate Worlds: Life Stories of Young Blacks, Jews, and Latinos.* Ann Arbor: University of Michigan Press, 1991.

Selznick, Gertrude, and Stephen Steinberg. *The Tenacity of Prejudice: Anti-Semitism in Contemporary America.* New York: Harper & Row, 1969.

Sharot, Stephen. *Judaism: A Sociology.* New York: Holmes & Meier, 1976.

Shokeid, Moshe. *Children of Circumstances: Israeli Immigrants in New York.* New York: Cornell University Press, 1988.

Sidorsky, David, ed. *The Future of the Jewish Community in America.* New York: Basic Books, 1973.

Silberman, Charles E. *A Certain People: American Jews and Their Lives Today.* New York: Summit Books, 1985.

Sklare, Marshall. *America's Jews.* New York: Random House, 1971.

_____, ed. *Understanding American Jewry.* New Brunswick, N.J.: Transaction Books, 1982.

Strober, Gerald S. *American Jews.* Garden City, N.Y.: Doubleday, 1974.

Strong, Donald S. *Organized Anti-Semitism in America.* Washington, D.C.: American Council on Public Affairs, 1941.

Tobin, Gary A. *Jewish Perceptions of Asntisemitism.* New York: Plenum, 1988.

Waxman, Chaim I. *America's Jews in Transition.* Philadelphia: Temple University Press, 1983.

Weinfeld, J., W. Shaffir, and I. Cotler, eds. *The Canadian Jewish*

Mosaic. Toronto and New York: John Wiley & Sons, 1981.

Wiesel, Elie. *Night.* Translated by Stella Rodway. New York: Bantam Books, 1982.

Wistrich, Robert S. *Anti-Semitism: The Longest Hatred.* New York: Pantheon Books, 1991.

Zenner, Walter P. *Minorities in the Middle: A Cross-Cultural Analysis.* Albany: State University of New York Press, 1991.

Zweigenhaft, Richard L., and G. William Domhoff. *Jews in the Protestant Establishment.* New York: Praeger, 1982.

LANGUAGE AND BILINGUALISM

See also Canada/French Canadians and the Quebec Question; Education; Hate and White Supremacy; The Media; Multiracialism and Biracialism

Bastarache, Michael, et al. *Language Rights in Canada.* Montreal, Quebec: Editions Yvon Blais, 1987.

Biegel, Stuart. "The Parameters of the Bilingual Education Debate in California Twenty Years After *Lau v. Nichols.*" *Chicano-Latino Law Review* 14 (Winter, 1994): 48-60.

Bourhis, Richard Y., ed. *Conflict and Language Planning in Quebec.* Clevedon, Avon, England: Multilingual Matters, 1984.

Bracken, Harry M. *Freedom of Speech: Words Are Not Deeds.* Westport, Conn.: Praeger Publishers, 1994.

Chiswick, Barry R., ed. *Immigration, Language, and Ethnicity: Canada and the United States.* Washington, D.C.: AEI Press, 1992.

Crawford, James. *Language Loyalties: A Source Book on the Official English Controversy.* Chicago: University of Chicago Press, 1992.

Cummins, James. *Empowering Language Minority Students.* Sacramento: California Association for Bilingual Education, 1989.

Daniels, Harvey, ed. *Not Only English: Affirming America's Multilingual Heritage.* Urbana, Ill.: National Council of Teachers of English, 1990.

De la Peña, Fernando. *Democracy or Babel: The Case for Official English.* Washington, D.C.: U.S. English, 1991.

Freedman, Monroe H., and Eric M. Freedman. *Group Defamation and Freedom of Speech: The Relationship Between Language and Violence.* Westport, Conn.: Greenwood Press, 1995.

Fu, Danling. *My Trouble Is English: Asian Students and the American Dream.* Portsmouth, N.H.: Boynton/Cook, 1995.

Gallegos, Bee. *English: Our Official Language?* New York: H. W. Wilson, 1994.

Gleason, America Philip. *Speaking of Diversity: Language and Ethnicity in 20th Century.* Baltimore, Md.: The Johns Hopkins University Press, 1992.

Green, Jonathon. *Words Apart: The Language of Prejudice.* London: Kyle Cathie, 1996.

Hakuta, Kenji. *Mirror of Language: The Debate on Bilingualism.* New York: Basic Books, 1986.

Hayakawa, S. I. *The English Language Amendment: One Nation . . . Indivisible?* Washington, D.C.: Washington Institute for Values in Public Policy, 1985.

Herbst, Philip H. *The Color of Words: An Encyclopaedic Dictionary of Ethnic Bias in the United States.* Yarmouth, Maine: Intercultural Press, 1997.

Lippi-Green, Rosini. *English with an Accent: Language, Ideology, and Discrimination in the United States.* New York: Routledge, 1997.

McPhail, Mark Lawrence. *The Rhetoric of Racism.* Lanham, Md.: University Press of America, 1994.

Matsuda, Mari J. "Voices of America: Accent, Antidiscrimination Law, and a Jurisprudence for the Last Reconstruction." *Yale Law Journal* 100 (1991).

National Education Association of the United States. *Official English/English Only: More than Meets the Eye.* Washington, D.C.: Author, 1988.

Piatt, Bill. *¿Only English? Law and Language Policy in the United States.* Albuquerque: University of New Mexico Press, 1990.

Ridge, Martin, ed. *The New Bilingualism: An American Dilemma.* Los Angeles: University of Southern California Press, 1981.

Tatalovich, Raymond. *Nativism Reborn? The Official English Language Movement and the American States.* Lexington: University of Kentucky Press, 1995.

Wardhaugh, Ronald. *Language and Nationhood: The Canadian Experience.* Vancouver, B.C.: New Star Books, 1983.

Wetherell, Margaret, and Jonathan Potter. *Mapping the Language of Racism: Discourse and the Legitimation of Exploitation.* New York: Columbia University Press, 1993.

LATINOS

See also Caribbean Americans

Abalos, David T. *The Latino Family and the Politics of Transformation.* Westport, Conn.: Praeger, 1993.

_____. *Latinos in the United States.* Notre Dame, Ind.: University of Notre Dame Press, 1986.

Acuña, Rodolfo. *Occupied America.* San Francisco: Canfield Press, 1972.

Borjas, George, and Marta Tienda, eds. *Hispanics in the U.S. Economy.* New York: Academic Press, 1985.

Butler, Rusty. *On Creating a Hispanic America: A Nation Within a Nation?* Washington, D.C.: Council for Interamerican Security, 1985.

Chávez, Leo R. *Shadowed Lives: Undocumented Immigrants in American Society.* Orlando, Fla.: Harcourt Brace Jovanovich, 1992.

Chávez, Linda. *Out of the Barrio: Toward a New Politics of Hispanic Assimilation.* New York: Basic Books, 1991.

De la Garza, Rodolfo O., ed. *Ignored Voices: Public Opinion Polls and the Latino Community.* Austin: Center for Mexican American Studies, University of Texas at Austin Press, 1987.

DeFreitas, Gregory. *Inequality at Work: Hispanics in the U.S. Labor Force.* New York: Oxford University Press, 1991.

Delgado, Hector L. *New Immigrants, Old Unions: Undocumented Workers in Los Angeles.* Philadelphia: Temple University Press, 1993.

Delgado, Richard. *The Rodrigo Chronicles: Conversations About America and Race.* New York: New York University Press, 1995.

Fox, Geoffrey. *Hispanic Nation.* Secaucus, N.J.: Carol Publishing Group, 1996.

Garcia, F. Chris, ed. *Latinos and the Political System.* Notre Dame, Ind.: University of Notre Dame Press, 1988.

Haslip-Viera, Gabriel, and Sherrie L. Baver, eds. *Latinos in New York.* Notre Dame, Ind.: University of Notre Dame Press, 1996.

Hayes-Bautista, David E., et al. *No Longer a Minority: Latinos and Social Policy in California.* Los Angeles: UCLA Chicano Studies Research Center, 1992.

Heyck, Denis Lynn Daly. *Barrios and Borderlands: Cultures of Latinos and Latinas in the United States.* New York: Routledge, 1994.

Kanellos, Nicolás, ed. *The Hispanic American Almanac.* New York: Gale, 1997.

Keller, Gary D. *A Biographical Handbook of Hispanics and United States Film.* Tempe, Ariz.: Bilingual Press, 1997.

Knouse, Stephen B., P. Rosenfeld, and A. L. Culbertson. *Hispanics in the Workplace.* Newbury Park, Calif.: Sage Publications, 1992.

McWilliams, Carey. *North from Mexico: The Spanish-Speaking People of the United States.* 1948. Reprint. New York: Greenwood Press, 1990.

Mirande, Alfredo. *Gringo Justice.* Notre Dame, Ind.: University of Notre Dame Press, 1990.

_____. *Hombres y Machos: Masculinity and Latino Culture.* Boulder, Colo.: Westview Press, 1997.

Mohl, Raymond A. "On the Edge: Blacks and Hispanics in Metropolitan Miami Since 1959." *Florida Historical Quarterly* 69, no. 1 (July, 1990): 37-56.

Moore, Joan, and Harry Pachon. *Hispanics in the United States.* Englewood Cliffs, N.J.: Prentice-Hall, 1985.

Moore, Joan, and Raquel Pinderhugh, eds. *In the Barrios: Latinos and the Underclass Debate.* New York: Russell Sage, 1993.

Padilla, Felix. *Latino Ethnic Consciousness: The Case of Mexican Americans and Puerto Ricans in Chicago.* Notre Dame, Ind.: University of Notre Dame Press, 1985.

Piatt, Bill, et al. *Black and Brown in America: The Case for Cooperation.* New York: New York University Press, 1997.

Schoem, David, ed. *Inside Separate Worlds: Life Stories of Young Blacks, Jews, and Latinos.* Ann Arbor: University of Michigan Press, 1991.

Shorris, Earl. *Latinos: A Biography of the People.* New York: W. W. Norton, 1992.

Sosa, Lionel. *The Americano Dream: How Latinos Can Achieve Success in Business and in Life.* New York: Penguin Putnam, 1998.

Suro, Robert. *Strangers Among Us: How Latino Immigration is Transforming America.* New York: Alfred A. Knopf, 1998.

Tienda, Marta, and Frank Bean. *The Hispanic Population of the United States.* New York: Russell Sage, 1987.

Weber, David J. *The Spanish Frontier in North America.* New Haven, Conn.: Yale University Press, 1992.

Weyr, Thomas. *Hispanic U.S.A.: Breaking the Melting Pot.* New York: Harper & Row, 1988.

Williams, Robin M., Jr. *Strangers Next Door.* Englewood Cliffs, N.J.: Prentice Hall, 1964.

Cuban Americans

Abel, Christopher, and Nissa Torrents, eds. *José Martí: Revolutionary Democrat.* London: Athlone Press, 1986.

Boswell, Thomas D., and James R. Curtis. *The Cuban American Experience.* Totowa, N.J.: Rowman & Allanheld, 1983.

Brock, Lisa, and Digna Castañeda Fuertes, eds. *Between Race and Empire: African-Americans and Cubans Before the Cuban Revolution.* Philadelphia: Temple University Press, 1998.

Croucher, Sheila. *Imagining Miami.* Charlottesville: University Press of Virginia, 1997.

Domínguez, Jorge I. *Cuba: Order and Revolution.* Cambridge, Mass.: The Belknap Press of Harvard University Press, 1978.

Fernandez, Damian, ed. *Scholarship on the Cuban Experience: A Dialogue Among Cubanists.* Gainesville: University of Florida, 1992.

Hamm, Mark S. *The Abandoned Ones: The Imprisonment and Uprising of the Mariel Boat People.* Boston, Mass.: Northeastern University Press, 1995.

Jorge, Antonio, and Raul Moncarz. *The Political Economy of Cubans in South Florida.* Miami: Institute of Interamerican Studies, 1987.

Langley, Lester D. *The Cuban Policy of the United States.* New York: Wiley, 1968.

Larzelere, Alex. *Castro's Ploy, America's Dilemma: The 1980 Cuban Boat Lift.* Washington, D.C.: National Defense University Press, 1988.

MacCorkle, Lyn. *Cubans in the United States: A Bibliography for Research in the Social and Behavioral Sciences, 1960-1983.* Westport, Conn.: Greenwood, 1984.

Masud-Piloto, Felix Robert. *With Open Arms: Cuban Migration to the U.S.* Totowa, N.J.: Rowman and Littlefield, 1988.

Mazarr, Michael J. *Semper Fidel: America and Cuba, 1776-1988.* Baltimore, Md.: Nautical & Aviation Publishing Company of America, 1988.

Moncarz, Raul, and Jorge Antonio. "Cuban Immigration to the United States." In *Contemporary American Immigration,* edited by Dennis Laurence Cuddy. Boston: Twayne, 1982.

Morley, Morris H. *Imperial State and Revolution: The United States and Cuba, 1952-1986.* Cambridge, Mass.: Cambridge University Press, 1987.

Paterson, Thomas J. *Contesting Castro: The United States and the Triumph of the Cuban Revolution.* New York: Oxford University Press, 1994.

Pedraza-Bailey, Silvia. *Political and Economic Migrants in America: Cubans and Mexicans.* Austin: University of Texas Press, 1985.

Perez, Louis A., Jr. *Cuba: Between Reform and Revolution.* New York: Oxford University Press, 1988.

_____. *Cuba Under the Platt Amendment: 1902-1934.* Pittsburgh: University of Pittsburgh Press, 1986.

_____. *Intervention, Revolution, and Politics in Cuba, 1913-1921.* Pittsburgh: University of Pittsburgh Press, 1978.

Smith, Wayne S. *The Closest of Enemies: A Personal and Diplomatic History of the Castro Years.* New York: W. W. Norton, 1987.

Stepick, Alex, and Alejandro Portes. *City on the Edge: The Transformation of Miami.* Berkeley: University of California Press, 1993.

Suchlicki, Jaime. *Cuba: From Columbus to Castro.* 3d ed., rev. Washington, D.C.: Brassey's (U.S.), 1990.

Thomas, Hugh. *Cuba: Or, The Pursuit of Freedom.* New York: Harper & Row, 1971.

Welch, Richard E., Jr. *Response to Revolution: The United States and the Cuban Revolution, 1959-1961.* Chapel Hill: University of North Carolina Press, 1985.

Williams, Eric. *From Columbus to Castro: The History of the Caribbean, 1492-1969.* London: André Deutsch, 1970.

Mexicans and Central Americans

Acina, Rodolfo. *Occupied America: The Chicano Struggle for Liberation.* 2d ed. New York: Harper & Row, 1976.

Bean, Frank D., Jurgen Schmandt, and Sidney Weintraub, eds. *Mexican American and Central American Population Issues and U.S. Policy.* Austin, Tex.: Center for Mexican American Studies, 1988.

Briggs, Vernon M., Jr., Walter Fogel, and Fred H. Schmidt. *The Chicano Worker.* Austin: University of Texas Press, 1977.

Brischetto, Robert R. *The Mexican American Electorate: Political Opinions and Behavior Across Cultures in San Antonio.* Occasional Paper 5. San Antonio and Austin: Southwest Voter Registration Education Project and the Center for Mexican American Studies, University of Texas, 1985.

Copp, Nelson Gage. *"Wetbacks" and Braceros: Mexican Migrant Laborers and American Immigration Policy, 1930-1960.* San Francisco: R&E Research Associates, 1971.

Craig, Richard B. *The Bracero Program: Interest Groups and Foreign Policy.* Austin: University of Texas Press, 1971.

Dunne, John Gregory. *Delano: The Story of the California Grape Strike.* Rev. ed. New York: Farrar, Straus & Giroux, 1971.

Fusco, Paul, and George Horowitz. *"La Causa": The California Grape Strike.* New York: Macmillan, 1970.

Galarza, Ernesto. *Merchants of Labor: The Mexican Bracero Story.* Santa Barbara, Calif.: McNally and Loftin, West, 1978.

Gamboa, Erasmo. *Mexican Labor and World War II: Braceros in the Pacific Northwest, 1942-1947.* Austin: University of Texas Press, 1990.

Garcia, Mario T. *Mexican-Americans: Leadership, Ideology, and Identity 1930-1960.* New Haven, Conn.: Yale University Press, 1989.

García, Juan Ramon. *Operation Wetback: The Mass Deportation of Mexican Undocumented Workers in 1954.* Westport, Conn.: Greenwood Press, 1978.

Gómez-Quiñones, Juan. *Chicano Politics: Reality and Promise, 1940-1990.* Albuquerque: University of New Mexico Press, 1990.

Grebler, Leo. *Mexican Immigration to the United States: The Record and Its Implications.* Los Angeles: UCLS Mexican-American Study Project, 1965.

Grebler, Leo, Joan W. Moore, and Ralph C. Guzmán. *The Mexican-American People.* New York: Free Press, 1970.

Hoffman, Abraham. *Unwanted Americans in the Great Depression: Repatriation Pressure 1929-1939.* Tucson: University of Arizona Press, 1974.

Jenkins, Craig. *The Politics of Insurgency: The Farmworker Movement in the 1960's.* New York: Columbia University Press, 1985.

Leon, Arnoldo de. *They Called Them Greasers: Anglo Attitudes Toward Mexicans in Texas, 1821-1900.* Austin: University of Texas Press, 1980.

Levy, Jacques. *César Chávez: Autobiography of "La Causa."* New York: W. W. Norton, 1975.

Marin, Marguerite V. *Social Protest in an Urban Barrio: A Study of the Chicano Movement, 1966-1974.* Lanham, Md.: University Press of America, 1991.

Meier, Matt S., and Feliciano Ribera. *Mexican Americans and American Mexicans: From Conquistadors to Chicanos.* New York: Farrar, Straus & Giroux, 1993.

Menchaca, Martha. *The Mexican Outsiders: A Community History of Marginalization and Discrimination in California.* Austin: University of Texas Press, 1995.

Meyer, Michael C., and William L. Sherman. *The Course of Mexican History.* 3d ed. Oxford, England: Oxford University Press, 1987.

Miller, Robert Ryal. *Mexico: A History.* Norman: University of Oklahoma Press, 1985.

Mirande, Alfredo. *The Chicano Experience: An Alternative Perspective.* Notre Dame, Ind.: University of Notre Dame Press, 1985.

Múrguía, Edward. *Chicano Intermarriage: A Theoretical and Empirical Study.* San Antonio, Tex.: Trinity University Press, 1982.

Noriega, Chon, ed. *Chicanos and Film: Essays on Chicano Representation and Resistance.* New York: Garland, 1992.

Norquest, Carrol. *Rio Grande Wetbacks: Migrant Mexican Workers.* Albuquerque: University of New Mexico Press, 1971.

Pedraza-Bailey, Silvia. *Political and Economic Migrants in America: Cubans and Mexicans.* Austin: University of Texas Press, 1985.

Post, Louis F. *The Deportations Delirium of Nineteen-Twenty.* Chicago: Charles H. Kerr, 1923.

Reisler, Mark. *By the Sweat of Their Brow: Mexican Immigrant Labor in the United States, 1900-1940.* Westport, Conn.: Greenwood Press, 1976.

Rodriguez, Consuelo. *César Chávez.* New York: Chelsea House, 1991.

Romo, Ricardo. *East Los Angeles: History of a Barrio.* Austin: University of Texas Press, 1983.

Taylor, Ronald. *Chávez and the Farm Workers.* Boston: Beacon Press, 1975.

U.S. Commission on Civil Rights. *Mexican Americans and the Administration of Justice in the Southwest.* Washington, D.C.: Author, 1970.

Puerto Ricans

Cabranes, José A. *Citizenship and the American Empire: Notes on the Legislative History of the United States Citizenship of Puerto Ricans.* New Haven, Conn.: Yale University Press, 1979.

Cardona, Luis Antonio. *A History of the Puerto Ricans in the U.S.A.* Rockville, Md.: Carreta Press, 1990.

Carr, Raymond. *Puerto Rico: A Colonial Experiment.* New York: Vintage Books, 1984.

Carrion, Arturo Morales. *Puerto Rico: A Political and Cultural History.* New York: W. W. Norton, 1983.

De Passalacqua, John L. A. "The Involuntary Loss of United States Citizenship upon Accession to Independence by Puerto Rico." *Denver Journal of International Law and Policy* 19, no. 1 (Fall, 1990): 139-161.

Fernandez, Ronald. *The Disenchanted Island: Puerto Rico and the United States in the Twentieth Century.* New York: Praeger, 1992.

Fitzpatrick, Joseph P. *Puerto Rican Americans: The Meaning of Migration to the Mainland.* Englewood Cliffs, N.J.: Prentice Hall, 1971.

Kinsbruner, Jay. *Not of Pure Blood: The Free People of Color and Racial Prejudice in Nineteenth-Century Puerto Rico.* Durham, N.C.: Duke University Press, 1996.

Lopez, Adalberto, and James Petras, eds. *Puerto Rico and Puerto Ricans: Studies in History and Society.* New York: Wiley, 1974.

Maldonado-Denis, Manuel. *Puerto Rico: A Socio-historic Interpretation.* Translated by Elena Vialo. New York: Random House, 1972.

Meléndez, Edwin, and Edgardo Meléndez, eds. *Colonial Dilemma: Critical Perspectives on Contemporary Puerto Rico.* Boston: South End Press, 1993.

Rodriguez, Clara. *Puerto Ricans: Born in the USA.* Boston: Unwin Hyman, 1989.

Rodriguez, Clara E., and Virginia Sánchez Korrol, eds. *Historical Perspectives on Puerto Rican Survival in the U.S.* Princeton, N.J.: Markus Wiener, 1996.

Rodriguez de Laguna, Asela, ed. *Images and Identities: The Puerto*

Rican in Two World Contexts. New Brunswick, N.J.: Transaction Books, 1987.

Thomas, Piri. *Down These Mean Streets.* New York: Alfred A. Knopf, 1967.

U.S. Commission on Civil Rights. *Puerto Ricans in the Continental United States: An Uncertain Future.* Washington, D.C.: Author, 1976.

Wagenheim, Karl. *Puerto Rico: A Profile.* New York: Praeger, 1970.

THE MEDIA

Bogle, Donald. *Blacks in American Films and Television.* New York: Garland Publishing, 1988.

_____. *Toms, Coons, Mulattoes, Mammies, and Bucks.* New York: Continuum, 1992.

Campbell, Christopher P. *Race, Myth and the News.* Thousand Oaks, Calif.: Sage Publications, 1995.

Center for Integration and Improvement of Journalism. *News Watch: A Critical Look at People of Color.* San Francisco: San Francisco State University, 1994.

Chideya, Farai. *Don't Believe the Hype: Fighting Cultural Misinformation About African Americans.* New York: Plume, 1995.

Dennis, Everette E., and Edward C. Pease, eds. *The Media in Black and White.* New Brunswick, N.J.: Transaction, 1997.

Dines, Gail, and Jean M. Humez. *Gender, Race, and Class in Media.* Newbury Park, Calif.: Sage Publications, 1995.

Ferguson, Robert. *Representing "Race": Ideology, Identity and the Media.* New York: Arnold, 1998.

Gabriel, John. *Whitewash: Racialized Politics and the Media.* New York: Routledge, 1998.

Gandy, Oscar H., Jr. *Communication and Race: A Structural Perspective.* New York: Oxford University Press, 1998.

Gates, Henry Louis, Jr. *The Signifying Monkey: A Theory of Afro-American Literary Criticism.* New York: Oxford University Press, 1988.

Gershoni, Yekutiel. *Africans on African-Americans: The Creation and Uses of an African-American Myth.* Washington Square, N.Y.: New York University Press, 1997.

Hutchinson, Janis Faye, ed. *Cultural Portrayals of African Americans: Creating an Ethnic/Racial Identity.* Westport, Conn.: Bergin & Garvey, 1997.

Kamalipour, Yahya R., ed. *Cultural Diversity and the U.S. Media.* Albany: State University of New York Press, 1998.

Keever, Beverly Ann Deepe, et al., eds. *U.S. News Coverage of Racial Minorities: A Source Book, 1934-1996.* Westport, Conn.: Greenwood Press, 1997.

Lhamon, W. T., Jr. *Raising Cain: Blackface Performance from Jim Crow to Hip Hop.* Cambridge, England: Cambridge University Press, 1998.

Lusane, Clarence. *Race in the Global Era: African Americans at the Millennium.* Boston: South End Press, 1997.

Mintz, Sidney W., and Richard Price. *The Birth of African-American Culture.* Boston: Beacon Press, 1992.

Morrison, Toni. *Playing in the Dark: Whiteness and the Literary Imagination.* New York: Vintage Books, 1990.

Roediger, David R., ed. *Black on White: Black Writers on What It Means to Be White.* New York: Schoken, 1998.

Rogoff, Edmond Marc. *Gaining a Voice: Media Relations for Canadian Ethnic Minorities.* Ottawa: Media Resources Advisory Group, 1991.

Rollock, Barbard. *The Black Experience in Children's Books.* New York: New York Public Library, 1984.

Ross, Karen. *Black and White Media: Black Images in Popular Film and Television.* Cambridge, Mass.: Polity Press, 1996.

Said, Edward. *Covering Islam: How the Media and the Experts Determine How We See the Rest of the World.* New York: Pantheon Books, 1981.

Silva, Fred, ed. *Focus on "The Birth of the Nation."* Englewood Cliffs, N.J.: Prentice-Hall, 1971.

Simon, Rita J., and Susan H. Alexander. *The Ambivalent Welcome: Print Media, Public Opinion, and Immigration.* Westport, Conn.: Praeger, 1993.

Torres, Sasha, ed. *Living Color: Race and Television in the United States.* Durham, N.C.: Duke University Press, 1998.

Twitchin, John, ed. *The Black and White Media Book: Handbook for the Study of Racism and Television.* Stokes-on-Trent, England: Trentham Books, 1988.

Tyler, Bruce Michael. *From Harlem to Hollywood: The Struggle for Racial and Cultural Democracy, 1920-1943.* New York: Garland, 1992.

MULTIRACIALISM AND BIRACIALISM

See also Census Issues; Language and Bilingualism

Arboleda, Teja. *In the Shadow of Race: Growing Up as a Multiethnic, Multicultural, and "Multiracial" American.* Mahwah, N.J.: Lawrence Erlbaum, 1998.

Azoulay, Katya Gibel. *Black, Jewish, and Interracial: It's Not the Color of Your Skin, but the Race of Your Kin, and Other Myths of Identity.* Duke University Press, 1997.

Berry, John W. "Psychology of Acculturation: Understanding Individuals Moving Between Cultures." In *Applied Cross-Cultural Psychology,* edited by Richard W. Brislin. Newbury Park, Calif.: Sage Publications, 1990.

Chiong, Jane Ayers. *Racial Categorization of Multiracial Children in Schools.* Westport, Conn.: Bergin & Garvey, 1998.

Darder, Antonia, ed. *Culture and Difference: Critical Perspectives on the Bicultural Experience in the United States.* Westport, Conn.: Bergin & Garvey, 1995.

D'Souza, Dinesh. *The End of Racism: Principles for a Multiracial Society.* New York: Free Press, 1995.

Forbes, Jack D. *Black Africans and Native Americans: Color, Race, and Caste in the Evolution of Red-Black Peoples.* New York: Basil Blackwell, 1988.

Funderburg, Lise. *Black, White, Other: Biracial Americans Talk About Race and Identity.* New York: William Morrow, 1994.

Fusco, Coco. *English Is Broken Here: Notes on Cultural Fusion in the Americas.* New York: The New Press, 1995.

Grow, Lucille J., and Deborah Shapiro. *Black Children, White Parents: A Study of Transracial Adoption.* New York: Child Welfare League of America, 1974.

Kaeser, Gigi, and Peggy Gillespie. *Of Many Colors: Portraits of Multiracial Families.* Amherst: University of Massachusetts Press, 1997.

Korgen, Kathleen Odell. *From Black to Biracial: Transforming Racial Identity Among Americans.* Westport, Conn.: Praeger, 1998.

Lazarre, Jane. *Beyond the Whiteness of Whiteness: Memoir of a White Mother of Black Sons.* Durham, N.C.: Duke University Press, 1996.

McBride, James. *The Color of Water: A Black Man's Tribute to His White Mother.* New York: Riverhead Books, 1996.

Minerbrook, Scott. *Divided to the Vein: A Journey into Race and Family.* New York: Harcourt, Brace, 1996.

Nash, Gary B. *Forbidden Love: Secret History of Mixed Race America,* 1999.

Pohl, Constance, and Kathy Harris. *Transracial Adoption: Children and Parents Speak.* New York: Franklin Watts, 1992.

Roberts, Dorothy. *Killing the Black Body: Race, Reproduction, and the Meaning of Liberty.* New York: Pantheon Books, 1997.

Root, Maria P. P., ed. *The Multiracial Experience: Racial Borders as the New Frontier.* Thousand Oaks, Calif.: Sage Publications, 1996.

_____, ed. *Racially Mixed People in America.* Thousand Oaks, Calif.: Sage Publications, 1992.

Rosenblatt, Paul, Terri A. Karis, and Richard D. Powell. *Multiracial Couples: Black and White Voices.* Thousand Oaks, Calif.: Sage Publications, 1995.

Scales-Trent, Judy. *Notes of a White Black Woman: Race Color Community.* University Park: Pennsylvania State University Press, 1995.

Schott, Judith. *Culture, Religion, and Childbearing in a Multiracial Society: A Handbook for Health Professionals.* Boston: Butterworth-Heinemann, 1996.

Simon, Rita J., Howard Altstein, and Marygold S. Melli. *The Case for Transracial Adoption.* Washington, D.C.: American University Press, 1994.

Spencer, Jon Michael. *The New Colored People: The Mixed-Race Movement in America.* New York: New York University Press, 1997.

Thomas, Richard Walter. *Under Interracial Unity: A Study of U.S. Race Relations.* Newbury Park, Calif.: Sage Publications, 1996.

Waters, Mary. *Ethnic Options: Choosing Identities in America.* Berkeley: University of California Press, 1990.

Williamson, Joel. *New People: Miscegenation and Mulattoes in the United States.* Baton Rouge: Louisiana State University Press, 1995.

Wright, Marguerite A. *I'm Chocolate, You're Vanilla: Raising Healthy Black and Biracial Children in a Race-Conscious World.* San Francisco: Jossey-Bass, 1998.

Zack, Naomi. *American Mixed Race: The Culture of Microdiversity.* Lanham, Md.: Rowman & Littlefield, 1995.

_____. *Race and Mixed Race.* Philadelphia: Temple University Press, 1993.

POLITICS

See also African Americans/Politics; Civil Rights; specific ethnicities

Arthur, John, and Amy Shapiro, eds. *Color Class Identity: The New Politics of Race.* Boulder, Colo.: Westview Press, 1996.

Aufderheide, Patricia, ed. *Beyond P.C.: Toward a Politics of Understanding.* St. Paul, Minn.: GrayWolf Press, 1992.

Babu, B. Ramesh, ed. *Minorities and the American Political System.* New Delhi: South Asian, 1990.

Bennett, David H. *The Party of Fear: From Nativist Movements to the New Right in American History.* Chapel Hill, N.C.: University of North Carolina Press, 1988.

Black, Earl, and Merle Black. *Politics and Society in the South.* Cambridge, Mass.: Harvard University Press, 1987.

_____. *The Vital South: How Presidents Are Elected.* Cambridge, Mass.: Harvard University Press, 1987.

Bonnett, Alastair. *Radicalism, Anti-Racism, and Representation.* New York: Routledge, 1993.

Boston, Thomas D. *Race, Class, and Conservatism.* Winchester, Mass.: Unwin Hyman, 1988.

Browning, Rufus P., et al., eds. *Racial Politics in American Cities.* 2d ed. New York: Longman, 1997.

Caditz, Judith. *White Liberals in Transition: Current Dilemmas of Ethnic Integration.* New York: Spectrum Publications, 1976.

Carmines, Edward G., and James A. Stimson. *Issue Evolution: Race and Transformation of American Politics.* Princeton, N.J.: Princeton University Press, 1989.

Carter, Dan T. *From George Wallace to Newt Gingrich: Race in the Conservative Counterrevolution, 1963-1994.* Baton Rouge: Louisiana State University Press, 1996.

Chang, Edward, and Eui-Young Yu, eds. *Multiethnic Coalition Building in Los Angeles.* Los Angeles: California State University Press, 1995.

Cortner, Richard C. *The Apportionment Cases.* Knoxville: University of Tennessee Press, 1970.

Dahl, Robert. *Who Governs? Democracy and Power in an American City.* New Haven, Conn.: Yale University Press, 1963.

Dahrendorf, Ralf. *Class and Class Conflict in Industrial Society.* Stanford, Calif.: Stanford University Press, 1959.

_____. *Essays in the Theory of Society.* Stanford, Calif.: Stanford University Press, 1968.

_____. *The Modern Social Conflict: An Essay on the Politics of Liberty.* New York: Weidenfeld & Nicolson, 1988.

De Conde, Alexander. *Ethnicity, Race, and American Foreign Policy: A History.* Boston: Northeastern University Presss, 1992.

Fuchs, Lawrence H. *The American Kaleidoscope: Race, Ethnicity, and the Civic Culture.* Hanover, N.H.: Wesleyan University Press, 1990.

Garcia, Ignacio M. *United We Win.* Tucson: University of Arizona Press, 1989.

George, John, and Laird Wilcox. *Nazis, Communists, Klansmen, and Others on the Fringe: Political Extremism in America.* Buffalo, N.Y.: Prometheus Books, 1992.

Goldfield, Michael. *The Color of Politics: Race and the Mainsprings of American Politics.* New York: New Press, 1997.

Guinier, Lani. *The Tyranny of the Majority: Fundamental Fairness in Representative Democracy.* New York: Free Press, 1994.

Hadjor, Kofi Buenor. *Another America: The Politics of Race and Blame.* Boston: South End Press, 1995.

Hurwitz, Jon, and Mark Peffley, eds. *Perception and Prejudice: Race and Politics in the United States.* New Haven, Conn.: Yale University Press, 1998.

Jennings, James, ed. *Blacks, Latinos, and Asians in Urban America: Status and Prospects for Politics and Activism.* Westport, Conn.: Praeger, 1994.

Kinder, Donald R., and Lynn M. Sanders. *Divided by Color: Racial Politics and Democratic Ideals.* Chicago: University of Chicago Press, 1996.

Kuzenski, John C., ed. *David Duke and the Politics of Race in the South.* Nashville, Tenn.: Vanderbilt University Press, 1995.

Lauren, Paul Gordon. *Power and Prejudice: The Politics and Diplomacy of Racial Discrimination.* 2d ed. Boulder, Colo.: Westview Press, 1996.

Lind, Michael. *Up from Conservativism: Why the Right Is Wrong for America.* New York: Free Press, 1996.

Lipset, Seymour M. *Political Man: The Social Bases of Politics.* Garden City, N.Y.: Doubleday, 1960.

Lipsitz, George. *The Possessive Investment in Whiteness: How White People Profit from Identity Politics.* Philadelphia: Temple University Press, 1998.

MacInnes, Gordon. *Wrong for All the Right Reasons: How White Liberals Have Been Undone by Race.* New York: New York University Press, 1996.

Merton, Thomas. *The Nonviolent Alternative.* Edited by Gordon Zahn. New York: Farrar, Straus and Giroux, 1980.

Mills, C. Wright. *The Power Elite.* New York: Oxford University Press, 1956.

O'Rourke, Timothy G. *The Impact of Reapportionment.* New Brunswick, N.J.: Transaction Books, 1980.

Persons, Georgia A., ed. *Race and Representation.* New Brunswick, N.J.: Transaction, 1997.

Pickens, Donald K. *Eugenics and the Progressives.* Nashville, Tenn.: Vanderbilt University Press, 1968.

Roy, Donald H. *The Reuniting of America: Eleven Multicultural Dialogues.* New York: Peter Lang, 1996.

Sanjek, Roger. *The Future of Us All: Race and Neighborhood Politics in New York City.* Ithaca, N.Y.: Cornell University Press, 1998.

Schlesinger, Arthur, Jr. *The Disuniting of America: Reflections on a Multicultural Society.* New York: W. W. Norton, 1991.

Sleeper, Jim. *The Closest of Strangers: Liberalism and the Politics of Race in New York.* New York: W. W. Norton, 1990.

Smith, J. Owens. *The Politics of Racial Inequality: A Systematic Comparative Macro-Analysis from the Colonial Period to 1970.* Westport, Conn.: Greenwood Press, 1987.

Sniderman, Paul M., and Edward G. Carmines. *Reaching Beyond Race.* Cambridge, Mass.: Harvard University Press, 1997.

Sniderman, Paul M., Philip E. Tetlock, and Edward G. Carmines, eds. *Prejudice, Politics, and the American Dilemma.* Stanford, Calif.: Stanford University Press, 1993.

Solomos, John, and Les Back. *Race, Politics, and Social Change.* New York: Routledge, 1995.

PSYCHOLOGY, ATTITUDES, PERSONAL RELATIONS

See also Racism, Prejudice, Discrimination

Adorno, T. W., E. Frenkel-Brunswick, D. Levinson, and R. Sanford. *The Authoritarian Personality.* New York: Harper Brothers, 1950.

Anti-Defamation League. *Highlights from an Anti-Defamation League Survey on Racial Attitudes in America.* New York: Author, 1993.

Apostle, Richard A., et al. *The Anatomy of Racial Attitudes.* Berkeley: University of California Press, 1983.

Aronson, Elliot. *The Social Animal.* 3d ed. San Francisco: W. H. Freeman, 1980.

Baron, Robert A. *Social Psychology: Understanding Human Interaction.* 6th ed. Boston: Allyn & Bacon, 1989.

Berkowitz, Leonard, ed. *Roots of Aggression: A Re-examination of the Frustration-Aggression Hypothesis.* New York: Atherton, 1969.

Berry, Gordon LaVern, and Joy Keiko Asamen, eds. *Black Students: Psychosocial Issues and Academic Achievement.* Newbury Park, Calif.: Sage Publications, 1989.

Berry, John W. "Psychology of Acculturation: Understanding Individuals Moving Between Cultures." In *Applied Cross-Cultural Psychology,* edited by Richard W. Brislin. Newbury Park, Calif.: Sage Publications, 1990.

Bethlehem, Douglas W. *A Social Psychology of Prejudice.* New York: St. Martin's Press, 1985.

Billig, Michael. *Social Psychology and Intergroup Relations.* London: Academic Press, 1976.

Block, N. J., and Gerald Dworkin. *The IQ Controversy: Critical Readings.* New York: Pantheon Books, 1976.

Bowser, Benjamin P., and Raymond G. Hunt, eds. *Impact of Racism on White Americans.* Newbury Park, Calif.: Sage Publications, 1981.

Brink, William, and Louis Harris. *Black and White: A Study of U.S. Racial Attitudes Today.* New York: Simon and Schuster, 1967.

Brown, Rupert. *Prejudice: Its Social Psychology.* Cambridge, Mass.: Blackwell, 1995.

Bryant, Brenda K. *Counseling for Racial Understanding.* Alexandria, Va.: American Counseling Association, 1994.

Carter, Robert T. *The Influence of Race and Racial Identity in Psychotherapy: Toward a Racially Inclusive Model (Wiley Series on Personality Processes).* New York: Wiley, 1995.

Dalton, Harlon L. *Racial Healing: Confronting the Fear Between Blacks and Whites.* New York: Doubleday, 1995.

Davis, Allison, and John Dollard. *Children of Bondage: The Personality Development of Negro Youth in the Urban South.* New York: Harper & Row, 1964.

DeMott, Benjamin. *The Trouble with Friendship: Why Americans Can't Think Straight About Race.* New York: Atlantic Monthly Press, 1995.

Dollard, John, et al. *Frustration and Aggression.* New Haven, Conn: Yale University Press, 1939.

Duckitt, John. *The Social Psychology of Prejudice.* New York: Praeger, 1992.

Eckberg, Douglas Lee. *Intelligence and Race.* New York: Praeger, 1979.

Ehrlich, Howard J. *The Social Psychology of Prejudice.* New York: John Wiley & Sons, 1973.

Erikson, Erik Homburger. *Childhood and Society.* 2d ed. New York: W. W. Norton, 1963.

————. *Identity, Youth, and Crisis.* New York: W. W. Norton, 1968.

Eysenck, H. J. *The IQ Argument.* New York: Library Press, 1971.

Fancher, Raymond E. *The Intelligence Men: Makers of the IQ Controversy.* New York: W. W. Norton, 1985.

Ferguson, Carroy U. *A New Perspective on Race and Color: Research on an Outer vs. Inner Orientation to Anti-Black Dispositions.* Lewiston, N.Y.: Edwin Mellen Press, 1997.

Fisher, Roger, and Scott Brown. *Getting Together: Building Relationships As We Negotiate.* New York: Penguin Books, 1989.

Flyn, James. *Race, IQ, and Jensen.* London: Routledge, 1980.

Fredrickson, George M. *The Black Image in the White Mind: The Debate on Afro-American Character and Destiny, 1817-1914.* Hanover, N.H.: Wesleyan University Press, 1987

Guthrie, Robert V. *Even the Rat Was White: A Historical View of Psychology.* New York: Harper & Row, 1976.

Haller, John S., Jr. *Outcasts from Evolution: Scientific Attitudes of Racial Inferiority, 1859-1900.* Carbondale: Southern Illinois University Press, 1995.

Hamilton, David L., ed. *Cognitive Processes in Stereotyping and Intergroup Behavior.* Hillsdale, N.J.: Lawrence Erlbaum, 1981.

Herrnstein, Richard, and Charles Murray. *The Bell Curve: Intelligence and Class Structure in American Life*. New York: Free Press, 1994.

Hilliard, Asa G., III. "IQ Testing as the Emperor's New Clothes: A Critique of Jensen's *Bias in Mental Testing*." In *Perspectives on Bias in Mental Testing*, edited by Cecil R. Reynolds and Robert T. Brown. New York: Plenum Press, 1984.

Hocker, Joyce L., and William M. Wilmot. *Interpersonal Conflict*. 3d ed. Dubuque, Iowa: Wm. C. Brown, 1991.

Howitt, Dennis, and J. Owusu-Bempah. *The Racism of Psychology: Time for Change*. New York: Harvester Wheatsheaf, 1994.

Issa, Ihsan al-, and Michel Tousignant, eds. *Ethnicity, Immigration, and Psychopathology*. New York: Plenum Press, 1997.

Johnson, Walton R., and D. Michael Warren, eds. *Inside the Mixed Marriage: Accounts of Changing Attitudes, Patterns, and Perceptions of Cross-Cultural and Interracial Marriages*. Lanham, Md.: University Press of America, 1994.

Jones, Edward Ellsworth. *Interpersonal Perception*. New York: W. H. Freeman, 1990.

Jordan, Winthrop D. *White over Black: American Attitudes Toward the Negro, 1550-1812*. New York: W. W. Norton, 1968, 1995.

Katz, Irwin. *Stigma: A Social Psychological Analysis*. Hillsdale, N.J.: Lawrence Erlbaum, 1981.

Kidder, Louise. *The Psychology of Intergroup Relations: Conflict and Consciousness*. New York: McGraw-Hill, 1975.

Kovel, Joel. *White Racism: A Psychohistory*. New York: Vintage Books, 1970. Reprint. New York: Columbia University Press, 1984.

Kroger, Jane. *Identity in Adolescence*. London: Routledge & Kegan Paul, 1989.

Lassiter, Sybil M. *Cultures of Color in America: A Guide to Family, Religion, and Health*. Westport, Conn.: Greenwood Press, 1998.

Leon, Arnoldo de. *They Called Them Greasers: Anglo Attitudes Toward Mexicans in Texas, 1821-1900*. Austin: University of Texas Press, 1980.

Locke, Don C. *Increasing Multicultural Understanding: A Comprehensive Model*. Newbury Park, Calif.: Sage Publications, 1992.

Lorenz, Konrad. *On Aggression*. Translated by Marjorie Kerr Wilson. Reprint. New York: Harcourt Brace Jovanovich, 1974.

Lott, Bernice E., and Diane Maluso, eds. *The Social Psychology of Interpersonal Discrimination*. New York: Guildford, 1995.

Mayer, Egon. *Love and Tradition: Marriage Between Jews and Christians*. New York: Plenum Press, 1985.

Messick, David M., and Diane M. Mackie. "Intergroup Relations." In *Annual Review of Psychology* 40. Stanford, Calif.: Annual Reviews, 1989.

Miller, Arthur G., ed. *In the Eye of the Beholder: Contemporary Issues in Stereotyping*. New York: Praeger, 1982.

Miller, Norman, and Marilynn B. Brewer, eds. *Groups in Contact: The Psychology of Desegregation*. Orlando, Fla.: Academic Press, 1984.

Mitchell, Susan. *The Official Guide to American Attitudes*. Ithaca, N.Y.: New Strategist, 1997.

Montagu, Ashley. *The Nature of Human Aggression*. New York: Oxford University Press, 1976.

_____, ed. *Race and IQ*. New York: Oxford University Press, 1975.

Múrguía, Edward. *Chicano Intermarriage: A Theoretical and Empirical Study*. San Antonio, Tex.: Trinity University Press, 1982.

Phinney, Jean, and Doreen Rosenthal. "Ethnic Identity in Adolescence: Process, Context, and Outcome." In *Advances in Adolescent Development*, vol. 4, edited by Gerald R. Adams, Thomas P. Gullotta, and Raymond Montemayor. Newbury Park, Calif.: Sage, 1992.

Porter, Judith D. *Black Child, White Child: The Development of Racial Attitudes*. Cambridge, Mass. Harvard University Press, 1971.

Raybon, Patricia. *My First White Friend: Confessions on Race, Love, and Forgiveness*. New York: Viking, 1996.

Reddy, Maureen T. *Crossing the Color Line: Race, Parenting, and Culture*. New Brunswick, N.J.: Rutgers University Press, 1994.

Richards, Graham. *"Race," Racism, and Psychology: Towards a Reflexive History*. Routledge, 1998.

Ridley, Charles R. *Overcoming Unintentional Racism in Counseling and Therapy: A Practitioner's Guide to Intentional Intervention*. Thousand Oaks, Calif. Sage Publications, 1995.

Robinson, James L. *Racism or Attitude? The Ongoing Struggle for Black Liberation and Self-Esteem*. New York: Insight Books, 1995.

Rokeach, Milton. *The Open and Closed Mind*. New York: Basic Books, 1960.

Schuman, Howard, Charlotte Steeh, and Lawrence Bobo. *Racial Attitudes in America: Trends and Interpretations*. Rev. ed. Cambridge, Mass.: Harvard University Press, 1998.

Scott, Daryl Michael. *Contempt and Pity: Social Policy and the Image of the Damaged Black Psyche, 1880-1996*. Chapel Hill: University of North Carolina Press, 1997.

Spickard, Paul R. *Mixed Blood: Intermarriage and Ethnic Identity in Twentieth-Century America*. Madison: University of Wisconsin Press, 1989.

Storfer, Miles B. "The Black/White IQ Disparity: Myth and Reality." In *Intelligence and Giftedness*. San Francisco: Jossey-Bass, 1990.

Swim, Janet K., and Charles Stangor, eds. *Prejudice: The Target's Perspective*. San Diego, Calif.: Academic Press, 1998.

Tatum, Beverly Daniel. *"Why Are All the Black Kids Sitting Together in the Cafeteria?" and Other Conversations About Race*. HarperCollins, 1997.

Taylor, Donald M., and Fathali M. Moghaddam. *Theories of Intergroup Relations: International Social Psychological Perspectives*. New York: Praeger, 1987.

Taylor, Ronald D., and Margaret C. Wang, eds. *Social and Emotional Adjustment and Family Relations in Ethnic Minority Families*. Mahwah, N.J.: Lawrence Erlbaum, 1997.

Taylor, Ronald L., ed. *Minority Families in America: A Multicultural Perspective*. 2d ed. Upper Saddle River, N.J.: Prentice-Hall, 1998.

Terkel, Studs. *Race: How Blacks and Whites Think and Feel About the American Obsession*. New York: New Press, 1992.

Thomas, Alexander, and Samuel Sillen. *Racism and Psychiatry*. New York: Bruner-Mazel, 1972.

Toch, Hans, ed. *Psychology of Crime and Criminal Justice*. New York: Holt, Rinehart and Winston, 1979.

Ward, W. Peter. *White Canada Forever: Popular Attitudes and Public Policy Toward Orientals in British Columbia*. Montreal: McGill-Queen's University Press, 1990.

Watson, Peter, ed. *Psychology and Race*. Chicago: Aldine, 1973.

Wiener, Eugene, and Alan B. Slifka. *The Handbook of Interethnic Coexistence*. New York: Continuum, 1998.

Williams, Vernon J. *From a Caste to a Minority: Changing Attitudes of American Sociologists Toward Afro-Americans, 1896-1945.* New York: Greenwood Press, 1989.

Willie, Charles V., Bernard M. Kramer, and Bertram S. Brown. *Racism and Mental Health.* Pittsburgh: University of Pittsburgh Press, 1973.

Woolfolk, Anita E. *Educational Psychology.* Needham Heights, Mass.: Allyn & Bacon, 1993.

Worchel, Stephen, and William G. Austin. *Psychology of Intergroup Relations.* Chicago: Nelson-Hall, 1986.

RACE DEFINITIONS

See also Racism, Prejudice, Discrimination

Allen, Theodore W. *The Invention of the White Race.* New York: Verso, 1994.

Augstein, Hannah Franziska, ed. *Race: The Origins of an Idea, 1760-1850.* Bristol, England: Thoemmes Press, 1996.

Banton, Michael. *The Idea of Race.* London: Tavistock Publications, 1977.

Banton, Michael, and Jonathan Harwood. *The Race Concept.* New York: Praeger, 1975.

Bean, Robert Bennett. *The Races of Man.* New York: University Society, 1935.

Bernardi, Daniel, ed. *The Birth of Whiteness: Race and the Emergence of U.S. Cinema.* New Brunswick, N.J.: Rutgers University Press, 1996.

Chase, Allan. *The Legacy of Malthus: The Social Costs of the New Scientific Racism.* New York: Alfred A. Knopf, 1977.

Conrad, Earl. *The Invention of the Negro.* New York: Paul S. Eriksson, 1967.

Corcos, Alain F. *The Myth of Human Races.* East Lansing: Michigan State University Press, 1997.

Davis, F. James. *Who Is Black? One Nation's Definition.* University Park: Pennsylvania State University Press, 1991.

Diamond, Jared. *The Third Chimpanzee: The Evolution and Future of the Human Animal.* New York: Harper, 1992.

Du Bois, W. E. B. *Dusk of Dawn: An Essay Toward an Autobiography of a Race Concept.* New York: Harcourt Brace, 1940.

Ferrante-Wallace, Joan, and Prince Brown, eds. *The Social Construction of Race and Ethnicity in the United States.* New York: Longman, 1998.

Gould, Stephen Jay. *The Mismeasure of Man.* 1981. Rev. ed. New York: W. W. Norton, 1996.

Hannaford, Ivan. *Race: The History of an Idea in the West.* Baltimore, Md.: The Johns Hopkins Press, 1996.

Kevles, Daniel J. *In the Name of Eugenics: Genetics and the Uses of Human Heredity.* New York: Alfred A. Knopf, 1985.

Malik, Kenan. *The Meaning of Race: Race, History and Culture in Western Society.* Washington Square: New York University Press, 1996.

Montagu, Ashley. *Man's Most Dangerous Myth: The Fallacy of Race.* New York: Columbia University Press, 1998.

Shipman, Pat. *The Evolution of Racism: Human Differences and the Use and Abuse of Science.* New York: Simon & Schuster, 1994.

Smedley, Audrey. *Race in North America: Origin and Evolution of a Worldview.* Boulder, Colo.: Westview Press, 1993.

Sollors, Werner. *The Invention of Ethnicity.* New York: Oxford University Press, 1989.

Stanton, William Ragan. *The Leopard's Spots: Scientific Attitudes Toward Race in America, 1815-59.* Chicago: University of Chicago Press, 1960.

Thompson, Richard H. *Theories of Ethnicity: A Critical Appraisal.* New York: Greenwood Press, 1989.

RACISM, PREJUDICE, DISCRIMINATION

See also African Americans/ The South and Segregation; Psychology, Attitudes, Personal Relations; Race Definitions

Aguirre, Adalberto, Jr., and Jonathan H. Turner. *American Ethnicity: The Dynamics and Consequences of Discrimination.* New York: McGraw-Hill, 1995.

Allport, Gordon W. *The Nature of Prejudice.* Cambridge, Mass.: Addison-Wesley, 1954.

Banton, Michael. *Discrimination.* Philadelphia: Open University Press, 1994.

Barndt, Joseph. *Dismantling Racism: The Continuing Challenge to White America.* Minneapolis: Augsburg Fortress, 1991.

Braham, Peter, et al., eds. *Racism and Antiracism: Inequalities, Opportunities, and Policies.* Newbury Park, Calif.: Sage Publications, 1992.

Brandt, Joseph R. *Dismantling Racism: The Continuing Challenge to White America.* Minneapolis: Augsburg, 1991.

Carr, Leslie G. *"Color-Blind" Racism.* Thousand Oaks, Calif.: Sage Publications, 1997.

Cohen, Mark Nathan. *Culture of Intolerance: Chauvinism, Class, and Racism in the United States.* New Haven, Conn.: Yale University Press, 1998.

Cross, Malcolm, and Michael Keith, eds. *Racism, the City and the State.* New York: Routledge, 1993.

Cruz, Hernán S. *Racial Discrimination.* Rev. ed. New York: United Nations, 1977.

Daniels, Roger, and Harry H. L. Kitano. *American Racism: Exploration of the Nature of Prejudice.* Englewood Cliffs, N.J.: Prentice-Hall, 1970.

Doob, Christopher Bates. *Racism: An American Cauldron.* New York: HarperCollins, 1993.

Dovidio, John F., and Samuel L. Gaertner, eds. *Prejudice, Discrimination, and Racism.* Orlando, Fla.: Academic Press, 1986.

Downs, Anthony. *Racism in America and How to Combat It.* Washington, D.C.: U.S. Commission on Civil Rights, 1970.

Eberhardt, Jennifer Lynn, and Susan T. Fiske, eds. *Confronting Racism: The Problem and the Response.* Thousand Oaks, Calif.: Sage Publications, 1998.

Essed, Philomena. *Understanding Everyday Racism.* Newbury Park, Calif.: Sage Publications, 1991.

Feagin, Joe R., and Clairece B. Feagin. *Discrimination American Style.* 2d ed. Malabar, Fla.: Robert Krieger, 1986.

Feagin, Joe R., and Hernán Vera. *White Racism: Basic Principles.* New York: Routledge, 1995.

Fix, Michael, and Raymond J. Struyk, eds. *Clear and Convincing Evidence: Measurement of Discrimination in America.* Washington, D.C.: Urban Institute Press, 1993.

Frederickson, George M. *The Comparative Imagination: On the History of Racism, Nationalism, and Social Movements.* Berkeley: University of California Press, 1997.

Holmes, Fred R. *Prejudice and Discrimination: Can We Eliminate Them?* Englewood Cliffs, N.J.: Prentice-Hall, 1970.

Jones, James M. *Prejudice and Racism.* Reading, Mass.: Addison-Wesley, 1972.

Katz, Judy H. *White Awareness: A Handbook for Anti-Racism Training.* Norman: University of Oklahoma Press, 1978.

Katz, Phyllis A. *Towards the Elimination of Racism.* New York: Pergamon Press, 1976.

Katz, Phyllis A., and Dalmas A. Taylor, eds. *Eliminating Racism: Profiles in Controversy.* New York: Plenum Press, 1988.

Kivel, Paul. *Uprooting Racism: How White People Can Work for Racial Justice.* Philadelphia: New Society, 1995.

Knowles, Louis L., and Kenneth Prewitt, eds. *Institutional Racism in America.* Englewood Cliffs, N.J.: Prentice-Hall, 1969.

Levin, Jack, and William Levin. *The Functions of Discrimination and Prejudice.* 2d ed. New York: Harper & Row, 1982.

Miles, Robert. *Racism.* London: Routledge, 1989.

Pascoe, Elaine. *Racial Prejudice: Why Can't We Overcome?* New York: Franklin Watts, 1997.

Pettigrew, Thomas T., George M. Frederickson, Dale T. Knobel, Nathan Glazer, and Reed Ueda. *Prejudice.* Cambridge, Mass.: The Belknap Press of Harvard University Press, 1982.

Powell, Thomas A. *The Persistence of Racism in America.* Lanham, Md.: University Press of America, 1992.

Reimers, David M., ed. *Racism in the United States: An American Dilemma?* New York: Holt, Rinehart, 1972.

Ropers, Richard H., and Dan J. Pence. *American Prejudice: With Liberty and Justice for Some.* New York: Insight Books, 1995.

Rutstein, Nathan. *Healing Racism in America.* Springfield, Mass.: Whitcomb, 1993.

Shepherd, George W., and David Penna, eds. *Racism and the Underclass: State Policy and Discrimination Against Minorities.* New York: Greenwood Press, 1991.

Smith, Robert Charles. *Racism in the Post Civil Rights Era: Now You See It, Now You Don't.* Albany: State University of New York Press, 1995.

Snowden, Frank. *Color Prejudice.* Cambridge, Mass.: Harvard University Press, 1983.

Solomos, John, and Les Back. *Racism and Society.* New York: St. Martin's Press, 1996.

Waller, James. *Face to Face: The Changing State of Racism Across America.* New York: Insight Books, 1998.

Weinberg, Meyer, comp. *Racism in Contemporary America.* Westport, Conn.: Greenwood Press, 1996.

Wellman, David T. *Portraits of White Racism.* Cambridge, England: Cambridge University Press, 1993.

Wright, W. D. *Racism Matters.* Westport, Conn.: Praeger, 1998.

REFUGEES

See also Immigration and Immigrants

Gold, Steven J. *Refugee Communities: A Comparative Field of Study.* Newbury Park, Calif.: Sage Publications, 1992.

Haines, David W., ed. *Refugees as Immigrants: Cambodians, Laotians, and Vietnamese in America.* Totowa, N.J.: Rowman and Littlefield, 1989.

Knoll, Tricia. *Becoming Americans: Asian Sojourners, Immigrants, and Refugees in the Western United States.* Portland: Coast to Coast Books, 1982.

Levinson, David. *Ethnic Relations: A Cross-Cultural Encyclopedia.* Santa Barbara: ABC-Clio, 1994.

Loescher, Gil. *Refugees and the Asylum Dilemma in the West.* University Park: Penn State University Press, 1992.

Loescher, Gil, and John A. Scanlan. *Calculated Kindness: Refugees and America's Half-Open Door, 1945-Present.* New York: Free Press, 1986.

Marrus, Michael Robert. *The Unwanted: European Refugees in the Twentieth Century.* New York: Oxford University Press, 1985.

Miller, Jake. *The Plight of Haitian Refugees.* New York: Praeger, 1984.

Stepick, Alex. *Haitian Refugees in the U.S.* London: Minority Rights Group, 1982.

RELIGION

See also African Americans/Religion and the Black Church

Abramson, Harold J. *Ethnic Diversity in Catholic America.* New York: Wiley, 1973.

Abzug, Robert H. *Cosmos Crumbling: American Reform and the Religious Imagination.* New York: Oxford University Press, 1994.

Barkun, Michael. *Religion and the Racist Right: The Origins of the Christian Identity Movement.* Chapel Hill: University of North Carolina Press, 1994.

Bassiri, Kambiz Ghanea. *Competing Visions of Islam in the United States: A Study of Los Angeles.* Westport, Conn.: Greenwood Press, 1997.

Billington, Ray Allen. *The Protestant Crusade, 1800-1860: A Study of the Origins of American Nativism.* New York: Macmillan, 1938.

Butterworth, Charles E., and I. William Zartman, eds. *Political Islam.* Newbury Park, Calif.: Sage Publications, 1992.

Dolan, Jay. *The Immigrant Church: New York's Irish and German Catholics 1815-1965.* Baltimore: The Johns Hopkins University Press, 1975.

Esposito, John L. *The Islamic Threat: Myth or Reality?* New York: Oxford University Press, 1992.

Findlay, James F., Jr. *Church People in the Struggle: The National Council of Churches and the Black Freedom Movement, 1950-1970.* New York: Oxford University Press, 1993.

Haddad, Yvonne Yazbeck, and Adair T. Lummis, eds. *Islamic Values in the United States: A Comparative Study.* New York: Oxford University Press, 1987.

Haddad, Yvonne Yazbeck, and Jane Idleman Smith, eds. *Muslim Communities in North America.* Albany: State University of New York Press, 1994.

Harvey, Paul. *Redeeming the South: Religious Cultures and Racial Identities Among Southern Baptists, 1865-1925.* New York: Oxford University Press, 1997.

Kelley, Robert. *American Protestantism and United States Indian Policy.* Lincoln: University of Nebraska Press, 1983.

Koszegi, Michael A., and J. Gordon Melton, eds. *Islam in North America: A Sourcebook.* New York: Garland, 1992.

LaBarre, Weston. *The Peyote Cult.* 1938. Reprint. Hamden, Conn.: Shoestring Press, 1964.

Lincoln, C. Eric. *Race, Religion, and the Continuing American Dilemma.* New York: Hill & Want, 1984.

Lippman, Thomas W. *Understanding Islam.* New York: Signet Books, 1982.

McKenzie, Steven L. *All God's Children: A Biblical Critique of Racism.* Louisville, Ky.: Westminster John Know Press, 1997.

Marty, Martin E., and R. Scott Appleby. *Religion, Ethnicity, and Self-Identity: Nations in Turmoil.* Hanover, N.H.: University Press of New England, 1997.

Mayer, Egon. *Love and Tradition: Marriage Between Jews and Christians.* New York: Plenum Press, 1985.

Mernissi, Fatima. *Islam and Democracy*. Translated by Mary Jo Lakeland. Reading, Mass.: Addison-Wesley, 1992.

Phan, Peter C. *Ethnicity, Nationality, and Religious Experience*. Lanham, Md.: University Press of America, 1995.

Piscatori, James P., ed. *Islam in the Political Process*. New York: Cambridge University Press, 1983.

Shearer, Jody Miller. *Enter the River: Healing Steps from White Privilege Toward Racial Reconciliation*. Scottdale, Pa.: Herald Press, 1994.

Turner, Richard Brent. *Islam in the African American Experience*. Bloomington: Indiana University Press, 1997.

Yinger, J. Milton. *Religion in the Struggle for Power: A Study in the Sociology of Religion*. Durham, N.C.: Duke University Press, 1946.

WOMEN AND GENDER ISSUES

See also Canada/Women in Canada

Abramovitz, Mimi. *Regulating the Lives of Women: Social Welfare Policy from Colonial Times to the Present*. Boston: South End Press, 1988.

Adleman, Jeanne, and Gloria M. Enguidanos, eds. *Racism in the Lives of Women: Testimony, Theory, and Guides to Antiracist Practice*. New York: Haworth Press, 1995.

Alcott, Louisa May. *Louisa May Alcott on Race, Sex and Slavery*, edited by Sarah Elbert. Boston: Northeastern University Press, 1997.

Allen, Paul Gunn. *The Sacred Hoop: Recovering the Feminine in American Indian Traditions*. Boston: Beacon Press, 1986.

Amott, Teresa L., and Julie A. Matthaei. *Race, Gender, and Work*. Boston: South End Press, 1991.

Asian Women United of California, ed. *Making Waves: An Anthology of Writings by and About Asian American Women*. Boston: Beacon Press, 1989.

Backhouse, Constance. *Petticoats and Prejudice: Women and Law in Nineteenth-Century Canada*. Toronto: Women's Press, 1991.

Bataille, Gretchen, and Kathleen Mullen Sands. *American Indian Women: Telling Their Lives*. Lincoln: University of Nebraska Press, 1984.

Bederman, Gail, and Catharine R. Stimpson. *Manliness and Civilization: A Cultural History of Gender and Race in the United States, 1880-1917*. Chicago: University of Chicago Press, 1995.

Bell, Linda A., and David Blumenfeld, eds. *Overcoming Racism and Sexism*. Lanham, Md.: Rowman and Littlefield, 1995.

Bradley, Harriet. *Men's Work, Women's Work*. Minneapolis: University of Minnesota Press, 1989.

Brown, Elaine. *A Taste of Power: A Black Woman's Story*. Garden City, N.J.: Anchor Books, 1992.

Burr, Virginia Ingraham, ed. *The Secret Eye: The Journal of Ella Gertrude Clanton Thomas, 1848-1889*. Chapel Hill: University of North Carolina Press, 1990.

Caraway, Nancie. *Segregated Sisterhood: Racism and Politics of American Feminism*. Knoxville: University of Tennessee Press, 1991.

Clinton, Catherine. *The Plantation Mistress: Woman's World in the Old South*. New York: Pantheon Books, 1982.

Clinton, Catherine, and Michele Gillespie, eds. *The Devil's Lane: Sex and Race in the Early South*. New York: Oxford University Press, 1997.

Collier, Jane Fishburne, and Sylvia Junko Yanagisako, eds. *Gender and Kinship: Essays Toward a Unified Analysis*. Stanford, Calif.: Stanford University Press, 1987.

Collins, Patricia Hill. *Black Feminist Thought: Knowledge, Consciousness, and the Politics of Empowerment*. Boston: Unwin Hyman, 1990.

Connolly, Paul. *Racism, Gender Identities and Young Children: Social Relations in a Multi-Ethnic, Inner-City Primary School*. New York: Routledge, 1998.

Cordova, Teresa, et al., eds. *Chicana Voices: Intersections of Class, Race, and Gender*. Austin, Tex.: Center for Mexican American Studies, 1986.

Crawford, Vicki L., Jacqueline Anne Rouse, and Barbara Woods, eds. *Women in the Civil Rights Movement: Trailblazers and Torchbearers 1941-1965*. Bloomington: Indiana University Press, 1993.

Cyrus, Virginia, ed. *Experiencing Race, Class, and Gender in the United States*. Mountain Valley, Calif.: Mayfield, 1993.

Davis, Angela. *Women, Culture, and Politics*. New York: Random House, 1989.

_____. *Women, Race, and Class*. New York: Vintage Books, 1981.

Diner, Sasia R. *Erin's Daughters in America: Irish Immigrant Women in the Nineteenth Century*. Baltimore: The Johns Hopkins University Press, 1983.

Dines, Gail, and Jean M. Humez. *Gender, Race, and Class in Media*. Newbury Park, Calif.: Sage Publications, 1995.

DuBois, Ellen C., and Vicki L. Ruiz, eds. *Unequal Sisters*. New York: Routledge, 1990.

Essed, Philomena. *Diversity: Gender, Color, and Culture*. Amherst: University of Massachusetts Press, 1996.

_____. *Everyday Racism: An Interdisciplinary Theory*. Thousand Oaks, Calif.: Sage Publications, 1991.

Evans, Sara. *Personal Politics: The Roots of Women's Liberation in the Civil Rights Movement and the New Left*. New York: Alfred A. Knopf, 1979.

Foerstel, Lenora, ed. *Women's Voices on the Pacific*. Washington, D.C.: Maisonneuve Press, 1991.

Fox-Genovese, Elizabeth. *Within the Plantation Household: Black and White Women of the Old South*. Chapel Hill: University of North Carolina Press, 1988.

Frankenberg, Ruth. *White Women, Race Matters: The Social Construction of Whiteness*. Minneapolis: University of Minnesota Press, 1993.

Friedman, Jean E. *The Enclosed Garden: Women and Community in the Evangelical South, 1830-1900*. Chapel Hill: University of North Carolina Press, 1985.

Giddings, Paula. *When and Where I Enter: The Impact of Women on Race and Sex in America*. New York: William Morrow, 1984.

Golden, Marita, and Susan Shreve, eds. *Skin Deep: Black Women and White Women Write About Race*. New York: Doubleday, 1995.

Gordon, Vivian Verdell. *Black Women, Feminism and Black Liberation: Which Way?* 1991

Gunew, Sneja, and Anna Yeatman, eds. *Feminism and the Politics of Difference*. Boulder, Colo.: Westview Press, 1993.

Guy-Sheftall, Beverly. *Daughters of Sorrow: Attitudes Toward Black Women, 1880-1920*. Brooklyn, N.Y.: Carlson, 1990.

Healey, Joseph F. *Race, Ethnicity, Gender, and Class: The Sociology of Group Conflict and Change*. Thousand Oaks, Calif.: Pine Forge Press, 1998.

Hibbert, Joyce. *The War Brides*. Toronto: PMA Books, 1978.

Higginbotham, Elizabeth. "We Were Never on a Pedestal: Women of Color Continue to Struggle with Poverty, Racism, and Sexism." In *For Crying out Loud: Women and Poverty in the*

United States, edited by Rochelle Lefkowitz and Ann Withorn. New York: Pilgrim Press, 1986.

Hill, Anita, and Emma Coleman Jordan, eds. *Race, Gender, and Power in America: The Legacy of the Hill-Thomas Hearings*. New York: Oxford University Press, 1995.

Hill, George, Lorraine Raglin, and Chas Floyd Johnson. *Black Women in Television*. New York: Garland Publishing, 1990.

Hodes, Martha Elizabeth. *White Women, Black Men: Illicit Sex in the Nineteenth-Century South*. New Haven, Conn.: Yale University Press, 1997.

Hooks, Bell. *Ain't I a Woman: Black Women and Feminism*. Boston: South End Press, 1981.

————. *Feminist Theory: From Margin to Center*. Boston: South End Press, 1984.

————. *Killing Rage: Ending Racism*. New York: H. Holt, 1995.

————. *Outlaw Culture: Resisting Representations*. New York: Routledge, 1994.

Horno-Delgado, Asunción, Eliana Ortega, Nina M. Scott, and Nancy Saporta Sternbach, eds. *Breaking Boundaries: Latina Writing and Critical Readings*. Amherst: University of Massachusetts Press, 1989.

Jones, Jacqueline. *Labor of Love, Labor of Sorrow: Black Women, Work, and the Family from Slavery to the Present*. New York: Basic Books, 1985.

Katz, Jane, ed. *Messengers of the Wind: Native American Women Tell Their Life Stories*. New York: Ballantine Books, 1995.

Kent, Ronald C., et al. *Culture, Gender, Race and U.S. Labor History*. Westport, Conn.: Greenwood Press, 1993.

Kirp, David, et al. *Gender Justice*. Chicago: University of Chicago Press, 1986.

Lagerquist, L. DeAne. *In America the Men Milk the Cows: Factors of Gender, Ethnicity, and Religion in the Americanization of Norwegian American Women*. Brooklyn, N.Y.: Carlson, 1991.

Libeau, Vera A. *Minority and Female Membership in Referral Unions, 1974*. Washington, D.C.: Equal Employment Opportunity Commission, 1977.

Lips, Hilary M. *Sex and Gender: An Introduction*. Mountain View, Calif.: Mayfield, 1988.

McClintock, Anne, ed. *Dangerous Liaisons: Gender, Nation, and Postcolonial Perspectives*. Minneapolis: University of Minnesota Press, 1997.

Madison, D. Soyini, ed. *The Woman That I Am: The Literature and Culture of Contemporary Women of Color*. New York: St. Martin's Press, 1994.

Makabe, Tomoko. *Picture Brides: Japanese Women in Canada*. Toronto: Multicultural History Society of Ontario, 1995.

Martínez, Elizabeth Sutherland. *De Colores Means All of Us: Latina Views for a Multi-Colored Century*. Cambridge, Mass.: South End Press, 1998.

Mirza, Heidi Safia. *Young, Female and Black*. New York: Routledge, 1992.

Moraga, Cherríe, and Gloria Anzaldúa, eds. *This Bridge Called My Back: Writings by Radical Women of Color*. 2d ed. New York: Kitchen Table: Women of Color Press, 1983.

Neidle, Cecyle S. *America's Immigrant Women*. Boston: Twayne, 1975.

Paul, Ellen Frankel. *Equity and Gender: The Comparable Worth Debate*. New Brunswick, N.J.: Transaction Books, 1989.

Pogrebin, Letty Cottin. *Deborah, Golda, and Me: Being Female*

and Jewish in America. New York: Crown, 1991.

Poling, James Newton. *Deliver Us from Evil: Resisting Racial and Gender Oppression*. Minneapolis: Fortress Press, 1996.

Riggs, Marcia Y. *Awake, Arise, & Act: A Womanist Call for Black Liberation*. Cleveland: Pilgrim Press, 1994.

Rittner, Carol, and John K. Roth, eds. *Different Voices: Women and the Holocaust*. New York: Paragon House, 1993.

Robinson, Jo Ann Gibson. *The Montgomery Bus Boycott and the Women Who Started It: The Memoir of Jo Ann Gibson Robinson*. Knoxville: University of Tennessee Press, 1987.

Rodgers, Harrell R., Jr. *Poor Women, Poor Families: The Economic Plight of America's Female-Headed Households*. Rev. ed. Armonk, N.Y.: M. E. Sharpe, 1990.

Rosser, Phyllis. *Sex Bias in College Admissions Tests: Why Women Lose Out*. 3d ed. Cambridge, Mass.: The Center, 1989.

Rothenberg, Paula S. *Race, Class, and Gender in the United States: An Integrated Study*. 2d ed. New York: St. Martin's Press, 1992.

Rothman, Robert A. *Inequality and Stratification: Class, Color, and Gender*, 2d ed. Englewood Cliffs, N.J.: Prentice-Hall, 1993.

Schecter, Tanya. *Race, Class, Women and the State: The Case of Domestic Labour in Canada*. Montreal: Black Rose, 1998.

Shukert, Elfrieda Berthiaume, and Barbara Smith Scibetta. *War Brides of World War II*. Novato, Calif.: Presidio Press, 1988.

Sidel, Ruth. *Women and Children Last: The Plight of Poor Women in Affluent America*. 2d ed. New York: Penguin Books, 1992.

Simms, Margaret C., and Julianne Malveaux, eds. *Slipping Through the Cracks: The Status of Black Women*. New Brunswick, N.J.: Transaction Books, 1986.

Smith, John David, ed. *Racial Determinism and the Fear of Miscegenation, Pre-1900*. New York: Garland, 1993.

Spelman, Elizabeth. *Inessential Woman: Problems of Exclusion in Feminist Thought*. Boston: Beacon Press, 1988.

Stephenson, Marylee, ed. *Women in Canada*. Don Mills, Ontario: General, 1977.

Swyripa, Frances. *Wedded to the Cause: Ukrainian-Canadian Women and Ethnic Identity, 1891-1991*. Toronto: University of Toronto Press, 1993.

Tarantino, Thomas Howard, and Dismas Becker, eds. *Welfare Mothers Speak Out: We Ain't Gonna Shuffle Anymore*. New York: W. W. Norton, 1972.

Taylor, Jill McLean, et al. *Between Voice and Silence: Women and Girls, Race and Relationship*. Cambridge, Mass.: Harvard University Press, 1995.

Wall, Steve. *Wisdom's Daughters: Conversations with Women Elders of Native America*. New York: HarperCollins, 1993.

Ware, Vron. *Beyond the Pale: White Women, Racism, and History*. New York: Verso, 1992.

White, Deborah G. *Ar'n't I a Woman? Female Slaves in the Plantation South*. New York: W. W. Norton, 1987.

Wiegman, Robyn. *American Anatomies: Theorizing Race and Gender*. Durham, N.C.: Duke University Press, 1995.

Wilson, Midge, et al. *Divided Sisters: Bridging the Gap Between Black Women and White Women*. New York: Anchor, 1996.

Zack, Naomi, ed. *Race/Sex: Their Sameness, Difference, and Interplay*. New York: Routledge, 1997.

Zack, Naomi, et al., eds. *Race, Class, Gender and Sexuality: The Big Questions*. Malden, Mass.: Blackwell, 1998.

Zinn, Maxine Baca, and Bonnie Thornton Dill. *Women of Color in U.S. Society*. Philadelphia: Temple University Press, 1994.

Racial and Ethnic Relations in America

Categorized List of Entries

Subject Headings Used in List

African Americans
American Indians
Arab Americans
Arts
Asian Americans
Canada
Caribbean Americans
Civil rights
Court cases
Demographics and housing issues
Discrimination
Educational issues

Employment and workplace issues
Ethnicity
Euro-Americans
Family
Governmental programs and policies
Identity issues
Immigration
Irish Americans
Italian Americans
Jewish Americans
Latinos
Laws, acts, and amendments

Movements
Organizations and institutions
Other minority Americans
Prejudice
Race and racism
Religion and religious issues
Riots, violence, and wars
Sociological theories, concepts, and
   issues
Theories of racial/ethnic relations
Treaties and agreements
Women

African Americans
Abolition
Accommodationism
African American-American Indian
   relations
African American Baptist Church
African American cowboys
African American literature
African American music
African American stereotypes
African American women
African Americans and film
African Americans in the Civil War
African Liberation Day
Afro-Caribbeans
Afrocentrism
AIDS conspiracy theory
*Alexander v. Holmes County Board of
   Education*
All African People's Revolutionary
   Party
AME Church
AME Zion Churches
American Anti-Slavery Society
American Colonization Society
American Council on Race Relations
Amistad slave revolt
Antislavery laws of 1777 and 1807
Atlanta Compromise
Baseball
Batson v. Kentucky
Black "brute" and "buck" stereotypes
Black cabinet
Black church
Black codes
Black colleges and universities
Black conservatism
Black flight
Black Is Beautiful movement
Black Jews

Black middle class/black underclass
   relations
Black nationalism
Black-on-black violence
Black Panther Party
Black Power movement
Blackness and whiteness: legal
   definitions
Bleeding Kansas
Body of Liberties
Bolling v. Sharpe
Brotherhood of Sleeping Car Porters
Brown v. Board of Education
Buchanan v. Warley
Busing and integration
Charleston race riots
Civil War
Clinton massacre
Colegrove v. Green
Colfax massacre
Colored Women's League
Compromise of 1850
Compromise of 1877
Confiscation Acts of 1861 and 1862
Congress of Racial Equality
Congressional Black Caucus
Cooper v. Aaron
Council of Federated Organizations
Critical race theory
Crown Heights conflicts
Cuban-African American relations
Desegregation: defense
Desegregation: public schools
Detroit riot
Disfranchisement laws in Mississippi
Dyer antilynching bill
Ebonics
Edmondson v. Leesville Concrete Company
Education and African Americans
Emancipation Proclamation

Employment among African Americans
Family and socialization: African
   Americans
Free African Society
Free blacks
Free-Soil Party
Freedmen's Bureau
Freedom Riders
Freedom Summer
Fugitive slave laws
Fusion movement
Goetz, Bernhard, incident
Grandfather clauses
Great Migration
*Green v. County School Board of New Kent
   County*
Greensboro sit-ins
Grovey v. Townsend
Guinn v. United States
Gullah
Harlem Renaissance
Harlins, Latasha, murder
Harper v. Virginia Board of Elections
Hawkins, Yusuf, murder
Heart of Atlanta Motel v. United States
Horton, Willie, incident
Hypogamy
"I Have a Dream" speech
Indentured servitude
Irish-African American relations
Jewish-African American relations
Jim Crow laws
John Brown's raid
Jones v. Alfred H. Mayer Company
Kansas-Nebraska Act
Kerner Report
Keyes v. Denver School District No. 1
King, Martin Luther, Jr., assassination
King, Rodney, case
Know-Nothing Party

Jury selection
Mainstreaming
Majority and minority
Meritocracy myth
Migrant superordination
Multiculturalism
Multiracial identity
Multiracial movement
Nativism
Nonviolent resistance
Oppositional culture
"Other" theory
Out-group
Panethnicity
Passing
Patriarchal system
People of color
Police brutality
Political correctness
Politics of hate
Positive ethnocentrism
Poverty and race
Power elite
Psychological theories of intergroup
    relations
Psychology of racism
Racial hierarchy
Resistance, cultures of
Sabotage
Self-determination movements
Sell-out
Sexual fears and racism
Social Darwinism and racism
Social mobility and race
Social perception of others
Social rearticulation
Socialization and reference groups
Stereotype
Stereotyping and the self-fulfilling
    prophecy
Subordinate group
Symbolic racism
Tokenism

Tolerance
Transnationalism and ethnonationalism
Triple oppression

Theories of racial/ethnic relations
Assimilation: cultural and structural
Assimilation theories
Attitude-receptional assimilation
Authoritarian personality theory
Behavior-receptional assimilation
Caste model
Civic assimilation
Class theories of racial/ethnic relations
Colonial model of racism
Competition theory and human ecology
Conformity theories
Conquest and annexation
Conservatives and racial/ethnic
    relations
Contact and adaptation patterns
Contact hypothesis
Cress theory
Cultural pluralism
Ethnogenesis theory
Frustration-aggression theory
Identification assimilation
Indigenous superordination
Internal colonialism
Marital assimilation
Marxist models
Melting pot theory
Moynihan Report
Multiculturalism
Pluralism vs. assimilation
Pluralism vs. particularism
Progressive inclusion theory of
    assimilation
Race relations cycle
Racial/ethnic relations: theoretical
    overview
Segmented assimilation theory
Separatism
Social stratification theories

Somatic norm theory
Split labor market theory
Structural assimilation
Syncretism
Transnationalism and ethnonationalism
Underclass theories
Urban underclass and the rural poor

Treaties and agreements
Alaska Native Brotherhood and Alaska
    Native Claims Settlement
Gadsden Purchase
Gentlemen's Agreement
Guadalupe Hidalgo, Treaty of
Trail of Broken Treaties
Treaties and agreements with Indians:
    Canada
Treaties and agreements with Indians:
    United States

Women
African American women
American Indian women
Asian American women
Colored Women's League
Ethnic identities of women
French Canadian women
Gendered racism
Immigrant women
Jewish women
Latinas
Million Woman March
National Association of Colored
    Women
National Black Women's Political
    Leadership Caucus
National Council of Negro Women
Triple oppression
War Brides Act
"Welfare queen" stereotype
Women and racism
Women of All Red Nations
Women of color

Personages Index

Index

A page number or range in **boldface** type indicates a full article devoted to that topic.